𝕿𝖗𝖆𝖓𝖘𝖋𝖊𝖗 𝖔𝖋 𝕰𝖗𝖎𝖓

Or The acquisition of Ireland by England

Thomas C. Amory

Alpha Editions

This edition published in 2020

ISBN : 9789354018992

Design and Setting By
Alpha Editions
email - alphaedis@gmail.com

TRANSFER OF ERIN:

OR

THE ACQUISITION OF IRELAND BY ENGLAND.

BY

THOMAS C. AMORY.

PHILADELPHIA:

J. B. LIPPINCOTT & CO.

1877.

PREFACE.

For a large portion of the period which elapsed from the Anglo-Norman invasion to the reign of Queen Anne, the history of Ireland was little else than a struggle to acquire or retain property and possession of the soil. Conflicts of race and creed, of rival dynasties and ambitious chieftains, of enterprising and unscrupulous adventurers, modified or disguised the issues and the strife, but the root of Irish discontent, resentment and resistance was the systematic spoliation which finally succeeded in divesting the descendants of the ancient proprietors of all interest in their native land. Loyalty to established rule and common nationality too often yielded to this sense of wrong, and had not statesmanship devised methods of readjusting what was objectionable and at times seriously imperilling the stability of the social fabric itself, Ireland would have continued to prove rather a source of weakness than of strength to the realm.

Parliament has been sustained by public opinion, in recognizing the duty of making amends, and the impolicy of leaving any just ground of jealousy to the millions who fight the national battles, and who in time must participate more largely in making the laws. The tenure act is an initial step, which if followed out in the same spirit will soon disarm what remains of disaffection. It cannot be denied that the present state of tranquillity and order is in striking contrast to the restlessness which prevailed before these measures were adopted. As Ireland under just legislation starts on a new era of commercial and industrial activity, without infringement on vested right or disregard of any reasonable pretension the future will discover ways of restoring to the masses, who till the ground, a larger share in its ownership. The plea on which the land is now held, that government may take from one and give to another for national security and consolidation, would justify redistribution, and the increasing value afford a fund for compensation. With the development of its natural resources under good government the wealth of the island would be increased manifold, and landlords derive from less extended areas or less absolute control revenues largely augmented.

Any such course, however, if within the bounds of eminent domain would be denounced as radical and agrarian, and happily is not called for to effect the object. Generations are of little account in the life of nations, and those who shape their destiny may safely leave results to time. With the more general diffusion of education and consequent equalization of property, with modified laws of succession likely to approve themselves to growing enlightenment, what is unreasonable will rectify itself. While, goaded by a sense of injustice, Ireland was ever on the verge of rebellion, the stranger might feel some reserve in intruding his researches into this department of her history. But now that faith in honestly intended reparation has appeased long cherished animosities, and that history, consisting largely of these successive spoliations, cannot otherwise be understood, the selection of the subject needs no apology.

CONTENTS.

TRANSFER OF ERIN.

I.

NATIONAL BIAS.

HISTORY, which formerly dealt almost exclusively with political revolutions and religious controversies, with kings and courts, war, its campaigns and battle-fields, of late has extended its province. It tells us more of the inner life of nations, the development of their industry and trade, progress in intelligence and civilization. It condescends to render more clear and intelligible the course and causes of events, by taking into view the origin, character and vicissitudes of families, classes and individuals. Under patriarchal governments like that of Ireland for twenty centuries, knowledge of what concerned the whole would be incomplete without some acquaintance with the annals of each clan, and of its leaders where they chance to be of note. It is also a help to know something of the place they inhabited, its geographical and other physical conditions, the extent of their possessions, and how they became from century to century enriched or impoverished. It is not easy to comprehend with precision the feuds and alliances of this ancient race, their hates and attachments, customs and traditions, for they form a tangled web. But they constituted an important part of what rendered them peculiar, and invest their history with a romantic interest as yet but partially improved.

2

Our population in America, and especially in New-England, is so largely composed of families of Irish birth or origin, that whatever relates to their history recent or remote, falls legitimately within the scope of our assumed obligations. It is of peculiar interest now, for Irish questions which have been for centuries fruitful sources of controversy, have attracted of late more than ordinary attention. Recent works, from imputed want of fidelity to truth, or from their gross partiality, have provoked resentment not confined to those whose country or ancestors have been maligned, but arousing every where the sympathy of the generous, who love fair play. All honorable minds, Irish, English or American, regard with indignation the paltry attempts of the wealthy and powerful for selfish objects to prejudice by misrepresentation the victims of that injustice on which rests their present preëminence.

Ever since the invasion of Ireland seven centuries ago, from Barry to Trench and Froude, Englishmen have been striving to justify their intrusion upon a people weaker than themselves in numbers and military resources, and to still their own consciences and the reproach of other men, for appropriating lands not their own simply because they coveted them, by misrepresentation. Throughout their writings, public documents, even acts of legislation, is exhibited a design to vindicate that intrusion, by disparaging or vilifying those they dispossessed. Ware, Stanihurst, Temple, Davis, Campion, Spencer, Wood, and a multitudinous throng of others of more or less reputation, hardly one of them but betrays, in relating his experiences, or stating the results of his investigations, his particular national bias, misrepresenting events and characters to uphold a theory, flatter a prejudice or justify a wrong. Many of them were the paid advocates of vested interests, of a government or class. Where passion or dishonesty thus poison the fountain head of information, whatever is said represents an opinion, an aggression past or intended, some conflicting claim. It comes consequently with suspicion, is obnoxious to criticism, and should be received with caution.

For the full and fair consideration of these questions, all the judicial attributes of impartiality and candor are demanded. One cannot be either a bigoted Protestant or a bigoted Catholic, English owner of Irish soil or dependent upon those that are, and weigh evidence so conflicting, or pretend arrogantly to be wiser than any body else. The authorities, however much they profess to be calm and dispassionate, are advocates not witnesses, invariably one-sided. Where there is occasion for praise or reproach, events and characters change their identity. Soldiers and statesmen, the most exemplary, lose all claim to respect as traduced by those seeking to disparage them; monsters of extortion and iniquity are portrayed as saints and heroes by their partisans. Vindication of one side involves reflection on the opposite. Temper begets recrimination, and even honest effort to ascertain the truth but leads farther astray. Though favorably placed here in America for impartial judgment upon contentions in another land, we can hardly hope to avoid altogether the paths beneath which are still smouldering the embers in their ashes. It is of little service to any one to disturb them, folly to fan them into fresh flame by discussion. But when injustice is added to injury by misstatement of fact or perversion of evidence, silence becomes pusillanimous.

No one of late has done more to exasperate the sensitiveness of Ireland, or aggravate its grievances by stirring up strife, at a moment when parliament and public opinion were alike combining to redress them, than Mr. Froude, and his statements have met with signal and eloquent rebuke from Father Burke, Mr. Prendergast, and others, from all sects and nationalities and from every standpoint.

II.

ENGLISH INVASION.

Interesting as it might prove, in the light of recent archæological discoveries in the old world and the new, it is not our present purpose to dwell on the early settlements of Ireland. Whether Caisser's or Partholan's, Nemidian, Formorian, Firbolg, Tuatha de Danaans, Belgian or Damnonian, they are no doubt in some measure fabulous, fact and fiction intermingled. Yet it cannot be disputed that long before the Christian era, strangers from Britain or Gaul, from Mediterranean or Baltic, brought into the island, early famed as flowing with milk and honey, diversities of race, of language and of law. Nor that later still, about the time that Troy fell and Rome was founded, from Scythia through Spain, with harp and battle-axe and an advanced stage of civilization, proceeded that remarkable dynasty of Milesian chiefs who for centuries formed its governing and enlightened class, moulded its institutions and shaped its destinies. Enough remains of tradition, entitled to equal faith with what has been transmitted of other nations of Western Europe, to inspire respect and interest curiosity. But passing over what has come down to us of the many among them who left their mark on their day and generation, over Druids, Ossian and the Sagas, Scotch kings, and by Scandinavian pirates, St. Patrick, Bridget and Columba, and those Holy men and women that gave Ireland its designation of the "Island of Saints," and "School of the West," by Norman and Dane, we proceed to dwell for a moment on that event of all others in its annals most pregnant with serious consequences to Ireland, the English conquest, a struggle which commenced seven centuries ago for national independence on one side and subjugation on the other, and which has lasted from that day to this. Many wrongs have been righted and grievances redressed, but much remains to be done before Irishmen will consider that struggle at an end.

Whether the bull of 1153 of Nicholas Brakespeare, the Englishman, known as Pope Adrian 4th, or that of Alexander 3rd, twenty years later, were genuine, or the fabrication of Barry or some other man clever and false, they profess to give Ireland to the English Kings. But the pope had no authority divine or human to dispose of lands or nations, no right actual or admitted over an unwilling bride. Nor were other enforced espousals of happier augury. Derforguill, daughter of the prince of Meath, when in 1153 attached to Dermod son of Morough, king of Leinster, was compelled to marry O'Rourke, prince of Breffney, and unhappy in her conjugal relations, she fled several years later to her early lover. Roderick O'Connor, king of Connaught and then likewise monarch of Ireland, ordering restitution, Dermod, who had succeeded his father as king of Leinster, refused to obey, and being consequently deposed, appealed to Henry II. to reinstate him. With Henry's sanction, he invited Strongbow, Richard Clare earl of Pembroke, younger brother of Gilbert, earl of Hertford, to help him, promising to bestow upon him the hand of his daughter Eva in marriage, and, what he had no right to promise, the succession after his death to the kingdom of Leinster.

It was natural for the sturdy and grasping race who had taken forcible possession of Normandy, England and Wales, to wish to extend their conquests. What had already been realized was only a greater incentive to farther acquisition to such as had had no lot or part in the original distribution, or who had already wasted what had been assigned them. The conqueror and his successors looked across the channel with covetous eyes to that great island in the west, which since Brian Boroihme, 150 years before, in 1014, expelled the Danes or greatly crippled their power, had been growing in wealth. The permission given by Henry to his nobles to aid Dermod was gladly improved, and besides Strongbow, the Geraldines, that remarkable progeny of Nesta, princess of Wales, and concubine of Henry the First, Prendergast, De Courcy, De Braose and St. Lawrence, with hosts of other stalwart men, readily volunteered, embracing with alacrity this opportunity for bettering their condition. Thousands

of adventurers from England and Wales joined or followed them;
and the strongholds and wall towns of Dublin and Wexford along
the shore belonging to Dermod's dominion, and Waterford and Limerick which had been built by the Danes and were still occupied
largely by their descendants, being taken possession of with little resistance, from their strength and accessibility for supplies and reinforcements from England, long proved a serviceable base of operations to carry out their projects.

That the invaders should have gained and kept with comparative
ease this base of operations, yet for centuries failed to complete their
conquest, is sufficiently explained, when we bear in mind how not
only Ireland with her clans or septs at this period, but Europe generally under the feudal system, was broken up and subdivided into
petty possessions and principalities each under its hereditary chieftain.   These chieftains were not merely rulers and leaders of their
people, but proprietors of the territory.   The actual occupants, in
their several ranks and degrees, were tenants as well as vassals, their
rights and duties being defined by established law and usages of
mutual obligation.   Their allegiance was not so much to the king
or country as to the immediate chief, who as liege of some superior
lord, emperor, or king, rendered him military service, rent in money,
arrows, roses, or spurs, and represented in his own person his
subordinates for whose proceedings he was responsible.   English
monarchs owed and paid this homage and fealty to the French, who
in a few instances in history in their turn held the reversed relation
to them as royal vassals.

Retaining their conquests by intimidation or superior military
force, it was the Norman policy to complicate so far as they were
able the network of feudal relations, to impart to them additional
strength, and better keep the people in subjection.   William after
Hastings had recompensed his principal followers with fiefs and
manors scattered broadcast over the land, interspersed among those
retained by himself, or bestowed upon his kinsmen and more devoted

adherents, that he might rely with more confidence on their fidelity, and they be enabled more readily to combine their forces from their different possessions for mutual support, or to repress disaffection. This policy strengthened the hands of the nobles in curbing the tyranny of evil-intentioned kings, and brought to bear upon the subjected races a power which they were too feeble and too little organized to resist.

The feudal laws regulating succession and inheritance, if not quite uniform, bore a general resemblance. When a proprietor died leaving daughters, but no son, his estates by the Norman rule were distributed among them in equal shares, and passed with the consent of his superior lord to their husbands and children of other names; titles of honor, if any, remaining generally in abeyance, or passing in some instances to male heirs more remote. As the same law regulated these successions and their own rights which were valuable, tenants were not inclined to risk the displeasure of those on whom they depended, and acquiesced in what they could not control. This change of masters without their being consulted came to be regarded as the natural course of events. When some stranger became invested by conquest, marriage, inheritance, gift or other recognized title with baronial or royal functions, the people claimed no effectual right to object, and allegiance and homage, the condition on which they held their lands, soon warmed into affectionate loyalty towards their new lord on whose favor their prosperity depended. These personal attachments to their feudal superior, through fear, self-interest or gratitude, for kindness received or expected, thus taking place of any patriotic love for their country at large, the sense of common nationality and of obligation to defend it grew weak.

Feuds and jealousies from disputed rights and rival pretensions between neighboring lords, clans or people, engendered resentments transmitted from generation to generation, discouraging any general rally of the clans or national forces, and rendering powerless every combination formed to resist aggression. It was only when peril was unusually imminent, and the sovereign sufficiently wise and popular to quiet these animosities, that it became possible to consolidate the national strength.   In 838 the Irish under Niall drove into the sea the earlier Norman invaders, and when the Danes were expelled a few years later by Malachi, and again in 1014 by Brian Boroihme, there existed more unanimity, and their efforts resulted in regaining the possession of the island.

The existing relations between kings and princes, chiefs and their clans in Ireland, corresponded in some essential points with the provisions of feudal law, in others they greatly differed.   All the chiefs derived from Heremon, Ir or Heber, sons of Milesius, or from Ith his uncle, and held their several territories by royal grants.   The people, unless forming separate communities like the Firbolgs in Connaught, or Danes in Dublin and other seaports, or later as the Flemings near Waterford, or Scotch in Antrim and Derry, through intermarriages with younger branches of princely families, gradually blended into one race.   When surnames were adopted by law at Tara, under Brian Boroihme, in the eleventh century, the clans generally came to be designated by those of their chiefs, or one of his ancestors.   If not all of Milesian blood they formed part of the clan which was governed by Brehon laws established under earlier kings. By these laws the land was regarded as belonging to the sept as well as to the hereditary chief, whose right to his castles and immediate domains was defined and passed by fixed rules to his heirs or to his tanist, who like our vice president was at the same time as himself elected to succeed him, in case his heirs at his demise were too young or infirm to administer the government.   Of these clans there were nearly a hundred in all, respectively subordinate to the several kings of the five or six provinces, who in their turn were feudatories to the monarch of Ireland, who mounted the throne sometimes by virtue of his superior power, sometimes by the consent of the princes.

III.

IRISH RESISTANCE.

Such was the political and social state of Ireland when the English came, and if we glance our eye upon its map, we shall find a clue to its sad destiny. Its area, nearly rectangular, about two hundred and eighty miles in greatest extension, by one hundred and twenty-five in breadth, comprised about thirty thousand square miles, or eighteen millions of English acres, in five chief divisions, Ulster, Connaught, Munster, Leinster, and Meath. At the time of the invasion, and for long ages before, the government was a confederated monarchy, not unlike that of the Saxon Heptarchy, as it existed a few centuries earlier in England. Roderick O'Connor, destined to be the last monarch, was on the throne, the several provincial kings acknowledging his supremacy. Munster was divided into two kingdoms, Thomond under Donald O'Brien, Desmond under Dermod McCarthy. The Leinster kings were McMurroughs, eldest branch of the Cavanaghs, princes of Kinsellagh. Ulster was under the O'Neils and O'Donnels. Meath, earlier set apart for the mensal domains of the monarch of Ireland, had been alienated by Laogaire in favor of the sons of his predecessor Daniel, and was under the McLaghlins, while the McMahons were princes of Uriel, a territory comprising the present countries of Louth, Armagh and Monaghan. These chieftains virtually independent were often at variance among themselves, and their country, fertile in soil and weak from their dissensions and at the same time exposed all around its shore to depredations, offered an irresistible temptation to its powerful and restless neighbors.

Two years before the invasion, on the demise of Turlough O'Brien, king of Limerick, after a long reign as monarch of Ireland, when Roderick of Connaught had been chosen to succeed him, at a convention of princes in 1167, to give in their allegiance, Dermod McCarthy king of Cork or Desmond, Donnel O'Brien king of

Limerick or Thomond, Dermod of Leinster, Dermod McLaghlin prince of Meath, Tiernan O'Rourke prince of Breffney, Duncan McMahon prince of Uriel, Eochaid prince of Ulad, Fitzpatrick prince of Ossory, Duncan O'Phelan prince of Decies, and others, in all thirteen hundred principal men and thirty thousand followers, assembled at Athboy. With them came Asculph, son of Torcal, prince of the Danes, from Dublin. The power of Roderick differed greatly from that of his predecessors. Meath with Tara having been alienated from the crown, Roderick had no national capital, officers, revenues, flags or forces. He was indeed little more than king of Connaught, his ancestral dominions.

He did what he could to prevent or stay the menaced invasion. He early anticipated what was impending, even before Strongbow landed, striving by remonstrance, concession and conciliation to divert Dermod of Leinster from an alliance fraught with such fatal consequences. He made an earnest appeal to the princes of Ulster and Munster and to his own lieges in Connaught to rally for their general defence, and urged the king of Man to prepare and forward his quota. In May, 1169, took place the first landing of Anglo-Normans near Wexford. Roderick assembled an army, and at Tara convoked a council of princes. Adjourning to Dublin, the king of Ulster, and McMahon prince of Uriel, disaffected, drew off their forces. The King led his army to Fernes, Dermod's stronghold, and compelled him to recognize his authority, and secretly to promise to send away his allies. Dermod proved a traitor, or utterly powerless to close the gates he had opened. Numbers of English knights and their followers were already swarming in to join their countrymen, and it was too late to organize against them with effect. Cormac McCarthy, son of the king of Desmond, repossessed his clan of Waterford, and after Dermod's death at Fernes, in 1170, Strongbow claiming to be heir to the throne of Leinster as husband of Dermod's daughter Eva, King Roderick defeated him at Thurles in Ormond, seventeen hundred Englishmen being slain. Such success did not, however, always or perhaps often attend the efforts of the chiefs to stem the tide of aggression on their territories.

The invaders were the flower of England's knighthood, younger sons with every thing to gain, depending for their subsistence and prosperity on their profession of arms, which they had studied in the best schools in the crusades, on the continent, or in civil strife. From her French possessions retained by naval force, and the development of her arts and trade, England had greatly the advantage over her sister isle, in all the implements and sinews of war. Her warriors, on powerful chargers, both alike invulnerable in steel, rode unharmed through battle-fields, on which the Irish without defensive armor, and with inferior weapons, too brave to retreat, fell a useless sacrifice. The forces that accompanied Henry the Second, October, 1171, were forty-five hundred knights and men at arms ; but the lower orders and ranks greatly exceeded that number, and there were already in Ireland as many more who had come over before the king.

Possibly from a sense of inability successfully to cope with this formidable armament, or that the chiefs, realizing the growing power of England, and the inadequacy of their own confederate government to oppose them or other foreign foes, regarded consolidation with England only as a matter of time, all but the O'Neils and O'Donnels of Ulster, whose remote position protected them from immediate molestation, even Roderick, on condition that his rights as king of Connaught and monarch of Ireland, and those of his subordinate kings and princes should be respected, recognized Henry perhaps as sovereign. Henry took a surrender of Leinster from Strongbow, and granted it back on condition of fealty, whilst Meath with Tara and eight hundred thousand acres was granted to DeLacy the chief justiciary. If the chiefs in putting faith in Henry's promise not to disturb their possessions expected to be protected from the rapacity of the adventurers, it was a fatal blunder, and they soon discovered their mistake. Dermod McCarthy, the aged king of

Desmond, whose territories were invaded by this formidable array, which he had no adequate force to resist, acknowledged Henry's supremacy. If in this disloyal to his country and its national independence, he was sufficiently punished, having been slain a few years later when nearly ninety, by Theobald Walter, at a friendly conference.

IV.

EARLY APPROPRIATIONS.

Dermot Mac Morrough died, as has been stated, the spring after the arrival of his English allies. He had given Fitzstephen, the city of Wexford, and made other liberal grants of territory. Upon his death Strongbow's claim to Leinster was of course disputed; it was contrary indeed to all law and precedent. Neither could Dermod give nor Eva take what belonged to the nation, and with their consent to the male representative of the McMorrough Cavanaghs, its hereditary chieftains. This vast domain, out of which many grants had also been made by Strongbow prior to his own death, six years later passed through Eva's daughter Isabel wife of William Marshal, earl of Pembroke, first in succession to her five sons, who each in turn became earl, married and died without issue, and afterwards was distributed in 1243 among her five daughters or their representatives. Carlow was assigned to the eldest, Maud, who married Mowbray duke of Norfolk, whose descendants never made good their claim against its Irish possessors. Joan carried Wexford, which seems to have reverted from Fitzstephen through Montchesney to William de Valence. With Isabel Kilkenny passed to the elder branch of the Clares, whilst through Sybil to William de Ferrers, earl of Derby, came Kildare, which went in 1290 through the De Vecies to that branch of the Fitzgeralds, created earls of Kildare, in

1316. Eva, who married William de Braose, had for her share Ossory, which through their daughter went to Lord Mortimer and merged two centuries later in the crown.

Meath, with its eight hundred thousand acres, given by King Henry to Hugh de Lacy, was subsequently divided by him into baronies, bestowed on his principal followers, Tyrrel, Petit, Fitzhenry, De l'Angle, Tuite, Chappel, Constantine, De Freigne, Nugent Nisset, Hussey, Dullard and Fleming. When slain in 1186, by an adherent of the dispossessed chieftain, his son Walter succeeded, and after Walter's death Meath went to his granddaughters, who had married De Genevil and De Verdon, and De Genevil's portion passed afterward through Roger Mortimer to the crown.

In direct violation of his agreement two years before with King Roderick, Henry at Oxford, in 1177, without any other pretext than his sovereign will and pleasure, gave Robert Fitzstephen and Milo De Cogan the kingdom of Cork, which belonged to the McCarthys. Of the millions of acres it contained, however, less than two hundred thousand, near Cork, was all of which they could then gain possession. Of his share of this, Robert Fitzstephen gave his nephew Philip de Barry, also descendant of Nesta, three cantreds or seventy-five thousand acres, which continued in Philip's line and name, ennobled as Viscounts Buttevant and earls of Barrymore, down to 1824. A year or two later De Cogan and his son-in-law, the son of Fitzstephen, were slain near Lismore by a chief of the Mac Tyres. Wexford, which Dermot McMurrough had given with the barony of Forth to Robert Fitzstephen on his landing in 1169, the king took away from him and bestowed it on Fitzadelm, ancestor of the De Burghs in Ireland.

No family connected with the English invasion, and the subsequent history of the island, is more renowned or more remarkable than that of the Geraldines springing from Nesta Tudor, princess of Wales. After attaching to her early maidenhood the affections of Henry the First, by whom she had two sons, Henry and Robert,

Nesta married Stephen, constable of the castles of Cardigan and Pembroke, by whom she had Robert Fitzstephen, who took a prominent part in the expedition into Ireland. She subsequently became the wife of Gilbert Fitzgerald, by whom she had three sons and a daughter. The eldest son, Maurice Fitzgerald, whose wife was Alice Montgomery, granddaughter of Morough O'Brien, king of Munster, formed also one of the company of Strongbow, his kinsman, and received from him what is now the county of Wicklow, then and for five centuries later the territory of the O'Byrns and O'Tooles, as also Naas and Offaly that of the O'Connors in Kildare. He received a few years afterward Connelloe, one hundred thousand acres in Limerick, the country of the O'Connels, who received an equivalent in Clare and Kerry, still possessed in part by their descendants, one of whom was the distinguished liberator. By marriage with the daughter of De Marisco, his third son, Thomas, acquired the territory of Wexford, and his grandson Decies and Dromenagh with the heiress of Fitz Anthony. His grandson Maurice married Margaret, daughter of De Burgh the third earl of Ulster, and was created, 1329, first earl of Desmond; his grandson the seventh earl bought of Robert de Cogan, half Desmond, part of Limerick, Waterford, Cork and Kerry, which was not, for John's gift at Oxford 1177, any more his to sell; and Gerald the sixteenth, four generations later, when slain in 1583, had nearly six hundred thousand acres in Munster to forfeit to the crown, to become the spoil of adventurers. Offshoots from this line, knights of Glynn and the Valley, Kerry and Fitzgibbon, of Dromanagh and Imokilly, and many more, held also vast domains in Munster, acquired by inheritance or marriage. From William the brother of the first Maurice descended Raymond le Gros, a distinguished commander, whose wife was Basilia, sister of Strongbow and widow of Robert de Quincy, and whose two sons were respectively the progenitors of the earls of Kerry, and the family of Grace. William received, besides Idrone, Fethard and Glascarrig, a large domain in

Kilkenny, which, transmitted by him to his second son, was long known as Grace's country. A tract of territory in Kerry given to Raymond by Dermot McCarthy, for aid in reducing to obedience his son Cormac, who disapproved of his father's acknowledging fealty to the English king, has been for seven centuries the estate of the Fitzmaurices, barons and earls of Kerry and marquises of Lansdowne. From William, the eldest son of Maurice, derived the lords of Naas in Leinster, ending in an heiress, who married David de Londres; while from Gerald the second, sprang the lords of Offaly, of whom one married the heiress of Rheban in Kildare, and another, receiving in 1291 a grant from King Edward, of that country, forfeited by De Vecies, was created, as before mentioned, in 1316 earl of Kildare, one of the titles of the present duke of Leinster, his representatives and their line having ever since possessed them.

Anghared, sister of Maurice and daughter of Nesta, became the wife of William de Barry, father by her of Gerald Cambrencis, the earliest English writer of note on Ireland, and of Philip, who as above stated receiving three cantreds of land in Munster from his uncle Fitzstephen founded the house of Barrys, viscounts of Buttevant and earls of Barrymore. The matrimonial alliances of the different branches of the Geraldines with the families of the Milesian chiefs materially strengthened the hold of the British crown. On the island they made common cause with the O'Briens and McCarthys, in opposition to any encroachments attempted on their independence from beyond the channel, were often themselves in rebellion, yet ever interposed an insuperable obstacle to any general and well organized plan of operations by which the British yoke could be shaken off.

John de Courcy and Amory St. Lawrence, brothers-in-law, also joined the company of adventurers, sworn brothers also, like D'Oilly and D'Ivry of Oxford, in the Norman conquest of England, to divide their spoils. They first attacked Ulidia, consisting of Down and Antrim, and later penetrated into other parts of Ulster, but after much hard fighting were driven out in 1178, by the O'Neils and their kindred chieftains. A few years afterward, however, after his marriage with Africa, daughter of Godred, king of Man, in 1182, De Courcy was in a measure more successful, and in consequence was created earl of Ulster. He died about 1229, but long before King John bestowed the province and earldom on Hugh de Lacy, second son of the justiciary, whose wife was King Roderick O'Connor's daughter, and they passed with Maud, the daughter of Hugh, to Walter de Burgh descended from Fitz-adelmn, head of that house in Ireland who had acquired extensive tracts in Connaught through or by marriage with a daughter of another O'Connor. By the marriage of the heiress of the De Burghs to Lionel, duke of Clarence, son of Edward the Third, these passed to Mortimer, his son-in-law, vesting finally in the crown, and among the royal titles that of earl of Ulster and that of Connaught are still preserved.

As some compensation for the lost earldom of Ulster, given to De Lacy, Milo son of John de Courcy was made lord of Kinsale in the south of Munster, both land and title having ever since been retained in the line of his descendants, of whom the present is the thirtieth viscount. John's companion, Amory St. Lawrence, was created lord of Howth, and for seven centuries his representatives have retained that title, now an earldom, and the estate then granted to their progenitors. A niece of St. Lawrence was wife to Roger le Poer, one of the most valiant of Strongbow's company, and their posterity with various fortunes, but generally prosperous, long ruled over Curraghmore, or Powers country in the county of Waterford, and were created earls of Tyrone in 1673, the third, who died in 1704, being the last. The De Prendergasts have ever been among the most honored races in Ireland, highly esteemed and connected. Barnwell was also one of the early invaders : his descendants obtained later a grant from the crown of Bearehaven, belonging to the O'Sullivans, who rose and destroyed them utterly, only a mother quick with child being spared. The O'Sullivans at about the time of the invasion, finding their possessions imperilled at Knoc Graffon, Tipperary, in the east of Munster, removed to the country about the Bay of Bantry, Bearehaven, Glanerought, Iveragh and Dunkerron in the southwest, and there among mountains almost inaccessible for four centuries remained substantially undisturbed and independent.

The rise and long continued power and prosperity of the Butlers in Ireland, has generally been supposed to have originated in the remorse of Henry the Second at the assassination of Thomas à Becket, whose disposition to subject the king to his ecclesiastical domination had provoked resentment. The sister of Becket was the wife of Theobald Walter, and to make amends he was appointed by that monarch Butler of Ireland, with prisage of all wines imported, he himself and his descendants taking their name from this office. Upon them valuable tracts of land were bestowed, which belonged to Carrols, Kennedys, Meaghers, Sheas, Donnellys, Fogartys, Ryans, in Kilkenny and Tipperary, and among these also Knoc Graffon. Their estates stretched from the Barrow to Lake Derg, and different branches of the name received titles of rank from the crown to which they were generally loyal in reducing Ireland to subjection. They were created lords of Carrick and Galmoy, viscounts Dunboyne, earls and dukes of Ormond, the greater part of their territory being forfeited in 1714, from the preference of the last duke for the house of Stuart to that of Brunswick.

The name of Burke is even more extensively multiplied than that of Fitzgerald. If not tracing their origin directly to Nesta, their founder married the mother of King William the Conqueror, Arlotta of the inn. Richard the Great, his descendant, had for wife Una, daughter of Hugh, son of King Roderick; and his son, Maud, daughter of Hugh de Lacy, earl of Ulster, by a granddaughter as before mentioned of another king of Connaught. The gr. gr. grandson, third or red earl, left for his heir a granddaughter, Elizabeth, who marrying the duke of Clarence, carried the title of earl of Ulster and lord of Connaught to the crown. When Phillippa Plantagenet,

4

daughter of this Elizabeth De Burgh and granddaughter of Edward the Third, married about 1360, Edward Mortimer, third earl of March and gr. gr. grandfather of Edward the Fourth, their united possessions according to English law covered the province of Ulster, and half of Connaught, her inheritance, half of Meath which had come to him through the marriage of his gr. grandfather with Joan de Genevil, granddaughter of Hugh de Lacy, and portions of Leinster and Munster, Ossory and Kilkenny from that of a more remote ancestor still, Hugh de Mortimer with Annora daughter of William de Braose. Theirs were, however, for the most part mere nominal titles, for they had hardly an acre of this territory in peaceable possession, and their son Roger, fourth earl, who inherited with this vast domain forty thousand marks ready money, and who was sent as lord lieutenant into Ireland, was treacherously slain there in 1398 by his own countrymen. Several generations earlier, Carthal O'Connor had been forced to yield extensive territory in Connaught, to the De Burghs his kinsmen, and on the death of the third earl this was taken possession of by the male representatives of the family, who giving up the name of De Burgh, for a while assumed the designation of Mac William Eighter of Galway, or Clan Richard, from whom derive the earls and marquises of Clanrickard, and Mac William Oughter, from whom proceeded the earls of Mayo. Another branch of the name were lords of Castle Connel and Brittas. Identified with the Milesian races by these matrimonial alliances, common interests and habits of life, as also by their language, they could often be of service to them by their support in perilous conjunctures. They became to all intents Irishmen, and probably in blood represent to-day equally their Norman and Milesian progenitors.

Ten has been usually stated as the number of principal leaders in the invasion, amongst whom Henry II. at Oxford in 1129 divided the island; and Sir John Davis, in his Historical Relations, enumerates Strongbow, Robert Fitz Stephen, Miles de Cogan, Philip de Braose, Sir Hugh de Lacy, Sir John Courcy, William Fitz

Adelmn, Sir Thomas de Clare, Robert le Poer, and Otho de Grandison as the favored individuals. The grant of Tipperary to the last mentioned, took place a century later, when the eminent crusader of the name returned with the first Edward from Jerusalem. Whether then or earlier, after passing through several of his representatives, the estate vested, 49 Edward III., in females. Any supposed grant of Thomond to Thomas de Clare at Oxford, would be an anachronism. If the best known of the name is intended, the son of the sixth earl of Hertford who married Amy daughter of the ancestor of the earls of Desmond, then called Fitz Gerald as his descendants afterwards, he took advantage of a family quarrel for the chieftainship of the O'Briens to gain possession, under his grant, of the northerly portion of Thomond called Clare, from his thus possessing it, and there about 1280, erected several strongholds and castles, among them Bunratty, where he dwelt and his sons afterwards. Early in the reign of Edward the First, he had been appointed governor of London, and appears to have been a favorite with the great Plantagenet. The Leinster estates which came to his grandfather, the fifth earl, with Isabel one of the five heiresses of Pembroke and which were then vested in Gilbert his elder brother, led probably to his connection with Ireland, and to his procuring this grant of Thomond. It was not a fortunate acquisition. His career there was stormy and violent, an incessant warfare. He showed a crafty, cruel and rapacious disposition, and the murder of his ally Brian, from jealousy or disappointment, was a crime without extenuating circumstances. His death and that of Fitzgerald occurred in 1286. His two eldest sons, Gilbert and Richard, left no issue, the latter and his son being both slain on the same battle field, in 1217, when the family of de Clare, burning Bunratty, left Thomond never to return. Margaret and Maud, daughters of Thomas, the third son, carried to their husbands, Lord Clifford and Lord Badlesmere, a barren inheritance, for the Dalgas resumed possession of their lands and have kept, if not all, large portions to a recent day.

The kingdom of Limerick had been bestowed upon Philip de Braose, of Brecnock, who not willing to brave the perils attending forced occupation of territory in possession of fierce and hostile septs disposed to dispute his pretensions, transferred his claims to his son William. In consequence of a quarrel with King John for murdering certain Welchmen, the wife and son of William were starved to death at Windsor, he himself escaping into France, where he died. His nephew William married Eva, daughter of the earl of Pembroke, and received for her share of Leinster, Leix and Ossory, the claim to which passed with their daughter and heiress to Lord Mortimer, but no claim was ever made to Limerick under this grant, which leads to the conclusion that it was forfeited when William fled into France.

Hervey de Monte Marisco, brother to the first earl of Pembroke and uncle of the son-in-law of Dermot McMorrogh, was one of the principal leaders in the invasion of the English forces and received his share of the spoils in Wexford. His wife was Nesta, daughter of Maurice Fitzgerald. After twenty years of activity, not attended with much success, or redounding to his glory, he parcelled out his estates, in part among his followers, retaining as was usual his signorial rights, and consecrated large portions of what remained, by gift, to the convent of Dunbrody, which he had erected, and of which he was the abbot. His nephew Jeffrey was lord lieutenant in 1215, and his descendants continued to flourish down to 1491. In the history of the Montmorencies Hervey is called constable of that house.

When in 1004, Brian Boroihme ordered the clans to adopt surnames, it was in consequence no doubt of some necessity specially felt at the time. Other European nations were gradually introducing this convenient usage, but it was of slow growth, and among the Normans and Saxons was far from being general. Even much later, several of the principal families of England were still designated in the ancient mode, and it was not for some years that Fitzstephen, Fitzgerald, or Fitzmaurice, about the time of Henry the Second, became family names. Thomas Fitz Anthony was an instance of a distinguished personage of wealth and power and large landed possessions of whose origin nothing is known. He was lord of Decies and Desmond, and held lands in Kilkenny. Four of his daughters married, their husbands being Gerald Roche, Jeffery de Norragh, Stephen Archdeken, and John Fitz Thomas. In one of the discontents against Henry III. for bringing over French nobles into England, the earl marshal took sides against the king. Orders were sent to the Fitzgeralds, De Lacies, Richard de Braose and Jeffery de Marisco to waste his lands and secure his person, whereupon all the son-in-laws of Fitz Anthony, except Fitzgerald, took part with the earl. In 1260 Fitzgerald applied to Edward, then lord of Ireland, for the shares of his brothers-in-law in the succession of Fitz Anthony, and Decies, Desmond and Dungarvan with other lands were so granted and constituted part of the territory forfeited by his descendant, the earl of Desmond, in 1583.

On Maurice Prendergast, one of the first to land upon the island, Strongbow bestowed Fernenegal, near Wexford, with lands besides in Kinsellagh. His son Philip had for wife Maude daughter of Robert de Quincy, who was slain by O'Dempsy in Ofaly, and who had been the first husband of Basilia, Strongbow's sister, afterwards the wife of Raymond Fitzmaurice. Of Philip's granddaughters, coheiresses of his son Gerald, Mary married John de Cogan, and Matilda, Maurice de Rochefort. William, brother of Gerald, before 1244, held valuable possessions in Iffa and Offa, in Tipperary, as also the barony of New-castle, and his descendants gaining many accessions along the Suir retained them till 1653, when driven into Connaught or across the sea.

Strongbow gave William de Birmingham Carbry in Ofaly, whose descendant John was made baron of Athenry and earl of Louth for killing Edward Bruce. To Hugh de Roche, he gave the cantred Roches country in Cork, which with accessions continued in that family, well connected by marriage, till viscount Fermoy was dispos-

sessed by Cromwell. The representatives of Archibald Fleming,
lords of Slane, Plunkets later barons of Dunsany, Killeen, Louth
and earls of Fingal, Nettervilles intermarrying with Lacies and
Veseys, viscounts Louth, Walshes, lords of Oldcourt, Dublin, one
of whom gained glory in crossing the Shannon under Raymond le
Gros, Aylmers and Whytes, in Kildare; Herberts, Colbys, Moors,
in Kings; Wale and Carew in Carlow; Devereux, Sinnott, Chee-
ver, Hore in Wexford; Louth, Foresters, Comerfords in Kilkenny;
Talbots of Malahide, Tyrrels of Castleknock, Warrens of Cordiff,
Luttrells, Ushers, Purcells, in Dublin; Husseys, barons of Galtrim,
Everards, Garlands, Griffins, Ivers, Allens, Cussacks, Garvys,
D'Altons, in Meath; Hurleys, Chases, Supples, in Limerick; Ver-
dons, Tates, Clintons, Dowdals, Gernons, Waltons, Brandons,
Moors, Chamberlains, in Louth; Russells, Anthonys, Savages,
Riddells, Mandevills, Jordans, Stantons, Copelands, in Down, are
all well-known names connected with the early days of English rule
in Ireland, and nearly all of them common here.

Camden also mentions as in the country, from the twelfth
to the sixteenth centuries, Wolwastons, Peppards, Wallaces,
Blacks, Redmonds, Esmonds, Chattans, Tobins, Allens, Gennits,
Wades, Sweetmans, Grants, Archers, Rochefords, Datons, Rothes,
Wares, Purfields, Smiths, Cooks, Hooks, Dens, in Leinster; Condons, Nagles, Morris, Keating, Johns, Pierce, Cummings, Rice,
Lombard, Tallon, Gold, Baggot, Skiddy, Coppenger, Porter, Denny, Terry, Gough, Picket, Dondon, Waters, Wolfe, in Munster;
Blake, French, Bodkin, Martin, Crofton, in Galway. These names
are multiplied in America, and mentioned as a help to students of
family history. At what precise period or under what circumstances
they originally settled in Ireland cannot in all cases be ascertained.
The family of Dillon created barons of Kilkenny and earls of Roscommon in 1622, and viscounts of Castle gillen in 1621, derive from
Hugh Slaine of the O'Neills monarch of Ireland in the sixth century. After being settled manifold generations in Aquitaine, they

came back to Ireland in the person of Henry secretary to King John. It would be vain to attempt to enumerate the families of adventurers and undertakers established in the island in periods comparatively modern, and there is not the same object.

V.

EXTENT OF POSSESSION.

These grants from Dermot. Strongbow, Henry, or his immediate successors, to the feudatories above mentioned, covering nearly the whole island, had neither by Brehon nor feudal law the slightest validity. If might makes right, if " they may take who have the power, and they may keep who can," if overrunning neighboring states by superior military power and confiscating private property, could rightly or justly affect its title, neither by conquest, submission nor continued possession by common, feudal, or Brehon law, as respects three fourths of Ireland, was it transferred before the seventeenth century. Parchments under royal seals could neither create nor transmit title which the grantor had not to bestow. Neither king of Leinster, Connaught, nor Desmond, could give or sell to strangers what belonged not to themselves, but to their clans. These gifts from Henry, after fealty accepted from Dermod and Roderick with its well known obligations and solemn pledges not to disturb their rights or those of the chiefs of the clans under them, were simply acts of perfidy, entitled " *in foro conscientiæ*," or by the rules of eternal justice, to no effect or consideration whatsoever.

Outside the pale consisting of portions of what are now Dublin, Kildare, Lowth and Meath, and the ports of Wexford, Waterford, Cork and Dundalk, or where Geraldines, Butlers, De Courcys, Powers and Roches in Munster, or Burkes in Connaught, were allied by marriage to Milesian families, and more Irish than the Irish them-

selves, in repugnance to English rule, with many interests in common,
speaking the same language and wearing the same dress, the clans
under their chieftains retained their ancient possessions, rarely paid tribute, much more often exacted it, were governed by their own Brehon
laws, retained their own usages, and instead of assimilating to the
English, it was the constant complaint of the English statutes, state
papers and works on Ireland, that the English assimilated to them.
Before the eleventh century, as already mentioned, surnames were
not customary any where, and it is reasonable to presume the Irish
adopted them slowly. The previous mode of distinguishing individuals by the line of ancestors in three or four generations by
christian names often led to embarrassment, especially as certain giv-
en names were of constant recurrence in particular families, and the
surname itself had originally been of this character. Mac and O
indicating descent, the strangers resorted to similar forms to render
less conspicuous their English origin. In the fourteenth century, the
De Burghs assumed the name of Mac William, Mac Hubbard and
Mac David; Berminghams took the name of Mac Yoris, Dexters
that of Mac Jordan, Nangles of Mac Costello, one of the Butlers,
Mac Pheris, and the White Knight, Fitzgibbon.

With these precautions taken in order that they might possess
their lands without disturbance from Milesian chiefs or English governors, though active lord lieutenants, deputies or justices made occasional forays out of the " pale " and by concentration of forces were
able to slaughter and despoil, after the first century of invasion to
the reign of Queen Elizabeth not one fourth part of Ireland was
in the possession of the English race. The victories of the Milesian
chiefs were as frequent as theirs. These chiefs were constantly on
the defensive against the evident design to appropriate their lands
and reduce them to subjection. They did what they could under
many discouragements and jealousies, constantly breaking out into
embittered warfare. Accumulation of capital, or its application to
agriculture or the useful arts, the pursuit of learning beyond what

could be obtained from the priests and monks, comfortable houses or garments, or many other appliances of civilization which Englishmen are apt to mistake for civilization itself, were not possible in the presence of the despoiler.

The clans tended their flocks and herds, raised their own corn, pursued the game with which the woods abounded. Religious, social and fond of music and similar recreations, and frequently at war among themselves, or with the English, the life they led was better fitted to make them brave, self-sacrificing and generous, quick-witted and wise, than one such as is commonly called industrious. The numerous beautiful castles erected by Irish chieftains, superb conventual establishments they founded, now mouldering all over Ireland with dilapidated walls mantled with ivy, testify to their taste and resources, to their devotion and determination to preserve their independence. If constantly in arms, punctilious and quick to resent aggression or insult or to espouse the quarrels of their neighbors, their history overruns with sanguinary conflicts, it was the part of wisdom, while so powerful a nation as the English occupied the sea-board, while fortresses about the island menaced their liberties and the security of their possessions, and they were themselves prevented by the disturbing presence and influence of a restless and treacherous foe from any national consolidation, to encourage wars which educated their people to resistance.

In the early part of the fourteenth century Edward Bruce, after conquering at the head of the Irish clans the English in sixteen battles, at last was slain. Ormond and Kildare, rivals for power, for two centuries after divided the pale with their disputes. In Munster, near Cork and Waterford, Fitzgeralds earls of Desmond, Roches, Coureys and Barrys occupied strong holds, while McCarthies kings of Desmond and their kindred chiefs bore actual sway. In Connaught, the O'Connors, O'Briens, Burkes, Macnamaras and McMahons, intermarried or fought. Meath and Leinster were incessantly traversed by armed men going to battle or maraud. Ulster kept

5

out the stranger for a time, but Scots crept in from across the channel or from the isles, McDonnels settling in Antrim, marrying O'Donnels and O'Neils. The government at the castle was at times severe or lax. Usurpation was as often requited by reward as punishment. Whatever authority England possessed was employed by the factions which chanced to be uppermost, York or Lancaster, Geraldine or Butler, to wrest more land from its previous owners, the welfare of the people or security of the state being secondary considerations to individual aggrandizement.

But still Ireland was Irish. Four centuries had made no more impression than the tide upon the shore. Ireland had cost the English treasury many times its revenues to keep Geraldines, Burkes and Butlers in their possessions, but still remained the weakness and embarrassment of England, and often curiously its reproach. It is sad to think that Surry's advice had not been taken. Had Ireland been left to the Irish, as Scotland to the Scots of the same original stock, the people, enjoying the same rights and privileges as Englishmen, would have soon sought, for mutual strength and protection, a union with the sister island. Irishmen, lords of their own soil, masters of their own destinies, and not tenants and bondsmen to strangers, would have become the honor and safety of the united realm; with education, the arts and refinements of life, industry and its developments, with religious liberty and toleration, they would have been in Ireland what they have proved themselves here, an intelligent, thrifty, law-abiding, patriotic, brave, generous and noble-hearted people; they would have vindicated their claim to be possessors of that best blessing of Providence, self-government which they have learned by sad experience at home how to enjoy in their adopted country.

VI.

HOMES OF THE SEPTS.

In order to understand the gradual transfer of ownership in the soil from the races in possession at the time of the invasion, before pursuing further the course of events that brought that transfer about, we must consider the geographical distribution of the clans of whom the population consisted. There have been times not very remote when researches in this direction might well have suggested suspicion of ulterior purpose: but it is not so now. Laws of limitation both for rights and wrongs are everywhere recognized as indispensable to public tranquillity, and the actual tenures are too intimately interwoven with the whole social structure for any pretention to disturb them. Without apprehension of misconstruction, whatever in this department of Irish lore can be turned to account to elucidate our subject is collected here for convenient reference. The authorities consulted if within reach of diligent inquirers are not equally accessible to all who feel an interest in their progenitors.

The districts occupied by the forty one Scotch clans three centuries ago have been recently mapped. For reasons sufficiently obvious there, not only the clans but the chieftains, in modified relations, continue to exist in their present representatives. In Ireland, from circumstances reflecting no discredit upon the chiefs who from fidelity to principle have been divested, the old race remains under unlineal lords. New conditions and bounds have effaced the ancient landmarks, but the same names familiar for centuries in their respective neighborhoods are still extensively multiplied. Rarely elsewhere can be found in these days more distinctly marked traces of that patriarchal system common to the early stages of social development, for the study of whoever is interested in human progress. In many parts of Ireland not even the incessant strife of ages or disturbing elements of industry and improvement in the arts have wholly removed them, though they have materially affected the character and modes of life.

Keating, the Four Masters, M'Geoghan, following the ancient
annals all place the arrival of Heremon and Heber more than ten
centuries before the christian era.   This great antiquity is disputed
by Woods and other English writers, but no good reason is advanced
to shake the probability of a period very remote.   In other lands
at corresponding epochs, legends too precious to be discarded inasmuch as if not true they are founded upon truth and point the
way to it, have been handed down by tradition or preserved in such
records as they had.   Tigernach in 1080 dated the earliest authentic
Irish history to which implicit credence could be accorded as three
centuries before Christ when Cymbaoth erected the palace of Emania,
near Armagh.   But before the colony from Spain, Firbolgs, whose
nine Kings from Slainge to Eochaid and Tuatha de Danaans, whose
eighteen from Nuadat to 2737 A.M. over two centuries ruled over
the land, were numerous and their posterity variously intermingled
are still represented in the present population.   Keating enumerates
three families known in his day as derived from the former, Gad-
braigh, Tairsigh, and Galvin.   Cromwells notion of hedging in the
conquered in Connaught was not original with him for there what
remained of the two previously subjugated nations had been rele-
gated by the Milesians.   They long remained as distinct communities till Muradach of the race of Heremon, one of whose grandsons
Brian was the progenitor of the Hy Brunes consisting of O'Connors,
Rourks, Reileys, Malleys, Flynns and kindred septs, and another
Fergus of O'Dowds, Shaughnessies, Clerys and others, was in the
fourth century the first king of Connaught after defeating the Clan
Morna warriors of the Firbolgs.   Conqueror and conquered intermingled, and both alike represented in the present inhabitants.

The early divisions of the island by Partholan, Nennins, and the
Firbolgs gave way to lines agreed upon by Heremon and Heber, to
the former of whom was assigned Leinster, and to the other Munster.
To the son of their brother Ir, drowned off the Skelligs in disembarking, was given Ulster and the Clan Rory, his descendants,

held it undisturbed till the fourth century, when the sons of Neal
the Great wrested away the larger part of it. To the descendants
of Ith uncle of Milesius, slain by the Tuatha de Danaans whilst on a
friendly visit to the island, and to revenge whose death his nephews
came over from Spain, a district was allotted on the southerly shore
of Cork, about Baltimore, where under the name of Driscolls they
are still to be found. Ugaine the Great, three centuries before Christ,
divided the island into twenty-five principalities, the names and
boundaries of which are little known unless they are in a few instances the same which from beyond memory have attached to certain
districts.

Tuathal in the first century taking a portion from the other provinces had set it apart for the special domain of the monarchs. It
did not long, as we have seen, remain inviolate. Near its easterly
bound was Tara where the chiefs and kings often assembled for conference and legislation, as they did at Tailtan for annual games
after the manner of the Greeks, attracting a large concourse of all
ages and conditions, and the occasion it is said was improved by the
chiefs who were much given to diplomacy in forming matrimonial
alliances for their children. Munster was divided by Oliol Olum in
the second century between Owen and Cormac Cas, the former receiving Desmond, the latter Thomond while Kian a third son was
provided elsewhere. The Keniads posterity of Kien embraced the
Carrols of Ossory, Meaghers of Kilkenny, Haras, Garas, Hen-
nessys, Caseys, Conors of Derry dispossesred by the Kanes, Breens
of Lune, Flanagans, Corcorans of Cleenish in Fermanagh, Lough-
lans of Moggalion in Meath and Clankee in Cavan.

VII.

SUBDIVISIONS OF THE ISLAND.

It was one of the prerogatives of the king and chiefs to bestow surnames on those subject to their rule. These may have exceeded two or three hundred in all. The number of Chieftainries was much more limited, computed variously at from sixty to a hundred and eighty-five. These subdivisions varied with the vicissitudes of war, marriage or inheritance. The whole island was divided into sixty-six thousand six hundred ploughlands estimated to average about one hundred Irish acres each.

As usually computed allowance being made for land less productive, one Irish acre was about equal in area to two English, but the more approximate difference is about two-fifths more for the Irish, or as twenty to twelve. This difference proceeds more legitimately from an Irish rod of long measure being equal to seven yards, the English to five and a half. But there is another embarrassment in estimating the extent of a plantation acre when mentioned in historical works. In grants from the crown, the quantity of prime or good land within certain bounds, or embraced in certain denominations was alone estimated, all less valuable thrown in. Under color of his grant of blackacre, whatever of whiteacre or inferior soil the patentee by force or fraud could appropriate, he was permitted to hold, and his title thereto confirmed and quieted. The average area thus passed has been estimated as high as thrice the quantity actually expressed in the grant. It was not before the seventeenth century that surveys were made on which any dependence could be placed, and then it is easy to see how deceptive they must have proved.

County lines established at different periods by the English, as they extended their rule, corresponded generally to the boundaries now existing. King John created twelve counties, Dublin, Kildare, Meath, Louth, Carlow, Wexford, Kilkenny, Waterford, Cork, Limerick, Kerry and Tipperary. 34 Henry VIII. Meath was divid-

ed in to two counties, the westerly portion becoming West Meath; and
the land of the O'Byrnes, before part of the county of Dublin, Wicklow. 3 Philip and Mary, Leix and part adjacent after the O'Moores
had been subdued, were formed into Queens; Offaly with part of
Glenmalire into Kings. In 1565 out of Annaly was made the county
of Longford by Sir Henry Sydney, who divided Connaught into Galway, Sligo, Mayo, Roscommon and Leitrim. Clare, before a part
of Munster, was added to Connaught in 1602 at the request of the
earl of Thomond. Ulster was divided in 1584 into the shires of
Armagh, Monaghan, Tyrone, Coleraine, now Londonderry, Donegal, Fermanagh and Cavan. Earlier mention is made of Down and
Antrim. Besides these thirty-two counties, the cities of Dublin and
Cork were separate shires. For centuries these lines were of
little significance. English authority was confined to the Pale as
it was first called under the Tudors. It embraced portions of Dublin, Louth, Meath and Kildare, extending along shore from Dundalk to Dalkey eight miles south of the Liffy and inland to Ardee,
Kells, Castletown—Delvin, Athboy, Trim, Maynooth and thence to
Clane and Ballymore—Eustace.*

County courts were established wherever protected by military
force; but their jurisdiction could not be sustained even over the
king's subjects. Against English rebels or Irish enemies his writ
was powerless. The former lords enumerated under Henry the
Eighth, as thirty-one in number held their courts palatine, baron or
leet, administering common and statute law, or in the Marches,
where both races dwelt, these combined with the ancient law of the
land and usages growing out of existing need. The latter acknowledged no authority or control over them except that of their chiefs,

---

* 1515. 6 Henry VIII. State Papers. Part III. Vol. II., pp. 9-22. The English
Pale doth stretch and extend from the town of Dundalk to the town of Dervor, to the
town of Ardye, always on the left side, leaving the marche on the right side, and so on to
the town of Sydan, to the town of Dengle, to Kylcoke, to the town of Clanne, to the town
of Nasse, the bridge of Kilcullen, to the town of Ballymore, and so backwards to the
town of Ramore, to the town of Rathenoo, to the town of Tallaght, and to the town of
Dalkey, leaving the march always on the right hand, from the said Dundalk, following the
said course to the said town of Dalkey.

were governed by their own laws enforced by their own tribunals. These independent chieftainries were, at that time, set down as fifty-eight in all : nine in Ulster, ten in Leinster, nine in Desmond, twelve in Thomond, fifteen in Connaught and three in the western part of Meath then not divided. English process, in a language few understood, if served no one obeyed, and levies where attempted on their cattle provoked reprisal on the nearest English families whose herds were exposed and resentment was only quieted in blood. This arbitrary exercise of power confused every distinction of right, and if in later days property in Ireland has been less inviolate, it is simply the poisoned chalice returned to the lips that sent it.

In the general view now proposed of the geographical distribution of the septs, an approximation to exactness can alone be attempted. If incomplete or occasionally incorrect, it may still afford some guidance amidst the perplexities of a difficult subject. In some instances the name may have become extinct in the locality designated, in more only to be discovered under circumstances greatly reduced. Dispossession, pursuit of employment, increased facilities of intercourse, have carried many into exile, or to other parts of the island. In great cities and larger towns nearly every Irish name may be represented. But generally numerous branches remain in their original neighborhoods, and by assigning each family group to the province and county where they formerly flourished, some idea may be formed of the dwelling places of them all at the time their possessions respectively passed to the stranger.

VIII.

ANCIENT FAMILIES OF LEINSTER AND MEATH.

The southeast corner of the island betwen the Barrow and the sea was the special domain of the Cavanaghs, and Fernes about twenty miles north of Wexford the early residence of the McMorroghs their chieftains, princes of Hy Kinsellagh and kings of Leinster. Along the easterly shore were Larkins chiefs of Forth, Murphys of Hy Felimy or Ballaghkeen, Doyles, McKeoghs, Dowlings of Ballynacor, Garveys, Horans, Cullen; and inland Ryans of Idrone, Cosgrys of Bantry, Nolans of Forth and Gahans lords of Shillelagh in Carlow. In Wicklow near the vale of Avoca and Glendalough were the O'Byrnes of Ranelagh, Newcastle and Arklow, and farther north and west O'Tooles of Fercular and Imaile, Kilkea and Moone. In Kildare were the O'Connors of Offaly, Carys of Carberry, Colgans of Ikeathy, Dunns of Great Connel, Murrigans of Moyliffy, Cullens of Kilcullen, Kellys of Reeban and Norragh. In Kilkenny dwelt Brodars of Iverk, Bolgers of Ida, Donaghoes of Knocktopher, Sheas of Shillelogher, Brennans of Idough. In Queens were O'Moores of Leix, Fitzpatricks of Ossory, Carrols of Ely; and in Kings, Dunns of Hy Regan, Molloys of Fercal, Mooneys of Garrycastle, O'Dempseys lords, viscounts and barons of Clanmalier. About Dublin the Danes had held for many years before the English invasion exclusive possession, so that nearer than Bray to the south where the O'Tooles retained their ascendancy few septs remained. North of the city Kellys of Bregia, and in Louth Carrols of Orgiel, Heas of Slane, Rorys of Moygallion, Branagans, and both north and south the MacGiollamholmoges of Cualan were at times formidable when allied to septs more remote.

Of the Meaths the McLaghlins of royal race were kings long after the invasion. or were recognized as sovereigns by their ancient sub-

6

ordinates. Their chief seat was early near Tara, but later farther west. The system adopted by De Lacy in subdividing his domains amongst his principal followers weakened the power of the chieftains, but the Connollys of Navan, Dunns of Lune, Finelans of Delvin, Kearnys of Fore, McGeoghans of Tertullagh and Moycashil, O'Ferrals of Annaly, Quins of Rathcline in Longford, Hennesseys of Moygoish, Higgins of Usneach, Tolargs near Athlone, Hanrahans of Corcaree, McCoghlins of Delvin Ara, were ready when occasion offered to assert their rights.

Besides the names already mentioned are many others, branches of Cahir More of the race of Heremon, whose posterity supplied the principal dynasties to Leinster and many monarchs and roydammas to the throne of Ireland. Many of them were distinct septs, subsequently dispossessed and dispersed among their neighbors. Others long retained their lands and independence, subject only to the more powerful chieftains. Heelys, Loughmans, Callans of Ormond; Gormans, Dorans, Lawlors and Dowlings in Queens; Brehans, Coghlans, Hartys, Bergins in Kings; McDonnels in Kildare, Deignans in Longford, Sculleys, Coffeys and Dooleys were at times of note, though not, it is believed, as important as the rest.

Within the bounds of these two more central provinces, besides some remnants of Danish race and name and a larger infusion than anywhere else of English, there are naturally to be found representatives of nearly every sept and family of the island, attracted to the neighborhood of the capital and its busy marts. Of thirty-six hundred thousand acres in Leinster three-fourths are under cultivation, of the nine hundred and fifty thousand in the Meaths less than one twelfth are mountain or bog. The climate is excessively moist, the yield in grass and grain heavy, and markets are at hand. The former province constituted the territory which Dermot McMorrogh instigated by resentment offered with Eva to Strongbow; the latter what Henry the Second bestowed on De Lacy his justiciary.

IX.

ANCIENT FAMILIES OF ULSTER.

This province, embracing what now constitutes the counties of Donegal, Londonderry, Tyrone, Antrim, Down, Fermanagh, Armagh, Monaghan and Cavan, was assigned to Heber Don, son of Ir, the brother of Heremon and Heber. There his posterity the Clan Rory* long dwelt, some of them passing away or finding abodes in other parts of the island. They gave twenty-five kings to Ireland. Cearmne and Sobhänce A.M. 2870, who reigned forty years, dividing the island between them by a line from Drogheda to Limerick, the latter having his residence at Dun Patrick. Olla Fodhla, an author and lawgiver of renown, who reorganized the administration of the government and established or revived the triennial assemblages at Tara; Ciombath 3539 who erected the palace of Emania at Armagh, which work his wife Macha, of a bold and enterprising genius, who ruled over and after him, would seem to have completed; Roderick the Great 3402; Fachtna the wise 3470; Mal. 109, and Caobdoch 550, were of most note. Thirty-five of this race were kings of Ulster, among whom Connor established or renovated the Red Branch Knights of Emania, one of three orders then existing in the island, the other two being in Connaught and Munster. The Clan Rory lost their supremacy in Ulster, in the third and fourth centuries, when two sons of Neil the Great of the race of Heremon, Owen from whom descended the O'Neils, Keans, MacSweenys, Donnellies of Tyrone, and Conal from whom descended the O'Donnels, O'Dohertys, O'Galaghers, Boyles

---

* The Rudricians, as the posterity of Ir were also called, consisted of the families of M'Guinnis, M'Carthan, More, Cronnelly, Dugan, Moran, Lennan, Corsan, M'Gowan or Smith, M'Ward, M'Scanlan, Kenny, Lawlor, Lynch, Mannion, Maginn, M'Colreavy or Gray, Carolan, Connor Core and Kerry, Loghlin of Burren, Kirby, Shanly, M'Brien, Ferral, Roddy, Gaynor, M'Cormack, M'Dorchy, M'Raghneils or Reynolds, Quinn, Mulvey, Conary, Diochalla, M'Keogh, Beice, M'Machisas, M'Rory or Rogers, Corca-Dallan, Corca-Antim, Dal-Confinn, Ciarruighe, Cinal-Brine, Gailenge, Liodan, Drennon and Duan.

and O'Dalys dispossessed them, and for more than twelve hundred
years retained their hold of the country.

This event deserves to be borne in mind, marking an interesting
epoch and serving as a starting point in unravelling many perplexities. Besides Owen and Conal, Neil, who was slain in 405 after a
prosperous and brilliant reign of twenty-seven years, had Carbrei
ancestor of that sept in Sligo, and Ende of Tir-Enda, in Donegal and
Meath. From these four sons proceeded the northern Hy Nials,
whilst from Laogaire the first christian monarch, ancestor of the
Kindellans in Meath, Conal Crimthan of the Melaghlins, Feacha of
the Macgeoghans and Molloys, and Maine of the Caharnys, Breens
and Magawleys, were derived the southern. From Laogaire to
Malachi, deposed by Brian Boru, the former branch gave twenty-six
monarchs to the island, the latter nineteen. To prevent jealousies it
was provided that these two branches should fill the throne alternately, the successor or roydamna being selected when the king was installed, a ceremonial attended with many rites and solemnized before
the assembled chiefs and people at the place and upon the stone kept
sacred for the purpose. The original stone, it will be remembered, was carried into Scotland for the coronation of Fergus in the
seventh century. After being long at Scone it followed the Stewarts
into England, where it is still preserved in Westminster Abbey as a
venerable relic and used on similar occasions.

This rule of alternate succession with its modifications of tanistry
may well have been suggested to Nial by one prevailing since Oliol-
Olum in Munster and brought home to him in his own family experience. His father Eochy Moyveon, by Mongfinn sister of Crimthan, sixth in descent from Oliol, had four sons : Brian, ancestor of the
O'Conors of Connaught; Fergus of the O'Dowds, Haynes and
Shaughnessys ; Fergus, and Oliol. His own mother was Carinna,
daughter of the king of Britain. When Eochy died, his children
being too young to rule, their uncle Crimthan raised to the monarchy

selected Conal of the Dalgais to succeed him on the throne of Munster. This incensed the Eoghanaeth, who claimed that their prince, Core was the next in succession by the alternate rule, and this being left to the states of Munster was so decided. To this decree Conal peaceably submitted, and when Core died, in 366, succeeded him. When Crimthan was poisoned by his sister Mongfinn, that her son might rule in his stead, it was Neil and not Bryan who was by the choice of the country called to the throne.

Tyreonnel now Donegal was the chieftainry of the O'Donnels, of whom Rory was created earl of Tyreonnel in 1603, and his descendants have been variously ennobled since for their distinguished military and civil services in Austria and Spain. Their feudatories were the O'Dogherties of Inishowen between Lough Swilly and Lough Foyle, under whom were the M'Gonigles and Donnellys, M'Davets and O'Coyles. The territory west and south was occupied by offsets from these stems—McFadden, Bradley, Laverty, Haggerty, Dornin, Sheeran, McCrosky, McCroissan, Curran, Duffy, Kernaghan, M'Bride, M'Ward, Gettyghan, Preel, Rafferty, M'Gowan, M'Hugh, M'Nulty, M'Closky, Dorrian, M'Gilbride, Clery, Muldory, Gormly, M'Lean, Kenny and Quiny. The MacSweenys, variously derived by different authorities from Swain, king of Norway, from Ir and from Heremon, were lords of Tuatha, Castle Duff, Finad, Banagh and the Rosses. Other principalities were Kilmacrenan, Raphoe, Boylagh, Tirhugh and Ballyshannon. At Donnegal, the capital, the Four Masters, one of the standard books on Irish history, was compiled.

The county of Londonderry, originally Coleraine, between Lough Foyle and the river Bann outlet of Lough Neagh, comprises the baronies of Tuckerin, Coleraine, Loughlinsholin and Keenaught which belonged to the O'Keans. Branches of Hara, Mullen, Maguin, McGilligan, Conor, Carolan, Mulligan, Brolihan, Cassidy, Quigley, McConnel Devlin, Keenan, McCracken, Scallan, McNamee occupied the territory, making way early in the seventeenth century for King James's settlers. After the destruction of Emania in the fifth century, the kings of Ulster had their principal abode at Aileach, six miles from the city of Londonderry.

Tyrone formed but part of the dominions of the O'Neils, which were called Hy Neil or Kinel Owen, of which the castle of Dungannon was the chief seat and its barony, and those of Clogher, Omagh and Strabane principalities. The O'Neils held sway at times over nearly all Ulster, and furnished many kings to the throne of Ireland. Their chiefs were created earls of Tyrone and barons Dungannon in 1542, and a branch viscounts in 1793, but the most noted were Shane and Hugh under Elizabeth and Owen in 1643. Rafferty, Mellan, Connellan, M'Shane, M'Rory, M'Taggart, M'Intyre, M'Guire, M'Owen, Croissan, Curran, Duvany, M'Golrich, M'Breen, M'Caghwell lords of Kinel Feradaigh, Tomalty, Etegan, Donnegan, Hagan, Laverty were their lieges.

Armagh, separated from Tyrone by the Blackwater, contains Fews, chieftainry of the second branch of the O'Neils, Clanbresail formerly of the MacCanns, Orior of the O'Hanlons, and its baronies are Armagh, Turany, east and west Neilland, upper and lower Fews and Orior. Larkins, Hanrattys, Heirs, Kiernans, Carneys, Tiernays, Callans, M'Evoys and Marrons are family names.

Antrim in the northeast, bounding south on Lough Neagh and Carrickfergus Bay, consisted of North and South Claneboy, belonging formerly to the O'Neils and later to the MacDonnels earls of Antrim. Carey, Dunluce, Glenarm, Kilconway, Toome, Masarene and Belfast were baronies. The family names not Scotch or English, most common within its limits, are Shiel, Hara, Flynn, Donnellan lords of Hy Tuirtree, Quillan, Keevan, Criordan, Magees of the race of Heremon of Oilean Magee, and north of Carrickfergus Bay, the M'Nallys. It was formerly also known as Dalrieda, the north portion of Dalaradia, and earlier as Endruim.

Down or Ulidia, part of what was formerly Dalaradia, consisted of Ards originally under a branch of the O'Neils, Iveagh, Lecale and Moylnis, patrimony of the Magennises of the race of Clan Rory, Castlereagh and Dufferin of the MacCartans, Kinelenty and Mourne. Among other names familiar in the county of ancient origin are Rooney, Lonagan, Colgan, Cormac, Moore, Garvey, Kelley, Rohan, Macken, Lawlor, Lynch, Moran, Heoghy, M'Rory, Colteran, and Dunlevy prince of Ulidia. A large share of the present population is of course Scotch and English. Arthur, chief of Magennis, whose wife was daughter of O'Neil, earl of Tyrone, was created viscount of Magennis of Iveagh in 1622. Bryan the fifth lord died in 1693 compromised in the war which proved fatal to most of the peers of Irish race.

Fermanagh surrounds Lough Erne. It belonged to the Maguires whose chief Bryan was made baron of Enniskillen in 1627, a title forfeited by his son Connor, attainted in 1644. Clonkelly, Lure, Magheraboy, Clanawley, Coole, Knockininy, Maghaira, Stephano and Tyr Kennedy are baronies. Mac-Tiernan, Fadagan lords of Tura, Magrath, M'Lenon, Mehan, Casey, M'Garahan, Corcoran, O'Keenan, Gorman, M'Enteggart, Mulrooney, Tracy, Cassidy, Corrigan, M'Manvs, M'Corishenan, Devins, Leonard and Muldoon chiefs of Lure, Tully, Gilfinnen, were the family names most multiplied.

Monaghan or Uriel formed with Armagh and Lowth, at the time of the invasion, the kingdom of Orgiel, of which M'Mahons lords of Dartry were chiefs. Its other principalities were Clankelly, Cremorn, Donagmain belonging to the O'Nenys, and Trough of which M'Kennas were chieftains. Other familiar names in this county were Hughs, Hoey, Heany, M'Gilvray, Connolly, Cassidy, M'Ardle, Duffy, M'Quade and Boylan.

Cavan with Leitrim formed Brefney, divided between two branches from Ard Fin of the race of Heremon, the O'Rourkes being princes

of Leitrim, O'Reillys of Cavan created by Queen Elizabeth earls
of Brenny and lords of Cavan.   Clanmahon, Clonkee, Castlerrahan,
upper and lower Loughtee and the three Tullaghs are among
the chief subdivisions, and Daly, Clery, Fitzsimmon, Gowan,
Brady, Conaghty, Tully, Mulligan, M'Hugh, Dolan, Sheridan,
Brogan, M'Cabe, M'Tiernan lords of Tullaghodonoho and M'Gowan of Tullaghar names most familiar.   In Clonkee dwelt a sept of
that name peculiarly warlike, a terror to their foes.   They are now
said to be extinct, and of the numerous proprietors of the princely
race of Cavan but one family, that of Heath House, is mentioned
by Walton as remaining.   There are more in Meath and Louth,
but Butlers, Bells, Cootes, Hamiltons, Hudsons, Lamberts, Max-
wells, Pratts, Sandersons, Singletons and Shirleys representing the
earls of Essex, with others of Scotch and English descent, have superseded the O'Reillys.   With Lough Erne which lays chiefly in Fermanagh and its river flowing into Donegal Bay, its lofty highlands
to the west, some reaching an elevation of two thousand feet, among
which rises the Shannon, and its other lakes, streams and mountains,
the country abounds in the picturesque.   Ample spaces are enclosed
in parks and pleasure grounds, but high rents and improving landlords have driven away the people, who now number less than two
hundred to the square mile.   Extremes of opulence and destitution
here as everywhere else in the country are disingenuously attributed
by English writers to race or sect, while mainly due to vicious legislation and to the exclusion of the people from interest in the soil they
till.   This is justified on the specious plea of the political necessity of
maintaining the union and protestant ascendancy.   But it is of no
practical utility for either.   What is true of this county is true of the
rest ; our limits forbid with regard to them the same particularity.

The province covered an area of over five millions four hundred
thousand acres.   Of 1,165,107 in Donegal, about one-half are improved ; of 518,425 in Londonderry, one-fifth only waste ; of

754,395 in Tyrone, nearly three-fourths. In Armagh nearly all its 328,000 acres are susceptible of cultivation ; in Antrim two-thirds of its 780,000 and in Down five-sixths of 611,404 are productive ; of 456,538 in Fermanagh, 327,048 in Monaghan, 477,360 in Cavan, the soil is generally good. Much of what is now waste if not stripped of its growth would have remained of value. That all the territory before its settlement by the Scotch was improved to advantage is plain from the amount expended by the O'Neils under Elizabeth in their campaigns,—eighty thousand pounds in a single year. At that period the revenue of the crown from such portions of the country as were subject to its collectors was far less than this, and the value of money several times greater than it is at present.

<hr />

X.

ANCIENT FAMILIES OF CONNAUGHT.

The westerly projection of the island into the ocean embraces the counties of Mayo, Sligo, Leitrim, Roscommon, Galway, and before 1602, of Clare. It was set apart by Heremon and Heber for the Firbolgs and earlier races, but in the fourth century was conquered by the descendants of Fiachra of the posterity of Heremon. Muradach, son of Fiachra, was its first king of that dynasty, and from his grandsons Brian and Fergus branched the Hy Brunes and Hy Fiachras ; the former consisting of O'Connors Don, Roe and Sligo, Rourkes, Reillys, MacDermots, MacDonoghs, Flahertys, O'Malleys, Flins and Flanagans, Hanlys, MacManus, Fallons, MacKiernans, MacBradys, Donellans, Garvys, Malonys, MacBrennans, Lallys, Creans, Fahys, Breslans, MacAodhs, Crowleys, Finnigans, Hallorans. The descendants of Fergus were the Dowds,

7

Shaughnessys, Haynes, Kilkellys, Keanaighs, Clerys, Ceads and Lennains.

In Roscommon, between the Shannon and the Suck, at Ballintobber, famous for its abbey, was long one of the chief seats of the O'Connors, kings of Connaught, from whom, through the De Burgs, descends the royal family of England. Another of their regal residences was at Cong, between lakes Mask and Corrib, on the borders of Mayo and Galway. This place was also famous for its abbey, founded by Domnal II., one of the O'Connor kings, who was monarch of Ireland. The duties and responsibilities of government demanding health and vigor, kings and chiefs, as they grew old or infirm, if they escaped the battlefield, retired to the cloister. Roderick, the last unfortunate monarch of the island, spent many of the last years of his life at one of these abbey retreats, dying in 1198 at the age of eighty-two.

In the fork between the two rivers, the Kellys, princes of Hy Maine, ruled over Athlone and Moycarne, part of Maineeh, which extended across the Suck into Galway. Dugans, Donegans, MacBrides, Meanys, Fallons, MacKeoghs and Nortons were septs under them. North of Athlone the barony of Roscommon, the more special demesne of the kings, were Donnalans, Bernes, Hanleys, Conroys, Monahans, Flannagans, MacDowells. Farther west were Baltimoe and Ballintobber, divided later between the O'Connors Don and Roe, Connellan, Moran and Fenaghty, and to the north MacDermots, princes of Moylurg. East of the Shannon and forming part of Brefney, Leitrim was the patrimony of the O'Rourks, comprising Dromanaine, Mohill and Carrigaleen under the Reynolds, and Rosselogher under the MacClancys of Dartry, with MacFergus, Meechan, MacGlom, MacKenny, O'Carrols of Calry, Fords, MacGowan of Tullaghar, MacGartlan, MacKeon, MacColreavy, Shanly, MacTeigue and MacDorchy for septs well known but not equally powerful.

Mayo, extending east to Lough Gara and south to Lough Corrib, borders for a long distance on the sea. A large portion of its territory was early under the rule of O'Dowds and O'Malleys, the former furnishing a dynasty of princes to Tyrawly and Ennis, the latter to Barrishole and Morrisk. Below, on Lough Mask, were domains of the O'Connor kings on the easterly side; the country of the Joyces, a fine race of men originally from Wales, tall and vigorous, on the west. North of the Lake is Curra, where Murrays and Tiernays were chieftains; and on the east Clanmorris, of which the Burkes, MacWilliams Oughtar, in later days earls of Mayo, were principal proprietors, and where the Prendergasts had possessions; farther east again, Costello of the MacCostellos or Nangles, and north of the Burkes, Athleathan of the Jordans de Exeter. Finnegans, Gearans, Connegans, Callaghans, Cahanys, Rothlans, Ronans, Bradys, Blighs, Quinns, Lennons, Milfords, Mulroys, Mulrenins, Mogahns, MacHales, Flynns, Cummins, Creans, Tooles, Duffys, Gradys, MacDarells, Dorchys, Lavels, Morans, Larissseys, MacGowans, Gormlys, with some other families of English patronymics, such as Lawless, Barret, Cusack, Petit, Lynch and Brown, held under them or succeeded to their possessions.

Sligo, on the north shore, embraced Tireragh, part of the large possessions of the O'Dowds, Gallen and Leny of the O'Haras, Cooltavin of the O'Garas, Corran and Tyrerrill of MacDonoghs, Carberry of O'Connors Sligo, and under them were Brogans, Flanellys, Colemans, MacGeraghtys, Morrisons, Morrisseys, Kernaghans, Howleys, Laughnans, Feenys, McFirbis, Morans, Keevans, Durkans, Spillane and MacConways.

The seven lower baronies of Galway, Longford, Clare, Dunkellen, Loughrea, Kiltartan, Athenry and Leitrim were early appropriated by the MacWilliams Eighter or Burkes of Clanrickard,—whose chief abode was at first the castle of Loughrea, and later that of Portumma. They held no exclusive possession, for the

O'Shaugnessys, connected with them by various matrimonial alliances, retained portions of Kiltartan, of which they once were chieftains, as did the Mullalys of Loughrea, the Hallorans of Clare or
Clan Fugail, Donnellans of Clan Brassail in Leitrim, Maddens
and Hoolaghans in Longford, Haverties, Haynes and Connollys in
Athenry. To the westward toward the Atlantic stretches a wilderness of rock and bog and mountain, with wild and romantic scenery,
intermingled with patches of luxuriant vegetation, kept fresh from
its proximity to the sea.   In this territory, well known as Connemara, the O'Flahertys once ruled in Ire Connaught and the Mac-
Conrys in Moycullen.   Farther north and east was Conmayne, the
Cross of Tuam, the seat of the archbishops, forming part of Dunmore, from which the Birminghams, barons of Athenry, expelled
the O'Connors and O'Flahertys, lords of Dunamore, after the fall of
Edward Bruce, at which time the Flynns were lords of Cloinmoel-
roin.   Tyaquin, Kilconnel, Clonmacnoon, Killian, Ballimoe, formed part of Maineech or Hy Maine, of which the Kellys of the
race of Heremon were princes, one of whom lord of Aughrim
forfeited his possessions. Cowleys, MacHughs, Duanes, Lees, Calla-
nans, Kirwans were other families of Connemara.   Heynes, princes
of Hy Fiachra, Sheehans, Cullens, Cahills, Fahys, MacTullys,
MacNevins, MacEgans, Traceys, Larkins, Coffeys, Doyles,
Daleys, Maginns, Cashins, Tourneys, Degans, Connollys, Mulroo-
neys and Mannings were also names much multiplied in Galway.

Though a large part of the four millions and a half of acres in the
five counties are not very fertile, and two-thirds of them only under
any cultivation, the population before the famine of 1849 and
exodus that followed exceeded fifteen hundred thousand, that of Mas-
sachusetts to-day on the same area.   It has of course greatly diminished since by emigration.   The traveller attracted into the country
by the beauty of its scenery and abundance of its salmon, will observe
in the various races traits and lineaments which afford abundant

evidence of their different origin. Here in Mayo were once preëminent the Clan Morna, said to be Dammonians as also the posterity of
Eadan in Roscommon and of Enda in Sligo.

XI.

EUEGENIANS AND DALCASSIANS OF MUNSTER.

After Mogha Nuadat or Angus (81), King of Munster, born A.D.
60, defeated Con of the hundred battles, they divided the island by
a line from Dublin to Galway, Con taking Leath-Con to the north,
Mogha Leath-Mogha to the south. Leinster or Ensellagh remained
subject to tribute for a time under the kings of Munster, but this
settlement was of short duration. When Oliol son of Mogha, and
son-in-law of Con (82), born in 92, came to die, he gave Fiacha son
of his elder son Owen, Waterford, Cork, Kerry and part of Tipperary or Desmond, and Cormac Cas his son next in seniority surviving
Limerick and Clare with the rest of Tipperary and part of Kings
county or Thomond, providing that the representative of each line
alternately should hold supreme sway in Munster.

It may prove serviceable to the reader to have at hand the respective main lines of the Eoghanaght and Dalcassians, from the time
this settlement was made to the coming of Strongbow. The former
consisted of : (84) Fiacha Mullathan b. 154 (85) Oliol Flanbeg
b. 190 (86) Daire Cearb and Luaghuaid b. 228 (87) Core b. 269
(88) Nadfraoch b. 320 (89) Angus b. 346, the first christian king
(90) Felim b. 386 (91) Criomthan b. 423 (92) Hugh Dubb father
of (93) Finghin ancestor of the O'Sullivans and of (83) Falvey b.
511 father of (94) Colga the generous chief b. 555 (95) Nadfraoch
b. 597 (96) Daolgiasa b. 640 (97) Donghaile b. 682 (98) Seach-
nusa b. 723 (99) Artgaile b. 764 (100) Lachtna b. 806 who lived

in the reign of Cormac son of Culenan king of Munster, who compiled the Psalter of Cashel (101) Buadhachan b. 848 (102) Ceallachan b. 886, who conquered the Danes (103) Justin b. 925 (104) Carthach b. 969 (105) Muireadach (106) Cormac b. 1054, who founded Cormac's chapel at Cashel, and (107) Dermod Morrna Cille Baine, king of Cork and Desmond, b. 1098, who married Petronilla de Bleete, an English lady of good family, and who made his submission to Henry the second and was slain in 1185, near Cork, by Theobald Fitzwalter.

The main lines of Cormac Cas who married the sister of the poet Oisin MacCumhale were : (84) Mogh Corb b. 167 (85) Fearcorb b. 198 (86) Angus b. 232, the peacemaker, (87) Luighaid b. 286, who dispossessed the Firbolgs of Clare (88) Conal Eachluath b. 312 (89) Cas (90) Blod (91) Carthin who had a son Angus progenitor of the Currys Cormacans and Seasnans, and (92) Eochy Balldearg, baptized by St. Patrick (93) Conal (94) Hugh Coiheme, or the comely king of Cashel and first christian king of the family. His son Congal was ancestor of the O'Neils of Clare and O'Noons of Thomond; (95) Cathal, from whose son Algenain derive the O'Mearas (95) Torlagh b. 641 (96) Mahon b. 683 (97) Core (98) Lachtna (101) Lorean (102) Kennedy (103) Brian Boru born at Knicora 926, who conquered the Danes at Clontarf April 23, 1014, driving them out of the island.   (104) Donogh was succeeded by his nephew (105) Torlogh, who died 1086. (106) Murtough d. 1119. (107) Dermod, whose wife was Sarah McCarthy daughter of Thaddeus, d. 1120.   (108) Conor d. 1142 was succeeded by his brother (108) Torlogh d. 1167. (109) Murtogh, slain by O'Brien whose eric was three thousand cows, exacted by his brother and successor (109) Donal King of Cashel who married Orlecam daughter of Dermod king of Leinster by a daughter of O'More of Leix. He founded the cathedral church at Cashel on the existing site. When Henry the second landed he tendered his submission, but in 1176, after that king violated at Oxford his pledge to king Roderick, Donal expelled the English from Limerick. He died in 1134.

The rule of alternate succession between the Eoghanacht[1] and Dalgais[2] was not observed with equal strictness and fidelity as that of a like nature adopted by the northern and southern Hy Nials to the central monarchy. The kings of the southern province, of Cashel as commonly called, while their seat of government was in that city, were more frequently selected from the former, their territories being nearer at hand. Between Conal of the Swift Steeds (87), and Lorcan (101), grandfather of Brian Boru, Dalgais furnished few kings to the throne of Munster. They sorely felt the injustice of this exclusion, and it led to desolating wars. When Cormac MacCuillenan, king and bishop of Cashel, in 908, was preparing for an expedition against Munster, which ended in disaster, he reminded the assembled princes of the law of Olioll Olum, and named Lorcan, king of Thomond, whom he had summoned from Kincora as his successor. But his wishes were not regarded, and though the two lines contended for the throne, seventy years elapsed before Brian Boru, son of Kennedy, conquered the Eugenians in 1078, and obtained the crown of Munster as the prize of victory.

It is not proposed at present to follow either line later down

[1] The Eoghanachts, or Engenian Families, are:—Mac Carthy Mor, Mac Carthy Muskery, Mac Carthy Carrignavar, Mac Carthy Aglish, Mac Carthy Cloghroe, Mac Carthy Na-Mona, Mac Carthys Mac Donogh, Mac Carthy Mac Donnell, Mac Carthy Reagh, Mac Carthy Duna, Mac Carthy Ballynoodie, Mac Cathy Glas, Keeffe, Mac Auliffe, Donoghue of Kerry, Donoghue of Cashel, Donoghue of Ossory, Collins, Connell, Daly, Mahony, Callaghan, Callanan, Moriarty, Cullen, Sullivan, Mac Gillicuddy, Quill, Riordan, Shea, Lyon, Cronan, Buadhachs, Cahalan, Maolins, Flathniadh, Flynn, Conal, Ceallaghan, Donnell, Duilgin, Hea, Ceanduibh, Mac Trialladh, Longadh, Dubhachain, Neill, Feichin, Flanlaoi, Dadhain, Leary, Rinn, Donall, Caomhloingsidh, Conall, Cronnelly, Dann, Ailgnin, Hooly, Ceitin, Meargan, Aignach, Canty, Eoghan, Agha, Maothagan, Maolerain, Glanihin, Berain, Loingseach, Angal, Finelly, Donovan, Feely.

[2] The Dalcassian Families are:—O'Brien, Mac Lysaght, Ailche, Ahern, Mac Nanara, Gunning, Kennedy, Meara, Mac Brody, Mulcahy, M'Einery, Liddy, Lenaghan, Lonergan, M'Clauchy, M'Coghlan, Mac Curtin, Grady, Morony, Molony, Griffin, Hanraghty, Hanrahan, Hehir or Hare, M'Innerney, Hartigan, Hickey, Hogan, Hurley, Lynch, Casey, Cudihy, Conolly, Cormacan, Crotty, Mac Mahon, Lanigan, Kirwan, Magrath, Neill, Dea, Spelman, Fogarty, Sheehan, Toomy, Regan, Kelleher, Shanahan, Hely, M'Arthur, Sexton, Reidy, Slattery, Kearney, Noonan, Quin, Mac Considine, Scully, Curry, Heffernan, Cahill, Hea, Finnellan, Gloram, Toler, Durcan, Silk, Mulchaoine, Heavy, Caisin, Noon, Larkin, Bowen, Alugidy, Maine, Flaherty, Conroy, Heynes, Hanify.

than the invasion. There are manifest reasons on the face of both
as we derive them from Cronelly, and from the interesting history
of the O'Briens by O'Donoghue, for doubting their absolute ac-
curacy. The intervals in the many instances are of undue length
for average generations; but possibly this may be accounted for by
grandsons, and not sons succeeding. From the similarity of names
in the two lists at about the same date, there seems also ground
for suspicion of possible confusion. But the historical incidents
with which they were severally connected are too well established
for any very important error. The mode of numbering the generations, though suggesting a degree of credulity far below the accepted standards of historical scepticism, in beginning at the cradle
of the race, is that common to all works of Irish genealogy, and is
too convenient not to improve.

XII.

ANCIENT FAMILIES OF MUNSTER.

How it chances that the Milesians are so peculiarly genealogical,
may possibly be accounted for from their having retained, down to
periods comparatively recent, the patriarchal system of government,
the earliest form of civil polity. With their property and independence constantly menaced by strangers ever at hand to take advantage of their weakness, their family ties were drawn closer for
mutual protection, and shut out from other pursuits, their shores
and larger towns in hostile occupation, clansmen went little from home
unless on military service. Their laws of succession, tenure of their
lands, hereditary castes and military organization, all demanded an
accurate record and transmission of descent, and officials specially
qualified and trained and in some instances hereditary were appoint-

ed and set apart for this duty. The family lore thus preserved is an important help for the elucidation of our particular subject, and with the tribal boundaries baronial and county lines might better perhaps be presented on map or in tables. Such are to be obtained, but are not everywhere accessible, and we are reduced to the necessity of placing here what information of this description our readers may require to bear in mind.

Enumeration of names and places may prove somewhat irksome and cannot of course pretend to be absolutely exact or complete. Many names are purposely omitted, as simply modifications or repetitions, others through inadvertence, but if we succeed in imparting the knowledge of which we have ourselves felt sorely the need in studying the history of Ireland, our end will be attained. Our subject is the social and political condition of two races, differing widely in character and circumstance, placed side by side for centuries, developing in their mutual relations whatever is good or evil in human nature. If not always at strife, their friendly intercourse was often fraught with greater peril to the weaker and more confiding race than when engaged in actual hostilities. They readily combined for common objects of ambition or resentment, but there was a natural antagonism engendering jealousy and contention, and when the immediate objects for uniting their forces were effected they revived in their original virulence. In this long struggle the chiefs and clans eventually succumbed. The stranger, with a powerful nation of larger and constantly augmenting resources to lend aid when needed, rooted himself in the soil, and like the parasite of the tropics, extended his deadly embrace over his less fortunate and persistent neighbors, absorbing their substance and gaining vigor from their decline, leaving, as time proceeded, his victims helpless. This was the course of events in many parts of the island, it was peculiarly so in Munster.

The northern province defended by bog and stream, with passes

8

impervious to hostile penetration, under its brave and sagacious rulers, kept its gates for centuries barred. If pressure from without aided by internal dissension ever swept in its tide of devastation, it soon ebbed, not again for long intervals to return. From the less homogeneous character of its people, and the hold the De Burghs early gained in Galway, the west if defiant of English authority was more under the influence of English interests. By Irish rules of succession, which excluded females, Eighters and Oughters had better claim than Mortimer or Plantagenet to the family lands of the De Burghs in Connaught, but if feudal law were to govern where it had never been accepted and could not be enforced, they were intruders, and if placed at disadvantage might be compelled to surrender. This led them to form for their security frequent alliances with the neighboring princes, and furnishes the key to the policy which long ruled in Connaught. In the central province and south toward the sea and St. George's Channel, the tenure of the representatives of Eva was constantly disputed and generally with success by the sons of Heremon.

The southerly shore was fringed with harbors, open to a maritime power and easily defended against land attack. We have seen how the map of Munster became curiously checkered with the demesnes of the two races, interspersed. There were septs of other stock than Hebers, English lords who did not trace to Nesta, but not many of either with sufficient extent of territory or influence to control events. From Waterford to Tralee, from Cashel to Derrynane, after assimilation in speech and dress had broken down the barriers which kept the races hostile and distinct, it was not so much two nationalities that were contending for mastery, as Fitzmaurice and Fitzgerald against Eugenian and Dalgais. Even these distinctions were constantly losing force as their houses became knit together by bonds of consanguinity. The line of Raymond lords of Kerry, now represented by the Marquis of Lansdown for seven hundred years,

have been gaining in territory and influence. Certainly no English
blood has been more largely tinctured by Milesian. It was in the
eighteenth century before a baroness of Kerry died of Saxon or pure
English stock. The first lord had for wife Grace Cavanagh, granddaughter of the noted Dermod McMorrogh, King of Leinster, father
of Eva, the second Mary McElligot of Connaught, the third,
fourth and eighteenth princesses of Thomond, the seventh Catherine
McCarthy, the ninth Maud O'Connor, the tenth Una McMahon;
the sixth, eighth and nineteenth Fitzgeralds, also widely connected
through Roches, Barrys and de Burghs with both bloods. The
wives of the second, ninth and eleventh earls of Desmond were
O'Briens, of the twelfth and thirteenth McCarthies, the fourteenth
espoused Mora O'Carroll.

Dermod McCarthys More (107) born 1098, king of Desmond at
the time of the invasion, had for his wife an Englishwoman, Petronilla
de Bleete. His great grandson Donal (110) b. 1204, also king,
espoused Margaret daughter of the third Kerry; Donal's grandson,
Cormac (112) born 1271, Honoria daughter of the sixth. In the
next generation Donal (113) b. 1303—1358 had to wife Joanna,
only child and heiress of the second earl of Desmond, and four
generations later the wife of Cormac (117) b. 1440 was Ellenor
Fitzmaurice, daughter of the ninth Kerry by Mora O'Connor. Of
the children of Donal an Druim in (118) b. 1481 Catherine married Finghin McCarthy Reagh, Honoria James fifteenth earl of
Desmond, Donal (119) b. 1518 created earl of Clancarre espoused
Honoria Fitzgerald, daughter of his brother-in-law. The house of
Kincora early selected their brides from O'Connors, O'Moores,
O'Cavanaghs, O'Kennedys, MacNamaras, Fogarties and McCarthies,
but Torlogh (116) who died 1460, his son (117), and great grandson (119) married Burkes, while the wives of Torlogh (118),
and Conor (121) third earl, were daughters of Kerry. Another
wife of Conor (119) was Alice daughter of Desmond; Donogh

(120) second earl of Thomond married Helena Butler, daughter of the earl of Ormond, and Donogh (122) the fourth Amy Roche and Elizabeth Fitzgerald, daughter of the eleventh earl of Kildare. The Carberry and Muskery branches were also as variously and intimately allied to the English race.

Their sons and daughters intermarried in each successive generation, forming a curious lace work of both races more or less harmoniously blended. With their territory coterminous and intermingled, their abodes not far apart, with constant occasion for social intercourse or friendly interchange, the marriage banquet or funeral rite, hostings, the chase, festivals of the church, to bring them into constant companionship, their stability and security depending in a great measure on mutual support, the religious sense extending far and wide, culture, refinement and civilization, earls of Desmond with their subordinate barons and knights of the Valley, Kerry and Glyn, white and black and five hundred established branches, Roches, Barrys, Condons and Barrets, the twenty powerful houses derived from the McCarthy More, Dalcassian chieftains subordinate to the kings of Thomond, O'Connors, O'Sullivans, Moriarties and Donovans held a singularly complicated sway over Munster.

They experienced strange vicissitudes of fortune, and not the least remarkable what we shall have occasion to allude to later, the last representatives of both earls and kings of Desmond, in the beginning of the seventeenth century, were caged in the tower of London. The Queens earl in 1601 and Sugan or earl of straw in 1608, seventeenth and eighteenth earls of Desmond died there, and Florence McCarthy Reagh, who had married without Queen Elizabeth's consent Helena, heiress and only child born in wedlock of Donal McCarthy More earl of Clancare, also ended his days after forty years' imprisonment more or less strict in London. The male representative of the eighth earl of Desmond, beheaded at Drogheda in 1467, ended in James Desmond descended from his fifth son who married an O'Brien and was living in 1687. The lineal representative of the McCarthy More, derives from an offshoot from the parent stem in the fifteenth century. Of the McCarthy Reagh there is a branch still residing in France. Justin of Cork represents the house of Muskerry, descended from Daniel of Carrignavar, second son of Sir Cormac of Blarney castle, and the line of Glenachroim now or not long since was represented by Charles Duna (124) whose principal abode is or was in the same city.

We have been tempted to loiter by the way to exhibit some of the modes by which the two races, naturally discordant and antagonistic, were gradually brought together and assimilated at the period under review. The same process was going on throughout the province and all over the country, more of course among chiefs and rulers and principal landholders with whom intercourse was more frequent, than lower in the social scale where the condition kept both sexes at home. It shows how difficult if not impracticable it becomes to expel a stranger race when it grows dominant and domineering, of what doubtful policy it may often prove to allow it to gain a foothold. Historical retributions find vent far apart from the original wrong, and at times the peace and order of America have been rudely shaken by the infusion of large numbers who do not understand how much its liberties and blessings depend for their preservation upon implicit obedience to wise laws justly and honestly administered; but this will probably correct itself.

XIII.

THOMOND.

Before crossing the Shannon, from what anciently was all Connaught, Clare, originally set apart with that province for the Firbolgs and other races the Milesians conquered, but which was wrested from them by Luighaid, one of the progenitors of Brian Boru, and, at the request of his descendant, third earl of Thomond, constituted 1602 part of Munster, spreads out its area of 802,352 acres, 500,000 arable land, the rest waste or pasturage. Embraced south and east by the river, its westerly bound extends a long distance by the sea into the bay of Galway. Its nine baronies, subdivisions established by the English government under Queen Elizabeth, and substantially the same in their limits as those previously existing, contained in 1841 three hundred thousand inhabitants, double its present population. In Tulla, its most easterly barony near the southeast corner of Lough Derg, once stood the celebrated palace of Kincora, near the pass of Killaloe, where the Kings of Limerick, when the Danes pressed hard upon them in that their earlier residence, took up their abode. Here Brian Boru was born and held his court as king of Thomond, Munster, or as monarch of the island; and there also dwelt other generations of his line, before and after him. At the other end of Lough Dearg, twenty-three miles to the north, was the castle of Portumna, one of the strongholds of the Burkes of Clanrickard, with which family the O'Briens were often at war, and as often in amity. The shores of the lake must have frequently resounded to the war cries of the chieftains, often returned the softer echoes of harp and other musical instruments of peace, as processions passed along the lake for festive entertainment or funereal rite. Kincora was frequently demolished and rebuilt, and only abandoned some centuries later, when the Kings of Thomond possessed more convenient residences, and more central as their hold relaxed on Tipperary, in Clonroad, near Ennis, their first castle constructed of stone, erected by Donogh Cairbreach about 1200, Claremore near Clare, Moy in Ibrickan and Bunratty.

The castle of Bunratty, erected by Thomas De Clare, soon after his grant from Edward the First, continued the abode of that family during its troubled possession in Clare. After the last fatal battle of Dysert O'Dee in 1318, in which were slain, his son and grandson, the wife of his son Richard gave it to the flames, and the family left the country never again to return. It has since stood many a siege, and experienced the fortunes of war: but its position in command of the pass of the river Raite was one of importance to defend, and after each fresh disaster it was restored. It was at one time the residence of General Ludlow, the favorite general of Cromwell, and passed away from the O'Briens in 1712, when the eighth earl of Thomond sold it to a kinsman, not of his own name, who conveyed it in 1728 to the family of its present proprietor. It still stands, its central mass little diminished by time, though long since abandoned as a dwelling except for the constabulary force which occupies its lower apartments. Round about buried in the turf are lines of walls, formerly part of out buildings enclosing its outer wards, or forming part of its defences. What remains of the castle consists of a large square tower, about one hundred feet in elevation, flanked at the corners by four of smaller dimensions and communicating, containing each many rooms. The main structure is chiefly composed of four or five large halls, the length of which is given by Thackeray as seventy feet, though it is probably less, the roof of the upper one now being reversed. On the walls as into the plaister decorations of the smaller rooms are wrought the armorial bearings of the O'Briens. At one end

between the towers have been constructed on several floors
modern apartments of the fashion of Queen Anne. Not draped
with ivy or environed by trees, this castle stands out stern and
grim against the sky, and from the solidity of its structure may
well, if undisturbed, remain for many ages an interesting historical
relic of the warlike age it has survived.

Near by Kincora in Tulla, once extended the territory of the
O'Gradys of Cinel Donghaile, supplying many dignitaries to the
church, contributing many works of value to the national annals.
They have long since passed from their ancient prosperity in
Clare, but are now represented by the O'Grady of Kilballyowen
Castle, in the barony of small county in Limerick, by Carrol of
Shore Park, and by the Viscounts Guillamore, connected with
the Blennerhassets. The northern portions of Tulla, and of the
adjacent barony of Bunratty, were long the domain of the
Macnamaras of the Clan Coilean, or Hy Caisin, one of whose
chiefs, Sioda, in 1402 founded the abbey of Quin, among the
largest mediæval ecclesiastical establishments, and the ruins of
which are considered the finest in Ireland. This line of chieftains
were hereditary marshals of Thomond, and its several branches,
two of whom are honorably represented among the present landed
proprietors of Clare, possessed no less than fifty-seven castles.
The lower part of Bunratty was called Hy-bloid, from the old
name of the O'Briens, and was the early home of the Shannons,
Kennedys, Creaghs and Kearneys, and near by were Moloneys,
Magraths, Griffins of the castles of Ballygriffy, and Moygowna in
Inchiquin. The Hehies or Hares of Hy Cormac possessed Magh-
adare between Tulla and Bunratty. Inchiquin or Hy Fermeic
was the patrimony of the O'Deas and O'Quins, the last now ennobled as earls of Dunraven, of Castle Adare, and there dwelt
the McBrodys, still celebrated as for many centuries earlier as
poets and historians; Hogans, bishops of Killaloe, Heffernans and

O'Neils of Finlora. In Ibrickan still dwell in prosperity the Moronys and Mac Consedines, derived from Consadan, son of Donogh Cairbreach, of the twelfth century. Kilfenora, along the bay of Galway, was the inheritance of a branch of Clan Rory, divided in the eleventh century between O'Connors Core, of Dough Castle, to whom was assigned the southerly half or Corcumroe; and O'Loghlins, lords of Burren, the northerly. The latter are still represented amongst the present landholders in Clare; but the lands of this branch of the O'Connor name, of which were the O'Connors Kerry, passed under Queen Elizabeth through O'Briens and Fitzgeralds to Gores, Stackpoles and other English families. There are now to be found Mac Lysaghts, represented by the lords Lisle, Cullenans, Davorens, Currans, Liddys, and Gormans, formerly chiefs of Hy Cormac. In the southwest corner of Clare are the Corkavaskins Moyarta and Clonderlaw, of which the MacMahons were long chieftains. From John, born in 1715, son of Patrick and Margaret O'Sullivan Beare, who became Marquis d'Equilly in 1763, descends Marshal MacMahon, duke of Magenta, present ruler of France. This house of MacMahon descends from Mortough More, king of Thomond, who died in 1119, and they are said to be the eldest extant branch of the O'Briens in representation of their great ancestor, Brian Boru. Sir William, late Master of the Rolls in Ireland, and his brother, General MacMahon, are of this race.

Across the Shannon, east and southwest of Clare, Tipperary, with its million of acres, four-fifths under cultivation, has at present but half the population within its borders before the famine of 1849. Its subdivision into eleven baronies corresponds very nearly to the ancient chieftainries. What is Lower Ormond was long under the rule of the Carrols of Ely, from whom descended the noble race distinguished on this side of the ocean,—Charles of Carrolton, being one of the signers of the declaration of indepen-

9

dence, and his brother the venerable archbishop of Baltimore, the descendants of the former having intermarried with Englishmen of the highest rank and note for public service. Kennedys were also its chiefs, Breslins, Quinlevans, MacGilfoyles and Donnellys had possessions, and there, as in many other parts of this kingdom of Thomond, McEgans and McClanchys held lands as brehons or hereditary judges. Upper Ormond was also the territory of the Kennedys, and there Sextons, Gleesons, Cullenans and O'Mearas had their abodes. O'Meaghers, of whom one has held in these present days an honored place in arms and literature, were lords of Ikerrin, Dermodys being their neighbors.

O'Fogartys were lords of Eliogarty, now represented by the Lanigans of Castle Fogarty, MacCormans, Meehans, Cahills being the names most multiplied. This country early vested in the Butlers, and near Thurles stands one of the most interesting ecclesiastical remains in the island, Holycross, with its beautiful windows, and which long boasted amongst its many relics a fragment of the true cross. O'Deas and Corcorans ruled in Slievardagh, whilst to the southwest, in what is known as Middlethird, was Cashel, with its sacred hill, crowned with abbey and round tower, and the chapel of Cormac, the last of beautiful proportions and of solid stone, dating back to before Strongbow came. Near by are the mouldering walls of Knockgraffon, abode as birthplace of eighteen of the Munster kings, and which, at the time of the invasion, was the chief seat of the O'Sullivans, eldest branch of the Eoghanatch; there also was Hy Rongally, and Shannahans, Slatterys and Kearneys had their home. In Iffa and Offa resided Keans and Morrisseys, and there is the present abode of the O'Callaghans of Shanbally Castle, Viscounts Lismore, of whom the first created in 1806, married Eleanor, daughter of the seventeenth Earl of Ormond. A branch of the Burkes were long paramount in Clanwilliam, whose castle of Cappa Uniac, memorable for many re-

markable incidents in their history, stood midway between Cahir
and Tipperary. Among their more powerful neighbors were
O'Cuires, lords of Musery Cuire, Dwyers, lords of Kilnemanagh,
Kellehers, Spillanes, Dineens and Lennahans. Along the Shannon,
in Owney and Arra, reigned the once powerful house of Mac-I-
brien Arra, derived from Brien Roe, whom De Clare murdered.
Of this territory O'Ryans and Donegans were previously chieftains
and near by were branches of the Hogans, Heffernans and Scullys.
This county early passed under the sway of the Butlers, being
created their special palatinate, and although its former chieftains
retained their lands and rule even as late as the sixteenth century,
sometimes exacting tribute, and sometimes paying it, the kings of
Thomond relinquished all pretension to sovereignty to a large
part of it not long after the invasion.

No part of the country more abounds in relics of the past.
Ruined castles and shattered fanes everywhere recall the days of
strife and persecution. It was border-land and the scene of many
hard fought conflicts. One of the most memorable was the successful defence of Clonmel, now a thriving city of twenty thousand
inhabitants, under Owen O'Neil, against Cromwell in 1652. The
marvels of the county are not all above the surface. At Mitchels-
town are caves of great beauty, extending nearly a thousand feet
into the bowels of the earth, turned no doubt to good account in
the days of persecution for the concealment of priest or rapparee
from the myrmidons of the law.

South of the Shannon extends the fertile region of Limerick, of
which the capital, sixty miles from the Atlantic, was a place of
strength and consequence in the days of the Danes. It was subsequently the regal abode of the kings and often beleaguered and now
and then burnt. Its present population of forty thousand souls
appears to be diminishing. Its lace works and other trades are on the
increase. The barony about the city is another Clanwilliam where

the Burkes of Castledonnel formerly flourished. East of the
town O'Briens were chiefs of Owney Beg, and west another branch
derived from Conor, second son of kings Mahon Moinmoy, and who
died in 1426, were chieftains down to the sixteenth century. On
the opposite bank of the river Kenny were the possessions of the
O'Donovans, and there Clerkins and Hannerys dwelt. West and south
was the broad domain of Connelloe, originally of the O'Connells lords
of Hy-Conal-Gaura, a branch of whom are still prospering in Enneis
as also at Derrynane and Dunloh. This was the earliest grant to
the Fitzgeralds in Desmond. Here near the Shannon is Askeaton,
one of their principal residences and burial places, and remains of
their grandeur abound in and around it. One of the five hundred
offshoots of the race that made the name of Geraldine famous, the
Knights of Glynn, held the northeast corner nearly twenty miles
square, and Sheehys, Hallinans, Scanlans, Kinealys, Sheehans,
Cullens, MacEninys, Mulcahys, occupied portions of the territory.
In Coshma and Small county ruled the O'Gradys, and Sarsfields
viscounts of Kilmallock took their title from that once splendid fortress
and abode of the Desmonds. The O'Brians lords of Coonagh derived from Morrogh of the Short Shield, grandson of Brian Boru and
grandfather of Devorghal, wife of Tiernan O'Ruare of Brefny,
whose family quarrels were fraught with such woe to her country.
Besides the septs or families already mentioned, Hartigans, Hon-
ans, Kerwicks, Conlans, Healys, most of them Dalcassians, are still
to be found in different localities. The Fitzgeralds then as now are
numberless, and intermingled with them are the families of the undertakers, who succeeded with Cromwell's ironsides and palatines from
Germany to the confiscated lands of Desmond.

XIV.

DESMOND.

Whatever forces were at work, whether of attraction or repulsion, assimilating or setting farther apart the two races in other parts of the country, their process and effects in Munster can be easily followed. Quite as much in Kerry, Cork, Waterford, and those parts of Tipperary which constituted the kingdom of Desmond, alternated between peace and war, much after the fashion of nations on a grander scale. English and Irish neighbors, with one unvarying and deplorable result for the latter. The land and political power which attends its ownership gradually drifted away to the former, not in consequence of any superior honesty, prudence or other deserving, but that the English crown and people at home lent them help and fought their battles.

In the north west corner of county Limerick, in Connelloe, spread the fertile plains of the knight of Glynn, one of the Fitzgeralds, extending over twenty miles. Further to the west, forming the southerly bank of the Shannon at its mouth, and sloping down toward Tralee bay and the waters dedicated to St. Brandon, was what in early days formed the kingdom of Cran (54) son of Fergus, of the Clan Rory by Maeva the celebrated queen of Connaught. From him it was designated Clarcaigh Luachaid, the former name attaching to the county. Here, for nearly forty generations, his posterity had ruled and dwelt, when Dermod King of Cork or Desmond, as lord paramount, gave the southerly portion to Raymond le Gras for aid in reducing his son Cormac, opposed to English rule, to obedience. Clanmaurice, the territory thus bestowed, has ever since belonged to Raymond's lineal descendants, the Fitzmaurices barons and earls of Kerry and now marquises of Lansdown, and some of the means have already been suggested in their intermarriages which have helped them to keep it. The upper portion,

known as Iraghticonnor, from Connor, of the race of Ir, continued
in the line of the O'Connor Kerry, down to the seventeenth century, and their matrimonial alliances[1] afford some clue to their power
and importance as chieftains.

Under divided sway Fitzgeralds knights of Kerry held land and
rule in the territory, which with what belonged to the O'Connors was
seized under the protectorate. Utterly disloyal to his sacred obligations to the families who had made such sacrifices for his own, Charles
the second granted in 1666 Iraghticonnor and part of Clanmaurice
to Trinity College. The O'Connors had various castles in these
fertile domains, earlier Listowel the chief abode of the lords of
Kerry, Ballybunion Minegalan Knocnacashel and Carrigasoil were
others. The last mentioned long withstood the attack of the protector, and when at last surrendered, his soldiers hung up its defenders
and with them six women and a child.

The earls of Desmond had many pleasanter abodes then Tralee.
Askeaton on the Shannon, Kilmallock on the southerly borders of
Limerick, Imokilly down by the sea, or Strancally, were more elegant and cheerful dwellings, but from its strength and favorable
position for resistance to English interference or native resentment,
this fortress throughout their troubled sway in Desmond was the
central seat both of their military power and civil rule. Marauders
of either race hardly cared to venture within the long peninsula of
Corkaguiney to the west with Tralee commanding its gates, and there
the Geraldine lords found safe retreat for their flocks and herds, their
vessels or themselves when sorely pressed. There were other septs
and chieftains there, Moriarties, Fahies, Doohns, and at Dingle,

---

[1] Core 92 had for wife an O'Keefe of Duhallow. Mahon 93 Johanna Moriarty of Lough
Lene. Dermod 94 Mora O'Donoghue. Mahon 95 Mora O'Mahony daughter of the lord
of Rathcullar. Dormod 96 Johanna Fitzmaurice of Kerry. Conor 97 Winafred MacMahon of Corcavaskin. Conor 98 Margaret Fitzgerald daughter of John of Lorcan. Connor
99, slain in 1445, Knathleen de Brunell. John 100, who founded Leslaghton Abbey in 1470,
Margaret Nagle. Conor 101 Johanna Fitzgerald, d. of the knight of the Valley. Conor
102 Margaret d. of the lord of Kerry and Slany of O'Brien of Killaloe. Conor 103 Honora
d. of second earl of Thomond. John 104 Julia d. of O'Sullivan More. Charles 105 Elise-
beth d. of the 19 Kerry, widow of Thomas Amory.

sheltered by its hills, Husseys, Trants and Hubberts. Ormond, after hunting down the last great Geraldine, obtained from the crown a grant of this tongue of land of magnificent proportions, but not long after it was restored to the knights of Kerry who for many generations had been its immediate lords under the earls. Trughenacmy, the barony of which Tralee was the capital, was partially possessed at times by the McEllygots and MacSheehys, MacSweenys, and the hereditary brehons, McEgan and MacClancy.

Of Kerry below, McCarthys More, whose principal residence was at Pallace, were lords paramount. Their supremacy was there rarely disputed, and their lieges contributed a chief rent to their treasuries and contingents to their array. But they were otherwise independent, except that they were bound to entertain their chief and his followers when they came to visit them. The answer in court under queen Elizabeth of a clansman that he knew no king but O'Sullivan More, cost him his ears, but goes to show that neither to the English crown, nor to the representative of these ancient kings, existed any very exacting obligations. Moriartys were early of the kings Eoghanact and O'Donaghoes, lords of Lough Lene and Ross Castle. O'Connals, O'Neils and Dalys were established in the barony of Masonihy, which passing from its former lords later became for the most part the property of the Brownes earls of Kenmare. One branch of the O'Donaghoes, that of Glenflesk, more fortunate longer retained their twenty-one ploughlands. The present member of parliament from Tralee is their representative. In 1556 Donal McCarthy More was created baron of Valentia and earl of Clancarre.

Under due subordination to their lords paramount the kings of Desmond the O'Sullivans More formerly of Knoc Graffon, actually the senior branch of the Desmond race, being derived from Finghin or Florence, elder brother of Faihlbe Flan (93), born 511, the progenitor of the MacCarthies—held all the rest of the county, if we except Iveragh of the O'Sheas and Mahonys from Dingle Bay—

Branches such as the Mac Gillicuddys of the Peaks or Tunacruacha, honored and prosperous, and the McFinnens, secured their share of the family territory, but throughout Dunkerron and Glanerought they were immediate if not absolute lords, holding the official position of hereditary marshals of Desmond. They intermarried with the various branches of McCarthies, O'Briens and Geraldines, Donovans and O'Callaghans. They lost their estates in defending them from spoliation in loyalty to the house of Stuart or in vindication of their religious liberties. Their representatives, by their military services to the united realm, the second baronet was killed at Bayonne in 1814, and by their civil career and contributions to literature, have done credit to an honored name.

In Glanerought on the east bank of the Kenmare close by its shore long stood the castle of Ardea, belonging to a branch of the O'Sullivans Beare, for so were designated the lords of Beare and Bantry whose domains extended north of and around Bantry Bay. If rocky and mountainous, upon them dwelt in the days of their prosperity a considerable population, and in the sixteenth century five hundred of their principal followers after their unsuccessful struggle for independence were included in the general amnesty. All the several branches of the name were intimately connected with the other leading families in Munster by marriage and consanguinity, with the McCarthies More, Reagh and Muskerry, O'Briens, Donovans, Butlers and Geraldines. Dermod chief of the Beare family was blown up in his castle of Dunboy in 1549, and that castle in the days of his grandson Donal, afterwards count of Bearehaven in Spain, stood a memorable siege for several weeks against a force of five thousand men under Sir George Carew. The defects in the system of government peculiar to Ireland and the efficacy of the English policy by dividing to conquer were both curiously illustrated in their fall.

Dermod, to whose fate we have alluded, married the daughter of

McCarthy Reagh by the daughter of the eighth earl of Kildare. Upon the death of his son Donal, whose wife was Sarah O'Brien of Thomond, Sir Owen second son of Dermod succeeded as tanist. His wife was daughter of the viscount Buttavant; his son's, of the fifteenth earl of Desmond. Other descendants of Sir Owen were widely connected and influential. Unwilling to yield up the rule and estates to his nephew Donal when he came of age, he surrendered them to Queen Elizabeth, as Morrough O'Brien had Thomond to her father, and received them back to hold by English tenure. Donal petitioned for his right; whereupon Bantry was given to Sir Owen, Ardea to Philip Owen's brother, Bearehaven to Donal, the rightful heir to the whole. Indignant at this injustice and the evident design of the English government to deprive him of his rights, and his country of its liberties, he appealed to arms. After the battle of Kinsale, which ended disastrously for the septs in 1602, he continued for a time in hostile defiance of the English forces, taking possession of his castles, but after a hopeless struggle he passed with his wife into Spain, where both he and his son received many acts of kindness from the king, but he was assassinated in 1618 by John Welsh. After the protectorate ended in the restoration, a portion of the estates were restored to the then O'Sullivan Beare, and the family for a brief period enjoyed their earlier prosperity. They were ardently attached to the faith of their fathers and naturally took part in 1689 with James the Second. For this, which no sophistry could construe into a crime or justification for sequestering their property, they were deprived of nearly all that remained of their domains. A revenue officer named Puxley obtained possession of Bearehaven and the castle of Dunboy. The race who had held for centuries were not of a nature to submit tamely to injustice; they made what resistance they could, but were forced to yield to the overwhelming superiority of English power.

All the westerly portions of the county of Cork long remained

10

under the McCarthy chieftains. Near Mizen Head the Mahonys whose several branches were scattered over Desmond, O'Driscolls of Baltimore, sons of Ith, Donavans of Clancahill, Horgans, Dugans, Crowleys, Regans, Hartigans and Fihilly were multiplied in Corgha Luic or east and west Carberry, but this large territory between the sea and the river Lee was bestowed by Donal McCarthy More NaCurragh, king of Desmond, on his second son Donal Gud with the castles of Dunmanway and Kilbrittain. This Donal Gud (109) the first McCarthy Reagh dethroned the O'Mahonys, chiefs of Ivaugh, but was himself slain in 1251 by John Fitzgerald of Callan. His grandson Donal the handsome (111) was the ancestor of the branches of Glenachroim and Duna Glas, and his grandson (113) espoused a daughter of Kerry, theirs (115) Catherine daughter of the eighth Desmond, and their son (116) Elinor, daughter of the eighth Kildare. The marriage of their grandson Florence to the only child and heiress of McCarthy More, earl of Clancarre, led to his forty years' imprisonment and forfeiture of a large part of her estates and his own. The direct line of Carberry still possessed, in the early part of the seventeenth century, the castles of Kilbrittain and Dunmanway, but lost them under the protectorate, recovering an inconsiderable part of their lands at the restoration. Donogh (121) purchased Springhouse in Tipperary, where he died in 1713, and his great-grandson, born there in 1744, died in 1812. The son of the latter married and dwelt in France, where his son Justin was born in 1811.

On the sea near the east of Carberry were the Barrys Roe and Oge, De Courcys lords of Kinsale, Mahonys lords of Kinel-mealky, Currys of Kerricurrihy, a Dalcassian family. Across the cove was Imokilly extending to Youghal, and farther north Hy Lehan where ruled the earls of Barrymore, west of which lay the Barretts, of English origin, and East Lismore and Kenataloon the former possessions of the earls of Desmond and now of the Dukes of Devonshire.

Between the Lee, running east before it changes its course south to the city of Cork and the Cove, and the Blackwater, which forming the easterly bound of the county empties its waters into the sea at Youghal, are the fertile fields of Muskerry, which Cormac, king of Desmond, whose father-in-law was the sixth lord of Kerry, bestowed on his younger son Dermod (113), 1310–1367, its first lord. His great-grandson (116), 1411–1494, built Blarney castle, and founded the monastery of Kilcrea, and his great-grandson Cormac (120), 1552–1620, described by Sir Henry Sidney as "the rarest man that was ever born among the Irishes and who possessed of many handsome castles was very hospitable," was father of Cormac Oge (121), 1564–1640. Cormack, whose wife was Margaret O'Brien daughter of the fourth earl of Thomond and who was ancestor of the earls of Kenmare and Kerry, was created viscount of Muskerry, and his son Donogh 1594–1666 who married Ellen Butler, sister of the first duke of Ormond, in 1558 earl of Clancarthy. His grandson Donogh was unjustly deprived of estates worth later two hundred thousand pounds annually, for taking part with the Stuarts, and Robert the fifth earl his son died at Boulogne in France, in 1774, aged 94. The estates forfeited were sold to the Hollow Sword Blade Company, Chief Justice Payne, Dean Davis and Sir James Jeffries and others, whose descendants still hold them.

North of Muskerry, extending to the boundaries of county Limerick, an elder branch of the McCarthies the MacDonoghs were long chiefs of Duhallow. They descended from the eldest son of Cormac Fionn McCarthy More, king of Desmond, born 1170, who was also the progenitor of the MacCartneys viscounts of Antrim in 1776. In the seventeenth century, the lord of Duhallow erected the castle of Kanturk, the completion of which was arrested by the order of the privy council, as too strong for a subject. With much of the territory the castle passed through the earls of Egremont to the Wynhams, lords Leconfield. The O'Keefes of Donogh castle, mar-

shals of Desmond, chiefs of Glenavon in Fermoy, Irebracken and of
Poble O'Keefe on the borders of Cork and Kerry, were long powerful in Duhallow, the present representative of the name being
Manus of Mount Keefe New Market in the county of Cork.   One
other family, the McAuliffes, chiefs of Clanawley, had possessions in
the mountains near the Limerick line, which were forfeited by the
last lord in 1641 with those of his nephew MacDonogh lord of Kanturk and Duhallow.   Noonan, Dugan, Herlihy, Desmond, were
names well known in Duhallow.

These principalities, Duhallow, Muskerry and Carberry, in possession of the three most powerful feudatories of the chief of Desmond,
protected the southwesterly portions of the island from encroachment; while along their easterly bounds Orrery and Kilmore in the
hands of the Barrys, Fermoy belonging to the Roches and Clangibbon to the white, Knight north of the Blackwater, the Barretts, Barrymore formerly Hy Lyhan, Imokilly, Kinnatalloon and
Kilmore, the domains of the earls of Desmond, which passed through
the Boyles and Cliffords, to the Dukes of Devonshire, protected Cork
from any hostile approach unless in considerable force.   The outer-
wall of the castle of Lismore remains with the interior restored, and
at Youghal at the river's mouth Myrtle Grove, the abode of Sir
Walter Raleigh, to whom was granted this property when forfeited by the earl of Desmond.   He sold it to Roger first earl of
Cork, through whose son it passed to the present proprietor.   With
so much of the picturesque and beautiful everywhere in Ireland it
seems out of our special theme to indulge in terms of admiration,
but the cove of Cork and the Blackwater from its mouth to Lismore
rank high in beautiful scenery, in graceful hills and luxuriant vegetation, lawns and pleasure grounds, varied by stretches of water.   This
great county divided into two ridings contains an area of nearly
two millions of acres, with a population of about seven hundred
thousand.   From Youghal harbor to Waterford and bounding east

on the Suir, extends the county of Waterford with less than half
a million of acres, about three to every one of its inhabitants. It
was for the most part early held under the kings of Desmond, by the
O'Phelans, but was too accessible to English power to be retained by them. The earls of Desmond had Coshmore and the
Decies, which coming to them from the Fitz Anthonys was settled by
the seventh earl on his second son. This earl had been by royal
permission entrusted for his training to the prince of Thomond, and
when he superseded his nephew for marrying Catherine Cormac he
gave Glenahiry to (114) Turlogh the ancestor of a branch of the
O'Briens, long settled in Waterford. There were numerous settlers
of English race in the county, but the family most honored and
prosperous from the invasion were the Poers, earls of Tyrone, now
represented by the marquesses of Waterford. Mullanys, Gearys,
Flannagans, Bries, Magraths and Conrans, if not extinct, have
greatly fallen away from their earlier prosperity, and the names associated with wealth and influence now are Lombards, Talbots, Whites,
Morrises, Daltons, Wyses, Barrons, Walls, Sherlocks and Comerfords, with others of English race.

Of the total area of Munster, 6,067,722 acres, 5,915,561 are
land, and 152,161 water. At the last census of 1871, 1,362,664
were under tillage; 3,326,035 plantation; 108,752 waste bog; and
mountain, 1,118,110. There were inhabited houses, 234,757; uninhabited, 7,183; building, 474. The population of the province
in 1871 was 1,393,485; in 1861, 1,513,588; in 1841, 2,396,161.
Of Cork, 85,000 in 1851; 80,000 in 1861; 78,642 in 1871.
Limerick had decreased to 39,353; Waterford slightly gained.
The constituency of Cork consisted of 4307 electors; Limerick,
2193; Waterford, 1404; Kinsale, 179; Mallow, 233; Ennis, 225;
Bandon, 253. Of the different religious sects, 1,304,684 were Catho-
lics; 74,213, Protestant Episcopalians; 4091, Presbyterians; 4758,
Methodist; and 5729 of other beliefs. 62,039 persons spoke Irish

alone; 483,492, Irish and English. There were 91,299 farmers;
126,013 farm holdings; 4 over two thousand acres, 2175 under
five. Between 1851 and 1871, 738,443 persons, 381,655 males
and 356,788 females, had emigrated from Munster; 15,561 in 1870.

XV.

GOVERNMENT AND LAWS.

We have thus endeavored to familiarize our readers with the
names of the tribes and septs most frequently mentioned in historical works, with the several ancestral stems from which they derived
their origin, places where they dwelt, and family ties that united
them. For reasons already made sufficiently obvious such matters
enter more largely into Irish history than any other, and without
this knowledge it cannot be understood. It has been also our aim
to individualize so far as we were able, chief or noble taking active
part in affairs military or political, although their special pre-emi-
nence was rather proportionate to the extent of their territories and
number of their adherents, than to their own personal character or
desert.

It remains, before resuming our narrative of events leading to the
exclusion of Irishmen from property in their natal soil, to allude
briefly to the light shed by recent publications upon the government
and laws of Erin, the language and literature, manners and customs
of its people from early ages through their various modifications and
changes until swept away or forced out of view by English ascendancy. For this flood of illumination upon what seemed not long
ago hopelessly wrapt in obscurity, we are indebted to the life-long
devotion of professor Eugene O'Curry, who through the judicious
selection of Mr. Newman its president, was called to the historical
chair of the catholic university, where his attainments in the Gad-

hailic tongue and intimate knowledge of its literary remains could be made best available for their elucidation. His lectures on the manuscript materials of Irish history, and on the manners and customs of the ancient Irish, delivered nearly twenty years ago, were published last year under the auspices and at the charge of the university. The second series has been edited by his associate professor, W. R. Sullivan, who, though in a different department of learning, has proved himself a proficient in this, greatly adding to their value by an introductory volume, and appendices rich with the later harvests from researches still pursued. Much we are told may be still gleaned from the materials worked by these zealous explorers, and as the field cannot be exhausted in a single generation, it has been wisely decided to communicate what has been already reduced to intelligible form and not to withhold it till the work is complete. The chief sources of information are manuscripts mouldering or fading into illegibility on vellum or more perishable paper, widely dispersed, and shame to say not all accessible even to scholars, and in a language passed for the most part into desuetude and difficult of interpretation for want of adequate dictionaries and glosses. More than ever of late attention has been given to these treasures, which like the Italian cities preserved under ashes and lava for modern instruction, are being revealed to us, fortunately at a time when investigation in similar fields of research has enabled us to appreciate their value and turn them to account.

What has already been imparted to the world in these lectures and other recent publications of the like nature, has tended less to satisfy than whet curiosity. The misapprehensions and errors which have grown out of imperfect information create an eagerness to be set right. Criticism has become especially exacting, and the learned men entrusted with interpretation of these ancient oracles have by frequent and often flagrant mistakes been taught to proceed with caution. What receives their sanction resting in no instance on conjecture or assumption, but drawn by conscientious and competent scholars from reliable and original sources, may justly claim implicit confidence. Before many years this whole mass of material, translated and in print, will no doubt be given to the public, and, after its due examination and study, the history of the country become a possibility.

Authentic accounts have come down to us in the pages of scripture and ancient historians of eastern civilization at the earliest date assigned to the colonization of the island. Offshoots from that Aryan stock, in the van of progressive development, carried from Asia around the borders of the great inland sea to beyond the pillars of Hercules and possibly to this western hemisphere, its arts and inventions, language and laws, and their nomad habits and reputed maritime facilities and enterprise justify the belief, that whatever enlightenment anywhere existed, Egyptian, Assyrian, Phœnician or Roman, had been, if not extended and adopted, at least heard of and more or less dimly reflected in the remotest confines of the then known world. Neither Nemidians, Firbolgs nor Tuatha de Danaans were savages. They belonged to this highest human type, and in natural endowment and intelligence equalled Jew or Greek. If their simplicity of life and polity harmonized with their pastoral pursuits, they for mutual defence and safety were gregarious, and wherever any large number gathered together the inherent elements of their nature implanted by providence for their improvement and happiness rapidly germinated in political institutions, education and refinement of manners.

No reason exists for believing that the Milesian colonies who found their way seven centuries before the christian era, or possibly earlier, from Spain, in sufficient force to overpower the nations then in possession of the land, were in any respect their inferiors. Coming from nearer the centres of existing enlightenment, the reverse would seem more probable. All that has been related of the Tuatha de

Danaans, their dwellings, arms, usages and magical incantations,
indicate a people well advanced in the modes of civilization then
prevailing, and among them, if we may credit tradition, there were
many sages and historians.   When after the conquest by Eber and
Eremon the island was divided between them, Ona one of their followers, a proficient on the harp, fell to the lot of the former; to the
latter, Cir famous in song; while Amergin, one of the brothers that
survived, gained celebrity as a lawgiver.   Ollamh Fodhla of Clan
Rory, establishing his court 4463[1] at Tara, appointed governors to each
cantred, chiefs to each village.   The instructions to his son of Moran,
of the golden collar which tightened round his neck if he made judicial blunders, or according to Sullivan choked the prisoner if guilty,
are still extant after nearly twenty centuries.

In what is known as the book of invasions, compiled by O'Clery
in 1630 from earlier manuscripts, it is stated that the laws brought
over by the Milesians were derived from the Jews.   But experience
of new wants led constantly to modifications adapted to their different condition and circumstances.   From time to time these laws
were revised, old and new consolidated into codes, and what had
been repealed or fallen into desuetude, if they left no historical trace
passed out of mind.   When St. Patrick under the monarch King
Leary introduced christianity, in order that the laws might better
conform to its precepts, a commission consisting of three kings, the
monarch, Daire king of Ulster and Core of Munster, three ollamhs,
Dubhtach of history, Ros of technical law, and Fergus of poetry,
with three bishops, Benen, Cairneck and the saint himself, revised
them.   They reported the code known as the Seanchas Mor, which
adopted by the collected kings and chief rulers at Tara remained in
force, of course with modifications, from 403 for a thousand years,
and as late in Thomond as 1600.   This code defined and punished

[1] The chronology adopted by O'Curry is predicated upon the following intervals or eras:
Adam to the Deluge, 2242 years; Deluge to Abraham, 942; Abraham to David, 949; David
to the Captivity, 485; Bondage to the birth of Christ, 599; together, 5199.   Orosius computed from Adam to Abraham, 3184; Abraham to Christ, 2015, with same aggregate.

11

crime, regulated contracts, social rank, military authority, land tenures and domestic relations, made provision for the poor, and at the instance of the saint, cries or compensation for life were substituted for the less merciful rule of blood for blood, tooth for tooth, laid down in the Mosaic law, and of which trace is found in the earlier laws and annals. The code of Justinian was established half a century later; but the saint, and probably many priests and laymen of Ireland had been brought in Rome or Roman cities to the knowledge of Roman law, and it is not surprising that many resemblances should be discovered between its provisions and those established outside the imperial limits in Erin or other lands.

Besides these statutes of general obligation called Fennachas or Cain laws, there were others of local or limited operation. The several subordinate kingdoms and tribes had laws and customs of their own for their special government, which formed part of the common law of the country or Urradas, and there existed besides certain contracts known as cairde between adjoining territories. The courts corresponded to territorial limits or distribution of power. The airecht fodeisin or king's court presided over by the chief ollamh and his "brethren no dolbeir," airechtaeb for settling disputes between different territories, the urnaide or common pleas, and foleith, had each its jurisdiction; and above all was the culairecht, one for each province and one at Tara, courts of appeal. Four grades of advocates duly qualified for fixed fees, practised under rules complicated and tending to the furtherance of justice, their process and proceeding suggesting their having been borrowed from the English or from an origin common to both. Landlords were responsible that their tenants should do right and prosecuted their plaints, and in evidence much weight was attached to character. After the central rule came to an end with Roderick, kings and chiefs maintained their several tribunals, but their decrees were less respected and the governing power became more absolute and arbitrary.

Land and office alike followed generally established rules of succession. Rigs and tanists, ollamhs and brehons, poets and physicians, even cerds or smiths, saers or carpenters and other artisans held their employments and their lands by inheritance, and ceilles bond or free held according to possession or descent, paying in kine or military service. The ceille bond took his land with stock and followed his lord to war, the ceile free found his own cattle. Of the aire or freemen the boeirech febhsa had twenty-one cows ; the bruigfer who seems to have been both judge and publican, sixty-three. The fothla became noble when he had amassed double the fortune required for the lowest order of nobility. The aire coisring represented his community, the aire fine his family, in responsibility to the laws, the king or his liege lord.

Of superior rank socially and politically to the bo-aries or bothachs seven orders of flaths or nobles had their special functions, privileges and obligations, holding their deis or estates free from rent, but subject to the tribal laws, and, of course, to military service. The lowest degree or aire desa embraced them all, and they were clothed with power to preserve order, and three together authorized to hear complaints at custom or urradas law, and act as magistrates. The term aire cehtai or high-constable of a tuath, aire-ard with manorial court and clothed with authority to hear in the first instance informations and plaints under cain or statute law, with duties as steward to his superior lord or king; the aire-tuisi, commander of the levies of the tuath, and the aire forgail or chancellor, with supervision of the rights of minors, family disputes, common land and other similar responsibilities, and among them that of presiding over the court of the chief whether king or other flath, were rather titles of office than of rank. A certain number of tenants fixed by law from twelve to fifty, of cencleithe or personal retainers, a certain following of personal attendants, dwellings or lisses of prescribed size and elegance, steeds with green, gold or silver bridles, brooches and other appointments, were the required qualifications or insignia of each degree corresponding to their respective consequence. The wife of a flath was to be his equal in rank and a maiden. Such rules if for a while observed would soon very naturally fall into neglect, and probably were greatly modified with the changing condition of the country. Besides these freemen or aires bœirech and flaths, fuidirs originally strangers, captives or the empoverished were tenants at sufferance of their holdings, and if sometimes acquiring by their industry or other worth property and consideration, were for the most part hewers of wood and drawers of water to the rest, at the mercy of the lord and his dependents. They had no rights known to the law, and for them as for his other tenants the flath was responsible in the courts and represented them in their claims for redress when aggrieved. If the power of the flath over his tenants and adherents as defined by law was abused by him, he was compelled to make amends. His duties were also prescribed, and as their protector in peace and leader in war, the relation was one of mutual obligation and reciprocal regard.

Above the five orders of flaths we have mentioned were two more, the Rig and Tanaisi Rig, king and his tanist. The office of king, whether simply of a single tuath of which there were one hundred and eighty-six, rig of a cluster of tuaths or king of companies, a rank military rather than territorial, rig rurech or bonad such as were the five or six provincial kings, and the Ard Rig or monarch of the island, who was generally if not always one of them, was essentially hereditary, and although of limited prerogative was one both of dignity and power. Inter arma silent leges, and when war became the constant occupation, law martial or military, or arbitrary mandates of the chieftain, took place of the well-ordered procedures of the tribunals. Still frequent instances are met in an-

cient annals of kings relinquishing the supreme power without hesitation when this was required by law from his loss of sight, of an eye
or other maim or infirmity, disqualifying for royal functions.

The regal office was elective as well as hereditary. The freemen
flaths and aires, after three days consideration at the house of the
bruigh fer or at some other central place, selected from amongst the
candidates, but always out of the family or line of the chief and out of
the roydamnas or such as came within the prescribed degrees, generally the nearest in blood to the deceased competent to rule. In most
instances the son or brother succeeded. This usage or law of election
engendered jealousies and led to bloodshed, but held under restraint
despotic tendencies. When elected, the chiefs were inaugurated with
form and ceremonial in special places consecrated from time immemorial for this purpose. In some instances the tanaisi or success-
or was chosen at the same time as the rig, but more often later in the
reign of the chief, though the uncertainties of life must have rendered it judicious to have him defined in case of emergency.
When other than the next in succession assumed the government as
tanist, it was not simply as regent, for he did not surrender the control to the immediate heir when of age or disabilities were removed.
His deis or territory was often that appertaining to tanists, besides
what more particularly belonged to himself, and the duns or castles
of which a king was bound to have three, consisting of double wall
of masonry and moat, were occupied by him as king. In cases
of alternate succession, such as of the Eoghanacht and Dalcas,
northern and southern Hy-nials, the tanaisi rig was naturally often
chosen with the Rig himself, but not invariably. Indeed however
specific the regulation, practice under it underwent constant modifications and was at no period or place very uniform. This usage
of tanistry was not confined to the royal power. Even among the
class of bo-aires, tanaisis at times took charge of the land and
represented its responsibilities, furnishing soldiers to the army,

and performing other duties requiring mature age and experience.

Besides subsidies from his flaths and stipends from his superior lord, fees, booty, waifs and escheats, the royal revenues consisted of the produce of his own demesne, rents of his daer and saer ceiles, and the maidens' marriage rings sometimes weighing an ounce of gold. Reciprocal payments were notable features in the relation of liege and lord in Ireland. Each paid the other stipends in token of their mutual obligations. A king was not permitted to engage in any derogatory employment or go about unattended, and the court of the more wealthy and powerful consisted of hostages pledged for the fidelity of vassals, and of numerous officials and dignitaries, who sat at his table and took part in his amusements and counsels.

In the Crith Gablach, an ancient law tract on the social and political relations of the Irish published with the lectures, there is little intimation given of any peculiar clan or family structure in the social organization, and as already suggested whatever at any time existed the influx of strangers and other causes were constantly tending to break up. In early days the inhabitants were of many races, and though under Brian Boru each tribe or nation took its name from its chieftain or one from whom he descended, they were not all of his blood. In course of time by intermarriages, larger numbers through lines paternal or maternal might derive from his ancestral stem. But as the law limited the succession to the immediate family of the deceased chief, and only recognized as belonging to it those within a few degrees, the tie of common name or even consanguinity became little else than a sentiment, chiefly operating in inspiring loyalty and devotion in the field, and rendering less disagreeable other services. In some parts of the land where there was little intercourse from without, the clan after centuries may have been not only of one name but essentially of the same stock.

In what is known of Tara and its triennial gatherings, the last in

554, there was consultation among kings and chiefs, and even assemblages duly constituted, perhaps organized by law for deliberation. It is probable that these gatherings were more like Polish diets for ratifying laws than framing them, the principal personages meeting privately together for that. Cemeteries of kings, heroes or men of note were the spots selected for the purpose. Aileach with its remains of fort and palace and tomb in stone masonry in Donegal, Carmen in Wexford, possibly Cruachan in Rosscommon, and Tailtan in Armagh, may date back to the Tuatha de Danaans. The former in an old poem is described as the mound of the assemblies of noble Erin and long before Ernania was a royal dwelling. What is transmitted of the arrangement and mode of construction of these abodes of the kings will be seen later.

This sketch of the government and laws of Ireland in remote periods, and which modified by time and circumstance, continued to prevail in some parts of the island down to 1605, is all that our limits admit. It is sufficient to show that the political condition was far removed from anarchy or despotism, well suited for the furtherance of justice and maintenance of right. It indicates considerable progress in civilization, love of order and appreciation of liberty. It certainly very conclusively proves that the people were able to govern themselves without help from Norman or Saxon. Under this rule they drove out the Danes, and if they had been equally fortunate with their selfish neighbors from across the channel they would have made as rapid strides in civilization of the baser sort, in luxury and art, as other nations. When the brehon-law-commission report, what these laws in reality were will be known. Meanwhile O'Curry and Sullivan are safe guides to what has been divulged.

If we may depend upon what they tell us of those ancient laws, and both laws and ballads help to show what people were, no evidence exists to warrant the reproach that the Irish were either more lawless or savage than their neighbors. Much on the contrary to show that they were sensible, devout and loyal, in their domestic relations kind conscientious and devoted. Their social and political system was the best suited to foster whatever is most respectable in human nature by its complications of reciprocal duty and obligation. Constant war and exposure to danger and weather invigorated their physical powers, rendering them industrious, patient of labor and fatigue, engendering noble and heroic sentiment. Many nations were less favorably placed for development of character, few would have been more so for material and intellectual progress, had they been left alone.

XVI.

LANGUAGE AND LITERATURE.

That the speech of the ancient Irish from long before our era was essentially that of the Gaedlic manuscripts still existing, no one pretends to dispute. It is substantially that used exclusively by hundreds of thousands of the present inhabitants of the island, and by one-sixth of the population who also speak English. Its origin can be traced to the Aryan ancestors of the successive waves of colonization spreading through the centuries from the Indus to the Atlantic Ocean. How this particular branch of the mother tongue assumed form and its own special development, is not now to be ascertained. In all probability it remained for ages a spoken language and of a very limited vocabulary before it was reduced to writing.

The manuscripts preserved are in Latin characters slightly altered, and O'Curry expresses the opinion that the Cuilmen, Saltair of Tara and Cin drom Snechta. the earliest known Gaedlic compositions, were originally written in this alphabet, which had been introduced into Ireland by Druids or poets who had travelled into other lands, or which through other means had found its way into the country. But that there existed besides and earlier a system of writing and keeping records, quite different from and independent of the Greek and Latin forms and characters, which gained currency in the country after the introduction of Christianity in the first part of the fifth century, if not known a considerable period before that era, admits of as little doubt. What these earlier characters, called ogham or oghnim, actually were has been only partially ascertained. Their knowledge was not confined to druid or ollamh ; other persons of high social rank were initiated into the mystery which attended their use. They were employed to perpetuate the memory of the dead or mark their sepulchres, to record historical events and even sustained historical or romantic tales, long before the Roman letters were used and probably afterwards. Bilingual inscriptions have been discovered in both Roman and ogham characters, of which brief passages are found in the manuscript volumes. Whether the ogham were hieroglyphics or some lost alphabet, they have not been sufficiently studied for much more than conjecture, and have proved as yet of no great value for linguistic investigation.

Before parchment, bark of beech or other trees, probably covered with wax like the Roman tablets, for such excavated from bogs are in the academy museum, or else rods or staffs stripped of bark and notched with a knife, served instead. The letters or feadha, Gaelic for woods, of the ogham alphabet, which was sometimes styled nin from its term for the letter N, were possibly named from the different trees of the forest, or, as has been also conjectured, the names of the trees may have been taken from them. With such writing materials and the embarrassment attending their transportation and safety under the circumstances of the times, abbreviations were important, and this may have affected the formation of the alphabet. Donald Mac Firbis, of the seventeenth century, speaks of having in his possession, when he wrote, ancient writing

12

tablets of the gael, in which could be distinguished some hundred and fifty different signs, besides others which were used on the rods alluded to. These are not to be regarded as distinct letters, but combinations or adopted forms of more or less general acceptance, equivalent to different vocal sounds or meanings, possibly of the nature of mnemonics, serving to aid the poet in his recitations or minstrel in his song. Staffs or tamhlorg, opening fanwise and covered with these cabalistic characters, were of convenient form for travelling from dun to dun as was their wont for use in the festal hall. By comparison of what is still extant of ogham with the corresponding equivalents where known in Latin, much yet may be gleaned. Dr. Graves, Protestant bishop of Limerick, has in preparation a work on this subject, and forming part of it will be a translation of the tract on ogham in the book of Ballymote.

Gaelic possesses many roots in common with the Sanskrit and other branches of the great family of Indoaryan language, such as Greek and Latin. Lottner, from inscriptions found in northern Italy and France, reached the conclusion that the ancient Celtic revealed forms which in antiquity yield in nothing to classic Latin, and that these languages as well as the old Germanic were as highly inflected as that or Greek. Such inflections, clipped or worn by long use, are found in ancient Gaedlic, which varies in grammatical structure as in strict adherence to rule at different epochs and under different conditions. It seems probable that laying side by side with classic language in the minds of scholars, both being equally familiar and in constant use, the vernacular may have gained in regularity, again lost when and where employed rather for speech than for literary composition. Dead languages embalmed in masterpieces generally known and interpreted by grammar and dictionary, remain fixed and constant like sculptured forms: while those living and in popular use continue in a transition state, new words and phrases being constantly adopted. They become more simple or complex, according as new wants are experienced, and diverging into dialects often wander far away from their original matrix, where tribes speaking them have little education or intercourse with one another, and no common standard.

How language thus improves or degenerates, expands or diversifies, is happily expressed by Sullivan in the introduction to the lectures : "like the life from which it emanates its decay being the cradle of new growth. Words coalesce, sounds are dropped or modified, to satisfy the feeling for euphony or greater ease of pronunciation, the same word is applied to express distinct ideas, these gradually cease to be used in the original sense, differences of physical nature produce corresponding effects upon the sounds and meaning of words, nay even the idiosyncrasy of individuals affects their language. These changes would not take place uniformly over a large area ; so that if a country of considerable extent were originally occupied by the same tribe speaking the same language, in process of time dialects would arise." This is illustrated by the different words and phrases coined or borrowed from new tongues to meet new needs, not only in different parts of the island, but in the Scotch Gaelic originally the same as the Irish. Not long ago neighboring counties in England differed greatly in their speech; and from Chaucer to Macaulay, Froissart to Thiers, simplicity in orthography and elegance of expression keeping pace with the copiousness required by expansion of knowledge, the earlier English and French seem to us now almost different languages from the modern.

In pagan days habits of life were not propitious to scholarly pursuits. Druids, ollamhs and files and even princes themselves who visited foreign lands attained what knowledge was to be had, and according to tradition diligently improved their opportunities. But the cloister offered far greater facilities for learning and its fruits. Copying the scriptures, sacred offices and lives of the saints, historical accounts of other times and lands, record of passing events in

their own as its importance was felt, employed their leisure and
added to their means. Accomplished scribes became as accomplished authors. To the ten centuries succeeding the conversion and
before the invention of printing, are attributed most of the manuscripts now known and the works which they contain. The number
of conventual establishments, education of the priesthood at Rome
or in countries deeply imbued with Roman civilization, their acquaintance with the great productions of human genius, explains the
reputation enjoyed at home and abroad by Irish scholars. Their
intimate relations with the laity under their spiritual guidance, rendered indispensable a thorough knowledge of their own language,
which was greatly improved from their attainments in others
living or dead. As late as the sixteenth century Gaedlic was the
customary speech not only in remote places or amongst the septs,
but with the Anglo-Irish whose safety in a measure depended upon
assimilation with their neighbors, and who effacing so far as they were
able every distinction of race not only spoke the language, but
cultivated its literature and were diligent collectors of its books.

This demand stimulated production. Each convent had its
scriptorium, many of them not merely obtaining copies of whatever
elsewhere existed of fiction or historical lore, but keeping up such
records of their own. In the volumes preserved, the same compositions are found with little variation, showing to what extent these
interchanges took place. As hundreds of such institutions were
scattered over the land, more of these works would undoubtedly have
come down to us, but for the Danish and Norman devastations,
wanton destruction attending the suppression of religious houses
at the reformation, and numbers carried away, purposely or heedlessly
destroyed by unscrupulous despoilers, ignorant soldiers and their narrow minded commanders, or as a solace in their exile by priests
in the subsequent persecutions. How many must have been hope
lessly lost in the vicissitudes of their wandering and impoverished

life, or its untimely or solitary close, can never be known. The old book of Lismore, discovered in 1814 walled up in an old door-way of the castle, shows to what shifts they often had recourse for their preservation.

Notwithstanding this sad havoc of ancient writings, which from the justly reputed learning of Irish scholars, and opportunities their education abroad afforded them, may well have embraced priceless treasures from other lands and times now lost, an extensive literature remains. More than what would be equivalent to three score thousand printed pages lays in manuscript in different libraries public and private. Portions have from time to time been translated and printed, but far more remains out of reach in an unknown tongue except to a few zealous devotees to the literary antiquities of their country, who have been rarely in condition from their other pursuits to turn their knowledge to account for the public benefit. Indeed, though the time is approaching, it has not yet arrived for reaping the harvest probably ripening for other generations, and the present must be content with such windfalls as vouchsafed.

When a large body exists of thorough masters of the language in all its forms modern and archaic, when glosses of greater perfection have been provided, writings faded from age or exposure subjected to strong lights, chemical restorers and the photograph, all or the important portions brought together in print and studied by many minds of various culture, their true value will be known. It is to be hoped that parliament will appropriate generously to this sacred duty, till these works in the original are transcribed, electrotyped, translated and multiplied in print, and supplied to every public library. Already the work has been commenced. The Senchas mor and other legal codes, fragments and tracts have been entrusted to the brehon law commission. Nearly eight thousand pages have been transcribed, and when thoroughly studied, will be placed, with faithful versions in English and adequate glosses and commentaries,

in the hands of the public. The tale of the " White Bull " is now
in the press, and the " Leabhar-na-uidhre," one of the oldest volumes
soon to be mentioned, was published during the past year.

The manuscripts consist of material, historical, genealogical,
topographical and religious, of science and medicine, law and poetry,
historical tales and romances, fairy legends, and other flights of
fancy, such as for the most part itinerant minstrels sang or
recited, to amuse chiefs and their retainers in the banquet hall, in
cloister or ladies' bower. These wanderers served also to gather up
and spread the news in the place of modern journals. As the best
known works are in many copies made at long intervals, modernized
in language and matter, and interpolated with additional portions,
much that is incorrect, lost or illegible, can only be amended, restored
or made clear by collation with other copies more exact and perfect.
These writings are on vellum or paper, some in Latin, some in
Gaelic, in many instances monographs on a single subject in the
original forms, in others compilations and collections of many separate works.

Many of the larger volumes, thus embracing various distinct compositions, consist probably of what once constituted the library of a
castle or convent. We can only hope in our brief allusion to the
more remarkable of them to direct attention to the interesting lectures
of O'Curry, that visitors to the institutions that possess these treasures, or those who are debarred that privilege, may better understand what they are.

The supposed oldest manuscripts are in the Royal Irish Academy :
the four gospels or Domhnach Airgid in Latin, given by St. Patrick
to St. Maccairthan, and the Cathach or mutilated copy of the psalms
of St. Columcille, handed down for thirteen centuries in the line of
the O'Donnels. The same institution, a perfect treasure house of
lay relics, gold and silver, arms and ornaments, instruments of music
and implements of toil, possesses vast numbers of shrines, crosiers,

bells and rings, spoils of the church. Trinity College Library owns
an illustrated copy of the gospels of the seventh century, called
Diomas book; another of St. Molaise, the Miosach in the college
of Columba near Dublin; several private collections, and especially
the Stowe formed and catalogued by Dr. Charles O'Connor, grandson
of the distinguished antiquarian, now belonging mostly to Lord Ashburnham who permits no one to see them, and numbers besides of
both books and relics are of inestimable value.

Of the six hundred volumes of manuscripts in the Dublin collections of the Royal Irish Academy and Trinity College, the latter
possesses one hundred and forty. The oldest belonging to the former
is the "Leahbar-na-H.-uidhre," only partially preserved with one
hundred and thirty-eight pages, written by Maelmura of Clonmacnois
in the eleventh century. It contains a fragment of Nennius translated into Gaelic, an elegy on St. Colum, Mesca uledh or the
burning of Tamhlar Luachra in Kerry by the men of Ulster
cattle spoils or marauds, poems by Flann of Monasterbois. This,
as already mentioned, has been printed. The book of Leinster,
T. C. L., compiled for Dermod MacMorrogh in the twelfth century,
comprises some of the above writings, besides, amongst much else
of historical value, relations of battles of Ross-na-Righ, Cennabrat,
Magh Machrumbi, of the Boromean tribute, poems on Tara, and
the Dinnsenchas, a topographical tract of A.D. 550, in all about
equivalent to two thousand pages. The book of Ballymote, compiled about 1393, begins with the Gabhala or book of invasions.
It contains many relations historical or imaginative of Conor Mac
Nessa king of Ulster, Cormac Mac Art, Crimthan Mor and Nial
of the nine hostages, translation of Nennius, grammar and proso-
dy, tract on ogham, history of the O'Driscols, the Dinnsenchas,
history of the Argonauts, the Trojan war and of Eneas afterwards,
the whole equivalent to twenty-five hundred pages. The Leabhar
Breac or speckled book, R. T. A., with one exception consists of

translations into Gaedhlic of a religious character, about equivalent to two thousand pages in print. The yellow book of Lecain T. C. D., equivalent to two thousand printed pages, written by Mac Donogh and Gilla Mac Firbis in the year 1390, like the other collections comprises many historical relations, poems and tales. Bound up with it, but forming originally no part of it, are family poems, of Kellys and Conors of Connacht and of the O'Donnells. It contains accounts of kings and battles, poems on Tara, the great cattle spoil or raid for the white steer, Maelduin's nautical adventures, legends relating to Conor Mac Nessa, Curoi MacDaire, Labhraidh Loinseach, Nial of the nine hostage and his poet Torna. The book of Lecain, equal to twenty-four hundred printed pages, 1416, by Gilla and Isa MacFirbis, resembles in its contents the book of Ballymote. There are eight other volumes in the college library, amounting to eight thousand printed pages, most of them without special name, of which the contents are varied and interesting. Its paper manuscripts are extensive, valuable, and embrace much not found anywhere else.

The Academy besides its vellum has many hundreds of paper manuscript volumes. It has an excellent copy of the book of Lismore, of which the contents are peculiarly interesting and varied, lives of saints, incidents in ecclesiastical history, battles and sieges, translations into Gaedhlic of the history of Charlemagne, of the Lombards, travels of Marco Polo, showing the acquaintance of priest and chief with ancient and modern history. The last piece is a dialogue of two old men, Caoilte son of Ronan and Ossian son of Finn, with St. Patrick, especially instructive from its local allusions. The Gaedhlic treasures of these two libraries are not to be valued by their extent, but there are in both together six hundred paper volumes, equal to thirty thousand printed pages.

The genealogies in these collections are extensive, as some of those in the book of Leinster date from 1130; but the most frequently quoted are those of Duald Mac Firbis, 1650, in which is found the often quoted distinction between the three races, Firbolgs, Tuatha de Danaans and Milesians. "The latter white of skin, brown of hair, bold, honorable, daring, prosperous, bountiful in the bestowal of property, wealth and rings, not afraid of battle or combat. Every one fair-haired, vengeful, large, and every plunderer, musical person, professor of musical and entertaining performances, adepts in Druidical and magical arts, are descendants of the second. But whoever was black-haired, a tattler, guileful, tale-telling, noisy, contemptible, wary, wretched, mean, strolling, unsteady, harsh, and inhospitable person, every slave, every mean thief, every churl, who loves not to listen to music and entertainment, disturbers of every council and every assembly, and the promoters of discord among people, were descendants of the Firbolgs." This of course was prejudice, and if such distinctions once existed, they have long since been effaced by amalgamation of the different races. If we may judge from their loyalty to country and church, generous sacrifices for parents and kinsfolk, comparatively few offences on the criminal calendar of the courts, their readiness to embrace the great reform of Father Matthew and their thrift and industry where they have had equal chance with other men, this amalgamation has worked favorably in the development of national character.

Of the annalists, after Cormac MacArd, by whom was compiled the saltair of Tara, Mac Amalagaith of the Dinn Senchas, Cennfalath and Angus Ceille, and later Maelmura, Cormac Mac Cuilanan king and bishop of Cashel and author of its saltair in the ninth, Mac Lonan, O'Flinn and O'Hartigan in the eleventh century, O'Lochain, O'Seasnan, Flann of the Synchonisms and Gilla Caemlain who translated Nennius into Gaedlic, the first in celebrity is Tigernac of the Murray race of Connacht, abbot of Clonmacnois and Roscommon and who died in 1085. His learning was varied and extensive, and his annals commencing with the foundation of Rome cover the centuries to his own time in excellent Latin. Seven old copies exist of his

13

work, some mutilated and one of them continued down by other hands for the four subsequent centuries. The annals of the monastery of Inisfail on the island of that name in the lake of Killarney, were commenced in the tenth century, and are generally attributed to O'Carrol, prince of Loch Lene, who died 1009. It was continued to 1215, the most perfect transcriptions being found in the Bodleian and Ashburnham collections. In the former are preserved the annals of Boyle from Noah to 1251, and of Ulster by Maguire about 1500, of Kilronan or Lochee 1014—1592, of Conacht, once from 911, now from 1224 to 1562, and the Chronicon Scotorum by Dualth MacFirbis, who compiled the pedigrees of Irish and Anglo-Norman families and who was murdered in 1670. He was descended from Isa, who prepared the book of Lecain, and his chiefs were hereditary poets to the O'Dowds of Tyreril in Sligo. The Chronicon appears to have been written for Sir James Ware who knew no Gaedlic, and extends from the earliest historical epoch to 1135. The only version of the annals of Clonmacnois known to be extant is an English translation made in 1627. It professes to be a history of the island from the creation to the English invasion. The principal compilation from these various books and others now lost is that known as the Four Masters, prepared by Michael O'Clery born in 1580, and Peregrin and Conaine O'Clery of Donegal, Ferfeasa O'Mulconry of Roscommon, and Duigenan of Leitrim 1632–1636, at Donegal. The succession of kings and saints and the Leabhar Gabla, or history of the early invasions by the same, and a valuable glossary of ancient words, date at this same period; almost the latest when many of their materials could have been had. These were destroyed in large numbers by Cromwell and his ironsides, and other vandals, or lost in the confusion attending the banishment into Connaught and later or earlier confiscations.

The Boromean tribute the monarch Tuathal exacted of Eochaid king of Leinster, in the second century, for marrying his daughter

Fithir in the life time of her sister Daraine whom he had previously taken to wife, become tired of, and imprisoned. Abolished in 680, it was revived in the eleventh century, giving name to Brian Boru. This tribute and the wars of the Danes and of Thomond are subjects of separate works. The book of Munster chiefly relates to the sons of Heber, but contains much also of general interest, more particularly connected with that kingdom. It was a sensible arrangement, that of old Erin, for learning its history, that the ollamhs whose qualifications demanded twelve years of arduous preparation, had imposed upon them this charge. They were required to be able to relate three hundred and fifty tales in prose or verse. Probably many of these were chanted, whoever were musical being proficient in lullabies, pathetic and comic strains. About equal to four thousand printed pages remain classed as destructions and preyings, courtships, battles, sieges and slaughters, caves, navigations, tragedies or deaths, expeditions, elopements and conflagrations, eruptions, visions, loves, hostings, and migrations, all shedding light on life and manners, and believed mainly to be truthful accounts of the incidents related. Among the most curious is the account of the visit of St. Brendan to the American continent.

Besides the above much fairy lore exists and many imaginative tales and poems. Of the latter known as Fenian several are attributed to Oisin and Fergus, sons of Finn Cummhal. These tales, and among them the Tain Bo Chuailgne or raid for the white steer and wars of Cuchulain, are considered by Rev. Charles O'Connor to be of the thirteenth and fourteenth centuries, the historical facts derived from Tigernac and the saltair of Cashel, but his grandfather Charles of Balenagar and O'Curry ascribe to them an earlier origin. Whether taken directly from Irish sources or indirectly as current in the highlands, MacPherson out of them unquestionably constructed his poems. The landscape and weather and other natural illustrations are taken from Scotland, but Oisin son of Finn the gaal or Fingal

son of Cumhall, Cuthullin, Temora, Thorna and nearly all his persons and places are unmistakably Irish.   Were we better acquainted
with the originals and the Gaedlic itself, could go back into the spirit
of the language and the times, we might find that not only in rhythm
but in poetic expression there was greater similarity.   What we have
of Irish poetry ancient and modern, dirges, lamentations, impassioned or emotional, displays a degree of feeling, elevated expression,
and a sensitiveness to natural beauty, surpassed by few other nations.
What distinguished their poetry as well as national traits from the
Scotch is not difference of race but of climate, soil, and political
condition.   The Fenian tales are of various sorts, but whether in
prose or verse they are not rhapsodies and rarely abound in pathos.
The Ossianic poems on the contrary are wild and often plaintive ;
steeped in the genius of Scotland, of a people who believed in second
sight, and whose natural gaiety was subdued by the sombre character of its scenery.   Their gloomy grandeur is at times suggestive of
the masterpieces of Salvator Rosa, and their majestic movement has
even recalled the inapproachable sublimity of the inspired prophet
of Israel.

It seems sad to think that these remarkable compositions, which
Dr. Blair and other competent critics rate high for their sublimity
and beauty, should have lost hold on popular favor.   Literary taste
is morbidly sensitive where any attempt is made to deceive.   As with
Chatterton, the poet's fame has been tarnished, not for having arro-
gated too much to his own genius, but less than was justly its due.
It ought not to be considered surprising that poems or legends founded
on Irish incidents and characters, should have been transmitted orally
or in writing to a kindred race speaking nearly the same language, of similar modes of life and habits of thought, not remote,
and for centuries in constant and intimate intercourse with the people amongst whom they originated.   Many might well have been
preserved there which had perished at home.   But MacPherson

never produced any manuscript such as he professed to have studied for twelve years, nor revealed any source from which he could have procured them. His characters and incidents are drawn from the Irish tales, but are not like them in structure or tone. The groundwork is borrowed, but the poems owe their principal charm to poetic fervor and fancy wierd and mournful, peculiarly his own or his country's. Their tender sentiment and simple illustration from natural objects and phenomena derive their inspiration from Scotland and from the Scandinavian sagas, and are much more in unison with their staid and solemn character, than with the cheerful sprightliness of the Irish.

Prophecies not always deceptions or delusions, but simply one mode of describing historical events, abound among these remains. They are some of them evidently very ancient. How far file or druid improvised is not known, but before an excited gathering wrought upon by grief or resentment, poetic fervor might well assume this form, and the love of the marvellous was as fervent among the Irish as the Scotch. The scriptures afforded example and sanction for prophetic declaration, and for an imaginative people amidst perils and calamity with all their heroic passions on the strain, eloquence could assume no more effective form. That which Barry mentions in 1200, foreshadowing turmoil and war and distant and eventual subjugation which the subsequent history for several centuries seemed to verify, might well affect the faith of the credulous. But De Courcy's from the same source, that a knight on a white horse and bird on his shield would conquer the land, betrays its inspiration.

Besides the manuscripts in Dublin there exist long lists of them in the British Museum, sixteen precious volumes in the Bodleian at Oxford, a few in the Advocates at Edinburgh, Burgundian at Brussells, and in the Franciscan at Louvain, most of the latter dispersed at the revolution, twenty at least being now or lately in St. Isidora at Rome. Very many are in private collections, the most important formerly at Stowe, which Lord Ashburnham withholds from Irish scholars. They are possibly in the main transcriptions from those already mentioned, but probably not one in competent hands would fail to afford new light on the history and antiquities of the island and valuable additions to its known literary treasures.

What have perished, many even within comparatively recent periods, is apparent from the numbers mentioned as existing in their time by Tigernac, the several Mac Firbises, Keating, O'Curry and other authors. The Cuilmen, saltair of Tara of the second century, that of Cashel of the eighth, Cin of Drom snechta of the fourth by Ernin son of Duach king of Connaught, books of St. Mochta, Cuana, Dubhdaleithe, Slane, O'Flanagan, Inis-an-Duin Monasterboise, Dungiven, Downpatrick, Derry, Saul in Down, Cavan ; of Saint Molaga, Saint Moling, MacMurragh, Armagh, Mac Aegan, Leithlin, Clonmacnois, Dromseat ; of Clonsost in Leix ; of Glendaloch, of Bally Mulconroy 1543, Bally Clery 1500, O'Duinegans, of Sligo, Loch Ree, Loch Erne, are all gone. The saltair of Tara was lost before the thirteenth century, but a copy of that of Cashel was known to have been in existence little more than a century ago.

These sketches might be indefinitely extended, but we must bring them to a close. That what constitutes the excellence of our English literature, proceeds from the component elements of character derived from its Celtic stock as much as from its Saxon or Norman, is ably illustrated by Matthew Arnold. In his work on the study of Celtic literature published in 1867, the substance of four lectures delivered by him as professor of poetry at Oxford, he attributed to their derivation from the ancient Britton of Celtic race the quick instincts, poetic sensibility, wit and sprightliness, that with more solid qualities are characteristic of the higher type of Englishmen. Their poetic style, rhyme and rhetorical forms, he traces back to the same source as well as that play of imagination which he terms natural magic. He ascribes to the like inspiration, much of the tenderness which pervades some of the most remarkable productions of their poetic genius, the vein of sadness or melancholy constituting so marked a trait of the Ossianic poems. He places as high an estimate on the unpublished manuscripts we have been considering as O'Curry himself, and advocates the founding at Oxford of a professorship of Celtic.

We should still leave, however, this branch of our subject incomplete without reference to the sources of information in print on which the student of Irish history must also depend. Our roll cannot pretend to embrace them all, but only those of greatest value or best known. One of the earliest authors was Giraldus Cambrensis or Philip Barry, whose account of the country, written about 1200, forms, translated, a volume of Bohn's Library. Its object was to justify invasion and conquest, and it is consequently unfair and abounding in misstatement. It is clever and entertaining, and considering his brief residence and limited opportunity for collecting knowledge, very instructive. Stanihurst published in 1584 four books on Irish affairs, pronounced by Mageoghan to be prejudiced and unreliable. The work of Lombard of Waterford, a commentary in Latin on the history of Ireland, published after his death in 1632, is better esteemed.

Keating, a parish priest, near Knocgraffon, from manuscript sources and diligent study of his subject, wrote about 1630, in Gaelic, his history of Ireland from early times to 1170. It was translated and published in 1727, and though perhaps following too closely the marvellous accounts related in his authorities, is replete with instruction and especially valuable as drawn from manuscript works then in his possession, no longer in existence. Philip O'Sullivan Beare published in Spain in 1621 his compendium of the Catholic war, 1587–1602. It is in Latin, and though reprinted has not been translated. To the O'Clerys, aided by Ward of Donegal, we owe the Four Masters, compiled in 1636–50, from early manu-

scripts, a standard authority as to events and dates, and greatly
enriched by the notes of O'Donovan, its editor. Carew, Stafford's
Pacata Hibernia published in 1600, Roth's Hibernia Resur-
gens in 1621, Morrison's account of events from 1599 to 1602,
in 1735, Usher's fifty letters on the Irish in 1630, Sir James Ware's
Irish authors of 1639 and his Antiquities in 1658, in which last
work he was assisted by Duald Mac Firbis, abound most of them
both in error and truth.

Lynch in 1652 as Lucius Gratianus published his Cambrensis
eversus in refutation of Barry. O'Flaherty's Ogygia in 1684 gave the
history of early times, and of course has little pretension to be precisely accurate. O'Reilly's case stated in 1692, King William said
contained too many truths. Kennedy who deduces the Scotch kings
from Fergus, Harris, Belling, Walsh and Porter, are mentioned by
Mageoghan with various praise. His own history of Ireland written
1736–50, in French, and translated by Kelly, is one of the best.
Camden's account of the island in his Britannia is brief. Hollinshed
published Barry and Campion, which with his own sequel were put
into English by the learned Hooker about 1600. He relates events
from his own national standpoint. Doctor Hanmar's Chronicle of
Ireland, collected in 1571, terminates in 1286, but was continued by
Henry of Marlboro' to 1420.

Of later histories Wright's is voluminous and elaborate, and generally candid, but is more occupied with what concerns the English
than the Irish. From Tom Moore, the poet whose exquisite lyrics
breathed profound affection for the land of his heroic progenitors,
much was expected, but in his four volumes of Lardner's Encyclopæ-
dia he bows too often to English prejudice. It is greatly to his
credit that with his tastes and temptations, a social favorite of English proprietors, he should have performed so well a task which was
not a labor of love. Halloran's work is scholarly and conveys much
information in succinct form, and Haverty's well calculated to impart

information to readers of little leisure. Thomas Leland's history is
frequently quoted, Taafe 1810 seems less known. Miss Cusack, the
nun of Kenmare, among other works of great interest has published
one of the brightest and most readable of Irish histories. Mitchell,
Magee, O'Meagher and O'Connell treat with ability different
epochs. One of the best and which has elicited much applause
from all parties is the Cromwellian Conquest, by Prendergast,
whose services on the record commission have done much to illustrate
the history of the country. Gilbert's viceroys brought down to 1509,
presents his subject from a different point of view from the rest and
is candid and well written. Mooney's history of Ireland contains
much that is peculiar to itself, especially in relation to Irish lyrics.

Among the most interesting books on Ireland, as it is his only
prose work, is the view of its condition in his day by Edmund Spenser
the poet written in 1596, after his unfortunate experiences at
Kilcolman in the county of Cork. It abounds in just observations
on the character of the people, but recommends their absolute subjugation. Dowcra's narratives of his military experiences are often
quoted. Sir John Davis attorney general under King James in 1612
printed his discovery of the causes why Ireland had not been sooner
conquered; it is one of the least prejudiced of the various works of
that class on the country. It is remarkably honest, not sparing his
own countrymen if occasionally unduly harsh in his judgment of the
Irish. A collection of other historical papers on the country by the
same author was published in 1787. Lord Castlehaven's memoirs of
the campaigns under the protectorate are interesting, and considered
a faithful recital of his own experiences.

Colgan and Bruodine dealt chiefly with matters ecclesiastical.
Sir Richard Belling under the name of Philopater Irenæus, in his
two books Vindiciarum Catholicorum Hiberniæ treats with fidelity
the events from 1641 to 1649, which praise cannot be accorded to Sir
John Temple's account of the rebellion which abounds in prejudice and

14

gross exaggerations. William Molyneux in his case of Ireland dedicated to the prince of Orange ably vindicates its right to self-government; archbishop King in 1692 defended the cause of the protestants.

John Curry's historical and critical review of the civil wars from the reign of Elizabeth to the settlement under King William, with the state of the Irish Catholics down to the relaxation of the popery laws in 1778, was published in 1786. The Hibernia Anglicana of Sir Richard Cox and his manuscript remains are often quoted. Desiderata Curiosa Hibernica, 1772, Harris' Hibernica 1770, and Matthew Carey's Vindiciæ Hibernicæ have their value and are mentioned together from their peculiar titles rather than from similarity of subject or treatment.

Vallancey's works have been harshly criticised perhaps with justice, but they are often suggestive. O'Brien, Betham, Lascelles, Hatchell, Erck, have been diligent explorers among the archives, and Hardiman is especially thorough and conscientious. Lodge's Irish Peerage and genealogical works of the present Ulster king of arms, so favorably known wherever the English tongue is spoken, are of indispensable help to historical research. Judge Barrington's historical memoir is a weighty work, Sir Jonah's rise and fall an impartial one and his reminiscences especially entertaining. The Castlereagh correspondence, Story's impartial history and the Charlemont memoirs, explain many obscurities.

Graves' St. Canice of Kilkenny, Gough's Antiquities, Ledwich's and MacCurtin's 1717, Crofton Croker's legends of the Lakes and similar works, Franciscan Monasteries 1870, and Mervyn Archdall's Monasticon Hibernicum now being published in parts by Bishop Moran, Irish names of places by Joyce 1870, Tribes and Customs Hy-Many and of Hy Fiachrach 1844, O'Flaherty's Iar Connaught, O'Connors, Annals of Tigernach, Inisfail, Ulster and Boyle, O'Daly's Tribes of Ireland 1865, Petrie's Tara and treatise on MacFirbis and the Domnach Airgid 1837, book of rights 1847, O'Brien's law of Tanistry and rudiments of English common law discoverable in the old brehon law or Senchas Mor by Ferguson 1867, are indispensable to a public library professing to be complete. The publications of the Royal Irish Archæological and Celtic Societies contain much that is precious, and the Dublin and Irish Penny Journals in five volumes scattered papers of O'Donovan and other writers nowhere else to be found. Dalton's Army List of King James and his many other works throw light on family annals, and the history of the Irish brigades in continental service by O'Callaghan is well known.

In the Harleian and Lansdowne manuscripts in the British Museum, is much relating to Ireland. Of the state papers under Elizabeth and James, calendars have been lately published and in the introduction to the latter by Russell and Prendergast, there is much information not previously accessible. Several volumes of the publications of the record commission, consisting of Irish inquisitions and fines, and two works entitled the Public Records of Ireland and our Public Records 1873 shed light on the subject. The treasures of the Birmingham tower in the castle at Dublin are being arranged and calendared by Sir Bernard Burke, and the record offices attached to the Four Courts contain vast amounts of historical material intermingled with what is of little worth. The manuscripts of Sir George Carew out of which was compiled the Pacata Hibernia published in 1633 by Stafford as already mentioned, fill twenty volumes in the Lambeth library. A calendar of this collection has been recently published.

Among local works of note are Piers' Chorographical history of West Meath in Collectanea 1770, Smith's histories of Down Waterford and of Cork, Stuart's of Armagh, M'Gregor's and Fitzgerald's and Ferrar's of Limerick, Hardiman's of Galway, and Miss Cusack's of Kerry, Ryan's of Carlow, Gibson's of Cork ; Highlands of Cavan ; Siege of Derry, by Walker, Graham and Charlotte Elizabeth, history

of Bandon, and Gilbert's streets of Dublin.   Topographical and other
works by Mrs. Hall and her husband are most elaborate and valuable,
though often offending Irish sense of justice.   Family histories of the
Earls of Kildare and Dalys of the Geraldines, Gormans House of
O'Reilly, O'Briens by O'Donoghoe, of the MacCarthies, and O'Sullivans Mor, O'Tooles and O'Byrnes, Ormonds by Carte, MacDonnels
of Antrim, Graces and Montgomeries, Cronelly's Dalcas Eoghanacht
and Clan Rory, and biographies of Usher, Perrot, Charles O'Connor,
Florence MacCarthy, of Art McMorrrogh by Magee, Hugh O'Niel
by Mitchell, of Tyrone and Tyreonnel, and later of the United
Irishmen by Madden, of Grattan, Curran, Emmett, Flood, Holt,
Wolfe Tone, O'Connel by Cusack and Father Matthew by the same
accomplished writer, are important auxiliaries to the student in his task.
Young, Inglis, Head, Trench, Godkin, give interesting sketches of
the country and of Irish questions from different stand points ; and
Froude's prejudiced abuse has elicited able responses from father
Burke, Mitchell, Prendergast and Thiboult.   Lecky's "Leaders of
Public Opinion in Ireland" is especially valuable, affording a key to
the views of the best men of both parties at the present day ; he
discusses Irish politics from truly national points while presenting
in vivid colors the careers of Swift, Flood, Grattan and O'Connell.

Of works that should not be forgotten, connected with the island,
not mentioned above, are Judge Finglas' Decay of Ireland, 1525–33 ;
Clarendons' statement of 1668, Borlase's Rebellion of 1641, and
Sir William Petty's political survey 1719, and his tracts 1769.
Plowden 1805, Crawford, Warner, Musgrave, Atkins, Anderson and
Campbell, Mahoney, Carew, and Lanigan in church history ;
O'Reilly's memoirs of Catholic martyrs, 1868, Sullivan's story of
Ireland, Mrs. Ferguson's before the conquest, Beaumont's tour and
Cardinal Wiseman's, Gaskin's varieties 1870, have each their value.
The publications of W. Cook Taylor are highly esteemed, his civil
wars being especially instructive.   Matthew O'Connor also wrote a

military history of the nation, including that of the Irish brigade in the French service. Charles O'Connor of Belenagare, published in 1766, dissertation on historical subjects, and another of the name important events from Heremon and Heber to the present time. The O'Connor published in 1822 the chronicles of Eri translated from the Phenician. Sir William Betham takes high rank as an author by his Etruria Celtica, Gael and Cymbri, and his antiquarian researches. Our limits forbid allusion to historical fiction, but it is pleasant to remember how much Lever, Lover, Griffin, Banim, Lady Morgan, Miss Edgeworth and Mrs. Sadlier have illustrated historical epochs by their prose productions, Moore, Davis, Mangan and Sullivan in verse.

This enumeration of books connected with Ireland has no pretention to be complete. What has been written on the many controverted points in its history would fill a library. Many bibliographical works, catalogues of public collections and of bibliopolists are much more comprehensive. The simple aim has been to render available for readers who have no access to such sources, information they may find useful in selection. It is believed to embrace what are regarded of highest authority and most worthy of perusal.

Credit is due to the catalogues of James Campbell of Tremont street, Boston, and of P. M. Haverty, Barclay street, New York, for information with regard to some of the works mentioned in the text not in our libraries. These well known bibliopolists make Irish literature a specialty.

The name of Stafford (p. 103) in connection with the Pacata Hibernia was from inadvertence not corrected. He edited the work in 1633, but from his preface it appears to have been prepared under direction of Carew but not by him.

XVII.

MANNERS AND CUSTOMS.

Careful study of the literary remains of the ancient Irish, has given more exact information as to their modes of life. For this we are mainly indebted to the learned lecturer and his accomplished commentator. Much also has been contributed by other competent scholars whom growing interest in the subject has prompted to similar research. When English ascendancy had crushed out national life, and Gaelic no longer employed for literary purposes and only spoken had become corrupt, rarely were found men of sufficient education with opportunity and leisure to make its literature their pursuit. It is not so now, and with the grammar already published and the dictionary promised when the Brehon law commission shall have completed its task, whatever the manuscripts contain not yet known will be revealed.

From what has already been divulged some idea may be gathered as to what manner of people they were, and how they lived from Heremon to Eva, and afterwards wherever they could keep themselves aloof from foreign interference. Such exemption extended to much the larger part of the population, and over considerable areas, even of Leinster, Meath and Munster, and nearly all of Connaught and Ulster, lasted even down to the seventeenth century. During this period, and this is no idle boast for it is admitted by Sir John Davis and other English writers, the people, class for class, if not superior, were quite equal in true civilization, intelligence and education, in integrity and honor, consideration for others, in politeness and hospitality, to any other. In the varied rites of their church and the social sports and intercourse which it encouraged, at mart or court, or in the halls of their chieftains listening to historic tales with which O'Curry has made us agreeably acquainted, or taking part in the ordinary avocations for subsistence or complications of their civil rule, whatever was good in them had chance for development. An existence spent much in the open air and wholesome beverage of beer or ale in the place of later deleterious concoctions, gave to good constitutions that perfect health which alone admits of complete enjoyment. Constant warfare and the impoverishment it entailed, precluded for those who could not go abroad for education many accomplishments and some cultivation, but this was not their fault and certainly not one for Englishmen to impute.

Fenachas or laws which provide for much that was elsewhere left to individual election, specify the number and size of buildings required to be possessed by the flaths and aires, mention the domestic utensils and implements of toil, regulate the relations of rich and poor, parent and child, husband and wife, landlord and tenant, vassal and chief. Architects and artisans, teachers and physicians received ample compensation for their skill. That poets were generously recompensed is indicated by the amount received in later days by the MacNamees, hereditary poets of Tyrone, whose lands yielded them a rental of three thousand pounds. Cerds or smiths, saers or carpenters, workers in bronze and gold, wood and leather were encouraged by wages fixed by law. The spinning wheel was an appendage to every household and had its appropriate place, and cloths of flax and wool woven by women of all degrees, were dyed and fashioned into apparel. The tales and poems are precise as to what was worn by the different sexes and classes, and their descriptions if drawn from imagination, were based upon what was usual and within reasonable bounds of probability.

From royal palace to herdsman's hut were many sorts of dwellings, and there seems no reason why the early Irish should not have been comfortably lodged according to their respective rank. The first need even in milder climes is shelter from the storm, and Cain is mentioned in scripture as building himself a city. As his family was not large, this of course signifies simply such a home as his circumstances

permitted.   Neither time nor element have wholly removed the ves-
tiges of early edifices on the island.   Tara in Meath was selected by
Slainge one of the Firbolg kings for his residence, but it derived
its name from Tea wife of Heremon who desired there to be interred.
It continued till the sixth century the abode of the monarchs, each of
them afterwards holding his court in his own kingdom.   Aileach
near Derry, erected by Dagda of the Tuatha de Danaan dynasty coeval
with Pharaoh, had an enclosure with edifices of hewn stone, but
when rebuilt by Frigind for his wife Ailech, daughter of the king
of Albion, the house was of red yew, emblazoned with gold and
bronze.   Four royal houses stood within the walls of Cruachan now
Roscommon, when Ailill and his queen Mebh ruled over Connacht.
The abode of the Ulster kings at Emania destroyed in the third
century, of the Leinster at Naas, Munster at Cashel, and Meath
near Mullingar, of the O'Briens at Kincora, where Brian and his
descendants held their court, were all on one general plan.

These structures were chiefly of wood.   Extensive forests furnished timber easily wrought.   Stone was occasionally used but not
preferred, except for defence, anywhere at the period.   Stone edifices exist, dating back eight hundred years.   The chapel of King
Cormac at Cashel, constructed of that material, though very moderate
in its dimensions is a model of elegant proportion and skilful handi-
work.

The terms applied to royal abodes, rath, dun, les, cashel or
cathair had each its peculiar meaning, the rath being often an enclosure for cattle, the dun two concentric walls of twelve to twenty
feet in thickness and height to prevent their being scaled with a moat
between, the les of smaller dimensions, the cashel with a stone enclosure and cathair wholly of mason work.   In the outer wall was a
cell for the warder who kept vigilant watch over the approach.   Even
in the early Norman castles such as Conway or Caernarvon the hall
was within the walls, though soon after improvements in architecture

both in England and Ireland, led to the apartments forming integral part of the structure, as at Warwick or Blarney. But in those now under consideration the dwelling place and offices were in separate buildings of wood or wicker work inside the walls. There were seven different duns within the raths of Tara, each containing several buildings, the principal one measuring about eight hundred feet across. The residence of the ard-rig seven hundred feet in length, banquet hall or mead house and other edifices occupied the enclosure, and there were besides accommodations for an army.

In all of the royal abodes, Tara, Aileach, Emania, Cruachan, Naas, there seems to have been the same arrangement. The hall consisted of several compartments separated by columns from the central space in which in cold or wet weather burned the fire to warm the whole, the smoke making its exit through an aperture in the roof.[1] The columns fronting the centre space were coated with bronze as were arches over them, evidently not so much for ornament as for protection against fire. King and ollamh and other officers of his court had each his special place assigned, and though sixteen windows with shutters and bars of bronze are mentioned as provided for one of these buildings, two doors sufficed. In early times people slept when tired, stretched on the floor, at least such tradition says was the case with Charlemagne, but feathers were plenty and used for couches and pillows, and even sheets and coverlids were not wanting in these Irish dwellings, or tubs for bathing. As refinement spread from cities or palaces, convenience led to separate apartments for men and women, old and young, master and servant, and early laws provided that at houses of hospitality they should be lodged apart. As the house of a flath was required to be at least twenty-seven feet, with an

---

[1] This method of warming the hall or gathering place for the family was the usual one everywhere in Northern Europe down to the fifteenth century. Trace of it is still to be discovered at Penshurst, the home of the Sydneys, and many other ancient edifices. Chimneys built into the wall for warming the apartments were common at least two centuries earlier.

15

addition of sixteen all on the same floor, these dimensions when not exceeded admitted of little privacy.

Food was plentiful and various and served at one table to all. Flocks and herds abounded, fish and game ; and eight kinds of grain supplied bread, cake, and porridge. Ale often mingled with honey, for bees then supplied the sugar, was freely quaffed, leather bottles, wooden casks of staves, wooden quaighs, cups of horn, silver or gold being used. Stronger beverages not being easily obtainable, intemperance which has brutalized and degraded later generations the world over, was hardly known. Metheghlin or honey and water was drank rather by women than by men, but milk was abundant, and butter and cheese buried centuries ago in the bogs are still preserved.

Their active habits in war or other pursuits, games such as took place at Carmen or Tailtaan or in the Curragh of Kildare practised at home, compelled repose, and after their campaigns they gathered under the roofs of the chief, each in his appropriate place, playing at chess or listening when the feast was over to harp, psaltery or viol, or to historic tales which related their own achievements or those of their progenitors. Although contrary to law in these legends to exaggerate, the temptation was too great to be always withstood, and marvel mingles with fact in many preserved. These stories were recited or chanted, the Gaelic being a musical language, the verses preserved serving often merely as groundwork for language and incident impassioned to suit the occasion and the audience.

Though Boeck traces a relation between the rhythm of Pindar and musical notes, and poetic measures may yet prove a key to ancient song, Sullivan who is at home in this science as in many besides, does not concur in his view. The earliest music which is known of the ancient Irish is homophonous for many voices in unison. It is in what is called gapped quinquegrade, and without semi-tones is well adapted to harp accompaniment. This characteristic betrays the origin of many melodies claimed by other people. How early

the instruments above mentioned were introduced is conjectural.   In
second century tales, the harp is alluded to and proficients in its use
were required to lull to sleep, excite to laughter or melt to tears.
It was earliest known in Egypt which the Milesians visited in
their migration west, but possibilities are not historic facts, and that
and other instruments may have been later brought over to the island.
In very early times harps and viols and pipes, corns or horns, buines
or trumpets, cloccas or bells, timpans, cymbols, and musical branches
were played upon, and probably from long before our era contributed to the festal entertainment in royal and princely halls.   Barry
in the twelfth century bore witness to the musical accomplishments
of the Irish, but there is ample proof that centuries earlier they were
distinguished for their skill and taste in the art.   Charlemagne when
perfecting his church choir is said to have sought for choristers from
Ireland for his cathedral, as he did professors for his colleges.

Every house of consequence was required by law to have its can-
dlestick, in palace halls were candelabra of many branches, and wax
was abundant for light.   Bronze and silver and bright colors deco-
rated the columns and arches, and when Ugaine Mor, Cormac Mac
Art, Con of the hundred battles, Nial of the nine hostages kept their
state at Tara, there was as much enjoyment, if not as great magnificence as at the courts of cotemporary monarchs.   Fergus who
died 331, was the last Ulster king who dwelt at Emania, Ragnallach
of Connaught at Cruachan 645, Cormac of Munster at Cashel 903,
Cearbhall of Leinster at Naas 904, and Muircheartack of the Hy-Nials
at Aileach in 941.   O'Conors removed from Loch En to Cluain
Fraich in 1309.   Dermot McMorrogh had his abode at Fernes at the
time of the invasion ; Dermod McCarthy at Cork.   But as the law
required each provincial king to have three duns and they all had
probably more, we cannot enumerate them all.   Their residences after
this event were much the same as those of the Anglo-Normans, and
while retaining many of their early customs, in others they followed
the example set by the invaders.

To Tigernmas, seventh from Heber and Heremon, who according to the generally accepted chronological authorities reigned fifteen centuries before our era, and who first melted gold and introduced cups and brooches, is ascribed a law regulating the colors to be worn in dress. His successor, Eochaid, ordained that servants should wear but one color ; rent paying farmers, two ; officers, three ; chiefs, five ; ollamhs and poets, six ; kings and queens, seven. O'Sullivan himself eminent in his specialty as professor of chemistry as for numerous other accomplishments, tells us that dye stuffs of many sorts, moss, bedstraw, madder, woad, alder, bogbean grew wild or were cultivated on the island, and when alum was not to be procured, saline incrustations on the western coast might well have served as mordants in its stead. He doubts the general use of saffron for shirts, unless limited to some particular clan or neighborhood.

Among garments mentioned in the manuscripts, the lena and camaisi composed of flax, silk or syriac or wool, white or variously colored, without sleeves and extending to the knees, were worn next the skin ; not by the poorer classes, whose brat or cloak and berrbroc or kilt covered them. In the museum are breece or trews of diamond pattern like the Scotch plaid, tight fitting and reaching to the ankle, over which were drawn hose bound with bands sometimes not reaching the assai or shoes. Both men and women wore a jacket called the ina of green, scarlet or crimson silk or other stuff with a cris or girdle round the waist, and over it the brat or fuan, a cloak of many colors fringed often with silver and gold, and fastened with a brooch or thong. Matals or mantles, coculs or capes with a hood much used by monks, served as protection from cold or wet. Females wore the lena longer but no trews, covering the head with veil or head cloth called caille. Culpaits, ats and bars, the latter a square cap, were used by men instead of the cowl. Besides torques and minds and spiral fastenings for the hair, crowns, bracelets, chains and rings used as ornaments have escaped the havoc of time.

Arms and tools of many kinds are described and preserved in the
Royal Museum, some of iron or steel, but more often of bronze made
of copper and tin. Craisechs, heavy and thick handled spears, maces,
manais, and fiarlan or curved blade of the Firbolgs, sleg or light
spear of the Tuatha de Danaans, goth manars or broad spear and
fogad of the Milesians, laigen or lance of Leinster, cletine or spear
of Cuculain, bir or spit, faga or fork, stegin or goth, with the claidem
or sword, claybin or little sword, and claymor or larger sword, and
skené or dagger, were their principal weapons. Hand stones, slings,
clubs and flails were also used. Bows and arrows are not mentioned
nor battle axes very early, but what are supposed to be the latter are
found in the royal collection. Shields, long or round, of iron, bronze
or yew were common and when of wood had metal rim and boss.
Reference is made to defensive armor of hide with iron rings sewed
on, but before the tenth century it was little used of any sort even
by the chiefs. Soldiers going to battle threw aside their cloaks as en-
cumbrances; the chiefs and some small portion of their followers
fought on horseback without saddles. In after times both kernes
and gallowglasses were armed as the English, as will be seen in the
sequel.

The importance attached in rude times to skill in arms and the science of war, led not only to the foundation of schools for military
education and to placing young men for their training with experienced chiefs, but to the orders of knighthood already mentioned such as
the red branch of Emania, the Clan Morna of Connacht and Deargnil
of Munster. Cormac Mac Art grandson of Con in the third century
organized the Fenians, a standing military force consisting of about
nine thousand men divided into caths or battallions, each under its
chief, with an officer to each nine men. They eat once a day and
half the year supported themselves by the chase. Barracks were
constructed for them at Tara, but they were quartered on the people
in winter. To marry for fortune, insult a woman, accept a bribe,

fly from a foe, disqualified them for its ranks. The family of the soldier gave pledge not to avenge his death. He was to be well read in poetry, able to protect himself from harm against nine assailants standing still in a hole or coursing through the forest, to keep his hair in its plaits, run lightly enough not to break a withered twig, jump a tree as high as his forehead, stoop beneath one as low as his knee, pluck a thorn from his foot without losing speed. He was under oath of obedience and fidelity to his king or commander. The Fenians did not outlast the century. At the battle of Gawla fighting with their leader Ossian his nephew for Mogh Corb king of Munster, against Cairbre, ard righ or monarch, who employed the Clan Morna in their stead, this force which had won so many victories under Cumhall and Finn were nearly annihilated, Oscar, Ossian's son, being slain. They were never reorganized, and the want of that steady and well regulated discipline provided for in these rules and which under good generals won Benburg and Fontenoy, has occasioned many a disaster to Irish armies.

Of what has been transmitted of Carmen and Tailtan and similar gatherings at the burial place of heroes where games were played, consultations held and laws promulgated, young men and maidens met from different parts of the country and formed their attachments, or were mated by parental authority. Equality of rank and condition controlled selection, and portions were fixed upon equitable rates and established custom. The bride-price paid after the wedding by the husband went in part to her father. Females had no share in the landed inheritance, except on failure of nearer'male heirs, and only half a share with their brothers in the personalty. Sons even of flaths in early times divided equally, some exception being made in the case of the elder who with his obligations as chief had a larger portion. Woman's rights were respected, and if falsely accused by her husband, abandoned, beaten or otherwise maltreated, neglected by him, or if he was unfaithful, had used undue means to gain her affections, or she was deprived of her full right in domestic and social matters, she was entitled to separation and to retain her coibche or bridal gift, tincur or portion and her tindscra or bride-price. The Boromean tribute, dethronement of Dermod Mac Mor-rough, show that both in pagan and christian times marriage obliga-tions were not violated with impunity and that the rules of the church were piously respected and generally obeyed. Only one queen ever sat on the Irish throne, Macra, wife of Cymbaeth, the third century B. C., who built Emania. They were of course excluded from the chieftainries, but from Eva Mac Morrough to Grace O'Malley, women stand out in bold relief in Irish story, for wisdom, courage, and heroic deeds, and the high eulogium, passed upon their feminine excellence by the annalists in noting their decease, indicate a dis-criminating standard often reached. Family trees show how much marriages were influenced by neighborhood and previous alliances, affording opportunity for meeting and forming attachments. Wo-men do not seem to have taken part in the family councils, an institution which obtained in Ireland and probably prevented or appeased many of the misunderstandings and quarrels which other features of their social system tended to engender.

Their social and gregarious tastes were variously indulged. Re-ligious rites, weddings and funerals brought them together, and at the aenachs or fairs all ranks and both sexes congregated. These fairs were held periodically and less for interchange of commodities than for amusement. Athletic games, dances and music, courting and matchmaking were the principal attraction; but laws were pro-mulgated, disputes adjusted and acquaintance made. Mathluagh were of more restricted attendance and called to protest against arbitrary acts of the rig, denial of justice by a court, distribution of property of deceased members of the fine, weapon shows, to take measures of defence or for battle speeches. The mithal flatha was the meeting of the tenants of a flath; mithal tuatha of the freemen of the tuath, dals of the nobles, tocomrach for election of kings, adoption of laws and ordinances. Inaugurations of rigs or chiefs were occasions of great ceremony. They took place in the open air, on special spots designated by some rock or tree, and the oaths of faithful service were administered with much solemnity.

In relation to Tara we are tempted to cite the following passage from Ancient Ireland, a magazine devoted to Irish antiquities published at Waterford in 1835. In connection with Ollav Fodla, who reigned according to accepted chronology, 921–42 B. C., it says : " This illustrious assembly was called in Irish by the name of Feis Teav-rach, or, 'the Parliament of Tara.' The object of assembling it was two fold. 1st. To revise the entire body of the established laws, and to correct or amend them, or to enact new laws, as the exigence of the kingdom might require. 2d. To examine and digest all the annals, historical records, and genealogies of the kingdom, so as to transmit down to posterity a correct history of the several emigrations, wars, and other memorable transactions of his royal ancestors, from the Phenician king Fenius Farsa, down to his own time. The nobility, gentry and learned men, who attended this great convention, took their places thereat, according to their dignity, rank, or office ; all of which were strictly defined and regulated by the heralds or genealogists. Irish writers are loud in their praises of this monarch, for his abilities, wisdom, virtue, and valor. This assembly of the states at Tara, subsequently took place every third year."

We shall not apologize for another extract from the same valuable repository, as it is a work extremely rare, at least in America. " The office of historian in ancient Ireland, was kept up by the State, without interruption or intermission ; and when a historian died, his place was filled immediately, in the same manner, and with the same regularity, as our office of judge is now filled up. The writing of the national history was not left as in modern countries to the whim, or

caprice, or prejudice, of individuals. All the learned professions
were *hereditary*, in particular families, in Ireland. Thus we find
repeatedly in the Irish writers, such a name mentioned as the
"hereditary judges" of a particular district; another name as the
"hereditary historians;" another as the "hereditary bards,"—the
"hereditary physicians,"—the "hereditary standard bearers,"—and
other offices, civil as well as military. All the provincial kings,
princes, and dynasts, kept up these "hereditary institutions" within
their respective territories, as well as the monarch. These professions were assiduously cultivated by the respective tribes or families
to whom they hereditarily belonged. On the death of any professor, his office was filled up from his own tribe; but it was not the
eldest son, or the nearest a-kin, that was appointed, but he, of the
tribe, who was proved to be the most eminent and most learned in
the particular profession. Thus the most active competition was
kept up, and, at the same time, the entire mind of a tribe or family
was kept fixed upon the cultivation of the one pursuit, without dis-
traction or wavering, from their infancy; circumstances eminently
calculated to produce a very high degree of cultivation in each.
Large estates and ample fortunes were settled upon the different professions, and thereby those who cultivated them left at ease and
leisure to apply. Camden, by no means favorably inclined towards
Ireland, attests this fact. He says that "the Irish have their judges,
whom they call brehons; their *historians* who record historical
events; their physicians, poets, and musicians, who instruct their
children or relatives, *each in his own profession;* and they always
have *successors.*"

Sir John Davis attributes to the laws of tanistry under which the
successor elect was always a rival of the ruling chieftain, and to the
custom of gavelkind, which vested no permanent or hereditary interest in the soil but left it to the discretion of the chief to redistri-
bute, much of the turmoil and calamities of the country. Irishmen
16

could not fail to perceive the advantage of the better defined estates
under feudal law where the rule worked for their personal benefit.
Any such distribution of land rarely however occurred and the law
did not everywhere prevail. Their main object in life was not accumulation, or even subsistence. These were secondary to their other
pursuits of duty or enjoyment. Their wealth consisted of cattle,
little effort sufficed to satisfy their wants, and less importance was
attached to landed possessions except among the chiefs for increase
of military strength or political influence.   Rank was virtually
hereditary yet followed as a consequence to territorial power and
resources, measured by the number of fighting men they could rally
to their banners. But both chiefs and people were so much more
indifferent to acquisition of property as the principal motive which
governed them, that they cannot be judged by the standards prevailing in modern communities.

Obligations assumed at the baptismal font, held sacred by good
catholics, when between the races were viewed by the home government with distrust. Such alliances between its rebellious subjects
and the chiefs rendered both too independent of its authority. Gossipred was consequently interdicted by various acts. Among the
Irish themselves it was a bond of fellowship from early Christian
times punctiliously regarded. Fosterage, also prohibited between
Irish and English to as little purpose, signified not simply taking infants to nurse, though this was one of its meanings and another tie of
peculiar sanctity, but also receiving children to educate. It was
wisely thought that young persons away from the pernicious effects
of parental indulgence and subject to stricter discipline, would be
more zealous for improvement, better under control. This system
of fosterage was not confined to any rank, but universal for both lofty
and lowly. Peasant girls were taught to grind, sift and knead, as
also needlework ; farmers' sons to rear cattle, dry corn, prepare malt ;
maidens of superior station to sew and embroider, their brothers to

play chess, to swim, ride, use the sword and spear; and all of them
such other culture as befitted their condition. Eochaid rig of Cliach
in Limerick had at one time under his charge forty pupils, sons of
the chiefs of Munster, who, mounted on steeds richly caparisoned,
attended him on a visit to king Ailill and his queen Medbh at their
palace of Cruachan.

The sacred rites of hospitality were often carried to excess,
not of intemperance, for there was neither the inclination nor the
appliances since beer was the chief beverage, but to extravagance.
Cosherings or visits to their vassals not extended beyond moderation were a reasonable charge or rent service among the Irish, but
became oppression when claimed as a right by English lords, and
enforced with insolence and cruelty. Before the reign of James the
first there were no inns so called, but houses of hospitality which
were kept by the bruighfer or other person entitled to no compensation, but who held his land on condition of entertaining travellers.
Their social position was one of eminent respectability, if we may
judge from what is said of them in obituary notices by the annalists.

Such visits to their own tenants or those of other persons by
English proprietors were fruitful sources of complaint and pro-
hibitory legislation. In a work entitled the presentment of Irish
grievances under Henry VIII. it is stated that the earls of Desmond,
Kildare and Ossory, with their wives and children, and a multitude
of people, resorted to monasteries or gentlemen's houses, taking
meat and drink at their pleasure, their horses and servants being
quartered on the poor farmers, paying nothing, and so stayed for
more than half a year, sparing their own houses. Other customs
originally not objectionable, degenerated into like abuse. Coyne and
livery, or quartering and cess of soldiers, bonaghts which generally
amounted to their support from the farmers on the line of march,
risings out and compulsory military service enforced by lords of
either race, were grievous burdens. Cuttings and cess and other rents
cheerfully paid to their own chieftains became intolerable when ex-

acted by strangers. The acts however to restrain coshery and bon-acht were passed not for the benefit of the Irish, but of the poorer English settlers who often escaped these impositions by abandoning their farms and leaving the country.

Raids and hostings were regarded by the young and enterprising as expeditions of enjoyment. They loved the adventure and companionship, coveted the distinctions awarded to signal bravery. Often the sept invaded averted attack by joining forces and assailing some common foe. The lays of their bards taught them to emulate the heroic deeds of their ancestors, and to this and the prevailing temperament of their race may be ascribed their noted indifference to danger and death. As they were always armed and easily provoked, they often slew nearer kinsmen than they ought.

At their funerals open house was kept and feasting mingled with dirges and lamentation. Chiefs were often carried long distances to be interred with their ancestors. James the ninth earl of Desmond, slain at Rathkeele in Limerick in 1487, was buried at Youghall more than a hundred miles away. These ancestral tombs were generally selected for dals and other gatherings, civil and military, the memory of the dead being perpetuated by the games, marts and marriages of the living. Great respect was paid to places of sepulture. The traveller about the island is frequently reminded of honored names by inscriptions on dilapidated monuments of ancient date crowding some ruined chapel or long neglected church-yard.

These customs and manners became greatly modified after the invasion, but they were the groundwork of the Irish social system to a much later period nor have they yet wholly disappeared. Whoever cares to understand the subject thoroughly must read Curry's lectures. Our purpose is simply to point the way. What has been said will only stimulate curiosity to resort to the fountain head for rich stores of knowledge which will not disappoint expectation. Much in relation to the habits of the Irish later, will find a place as we proceed.

XVIII.

IRELAND UNDER THE PLANTAGENETS.

In our earlier chapters the historical events connected with the invasion were recalled to the reader. Its easy and early success was explained by the political state of the island, divided amongst many independent septs and chieftains comparatively powerless to cope, even if united, with soldiers trained in the best schools of warfare, better armed and equipped, and drawing their reinforcements and supplies across the channel from a nation vastly superior in numbers and resources. Some account was attempted of the more prominent leaders, and the share each received of the spoil. It was shown, how, establishing themselves in the seaports long occupied exclusively by Danes and other strangers, they contrived to preserve and extend their conquests by more thorough military discipline, and occasionally by their favorite policy of stirring up strife among the septs, of dividing in order to conquer. We then endeavored to group in forms convenient for reference all that local and family lore, whatever concerns the political, intellectual and social condition of the country in early times, without some knowledge of which its history is a puzzle. Resuming the narrative at the close of the first century from the landing, at the death of Henry the Third, we pursue the course of events bearing on our subject down to the epoch when the battle of Bosworth transferred the English crown from Plantagenet to Tudor.

Even in the early period of occupation the pressure of English power was not constant, and when opportunity offered the septs resumed possession of their territories, driving out the intruders. In Ulster, except near the eastern shore in Antrim and Down, the English retained no foothold; and in Munster, McCarthy More confined them to their castles. Hugh O'Connor of Connaught, after defeating the English under De Burgh at Moynise in 1270, with

great slaughter, reduced Roscommon, which with Athlone, Rath-
done, Carrickfergus and other cities along shore were their principal
strongholds, demolishing that and destroying other of their settlements.

Under a grant of Thomond, from Edward the First Thomas de
Clare brother of the Earl of Hertford, and whose wife Juliana was
daughter of Maurice Fitzgerald, taking advantage of a disputed succession between two of the O'Briens, made his way into the country
and erected fortifications.   Beset by the exasperated clans whom he
sought to subject, from jealousy or an ebullition of temper he cruelly
murdered Brian Roe O'Brien, who had befriended him, and to whom
he was indebted for what measure of success had attended his enterprise, ordering him to be torn asunder by horses.   In 1280 when
captured with his father-in-law by the O'Briens, no other reparation was exacted of him but the surrender of Roscommon.   He died
1286, and thirty years later, two of his sons being defeated and slain,
the remaining members of his family, burning Bunratty Castle which
they had erected for their abode, quitted Thomond never to return.

John Fitz Geffroi, in 1266 justiciary for the third time, obtained
a grant of the Barony of Islands in Clare, seventy thousand acres.
In 1281 the O'Neils, aided by the English, defeated the O'Donnels
at Desertcreigh in Tyrone.   De Burgh, two years later, invaded
Ulster, but in 1285 was overcome by the men of Connaught at Ballys-
adare, sustaining great loss.   The endeavors of O'Hanlon and
McMahon to expel the intruders were attended with partial success,
and McLaghlin of Meath defeated and slew Richard Tuite the great
baron.   The O'Connors of Offaly sacked the Castle of Kildare.
At a later period, in 1305, their chiefs, invited to a banquet at the
Castle of Sir Pierce Birmingham, were massacred.   Birmingham
was arraigned for the crime, but no justice was done.   He was
soon after defeated at Ballymore.   The hard fought battle of Glen-
fel was won by Mandeville, but the O'Byrnes and O'Tooles gained
a decisive victory at Glendalough.

The presence within their borders of a power ever aggressive bred distrust and stirred up strife among the septs and sometimes from temper or jealousy, often through the ingenious machinations of the stranger, they imbrued their hands in fraternal blood.   Their laws ceasing to restrain their passions when aroused, their only recourse was the arbitrament of arms.   The English had their quarrels, but the royal authority was invoked to adjust them, or interposed with its strong arm.   Under weak kings it was less respected, and the red earl of Ulster from his castle of Trim set at defiance Piers de Goveston at Dublin who proved an over active governor, but in 1311 the earl was defeated and taken prisoner in Thomond by Richard De Clare at the head of the Geraldines.   De Wogan sent again as governor, found Deverdon as troublesome as the Byrnes and O'Tooles. De Verdon had inherited half of Meath from his mother Margaret heiress of Walter Lacy.   This turbulent lord of both parliaments and viceroy in 1314 married Elizabeth De Clare after the death of her first husband son of the earl of Ulster.   His death took place in 1317 and his four daughters, one Isabel by his second wife, carried his moity of Meath into the families of Furnival Burghersh, Devereux and Ferrers.

After the battle of Bannockburn, 1314, Edward Bruce, brother of King Robert, was invited to become king of Ireland.   Robert's wife was daughter of the Earl of Ulster: her sisters married Fitzgeralds of Offaly and Desmond, De Clare and Multon.   De Laceys and De Bissets lent aid to the project, but soon sought pardon for their imprudence and returned to their allegiance.   Ulster gathered an army, but lost it at Coleraine where the Scots gained a decisive victory.   Felim O'Connor of Connaught at first took sides against Bruce, but after defeating his kinsman Roderick, who sought to supplant him with his sept, he went with his countrymen, nearly all of whom favored and sustained the movement.   They were profoundly disgusted with English rule, of which the manifest policy

was to dispossess them of their lands and subject them to servitude.
In an admirable address to the Pope, signed by the O'Neil and other
chiefs, they state that they were treated as enemies, not subjects;
that any Englishman might take the law against an Irishman, but
if he killed an Irishman, falsely and perfidiously, as often happened,
he could not be brought before the English tribunals. They had
urged on Edward I. the extension to them of the laws of England,
and though the king had consented the measure had come to naught
from the opposition of the English settlers.

Bruce was one of their own race.[1] For two years he was eminently fortunate, defeating the English forces on eighteen battle-fields.
His brother Robert joined him from Scotland, and they marched into
Connaught. Circumstances seemed propitious, for Edward the Second was a weak king, and the nation apparently of one mind. But
when all promised success, Robert was called back to Scotland, disputes arose among the chiefs, and the Irish having wasted their
strength in mutual slaughter were defeated with great loss at the
fatal battle of Athenry, helped by Birminghams and De Burghs.
After waiting in vain for happier auspices, Edward Bruce marched to
meet the English forces, and fell at the battle of Faughard near Dundalk in 1318. Thus faded away for Ireland the hope of escape, by
uniting the two branches of the Milesian race against foreign domination, from a connection she had every reason to dread. The event
gave strength and stability for a time to English rule, but even in the
ten counties and liberties it was mostly nominal, the preponderance
of the natives setting at naught any effort to molest them. The
power of the kings of Connaught, however, was broken at Athenry,
their territories after a few generations being divided between two
branches of the race, O'Connors Don and O'Connors Roe.

[1] In 1240 Robert Bruce, grandfather of Robert and Edward, married Isabel De Clare descended from Eva.

XIX.

REIGN OF EDWARD III.

If sire and son of the second Edward were energetic monarchs, his own weak and vacillating character brought contempt on royal station. Governed by worthless favorites, overawed by turbulent barons, he was dethroned and murdered at Berkeley castle in 1327 at the instigation of his queen and her paramour Roger Mortimer. At Bannockburn in 1314 had ended all hope of adding Scotland to his realm, and though at Faughard Edward Bruce proved less fortunate than his brother, the island was not subdued and hardly more dependent on the English crown. Two years after the latter combat O'Connors and McDermots, near neighbors, were at war in Connaught. Roderick king after Feidlim had been killed by Cathal, who in turn yielded life and throne to his kinsman Turlogh. English in Meath defeated O'Connors of Offaly and in Thomond were put to rout by Brian O'Brien. MacGinnis of Fermanagh, Ferrals in Analy, Rourkes, Reillys and O'Neils were rioting in mutual bloodshed, and Geraldines in Desmond were vanquished by McCarthies as disastrously as sixty years before at Callan.

The English among themselves were restless and quarrelsome. Grasping and domineering, like birds of prey they pounced down upon whoever were weak, their allies of to-day being their enemies on the morrow. There was, perhaps, often more of policy than temper in their course. The Geraldines with Butlers and Birminghams warred with Powers and De Burghs. Talbots and Birminghams were butchered by Gernons and Savages, Bodnets and Condons by Barrys and Roches. Fighting, indeed, was the business of life at the period, not in Ireland alone, but in England, France and everywhere else. Bermingham had been created earl of Louth in reward for conquering Edward Bruce. At his death in 1330, when he was

17

slain by his own countrymen, his earldom became extinct, and three years later that of Ulster passed away from the De Burghs.

When Bruce in 1315 set up his standard, Richard red earl of Ulster and father-in-law of king Robert rallied an army to stay his progress. When repulsed his defeat was attributed by himself to the defection of Feidlim O'Connor. But his haughty rejection of help from Edmund Butler exciting suspicion of his own disaffection, the mayor of Dublin arrested him at his abode in that city, and when set at liberty by Roger Mortimer sent over to assume command, he was watched. Feeling the approach of infirmity in 1326, he sumptuously entertained his kindred and friends at Trim, and formally surrendering his estates to his grandson William, son of John and Elizabeth de Clare, entered the cloister at Athassel, where William Fitzadelim his first Irish ancestor and the founder of the family had been interred. Upon his death soon after, this grandson, known as the dun earl, succeeding to his honors inherited with the earldom one fourth the island. Galway and Trim were the chief abodes of the De Burghs, but Ballymote, Corran, Sligo, Castleconnel and green castles at Carlingford Bay and Lough Foyle were other of their strongholds. The annual revenue of what they actually possessed of this vast territory had exceeded ten thousand pounds.

The young earl under these extraordinary responsibilities was active and enterprising but unfortunate. With Turlogh king of Connaught, and Mortogh king of Munster, he joined in an attack upon Brian Bane O'Brien, but they were badly defeated. He was accused of starving to death one of his kinsmen, and this is said to have been the provocation which led to his own taking off. His disposition if exhibiting many generous traits was imperious, and when his kinsman Walter for some wrong to the earl's mother was suffered by him to die of starvation in his red castle at Inishowen, Mandeville under the influence of his wife, sister of the victim, watching his opportunity slew him as they were riding together to mass at

Carrickfergus. His infant heiress by Maud, daughter of the earl of Lancaster and Maud Chaworth, by her marriage with Lionel son of the third Edward, transmitted, as already stated, Ulster and Connaught through the Mortimers to the crown a century later in the person of the fourth.

Offshoots from the race of the De Burghs descended from the brother of the first earl according to Lodge, but sons of the red earl to the annalists, claimed the estates as male fiefs by Irish tenure, taking respectively William the name or title of Mac William Oughter of Clanrickard, Edmund that of Mac William Eighter or the lower of Mayo. In the existing state of the country even the crown was powerless to resent this intrusion, and possession somewhat shorn of its original pretensions and with many vicissitudes has continued with little interruption to the present day in their descendants. The O'Neils resumed Clannaboy in Antrim, portions of which about Shanes Castle remain in that name; nearly all the residue of its ancient domains in Ulster having long since passed to the stranger.

Disputes arose over the spoils of the late earl, between two Burkes named Edmund, and one drowned the other in Lough Mask. Turlogh O'Connor thereupon drove the Burkes and English generally out of Connaught. Unfortunately Turlogh was not proof against feminine enticements. Enamored of the widow of. the drowned Edmund, daughter of his brother king of Thomond, and repudiating Dervail O'Donnel, his lawful spouse, "whom no woman of that race prolific in female excellence surpassed in goodness," he took her instead. He did not keep her long, for indeed both wives died the same year in 1343. Nor was he otherwise prosperous. The Sil Murray, MacDermots of Moylurg, O'Rourkes and Burkes rose against him, and with the chief of Tirconnel who was incensed at the wrong to his daughter, set up Hugh son of Hugh son of Cathal as king, with Hugh son of Felim for tanist. He was reinstated, and when slain in 1345 his own son Hugh took his place. Hugh was deposed by the tanist in 1351, but restored the next year. Unfortunately endowed with the fatal proclivities of his father he abducted in 1356 the wife of O'Kelly of Hy-Many, and dethroned the tanist Hugh reigned in his stead. This king foremost among his countrymen for valor and prowess, seems to have inspired their confidence, though in 1362 he burned fourteen churches in Kilkenny and Meath used by the English as fortresses. His last warlike expedition was with Mac William of Mayo and William O'Kelly against Clanrickard, from which he returned triumphant, and when two years later in 1368 he died after penance at Roscommon, another Roderick son of Turlogh ascended the throne by consent of the people. These successive transfers of the supreme authority in Connaught afford some insight into the working of brehon institutions.

Other earldoms, destined from the power and influence which attached to them to further English ascendancy, were created at this period. John Fitzgerald in 1316 was made earl of Kildare. Two contradictory versions of the wager of battle which transferred to him from Vesci a large part of what is now the county of that name, are given by Hollinshed and Gilbert, and probably neither is correct. In 1327, James Butler on his marriage with Eleanor de Bohun was created earl of Ormond, and in 1329 Maurice Fitzgerald earl of Desmond, and for several centuries earls of Ormond, Kildare and Desmond were principal powers in the land. They signalized their new rank by expeditions against their neighbors, selecting their opportunity so as to guard against defeat.

The matrimonial alliances of the De Burghs and Butler with the royal family of England became too important an element in the subsequent history of the island to be overlooked. From Joan d'Acres, born to Edward the First on his crusade, wife of Gilbert De Clare, earl of Gloucester, descended Elizabeth De Burgh the heiress of Ulster. Joan's sister Elizabeth married Humphrey de Bohun, earl of Hereford, and their daughter Eleanor James earl of Ormond, who in consequence of this alliance was made lord palatine of Tipperary. Their daughter espoused Gerald the poet, fourth Earl of Desmond, and their descendants thus transmitted the blood of the Plantagenets, of Charlemagne and Alfred to most of the ruling families of Ireland,—English and Irish. For the first earl of Desmond, son of Thomas Simiacus so called from a domesticated ape having carried him an infant in 1260, up to the battlements of the castle of Tralee, after his father and grandfather were slain by the McCarthies at Callan, Kerry had been created in 1330 a palatinate. It was the eighth so constituted, with power to make barons and knights, establish courts, choose judges and sheriffs, and within their limits the king's writ did not run. As their jurisdiction could not be maintained over the septs, it was limited, but the Munster Geraldines gaining gradually in power, their court at Tralee was said later to have been better administered than that of the king at Dublin, and was attended by both races. Lands ecclesiastical, called the crosses, had sheriffs of their own and their tenants were subject to special regulations.

These tribunals, with their conflicting modes and process, governed by common law and statute, march law and usage, bred confusion. Attached though they were to their own ancestral code, greater uniformity was to be wished, and the Irish, who when within reach of the English law were subjected to its oppressions without enjoying its benefits, would gladly have seen it universal. The protection extended to the five bloods, O'Neils, O'Connors, O'Briens, Cavanaghs and McLaghlins, was very naturally coveted by the rest. The request to the first Edward and his grandson for its extension led to an ordinance of Parliament that there should be one and the same law for both races. It was frustrated by landholders, who recognized in their own race alone any rights to be respected. Where they could with impunity, they shot down the Irish as game upon the mountains, despoiling them of their cattle, their lands or their children, leaving no redress but retaliation. That these atrocities engendered no implacable animosity can only be explained by the lawless state of the country and incessant warfare. Memory of them, even when preserved in the cloister, passed out of mind among the people, and each generation, as it succeeded, received what existed as the natural condition of affairs, and, powerless to improve, acquiesced in what could not be remedied.

Our Salem witchcraft of 1691 finds curious parallel at this period in Irish history. Practice of the black art in various lands having provoked papal decrees against sorcery from John XXII., the bishop of Ossory professed to discover sorcerers in his diocese, and among them Alice le Kyttler who from her four husbands and her own inheritance had derived a plentiful fortune. Three thousand pounds entrusted to her son William Outlaw for safe keeping had been buried in his garden at Kilkenny, but carried off by the sheriff and confiscated to the king as treasure trove. Her efforts to recover her property led in 1325 to charges against her and twelve other persons her accomplices of denying Christ, sacrificing to demons, obtaining from them revelations, profaning the sacred offices, and practising incantations. It was further alleged against Alice that she had compassed the death of her three first husbands after procuring them to leave her their estates, reduced her surviving husband Sir John le Power to a miserable condition by her powders and ointments, and held unholy intercourse with Robert Arturson "one of the poorer sort of hell."

As the lord chancellor kinsman to Outlaw and Arnold le Poer seneschal of Kilkenny were her friends, Dalrede the bishop proceeded with some hesitation. The accused claimed to be heard by counsel, but when the bishop overruling her plea was about to arrest her, the seneschal seized upon him and held him in confinement till the return day was past. Alice disappeared. The angry prelate being set free placed his diocese under an interdict, but came off second best in the quarrel. He was sued for defamation, excommunicated, imprisoned till 1328 in the castle at Dublin, and later accused of the same crime himself was compelled to escape into Italy. All the witches had not been so fortunate as Alice. One Petronilla of Meath, confessing under torture and accusing her mistress was flogged and burnt as were others of "her pestiferous society." Some were whipped in the market place, a few banished. We are more enlightened now, sorcery has become a lucrative profession patronized by our educated classes.

Some idea may be gathered of the actual condition of the people from what affected its chiefs. In the north-east corner Hugh lord of Tirconnel, Kinelmoen, Inishowen, Fermanagh and Brefney, eminent for his laws and their administration, hospitality and munificence, after reigning half a century died in 1333, victorious over the world and the devil. He had assumed the habit of a monk, a custom not unusual upon approaching dissolution, as in the instance just related of the earl of Ulster. His sons contested the succession. Conor slew his brother Art, and in 1342 met his own fate from Nial, who driven out by Angus was made way with by Manus in 1348, as was also Angus five years afterward. Felim son of Hugh was killed in 1357 by John son of Conor, who in 1380 fell at Assaroe in combat with Turlogh son of Nial. In Tyrone after Donnel expelled by the English in 1325 reigned Hugh, "best of his time, and bearing the palm for humanity, hospitality and valor." Nial his son followed in 1364, and when he died in 1397 he is described "as aspirant for the Irish crown, pillar of the dignity and preëminence of his own principality, destructive to the English, uniting his own countrymen, exalting the church and the sciences."

Strange to say Brian Bane, grandson of the chief cruelly murdered in 1277 by Thomas De Clare, commanded the native auxiliaries of

Richard de Clare in 1318 at Dysart, which fatally terminated the intrusion of that family into Thomond. Banished east of the Shannon by his victorious kinsman, his branch known later as the Mac I'Brien Ara became powerful, he himself till the middle of the century taking active part in military operations, When Mortogh after ruling thirty-two years died in 1343, Brian succeeded to the crown and seven years later he was slain by the sons of Lorcan. Dermod brother of Mortogh reigned fourteen years, and then the son of that chief, Mahon Moinmoy, who in 1369 made way for his own son another Brian, Cathan an Oinaigh, rivalling Brian Boru in stature and vigor. He defeated the English in Munster, taking the earl of Desmond captive, and burnt Limerick and exacted black rent throughout Munster. He made close alliance with the Burkes of Clanrickard, and gave to their chief his daughter in marriage. He was one of the four kings entertained by Richard the second at Dublin, and after a reign of forty years ended his life with the century.

In 1328 Donald McMorough, representative of the ancient king of Leinster, then for the most part regained by McMoroughs and O'Moores, declaring his right to its throne and marshalling his clan, Desmond and O'Brien attacked him and his allies, O'Nolans and O'Dempsys. He was taken prisoner, but escaped from the tower by means of a rope provided for him by Adam Nangle who was executed for his generosity. Other chieftans were more fortunate. The Mageoghan gained a complete victory over Thomas Butler, who was slain with one hundred and forty men at Mullingar. O'Brians burnt Athassel, Bunratty and Tipperary. Inasmuch as both races were represented on either side of many hostile encounters at this period, neither could claim any special glory, and both were equally responsible for the inhumanities of war. An English army with auxiliary septs invaded Clancuilen, subduing Macnamara and burning a church and one hundred and eighty persons who had taken refuge therein. Another under Desmond in 1339, overcame the men of Kerry slaying twelve hundred of them. Among the prisoners was Maurice Fitz Maurice, fourth baron of Kerry, who was fighting on the side of the native chiefs. This is the more remarkable that having been attainted for some atrocious deed of violence in 1325, he had murdered Desmond son of McCarthy More in the court room at Tralee.

Farther south there were few incidents to be recorded. Three Donals successively McCarthy More maintained their ascendency, intermarrying with the Geraldines of Kerry and Kildare, and branches of the race under them ruled over Duhallow, Carberry and Muskerry. O'Donoghues kings of Lough Lene were paramount about Killarney, Sullivans in Dunkerron, at Beare and Bantry. O'Driscolls, Mahonys, Callaghans and Donovans being rarely molested retained in peace their laws, customs and possessions. Nearer the centre hostilities were of more frequent occurrence. O'Carrols, O'Reillys, Mac Mahons and Cavanaghs possibly from motives of policy kept the country in a turmoil to discourage English settlement, and the English on their part addicted themselves to strife that they might be ready to defend what they had.

Edward dissatisfied that his subjects should squander blood and treasure needed for the successful prosecution of his wars in France, issued a decree that all lands granted by his father or himself should be resumed. It was easier even for him, though sufficiently strong in purpose, to order than to accomplish, and what were seized he was compelled to restore. However eager for contention with Irish sept or their own countrymen, the English banded together as one for their own security, and were too remote to be much endangered. ·

Growing independence of the crown excited the jealousy of its representatives and led to a distinction between those of English birth and English blood. Edward the Third, in 1342, instructed Darcy his justiciary to remove from official position whoever had

18

married or held lands only in Ireland, and replace them by such as having estates in England were more within reach of the royal displeasure. A long course of similar orders and decrees, as well as of acts of legislation, proved how utterly ineffectual such measures were to prevent what they prohibited.

The resentment provoked by this interference with the estates of the great landholders, to whom the crown was indebted for what hold it still retained of the island, was not easily appeased. Refusing to attend the parliament called by Darcy at Dublin they assembled at Kilkenny, and with Desmond to preside over them passed a remonstrance to the king inveighing against the maladministration and extortion of the government officials. It was attributed to their rapacity that the royal revenues had become reduced and many arbitrary measures against loyal subjects, exactions and imprisonments without cause were enumerated. The change of policy wrought by this spirited opposition, and conciliatory answer of the king served to allay the growing disaffection. When Dufford as deputy summoned another parliament in 1345 the barons still kept aloof, and Desmond called an opposition meeting at Callan which from apprehension of possible consequences was not so largely attended. The deputy marched into Munster, issued orders that the estates of the earl should be seized and his rents distrained into the exchequer. He contrived to gain possession of the castles of Inniskelly and Castlemaine and hung Poer, Grant and Cottrell their warders. The earl surrendering gave bonds for peaceable behavior, but not submitting to the imperious commands of the governor, his bail given in 1333 was declared forfeited and his bondsmen, more than a score in number, were reduced to poverty. Some years after when he had regained the royal favor by submission and surrender, their sequestered estates were restored in most instances, though some of them were irretrievably ruined. Dufford summoned Thomas earl of Kildare to join him with his forces, sending at the same time Burton with a writ to arrest him.   His followers gathered too speedily for his arrest to be effected, but Burton persuading Kildare to accompany him to Dublin he was there seized in the council chamber and kept in close confinement.

To meet the vast expenditures of his wars in France soon after the battle of Cressy both laity and clergy were taxed by Edward, and in both kingdoms the latter refused to pay.   Ralph O'Kelly archbishop of Tuam with his suffragans issued a decree, that any beneficed clergyman in their dioceses who paid the tax should be deprived and incapable of future preferment.   They presented themselves in their pontifical robes in the streets of Clonmel and excommunicated the royal commissioner and his subordinate tax gatherers. When informations were exhibited against them they pleaded magna charta that the church should be exempt from taxation.   It was ruled against them, but they were not farther molested.

The clash of arms was not incessant, and an event to which we have already had occasion to allude took place at this period. William O'Kelly when sorely beset in 1340 by his enemies, not knowing he was beaten, retrieved the fortunes of the day, gaining that chieftainship of Hy-Many in Connaught which he retained for forty years, and when he died received praise from the annalists for his great worth and preëminent hospitality.   This last virtue was signally displayed at the Christmas holidays of 1352 in his entertainment at his castle near Athlone of two thousand ollavs, poets, brehons, harpers and other learned men that chose to attend, to their great content.   His piety was equally conspicuous in the foundation the next year of Kilconnel for Franciscan friars.   Amongst his guests at his memorable festival were O'Dugan his own historian, Davoran, Mac Firbis, O'Curnin of Brefny, Sgingan of Tyrconnel, Mac Egan, O'Nain, all scholars of renown, and the scarcely less famous minstrels Finnaghty, Conway and Mac Carrol.

When in September 1361 Lionel the Duke of Clarence came

over as deputy and issued a proclamation that the old English should not come near his camp, they kept away, but when defeated in Munster he rallied them back to his standards. He seized Art Mac Morrogh king of Leinster and his son in their own residence and while in prison they were both put to death. After an arbitrary rule of three years he was recalled, but sent back a third time in 1367, and prompted it is said by his resentment against the Burkes of Connaught for withholding the inheritance of his wife, he procured the enactment of the famous statute of Kilkenny already mentioned. This law constituted intermarriages, gossipred or fostering with the Irish, adopting or submitting to Brehon law, treason. Assuming an Irish name, using the Irish language, apparel or customs, worked forfeiture of estate. The act further forbade the English from making war without permission of the government, allowing Irish to pasture cattle on their lands, admitting them to benefices or religious houses, or entertaining their minstrels, rhymers or newstellers.

These unfriendly dispositions towards the septs, expressed in a language they did not comprehend, if known to them produced little effect and went soon out of mind. When a chief was inaugurated, to enure them to their vocation of war he led his new subjects against some neighboring sept of either race against whom there was a score to be paid. When the maraud was over, little rancor remained, the despoiled biding their time for retaliation, and their general policy being simply to dislodge the intruders.

The moral sense of the people displayed in the dethronement of Turlogh and his son O'Connor king of Connaught twenty years before for their disregard of sacred obligations finds another example farther north. Brian Mac Mahon lord of Oriel in 1365 induced Sorley prince of the Hebrides to divorce the daughter of O'Reilly and marry his own, and afterwards drowned his son-in-law when partaking of his hospitalities. All the other chiefs of Ulster confederated to punish him, and driven in disgrace from Oriel he was slain by one of his own gallow-glasses.

Two years later when William de Windsor was lord lieutenant Gerald Mac Morrogh, heir presumptive to the throne of Leinster, rallied his sept but was slain by the black knight an Englishman of Dublin, and Dermod the king then also a captive was put to death. O'Briens and O'Connors defeated and slew in 1370 the earl of Desmond and several of his principal followers and captured Limerick, placing there as governor the chief of the Macnamaras. That the exercise of arbitrary power was not the true policy for Ireland is clear from its effects. Nearly all the septs were in revolt or alienated and only the four shires about Dublin actually under royal authority. When Pembridge was selected to try his hand as governor he absolutely refused the responsibility, and successfully controverted the right of the crown to send him against his will. De Windsor reappointed with a revenue of more than eleven thousand pounds effected nothing, and was not even able to approach the territory of the Irish chieftains.

An incident is related by the annalists of Sir Robert Savage of Ards in Down which speaks well for his nobleness of nature. When going to battle with his army of retainers he spread his hospitable board against their return. It was suggested that in case of defeat they would have been making preparation for the enemy, and it would be more prudent to conceal their effects than thus expose them to depredation. But he replied that the world was an inn, of which they were only tenants of will to the Lord. If it please him to command us from it as if it were from our lodging and to set other good fellows in our rooms, what hurt shall it be for us to leave them some meat for supper? If they enter our dwellings good manners would do no less than welcome them with such fare as the country breedeth, and with all my heart much good may it do them. Notwithstanding I presume so far upon your bravery, that verily my mind giveth me assurance that we shall return at night and feast upon our own provisions. He was not deceived and gained the victory. When building a castle and enjoining it upon his son to complete it, the reply made exhibited the like noble spirit. Better, he said, a castle of bones than of stones. Where strength and courage of valiant men are ready to help us, never will I with God's grace cumber myself with dead walls. My foot shall be wheresoever young bloods are stirring, and where I find room to fight.

A chance chat in the royal ante-chamber at Eltham with Froissart, who was bringing a poem of his own composition to king Richard rather to be appreciated by him for its splendid binding than its meaning, affords us one of his bright glimpses into the social ways of distant generations. His companion was Christedé from Bristol, who related to him his experiences many years before when under the earl of Ormond, in battle with border foes, his horse ran away with him into the hostile ranks and he was captured by Brian Costerea. This noble looking personage as he is described in the narration gave his daughter, also possessed of great personal attractions, to the stranger, who for many years made his home in the country, acquired its language, and adopted its modes of life to which he became greatly attached. In process of time another occasion of the kind was improved by the steed to deliver Costerea to the English, and the horse being recognized led to explanation. Brian reluctantly consented to part with his daughter and her husband, who left one of their children to console him and marry in Ireland, whilst her sister going back with their father to his home in Somersetshire raised up descendants for him there. This talk of a few moments whilst waiting the pleasure of the king for an audience, jotted down by the prince of annalists and gossips, sufficiently refutes the charge studiously urged by prejudice that one race was in any way superior to the other under like conditions.

Impatience at events led to frequent change of rulers, more than twenty in this single reign selected for their abilities and station, and in most instances with estates on the island, took their turn in rapid succession, and with equal inability to effect what was expected of them. Not one was permitted to remain long enough to gain wisdom or experience, and however sanguine when accepting office they were all glad to surrender its responsibilities. It may be of convenience to our readers to pass once again over the period under consideration to gain a clearer idea of the chronological order in which they exercised their functions.

Roger de Mortimer, with an inheritance both in Meath and Leinster, had been defeated with his predecessor Edmund Butler in 1316. He five years later gave place to the new earl of Louth who had conquered Bruce at Faughard, but after a single year Ralph de Gorges and John Darcy were appointed governors. In the new reign the second Kildare died in office, and Roger Utlagh, prior of Kilmainham, kinsman of the victim of the witchcraft persecutions, succeeded. The rule of Ulster ended before his assassination by Mandeville, and Darcy who had married his aunt, widow of Kildare and daughter of the red earl, was appointed viceroy, but his services being needed at Hallidon Hill and in France, he left his brother-in-law Thomas de Burgh as his deputy. The language used by Edward in reproof of this deputy's unfaithful administration sounds well for the king, who might well have profited himself by his own discourse. He reproached him with favoring persons of power, yielding to men and not to right, making one law for the rich and another for the poor, allowing the strong to oppress the weak, usurping the royal authority, detaining debts due to the crown, perpetrating heinous crimes; instead of protecting the poor, who were willing to be obedient subjects, he had harassed and grieved them against all justice, thereby giving a pernicious example to others. Considering therefore, he adds, that princes are appointed by God to punish evil doers and reward the good, we expressly command you to treat and judge equitably all those under the law of England, both small and great, rich and poor, so as to silence those who blame you and to merit our approbation.

Bishop Charlton, superseding his brother in 1337, by arrest of truculent nobles and his memorable cattle prey in Carlow, by marching about the land with horse and foot, gratified the king, who ordered that his salary should take priority of all other payments. Under Sir John Morris, deputy of D'Arcy, appointed for life in 1340, the septs regained possession of at least one-third of what had been wrested from them, reducing Athlone, Roscommon and even Randown, which from its strong walls and position on Lough Rea had been deemed impregnable. O'Neils were spreading again over Antrim; settlers in Louth paying tribute to O'Hanlon; Leinster from Carlow to the sea reverted to O'Byrnes, O'Tooles and Cavanaghs, the chief of the latter receiving an annual payment from the authorities at Dublin not to molest them.

The next choice Sir Raoul D'Ufford had espoused Maud, widow of the murdered Ulster. His progress towards the north ended in disaster, Mac Artan giving him a humiliating overthrow in Down. He rendered himself universally detested, when to the general joy disease malignant as his temper brought relief to the land, and he died in 1346.

Lord Athenry, brother of the Bermingham, executed by De Lacys in the castle in 1332, and from whom its famous tower derived its name, next in succession, warred with Kildare against O'Moores and O'Dempseys, and was followed in 1349 by the model governor Rokeby, who checked extortion and conciliated the septs. It was he who preferred to be served on wooden platters rather than not pay in gold and silver the wages of his men. Desmond, appointed for life, for a few months proved an efficient and just governor; but on his death in 1356, St. Amand, lord of Gormans-

town, inherited through the De Verdons, was sent over with increased appointments. His report home exhibited the sorry plight
of the land under misrule, which he for three years did what he
might to reform. The second Ormond was followed by Lionel,
created duke of Clarence, who rendered his third visit to the island
memorable by the passage of the act of Kilkenny. Having lost
his first wife, heiress of Ulster, immediately after the passage of this
law, he betook himself to Italy to marry his second, Violante Vis-
conti, and there died.

The fourth Desmond Gerald "the poet," from his attainments in
many arts regarded as a magician, was in 1369 replaced by Windsor, who when Edward died in 1377, espoused Alice Piers the
royal favorite. Kildare appointed in 1371, was succeeded by the
chancellor William de Taney. Then came Windsor again, who
with an exhausted treasury and the island in arms, effected little, and
made way in 1375 for the fourth Kildare, whose successor the second
Ormond in 1376 proved the last of Edward's viceroys.

XX.

REIGN OF RICHARD II.—1377-1399.

The black prince, hero of Cressy and Poictiers, than whom for
nobleness of nature or heroic action no character in English history
shines with more brilliant lustre, died the year before his father.
His son Richard, by Joan the fair maid of Kent, grand-daughter
of the great Plantagenet, at the age of eleven years, succeeded to
the throne. With such progenitors, if dependence could be placed
on transmitted trait, the young king should have proved one of
the best of monarchs, instead of the worst and weakest. In vanity,
extravagance and foolish fondness for favorites, his career certainly
exhibits curious parallels to those of his ancestors the second Edward
and third Henry, but there was little resemblance to be found in him

19

to the wise or strong of his race.   Brought up in the purple, without restraint or counsel, his kinsmen powerless to control him, and
no courtier disposed to risk his displeasure by opposing his caprice,
he developed slowly but surely into a frivolous voluptuary.   Wasting thirty thousand marks on a single garment, decking himself
with trinkets, three hundred servants employed to pamper his appetites, his days passed in feast and pageant.   In administration of
affairs, self-willed and arbitrary, the affectionate loyalty which
greeted his accession, due in a large measure to the respect attaching to the memory of his father, and which reluctantly yielded its
hold, since there was much in his personal appearance and manner
to prepossess, changed into contempt.   His uncles York and Lancaster, able men, endeavored in vain to exercise some influence over
his wayward courses, but soon mortified and disheartened withdrew
into retirement, and Gloucester who longer persevered, nobly actuated by affection for the king and solicitude for the welfare of the
realm, was cruelly and treacherously murdered at Calais in 1397 by
order of his royal nephew.

For the first year of this reign, James the second earl of Ormond,
1331–1383, continued viceroy, followed by Balscot and Bromwich.
English rule was at a low ebb.   Ireland was indeed nearly lost.
Absentee landlords abandoned estates, which they could not enjoy in
security, to the older titles of the septs sustained by adequate force,
and went home making such composition as they might.   They
were ordered to return or find substitutes under penalty of forfeiting
two-thirds of their revenues, or one-third if students in English
colleges.   Permission was given them to dig for gold and coin it
and to import wines free from Portugal.   But these gracious boons
offered no compensation for discomforts and perils to which they
were not inclined to expose themselves or their families.

When Art McMorragh claimed arrears of tribute and eric for his
brother Donald, they were promptly paid, as also subsidies to

O'Connor and O'Brien by assessment on royal functionaries. In 1380 the government was entrusted to Edmund Mortimer, who at the age of twenty-nine had already gained reputation for ability and discretion by negotiations in France and Scotland, and who by right of his wife lord of Ulster, Connaught and Trim, seemed especially fit to cope with the embarrassments attending administration. He went over with a numerous following and full purse. Several chieftains hastened to welcome him and showed their disposition to accede to propositions which he offered. But want of good faith in making prisoners of Magennis and O'Hanlon whilst his guests, checked their misplaced confidence and barred his further progress into Ulster. He constructed a bridge over the Bann in Coleraine with oak from his lands at home, fortifying it with three castles ; he plundered clergy and laity of cattle and other spoils ; captured St. Aubyn of Cumpsy, confining him in the castle of Kilkenny, and reduced Athlone ; but taking cold crossing a river, died at Cork on the twenty-sixth of December, 1381.

De Colton chosen in his place by the council was shortly after superseded by Roger de Mortimer then but eleven years of age, son of the deceased Edmund, with his uncle Thomas for his deputy. They made way in 1385 for Philip de Courtenay, another cousin of the king, who for alleged rapacity and arbitrary rule was taken into custody, dispossessed of his official functions and severely punished. Records exist to show that his oppressions if not inventions in the interest of his successor were grossly exaggerated. That successor, Robert de Vere, ninth earl of Oxford and grandson of Dufford, the abuses of whose administration have been already mentioned, by his personal attractions secured an ascendancy over the mind of Richard, the one steadfast passion of his life. In 1385, with the consent of his council, the king bestowed upon his favorite the whole of his Irish dominions with the islands round about, and whatever else he could conquer, creating him first marquis of Dublin and then

duke of Ireland. Not willing to lose his companionship, Sir John
Stanley, lately enriched by marriage with the heiress of Lathom,
was sent over as deputy, De Vere himself never setting foot on the
island. Levying war against the duke of Gloucester, whose niece
Phillippa de Couci, he repudiated for the daughter of a Portuguese
joiner, or for a German landgravine, both stories are told, he was defeated in Oxfordshire. He escaped on to the continent, and attainted in 1388 was killed in hunting by a wild boar four years later in
Louvain.

Stanley again governor in 1389 was not inactive. He contrived
to capture Nial Oge O'Neil, but soon surrendered him. The English
in Waterford, Cork, Limerick and other cities dared not leave
their walls. Kildare was laid waste, its principal towns were sacked
by the neighboring septs, and Carlow overrun. Two years later James
the third Ormond, who succeeded his father as earl in 1383, was appointed viceroy with three thousand marks allowance. The Butler
abode at Nenagh having been wrested from them by its earlier proprietors, he had built the castle of Gowran, but the year of his appointment he purchased of the Spensers, heirs of Isabel de Clare,
the castle of Kilkenny, which has been ever since the chief abode
of his line. In 1393, the duke of Gloucester nominated as his successor made preparations to go over, but his loyalty being suspected
his commission was revoked, and the king announced his intention
of proceeding to Ireland in person. The death of his wife Ann of
Bohemia caused delay; but in October with four thousand men at arms
and thirty thousand archers he landed at Waterford. His troops
were discomfited in Offaly and Ely, and Art MacMorrogh, king of
Leinster, molested his march to Dublin where he passed his Christmas.

Of Art the Four Masters tell us in noting his death in 1417
that he had defended his province against Irish and English from
his fifteenth to his sixtieth year. Hospitable, well informed and
chivalric, right royal and prosperous, he enriched churches and

monasteries by his alms and offerings. Succeeding Donogh, slain in 1775, his reign lasted forty-two years, and by his activity, wisdom and valor, he acquired and retained such ascendancy over the descendants of Cahir Mor that they willingly accepted him for their leader and king. His wife was an Englishwoman, baroness of Norragh, whose estates were within reach of the government at Dublin. They were confiscated on the plea that she had married an Irishman. Thus with monstrous ingratitude the representative of Dermot McMorrogh, who with his daughter Eva had given all Leinster to Strongbow and the English, was deprived of the small portion of the land of his ancestors which had returned to him by virtue of English law under a like title.

The decease of Roderick king of Connaught by the plague in 1484, after a reign of sixteen years, led to a disputed succession which embroiled the country in blood for many years. Two Turloghs, Don and Roe, brown and red, contended for the throne of which the former held uneasy possession twenty-two years. Whether he or Roderick his uncle was the last king of Connaught is a subject for dispute ; but when he was slain in 1406, the partition of the family domains of Roscommon was carried into effect under compact made some years before. From this epoch the power of the royal family of O'Connor greatly declined. To follow out the vicissitudes of their incessant strife would occupy more space than our limits permit ; but the waste of strength in such unnatural warfare and subdivision of territory paved the way to eventual subjugation. O'Dowds, O'Malleys, O'Flahertys, O'Kellys, McDermots, O'Haras, McMurtoghs, MacJordans d'Exeter, both houses of the Burkes and other septs of Connaught took part, and O'Rourks, O'Reillys, O'Ferrals, O'Rannals engaged on either side, O'Donnels interposing to allay or aggravate the turmoil.

Brian Catha an Aonaigh ruled over Thomond for thirty years, dying in 1399. With his son-in-law Ulick de Burgh of Clanrick-

ard he levied tribute upon the English of Munster, and proved
both an able and successful ruler. In 1380 Murrogh the tanist of
Thomond plundered Fitzgeralds and Fitzmaurices, defeating the
English under Mortimer at Athlone, and in 1395 Bryan, son of
Mahon, made war upon the O'Brien whom he drove out from
Thomond, taking John fifth earl of Kildare and Dermod O'Brien
prisoners. In 1398 McCarthy Reagh defeated O'Sullivan; his two
sons, and Owen and Conor O'Sullivans Beare being slain. The Barrets and some branches of the Geraldines were at strife, but for the
most part the lords of Munster of either race were too sensible to shed
each other's blood. The fourth earl of Desmond called the poet
left his camp one evening in 1396 and disappeared for ever. His
son John the fifth was drowned in the Suir in 1399; and another
son James who in 1388 by special permission of the crown was
placed at fosterage with Conor O'Brien, became later the seventh
earl by usurpation, Thomas the son of the fifth being set aside for
selecting his wife for her beauty.

At this period two sage monarchs ruled over Tyrone and Tyrconnel. They had occasionally to contend with discontent at home or
attack from without, but allied by marriage they were generally careful not to waste their strength upon each other. Nial defeated the
Maguires in 1379, depredated Orial in 1383 and invaded Savages of
Down, and the next year burnt Carrickfergus. In an interval of
peace he rebuilt in 1387 Ermania two miles west of Armagh,
the ancient palace of the Clan Rory monarchs destroyed a thousand
years before, and appropriated it to the entertainment of the
learned men of the country. In 1392 he conquered the English at
Dundalk and later invaded Tyrconnel, but after the two armies lay
opposed at Fearsat More, they made peace, and again in 1397
separated without fighting. This was the last expedition of Nial,
for "the contender for the crown of Ireland, pillar of the dignity and
preëminence of his principality and of resistance to every attack,

destroyer of the English, uniter of the Irish, exalter of the church and sciences, died after the victory of unction and penance, and his son Nial Oge assumed his place." His son Henry Aimreigh who was called the contentious died five years earlier. Whilst he lived he took an active part in the affairs of Tyrone, as did later his sons not always on the side of their grandfather. Along the southern border of Tyrone and to the west, O'Rourkes and O'Reilly's, Mac Kennas and Mageoghans, O'Ferralls O'Molloys and Maccoghlans of Delvin were constantly in contention, generally amongst themselves, but often also against the English in Meath, who in 1385 sustained a disastrous defeat from O'Connor of Offaly.

In one of those family quarrels which grew out of the social condition of the septs, Turlogh O'Donnel son of Nial Garve with his followers in 1380, attacked at night in his camp John lord of Tyrconnel, g. g. s. of Donnel Oge. John fell in the combat. Turlogh inaugurated in his place continued chief forty-two years, when he resigned in favor of his son Nial Garve, and entered the monastery of Assaroe, near which John was slain. "He was a peaceable, affluent and graceful man, and died in the habit of a monk after victory of unction and penance." If peaceably disposed and this epithet justly attaches to his career, he was frequently engaged in warfare with his neighbors. When Murtogh O'Connor made an onslaught upon him, killing his chiefs O'Boyle and O'Gallaghar and capturing MacSweeny and his son, with great prey of horses, arms and armor, he led his army into Carbury and spoiled the Clan Murtogh Thereupon Donel son of Murtogh made submission, yielding what was demanded of him and surrendering the prisoners and hostages taken on the previous expedition. Four years afterward his neighbor Nial king of Tyrone invaded Tyrconnel as did also the Clan Murtogh. The latter Turlogh defeated and at Fearsat Mor took place the reconciliation already mentioned with O'Neill, whose daughter Graine was Turlogh's wife. In 1395 O'Donnel defeated her

nephews, sons of Henry O'Niel at that time at war with their grandfather, and the next year the Clan Murtogh in Carbury, burning
the town of Sligo with its splendid edifices of stone and wood.
Quick to take offence Nial the next year, and the last of his life,
made an incursion into Tyrconnel, but withdrew without sustaining
much loss. Turlogh then invaded Fermanagh spoiling land and
castle but sparing churches, and likewise invaded Carbury, expelling
Donnel and setting up O'Connor his grandson in his stead. The
same year he again defeated the men of Carbury and concluded
peace with them, but soon after was taken at disadvantage at Brena-
oge. This reverse alienated his chieftains, and Nial Oge now king
of Tyrone aided by some of his own lieges, O'Doherty and the
Clan Sweeny, plundered Assaroe of its riches and reduced him to
straits, but in 1400 the Kinel Owen again invading Tyrconnel they
were driven out and many of them slain.

The plague of 1383 was peculiarly fatal to the magnates of Ire-
land. Art Magennis, Roderick of Connaught, Murrogh the tanist
of Thomond, Mora O'Madden wife of Clanrickarde, Joanna daugh-
ter of Ormond and wife of O'Carroll of Ely, O'Kennedy, the lord of
Corcovascain, the Gilpatrick and the son of his tanist of Ossory,
O'Conor Kerry, Magauran tanist of Tullyhar, O'Farrell lord of
Annaly, the son of Fircall and many more were its victims.
William O'Kelly the hospitable lord of Hy-Many died in 1382, and
Quintin O'Kane whose tomb is at Dungiven in 1395. Among the
prominent personages whose deaths are recorded, were many of the
Mac Sweenys originally of the northwest corner of the island, where
they flourished in great power as feudatories of O'Donnel, but who
for their military skill and prowess became hereditary constables to
the kings of Connaught, Desmond, Thomond, Clanrickard and
of many other chieftains, their duty being to marshal the septs and
attend to all the functions of war.

The number of learned men who are mentioned in the annals as passing away from life during this last quarter of the fourteenth century gives us some notion of the general intelligence of the people. O'Donnellan ollav of Sil Murray the most learned man of the island, O'Beaghan, MacCurtin historian of Thomond, O'Rooney poet to Magennis, O'Mulvany ollav to O'Kane, Donogh MacFirbis a good historian, Ruarean O'Hamill poet to O'Hanlon who had kept a house of general hospitality and never refused to receive any one, O'Rodaghan a general scholar and Fiutan a good poet, acquired reputation and slept with their fathers. O'Sgingan ollav of Kinel Connel in history, Mac Egan chief brehon of Lower Connaught, sage without contention or reproach, another MacFirbis, MacCarrol most eminent of the Irish in music, another Sgingan intended ollav of Kinelconnel, O'Duiganan chief historian of Conmaine in Leitrim, left if not monuments of their genius at least its memory. O'Mulconry chief of Connaught in history and poetry, O'Daly chief poet of Ireland, O'Keenan a learned historian and ollav of Oriel, Mac Egan ollav of Brefny in judicature, Matthew O'Luinin eranagh of Arde in Fermanagh, two Mac Egans in 1400, one skilled in Fenecha law and music and who had kept a celebrated house of hospitality, and the other arch ollav of Fenecha law, added futher lustre to names already familiar in connection with Irish literature.

The meagre materials afforded by the annalists at this period shed little light upon the condition of the people beyond what we have gleaned. Froissart describes the country as one of the most evil to make war upon or bring under subjection. It was closely, sharply and widely covered with high forests, great waters and marshes, and places uninhabitable and hard to enter to do damage. There were no towns or persons to speak withal. The men drew to the woods and dwelt in caves and small cottages under trees and among bushes and hedges. A man of arms might be ever so well mounted, yet run as fast as he might the Irishman would overtake him, leap up be-

20

hind his horse and draw him off. The chiefs were better lodged, but for safety selected islands in the lakes of which a well known instance is the majestic ruin of Ross Castle in Killarney the home of the elder branch of the O'Donoghoes.

It is difficult in the changed condition from good roads, large cities and rapid locomotion to realize the isolated existence of the septs at this remote period. We know enough of their habits of life and occupations to know they did not stagnate. Their constant warfare with their neighbors was a grim struggle for honor as well as for spoil; it developed manly and generous sentiment, induced social tastes and brought them into companionship in their sports, occupations and religious rites. Enough has been said in former chapters of what their duties and pleasures consisted. They had resumed possession of much of the land. The lords of English race had assumed their language and dress, and related by blood were regarded simply as chieftains like their own. The government at Dublin was looked upon as little else than another sept, an English colony planted on the shore like Waterford or Kinsale.

What had long existed occasioned no surprise, but the arrival of king Richard in 1394 with his large army must have attracted attention and produced some consternation. The manifest intention of the king to subjugate the island at a time when no unusual provocation had been given for a long previous period, proves the prudence of the chiefs in the precautions which they took for safety. Many of the more powerful, realizing their inability, divided as they were, to make head against the formidable armaments he brought with him, accepted the situation and made overtures of peace. The king at Drogheda received in person the homage of O'Niel and other chiefs of Ulster, and Art of Leinster and MacCarthy of Desmond near Carlow tendered similar submission to Mowbray earl of Nottingham.

Seventy-five chiefs entered into bonds payable in the apostolic chamber to keep the peace. O'Connor king of Connaught, O'Brien of Thomond, O'Nial of Ulster, and Art of Leinster were entertained by Richard in Dublin and received knighthood at his hands, Henry Crestede already mentioned and the earl of Ormond initiating them in the mysteries of the rite. Art in giving in his adherence made it conditional on the restoration of the lands of his wife in Kildare, but when this condition was not complied with, he considered himself absolved from any obligation.

The king in reporting to his council the success attending his progress wrote that there were in Ireland three kinds of people, the wild Irish our enemies, the rebel Irish and the English who are in obedience; that the Irish had been driven into rebellion by injuries and wrongs for which they had no remedy, and if not more wisely treated and placed in hope of favor they would join the enemy. He had therefore granted them a general pardon and taken them under his special protection. There was disappointment at home that the costly array in Ireland should not have been employed to better purpose in subduing more effectively the septs as had been his intent, but the council yielded their assent to the course adopted, provided fines and penalties were exacted to defray the expenses incurred. They soon after urged his return to repress the Lollards and take measures against hostile menace from Scotland and in 1395 he went home to receive the plaudits of his English subjects for his achievements.

Roger de Mortimer presumptive heir to the throne, then approaching his majority and married to the niece of the king, daughter of the duke of Surrey, once more was appointed viceroy. His vast estates in both countries and twenty thousand marks of accumulated rents made him rich. He was "a stout champion at tournaments, a famous speaker, a bountiful giver, in conversation affable and jocose, in beauty and form surpassing his fellows, but although warlike and

renowned and successful in his enterprises, he was disolute and re-
miss in matters of religion." His brother Edmund married a
daughter of Owen Glendower, his sister Elizabeth Henry Percy,
more familiarly known to readers of Shakespeare as Hotspur.
Soon after his appointment appeared Romin de Perellos, a Spanish
magnate on his way to visit the purgatory of St. Patrick in Donegal.
Mortimer tried to dissuade Ramon from his enterprise but without
effect, and the Spaniard was hospitably entertained by the chiefs
who remembered that their progenitors came also out of Spain.

Le Scrope, justiciary of Leinster, to whom the king had confided
his hostages, was rapacious and cruel till his wife refused to live
with him unless he changed his course; whereupon he became
generous, promoted the public welfare, and died generally beloved.
Sir Thomas de Mortimer, uncle of the viceroy, not so easily converted from the error of his ways, perhaps having no wife to save
him from the bad, was impeached, declared a traitor, and forced to
seek asylum beyond the pale. Gerald fifth earl of Kildare taken
prisoner paid large ransom to O'Connor of Offaly. The viceroy
himself soon afterwards fell at Kenlis in Carlow, where his army
was put to rout and cut to pieces. Surrey succeeded, but the king
giving him the lands of Art's wife in Kildare, neither he nor Janico
d'Artois his gascon general could make any impression on the
septs, and Richard in 1399 returned with like numbers as before.

After three weeks at Waterford he marched, on the 23d of June,
against Art who claimed to be king of Ireland, and who with three
thousand men set his brother king at defiance. Richard burnt his
villages and woods and by the blaze knighted Henry of Lancaster
afterwards the hero of Azincourt. The army after eleven days of
fruitless effort to take McMorrogh at disadvantage or to penetrate
within his domains would have famished had not three vessels brought
supplies from Dublin. They rushed into the waves to satisfy their
craving, drank the wines till intoxicated and quarrelsome, and

Richard made what haste he could to Dublin. Mac Murrogh proffered peace and the earl of Gloucester was sent to parley, when Art on a splendid steed, valued by the prevailing standards at four hundred cows, rode down the mountain, a fine large able man, wondrously active, of stern indomitable mien. A long dart which he held in his hand he threw from him as he approached. The conference was long and earnest, but, as the chief insisted upon peace without condition, led to no result.

The king vowed he would not depart from Ireland till he had Art alive or dead; but soon arrived the tidings that Henry of Lancaster had taken possession of his own throne. The duke of Albemarle his nephew, in the plot, discouraged his immediate return, and when in September, 1399, he reached Milford the mischief was done, and Henry the fourth ruled in his stead. His crazy and wicked obstinacy in seeking to dethrone Art brought fitting retribution in his own deposition. The murder of his uncle Clarence, spoliation of the son of his uncle Lancaster, his heedless extravagance and oppressive taxes alienated the affections of his people, and a violent death, in what manner has never transpired, closed at the age of thirty-four his reign of twenty-three years.

XXI.

REIGN OF HENRY IV.—1399-1413.

The nearest in lineal succession after Richard II. was not Henry, but Edmund Mortimer then seven years of age, son of Roger, slain at Kenlis in 1398, and representative of Lionel duke of Clarence third son of Edward III.; while the new king derived from John of Gaunt the fourth. This usurpation proved for eighty years a fruitful source of contention and jealousy between the houses of York and Lancaster, the white rose and the red, drenching England

in blood. Richard of York, son of Edmund Langley, fifth son of
Edward III. married Ann Mortimer the rightful heir after the
death of her brother, Edmund the last earl of March, who while
viceroy in 1424 died of the plague. From them descended the
house of York.

Henry's wars with Scotland led to repraisals, and the north-easterly
shores of Ireland were exposed to depredation from the isles. A
fleet fitted out by the Anglo-Irish at Dublin encountered the
enemy near Strangford, but met with disaster. Expeditions from
Drogheda with better fortune, took many prizes; and privateers
from the capital emulated their example, plundering Wales and
carrying off to their cathedral the shrine of St. Cubin. Royal
license was given in 1400 to merchants of Bristol to make war with
four vessels against the De Burkes, who aided by Ormond had
seized Galway, but there is no record of their design being carried
out.

Soon after the accession of the new monarch Stanley was appointed for three years for the fourth time viceroy, Balscot, bishop
of Meath, his brother William and Scrope representing him in turn
as deputy. Thomas of Lancaster, second son of the king, commissioned for twenty-one years as lord lieutenant, but who was still
a youth, reached Dublin in November, 1402. O'Byrnes the next
summer rose in arms four thousand strong, but were defeated near
Bray by Drake, mayor of Dublin. The royal treasury running
low, the soldiers unpaid became discontented, and the duke after
compacts with O'Byrne, O'Reilly, O'Connor and Mac Mahon to
keep peace went home. Scrope left as deputy soon made way for
the third Ormond, kinsman to the king, "a mighty man" who
after holding a parliament to confirm the statutes of Dublin and
Kilkenny, died at Gowran in 1405. The fifth Kildare chosen by
the council was removed in favor of Scrope, whose life was also
brought by the plague to a premature close at Castle Dermod in

1408. Lancaster again came over, and among other severities threw Kildare into prison for appointing a prebendary to Maynooth. He was seriously wounded in an engagement at Kilmainham with tenants of the crown, barely escaping with his life, and in 1410 left Ireland in charge of Thomas Butler son of the third Ormond. His only exploit was an invasion with fifteen hundred Irishmen against the irrepressible O'Byrnes, when more than half his army deserting him he succeeded with difficulty in effecting his retreat.

Wright, whose relation of events is tinctured by his national bias, tells us " that the island seemed sinking into barbarism and confusion amid the domestic quarrels of the septs, and their wars with one another and the English, that its history at this period was a continuous story of chiefs deposed, imprisoned and slaughtered, towns and villages rifled and burnt and outrages of every description." Gilbert, with better opportunities for information, comes to an exactly opposite conclusion, and historical candor will, no doubt, concur with his views even though the relation of events by the former writer should be accepted as generally correct.

Indeed this fifteenth century was comparatively for the native septs their golden age, their best certainly since Scandinavian pirates disturbed the saints' rest which St. Patrick brought with christianity. The ancient laws and institutions, that Brehon code which with minute precision laid down rules for adjudicating on almost every variety of dispute, encroachment or breach of law, were in full operation. Justice was enforced, religious observances respected, institutions of learning received generous support. Their intimate relations with Scotland and frequent pilgrimages to France, Spain and Italy rendered the chiefs conversant with the affairs of the continent, with which constant communication was maintained by their clergy and ecclesiastical students. Elegancies of life found their way into the castles of the chieftains, and as these were the gathering places of the

clans the people generally participated in their refining influence.
Castles were built by MacDonogh and MacDermots; the abbey of
Quin by MacNamara, Portumna by O'Maddin.

The septs had been gradually gaining on the English race, so that
only portions of the four counties of Dublin, Meath, Kildare and
Lowth were subject to the crown. Nor were these limits to be extended during the next hundred years. Lowth or Oriel paid O'Niel
forty pounds, Meath three hundred and Kildare twenty to O'Connor of Offaly, the royal exchequer eighty marks to Art MacMorrogh as tribute, and large portions of the common people within
reach of English rule were of Irish birth, habit and language. Beyond this limited space of twenty miles square stretched what were
called the marches, and only there by payment of black rent could
proprietors of alien race retain any part of their possessions.

All around the English precincts, the liberties swarmed with kerns,
light armed infantry with "javelins, darts and skeynes," or with
gallow-glasses "with iron helmet, coat of mail, cuirass and battle
axe," formidable antagonists even for men-at-arms, "with bas-
nets, sallets, visor, spear, axe, sword and dagger," or for archers
"with jack of defence, salet, sword and sheaf of forty arrows."
The Irish soldiers were not always arrayed upon the side of their
countrymen, but retained for protection against their forays and
marauds by the few colonists that ventured to remain in positions so
exposed. Beyond the marches, accessible to enemies only through
dense forests and passes easily defended, dwelt the septs with fields
well tilled and well stocked pastures. Their laws were framed with
ample provisions to prevent disagreement, and their chieftains, whose
election depended upon their consent, led them in war and studied
their interests. It is not surprising that they should have preferred
their own system to the venality and corruption which marked every
department of English administration, or that, at one period in
Munster, the English themselves should have adopted it in preference
to their own.

The O'Connors were still restless. Circumstances already stated and many foreign elements besides contributed to stir up strife. They captured in 1400 the castle of Dunamon from the Burkes. For Mulconry the renowned historian of Sil Murray accidentally slain in the assault, an eric of one hundred and twenty-six cows was paid to his family by Gary who slew him. O'Hanly, O'Kelly, O'Mally and many other chiefs after long periods of prosperous rule died at advanced ages in their beds. McDermot in asserting his supremacy over his sept fell at Lough Lonbain in 1405. The next year Turlogh Don king of Connaught was slain by Cathal son of O'Connor Roe and the Burkes. Cathal son of Roderick succeeded, but his rule was contested. He was captured after the battle of Killeachy by the O'Kellys and MacDermots in 1407, and though he lived a third of a century longer he was of little account, his sept having been broken up into feeble fragments.

A curious incident is related connected with the marauds of the period. A party of English had invaded Offaly, and Calvagh son of its chief went in pursuit. It chanced as he was overtaking the plunderers who were not aware of his approach he met a kern bringing back to him a brazen cauldron used for brewing beer which he had lent to one of his neighbors. Calvagh flung a stone, possibly the missile earlier described as part of the military equipment, at the cauldron, and the deafening sound of its reverberations startling the marauders, they incontinently took to flight, three hundred of them being put to the sword in the pursuit. The mitre of St. Patrick a precious relic kept at Elphin was recovered on this occasion from the English.

Turlogh the peaceable still ruled over Tyreonnel, defeating the Kinel Owen who invaded his territories. Two years later he made peace with their chieftain at Cael Uisge. In 1402 he drove out from his dominions Brian O'Neil son of Henry, who lost his life in the expedition, spoiling the O'Kanes and Carbury, and in 1411 the

21

O'Rourkes. On the death of Nial Oge of Tyrone, his son Owen was not accepted as chieftain, but Donnel the son of Henry, his cousin, succeeded by the rules of tanistry. In 1410 Donnel was captured by Mac Mahon of Oriel and surrendered to his son-in-law Owen, who entrusted him to Maguire, by whom he was delivered up to the English. His brother Hugh had been ten years a captive in the castle of Dublin. They both escaped. Donnel was reinstated to be again driven out seven years later by Owen, aided by Turlogh of Tyrconnel, and when in 1432 Donnel was slain, Owen was inaugurated, and reigned twenty-four years.

Art was not to be trifled with; he renewed the war till reparation was made him for his wife's inheritance, and in 1402 took part with the Geraldines against the Butlers. In 1404 O'Moore defeated the English at Athdown, and the next year Art harried Wexford and Carlow, but with O'Nolan was routed in 1407 after a hotly contested combat by Scrope, Ormond and Desmond, who then attacked O'Carrol of Ely at Callan, that chief and eight hundred of his followers falling in the fight. This success was attributed by English chroniclers to a special miracle in their favor, the sun standing still that day as related in Holy Writ for Joshua. O'Carrol a patron of learning had been on a pilgrimage to Rome, and on his return been entertained by king Richard at London. The next year Art came off again victorious, and in 1413 he gained a decisive victory in Wexford. O'Byrnes were equally successful against a force from Dublin, and O'Connor Faly captured the sheriff of Meath and many knights and gentlemen, holding them to ransom.

O'Sullivan Mor at war with McCarthy, lord of Desmond, was drowned in a naval engagement, but his successor with better fortune drove McCarthy out of Munster. Later taken prisoner, he was deprived of his sight by Donnel Duv, and his son Owen was slain. Gilla Mochuda, grandson of the first lord of the Reeks of Killarney, fell in a family feud in 1411. Such incidents would

seem to confirm the view taken by Wright, but quarrels ending in
bloodshed were not confined to the Irish. Dowdall, sheriff of Louth,
was set upon and killed by Whites and Verdon, who were pardoned
by the king. Donnel O'Brien fell in combat with lord Barry,
O'Connor of Offaly with Meiler Bermingham. Gilmory burnt
forty churches, held Savage to ransom, and then put him to death,
but was himself slain by his kinsmen in a church. Magennis was
killed by his own people. But this period when the septs had regained most of their possessions was marked by few instances comparatively either of family feuds or deaths by violence.

During the previous century alien lords had abounded in Munster. Besides Ormond and Desmond, the marquis of Carew had
enjoyed revenues of twenty-two hundred pounds sterling, Barnwall
sixteen hundred, Cogan of Green castle thirteen thousand, Bahram
of Enfort thirteen hundred, Courey of Kilbritton twelve hundred,
Mandeville of Barrenstallie twelve hundred, Arundel of the Strand
fifteen hundred, Steiney of Baltimore eight hundred, Roche of
Poole one thousand, Barry eighteen hundred. There were moreover knights, esquires, gentlemen and yeomen, to a great number
who might expend yearly from eight hundred to twenty. The inhabitants of Youghal, Cork and Kinsale, were now complaining
that these proprietors had fallen at variance and called in the Irish
to help them in their quarrels, who soon became the stronger, and
drove them out or reduced them to subjection. Before this century
closed, besides Desmond, Courey and Barry, few were to be left
of any account.

What Gilbert tells us of English rule in Ireland at this period
sufficiently explains how it came to naught. He says: "The
internal condition of the settlement, and the manifold injustices
perpetrated by the officials of the colonial government on every
one under their control tended to repel, rather than to attract,
the independent Irish towards the English system, as then ad-

ministered. Many of the judges and chief legal officials of the
colony were illiterate and ignorant of law, obtained their appointments by purchase, and leased them to deputies, who promoted and
encouraged litigation, with the object of accumulating fees. Commissioners of Oyer and Terminer were multiplied, before whom
persons were constantly summoned, by irresponsible non-residents,
to such an extent, that no man could tell when he might be indicted
or outlawed, or if a process had issued to eject him from his
property. The king's officers often seized lands, and appropriated
their rents, so long as legal subterfuges enabled them to baffle the
claims of the rightful proprietors; and thus agriculture and improvements were impeded. Ecclesiastics, lords and gentlemen,
were not unfrequently cast into jail by officers of the crown, on un-
founded charges, without indictment or process, and detained in
durance till compelled, by rigorous treatment, to purchase their
liberation. The agricultural settlers and landholders were harassed
by troops of armed 'kerns' and mounted 'idel-men,' who levied
distresses, maltreated and chained those who resisted, and held
forcible possession of the farmers' goods, till redeemed with money.

"The troops, engaged for the defence of the colonists, became little
less oppressive than enemies. Under the name of 'livere,' or
livery, the soldiery took, without payment, victuals for themselves,
and provender for their horses, and exacted weekly money payments, designated 'coygnes.' It was not unusual for a soldier,
having a billet for six or more horses, to keep only three, but to
exact provender for the entire number; and on a single billet, the
same trooper commonly demanded and took 'livery' in several parts
of a county. The constables of royal castles, and the purveyors of
the households of the viceroys, seldom paid for what they took;
and for the purpose of obtaining bribes, to release their seizures,
they made exactions much more frequently than needed. These
grievances, wrote the prelates, lords and commons, to the king of

England, have reduced your loyal subjects, in Ireland, to a state of destruction and impoverishment, and caused them even to hate their lives.

"Most of the king's manors, customs and other sources of revenue, having been granted or sold to individuals, but little came into the treasury of the fees, fines, and crown profits, which previously had defrayed part of the expenses of the colonial government. These reduced finances were nearly exhausted by pensions and annuities, paid to propitiate the chiefs of the border Irish, and to secure the settlement against their inroads. Various good towns and hamlets of the colony were destroyed, while several royal castles and fortresses became ruinous, as those in charge of them embezzled the rents and profits, allocated for their maintenance, repairs and garrisons."

Thus corrupt, English authority relaxed its hold on the people it was powerless to restrain, and secured partial immunity from molestation by paying tribute. Its exclusive policy yielded to necessity. Encouragement to trade with the septs took the place of prohibition. English proprietors on the borders gladly leased their lands at moderate rents to Irish tenants, who were thus enabled often to regain their own. Fosterage of English children with Irish nurses, and intermarriages between the races, became common, and were openly sanctioned. Mac Mahon in Louth and other chieftains did what seemed to them good with impunity, and Tibetot, speaker of the house of commons, admitted that the greater part of Ireland had been conquered by the natives.

The Irish annalists dwell little on details of domestic life, but mention many deaths of chiefs and scholars. They tell us that O'Rourke, heir to Breffney, powerful, energetic and comely, was slain in his own house by the Danish clan of MacCabes; that O'Dowd, universally distinguished for his nobleness and hospitality; that Conor, son of the lord of Hy-Many, the serpent of his tribe and of all Ireland; that Conor MacDermot, a bear in vigor; that Mahon MacNamara on his way to Rome; that O'Gormly, heir to Kinalmoen; that O'Kelly, archbishop of Connaught, eminent for wisdom, hospitality and piety; that Conor, son of Ivor O'Hanly, of Kinel Dofa, on the Shannon; Donnel O'Hara, heir to Leyny; that O'Farrell who had never been reproached; Conor O'Doherty, lord of Inishowen, generous to the wretched and poor; besides numberless other chiefs, poets and brehons, passed out of life. Another death is mentioned of a different character.

When whiskey or usquebaugh was first introduced into Ireland does not appear, but its earliest recorded victim, Richard Mac Rannall heir to the chieftainry of Muinter Eolais, died in consequence of drinking too much of it at Christmas tide in 1405. It is subject of controversy whence the name was derived. Uisge, in Inishowen in Donegal, the burial place of Owen son of Nial of the nine hostages, who died in 465 of grief for the loss of his brother Conal, and from whom his descendants took the name of the Kinel Owen, lay not far removed from the abode of the Mac Rannals. Human ingenuity readily devises what suits its needs, and the humidity of the climate and soil of the island affecting the vegetable products used for food required correctives tonic in their nature, drying up moisture, and less inflammatory than the distillations of the grape. Such beverages adapted to a wet climate prove deleterious in a dry, and Americans are losing their taste for what experience proves prejudicial to health, and if in Ireland from poverty and inadequate nourishment its use was once carried to excess it is less so now. It is not supposed that in the fifteenth century potations stronger than ale and wine were common. But that the latter might prove a dangerous temptation is indicated by the following incident.

The sons of Ith at Baltimore were troublesome neighbors to Waterford. Christmas night its mayor arrived off the castle of

O'Driscoll with a cargo of wine, and bringing presents and claiming hospitality his purpose was not suspected, and he received cordial welcome to the family banquet. In the midst of the dance which formed part of the festal entertainment a force sufficient to overpower the host and those of his kinsmen who were present, contrived to take them at disadvantage and carried them prisoners to Waterford.

XXII.

REIGN OF HENRY V.—1413–1422.

Stanley for the fifth time viceroy landed at Clontarf in September. Age had not improved his disposition. Enriching himself by his rapacity he yet left his debts unpaid. Neither clergy, laity, nor men of science received mercy at his hands. Plundering Nial O'Higgin hereditary bard at Usnagh in Meath, the poet, with his own special weapons of retaliation, lampooned him to death. Henry D'Alton, indignant at any injustice to a class so sacred as the poets, swept down upon the pale and from his prey made ample reparation. This was not Nial's first exploit of the sort. When the Clan Conway wronged him at Cladan, his venomous shafts turned them all grey in a night.

Crawley, archbishop of Dublin, "greatly praised for his liberality, a good almsman, a great clerk, a doctor of divinity, an excellent preacher, a great builder, beautiful, courteous, of a sanguine complexion and of tall stature, was elected by the council to fill the vacancy caused by the death of Stanley. But being nearly fourscore he prayed at castle Dermod whilst prior Butler and the bishop of Ferns marched against the septs. O'Connor of Offaly and Mageoghan put the priests to rout, carrying off many prisoners, slaying a baron and receiving fourteen hundred marks ransom for his son.

Sir John Talbot lord of Verdon lands in Meath, then forty-one years of age, came over in November, 1414. Calling out the whole English strength he organized it into bodies of twenty, one hundred and a thousand, arrested outlaws, seized upon children at fosterage, plundered Dalys, Magrath and Mac Keogh the poets and spared neither church nor sanctuary. He twice harried Leix for six days, razed two castles, built a bridge at Athy duly defended, forced the O'Moore and O'Keating to sue for peace. He compelled the former to march with him forty leagues to assist in reducing the MacMahons who in their turn were forced to join him in reducing the O'Connors. O'Byrnes, O'Tooles and Cavanaghs, O'Dempsys, O'Molloys, O'Ferrals, O'Reilys, O'Hanlons, even the O'Neils and O'Donnells submitted. Talbot's strong arm laid heavy on English lord as on Irish chieftain. His extortions, the coin and livery he exacted, his raid on the Geraldines who held as prisoner the unfortunate earl who had married for love, provoked resentment. His return home in 1415 gave but brief respite. Art McMorrogh grown old died in 1417, and Talbot soon after seized upon his son and successor Donogh, who was imprisoned in the tower of London, Talbot being allowed by the king to extort from him what ransom he could. He purchased O'Connor of Offaly from De Freigne who had captured him, but O'Connor escaped and his venture was lost. In Ulster Magennis and O'Neil of Clanaboy gave him a check and many of his soldiers were slain.

His services being needed elsewhere his brother Richard, now archbishop of Dublin left as deputy, arrested Kildare, Preston and Bellew, for conniving with the prior of Kilmainham to subvert his authority. Richard made way in 1420 for the fourth earl of Ormond, before whom upon his arrival two of his kinsmen fought a wager of battle, one being killed and the other grievously wounded. The earl invaded Leix with some success and De Burgh in the west defeated the O'Kellys. At the same time, O'Connor Faly gained a

victory over a portion of the English troops, obtaining considerable
spoil and what they especially valued, arms and armor and accoutre-
ments.   Parliament when convened harped on the old grievances of
maladministration and extortion, illegal arrests, illiterate officials,
plurality of offices, and that the inns of court at London allowed no
Anglo-Irish to study law.   In 1416 statutes forbade all ecclesiastical
preferment to Irishmen, prohibited their leaving the island without
permission, and ordered all Englishmen holding official positions in
Ireland to return to them.

It enforced the old law aganst intermarriages between the races, a
rule now unjustly applied to the earl of Desmond.   After Gerald
the poet disappeared in 1398, or according to another account was
slain by the O'Briens, John his eldest son the fifth earl succeeded,
and after holding the earldom for a year was drowned in the river
Suir.   His only son Thomas, the sixth, hunting near Tralee, and
benighted, took refuge under the roof at Abbeyfeale of William
Mac Cormac, with whose beautiful daughter Catherine he became
enamored.   This imprudent marriage with one of inferior rank
alienating from him the respect and favor of his worldly-minded kinsmen and followers, it afforded an opportunity to his ambitious and
stronger minded uncle, James the seventh earl, to supplant him.
Thomas, after long and obstinate resistance twice driven from his
estates and detained in durance, on the plea that his marriage conflicted with the law prohibiting such connections between the races,
was deposed in 1418, and by the interposition of Ormond had assigned to him with Moyallow and Broghill, Kilcohnan, afterwards
the abode of Spencer, and which his descendant Raymond forfeited
with his life under Elizabeth.   The elder branch still continues under
the name of Adair in Scotland and Ireland.   The unfortunate
Thomas repaired to France, perhaps to procure redress from the
king, who attended his funeral obsequies as a kinsman when he died
soon after at Rouen in 1420.   They were not very nearly related,

22

Henry's mother Mary de Bohun having been niece once removed of Elinor wife of the first Ormond, from whom the earl of Desmond descended.   The new earl was already in the prime and vigor of middle life when he succeeded his nephew.   His marriage with Mary daughter of Ulick lord of Clanrickard strengthened his position. He was appointed by the lord lieutenant, seneschal for life of Imokilly, Inchiquin and Youghall; and in 1422 made constable of Limerick.

Ormond in 1419, invested with ample powers as viceroy, used them in repressing alike the septs and the refractory English.   His parliaments granted liberal subsidies.   He vanquished O'Moore and his "terrible army" at the red bog of Athy, reduced O'Dempsy who had taken possession of the castle of Ley belonging to the earl of Kildare; and MacMahon of Orgial who had spread havoc over the English possessions.   Whilst employed in these military movements, the clergy of Dublin went twice each week in solemn procession to the cathedral to pray for his success.   Submission under coercion lasted only so long as power overawed.   In 1420 the parliament represented that little more than the single county of Dublin remained in the undisturbed possession of the English, that Limerick, Tipperary, Kilkenny and Wexford, Meath, Orgial, Carlow and Kildare were in the possession of native chiefs or degenerate English or under tribute to them.

In the last parliament of this reign Richard O'Hedian, archbishop of Cashel, was tried on thirty articles of accusation brought against him, chiefly for partiality shown to his own countrymen in promoting Irish clerks to benefices, for harboring the design of making himself king of Munster and giving his concubine a ring, the pious offering of Desmond to St. Patrick.   In representations to the king on the state of the island, the oppressions and extortions of the deputies and their appropriating to their own use the royal revenues are especially dwelt upon.   They urged the prosecutions of the bonds given to the apostolic chamber, and complain that landholders, artificers and workmen were deserting the country.

Among feminine accomplishments in vogue at this period one is noted for which the lakes that abound in the island afforded peculiar facilities. Richard O'Reilly king of Cavan with his son and many distinguished persons, whilst on an expedition to meet the English in 1418 in the royal barge, met with disaster from squall or other peril on Logh Finvoy, and were all drowned. Finola Mac Rannall, wife of Richard, escaped by swimming.

XXIII.

REIGN OF HENRY VI.—1422-1461.

An order simply chronological in presenting the history of Ireland is not calculated to convey to the reader the fullest information or very clear impressions, either as regards character or events. So little connection is found to exist between what was taking place in different parts of the island, that whilst it has been thought best to follow the generally accepted division of the subject into periods embraced by the reigns of the English monarchs, what concerns the administration at Dublin, or affects Anglo-Irish lords or sept and chieftain, will be kept as distinct as its complications permit.

The succession of viceroys as a guide to the course of affairs has the first claim to attention, since it enters as an element of greater or less importance into occurrences all over the island, but their authority was so circumscribed and so little respected as to be hardly felt beyond the immediate vicinity of the capital. Ormond was soon superseded by Richard Talbot archbishop of Dublin, followed by Edmund Mortimer for whom Dantsy bishop of Meath acted as deputy. On the defeat of an English army in Meath, Ormond sent over

with a strong force checked for a time the chiefs of Ulster. Mortimer arrived soon after, but died of the plague at his own castle of
Trim in February, 1424. Talbot again lord lieutenant remained for
a year, and upon his departure Ormond pursued the same repressive
policy. MacMahon and O'Toole surrendered the lands they had
taken from English settlers, relinquishing their black rent, and
O'Neil, Donnel the Soft, the revenues belonging to the earls of Ulster, and after the death of Mortimer acknowledged fealty to his
nephew and heir the duke of York.

This submission was in latin, with which language it is not unreasonable to suppose O'Neil but imperfectly acquainted, and it is quite
probable that in this as in many similar transactions of the kind
with Irish chiefs, the covenants and obligations set forth in the in-
strument, even though signed and sworn to, were not understood.
If assumed under duress or with any misrepresentation as to their
meaning, he may not have considered them of any binding validity either in honor or conscience. It is incredible that under the
actual circumstances he should have known their purport.

Sir John de Grey held the office of viceroy for a year spent in
feeble efforts to repress the MacMorroghs, followed in 1428 by Sutton, lord Dudley, who diligently warred with the O'Byrnes, " burning and destroying corn and houses, breaking down castles, cutting
their woods and passes, making great slaughter," but it was intimated that notwithstanding these active measures the country was in
great danger of being lost. The enemies of Ormond gave it to be
understood secretly to the council at home that his courses were destructive and ruinous, and that he ought to be removed. To guard
the borders of Louth, peculiarly exposed to forays from the Ulster
septs, ten pounds were offered to any subjects who within five years
should erect castle or tower, twenty feet long by sixteen broad and
forty high. English merchants and the colonists generally were
prohibited from resorting to fairs or markets of the Irish, or sending them commodities unless for ransom to redeem prisoners.

Meanwhile, the colonists, despoiled by both friend and foe, were deserting the island. Representations were made that the deplorable state of the country resulted less from maladministration, which was sufficiently bad, than from enormities practised by the Irish, instigated by the nobility and gentry. Stanley, sent over in 1431, found Butlers and Talbots at variance, Dundalk paying tribute to O'Neil, Armagh to O'Connor, Waterford in ruins, one hundred and forty-eight castles lately defensible in Carlow demolished. Munster was in possession of the enemy, and the walled towns of Kilkenny, Ross, Wexford, Kinsale Youghall, Clonmel, Kilmallock, Thomastown, Carrick, Fethard and Cashel on the point of famishing, their supplies being cut off. Connaught had relapsed under Irish control, for Burkes and Birminghams were virtually Irish, no governor having been seen in Galway or Athenry for forty years. Even Ormond, whose kinsmen had intermarried with the McMurroghs, O'Carrols and O'Reillys, and who was personally popular with the septs, had lost most of his domains. O'Neil, aided by Connors, Molloys, Maddens, McLaghlins and McGeoghans, warred successfully against the English, and McMorrogh, who for seven years had been prisoner in the Tower and had recently escaped, marched an army to the walls of Dublin.

When in 1432 Stanley contrived to capture Nial chief of Tyrconnel, O'Connor his son-in-law resenting his long imprisonment in London obtained possession in 1438 of William Welles soon after his appointment as his brother's deputy. In order to effect the release of the viceroy several prisoners in Dublin were set at liberty and Nial sent over to the Isle of Man to be included in the arrangement, but he died the following year before it could be consummated as regarded him. Lord Welles held his office till 1442, Ormond his kinsman performing its functions as deputy when he was absent from the island. The Talbot faction fearing that Ormond would be appointed lord-lieutenant and their influence prevailing in the parliament of 1441, charges were brought against him and representations made to the king that some English lord not born in Ireland could execute the laws with more efficiency and justice than any Irishman, and that his interests demanded a man of vigor and activity in the field as well as council; that Ormond was aged, unwieldy and unlusty to labor, and had lost in substance all his castles, towns and lordships; and it was not likely that he should keep, conquer or get any grounds to the king who had thus lost his own. Instances were adduced of tyranny and injustice perpetrated by the earl during his administration. The articles drawn up by Talbot were not entitled to weight, and Ormond in 1442 was appointed lord lieutenant, and with James of Desmond as his friend and confidant set at defiance the machinations of his enemies. Little discouraged by their recent failure, however, they persevered in their efforts to undermine him in the favor of the young king.

They found unexpected aid. Desmond had become too powerful for the viceroy. In 1438 he had purchased of Robert Cogan all his lands in Ireland comprising half the county of Cork which belonged of right to the heirs general, De Courcy and Carew; in 1444 he obtained a patent for the government of Limerick, Waterford, Cork and Kerry, with license to absent himself during life from attending all future parliaments sending a sufficient proxy, and to purchase any lands he pleased by what service soever they were holden of the king. The family of the Gherardini of Florence sent to acknowledge him as kinsman. His daughter Honora had married the eighth baron of Kerry, and Joan the seventh earl of Kildare. Occasions naturally arising for question and dispute between him and the viceroy, controversy led to jealousy and resentment. Force was tried and conciliation. A truce between them was agreed to for a year, but the breach grew wider and Desmond went over to the enemies of Ormond and intrigued with the council and parliament to secure his downfall.

Fifteen fresh charges were brought against him; among them, that he prevented petitions reaching the king and had proposed a bill punishing with forfeiture of land and goods all who should make complaint not under the great seal; that his real object was to enrich himself by these forfeitures, and that he had appropriated to his own use the public monies. He appealed to a parliament at Drogheda, calling upon them to declare in what he had offended, to point out any instance in which the subject had suffered from his injustice or the state from his neglect. The parliament convinced of his innocence bore witness to the integrity of his administration and to his fidelity and services, and an address being presented to the king he was left in office.

In this angry contention at this inopportune moment for English interests, between him and archbishop Talbot, it is not easy to determine which was right, if either. The conclusion of Sir Giles Thornton, sent over to investigate, was that the prevailing misrule was equally attributable to both. The enemies of Ormond were not silenced. He was summoned to London, in 1444, and Thomas Fitzgerald, prior of Kilmainham, maintaining the truth of the charges against him, proffered wager of battle, which was accepted. The combat was prohibited by the King, who, examining the parties, decided in favor of Ormond. Henry confided the government, however, to one of the opposite faction, Sir John Talbot, created earl of Shrewsbury as also now of Waterford and baron of Dungarvan, for his distinguished services in France. He was a good soldier, but sorry knight; for, inviting O'Reilly to Trim, he held him to ransom. The thirty years since his former viceroyalty had not improved his temper, and it was said of him, that since Herod, there had been no man more wicked.

Bermingham lord of Louth, in 1443, insulted by Barnwall son of the treasurer of Meath, by a caimin or filip on the nose, resorted to O'Connor Faly. Calvagh gladly undertook to punish the offend-

er by a foray against the English which proved eminently successful.
Three years later Talbot forced Calvagh to make peace and to ransom his son who had fallen into his possession.   This was a source
of considerable income to successful warriors in fighting days, and one
we have already seen turned to good account by this famous captain
who preserved for a while to the English crown its possessions in
France.   His forty-eight battles in that country had secured him
not only renown but the earldoms of Shrewsbury and Waterford.
He perished there at the age of eighty in besieging Chatillon, and with
his death began the downfall of English rule in France.

The successor of John Talbot was Richard, duke of York, earl
of Ulster, lord of Connaught, Leix, Meath and Ossory, which
titles he had inherited from Ann Mortimer, his mother.   He came
over in the summer of 1449 with his wife, Cecilia Neville, the Rose
of Raby, mother of Edward IV. and Richard III., and adopting a
conciliatory policy, Maginnis, McMahon, McArtan and O'Reilly
joined his army with three thousand of their clansmen.   O'Neils,
O'Farrels, Mores, Dempsys, McMurroghs and Byrnes, with nearly
all the English lords, swore fealty to Henry and the duke.   This
friendly spirit may be attributed to their appreciation of Richard's
claims as the true heir.   It could have proceeded from no sense of
his superior power, for when McGeoghan, who soon after took
offence at some injustice, advanced with a large force of cavalry to
Mullingar, he made concessions and amends.

James the fourth earl, or white Ormond, died in 1452, after sack-
ing the fortresses of the Mulryans in Limerick and of the O'Dempsys
at Leix, making a successful raid into Ulster and as far as Longford, the last few months of his life.   His son was appointed viceroy for ten years, but the inveterate strife between Butlers and Geraldines "causing more destruction in Kildare and Meath than any
inflicted by Irish or English enemies, so that neither life nor property
were safe," the Duke was re-appointed, after St. Albans in 1455 be-

coming protector of the realm. Deserted by some of his adherents at Ludlow, he betook himself to Dublin, where, supported by the Geraldines, he was recognized as viceroy, the parliament declaring its independence of that of England, and English laws and process of no force within their borders.

Neither Henry nor his ministers took much thought of Ireland. France had slipped away from his incompetent fingers, which now and then by some feeble clutch sought to recover firmer hold of the island. To him Irish administration consisted of occasional marauds upon chieftains within reach and off their guard, and when a few lives were taken and villages burnt its duty was done. That government existed for the benefit of the governed, rarely crossed the threshold of medieval statesmanship. Its ends were answered when the territory of the sovereign was extended and his courtiers conciliated by gifts and place. Spasmodic efforts of useful legislation in England to prop a tottering throne were rarely wasted across the channel, and governors set over Dublin and its immediate neighborhood indulged no other aspirations than to improve their own condition. That fifteen hundred pounds more than the revenues of the kingdom for the year were required to pay the viceroy and his officials, affords some criterion of the boasted blessings of English rule and the extent of its power.

Had respect for their own ancient laws more generally actuated chief and sept, this wretched rule would have been driven out. Unfortunately English laws of inheritance to positions of authority were more in accordance with human nature, contrasted to the disadvantage of their own in the eyes of disinherited sons of deceased chieftains, whose friends often helped them to set aside their legally elected tanists. Ulster and Connaught lost strength by such disputed successions, which had led to disintegration in Munster of the originally consolidated territory of the O'Briens and MacCarthys. They wrought infinite harm all over the island. At the same time when

23

the roll of chieftains of the several septs is examined, it occasions
surprise that there prevailed so late as the fifteenth century such strict
observance of the law, and that so many of them lived to a good old
age at peace with their kinsmen and neighbors. If we select
Analy, the Breifnys, Oriel and Fermanagh, all exposed to aggression, or even Ulster, and group the facts related with regard to each
of them, the imputation that they were constantly engaged in mutual
bloodshed cannot well be sustained.

John O'Farrell, lord of Analy, who had erected in 1377 the castle of Lasadawla, "learned and able," died in 1399 ; and Donnel
his son in 1435.   Ten years later upon the death of William "after
a long and virtuous life," Donnel Boy and Rossa contested the succession and the territory wasted by their dispute was divided between
them.   Tiernan O'Rourke, who had been lord of West Breifny for
forty years, died at a great age in 1418. His son Owen died before
him at the age of sixty-three, and on the death of another son Hugh
Boy, eighteen months after, Teigue and Art contended for the mastery.   When the former died in 1435, Donogh son of Tiernan ,
was proclaimed, and when he too passed away in 1455 Loughlin son
of Teigue his competitor succeeded.

Thomas Maguire, lord of Fermanagh, "a man of universal hospitality toward poor and mighty, founder of monasteries and churches,
and giver of images, peace-maker for many chiefs and septs, beloved
by all conditions for the excellence of his administration," ended
his days in 1430. His son Thomas Oge was installed in his place
by the laity and clergy who chose his kinsman Phillip tanist.   For
reasons not assigned the tanist in 1438 incurring the displeasure of
his chieftain was cast into prison.   The clan disaffected rose in
arms, and taking possession of the castle transferred the fetters from
the limbs of the tanist to those of the chief.   Henry O'Neil hastened to the relief of his vassal, for whose release his wife, daughter of
Mageoghan, and his son Edmund were detained as hostages, and

Enniskillen surrendered to his uncle Donnal who had sided with the tanist. Upon the release of Edmund that castle was given to Phillip whose son slew the aggrieved Donnal. Whilst the chief was on a pilgrimage to Rome in 1450 his son Cathal was put to death by his uncle Donogh, for which atrocity his brother Edmund maimed Donogh, cutting off his hand and foot.

Phillip the tanist for the rest of his life continued loyal to his chief. "Charitable and humane and the best warrior of his time," he led the clan in 1457 against Magauran, invaded Monaghan, and when the lord of Leitrim took advantage of a proposed conference to assail him with superior forces, he defeated him also, adorning his castle bawn with the heads of sixteen O'Rourkes. He fell in battle with the O'Kanes, and soon after his death in 1470 the chief who had taken an active part in all the wars of Tyrone surrendered the chieftainship to his son Edmund, appointing another son Donogh tanist. Eight years later he closed his long and prosperous career and was buried in the monastery at Cavan, receiving from the annalist like praise to that accorded to his father half a century before, "that he ruled over Fermanagh for half a century, the most charitable, pious and hospitable man of his time, founding churches and monasteries and bestowing upon them chalices." Besides his pilgrimage already mentioned to Rome he had been twice to the shrine of St. James of Campostella.

Turlogh an Fhina O'Donnel, after reigning forty-two years retired in 1422 into the monastery of Assaroe, where he died the following year. His son Nial inaugurated chief of Tyrconnel celebrated his succession by an expedition into Fermanagh, subjugating Maguire, MacMahon, Magennis, Clanaboy and Bisset, and taking possession of Carrickfergus. Owen O'Niel tanist of Tyrone in 1421 had been taken prisoner by Clanaboy, on his way to visit Ormond at Dundalk, but the next year was ransomed by his wife and sons. Nial O'Donnel and Donnal O'Neil invaded the territories of Clanaboy to punish this high handed procedure, and thence marched into Connaught to protect the young MacDonoghs against an uncle who had erected a fortress within their rightful possessions. O'Dowd submitted to them and O'Rourke was taken captive. The next summer these two great chiefs of Ulster still in amity defeated the English in Meath. the commander of the enemy being killed by Maelmora MacSweeny, O'Donnel's constable. Dundalk was laid under tribute. Nial upon his accession to the throne of Tyrconnel erected the noble castle of Ballyshannon, which long continued the principal residence of the chieftains of his line.

When Edmund Mortimer came over as lord lieutenant in 1425, the three O'Neils, Donnel the Soft, Owen son of Nial Garve the tanist and Clanaboy, with Naghtan brother of the O'Donnel, Mac Quillin and O'Mellen, keeper of the bell of St. Patrick a relick still preserved, went to his castle of Trim to give him welcome. Whilst there, Mortimer died of the plague and Talbot his successor contrived to take them prisoners. Held to ransom Donnel O'Neil, Clanaboy and Mac Quillin paid forthwith, but Owen and Naghtan were taken to Dublin. They also were soon ransomed, Naghtan by his brother. There had long existed an unfriendly feeling between O'Neil and his kinsman and tanist Owen. A reconciliation was now brought about. They probably realized from this late act of perfidy the importance of union, and coöperating they soon recovered the lands which had been lost by their disputes. Clanaboy had been deprived of sight by one of his kinsmen, and soon after to aid his sons Nial O'Donnel in 1427 invaded Tyrone. Two years later O'Rourkes and O'Reillys being at feud the latter called upon his chief O'Neil to assist him and O'Rourke was defeated. In 1430 Owen the tanist in one of his raids burnt Dundalk, exacting tribute from the English, and thence proceeded into Annaly and through Meath; Calvagh O'Connor of Offaly, O'Molloy, O'Madden, Mageoghan, McLaghlin accepted stipends from him as acknowledgment of fealty; and Nugents, Herberts, Plunkets and other English colonists paid him what he demanded. The next year with Maguires and O'Reillys he spoiled the MacQuillins, and in 1432 Donnell the Soft being slain by the O'Kanes, he was inaugurated chief of Tyrone.

That same year he visited O'Connor Sligo in Connaught, and Nial O'Donnel jealous of this proposed conference with his neighbor and liege, interposed to prevent their meeting, which led to resentment and hostilities between them. Owen invaded Tyrconnel with Maguire and Clanaboy, but after his army had confronted for some time that of O'Donnel without coming to blows, excepting in slight skirmishes, he withdrew. The next year MacDonnell of the isles, taking sides with O'Neil, first assailed and subdued the Savages of Antrim and then sailed to Inishowen whither O'Neil proceeded by land. The wife and sons of O'Donnel without his permission submitted. O'Donnel making terms with the English and marching with considerable force through Meath, by Athlone, Hy-Many and Moylurg, O'Neil and Maguire came to meet him and " a charitable peace " was brought about.

Naghtan being implicated in the taking off of Owen one of the subordinate chiefs of the O'Donnells, Tyrone and Tyrconnel besieged his stronghold Castlefinn. It proved too strong for them, and unable to reduce it they proceeded into Meath to collect tribute of Dundalk. Whilst Henry and Hugh sons of O'Neil were engaged in destroying Nobber, the deputy dropped down upon them but they effected their retreat. The chief of Tyrconnel was less fortunate. Whilst similarly engaged a force of English cavalry surrounded him. His son and heir Turlogh fell in the fight and Nial himself was taken prisoner. Delivered up to Sir Thomas Stanley then deputy, in 1435, he was sent over to London and died four years later at the Isle of Man whither he had been sent to be released. He is highly extolled by the chroniclers.

O'Neil showed little sympathy for the misfortunes of his brother chieftain. Soon after his capture he proceeded through Fermanagh into Tyrconnel upon a predatory expedition The O'Donnels, Brian and Naghtan collected their forces, attacked him in his camp among the wild mountain tracts of Donegal, called the Rosses, and drove him out of his entrenchments of which they took possession. Henry son of O'Neil mortified at this disaster exhorted his warriors to retrieve it, and selecting their time they broke in upon their enemies at night. The description in the annals of this nocturnal combat recalls the stir and lurid glow of Ossian. The closeness of the combatants, sparks of fire that flash from the helmets of the heroes and armor of the champions, the personal encounter of Hugh and his kinsman Brian cause regret that such flights of fancy so rarely lend animation to their recital. Victory declared for the O'Neils, and the O'Donnels disappeared into the darkness. If not very chivalric to invade Tyrconnel whilst its chief was absent and a captive, Owen punished severely by maiming one of the O'Donnels who entrusted by Naghtan with the keeping of the castle of Ballyshannon proposed to surrender it to himself. Later in the summer when Brian son of Henry O'Neil invaded Tirhugh on a predatory incursion, the household of Nial the captive chief overtook and slew a great number of his followers.

Naghtan succeeded to the chieftainship upon the death of his brother and continued lord of Tyrconnel till slain in 1452 by the sons of Nial. His son Roderick disputed the succession with Donnel, son of his brother Nial Garve, who was imprisoned by O'Doherty at Inis. Rory with the O'Kanes and MacQuillins endeavored to destroy Inis and had burnt down the gate and set on fire the stairs, when Donnel praying to be released from his fetters, ascended the battlements, and seeing Rory beneath cast down upon him a large stone which crushed him. Donnel was thereupon acknowledged chieftain. Henry then lately inaugurated lord of Tyrone, espousing the cause of Turlogh, son of Naghtan, in 1456 waylaid Donnel and slew him, and two years after joined Turlogh in a hosting into Brefny. In 1460 he released Hugh, son of Nial, who the next year with his brothers Con and Owen and the MacSweenys, defeated Turlogh at Kinnaweer in Donegal, cutting off his hand and foot to disqualify him for the chieftainship. Inaugurated at Kilmacrenan Hugh reigned forty-four years. He proposed in 1497 to resign in favor of his son Hugh, who would not consent. He died at the age of seventy-eight in 1505, and his widow Finola daughter of Conor na Srona O'Brien in 1528.

Owen O'Neil with his son Henry in 1442 with the English to aid them attacked Castlefin, the stronghold of Naghtan O'Donnel, who outnumbered made peace, giving up Kinelmoen and the tribute of the O'Dohertys in Inishowen. Two years later Owen was discomfited by Clanaboy in Dufferin, but an expedition against the English of Oriel was attended with better success, sixty marks and two tuns of wine being the ransom of unhappy Dundalk. In 1452 the English and MacMahon combined against him and he was worsted in the Fews, but MacMahon submitting made peace paying an eric for Sorley Mor McDonnel who was slain. As age overtook him Owen became less reasonable, and the year before his death in 1455, he was deposed by his son Henry, who but for this act of filial impiety would have left a brilliant record, having been already for twenty-five years the hero of Tyrone. His first hosting as chief was against O'Donnel, who in 1458 joined him in an expedition into Connaught, and the next year he attacked Omagh the castle of the sons of Art O'Neil. In 1462 Edward IV. sent him a chain of gold and forty-eight yards of scarlet cloth as a peace offering. He subdued the O'Kanes, defeated and banished the Savages, constituting Patrick White lord of Leeale. In 1470 he conquered the Mac-Quillins, the next year took the castle of Omagh, and in 1482 ransoming his son Con from the O'Donnels transferred to him his chieftainry. He died in 1489 after a prosperous career, having been as chief or prominent leader a power in Tyrone for sixty years.

John O'Reilly, "most noble of his name," died at Cavan in 1400 ;
Maelmora in 1411. John, son of Owen, was slain in 1460 by
the English, Cathal taking his place. Richard who succeeded
as tanist died in 1469, and Turlogh, grandson of Owen, in
1487, his son John succeeding. Occasional contention arose
between different branches of the family, but the regular order of
succession was little disturbed. In Oriel, Ardgal died in 1416,
and his son Brian in 1442. Hugh, son of Rory, "affable and
pious, well skilled in every art, distinguished for his valor and noble
deeds," died in 1453 at his castle of Lurgan ; and Felim, son of
Brian, elected to succeed him, ruled over the Oriels to his death in
1466. During the next century Monaghan was parcelled out between four different branches of the MacMahons. The long reigns of
these chieftains, as the case with so many more over the island,
speak favorably for the stability and wisdom of their institutions.

Calvagh O'Connor, of whom the adventure of the cauldron has
been related, chieftain of all Offaly, "who had won more wealth
from both races than any lord in Leinster," succeeded his father in
1421. His wife Margaret was daughter of Teigue O'Carrol of Ely,
slain by the English in 1407, whose pilgrimage to Rome has
been noted and whose fame as the patron of learned men was
sufficiently conspicuous to be mentioned by the annalists. Margaret
derived from her father similar tastes for literature and interest in
the welfare of its professors, which were also shared by her noble
husband.

In 1433, the year of famine, known as "the season of slight
acquaintance," in the spring season and again at the time of harvest
she entertained all persons "of science and literature, in poetry, music
and antiquities" from every part of the country at Killachy. Mac
Egan, chief judge to her husband, made out the roll of the guests
to be invited, twenty-seven hundred in number. She received them
clad in cloth of gold, surrounded by her clergy and judges in the

church of De Senchal, the patron saint of Offaly, her husband outside mounted on his charger bidding them welcome. The entertainment began by her offering on the altar of the church two golden chalices to God, and by taking upon herself the charge of two young orphans to support and educate. She then bestowed sums of money or other suitable gifts upon each of her guests, who after receiving them proceeded to the banquet. It is added "that never was seen or heard the like of that day nor comparable to its glory and solace." It will be remembered however that a century earlier William O'Kelly the admirable chief of Hy-Many held high festival for scholars and the poor, and in that which followed, Hugh O'Neil rebuilt for similar purposes the palace of Emania. Margaret was also famous "for repairing highways, erecting bridges and churches, for the making of mass-books, and doing all manner of things profitable to serve God and her own soul,"—so that the annalists add that not only these but while the world stands her very many gifts to the Irish and Scottish nations shall never be forgotten. In 1451 cancer in the breast brought her life to a close, her son Felim dying the night before his mother.

Her daughter Finola, wife of Nial O'Donnel, who made for her husband the peace with the O'Neils, and who after his death married Hugh Boy, son of Brian O'Neil, "the most beautiful and stately, the most renowned and illustrious of her time in all Ireland, her own mother only excepted," when again a widow retired into the convent of Killeigh, and there died in 1493, nearly half a century later. Her father Calvagh, the great king of Offaly, prosperous in war and munificent in bounty, having designated his son Con to supply his place, in 1458, went to his fathers and was buried within the sacred enclosure which Finola had selected for her retreat.

During all this reign in Leinster comparative tranquillity prevailed, for the reason that the septs were little disturbed. Soon after Donogh MacMorrogh son of king Art was redeemed from his nine

24

years captivity in London, he led in 1431 an army to the walls of Dublin, where after success in the earlier part of the engagement he was at last defeated. Two years later he routed the English. When his son Murtogh was slain in 1442 in Wexford, the chief compelled the English to pay him an eric of eight hundred marks. His tribute from the English treasury depending upon his peaceable demeanor—perhaps explains why so few incidents are related which concern at this period this part of the island. In 1456 Mageoghans discomfited a party of English fish merchants, scattering their fish, but in a battle not long after Farrell Roe chief of the sept was slain, and the next year a victory was gained at Ardglass by the English over Clanaboy. Immediately after the death of his father Calvagh, Con of Offaly sustained a defeat from Kildare, which in the following campaign he paid back on the baron of Galtrim. With the Butlers he ravaged Meath; and the MacMahons and O'Neils levied tribute on many of the English proprietors, who were driven from their abodes, their lands being re-occupied by the septs.

Munster remained comparatively tranquil. In Thomond in 1426 after Conor's decease his nephew Teigue O'Brien succeeding was deposed by Clanrickard in favor of his son-in-law Torlogh the Soft, who by his aid retained the throne till his death in 1459, when Mahon's son Donogh ruled for a year and then gave place to Teigue son of Torlogh. Contentions occasionally occurred between McCarthies and O'Sullivans, but the septs pursued the even tenor of their way, with none to molest unless for a brief period the earl of Desmond. Donal McCarthy Mor born in 1373, and his son Teigue in 1407 and slain in 1490, ruled over Desmond. In Muskerry Teigue born in 1380 reigned twenty years to 1448, and his son Cormac, who built Blarney and the abbey of Kilcrea in the middle of the century died in 1494. The contemporary lords of Carbery were Donal Glas who lived to a great age, Donal Reagh, and Dermod an Duna who succeeded in 1452. The O'Sullivans Mor lords of Dunkerron were

Roderick and Donal; of Beare, Dermod Balbh, who founded the monastery at Bantry, and his son Donal who died in 1485.

To other chieftains besides those already alluded to tributes of respect are paid by the annalists as they ended their days. Mention is made among others of Tomaltagh MacDermot patron of the learned and bountiful lord of Moylurg; O'Boyle who died in 1458; Hugh Maguire on his return after pilgrimage to Campostella at Kinsale the night of his return; O'Dowd, lord of Hy-Fiachra in Connaught, who had restored to their lawful proprietors in his territory, their hereditary possessions both lay and ecclesiastical; Conor MacDonogh, lord of Tireril, another patron of learned men; Dermod king of the O'Tooles, best horseman in his province, taking a prey at the age of eighty; Brian O'Conor of Connaught, star of the bravery of the Irish after reigning thirty-seven years; William O'Farrell of Analy after a long and virtuous life; Edmund Burke in 1458, the only Englishman in Ireland worthy to be chosen chief for his personal comeliness, generous hospitality, constancy and truth, gentility of blood, martial feats and all qualities which merit praise; Felim O'Neil, son of Nial Oge, who had purchased a larger collection of poems than any man of his time; and lastly of Hugh son of Torlogh Oge O'Conor, half king of Connaught and well worthy of the kingdom of Ireland, for his personal shape and comeliness, his valor, warfare, hospitality to learned men and all who stood in need of it. He died in May, 1461, at Balintober in Roscommon in the sixty-third year of his age. Ollavs, brehons, poets and historians are also noted as ending their labors, but the same names are still found attached to them, and they bear the same relation to the different chiefs as in previous generations.

Under Henry VI. there were few changes in the three English earldoms. James seventh Desmond who deposed his nephew in 1418 survived the king, and his son-in-law Thomas seventh Kildare who succeeded his father in 1429 possessed that earldom fifty years.

James fourth Ormond held the title nearly as long, having succeeded in 1405. His son James an ardent Lancastrian and able officer by sea and land, and who had done good service in France, was decapitated after Towton in 1461. All these personages for a time held the office of lord-lieutenant or deputy. The other son-in-law of Desmond and who acknowledged fealty to him, Thomas eighth lord Kerry in 1410 succeeded his father and died in 1469.

The civil war in England was a blessed boon to the sister kingdom. While it lasted it engaged the support of the English lords of Ireland on either side, Butlers for Lancaster, Geraldines for York. Relieved for a time from the heavy hand of oppression, chief and sept enjoyed a brief respite of repose to recover their strength and to use it. Instead of adding to their acquisitions the English gradually lost what they had gained. Berminghams slightly increased their territory in Connaught, Desmond purchased half of Cork from De Cogan, Clennish and Kilsellan from Grandison, in Tipperary. Ormond over-ran and for a time subjected the Barrets. Kildare received by marriage and by grant other portions of the inheritance of Sybil Marshall, one of the five co-heiresses of Leinster. But they were titles rather than possessions. Many of the other proprietors, sixty-three are enumerated in 1461, never visited their estates, but extracted from them what they could which was not much.

The year after his father fell at Wakefield, Edward of York entered London and was proclaimed king in 1461. His victories over sixty thousand Lancastrians at Mortimers Cross and Towton, in which last engagement nearly forty thousand were slain, established his throne. The deposed Henry was sent to the tower there to remain till Warwick after ten years replaced the crown upon his head for a brief period. Barnet and Tewkesbury won by Edward sent him back to his dungeon, and in all probability to a bloody death. The war in which more than one hundred thousand fell brought to a close the hopes and almost the existence of the house of Lancaster, so many perished by axe or dagger, on the block or battle-field.

During this period of comparative immunity from foreign domination, religious houses multiplied over the land. Record of their institution being kept in the apostolic chamber, their date and the name of their founders can be ascertained. More than two hundred are to be credited to the era of the Plantagenets, twenty to this reign of Henry the sixth. English proprietors did their part, but very many of the Irish chieftains are mentioned as founding one or more such establishments. The number of these chieftains and members of their families mentioned as retiring into the cloister, as life drew to its close, as well as the tribute paid by their historians when it was over to their piety, penitence and other christian graces, testifies to the ascendancy of the religious sentiment over their minds.

Askeaton was erected by Desmond, Dunmore and Kaltragh by the Berminghams, Kilcarbain by the Burkes, Holywood by the Audleys, Kilmichail by the Pettits.* O'Donnel founded Kilmacrenan and Magheri-Beg; Con O'Neil, Dungannon; MacSweenys, Ballymacsweeny and Rathmullian; Dowells, Tulks in Roscommon; O'Malleys, Morrisk; Gerald Cavanagh, Enniscorthy in Wexford; Florence O'Driscoll, Inishirean near Baltimore; O'Donoghoe, Moyen in Mayo; O'Sullivan Beare, Bantry; and Donogh McCarthy, Irrelagh or Mucruss Abbey on the borders of lake Lene or Killarney, the remains of which in good preservation attract the attention of visitors to that region. Cormac of Muskerry erected the abbey of Kilcrea nunnery of Ballyvacardane besides five churches. The O'More in 1447 founded Abbyleix of which no vestige remains, and in 1464 Adare was erected by Kildare. To many churches now in use were attached conventual establishments that date from this period.

Pestilence in the form of the black death which in 1348 swept from the earth twenty five millions of human beings proved more fatal in Ireland in the towns than in the country, fourteen thousand dying in Dublin alone. It spared neither race nor condition and reappeared four times in that century. In the fifteenth, few years passed without numerous victims to what is called the plague. It raged with especial violence in 1439, three thousand perishing within two months in the capital, and in 1447 seven hundred priests, who did not spare themselves in taking care of the sick.

XXIV.

REIGN OF EDWARD IV.—1461—1483.

By the established rules of succession no one had better claim than Edward to the throne. Through him vested in the crown the inheritance derived to his father from Anne de Mortimer, Ulster, Connaught and portions of Leinster and Meath. To the greater part of this vast domain no valid title subsisted, since by English law whatever his ancestors had acquired by grant or prescription had been divested long before by disseizin and returned either to the septs from whom it had been originally wrested, or passed to the Burkes who had been beyond legal memory in possession of the Connaught lands, though not one very peaceable.

Thomas seventh earl of Kildare after the death of Richard of York at Wakefield chosen governor by the council was confirmed in that office by the king. From no want of affection or confidence, since Kildare had ever been steadfast in his devotion to himself and his house, but from motives of policy in the hope of inspiring a more loyal feeling among the Anglo and Irish nobles to the throne, George duke of Clarence his brother was commissioned as lord lieutenant for seven years. Fitzeustace appointed his deputy yielded the office that same year to Sherwood bishop of Meath.

Acts were passed in parliament confirming the attainder of the late earl of Ormond beheaded at Newcastle, and subjecting his

brothers John and Thomas and other prominent Lancastrians to the
like forfeitures. John next in succession to the title took refuge
with several of his friends and adherents in the fastnesses of the
family domains, and raising his standard as earl of Ormond collected
a considerable army. Thomas the eighth earl of Desmond who had
that very year succeeded his father marched against them with twenty
thousand men but with little result, his brother Gerald being taken
prisoner. The Butlers swept havock through Leinster and occupied
Waterford, but at Pillstown near Carrick on Suir in Kilkenny sustained a disastrous defeat, having come to an engagement on a
Monday, considered an unlucky day for the purpose, contrary to the
advice of Ormond. Many were slain and their leader MacRichard
Butler, "the most famous English chieftain in Ireland," was captured. His ransom, strange to relate, consisted of two manuscript
volumes: a portion of the celebrated psalter of Cashel, a collection
of histories, poems and tales transcribed for him by O'Clery, which
copy with this incident connected with its history entered on one of
its leaves is now in the Bodleian library at Oxford; the other was
the book of Carrick of a like nature which he had also had copied.

Ormond after his defeat withdrew into the mountains awaiting re-
enforcements, which reached him shortly under command of his
brother, who had captured on his way four vessels of Desmond's.
Peace was made and the Butlers discouraged for a time remained at
rest. Desmond was appointed deputy to Clarence. He was nearly
forty years of age, described in the annals as "valiant and successful
in war, comely in person, versed in Latin, English and Gaelic lore,
affable, eloquent, hospitable, humane to the needy, a suppressor of
vice and theft, surpassingly bountiful in bestowing jewels and wealth
on clerics and laymen, but especially munificent to the antiquaries,
poets and men of song of the Irish race. He founded a college
church at Youghal, and at his suggestion parliament passed an act
to establish a university on the plan of Oxford at Drogheda, which

for want of endowments never grew up. He was ostentatious and
liked to be surrounded by Irish chieftains who attended his court
and were attached to him for his personal qualities, hereditary gossipred, fosterage or similar ties. His wife was Elisabeth Barry
daughter of the viscount Buttevant, and her sister had married Cormac Ladir McCarthy. The mother of Desmond was a Burke of
Clanrickard, and that chief helped him to subdue five thousand
of the English of Meath who were disaffected, and an assessment of
one hundred marks being laid upon them to pay O'Connor of Offaly
for his prisoners. The Butlers became from time to time less quiet,
and for seventeen days he wasted their territory. He twice invaded
the O'Byrnes inflicting the usual amount of mischief and doing his
part to encourage that habit of destruction in the conflagration of
villages and houses which perhaps more than anything else tended
to barbarize the habits of life at that period.

Similar rivalries to what had alienated Ormond and archbishop
Talbot in the previous reign, and led in the following century to the
taking off of archbishop Allen by the Fitzgeralds of Kildare, stirred
up strife between Desmond and the bishop of Meath, whose followers
had slain in Fingal nine of the viceroys. Parliament sided with
Desmond, enumerating in an address the services he had rendered to
the king at the jeopardy of his life and lands, and his many
other claims to royal confidence. After hearing both parties summoned to his presence, Edward sent back the viceroy to his post with
gifts and assurance of continued favor. Parliaments at Wexford
and Trim relaxed the laws prohibiting trade with the Irish, but
made it lawful "to capture and kill thieves, robbing liege people by
day or night, having no faithful Englishman of good name or fame
in their company in English apparel," it appearing from this no
offence in their eyes to rob in good company. The heads of the
captured were to be cut off and set upon stakes, a practice which the
Irish would seem to have borrowed from this source in the like in-

stances related of the Maguires and MacMahons. It was further ordered that Irishmen dwelling in the four counties should adopt the English garb, shave the upper lip, and take a surname from some town, color, art or office. Every Englishman and friendly Irishman speaking English was to keep a bow of yew, hazel, ash, auburn or other reasonable tree, with twelve shafts and shoot thrice before their constables, on each festal day. Foreign fishermen were forbidden without license from the governor in Irish waters, an order not easily enforced, for the chiefs derived considerable revenue from the permission which they gave strangers to fish along their shores. Court fees were regulated and penalties imposed for clipping money, but in this the government set but a poor example as they debased the coin to half standard and fixed prices at half value.

The period was approaching when gold and silver from abrasion and use in the arts were to reach their lowest point in quantity, estimated at little more than fifty millions sterling in Europe, before additional supplies from America changed the standards. The process was slow and there was but little perceptible change in prices till a century later. But as parliament endeavored to control them by this act, what they attached to the principal commodities it may be worth while to note. A peck of wheat was placed at sixteen pence, barley at eight and oats at four; an ox was valued ten shillings, a cow at six and eight pence, sheep eight pence, a good hog at three and four pence: a couple of capons four pence; a pair of shoes four pence; a gallon of the best ale three half pence; wine of Rochelle six pence, of Gascony eight and Spanish ten, a barrel of herrings six and eight pence. Trade generally was by barter and cows the most common equivalent, for Ireland from the moisture of its climate and luxuriant pastures ever abounded and excelled in cattle.

Some of the Melaghlins seized by the Pettits whilst on a visit to Mullingar were rescued by O'Connor. This led to commotion in Meath. Desmond in 1466 with a large force was defeated, and with

25

Plunket and many other personages of consequence was captured by Con of Offaly, whose brother after entertaining them kindly, from some obligation he was under to the earl, set them free without ransom. Teigue O'Brien crossed the Shannon with a great army spoiling West Munster. After making influence with the Leinster chiefs to help his inauguration at Tara as successor of Brian Boru, he obtained from Desmond a surrender of the county of Limerick and Clan William, subjecting the city of Limerick to a perpetual tribute of sixty marks. He went home and died, not without suspicion of being made away with. Hugh O'Niel son of Owen gained a great victory in Orgial over the English, who later in the year defeated the MacMahons taking Art prisoner. The septs wasted the country up to the gates of Dublin, and the colonists lived in constant consternation.

Warwick not content with placing Edward on the throne, selected for him a wife suitable to his station in Bona of Savoy, sister of the queen of France. He himself negotiated the match. Unfortunately the royal eye had rested with favor on Elizabeth Woodville, widow of Sir John Gray, who became queen. The kingmaker disgusted left the court, and his discontent led a few years afterwards to the restoration for a few months in 1470 of the dethroned Henry. Desmond when in England and engaged in confidential chat with the king had been questioned by him as to what the people thought of this marriage. He replied that he had lost by it the favor of his subjects, but that it was not too late to retrieve his mistake by repudiating Elizabeth, and marrying some daughter of a royal house. This view was the more natural to him that his own father had been indebted for his elevation to the earldom to the dissatisfaction created among the Fitzgeralds by the sixth earl marrying one of inferior rank. What seems quite improbable, it is also related that he spoke of the queen to her husband as a tailor's widow.

Curtain lectures occasionally disturb the slumbers of majesty, and it was whispered that the king in some moment of conjugal temper expressed regret he had not taken the advice of Desmond. The infuriated queen did not rest till she found occasion to wreak her resentment. On the pretext that Desmond was the favorite of Clarence whom the king suspected of disaffection, she contrived to have him removed from the office of deputy, and Tibetot earl of Worcester sent over in his stead. The new governor had claims growing out of the marriage of his father with an heiress of Talbot to Dungarvan, which given to the earl of Shrewsbury had been restored to Desmond. With Sherwood and the queen to aid him he proceeded without hesitation not only against Desmond himself but against Kildare his brother-in-law and Edward Plunket, arraigning them before the parliament at Drogheda, for alliances, fostering and alterage with the king's enemies, and furnishing them with horses, harness, and arms.

Desmond never suspecting the fell purpose of his adversaries and responding in person to these accusations, was arrested and decapitated on the 15th of February, 1468, the queen attaching, surreptitiously it is said, the royal seal to the warrant. The remains of "the great earl" were carried across the country to Tralee for interment, and his death was greatly mourned by the people. Even Richard III. wrote in 1485 that "the earl had been murdered by color of law against all manhood, reason and conscience." Three of Desmond's sons were earls after him, and Gerald, who in 1583 forfeited the family domains, was grandson of another, the fourth. His daughters married McCarthy Reagh and Mac Ibrien Ara. Kildare proceeding to England convinced the king of the injustice of this persecution, and the sentence against himself was annulled and he was appointed governor.

Worcester soon after was appointed lord-lieutenant with Edmund Dudley for his representative. After the rising of Clarence and Warwick he was appointed by the king to sit in judgment on the prisoners, and the cruelties practised by his order on twenty that were condemned, attached to him the title of "the butcher of England." Upon the restoration to the throne of Henry he was discovered by the Lancastrians in a tree in the forest of Havering, and beheaded on Tower Hill was cut to pieces by sentence of John de Vere earl of Oxford, whose father had been executed by his command in the same place four years before. He was a strange compound of considerable learning, intellectual gifts and malignant cruelty. He translated several of the classics, and at Rome by a latin oration moved to tears the second Pius. His estates upon his execution were given to Kildare as amends for the injuries sustained at his hands.

It was harder on Desmond to cut off his head. He had fought nine battles for the house of York, been instrumental in raising Edward to the throne, and in saving the island held by a slender thread from irretrievable loss to the realm. Gilbert charged him with entertaining the design of making himself king of Ireland, but without proof or probability. Such a project could justly be imputed to Teigue O'Brien his relative by marriage, whose death had rendered it abortive; or with some reason to Henry of Tyrone who had supplied Teigue with means for his late raid into Munster. But both Desmond and Tyrone understood too well the character of the Irish chiefs to have any confidence in their willingness to yield up their valued independence to any master. Desmond in personal graces and mental endowments surpassed most men of his time, and it was probably his general popularity and vast possessions which engendered jealousies and brought him to the block. His children were too young to resent his murder. Their uncle Gerald gathered a powerful army and spoiled the English settlements in Munster and Leinster, whilst Meath and Louth were at the same time devastated by another Englishman, John Hadesor, who having married a daughter of MacMahon chief of Farney, harried the settlers, hanging those he captured on trees by the roadside.

On this Gerald his second son, the seventh earl of Desmond had bestowed lands in Waterford about Dungarvan across the Blackwater from Youghal. They consisted of north and south Decies from which comes the name of Desmond, property which his ancestor derived two centuries before by marriage with Margaret Fitzanthony, and which another heiress Margaret Fitzgerald carried two centuries later to the Grandisons. John son of Gerald by Margaret daughter of Mac Richard Butler had by Ellen Fitzgibbon Catherine widow of Thomas Maol twelfth earl of Desmond. This remarkable personage whose span of life is said to have extended over seven score years, from 1464 to 1604, is mentioned by Morrison and Bacon as also by Raleigh whose residence at Youghal in 1589 was but five miles from the castle of Inchiquin, which the old countess occupied and of which he owned the reversion. Raleigh says that she married in the reign of Edward IV, and had held her jointure ever since under seven earls. Her husband, seventy-eight years old when the earldom fell to him in 1529, was ten years her senior but not of age when his father was beheaded at Drogheda in 1468. Horace Walpole relates that she danced with Richard III. at the court of his brother Edward, and that she found him a "marvellous proper man" notwithstanding the tradition. Her great aunt widowed countess of Kildare survived till 1486, the earl her husband, lord deputy, to 1478, and the attendance of Catherine at the English Court even at an early age would not have been remarkable. Her second visit to London more than a century later, mentioned in 1640 by Robert Sydney, second earl of Leicester, is generally regarded as apocryphal, and her fall from the cherry tree which hastened her end is open to doubt.

Some degree of incredulity as to an age so exceptional has been thought warranted by the discovery of a lease of land made in 1505 to Julia daughter of Cormac Ladir (1411–1494), who built Blarney, in which Julia is described as wife of Thomas Maol. As his son Maurice by this lady, deceased in 1529, left a son James called the

court page, thirteenth earl, married when slain by his kinsman
Maurice in 1540, this first marriage must have taken place at least
as early as 1490. If Julia died in 1505 the date of the lease, her
widowed husband may have then or later married his second cousin
Katherine who ten years younger than himself had considerable life
still left in her. The statement of Raleigh that she had held her
jointure from the reign of Edward, if this hypothesis is the true one
would of course be a mistake, but one not surprising considering the
lapse of time. Margaret O'Brien widow of the ninth earl lived long,
and Elinor Butler widow of the unfortunate Gerald the sixteenth,
but neither of them could have been "the old countess of 1589."
Sainthill supposes Julia was divorced from her husband, but it is conjecture without ground to rest upon, and his grandson married her
niece Mary daughter of Cormac Oge (1447—1536). Sound constitutions, active habits and excellent climate probably conduced to
longevity, quite as much as the baths of salt butter to which it
was ascribed by Bacon. It may well be that the place of Catherine
on the family tree is lower down, but the legend as it stands does
not materially conflict with any well known or established fact or
date. The old countess is not only a puzzle on the score of her extraordinary span of existence, but also as a genealogical problem,
and they both have since been made the subject of several essays and
volumes.

The king sought to conciliate the sons of the murdered Desmond.
To James who succeeded as ninth earl he restored the confiscated
estates of his father, adding the castle of Dungarvan. After flourishing twenty years in riches, honor and power, he came to a tra-
gical end, leaving by Margaret O'Brien, daughter of the prince of
Thomond, a daughter who married lord Fermoy. The estates of
Ormond were remote enough not to be much disturbed, continuing
in possession of MacRichard and his descendants, nearly allied
to the MacMorroghs, O'Carrols and O'Reillys. Sir John kept aloof

for awhile when Edward took him into favor, declaring he was the goodliest knight he ever beheld and the finest gentleman of Christendom, and that if good breeding, nurture and liberal qualities were lost in the world, they might be found in the earl of Ormond. This paragon was master of all the languages of Europe, and there was scarcely a court in it to which he had not been sent as ambassador, when he died in 1478 at Jerusalem. Edward had bestowed the office of butler of Ireland on lord Welles and a portion of the prisage of wines on lord Dunboyne for taking O'Conor of Offally prisoner; but an act reversing the attainder of Ormond passed in 1474, and in 1481 Thomas his brother and successor was also restored in blood. Margaret, daughter of Thomas and his co-heiress when he died in 1515, married Sir William Boleyn and was grandmother of Ann who married Henry VIII.

False, fleeting, perjured Clarence, son-in-law of Warwick, took part with that restless spirit in all his plots against Edward, and when upon the brief restoration of Henry the sixth in 1470, co-regent with him of the kingdom, he was reappointed lord lieutenant of Ireland. When Barnet and Tewksbury replaced his forgiving brother on the throne, he was confirmed in that office for twenty years. The close of his feverish career in the butt of Malmsey, execution on Tower Hill of his son Edward the last male Plantagenet in 1499, and of his daughter Margaret in 1541 at the age of seventy, have no other connection with Ireland than from his having held so long its lord-lieutenancy. From 1468 to 1475 the seventh Kildare administered the government as his deputy, and to him may be attributed the origin of what has since been known as the English pale. Dikes were constructed to defend the county of Dublin, and palisades and trenches about the borders of the four counties. A force of men at arms and archers was organized to protect the capital from sudden inroads, and in 1474 the St. George society established, consisting of Kildare as president, Fitzeustace, Plunketts,

St. Lawrence, Dowdals, Barnewal, Bellew, Preston and Lacy, with
the mayors of Dublin and Drogheda, and a force of two hundred
men at arms, with the same object. It was given up ten years later.
The earl had his enemies, and Sherwood one of them replaced him
in 1475.

When the earl died two years afterwards, Gerald his son the
eighth Kildare was appointed deputy, to give place in a few months
to Lord Henry Grey. His letters of dismissal being under the
private seal of the king, with the connivance of the chancellor Portlester his father-in-law who carried away the great seal of Ireland,
he continued to exercise his official functions, summoning and pro-
roguing the parliament at Naas, Grey deputy to the infant lord-
lieutenant prince George holding his parliament also at Trim.
Strange to say the king was powerless to stay or resent this unseem-
ly disregard of his authority. A new seal was ordered, the laws of
Naas were repealed and annulled by those of Trim, there issued
plentiful decrees and proclamations, but Gerald knowing his hold on
popular favor persisted. One infant viceroy by his death made
way for another Richard his brother not much older, but who was
already contracted to Ann Mowbray heiress of Carlow, and to him
Preston, recently created viscount Gormanstown which manor his
great grandfather had purchased of St. Amand viceroy under Edward III., was appointed deputy. Preston by his wife Margaret
Bermingham had claims in Carbery and Naas and was lord of Kells
in Ossory. Roche was created viscount Fermoy the same year,
a rank the Barrys had held for two centuries before.

Among other acts of legislation at this period by the two parliaments, selections from which received the royal sanction, one
added to the council, the archbishops of Dublin and Armagh,
and lords spiritual and temporal of the four counties to fill any vacancy in the supreme authority; and provided that the office should
not be vacated by the governors visiting the neighboring islands.

Power was given to the mayor and council of Waterford to elect a sheriff for the county, Richard Poer who had held that office for twenty years "having kept the place in terror, robbing and spoiling, until the whole neighborhood had abandoned English speech, dress and habits and obeyed the wicked and damnable brehon law." Another statute authorized Englishmen sustaining damage from an Irishman, to be reprised out of his sept, according to the discretion of the viceroy and council. St. Patrick's Cathedral was empowered to sell lands it could not hold to Irishmen. Members of parliament, as travelling about was attended with many perils, were no longer required to be residents of places they represented. Rhymers and hermits were prohibited near the capital, trade at Irish fairs was interdicted; but ecclesiastics attached to religious houses were allowed to traffic with Irishmen and be godfathers to their children with a view of procuring intelligence of their plans and movements.

Kildare was too generally popular to disaffect. He was soon restored to his office which he held for thirty-three years with brief intervals. To strengthen his own position and English rule it is said he gave his sister at this time to O'Neil. Statements vary as to this alliance. Henry MacOwen, whom the annalist of the house of Kildare designates as brother-in-law of the earl, ruled over Tyrone from 1455 to 1482, dying seven years after his resignation in favor of his son Con Mor. The decease of Gormlaih daughter of MacMorrogh left him a widower in 1465, but he was then well advanced, and it seems more probable that Eleanor Fitzgerald married Con who succeeding his father was slain in 1493. Her death took place in 1497, and her son Con Baccagh, first earl of Tyrone, espoused his cousin Alice, daughter of Kildare. By an act passed in 1481, to Con Mor was extended the benefit of English law rigorously withheld from his countrymen. That same year his brother-in-law had been confirmed as deputy for four years with six hundred pounds allowance, the revenues of absentee estates and

26

authority to occupy Carlow and keep it, unless repaid within a
twelvemonth by its recreant lords his advances for recovering it.

Confusion reigned in Connaught.   Its half kings and other
O'Connors, MacDermots, MacDonoghs, O'Kellys, O'Hara, O'Gara,
Flahertys and the two houses of Burke were often at feud.   In 1461,
Hugh son of Turlogh Oge worthy to be king for his comeliness,
valor and liberality to learned and poor, died in his sixty-third year.
MacWilliam ransomed Felim out of his fetters and carrying him to
Carn-fraich, Mac Dermot "put on his shoe after buying it."
O'Conors Roe not to be outdone gave O'Connor Don half the town
of Clare for his prisoner Teigue, and MacDermot was invited also to
his installation.   Discussion led to strife, which ended only when the
combatants at night were too weary to fight any longer.   Teigue
soon after whilst resting for refreshments and food on a Sunday, was
attacked by the sons of Brian Ballagh, but as the annalists say
they were fittingly punished for breaking the Sabbath.   He drove
them from their houses into Analy where the O'Farrels gave them
shelter, and when they returned on a predatory expedition into his
country, he routed them, and took MacBrannan prisoner, releasing him
for eighty marks ransom, the chief of his sept shortly dying at an
advanced age impoverished.   Teigue next year killed Dermot son of
Dermot at Oscelin, and when he himself died in 1464, the Sil Murray buried him as never king was before, so many horse and foot
attended his obsequies, so many herds and horses and so much
money were given for his soul.

Felim in 1468 took great preys from O'Connor Don and Hy-
Many, and carried them into Moylurg to join Burke of Clanrickard,
but after remaining a week together they parted.   On his way home
Felim was overpowered by Edmund MacWilliam and forced to surrender his spoils.   Not disheartened, with MacDermot he attacked
Balintober and defeated that branch of his name and the ClanConway
at Skurmore.   In 1470 he made peace with O'Conor Roe and all

other of his enemies, but four years later a conference with O'Kelly and O'Connor Don ended in an engagement in which he was slain. Donogh the blackeyed, and Teigue, son of Owen, became rival competitors for his throne.

The year after, Tyrconnel with his chiefs joined by MacWilliam of Mayo marched against Clanrickard to revenge his defeat at Crossmacrin two years before. They burned Clare Galway. Ulick with his ever steadfast friends the O'Briens and other chiefs of the Dalgais at Ballinduff attacked O'Donnel, whose cavalry put their army to rout there and again when another onslaught was attempted at what was called the defeat of Glanog.

In 1470 O'Donnel after a long siege compelled Donnel son of Owen O'Conor to surrender the castle of Sligo and to stipulate that tribute should be paid him from lower Connaught. On this occasion he recovered two volumes the Leabhar Gear and Leabhar Na-h-Uidri which had been brought into Connaught in the time of John son of Conor, son of Hugh, son of Donnell Oge O'Donnel. Since their capture they had remained in the possession of ten successive lords of Carbury. What is left of the latter book, transcribed at Clonmacnois, from earlier collections, has been mentioned as among the treasures of the Royal Academy.

Five years later O'Donnel with Maguire, O'Rourke and the chiefs of lower Connaught went on a circuitous hosting. In Cavan he rescued Brian O'Reilly and made peace between that chief and O'Rourke. MacRannall joined him and he burnt Analy to assist Irial O'Farrel and then Delvin, receiving the submission of Daltons and Dillons. He staid long enough in Offaly to avenge Nial Garve, captured in 1435, ravaging the English on either side. He demolished castle Carbury and castle Meyler, spoiled the Melaghlins, defeating them at Esker, and burnt Moyelly and another castle in what is now King's county. On the same day he gained a battle at Ballyloe six miles from Athlone, over the Magawleys. Crossing the

Shannon into Hy-Many he rested his army, and marched home through Clanrickard, Conmaine, Costello and lower Connaught, his expedition having been attended throughout with success. In 1476 the Burkes were on the war path helped by the McDonoghs. O'Donnel with the MacDermots opposed them. They made peace without fighting, to the disadvantage of their neighbors, Burke taking for his share the O'Dowd country, Leyny and one half Carbury and O'Donnel the other half.

In Tyrone no sooner had Con been installed in the place of his father Henry, than O'Donnel pounced upon him, probably in anticipation of the inaugural foray which Con would have otherwise inflicted upon Tyrconnel. With Clanaboy, always at feud with the elder branch of his race at Dungannon, Hugh plundered Dundalk, defeated Kildare who hastened to the relief of his brother-in-law, placed Louth under tribute and devastated Oriel then subject to O'Neil. Felling the dense and impervious forests along the Blackwater he made a road for his army, throwing across that river a wicker bridge, which when his horse and foot had crossed he floated down stream. Returning home in triumph he had hardly reached Ballyshannon, before he again started on another expedition into Fermanagh, bringing back from the Maguires who had taken advantage of his absence to raid his country, considerable booty.

Order and tranquillity prevailed throughout the south. Frequent remains of castle and abbey then recently constructed and in their elegance and strength, now mouldering, bear witness to the devotion and prosperity of that interval of freedom from foreign domination. Desmond soon after his accession resorted to measures to assert his hereditary rights or to extend them, which exasperated his neighbors, and for a year the McCarthies kept him in captivity. When released in 1472, his uncle Gerald, lord of Decies, who had taken part against him, felt the weight of his displeasure, and five years later with eighteen other Geraldines of note was slain. At that particular epoch Munster was momentarily disturbed. Finghin McCarthy Reagh, prince of Carbery, son of Dermot-an-duna, and brother-in-law of Desmond, seated near the sea in his castles of Kilbrittan and Kilgobban was at that time the most powerful chieftain of the south. Cormac, one of his cousins, having provoked his maternal uncle Cormac Ladir, lord of Muskerry, by some wrong to that chief or to his nephews, other sons of Dermot-an-duna, he was taken captive and incarcerated possibly within the lately erected walls of Blarney, and by blinding or otherwise rendered "harmless." What warranted this ill usage does not appear, but his death or mutilation went not unavenged. Resentment at what his friends considered excessive cruelty led to general war, not confined to the immediate parties to the quarrel, but destructive throughout the whole southern part of the island and alike to both bloods.

It did not last long, and chief and sept resumed their usual avocations. About Killarney, McCarthy Mor and the O'Donoghoes, O'Sullivan Mor near Kenmare, O'Sullivan Beare around the Bay of Bantry with their kinsmen lord of Kerry, O'Connor, Donavans, Mahoneys and Driscols, all prosperous and at peace, maintained their independence, and their clans acknowledged no chieftains but themselves. They had reason to be contented, possessing so goodly an heritage. Sea and shore rendered them plentiful harvests and the forest abounded in game. Ireland was famous for its hounds and also for its goshawks and tercels, which demand from other countries rendered sufficiently scarce to require their exportation to be discouraged. Enough were left, however, for the gentle science of falconry where feathered game abounded as in Munster; and when the chief engaged in the sport his followers shared in its excitement. That minstrels abounded may be presumed from acts of parliament at this time to repress them, and there were other pleasant pursuits to develop faculty and elevate taste, above the mere gratification of physical need. The brehon law with its social customs and nice distinctions of right and wrong inculcated the loyalties of reciprocal obligation, fostered a due sense of their duties and responsibilities, whilst an educated and intelligent priesthood inspired sentiments of piety and promoted religious observance. If in Ulster and Connaught under Edward, war appears to have been the rule, and not the exception, it was far otherwise in Munster and Leinster, where profound peace cherished the growth of culture and refinement and diffused the blessings of plenty and prosperity.

With such numbers of independent clans, however, whose active energies found no more congenial employment than war, and for whom abounded many elements of strife at home and with their neighbors, absolute peace never reigned throughout the island unless in the dead of winter, and not always then, for O'Neil in 1471 besieged Omagh from autumn to spring. Still there were intervals of repose for all. War made widows and orphans, pestilence contributed to the work of death. The plague brought from abroad to Assaroe in Donegal spread over the land poverty and distress. The cloister furnished fitting refuge for the bereaved and feeble, and more monasteries were in request. McMahon of Oriel built one at Monaghan in 1462; John O'Connor Kerry, Lislaghtan in 1470; Hugh Roe O'Donnel, Donegal in 1474; O'Madden, Michial in 1479; Kildare, one at Athenry. Others were founded by Ormond at Callan and by Bisset at Glencairn.

Edward but twenty years of age when he ascended the throne, was little more than forty when he left it for the tomb. Brave, sagacious, of a noble presence, affable and popular, he proved a match for Warwick in intrigue, equalled in ability the first and third Edwards his progenitors, Louis XI. of France, or Ferdinand of Aragon his cotemporaries. Whilst king, one fifth of his realm, spoils of the Lancastrians, of whom more than one hundred nobles or great proprietors were attainted, vested in the crown. Subsidies and enforced loans poured into his coffers, running over with the profits of com-

mercial adventure in which he extensively engaged. His accumulations were millions. He expended little in war, and though his wife's
relatives partook of his bounty he was not lavish and had no favorites.
Parliament submitted to his orders and he ruled England with an iron
will. Why no effort was made to extend his authority in Ireland
can only be explained by his jealousy of the Lancastrians in the
earlier part of his reign, and his unwillingness to expend his hoards
as he grew older. Possibly the exhausted state of England from
the effects of the civil war may have in part dissuaded more active
measures. He had a numerous progeny, but proved no exemplary
husband, and Jane Shore was not the only rival of the queen in
his affections. Fond of literature from his reign dates the introduction by Caxton into England of the printing press, destined to work
such momentous changes in the civilization of the world.

XXV.

REIGN OF EDWARD V.—1483.

In the palace of the doges at Venice a black veil covered the space
upon the wall where should have hung the portrait of the beheaded
Marino Faliero. In English history the ten weeks from the ninth
of April, when the late king closed his career, to the twenty-second
of June, when his brother Gloucester usurped the crown, form a
blank equally suggestive, left to the marvellous genius of the great
dramatist, perhaps the best also of England's historians, to fill. In
Ireland, if we may judge from the silence of the annalists, it proved a
period singularly uneventful. Robert St. Lawrence, lord of Howth,
was appointed chancellor, but neither within nor without the pale, did
ought of consequence occur, to be assigned with any degree of cer-
tainty to the reign of the unfortunate youth, who hurried from the
palace to a dungeon was with his brother smothered by the myrmidons of his wicked uncle.

XXVI.

REIGN OF RICHARD III.—1483—1485.

The natural guardian of his nephew and protector of the realm, it proved no difficult task for one so shrewd and unscrupulous as Gloucester to gain adherents, and the unpopularity of the late king towards the end of his reign from his arbitrary exactions he contrived to turn against the son. To send Hastings to the block, to declare illegal his brother's marriage on the plea of previous contract, to denounce the late extortions, and convoke parliament rarely convened by Edward, were successive rounds for an ambition which with slight show of reluctance clutched the proffered sceptre. Reversals of attainder, restoration of confiscated property, pardons judiciously extended where favor could be won, erased remembrance of the means employed to gain his elevation, and by fostering trade and patronizing learning, emancipating bondsmen on the estates of the crown, and assuring the liberties of the subject, Richard gained like ascendancy over the affections of his people as over Ann in the play, who, the child of Warwick and widow of that Edward whom he stabbed in his angry mood at Tewksbury, became his wife.

His Irish policy was equally sagacious. Lacy was sent to sound Kildare, and if his intentions proved friendly, to confirm him for a year as deputy under Edward, son of the king, then eleven years of age, nominated lord lieutenant. Kildare accepted the appointment, but equally politic and wary solicited guaranties for his personal safety, extension of his office for nine or ten years, an annual salary of one thousand pounds, the manor of Leixleip and custody of the castle of Wicklow. To these terms Richard signified his assent, sending him the safe conduct he demanded and requesting his advice how best to bring the island to subjection and obedience. The following year Richard sent over Bishop Barret to remind the deputy of his influence over his brother-in-law, Con of Tyrone, and urge his active efforts to bring that chief and O'Donnel to peace and allegiance, that Ulster might be reduced to possession. Royal despatches to Barry and Roche, Powers, Fitzeustace, Plunket, Delvin and Gormanstown, Staunton, Dexeter, Nangle, Bermingham, and Barret, enjoined it upon them to assist. The king sought to conciliate Desmond, who had not forgiven the execution of his father, apprising him of his intention to provide for him an eligible consort, praying him to assume the English dress, maintain the rights of the church, repress spoliation and extortion, and render the highways safer for travel. His exhortations were seasoned by gifts, "a golden collar and robe embroidered with gold and lined with damask, two doublets of velvet and crimson satin, three shirts and kerchiefs, three stomachers, three pair of hose, scarlet, black and violet, three bonnets, two hats and two tippets of velvet." The earl accepted the gifts but paid little heed to the counsel. He selected his bride from the house of Thomond and ruled his people rather as an Irish chieftain than as an English earl. How completely his family had assimilated in speech and taste to their neighbors is curiously exemplified. A vellum volume of Gaelic writings is in existence, transcribed for the use of his sister Catherine, wife of Finghin of Carbery, by O'Calladh, which found in 1805 walled up in the castle of Lismore takes its name from the place of its concealment.

Kildare well understood the value of his allegiance and improved it to his own advantage. He obtained permission to fortify his county of Kildare, privilege for a market at Maynooth, with tolls on all merchandise exposed there for sale, a grant of thirteen and six pence for every ploughland to defend the pale, the profits of the mint, and a subsidy for his brother Thomas the chancellor wherewith to build his castle of Laccagh. The account given of "the great earl" by English and Irish chroniclers shows how well he merited that appellation. He was one of the wisest statesmen of his age, and since Warwick and Edward without superior in the management of men.

27

"He was a mighty man of stature and goodly presence, liberal and merciful, of strict piety, mild in his government, and if passionate easily appeased. A knight in valor, princely and religious in his words and judgments, frank and outspoken, and of little seeming self-control, he was honest, wise and persistent." Whilst studious of his own aggrandizement he was never unmindful of English interests, erecting castles, planting colonists and rebuilding ruined cities, and by his wise administration preserving the island from being absolutely lost to the crown. Beloved generally by the English, though unreserved toward such as he did not fancy, he repressed rebellion with a reckless boldness which inspired respect from friend and foe.

But what especially marked his policy was his conciliating the powerful chiefs by family alliances. By his first wife, heiress of Portlester by the daughter of the great soldier Jenico d'Artois, so well known in the pages of Froissart, he had six admirable daughters for this purpose, whom he turned to good account, contriving to attach to himself the most influential families of the four provinces by the disposition which he made of them. Eleanor the eldest was second wife of Donnal Reagh, son of Finghin of Carbery, and we shall find her later also spouse of Tyrconnel; Margaret the second, called "the great countess and wise enough to rule a realm," he gave in 1485 to Pierce Butler, grandson of MacRichard, who became afterwards eighth earl of Ormond, and whose maternal ancestors had been conspicuous among the great chiefs of Leinster; Elizabeth married Lord Slane; Alice, Con Baccagh her cousin of Tyrone: and Eustachia less fortunate, Ulick of Clanrickarde, one of the most considerable of the Connaught chiefs, but not of an amiable disposition. In this short reign Kildare was still in the early part of a career which lasted for thirty years longer increasing in glory and power, but what he was and had already accomplished, fully justified the king in his faith that while sure of Kildare he was sure of Ireland.

Richard neglected no measure that would strengthen his hold.

Charters were granted to Youghal and Galway, the latter through the influence of Dominick Lynch, whose brother was its first mayor; Dominick also procuring from the Pope Innocent VIII. for the burgesses the right to elect the warden and vicars of their church of St. Nicholas. Under other concessions from the king, Irish clerics received preferment, the friends of his father rewards, and the rights and claims of the chiefs were respected. At a parliament in 1485, after his nephew De la Pole earl of Lincoln succeeded his deceased son Edward, forty pence from every ploughland in Meath were levied to pay Cahir O'Connor of Offaly his dues for faithful service. That same parliament authorized Kildare to impress wagons and horses in Dublin and Meath for the construction of Castle Dermot, to overawe and reduce Carlow which had been given him by king Edward.

XXVII.

REIGN OF HENRY VII.—1485—1509.

What is generally termed Irish history is not so much the history of Ireland or its people, as of the English colonists. Works relating to them have naturally little to say to the advantage of a nation whom they had provoked by aggressions and spoliations, and whose resentment they often experienced and constantly had reason to dread. What bechanced the Irish themselves is more meagrely related by their own historians. In the existing state of the country few were in condition to record what occurred had it been prudent, and after the introduction of printing the English turned it immeasurably to better account in gaining credence for the version that favored themselves.

When the roses, emblems of the two branches of Plantagenet, white of York, and red of Lancaster, stained and drenched in many sanguinary conflicts, decked at last the throne of the Tudors, England seemed sufficiently exhausted to leave at least for a time her sister island at peace.   The new king, who now wore the crown of his ancestor in the fourth remove, Edward the Third, as the issue of John of Gaunt with Catherine Roet had been legitimated by act of parliament without exclusion from the succession to the throne, represented the house of Lancaster, though not its eldest line. Henry strengthened the position, gained by his victory at Bosworth and upheld by popular favor, by his union in 1485 with Elizabeth the eldest daughter of Edward the Fourth, who as her two brothers had been murdered by their uncle Richard in the tower, according to accepted rules was the rightful heir.   Pursuing the policy of his family, one not uncommon anywhere at that period under similar conditions, but which in instances paralleled or approached amongst Irish chieftains has been inconsistently made subject of reproach, he confined the last male of the house of York, Edward, earl of Warwick, son of that duke of Clarence drowned in the butt of malmsey, to the tower.

The king was not a devoted husband, and whether it was from this slight put upon her niece, or from implacable animosity against the house of Lancaster too long cherished to be readily appeased, Margaret, sister of Edward the Fourth, and widow of Charles the Bold of Burgundy, engaged in a course of systematic efforts to subvert his throne, not easily explained unless by some trickle in her veins from that ancient sorceress of Anjou from whom her race are said to have descended.   It seems equally incomprehensible that the Anglo-Irish lords, who were receiving from the king every mark of favor and confidence, little deserved at his hands by their late behavior, should have lent themselves to these intrigues.   Gerald, earl of Kildare, who since his father's death had held the post of deputy, was retained in that office. Thomas, seventh earl of Ormond, whose family were all along Lancastrians, was restored to honor and

estate. He succeeded his brother James, who had died upon a crusade to the east in 1478, and appointed one of the privy council was
honorably employed in military and diplomatic service, residing however for the most part of his time at court.

James ninth earl of Desmond after a general reign of prosperity,
rich, influential and powerful, had been murdered by his own servants at his castle of Rathkeale in 1487, and was buried at Youghal
a hundred miles distant. His brother Maurice, tenth earl 1450–
1520, whose wives were Ellen Roche and Honor Fitzgibbon, was
still disaffected in consequence of the execution of his father the
eighth earl at Drogheda. Henry had some friends among the
chiefs of Munster. He empowered Finghin McCarthy Reagh of
Carbery, son-in-law of the Desmond of Drogheda, and Cormac Mac
Teigue of Blarney who bore that relation to the ninth Kerry, to
receive the homage of the rest, and few took part with Simnel. The
other English lords were of less influence or power, but seemingly of
sufficient intelligence not to have been betrayed into such hazardous
courses without faith and reason for it to rest upon. Some writers
entitled to respect are of opinion that the young man who appeared
in Dublin, in 1486, as the earl of Warwick, was actually that
personage.

The pretender was crowned in Christ church in Dublin, and the
next year in July, 1488, with his kinsman Lord Lincoln, Lord
Lovell who perished in the secret chamber, Thomas Fitzgerald and
Michael Swartz with two thousand Flemings sent over to his aid by
the duchess of Burgundy, repaired to England, where his army was
defeated at Stoke and himself captured. The king displayed much
magnanimity in the treatment of his prisoner, who was employed
in the royal kitchen, and later promoted to the post of falconer.
The English nobles and men of property and consequence implicated in the rising were attainted, heavily fined or their estates
confiscated. But the hold on the island depended so absolutely

upon the Anglo-Irish, who had originated the movement and were
the most guilty, that no similar severities were ventured against
them. Edgecomb was sent over to take their submission and
oaths of future allegiance and grant them pardon. The following year, 1489, Henry summoned them to court, and the earl of
Kildare, Barry Viscount Buttevant and Roche of Fermoy, Birmingham Lord of Athenry, DeCourcy of Kinsale, Preston of
Gormanstown, Nugent of Delvin, St. Lawrence of Howth, Fleming
of Slane, Barnewal of Trimleston, Plunket of Dunsany, were entertained by him at Greenwich, Simnel waiting at the table as their
cupbearer. It is safe to conjecture that the sagacious monarch, when
closeted with the representatives of English rule, forcibly impressed upon them the importance of the policy best calculated to
preserve what estates they had by consolidating the government and
contributing by their harmony to its strength. Whatever measures
were suggested or recommended of course naturally tended to subject
the Irish to greater thraldom.

The duchess not discouraged by the failure of her earlier scheme
was now engaged in another, and in 1492, while the king was at
war with France, sent Perkin Warbeck to Munster, to represent
Richard duke of York, second son of Edward the Fourth. It was
pretended that he was not murdered by his uncle, but had escaped
from the tower. He was invited into France and treated with great
consideration. Upon peace taking place soon after, he repaired to
Flanders, where as the White Rose of York, he was made much of
by Margaret who professed she was his aunt. He remained at her
court till another treaty between Henry and the Netherlands drove
him first to Ireland and thence to Scotland, where James the
Fourth bestowed upon him the hand of Catherine Gordon, the beautiful daughter of the earl of Huntley and granddaughter of James
the First. In 1497 he was again at Cork with his wife, where
Desmond joining him with twenty-four hundred men, he invested

Waterford. but being unsuccessful, Warbeck sailed for Cornwall. He raised his standard at Bodmin as Richard the Fourth, and with a few thousand hastily collected followers besieged Exeter. Disheartened, he withdrew to Beaulieu in Hampshire, and soon after surrendered. but escaping from the tower was again captured and executed in 1499 at Tyburn with John Waters. mayor of Cork, his earliest and steadfast adherent, while Desmond according to English policy was pardoned and received into favor.

These plots. although their theatre of operation was partially if not principally in Ireland, and they derived much of their importance from the support they received from the colonists, have but indirect connection with its history. Kildare was suspected of connivance, but though prominently engaged in the cause of Simnel, there is no good ground for supposing he took any part whatsoever in that of Warbeck. His relations with the house of Ormond were not friendly, and their enmity was at no loss for expedients to undermine him at court. Sir James Butler, natural son of the sixth earl, had been sent over in 1492 by his uncle Thomas the seventh as his representative. With the aid of the Burkes and O'Briens, he compelled the retainers of Ormond to recognize his authority and accept him as their chief, the relation of an English lord to his tenants and vassals in Ireland being much the same as that of the chieftain to his clan. After obtaining pledges of submission, their forces marched through Leinster and Meath. Whilst the adherents of Sir James were quartered in Ship street, in Dublin, some commotion occurred, and it was said that the conflagration which ensued was purposely set by Kildare. His course, whatever it may have been, was no doubt mainly controlled by his wish to maintain the royal authority. But there may have been other motives for hostility. It was in contemplation to legitimate by act of parliament Sir James, who was well liked for his popular qualities and respected for his talents. The next in succession was a distant kinsman of the earl, and even more intimately

connected by consanguinity and friendship with the Irish chiefs than
Kildare, who had given him his sister Margaret in marriage. Sir
James was appointed with Garth, sent over as commissioner, to the
military government of Tipperary and Kilkenny, and received a
grant of all land in those counties belonging to the earldom of
March, then vested in the crown. Garth causing Calvagh son of
O'Carrol of Offaly to be put to death, Kildare his kinsman hung the
son of Garth. Quarrel existed between the Archbishop Fitzsymons
and Rowland Eustace father-in-law of Kildare, who for nearly half
a century had been treasurer. These complications led to the removal of Kildare, the archbishop replacing him, and also of
Eustace, who was called to rigorous account for his administration of
the finances. Kildare was sent over to London, but was again in
Ireland in 1494.

In that year Sir Edward Poynings, an able statesman and accomplished officer sent over as deputy, inaugurated his administration by
an inroad on O'Hanlon and Macginnis on the borders of Ulster
and not far from the pale, and when they withdrew into their fastnesses he destroyed twenty-five of their towns and villages. The
castle of Carlow having been seized by Thomas Fitzgerald, brother of
Kildare, a diversion designed in favor of the Ulster chiefs, the deputy
making the best terms in his power with them, marched south with his
forces and retook it. A few weeks later he convened the parliament
at Drogheda, composed of members under his control, and there was
enacted the famous statute known by his name. It was established
by this law that no session should thereafter be held of the Irish
parliament without express consent of the king, and after first submitting for royal sanction all acts proposed to be passed. It was also
provided that all general laws of the English parliament should take
effect and be enforced in Ireland. The statute of Kilkenny was
confirmed except the clauses prohibiting the use of the Irish language.
Pales and moats were ordered to be constructed for the protection of

the four counties, and proprietors in the marches were ordered when absent to leave sufficient deputies in their place. Colonists were to provide themselves with bows and arrows, and butts for practice to be erected in the towns and villages. It attainted Kildare for collusion with O'Hanlon. Family war cries, such as Crom-a-boo of the Kildares, Seanaid-abu of the Desmonds, Butler-abu, Lamh-dearg-abu of the O'Neils, Lamh-laider-abu of the O'Briens, McCarthies and Fitzmaurices, were forbidden, and coyne, livery and purveyance. It ordered the resumption of land grants since the reign of Edward the Second, repealed the privilege of sanctuary in the island for rebel refugees, and constituted the lord treasurer governor in case of vacancy. In 1498 the previous arrangement was restored which vested the election in the council as then constituted. These laws passed by a few English colonists, and not all even of them represented, had no authority outside the pale, but as English rule extended over the island, they became of more general obligation and observance.

It is worthy of note that although cannon had been used at Cressy in 1346, a century and a half later fire arms were little known in warfare, and bows and arrows, axes, swords and spears the principal dependence. The first mention of hand guns in Ireland is under date of 1487. Brien O'Rourke was killed by Hugh O'Donnel Gallda or the "Anglicised" by a shot from a gun. Kildare the following year battered down the castle of Balerath in Westmeath belonging to the Mageoghans with artillery, and about the same time received from Germany six hand guns which his sentinels bore on guard at Thomas Court his residence in Dublin. The septs realizing their disadvantage in fighting without adequate protection against enemies encased in iron or steel, had gradually accustomed themselves to the use of defensive armor, and O'Donnel in a raid into Tyrone carried off seventeen complete suits. The substitution of the new weapons was gradual and became general more than a century later, but the

28

change worked in favor of the English who could more easily procure them, and their improvement led in time to the abandonment of all armor as worse than useless. This innovation revolutionized military science and feudal methods of warfare slowly passed into desuetude. Trains of artillery from their cost were confined to the government or wealthy lords. The lower orders were left powerless to resist oppression. Combats again depended not so much on personal valor, as, at the invasion, upon superior weapons, and the richer nation had less difficulty in subjugating the weaker whose comparative poverty prevented their procuring as good. Development of commerce from the discovery of America and influx later of the precious metals, the changed standard of right and wrong from the accepted doctrine that might made right, lessened respect for property and helped along Irish subjugation effected under the Tudors.

Kildare after his attainder was sent prisoner to London, but his reply to the king, when charged with burning the cathedral of Cashel, that he thought the archbishop was within, and when advised by Henry to retain good counsel, that he had chosen the best, for he had selected himself, gained the monarch's good will, who when told that all Ireland could not govern Kildare, exclaimed that he was fitted to rule Ireland. He was restored to his dignities and possessions, and Henry gave him to wife his cousin Elizabeth St. John, in place of his countess, Portlester's daughter, who had died from anxiety at his imprisonment. He was sent back in 1496 to Ireland as deputy. His eldest son Gerald, with whom was matched a daughter of lord Zouche of Codnor, retained for a time as pledge for his father's fidelity, was soon allowed to join him, and in 1503 appointed treasurer.

The earl upon his return marched into Thomond in the interests of his brother-in-law Piers, afterwards eighth earl of Ormond. Conor Na Srona O'Brien, chief of the Dalgais, defeated him at Ballyhickey, and recovered back the castle of Felyback which he had taken from

Florence MacNamara. Conor's daughters were wives of the chief of Tyrconnel, of Clanrickard and O'Ruare of Breffny. Upon his death soon after he was succeeded not by his son Donough, but by his brother Torlogh Oge, and this chief by their nephew Torlogh Don, who favored the pretentions of Sir James as head of the Butlers. Piers were forced to lurk in the forests for safety and reduced to impoverishment. His wife suffering from want of the usual comforts of life and limited to a milk diet when her health required wine, expressed her discontent. Piers learning that Sir James was on his way to Kilkenny accompanied by six horsemen, though himself having but a single attendant, attacked and slew him, and from that time until the death of earl Thomas, twenty years later, as next in succession to the earldom to which he eventually succeeded, was the recognized head of the family in Ireland.

Soon after James was slain Kildare commenced hostilities against Thomond. Torlogh rallied his forces, and the Butlers were defeated at Moyalis in Ormond after a fiercely contested engagement. Obtaining reinforcements, the earl, later in the year 1498, made an incursion into Connaught, took Athleague from the Kellys of Hy-Many, Tulsk, Roscommon, and Castlerea from O'Conors, bestowing them upon disaffected chiefs of their respective families. This exercise of authority by virtue of superior force was characteristic not only of the earl but of his line, eager to impress upon the less powerful their own superiority. He was prompted, however, by another motive; his daughter had married the third Ulick of Clanrickard, who had provoked his paternal resentment by harsh treatment of his wife.

It was said to have been in consequence of this conjugal infelicity and unpleasant relation between the earl and his son-in-law, that these two representatives of foreign race brought about one of the most sanguinary conflicts of the period, in which, though Englishmen directed the military movements, not an Englishman was slain. This strange fact and others not dissimilar suggest treachery, hardly credible, however, as the recommendation of Gormanstown after the battle, to slaughter their Irish auxiliaries, would appear to have been rather in grim humor than in earnest. The immediate circumstance that led to the battle of Knocktow, Aug. 19, 1504, was the demand at Dublin of the O'Kelly, whom Kildare had placed in possession of Hy-Many and who had been subsequently driven out by Clanrickard, to be reinstated. The deputy collecting a large force from Leathcon, or the north part of the island, O'Donnells, O'Conors Roe, MacDermots of Moylurg, O'Neils, all but the O'Neil himself, Magennis, MacMahons and O'Hanlons, O'Reillys, O'Farrells, O'Conor Faly, MacSweenys, and Burkes of Clanwilliam, marched into Connaught. They were opposed by Clanrickard, O'Briens, MacNamaras, O'Carrolls of Ely and the leading warriors of Ormond and Ara. It was a struggle between the septs north and south, of Leath Con against Leath Mogha; and of nine divisions in the army of the latter there remained after the action but one battalion and that disorganized. The fight long and bloody, from two to nine thousand being the statement of the slain, is described with much animation in the annals of Ulster, and defects of expression may be ascribed to difficulty of translation. "Far off was heard the onset of martial chiefs, the vehement efforts of the champions, royal heroes rushing to the charge, battle cries of leaders, calls of endangered battalions, shouts of victory, the clang of the dead as they fell, the rout of the multitude by nobles invulnerable in steel. The plain was covered with mangled carcasses, spears, shields, and swords, shattered or cloven, beardless youths lying unsightly in death." Victory declared for the north, but they paid dearly for their triumph, for when after the fight it was proposed to march on to Galway, O'Donnell objected that a considerable number of their forces had been overpowered or slain and others of them scattered, and that it was advisable to remain for the night on the field in token of victory, and for the dispersed to rally round their banners. They took Galway on the morrow, and after some days rest went to Athenry which also surrendered.

To this internecine warfare, which like that of Athenry two centuries before was mainly of clan against clan, is generally attributed Ireland's final decline and subjugation. Thus easily persuaded to mutual slaughter by crafty and treacherous enemies, who, however individually honest, were by the course of events instrumental in carrying out the diabolical policy of English interests, all mutual confidence was lost amongst the chieftains, and efficient combination against their common danger rendered impossible. A brief interval of repose after this bloody conflict extended to the close of Henry's reign in 1509.

It will be observed that Kildare, excepting for the brief rule of Fitzsymons, archbishop of Dublin, appointed to supersede him in 1492, of Preston left at the head of affairs when the archbishop went to England, and the eventful administration which followed of Sir Edward Poynings closing in 1496, retained the office of lord deputy or justice throughout the reign of Henry VII., soon after whose accession Jasper duke of Bedford was nominated lord lieutenant. The son of the king, afterwards his successor as Henry VIII. in 1494, at the age of four succeeded his uncle, but neither of them took any part in the government.

This victory at Knoctow, in which he was the principal leader in the actual battle, proved the last exploit of Hugh O'Donnel, since his reign of forty-four years soon after ended with his life at the age of nearly four score. We left him in 1483 engaged in expeditions against Con More of Tyrone and Maguire[1] of Fermanagh. The great clans of Kinel Owen and Kinel Connel were too near neighbors to remain long at peace; but the two following campaigns were simple marauds, and either chieftain had for allies

---

[1] Page 204.

members of the opposing sept. In 1488 O'Donnel concluded
the peace of Sil Murray with Clanrickard and Felim Finn O'Connor, an active chieftain ambitious of consolidating under his rule
the severed branches of the O'Conors of Connaught. O'Donnel
that year defeated MacWilliam of Mayo in Tyrawley, and the
next invaded Breffny to adjust a quarrel of the O'Rourkes. He
thence proceeded into Moylurg, where one of the MacDermots in
his army despoiling a church, he compelled restitution, and one of
the O'Rourkes being guilty of a like depredation on the church of
Drum, he delivered him up as a pledge till satisfaction was made.

In 1490 he invaded the MacQuillans and with his spoils proceeded to Belfast which he reduced and demolished the castle.
Elate with success, he was in no humor to submit to the arrogant
pretensions of Con Mor of Tyrone, and to his demand to "send him
tribute or else—" replied that "he owed him none, but if—." They
gathered their forces and for several weeks lay opposed, O'Donnel
at Drumbo in Donegal, Tyrone three miles south of Londonderry,
retiring to their respective abodes at Christmas, without peace or
armistice, or coming to battle. Early the next year disposed to
reconciliation, they submitted in person their grievances to the
deputy, but during their absence one of the O'Donnels fell in a
skirmish with Henry O'Neil, Tyrone's lieutenant, which widened
the breach. They were both however too sagacious to waste
their strength in fruitless bloodshed, and in 1492 an armistice
was concluded to continue till the following May. But in January
Con Mor was slain by his brother Henry Oge, who supported
by the Kanes and Mellans, claimed the chieftainship. O'Donnel
interposed for Donnel the elder brother, and next in succession,
but who was defeated at Glasdrummond.

The chief of Tyrconnel rallied an army in Connaught, and with
O'Conors and O'Rourkes marched across the Island to Clanaboy.
At Mourna in Down his army was overtaken and surrounded by

O'Neil's; but he pressed his way through them till he gained a large plain favorable for an engagement and there drew up his forces in battle array. A fierce and obstinate conflict ensued, "in which they bore in mind all their old enmities and new hatreds." O'Donnel conquered, but the darkness of the night prevented pursuit of the vanquished. He had that year lost his chief ollav in literature, poetry and history, O'Clery, who kept a house of hospitality for rich and poor. He compelled the Melaghlins to submit to the O'Rourke and beleaguered Sligo. In 1494 he paid his famous visit to the king of Scotland, James the Fourth, and returned to find his son Con beset by O'Conors and MacDermots. He hastened to his relief, defeating their forces, MacDonogh lord of Tirerill, O'Dowd and O'Gara falling in the battle that ensued.

Con coveting a fine steed of Bisset or MacKeon of the Glinns, who had also wife and hound equally famous, proceeded with six score axe men and as many horse to his house to capture them, which he effected, releasing all but the horse and some prey of cattle which he carried off. He then gathered larger numbers of his father's retainers, crossed the Shannon into Munster and spoiled Magonihy, a country of MacCarthy Mor, and returned with his spoils into Donegal unopposed.

His father next year went into Oriel to assist Brian to obtain the chieftainship, and spoiled the O'Reillys and the English settlements in Louth. He made peace for Carbury, placing Felim in possession of the chieftainship. During his absence his son Hugh Oge took possession of Ballyshannon. Con hastened to retake it, but was driven off into Donegal by Hugh and Maguire, in their turn defeated by Con, who had mustered a larger force and took for spoil on this occasion one hundred and ten horses, besides Maguire himself. Hugh Oge soon after slew a number of his kinsmen in his camp, and the aged chieftain disgusted at the froward behavior of his sons resigned the chieftainship of Tyrconnel to Con. Hugh defeated Con, and Con Hugh who was sent prisoner to Conmaine Cuilla in Connaught. Con then invaded Moylurg, but was vanquished at Ballaghboy, the pass to Sligo through the Curlew mountains, losing in the fight several of his chiefs, Mac Sweeneys, O'Gallaghers and O'Doherty, as also the Cathach a sacred box containing the Psalter of St. Columba, always carried at the head of the Kinel Connel army on their expeditions, as a palladium of success. Con hurried back to Donegal to be slain by Henry Oge O'Niel, several O'Donnels Boyles and O'Gallaghers falling with him in the fight.

Hugh Roe resumed the chieftainship, proffering it to Hugh Oge who declined it and who, his rival now removed, proved ever afterwards a loyal son, aiding to put down their neighbors who had taken advantage of these family quarrels. Whilst his father visited Kildare to receive that earl's son Henry Fitzgerald into fosterage, Hugh Oge attacked Art O'Neil and took from him Castlemoyle. Another son of Tyrconnel, Donogh, had risen in rebellion and seized Bundrowes, but captured by his father and brother was delivered up to Maguire. Hugh Roe then reduced Moylurg, recovering the Cathach now in the Irish academy; the next year he demolished Dungannon, and joining forces with Kildare took the castle of Kinard from John Boy O'Neil and gave it to Turlogh the earl's nephew from whom Donnel O'Neil wrested it a few weeks later. Donogh still giving his father trouble he was maimed and died in consequence.

A twelve month after the battle of Knoctow, Hugh Roe ended his active career. The chroniclers make mention of him "as lord of Tyrconnel, Inieshowen, Kinel Moen and lower Connaught, a man who had obtained hostages from the people of Fermanagh, Oriel, Clannaboy and the Route, from O'Kanes and also from the English and Irish of Connaught, except Clanrickard, and his territory from the river Suck to Kinel Aedha he made tributary. This O'Donnel, the full moon of the hospitality and nobility of the north, the most jovial and valiant, the most prudent in war and peace, and of the best jurisdiction, law and rule of all the Gaels in Ireland in his time, for there was no defence of any house except to close the door against the wind only; the best protector of the church and learned men, who had given great sums in honor of the Lord, who erected the castle and monastery of Donegal; who had made many predatory excursions throughout the land, and might be justly styled the Augustus of the north-west of Europe, died at the age of seventy-eight at his fortress at Donegal." The encomiums lavished on this chief may be somewhat extravagant, but that he was a wise ruler and an excellent commander, besides possessing many noble traits of character, as shown throughout his career, cannot well be questioned. His frequent military expeditions were for the most part to prevent injustice and grew out of the state of the times.

Henry O'Neil in 1483, as has already been mentioned, resigned the chieftainship to his son Con Mor, surviving his abdication six years. Two other of his sons Donnel and Henry Oge in turn held sway over Tyrone. In 1470, Con who succeeded his father had avenged the death of his brother Rory by slaying six of his kinsmen implicated in his taking off, and ten years afterwards we find him occupied in negotiating a treaty of peace with the chief of Tyrconnel at Castlefin in Donegal. The treaty effected proved of little avail, for the following year taken prisoner by the O'Neils of Clanaboy, Con Mor was given in charge to O'Donnel, remaining in captivity till ransomed by his father, and with the consent of the sept inaugurated its chief. At what period his marriage with the daughter of Kildare occurred does not appear, but their sons in 1498 were already grown to manhood. Kildare his brother-in-law soon after his inauguration came to assist him in battle with O'Donnel, but they were badly defeated near Dundalk. War continued for several years with little actual bloodshed, when Con in 1488 repairing to the house of O'Donnel, it was brought to a

29

close for a brief respite. Two years before he had invaded Louth, and after that took hostages from O'Kane.

This peace proved like the rest delusive, and their armies were confronted for a time without a battle. Kildare's efforts to bring about a reconciliation were unavailing, though an armistice for a few months was concluded. In 1493 Con a brave and warlike man and generous was killed by his own brother Henry Oge. Their elder brother Donnel nominated chieftain was routed by Henry, who sustained a defeat at Beanna Boirche from O'Donnel, that chief exerting his influence in favor of Donnel who still claimed the headship of Tyrone.

In 1497, upon the release without ransom of his son Hugh, who had been captured, and in consideration of great gifts of land, steeds and armor, he yielded the supremacy to Henry. That chief the same year invading Tyrconnel returned victorious, to be slain the next by Turlogh and Con, sons of Con Mor whom he had murdered five years before. Donnel resumed the sovereignty. Surprised at Dungannon by Felim, son of Henry, he sustained some loss, but Kildare coming to the rescue took Dungannon "with great guns," leaving Donnel in peaceable possession, and in 1500 likewise reduced Kinard. This he gave to his nephew Turlogh O'Neil, soon after driven out of it, "which led to much war in Tyrone." Donnel was invaded by O'Neil of Clanaboy. Dungannon taken by O'Hogan was speedily recovered and the assailants hung, but the year after it was burnt by O'Donnel, and in 1507 again invested when Donnel made peace. His nephews, sons of Con, left him little repose, and in 1509 took from him Dungannon whilst Kildare demolished Omagh. That year, Donnel, "who had destroyed many men and committed many depredations to gain and keep the chieftainship," went to his fathers; and Art, son of Hugh son of Owen, roydamma or tanist, at whose house the sons of Con Mor slew Henry Oge, was installed in his place.

In Oriel, Redmond MacMahon succeeded his brother Owen son of Rury in the chieftainship in 1467, but taken prisoner by Hugh Oge and the English in 1478, ended his days six years later in the prisons of Drogheda. Hugh Oge son of Hugh Roe son of Rury succeeding burnt twenty-eight English villages. After other exploits he died blind in 1496, making way for Brian son of Redmond, when for several years war raged between the rival branches of the name. In one of the combats fought between them, at Ath-an-Choileir, Turlogh O'Neil nephew of Kildare was slain. In Fermanagh Edmund followed Thomas Oge in 1472, and sixteen years after resigned in favor of John, son of Phillip the former tanist, who, "merciful and humane, best in jurisdiction, authority and regulation, in church and state," died followed by Connor, who in 1527 was succeeded in the chieftainry by Cuconnaught. Turlogh O'Reilly son of John was elected lord of Breffny in 1468 upon the death of Cathal son of Owen. His own castle Tullamongan was burnt that year by the English, and in 1485 he burnt that of the Magaurans. His son John, "a young man kind and bountiful, passed away in 1491 at the beginning of his prosperity," and John son of Cathal son of Owen succeeded and invaded the Maguires. Catherine his wife, daughter of Hugh Roe MacMahon, died soon after his accession, and the next year the bereaved husband and brother sought consolation in defeating the English with considerable slaughter. John's rule and life closed in 1510.

In west Breffny or Leitrim, after Tiernan Oge O'Rourke head of the Hy-Brunes died in 1468, Donnel claimed the chieftainship as next in rightful succession, but Donough Lose was inaugurated. In 1487 the castle of Felim, son of Donogh, being captured by his kinsmen, O'Donnel restored it. After the death of Felim Owen son of Tiernan succeeded. In Analy, when Donnel Boy O'Farrel, son of Ross, son of Conor, son of Cathal died, Irial succeeded. Rury son of Ross, as he was taking possession deceased in

1475, and Rury son of Cathal ruled to 1496. Con, lord of Clannaboy, son of Hugh Boy killed in 1444, died at Shane's castle or Eden-
duffcarrig in 1482. His son Nial Mor, chief after him, espoused
Inneen MacDonnel, sister of Donald Balloch, whose wife bore
the same relation to him. It would be interesting to follow other
lines of chieftains in Ulster, MacSweenys, O'Dohertys, O'Kanes,
O'Boyles, Rannals and O'Hanlons, and also the Maginness, head
of the Rudricians, but they were not so prominent or as frequently
mentioned and they are reserved for notice later.

The MacDonnels had already become by their possessions in the
north-east corner of the island, later three hundred and thirty-three
thousand acres in extent, a power in the land. John Mor of Isla,
grandson of king Robert I., married Margery heiress of the Bissets
at the close of the fourteenth century. That family in the person
of two brothers John and Walter had been forced to quit Scotland
in consequence of supposed complicity in 1242 with the murder at
Haddington, after a tournament, of Patrick Galloway, the popular
earl of Athol. It was said they set fire to his house in order to
conceal their crime. They purchased large tracts of territory on
the shores of Antrim from Richard de Burg, earl of Ulster,
holding among other estates the seven lordships of the Glinns. It
will be remembered that in 1316 they took a leading part with
the Lacies in the attempt to place Edward Bruce on the Irish
throne. By marriage with their neighbors they maintained their
position, Sabia O'Neil, mother of Margery, being especially famous in
her day for the graces and sterling qualities befitting a noble matron.

. It was in 1399 in the fifth generation, that this marriage of Margery, sole daughter of the house, transferred with her hand its large
possessions to John Mor, who in 1425 was killed with the connivance
or by the order of James the First. Their son Donald Balloch
at the battle of Inverlochy defeated the royal forces. Dwelling
much in Ireland, he espoused a daughter of Con O'Neil of Clana-

boy, who when directed by king James to send him the head of
Donald, then the accepted suitor of the maiden, sent somebody's
else.   Donald died in 1480, and his son John and Sabina, daughter
of Felim O'Neil, son of Nial Mor, were parents of Sir John called
Cahanagh, from his fosterage with the O'Kanes, whose wife was
Cecilia Savage.   Betrayed by a kinsman at the instigation of the
earl of Argyle, in whose service originated "the far cry to Lochaw,"
he was executed at Edinburgh.   This kinsman, MacIan, was also
employed to destroy Alexander son of Cahanagh, but his daughter
fascinating his intended victim, he changed his purpose and their
marriage perpetuated the race, Sorley Boy afterwards famous being
the youngest of their six sons.   Down to the death of James IV.
at Flodden in 1513, Alexander was prohibited from visiting or
holding a rood of land in Scotland.

Four distinct immigrations of the Clandonnel from that country
or its islands into Antrim in the fifteenth century established
their foothold in Ulster.   The first took place after the death of
John Mor in 1425; the second after the battle of Inverlochy in
1431; the third after the formal surrender of the lordship of the isles
in 1476, which the then lord his son and grandson forfeited by entering into covenants to assist King Edward in the subjugation of Scotland; and the last in 1493, when the estates still left to their family
of Isla and Cantire in that kingdom were confiscated.   During the
next century they took an active part in the wars of Ireland.

To historians or genealogists the O'Conors in their various
branches are a constant perplexity.   Don, Roe and Sligo of the
Hy-Brunes, Core and Kerry derived from Rury, of Offaly from
Cahir Mor recur in the pages of Irish history, and often without
any mark to distinguish one from another.*   The four first men-

---

* The double N seems not to attach with uniformity to any branch of the name. The
Four Masters spell all alike with one.   O'Conors Kerry and O'Conors Core are spelt in the
same way by Cronelly.   The present representatives of Sligo adopt the double n, which
also distinguishes a family in Kerry, and which at different periods the O'Conors Don seem
also to have assumed.

tioned of Connaught were too restless to be long at peace, and
multiplied too numerously to render it easy to follow the fortunes
of the various subordinate branches in all their experiences. With
the death of Cathal, son of Rory, in 1439 came to an end that long
dynasty of kings, which since Eocha in the second century of our
era had borne sway in Connaught. Turloghs, Rodericks, Conor,
Dermots, Hughs followed each other in succession, more than
fifty from the coming over of Strongbow to the last, but in no very
regular order of succession, the strong man of the period proving
generally the successful competitor for the throne. Occasionally
the actual possessor losing popularity was deposed and perhaps
again restored, creating confusion, and baffling any attempt even to
enumerate this long line of monarchs, many of whom were justly
distinguished for character and ability.

Upon the death of Cathal, Hugh Don and Teigue Roe claimed
his throne as the rightful O'Conor, but the estates of the royal
branch of Roscommon having been partitioned between their two
families towards the close of the preceding century, authority followed this subdivision, and for a time the respective chiefs were
entitled half kings. Owen Don, son of Felim, was succeeded in
1485 by Hugh, son of Hugh, who held the chieftaincy for two
years, and upon the death of Turlogh Oge in 1503, at Balintober,
there was another subdivision of territory. That castle long the
abode of the kings, through the influence of the neighboring lord
of Hy-Many, was assigned to the family of his kinswoman Graine
an Kelly widow of one of them. In 1487, the feverish condition
of affairs had been calmed down by the treaty of Sil Murray, and
for a while greater tranquillity prevailed. The year after, upon the
decease of Donogh Roe of that branch, at an advanced age, Felim
Finn, son of Teigue, son of Turlogh Roe, brave and warlike, who
for his energy and talents had for thirty years taken a leading part
in affairs and been expected to reunite the divided kingdom, suc-

ceeded, inaugurated by O'Donnel and MacWilliam of Mayo,
McDermot according to ancient custom putting on his shoe.
But he was already too far advanced in years to effect any such
consummation as that contemplated, and after a brief reign of two
years his son Rory, "happy in peace and brave in war, already venerable," took his place, to make way in 1492 for his brother Hugh,
who led the sept at Knoctow.

In Carbury, Donnel Sligo, son of Murtogh, son of Donnel, in
1461 fell in battle with the sons of Owen, and thirty years later his
grandson of the same name as his own, valiant and vigorous, when
his fortunes seemed especially prosperous, perished at night amidst
the flames of his castle of Bunfin, slain by John and Brian, the
sons of Rory, who succeeded to die the next year. Upon his decease contest arose amongst the several branches of the race,
which should give a chief to Carbury ; but Felim, son of Maurice,
son of Brian, son of Donnel prevailed. Through the influence of
Tyrconnel, who claimed sovereign rights over Carbury, the castle
of Sligo was assigned to Calvagh Caech son of the murdered
Donnel. In the estimation of the sept this was contrary to established usage, and engendering discontent afforded a favorable
opportunity for his kinsmen to stir up strife. In 1501 the aged
Calvagh was aroused at night by the announcement that his hostile
kinsmen were clambering over his battlement walls by ladders into
the castle, and in making such defence as he could, he fell mortally
wounded, having first killed John, one of the sons of Rory, who slew
his father Donnel.

Of the same name substantially but of another race, from their
remote possessions along the western shore of Connaught less
embroiled in its incessant turmoils, but engaged in many of their
own, Dermot O'Connor succeeding Donnel, son of Rury, son of
Conor, became lord of Corcumroe in 1482. Their neighbors equally
remote, Loghlins of Burren, Flahertys, O'Haras, O'Garas,

O'Dowds and O'Malleys, Birminghams of Athenry, and Jordans Dexeter of Athleathan, took part in the wars of the period, but were less powerful and less frequently mentioned, and little can be gleaned from the annals that relates to them.

The hospitable chief of Hy-Many, William son of Donogh, who in the middle of the previous century entertained all the scholars of the land, was succeeded after a protracted life by his son Melaghlin of like estimable character and who survived his father twenty years. His sons Conor, Teigue, Donogh and Hugh in turn held the chieftainship, and William another when he died in 1420 full of prosperity and prowess was the expectant heir. In 1462 Breasil son of Donogh and Melaghlin son of William contesting the succession, the former summoned his rival to meet him in a week before a higher tribunal, and they both died in season to attend. Hugh son of William, also preëminent for his hospitalities and who never turned his face from any one in need, shared in the defeat three years later given by Clanrickard at Crosmacrin, and in 1469 was treacherously slain by descendants of his uncle Donogh. Upon his death William son of Hugh son of Brian and Tiegue the blind, son of William, strove for the mastery. The latter betook himself to the cloister, and William in 1487 taken prisoner by his kinsmen perished in his chains.

Such numerous competitors for the chieftainship naturally led to continual strife and frequent bloodshed. The coveted sceptre wrenched from chiefs more energetic to get than prudent to hold, exposed the land to devastation and encroachment by neighboring powers. As the century ended, Kildare took Athleague from the sons of William who were banished across the Suck, and gave it to Hugh son of Brian, at the same time that he transferred the castle of Tulsk from Felim to Hugh O'Conor, taking also into his possession the castles of Castlereagh and Roscommon. The Sil Murray incensed at this interference drove Hugh O'Conor across the Shannon.

Mac William came to the defence of the dispossessed chieftains. He restored Athleague to the sons of William O'Kelly and delivered Conor "second lord" of Hy-Many a prisoner to Melaghlin son of Teigue, son of Donogh, son of Melaghlin, son of William the hospitable, who became sole chief. To protect his dominions the new lord constructed in Galway three castles, Gallagh, Tarbelly and Monivea. These Ulick of Clanrickard demolished, and Melaghlin resorted for reparation to Kildare, who as already stated entertained resentments of his own against his son-in-law, and collected the army which fought the battle of Knoctow. Melaghlin left, as many of his progenitors, an excellent reputation for goodness of heart and love of learning. His son and successor Teigue, who survived him two years, died in 1513.

Turlogh of Thomond, "worthy sire of Brian Boru in waging war against the stranger," took, at the close of the century, the place of his brother Gilla on the throne, and there for nearly thirty years when not otherwise occupied, sat administering justice and dispensing hospitality to an attached and loyal people. His defeat at Knoctow, where fell his chief commander Murrogh of Ara, did not dishearten him. We find him engaged immediately after in the construction of his famous bridge over the Shannon at Porterush. This master-piece of engineering consisted of fourteen arches, and was protected at either end by towers or fortifications of hewn stone, for which the term in Gaelic Kincora or bridge-head is familiar as the name of the royal residence of the kings of Thomond. In this work of stupendous magnitude for the times the bishops of Killaloe and Kilfenora helped. They were both O'Briens. The great preferments of the Irish church being sustained by endowments from princely families were often considered as their private inheritance, and incumbents were elected and confirmed with due regard to this consideration. Religious vows interfered but little with the warlike habits of their race, and Terence who held the see of Kila-

loe forty-two years down to 1525, took part, at the head of his
retainers, in many sanguinary conflicts. Maurice of Kilfenora,
whose remains were interred in that Cathedral in 1510, had like
tastes. When the bridge was completed, Turlogh gathered his
clans for a hosting, and marched down upon Limerick, which he
took and burnt, a great number of its inhabitants perishing in its
defence and capture.

Two other independent branches of the O'Briens flourished at
this epoch. In 1502, Donogh son of Brian, son of Conor, "fountain of prosperity and affluence for all Munster," lord of Pobble-o-
brien and Carrigonel and other lands south of the Shannon, was
gathered to his fathers. The old brehon law of gavelkind dis-
tributing anew the territory of the sept among the family fines,
when one of the members passed away, if ever existing to any
great extent, had fallen into neglect. In families near the line of
succession to the chieftainship, and more or less generally among
the clansmen of degree, the custom had yielded to that of primogeniture, modified by the laws of tanistry, as they existed for the
chiefs. It was their first duty to be strong, and for self-preservation
it became indispensable to consolidate in them the family property
that they might better cope with the English lords, whose power
of aggression and disposition to use it grew with their possessions.
Donogh, influenced rather by parental instincts than regard for
worldly policy, divided his own territory in his life time equally
among his eleven sons, retaining for himself for what remained of
his existence, his castle of Carrigonel and its demesne. Before the
century had ended, perhaps in consequence of this distribution,
the castle had passed to an English name, and his descendants
fallen into impoverishment. Mora his daughter married that hard
man John fourth son of the eighth earl of Desmond, and they
were parents of James the fourteenth. The decease of Donnel
Mor Mac-i-brien-arra, "a distinguished Captain, kind to friend

and fierce to foe, after a life of one hundred years spent in noble and illustrious deeds," is mentioned by the annalists as occurring in 1508. This great age, not uncommon in a climate so salubrious for the strong who escaped pestilence and war, was also nearly reached by his grandson Turlogh under Elizabeth.

After the murder of James ninth earl of Desmond at Rathkeale by his servants at the instigation of his younger brother John, Maurice, next in order of the sons of the beheaded Thomas, succeeded as tenth earl. Called from his lameness Baccagh, and carried to the battle-field in a horse litter, he was brave and warlike, flourishing for a third of a century in great prosperity as an Irish chieftain. Often at war with his neighbors, in various engagements, from which he came off victorious, fell O'Carrol of Ely, Teigue McCarthy Mor at the age of eighty-three, and Dermot his son, as also Murrough son of Rory McSweeny. The earl sided with Warbeck and with twenty-four hundred men besieged Waterford, but making submission received from the king a grant of the prisage of wines in several ports of Munster.

Cormac McCarthy, son of Teigue, who was born in 1440 and became after his father's death prince of Desmond, had for wife Elinor Fitzmaurice daughter of Edmund ninth lord of Lixnaw by Mora daughter of O'Conor Kerry. Cormac of Muskerry who built Blarney and Kilcrea and "ordered the Sabbath to be strictly observed throughout his territory," was slain in 1495 at the age of eighty-four by his brother Owen of Rathduane, who followed him in the chieftainship. Three years later assailed by Fitzgerald, afterwards twelfth earl of Desmond and Cormac McCarthy, Owen atoned for his crime, falling in the strife with his two sons, Philip son of Dermot O'Sullivan Beare and other chieftains. This period proved especially fatal to his name. Donogh Oge lord of Duhallow,[1]

---

[1] Son of Donogh (113), son of Cormac (112), son of Donogh (111), son of Dermot (110), first lord of Duhallow and eldest son of Cormac Fion (109), b. 1170, king of Desmond, son of Donal Mor NaCurragh (108), b. 1138, son of Dermod Mor (107), b. 1098, son of Cormac (106), b. 1054, son of Murradach (105), b. 1011, son of Carthaigh (104), son of Justin (103).

Teigue son of Donnel Oge of Desmond, Cormac who had been tanist of Carbery, Fineen Reagh with his wife Catherine, sister of Desmond, "a truly charitable and hospitable woman who erected the castles of Banduff and Dunmanway," and Donnel Mor son of Teigue, "a comely and affable man who had knowledge of the sciences," besides eighteen score slain in family feud for his succession, ended their days in this decade.

Mageoghans of Kinel Fiachra bravely defended their possessions about Moycashel, and the death-bed of their chiefs was for the most part the field of battle. Not invariably, for the son of Hugh Boy in 1478 was murdered in his sleep in his castle of Leathratha by two of his sept who were burnt to death for their crime. James died in 1493, and his brother Laighneach succeeded. But the power which in the previous century warranted Farrel Roe in his boast that he had given peace to the lord lieutenant, gradual but steady encroachment on the part of his neighbors in Westmeath had greatly circumscribed. Cahir O'Conor, son of Con, son of Calvagh, maintained his authority nearly forty years in Offaly. O'Carrols of Ely, O'Moors of Leix, cautiously avoided entanglements that could endanger their stability. The chiefs of Leinster received tribute money and kept the peace. Donnel MacMurrogh Reagh son of Gerald in 1476 made way for Donogh, son of Art, who in 1488 slew his neighbor Murphy, lord of Hy-Felimy. Edmund O'Toole fell in battle with O'Byrnes.

This is a dry detail ; but serves to correct the impression conveyed by prejudiced historians, that the septs were incessantly engaged in mutual slaughter. It serves also to show what led to their contentions and what was the general result of them. Sixty independent powers, with no tribunal to adjust their disputes, always armed and organized in order to repel or discourage aggression, often had occasion to appeal to the arbitrament of arms. Laws lost their restraining influence. Authority uncontrolled vested in chiefs with little other rule for their selection than popular caprice or the selfish interests of their leading subordinates. Is it surprising that the septs for the most part with little else than pastoral pursuits to occupy them should have been occasionally at war? Still war led to no great bloodshed. At times a few hundred warriors crossed their own borders with hostile intent against their neighbors, but after slight skirmish or cattle prey went home content. When all the strife of these different tribes for a series of years is massed in a single page, it suggests the prevalence among them of dispositions savage and sanguinary. But battlés like Knoctow strewing the field with carnage rarely occurred, and are to be attributed to the angry passions of English lords. The Irish were naturally brave and warlike: their fondness for companionship, their spirit of adventure rendered war a pleasurable excitement, yet measured by the standard of the times, combats deserving the name were not more frequent or bloody than in other lands.

During this reign Mulconry ollav of Sil Murray "head of the cheerfulness and joviality of the island," another of the name teacher of poetry, and yet another "bard errant of Munster"; Lorcan ollav to Madden, Clery to O'Donnel, Duigenan of Maguire, Mac Namee of O'Neil, two Higgins chief preceptors of poetry, Rodoghan "whose goodness could not be well surpassed," Keenan a learned historian, are recorded when they died. Charles Maguire "a learned philosopher, deep theologian and well versed in history," as also O'Fihely archbishop of Tuam, wrote annals of Ireland which though seen in London by Ware, are not known to be extant. Con O'Neil founded a convent at Dungannon, O'Conor Roc one at Clonrahan. Invert in Antrim, Rosrelly in Galway, Kildonnel founded by O'Donnel, Killibegs and Fanegara by Mac Sweenys in Donegal, date also from this period. Besides war there were other calamities to inspire devotion, pestilence and famine destroying man and beast.

Henry who died in his fifty-second year, in April, 1509, was an able but not an amiable king.   Empson and Dudley his creatures, in their legal iniquities sparing neither class nor condition, accumulated for the royal coffers nearly two millions sterling; and though the dying monarch in his will ordered restitution, none of course was made.   He was fond of diplomacy and engaged largely in continental intrigues.   A mercenary match for his eldest son with Catherine of Aragon, excellent but unattractive, forced to save her dowry, when Arthur died, upon his surviving brother Henry, led to estrangement, infidelity and divorce.   If emancipating England from papal supremacy, the reformation, which in that country grew out of these complications, subjected her people for several generations to religious despotism, far more cruel and relentless than any which they thought to escape.

XXVIII.

REIGN OF HENRY VIII.—1509—1547.

This young monarch, who at the age of nineteen ascended the throne without competitor to dispute his pretensions, derived from nature a vigorous constitution and noble presence.   His manners were gracious and affable, his mental endowments above mediocrity. His education had not been neglected and he was considered the most learned prince of his day.   His career opened with the laudable ambition of proving an estimable king, and he selected able and honest counsellors.   His sway was nearly absolute, for what liberties his people had enjoyed under his predecessors had been crushed out by arbitrary measures and all classes intimidated into abject submission.   The great nobles, long a counterpoise to the regal power, had melted away in the civil wars, and their substance confiscated heaped to overflowing the royal treasury soon to be drained by reckless extravagance.   What demoralized the king's nature as it blighted his happiness, was his ill assorted marriage, for Catherine with many admirable traits had lost the attraction of youth and failed to gain his affections. Restless and discontented without curb to lawless passions, he plunged into excess. His lusty temperament found occupation for a time in "field of gold" or costly tournament. His love of pleasure, of pomp and pageant soon took entire possession of his soul, and what little self-control he ever had yielding to entice-ment, he rapidly degenerated into the heartless voluptuary and mer-ciless tyrant.

It was long before he paid other heed to Ireland than to confirm Kildare as lord justice. Age had not cooled the ardor of the earl, who notwithstanding his three-score years and ten was incessantly on the move. Attended by the chiefs of Leinster, English as well as Irish, he led an army into Munster, and without effectual opposition erected the stronghold of Carrigkettle in Small County near Limerick. O'Donnel came down through Meath to join him, and they together took Kanturk in Duhallow, Pallis and Castlemagne from MacCarthy More. His son-in-law Donal-Reagh McCarthy of Carbery, Cormac Oge of Muskerry, James, son of Maurice earl of Desmond, and all the English in Munster rallied to his banners, and they proceeded to Limerick.

Turlogh Don of Thomond with MacNamara and Clanrickard and another James of Desmond son of John the fourteenth earl mustered in force to oppose them. The hostile hosts encamped, near enough to hear each other's voices, at Porterush where O'Brien had erected his bridge, which Kildare after crossing over, destroyed. In the morning the earl marshalled his forces, the men of Munster in the van, with the Leinster contingents and O'Donnel in the rear, intend-ing to "take a short cut to Limerick," but before they reached the river at Monbraher, O'Brien attacked them. The battle lasted till night and was bravely contested. The earl encumbered with spoil sustained heavy loss, barons Kent and Barnwall and other personages of condition being among the slain. The defeat would have been even more complete and disastrous, had not O'Donnel, who gained great glory that day, extricated the army from its perilous position. It effected its retreat with difficulty, leaving the prey gathered in Munster to their enemies.

O'Donnel, soon after on a pilgrimage to Rome stopped on his way sixteen weeks in London, and as long upon his return, received on both occasions with marked attention by the king. His son Manus, left in charge of Tyrconnel, imprudently exchanging Art O'Neil son of Con his hostage for Art's son Nial Oge, Con the next year invaded Tyrconnel but was driven out. O'Donnor went into Connaught and forced the Burkes to peace, and then into Tyrone, taking Omagh in pledge of submission. After an unsuccessful attack upon Sligo he passed three months in Scotland courteously entertained by James IV., whom it is said he dissuaded from a project of invading Ireland.

Kildare meanwhile as ever indefatigable took Belfast, devastated the Glyns and on a second expedition harried as far as Carrickfergus. Learning that the O'Briens threatened disturbances in Munster, he marched to Killarney, reduced Pallis and thence proceeded into Ely to Leap. This fortress proved too strong for him and he raised the siege to procure heavier ordinance. On his way back, wounded by an O'Moore of Leix near Athy, he went home to Kildare to die in September, 1512. His remains were interred in St. Mary's chapel which he had just constructed for the purpose at Dublin. We have taken occasion earlier to portray the character of this strong earl, who for the third of a century ruled over Ireland, partly by force, and in a larger measure by his sagacity, with great prudence and success.

Whilst almost exclusively English through his own progenitors he pursued the policy of his house in strengthening their position by alliances with Milesian stock. His sister Eleanor had married Con Mor O'Neil. Of his own fourteen children, seven by his first wife

Alison Eustace and seven by his second Elizabeth St. John, Eleanor married Donal Mac Carthy Reagh and afterwards Tyrconnel, Margaret Piers the eighth Ormond whose blood was largely compounded of Mac Murroghs, O'Carrols and O'Reillys. Alice married her cousin Con Baccagh first earl of Tyrone, Eustachia Ulick first earl of Clanrickard, and Oliver, his fourth son by his second wife, Meva daughter of Cahir O'Conor of Offaly. Granddaughters of his own name, children of his son Gerald, had partners for life selected for them later in Ferganaim O'Carrol of Ely, son of Mulrony, and Brian O'Conor of Offaly.

Both of these names are familiar to our readers, but the latter has been most frequently mentioned. The O'Carrols of Ely, descended from Kian, younger son of Oliol Olum, and head of the Kianacht, as his posterity were called, possessed early vast tracts of territory in the northerly portion of Munster. Over the Ormonds, Hy-Regan, Fireal, Ikerren, and portions of Leix their sway extended from the Nore to the Barrow, from Kilkenny to Slieve Galy, in the southeast of the present county of Queens. They gave many archbishops to Cashel. David invested in 1289 was followed by Maurice in 1303, who six years later took an active part in that first parliament of Kilkenny which passed laws to prevent consolidation of the two races. He denounced from his altar who ever should infringe its prohibitions by intermarriage or gossipred, use the language, dress, or laws of the Irish, allow them to pasture cattle upon their lands, or advance them to any preferment in the church. John occupied the see in 1327, and in 1365 Thomas was translated to it from Tuam.

Refinement, culture and character distinguished both men and women of the race. Margaret O'Carrol wife of O'Conor of Offaly will be remembered for her munificent entertainment of the learned, and also Finola, her lovely and accomplished daughter, widow of O'Donnel and of O'Neil of Clanaboy. Her cousin, Mulrony, lord of

31

Ely, with his spouse Bibania O'Dempsy of Clanmalir, founded Roscrea, and with his son John fought at Knoctow. His grandson of the same name died in 1532, according to the annalists "the most distinguished of his family for renown, valor, prosperity and excellence, to whom poets, travellers, ecclesiastics and literary men were most thankful, who gave most entertainment and bestowed more presents than any other who lived of his lineage ; the supporting mainstay of all persons, the rightful victorious rudder of his race, the powerful young warrior in the march of tribes, the active triumphant champion of Munster, a precious stone and carbuncle, the anvil and golden pillar of the Elyans." This very remarkable personage was the father of Ferganim, who before 1530 married Elizabeth Fitzgerald.

Ferganim, although not entitled by the accepted rules of the brehons, succeeded his father, but the following year old and blind was slain by his cousins, leaving two sons, Teague, created in 1551 baron of Ely, and William Ower who recovered the castle of Leap and gained a victory over Mac-I-brian Ara, but who sustained a defeat from the English at Kincora in 1558 and again two years later. His rule occasionally contested proved generally prosperous. In 1581 he was taken prisoner by the English and confined in Dublin Castle, but soon released, fell in fight with the O'Conors of Offaly his implacable enemies. Calvagh, son of William, was knighted in 1585 and attended Perrot's parliament, which confiscated the Desmond dominions, but met the natural death of his line at the hands of the O'Meaghers of Ikerrin in 1600. A younger branch of the name ruled over Ossory. The Flanagans of Oughter Tir in Tipperary and Cinel Aiga in Ely were correlatives and subordinate chiefs. The distinguished position held in American history by the O'Carrols of Maryland will explain this particular relation of their origin and of their fortunes, which there will be further occasion to notice in the subsequent centuries.

Other descendants of Kildare in his life time or later intermarried with the three branches of the Mac Carthies, both O'Sullivans Mor and Beare, O'Meagher, O'Callaghan, O'Donovan and various families of the Munster Geraldines.   Had this powerful house indulged ambitious aspirations for the Irish throne, when nearly all the chiefs had thus become their kinsfolk, it would not have been difficult to accomplish.   Gerald the ninth earl, who succeeded his father Gerald the eighth also as lord deputy, the handsomest man of his time, was active, brave and sensible, but not the equal of his father in political wisdom.   His enemies were many and influential. His sister's husband, the eighth Ormond, who succeeded in that earldom a distant relative in 1515, proved his most unscrupulous rival striving to supplant him, and in this was aided by his countess, the clever Margaret, naturally more loyal to her husband than to her brother.

This ninth Kildare, if not as politic as his father, had like taste for war.   He drove O'Moore to his forests, stormed Cavan, slew the chief Hugh O'Reilly with eighteen of his followers, and Shane O'Toole of Imaly.   Joined by his brother-in-law Ormond and James son of Desmond, he invaded Ely, demolished Leap and reduced Clonmel.   The next year, 1517, he sacked Dundrum in Lecale capturing Phelim Macgennis, and burnt Dungannon, wasting the country with fire and sword.   Rewarded by the king for his services by grant of the customs of Strangford and Ardglas, he obtained license in 1519 to found the College of Maynooth.   Proceeding later into Delvin at the request of the Melaghlins he protected them from the O'Carrols, who had plundered Kincora.

These expeditions, often without provocation as without notice and with superior force, were often attended with success exaggerated by English writers, occasionally with disasters to their armies about which nothing is said.   Crops were destroyed, castles and towns put to the flames, young and old indiscriminately slaughtered, engendering animosities, only waiting opportunity for retaliation. It was a worthless policy so far as regarded national consolidation, and it was supremely unjust and wicked.

Family quarrels stained with bloodshed recur with equal frequency and from like motives in both races. The royal example of the Plantagenets was bettered by Barrys, Butlers, and Fitzgeralds, who slew brothers and cousins as often as O'Connors or O'Neils. Ambition, revenge, jealousy, unrestrained by law and unchastened by religious obligation, grew to vigorous type. Standards of honor and integrity, of fidelity to engagements or respect for right, were not much higher among the chiefs than among the lords. Lust for land or consequence was a controlling force sufficiently obvious, but others more easily concealed excited suspicion and distrust. Kildare occasionally made military inroads as deputy on his friends and kinsfolk, gaining easy victories which strengthened his hold on royal confidence. War itself thus often proved a cheat. Sire to the bough, son to the plough, kept broad acres in the same name and blood for generations across the channel; if not working always exactly in the same way in Ireland, the rule was there understood and often exemplified by the same results. Members of princely families, sons or brothers, were frequently found on opposite sides, and whichever prevailed, the family domains or dominions were not forfeited, but simply shifted for a while, eventually following the accustomed course of succession.

Hugh Oge of Tirconnel, restless and indefatigable, his warlike clans as impatient of repose, kept on the alert, now engaged in reducing Coleraine or Dunluce, at Enniskillen subjecting to his allegiance the refractory Maguires, or levying tribute in Connaught. His principal antagonist still continued to be the lord of Tyrone, and in 1514 after their two armies both alike strengthened by mercenaries had long lain opposed, by divine grace and the advice of their chiefs on the bridge of Ardstraw they became friends and gossips. Art confirmed the charters, and his son Neal Oge detained as hostage being released, this alliance was still farther cemented by Manus son of Hugh espousing Judith sister of Art, youngest child of Con Mor, then at the age of twenty in her bloom. The effect of this reconciliation was not very lasting, for two years later hostilities were recommenced and Manus invaded Tyrone.

Hugh still chafed under the loss of his castle of Sligo, which had baffled all his attempts, when aid from an unexpected quarter restored it to his possession. Pilgrimages at that period afforded occupation for the idle and devout, and a French knight on such quest to the purgatory of St. Patrick in Donegal, received hospitable entertainment from its chief. He proposed an attack upon the castle from the sea, and measures being concerted between them, upon his return home he sent a vessel of war armed with great guns to batter down its walls, whilst O'Donnel assailed it by land. After its surrender the country round about was overrun and several strongholds reduced. At this time war broke out in Munster. Maurice the warlike, tenth Desmond, approached the close of his life and reign. John his brother and fourth son of Thomas of Drogheda, at whose instigation their elder brother had been slain at Rathkeale, although another brother Thomas had superior claims from seniority, endeavored by intrigue to supplant James son of Maurice the next in regular succession. His wife being an O'Brien that family supported his pretensions. It led to sanguinary engagements, in which each in turn came off victorious, John aided by the Butlers taking Limerick. He did not effect his object, and died a monk in penance twenty years later just before the earldom devolved upon his son.

Elated with his success in the field and relying upon his popularity with his Irish kinsfolk, Kildare indulged an overweening confidence in the strength of his position, considering himself too indispensable to English rule to be disturbed. His independent spirit gave offence where prudence dictated conciliation, and his enemies found credence at court for representations that his course was exclusively governed by selfish motives for his own aggrandizement. It was urged against him that content with maintaining the pale within its existing limits, he made no effort to extend it, and intimated that if he were removed from office he would throw off his allegiance. His own professions of fidelity served for the moment to render abortive these attempts to undermine him. But his frank and unguarded expressions and proceedings equivocal in policy or open to misinterpretation kept alive the jealousy of the government, and in process of time supplied his rivals with opportunities they were constantly seeking to weaken his hold upon the king.

Wolsey was in the ascendant. He loved power too dearly himself to be indulgent to the deputy, who in 1519 was summoned over to explain his audacities. Kildare obeyed, leaving his kinsman Sir Thomas deputy in his place, writing O'Carrol "to keep quiet until an English deputy should be sent over, and then to make war upon all who were not his friends." Effort was made to obtain more positive proof of this letter, but without success. The earl attended the meeting of the monarchs on the "field of the cloth of gold" with fitting splendor for the occasion, and becoming the accepted suitor of Elizabeth Grey, daughter of Dorset and cousin of the king, married her. By the aid of her influential relations, he for a while was enabled to set at defiance the machinations of his enemies.

The earl of Surry, son of the hero of Flodden, able alike in field and cabinet, was appointed lord-lieutenant, and during his administration, among other enactments, exportation of wool or flocks was prohibited. He had brought over eleven hundred men whom he employed against the irrepressible O'Tooles who from the Wicklow mountains harried the pale. Either from discontent at the removal of Kildare, or his apparent intent to molest them, the septs laid aside their private quarrels to oppose the lord-lieutenant. He found the task he had undertaken neither easy nor pleasant. Without any special cause or provocation he demolished the castles of O'Moore and laid waste his dominions. O'Carrol did not obey the injunctions of his father-in-law, for he kept the peace and was not molested, and Surry marched into Tyrone. Art, "intelligent, powerful, noble, scientific, brave and majestic," son of Hugh the tanist, and "seldom before had the son of a tanist ruled over the Kinel Owen," had given place in 1514 to Art son of Con, "a distinguished captain, sensible and humane," followed five years later by his brother Con Baccagh, first earl of Tyrone. It was probably whilst Con was in preparation to signalize his accession according to usage by an inroad into Meath, that he found the enemy within his gates. Surry did not like his work. The Irish left open his path to harass his flanks. He wrote home that it was only by conquest the land could be reduced to subjection and order, and that, if possible, which he seemed to doubt, it would require money and time. He advised conciliation and was authorized to confer knighthood on the chiefs, and the king sent a collar of gold to O'Neil.

The state of the country was not encouraging to English aspirations. A tract of the period entitled "Salus Populi" by Pandarus shows what it in reality was. Seven hundred and forty pounds were paid as annual tribute to Irish chiefs. The king's writ was respected over little more than half of Louth, Meath, Dublin, Kildare and Wexford, and this chiefly occupied by Irish but partially under English rule. The rest of the island belonged to degenerate English or Irish septs, the larger portion consisting of sixty "regions some as big as a shire, some more, some less, under independent kings, princes, dukes or captains, that lived by the sword and obeyed no temporal power but only him that was strong." In Ulster, O'Neils of Tyrone and Clanaboy, O'Donnel of Tyrconel, O'Cahan of Coleraine, Doherty of Inishowen, Maguire of Fermanagh, Ma-

gennis of Upper Iveagh in Down, Hanlon of Armagh and Mac-
Mahon of Monaghan. In Leinster, MacMurrogh of Hydrone and
Nolan of Carlow, Murphy in Wexford, Byrne and Toole of Wick-
low, Gilpatrick in Upper Ossory, Moores of Leix, Dempsys of
Clanmelir, Conor of Offaly, Dunn of Oregan. In Munster, Mac
Carthies Mor, Reagh and Muskerry, Donoghue of Killarney, Sulli-
van Beare, Conor-Kerry, Driscol of Corca-Laighe, two Mahonys in
Cork, Briens of Thomond, Kennedy of Lower Ormond, Carrol of
Ely, Meagher of Ikerren, MacMahons of Corca-vaskin, O'Connor
of Corcumroe, O'Loghlens of Burren, O'Grady of Bunratty in Clare;
Mac-I-brien-Ara, Regan of Owney, Dwyer of Tipperary, and
O'Brien of Coonagh, in Limerick. In Connaught, O'Conor Roe
and MacDermot in Roscommon, Kelly, Madden, Flaherty in Gal-
way; Farrel, of Analy, Reilly and Rourke of Breffny; Malley of
Mayo, MacDonoghs of Tyreril and Corrain; O'Gara of Coolavin,
O'Hara of Leney, O'Dowd of Tireragh, O'Conors of Carbury in
Sligo. In Meath, Melaghlin, Mageoghan and O'Molloy.

The degenerate English or great captains that followed Irish rule
were in Munster: the earl of Desmond, his brothers Thomas and
John and kinsman Gerald of Decies, the knights of Kerry and
Glynn, white knight and other Geraldines; lords Barry, Roche,
Courey, Cogan, Barret, Power of Waterford, Burke of Limerick;
Pierce claiming to be earl of Ormond, and all the Butlers of Kil-
kenny and Fethard. In Connaught, lords Burke of Mayo and
Clanrickard, Bermingham of Athenry, Staunton of Clanmorris and
MacJordans, descendants of Jordan Dexeter in Mayo; Barrets of
Tyrawley. In Ulster, Savages of Lecale in Down, Fitz Howlins of
Tuscard, Bissets of Antrim. In Meath, Dillons, Daltons, Tyrrels
and Delamares.

All the English folk except in the cities and walled towns were of
Irish habit and condition. There were other lords not enumerated
and many smaller septs making war or peace at their own pleasure,

and often in rebellion against their own chieftains. The largest sept mustered but five hundred spears, as many galloglasses and a thousand kernes, the average army being hardly a thousand fighting men, the common sort not being counted. Pandarus attributes the prevailing disorder to the lords of either race, and advises that the yeomanry should be better armed and drilled, and forts erected for their protection. He says that "so the land would be a paradise, delicious of all pleasaunce; that no alien or stranger great or small left it willingly notwithstanding its disorder if he had the means to dwell there honestly, and that much greater would be this desire if the land were once put in order." In the summer of 1521 Surry invaded Offaly and took after some days delay Monasteroris, the castle of the chief, who to carry the war away from his own dominions wasted West Meath. The campaign was not a success for the viceroy, and his lieutenant Plunket was slain.

The year before Surry came over Maurice of Desmond died, leaving the earldom to his son James, who to display his power and prowess, or possibly from another motive which prompted such expeditions, to assert his claim to supremacy in Desmond, invaded Muskerry and Carberry. Cormac Oge and Donnel Reagh rallied their forces, and with Thomas of Desmond, uncle of James and his successor as twelfth earl, to help them, at Mourne Abbey in Muskerry defeated him. His loss amounted to eighteen banners of galloglasses and twenty-four of horsemen, together nearly two thousand men. The lord-lieutenant, whose avowed policy was to appease animosities between English lords and stir up strife amongst the Irish, fostered hostilities in Ulster, whilst he adjusted disputes between Ormond and Desmond. He visited Munster to reconcile the Geraldines, but was forced to admit in giving the king an account of his proceedings that he found Cormac Oge and Donnel Reagh "wise men, more conformable to order than their English neighbors." At the close of 1521 Surry, without means and strick-

32

en with disease, prayed to be recalled, and carrying home what
remained of his eleven hundred men and consigning the government
to his friend Ormond, left for duties more to his mind.

The new deputy invaded Ely adjoining his own territory.   Torlogh
O'Brien, king of Thomond, hastened to the aid of O'Carrol, between whom and himself still remained some of the ancient obligations of dependence and protection.   A drawn battle took place
at Camus, on the Suir near Cashel, in which Torlogh's son was
slain.   Kildare, absent at the north engaged in destroying Belfast and laying waste twenty-four miles of country, came back
to find his own tenants despoiled by Ormond who had made peace
with O'Carrol the better to effect his object.   Fitzpatrick of
Ossory had also been harassed by Ormond and sent over one of
his followers to Henry for redress.   The messenger stopped the
king on his way to his devotions, and addressing him in Latin
gave him to understand from his master that if the king did not
punish Peter the red for these aggressions the chief would
make war upon himself.   The haughty monarch, more amused than
provoked, took in good part the defiance of the chieftain, but was
neither sufficiently wise nor strong to interfere with effect.

Ormond used his official powers quite as exclusively for his own
private objects as Kildare, and when the latter returning with his
other brother-in-law O'Neil invaded Offaly and Leix, their old jealousies resumed their wonted rancor.   Robert Talbot on his way to
the Christmas festivities at Kilkenny was waylaid and slain by James
brother of Kildare.   Complaints home bringing over commissioners
to investigate, selected by Dorset, they reinstated his son-in-law, and
at the ceremonial ending in a sumptuous entertainment given them at
St. Thomas' Abbey, Con O'Neil bore before the governor the sword
of state.

Again in power, Kildare exerted it with vigor in repressing his
restless neighbors, and occasionally exercised his authority in a very

summary manner. Maurice Doran, bishop of Laughlin, of exemplary life and conversation and an eloquent preacher, had
excited the ill-will of certain ecclesiastics in his diocese, and among
them of Maurice Cavanagh, one of his archdeacons. They murdered
him in Glen Reynold in 1525, much to the horror of the land. The
perpetrators of this sacrilegious act being apprehended, by order of
Kildare were carried to the spot where the crime was committed
and then flayed alive, their bowels being first taken out and burnt
before them. So say the annalists, but probably the culprits ceased
to be conscious long before this just but barbarous penalty was
consummated.

Desmond as lawless and ambitious believing the conjuncture propitious for throwing off a yoke which fretted his haughty temper, held
secret correspondence with Francis the French king, proposing to
furnish ten thousand men in case of invasion. This becoming known
after Pavia to Wolsey, the king ordered his arrest, which the deputy
from inability, neglect or collusion failing to effect, he was summoned
over to answer for his disobedience as also for combining with Irish
chiefs to waste the lands of the Butlers and hanging their adherents.
Rudely questioned by the cardinal before the council, he was incarcerated in the tower, and barely escaped execution, on which Wolsey
seemed set, by interposition of Dorset and Surry, now duke of Norfolk,
upon whose pledge for his fidelity he was set free in 1527. His
brother James left as deputy had been replaced by Nugent lord of
Delvin, who refusing O'Connor his annual tribute was captured by
that chief and held for ransom. James Butler afterwards ninth earl
of Ormond visited Delvin in prison, but the conference was in Gaelic
and in the presence of the chief. O'Connor over-estimated his advantage in having the representative of royalty in his clutch. To
Delahide who brought him a letter from the king, he inquired from
what king, and when answered from the king of England, replied
if he lived a year he trusted there should be no more name of king

of England in Ireland than of king of Spain. Unable otherwise to rescue Delvin the council eventually yielded to the demands of O'Conor, paying him the arrears of his tribute. These payments were not much longer continued, and a few years later it was ordained by law that no more should be made.

The north was in more than its usual ferment. Con Baccagh, the new lord of Tyrone, in the full vigor of maturity when he attained the chieftainship, displayed an energy of will and spirit of enterprise giving indication of a busy career. But his neighbor Hugh Duv of Tyrconnel, as active and more domineering, in military capacity and political wisdom stands out boldly as the prominent character of the period. His natural endowments had been improved by study and travel into many lands; and residence at Rome, London and Edinburgh, opened to him fields of experience, quickening aspirations which alone can explain much that otherwise would appear inconsistent in his course. His incessant hostings against his neighbors of Tyrone and Connaught may have been partly to gratify his sense of power, train his soldiers or find them occupation, perhaps to collect his tribute money, but the traditional path to the throne of Ireland was by success in the battle-field, by compelling its other princes to give hostages and recognize supremacy, and realizing Irish independence could only be maintained by a strong central government, which he was best able to establish, this would seem to have been his governing policy.

This policy depending for success upon intimidation and frequently discouraged, he pursued as occasion allowed. If more had been transmitted of the obstacles which he had to encounter, his course might be better understood. His sagacity hardly admitted of mistake, his persevering temper knew no fickleness of purpose. If often seeking his objects by tortuous paths the times and not want of integrity taught him to dissemble. In 1521 he visited the lord lieutenant at Dublin, making merit of his refusal to take part with Con

O'Neil, whose sister was wife of his eldest son Manus, in invading the pale. Surry seemingly placed more reliance upon his professions than they deserved, for soon after the two chiefs being reconciled were ordered to coöperate with the English forces in subjugating their refractory neighbors. Disputes, real or pretended, immediately led to demonstrations of hostility between them, which the disgusted viceroy was forced to accept for explanation, why his intended foray could not come off. But whilst not disposed to abet English governors in molesting his brother chieftains, Hugh lost no opportunity himself of impressing them with a sense of his power.

The chiefs he assailed, not appreciating designs which if patriotic menaced their autocracy, instead of tamely submitting to his exactions, laid aside their feuds and jealousies and leagued together to oppose him. In 1522 nearly all the chiefs of the north and west formed such a combination with Con O'Neil at its head. The time designated for their rendezvous was Lady-day, and the place Tirhugh. Maguire, Magennis, MacMahon, O'Reilly, the Scots under Alexander MacDonnel, son of John Cahanagh, the Clan Donnel and MacSheehy of Meath and Leinster, the adherents of Kildare from whose house came Con's mother and wife, joined the clansmen of Tyrone; whilst in Connaught gathered another army led by Clanrickard, the sons of Thomond, the bishop of Killaloe, O'Carrol and O'Kennedy, O'Conors Don and Roe and MacDermot, a host which had it been united and well led would have proved too formidable even for Tyrconnel to withstand.

O'Donnel not dismayed summoned his chiefs, O'Boyle, O'Doherty, three MacSweenys, Fanad, Banagh and Tuad, and the O'Gallaghers; and took post in a mountain defile at Portnatryod by which Con was expected to pass. But marching by Lough Erne and Termon Davog to Ballyshannon, he reduced that castle, Bundrowes and Belleck. O'Donnel directing his son Manus to invade Tyrone, pursued O'Neil to defend Tirhugh. Con, learning what havock Manus was com-

mitting within his own borders, hurried home and encamped at Knocavoe.   Hugh and Manus, joining forces at Drumleen near Lifford,
concluded upon immediate attack before the Connaught army could
come to Con's assistance.   Leaving their horses they approached at
night silently, till they reached the sentinels, who retreating, the
Kinel Konel broke their ranks to gain the entrenchments before alarm
could be given, and entered them simultaneously with the fugitives.
With great clamor the opposing warriors engaged in the strife, unable in the darkness to discern each other's faces.   They fought long
and bravely on both sides, but the assailants finally gaining the victory, Con and his allies leaving dead behind them nine hundred
of their followers, many of them Scots, made good their retreat.
It was one of the bloodiest battles ever fought between the Kinel
Konel and Kinel Owen.   Horses, arms and armor, provisions and
wine, cups of silver and pitchers of brass with much else of value,
fell as spoils to the victors.   O'Donnel not permitting his men to
carry home their plunder as they wished, proceeded forthwith in pursuit of the army of Connaught then engaged in the siege of Sligo.
When they heard he was at hand and of his victory at Knocavoe,
they sued for peace, the terms to be left to Manus and O'Carrol; but
without waiting the return of their messengers, the chiefs, both Mac-
Williams, O'Conors, O'Briens, Mac Dermot, O'Carrol and O'Kene-
dy raised the siege, crossed the Curlew mountains and went home,
this bloodless triumph adding fresh laurels to the glory of the conqueror.

The next spring Hugh Duv remained encamped at Glenfin, and
when his son Manus returned from a visit to Scotland they together
ravaged Tyrone.   They destroyed an herb garden of note and much
kine, and on a second maraud that year, O'Neil making peace, they
wasted Breffny O'Rourke.   The sons of O'Donnel partook of his
impulsive disposition.   Contention between Nial Garv and Owen
for a castle led to a combat in which both were slain.   In 1524 Con

with his brother-in-law the deputy marched into Tyrconnel. Hugh
with a large force of his clansmen and kinsmen, the MacDonnels,
hastened to meet them and preparation was made for an engagement
on the morrow. Manus wished to repeat the night attack of Knocavoe ; but his father objecting as Kildare was strongly posted and had
ordnance, the son harassed the enemy with showers of arrows so that
they could neither slumber nor rest. The earl finally proposed a conference and peace was made, Kildare and O'Donnel entering into
gossipred. Returning, Con and his allies found Hugh son of Nial,
son of Con, son of Hugh Boy, lord of Clanaboy and brother-in-law
of O'Donnel, devastating Tyrone. Him they slew, his wife Gormley dying the same year.

A few months afterwards the two chiefs went to Dublin to confirm their covenants of amity. Probably neither of them were very
reasonable, and parting more embittered than before, O'Donnel
invaded Tyrone. That autumn more amiable they agreed to abide by
the arbitration of Manus and Kildare. In 1526 they visited the deputy to adjust their differences, but, no concession possible, after angry
altercation Tyrone was again invaded. That it was O'Donnel who
was at fault and unreasonably exacting may be inferred from the confederacy formed at this time against him in Connaught by the O'Conors
and MacDermot, which resulted in a foray into Moylurg and their
army being put to rout. O'Donnel could be just for others if not
where his own interests were concerned, and he made a lasting peace
between the Burkes and Barrets. He strengthened his frontier,
Manus erecting the strong castle of Lifford. Each of the three
subsequent years Hugh Duff made his annual hosting into Connaught, destroying many castles in Galway and Muinter Eolais of
the MacRannalls, and where his tribute was refused taking prey.

As he began to show symptoms of a strong man failing, Hugh Boy
contested the succession to the chieftainship with Manus by gaining
adherents in the sept. Their father called in Maguire to reconcile

them, but it only led to further strife and bloodshed. The next year O'Donnel and Maguire went to Skeffington, then deputy, and coming to terms of agreement the three invaded Tyrone. In 1537, on a hosting by Hugh into Connaught, his chief O'Boyle being mistaken at night for an enemy by another detachment of his army, was slain, after heavy loss on both sides. Grieved at this untoward event, for O'Boyle was greatly beloved, Hugh Duv marched on to Finved.

In an encounter at Doonierin between a portion of his cavalry and the O'Harts, feudatories of O'Conor Sligo, and also mounted, one of the principal warriors of the latter force fell. O'Connor had marshalled the men of Carbury to dispute his passage over the river at Fearsat, but not sufficiently strong, Hugh crossed unopposed and proceeding along the strand into Tireragh destroyed corn and villages, capturing the wife of O'Dowde daughter of Burke with all her property. He swept the country so completely of its kine that two beeves sold in his camp for a groat. Mac Dermot gathered his sept and neighbors to stay the progress of the Ulster army, and a skirmish took place in which Hugh son of the Moylurg chieftain was wounded. The hosting ended without rent or submission from lower Connaught, an unusual occurrence for O'Donnel, who sad at heart went home to die, his last moments embittered by the contention of his sons for his chieftainship.

History repeats itself, and in this remote corner of the island much variety was not to be expected. Not that the progress of events was dull or without interest; they were peculiarly stirring, heroic and picturesque. Yet in the experiences and characteristics of its chiefs as summed up in their obituaries by partial annalists, the uniformity often becomes monotonous. When Hugh Oge in 1537 realized from his dimmed sight and feebler footsteps that he was approaching the gates of judgment, he shuffled off his harness and assumed the cowl, bemoaned his crimes and iniquities, did

penance for his transgressions, and passing through, left his earthly
tabernacle to be interred with such honors as were meet. His four
score years had proved all too brief for the accomplishment of his
self appointed mission, the regeneration of his country under the
dynasty of its ancient monarchs in his own person, but all the chiefs
of Connaught of both races, and even the O'Kanes, MacQuillans
and far-away O'Neils of Clanaboy had paid him tribute, and four
lords of Tyrone by charter acknowledged his supremacy over Inishowen, Kinel Moen and Fermanagh, "so that he had quiet and
peaceable lordship over them, and commanded their risings out.
This was not to be wondered at, for never was victory seen with his
enemies, never did he retreat one foot from an army, great or
small. He was the represser of evil deeds and evil customs, the
destroyer and banisher of rebels and thieves, an enforcer of the
laws and ordinances after the justest manner. In his reign both sea
and land were productive. He established every one in his proper
hereditary possessions that no one might bear enmity towards
another. He did not suffer the power of the English to come into
his country, and formed a league of peace and friendship with the
king of England, when he found that the Irish would not yield
superiority to any one among themselves, but that friends and blood
relations contended against each other. He moreover protected
their termon lands for the friars, churches, poets and ollavs."

The power of these chiefs of Tirconnel is easily explained. Their
strength consisted of clans enured to war, hardened by exposure on
sea and shore in a rigorous clime. The three branches of Mac
Sweeny were conspicuous for valor and military talent, and scions
of their heroic stock will be found later, constables in all the armies
of the west. In 1513 an O'Malley from the western shore of Connaught, entering the harbor of Killybegs with three ships with hostile intent, the youthful Brian Mac Sweeny rallying from round about
shepherds and farmers, captured two of the vessels and slaughtered

33

sixty of their company. Three years later warder of Ballyshannon,
he fell in its defence against O'Neil. Castles constructed in part of
timber decayed; and Rathmullan on Lough Swilley shaken by war
and age mysteriously dropped into a heap. It was replaced by another, which with the abbey attached for the safety and instruction of
the youthful members of the race, still forms part of an habitable
dwelling. Rory Fanad, "rock of support in defence of his lord and
country and bestower of jewels and wealth," was succeeded in 1518
by Donnel Oge, whose reign continued eleven years. In 1544,
Turlogh son of Rory, "energetic, fierce and vivacious," was killed in
prison by Rory Carragh and Daniel Gorm, sons of Donnel Oge when
Rory succeeded. Nial Mor son of Owen, lord of Banagh, "of
hardiest hand and heroism, of boldest heart and counsel, best at withholding and attacking, first alike in feast and fray, who had the most
numerous and vigorous soldiers and who had forced the greater number of perilous passes," died at his castle of Rahin in 1524, and in
1535 his son Maelmory Mor was killed at its gate by his brother
Nial. This fratricidal act was avenged twelve years afterwards by
his son Donnel Oge who slew Nial in his prison in the new Badh
bawn. The sons of Maelmory son of Colla had been driven from
their habitations for some such deed of violence, and in 1542 en-
listed by O'Kanes to fight their battles they so effectually routed the
MacQuillans, that in a subsequent campaign the chiefs of that sept
engaged them in their service. This gave umbrage to their clansmen, who taking the clan Sweeny at disadvantage made sad havoc of
its warriors.

Gerald O'Doherty, chief of Inishowen, died in 1540 at a great
age; and the next year Tuathal O'Gallagher another of the most
powerful of the sub chiefs of Tirconnel. Conscientious as brave, he
never killed in battle, but devoted his efforts to capturing prisoners.
When a youth and listening to a sermon, the friar inculcated the doctrine that to obtain eternal life one must not shed blood, whereupon he

resolved never to wound his enemies, and thus kept his vow. Brian O'Rourke built the castle of Leitrim, and harried Moylurg where the sons of Rory were contending with sons of Owen for the rock of Lough Key. Cuconnaught of Fermanagh, "renowned for skill of hand and nobleness," Nial O'Boyle and Felim O'Coghlan of Delvin fell in family feud. These flagrancies speak sadly for human nature when not subjected to government, and where family property, instead of being equally divided under just laws impartially administered, passed by English rules to the eldest son, or by Irish to the nearest of kin strong enough to take and hold.

According to the annals of Donegal, besides his liegemen in Ulster, Hugh Duv claimed supremacy also over large portions of Connaught. But this was never peaceably conceded by the chiefs, who if frequently subdued by superior force, and compelled to pay tribute or give hostages, never long submitted. Their whole "rising out" consisted in 1515 of about six hundred horse, eight hundred galloglasses and thirty-three hundred kerns. Of these O'Conor supplied one hundred and twenty horse and about five hundred foot; Carbury, forty horse and two hundred foot; O'Rourke, forty horse and four hundred foot; M'Rannals, eight horse and three hundred kerns; O'Reillys, sixty horse and five hundred foot; Mac Dermot, forty horse, eighty galloglasses and two hundred kerns: but these numbers represent but a small part of what gathered to their armies upon great emergencies.

XXIX.

REIGN OF HENRY VIII.—1509-1547.—(Continued).

Piers the red, earl of Ormond, in 1527 resigned that title in favor of Sir Thomas Boleyn, grandson of his predecessor, taking instead that of Ossory, by which for the next ten years he is known in history. After that period, upon the decease of Boleyn without male heirs, the ancient title of his family was restored to him. As he was engaged in hostilities with Desmond and O'Brien, and no immediate prospect appeared of Delvin's release, eventually effected by concession to O'Conor of all his demands, the council appointed Thomas half brother of Kildare as his vice deputy. Norfolk, whose advice upon administration in Ireland was valued from his two years experience as viceroy, under his better known title of Surry, wrote Wolsey, "that in his opinion the only cause of the ruin of that poor land was the malice between Kildare and Ossory," and later that the latter if governor would be diverted from defence of his own possessions, and his army brought into the pale would prove a burden upon it. He advised that the appointment by the council should be confirmed, and that three or four hundred men under able captains should be despatched to strengthen the army, or else money to hire Irishmen to serve as soldiers, or keep quiet and prevent others passing through their borders to hurt the king's subjects.

Wolsey, if not partial to Kildare, as a statesman allowed no personal prejudice to influence his administration and advised his royal master against his removal lest the septs in resentment should overrun the pale, as they then could without resistance, and destroy the crops; that whilst encouraged to hope for his return they would refrain from whatever might operate to his disadvantage, and that continued deputy he could be held responsible for the preservation of peace. The king, unwilling to oppose his ministers and yet favorably disposed towards the Butlers, adopted a middle course, retaining Kildare still deputy at court, and sent over Ossory as his representative. This apparent distrust and preference for his rival rankled in the breast of Kildare, who despatched his daughter Alice, lady Slane, to stir up strife, and his friends forthwith harried Ossory. Could these marauds have been traced home to his instigation he was too powerful to punish, and what was then done in secret transpired afterwards. In June, 1529, the king constituted his illegitimate son Henry Fitzroy duke of Richmond lord lieutenant and Sir William Skeffington deputy, with whom Kildare went back to conduct military operations. James, eleventh Desmond, who had two years before negotiated with the emperor Charles V. an invasion of Ireland, was now dead, and his uncle Thomas his successor at the age of nearly fourscore was better disposed to be loyal. The three earls were enjoined to lay aside their mutual animosities and coöperate in the general defence, but it was not many months before Kildare and Ossory were snarling and eager for the fray.

Skeffington in presenting Kildare to the citizens upon their arrival in the capital, turned his popularity to account. He congratulated them " on having again one they had sore longed for ; who after many storms by him sustained, to the comfort of his friends and confusion of his foes, had subdued violence with patience, injuries with suffering and malice with obedience ; the butcher," signifying Wolsey, " who had thirsted for his blood, being now an outcast." The earl was received with joyful acclamations, and two hundred archers from the municipal forces were placed at his disposal to punish the O'Tooles who had taken advantage of his absence to plunder his tenants. With the deputy he brought to terms the O'Moores and captured O'Reilly. O'Donnel tendering submission they drove the Mac Mahons out of Monaghan and demolished Kinard. But O'Neil having mustered his forces and appearing in powerful array, they did not wait to be possibly defeated.

In this general hosting against Tyrone, Ossory had taken part, and made complaint to the king that after marching one hundred and forty miles with a well appointed force to assist the deputy, and abroad foraging, as he depended upon the country for supplies, Kildare's people plundered his lodges of harness, provisions and money. The deputy had other grievances of his own which were duly represented; but not to much effect, for Kildare proceeded to court and removing all impressions to his prejudice returned as deputy. In his elation he was not very prudent, and his predecessor having in his absence without any special provocation demolished Dungannon, the chief abode of his kinsman O'Neil, he treated him with scant courtesy. From another of his enemies Allen, archbishop of Dublin, he took the seals, thus rendering him more inveterate as an enemy, and bestowed them on George Cromar primate of Armagh, in whose devotion he could repose implicit confidence. James Butler son of Ossory, afterwards ninth Ormond, was appointed treasurer, but upon the decease of Mulrony this year in Ely, the deputy sided naturally with his son-in-law, the Butlers with the son of John, rival aspirants for the chieftainship, and in the warfare which ensued the lands of Ossory sustained considerable damage.

After reducing Ballinduna, Eglish and Killurin, the deputy laid siege to Birr which he forced to surrender, but not before his farther military operations were arrested by a musket shot from the castle, which penetrating one side of his body worked itself out on the other by the following spring. He did not take it very kindly, nor receive courteously the efforts of an attendant to console him. It is also said to have exasperated his temper and thus to have accelerated his downfall. Whilst crippled with his wound, O'Tooles burnt out three of his brothers, two of whom escaped in feminine attire, another was driven out of Monaghan, and his eldest son Thomas sustained defeat from O'Reilly. Con Baccagh with another brother, John Fitzgerald, committed sad havoc in Louth, plundering

English settlements; and Edmund Oge O'Byrne carried off at night prisoners and plunder from the castle of Dublin, creating trepidation and keeping the inhabitants on the alert.

Around the council board sat too many enemies of Kildare, secret or avowed, for this untoward turn in his affairs to pass unimproved. The treasurer, his nephew but still a Butler, archbishop Allen, whom he had displaced as chancellor, and several more with wrongs, real or imaginary, to create ill-will, watched his course with inimical purpose. They despatched their secretary, John Allen, kinsman of the archbishop, and who was also afterward chancellor, across the channel to represent their discontents to the king. A memorial, signed by several members of the board, intrusted to Allen, followed by others more or less official, besides private correspondence of great variety and interest, are still preserved in the public archives.

The condition of the country at this period and that immediately before may be gathered from these reports home. They show how little four centuries of spoliation, tyranny and corruption had accomplished for alien rule. Neither the English language nor its dress were used, its order or peace established, crimes against person or property punished, or the laws obeyed beyond twenty miles square, and even that much was in jeopardy. This mortifying state of affairs was attributed in great measure to royalties enjoyed by a few absolute lords, Desmond in Kerry, Cork, Limerick and Waterford, Ossory in Kilkenny and Tipperary, Shrewsbury's agents in Wexford, whose own rule was partial and occasional but effectually shut out that of the crown. Carlow which had then come to Norfolk was a desolate wilderness. Blackmail was levied by the chiefs; tributes paid them by government. O'Byrne carried off prisoners from the castle, keeping the pale in constant trepidation. O'Brien, over his new bridge across the Shannon, harried Limerick at will. Two thousand Scots from the isles were gaining possession of Antrim and Coleraine.

Crown lands were alienated, and the revenues thus reduced were utterly inadequate for the ordinary purposes of government. The Irish still improved their opportunities for inroads, but the opinion is advanced "that if justice were done them they would be as civil, wise, polite and active as any other nation."

Illegal exactions on English tenants had driven them from their settlements. Disaffected Irishmen replaced the once well conditioned yeomanry that tilled the ground and garrisoned the castles. Neglect of the records, frequent changes of government, were other abuses requiring reform. They recommended that the charge of affairs should be intrusted to English viceroys, the colonists be organized for military service under fixed captains, and that no English lord should enter into covenant or league with Irish chief except by permission of the crown. Tributes and eries should no longer be paid, and public revenues improvidently given away should be resumed. Dethyke the priest wrote that for want of meat Dublin fasted five days in the week, and in the same letter states that the deputy hath conveyed all the king's ordnance out of the castle to fortify his own strongholds.

Among other illustrations of the disloyalty of the Geraldines, against whose long continued supremacy these missiles were especially aimed, it is alleged that Sir Gerald Shaneson stood high in the confidence of Kildare, and was employed by him in the conduct of his intrigues. In his endeavor to work to his purposes Thomas, the eldest half brother of the earl, to take part against the king, he urged "that if his father had not crowned Simnel, imprisoned Garth, hung his son, resisted Poynings and the other deputies, killed them of Dublin on Oxmantown Green, and suffered no man to rule but himself, the king would not have made him deputy or married his mother to him, and he would not have had a foot of land, where now he could spend four hundred marks a year."

Summoned, as the year 1533 came to a close, to answer these charges, and justify his administration of affairs, Kildare endeavored to ward off the impending blow by sending over his countess, trusting that the influence of her family at court might once more stand him in stead. But his danger was greater than he knew. Surry when he returned from his vice-royalty in 1522 had cautioned the king against him, and subsequent events had not changed his opinion. Cromwell who had taken the place of Wolsey, in the royal counsels, in this instance coincided with his views. Skeffington whom Kildare had displeased and supplanted, Ossory his hereditary foe, with resentments and aspirations of his own to prompt him, and who was connected with the Boleyns, were both set upon his overthrow, whilst his brother-in-law the marquis of Dorset no longer lived to befriend him. The royal temper had not been improved by battle with the pope, parliament was feeble and obsequious, the people intimidated. Absolute power vested in a merciless tyrant, whose thirst for blood, soon to be slaked in that of Fisher and More, was not likely to be scrupulous in dealing with his refractory satrap. Kildare might well have hesitated to place himself in his power. Resistance was still possible. It is said he intended it. Ossory wrote Cromwell that it was thought all the parchment and wax in England would not bring Kildare there again, and this of course led to more peremptory orders which he dared not disobey.

Recognizing the gravity of the crisis, he held many consultations with his brothers and principal adherents, and recommending his eldest son then coming of age to their care, he enjoined it upon him to be governed by the advice of the Delahides, Eustace and his uncle James. Directed to appoint some fitting substitute to act during his absence, he called his council of state to meet him at Drogheda, and nominated to them this son as deputy in his stead, explaining the reasons which governed him in the selection. In February, 1534, he left Ireland never more to return. Upon

34

his arrival in London he was informed of the charges against him and committed to the tower, where before the year had elapsed his life came to a close.

Ossory hastened to court.   But the king hesitated to commit the government at this critical conjuncture to another Anglo-Irish noble against the advice of both his councils, and gave the appointment of deputy to Skeffington.   Reports of the incapacity of Silken Thomas, as the young Fitzgerald was called from the splendid suits, fringed with silk, of his body guard, crowded over from his enemies. That he might compromise himself beyond retrieval, they manu-factured and circulated plausible tales of his father's execution. Distracted by intelligence not at once corrected, or tormented by filial solicitude lest if not already true such an event impended, sure of losing his office, and if so, at the mercy of his foes, likely to lose besides both life and land, at the same time confident of sup-port from nearly all the septs, from Pettits, Tyrrels, Daltons and all the Geraldines, following moreover under advice of De-lahide, selected by his father as his guide, the traditional policy of his family to make themselves indispensable to the maintenance of English rule, he summoned the council to meet him on the elev-enth of June, at the abby of St. Mary's in Dublin.   Traversing the city streets at the head of seven score of his brilliant guardsmen with the usual following on foot, he entered the chamber where the council were assembled, the rest pressing in for his protection.   After brief explanation he divested himself of his robes of office and surrendered the sword of state to the primate chancellor Cromar, his friend and his father's, who with many tears sought to change his purpose. Amidst his discourse, an Irish bard not understanding or perhaps hearing what was said, struck his harp and commenced to chaunt aloud the praises of the youthful Geraldine, inciting him to resent-ment and resistance, who thereupon left the hall with his followers, and remounting they rode away.

It was an opportune moment for the movement. Dublin had been nearly depopulated by the plague. From Wicklow, tempted by opportunity, O'Tooles rushed down upon the grain fields of Fingal, upon which the city depended for food. Upon their return with spoil, the citizens tried feebly to intercept them, losing eighty men. Allen and Finglas and others peculiarly obnoxious to Geraldine resentment retired into the castle, which White its constable prepared to defend. Fitzgerald gathering his levies defeated the forces of the pale, and entering the city unopposed imprisoned whoever refused oath to be faithful. Powerless to resist, the authorities, after consulting with the constable, who improved the occasion to strengthen his garrison and replenish his magazines, consented that Fitzgerald should occupy the city, in order to reduce the castle.

Allen not satisfied of his safety if he fell into the hands of his enemies, whom he was conscious how much he had injured, embarked for home, but the vessel grounding near Clontarf he took refuge at Howth. Dragged from his concealment at Artane, a village near by, and brought into the presence of Fitzgerald, by whose side sat mounted his uncles Oliver and James, he implored on his knees for life. Remembering that the imprisonment of the earl was owing to the intrigues of the archbishop, lord Thomas exclaimed, "away with the churl," which interpreted by Terling and Wafer, his attendants, as an order to put him to death, they despatched him with their skeines.

Froude cites this as proof of Irish barbarism, but if Fitzgerald is to be held responsible, he had hardly a trickle of Irish blood in his veins, the mothers of his line being English, as was also his own education. Judging from his grandfather's speech to Henry VII. respect for bishops formed little part of their composition, and the hierarchy of the period were noted rather for corruption and intrigue than for sanctity. This event proved a serious prejudice to the rebel cause. Anathemas excommunicating all present were fulminated by the ecclesiastics of the see, and a copy sent to Kildare in the tower of

London is said to have accelerated his dissolution. He had been struck with palsy when he heard of the rebellion of his son. Allen was slain on the twenty-eighth of July, and as before five months were over he was dead, it came late. In 1580 his coffin with his name inscribed upon the lid plate was discovered in the chapel of the tower.

Thus closed the chequered career of Gerald Oge, "most illustrious of either race in Ireland of his time, for not only had his name and renown spread at home, but his fame and exalted character were heard of in distant lands." More than twenty years he had held the earldom, nearly as long administered the government. The controlling principle that governed him, to confirm his own hold on power, saved English rule from extinction as the septs became conscious of their strength, and alive to their danger sought by consolidation to escape it. Of abilities above mediocrity the situation in which he was placed afforded congenial employment for both his physical and intellectual powers. When not at court explaining his conduct or counteracting the intrigues of his rivals, war, and diplomacy occasionally indirect, engrossed his attention, and sad to say such opportunities as offered for ameliorating the condition of his countrymen, were not always improved. If his popularity with chiefs and septs grew out of relations already understood, their respect and affection for him must be also ascribed to his excellent personal traits. Had he been more politic or less imperious, he might have disarmed or safely defied the hatred of Ossory, the resentment of the displaced archbishop, and steering his bark safely through troubled waters, averted the tragic downfal of his house, stood high in its annals for military talent and statesmanship.

Negotiations with Scotland and Spain before the rebellion broke out resulted in encouragement of aid, and Fitzgerald sent messengers to Charles V. to hasten its coming, and to the pope to extenuate or excuse the death of Allen. His main dependence was upon his own

countrymen. Hugh Duv stood aloof, but his son Manus joined his
brother-in-law Con O'Neil whose promised contingents were delayed
by a competitor for his throne. Brian O'Conor of Offaly, who
bore a like relation to Fitzgerald, was at feud with his brother
Cahir. Donogh O'Brien afterwards second earl of Thomond, loyal
to Ossory, whose daughter he had espoused, crippled the efforts of
his father Conor ; and in Munster the death of the ancient Thomas
twelfth earl of Desmond while his grandson and lawful successor
was in London a page to the king, afforded opportunity to John
great uncle to James to take possession of land and rule.

For the actual conjuncture, Skeffington was the worst possible
choice. Broken in health, with neither taste nor aptitude for his
task, he wasted the summer in dilatory preparation, not even reaching Ireland till towards the close of October. Three months before,
royal missives spurred Ossory to muster his men, and in August his
forces took the field. He was old and heavy, but his untiring energy,
great practical sagacity, knowledge of men, and of the places and
complications with which he had to deal, rendered him more than a
match for his inexperienced nephew. He spoiled Carlow and Kildare. Fitzgerald with part of his army left the siege of Dublin
to oppose him, taking Tullo, and encamping on an island in the
Barrow, strove to bring him to an engagement at disadvantage,
but Ossory, wary and strongly posted easily foiled his manœu-
vres. After five such efforts on successive days without result,
during the last of which the earl pounced upon his camp and carried
off much spoil, O'Neil announced his approach. Possibly to gain
time to effect their junction, consolidate their forces and concert
measures of coöperation, the Geraldine proposed to divide the island
with the earl, who replied that if his country were wasted, his castles
won or prostrate and himself an exile, he should persevere in his
duty to the king. Menaced however in his rear by Desmond, he
assented to a truce, and soon after drawn into an ambush suffered a

defeat from the enemy reinforced; his son James subsequently ninth
earl being dangerously wounded, and a son of O'Moore on the other
side losing his life.

Meanwhile the siege of the castle went on. Three falcons,
all the rebel artillery, proved ineffective against its massive walls and
heavier guns. Threats were made, not probably in earnest, to protect the trenches by the children of the citizens. This provoked
their resentment, and encouraged by promises of speedy succor,
they shut the gates, imprisoning all the Geraldines they could, a
few effecting their escape by swimming the Liffey. Fitzgerald
alarmed left the war in Kildare to his allies and marched on Dublin. On his way he took into his possession as hostages many
children of the better sort, sent out of town to avoid the dangers of
pestilence and war. He burnt ships in the haven, cut off the con-
duits. His efforts to regain his position were attended with little
success. His troops driven out of Ship street and assembled in large
numbers in St. Thomas's court, endeavored to cut their way through
the houses along Thomas street to the new gate, which they set on
fire. Many of them had been compelled to take arms. Arrows without point, and some with letters attached of encouragement, promises
from Ossory of his speedy march to their rescue, emboldened the
citizens, who spreading a report that the expected reinforcements
had arrived, sallied out through the burning gate. They put to rout
the beleaguering force, who lost many men and all their artillery;
their commander, after concealment all night in a convent, barely
succeeded in reaching his camp.

Fitzgerald, discouraged by his failure and at the arrival of the fleet,
and disturbed by tidings that his tenants were sore bested by Ossory,
proposed to raise the siege upon release of his men, delivery in
money and wares of fifteen hundred pounds, artillery and ammunition, and of promised intercession with the king for the pardon
of himself and his confederates. The citizens were willing to ex-

change his men for their children, but were too poor to give him what he asked, and told him that wax and parchment would better answer the purpose for his pardon than powder and guns. When the deputy arrived and Brereton and Salisbury landed, a truce of six weeks had however been agreed upon, the authorities promising to petition not only for his pardon but that he might be appointed deputy for life. Fitzgerald sought without result to prevent the landing of the troops. He gained an advantage at Clontarf, but finding himself outnumbered, hastened towards Carlow to join O'Conors and O'Moores. Ossory with St. Loo from Waterford had taken Knocgraffon, and after waiting in vain the promised junction of the deputy at Kilkee contrived to detach Mac Morrogh from the cause. The deputy started the middle of November, and encountering the rebel army on the borders of Meath, he regained the city in haste, after a week's absence, harassed by the hostile cavalry on his march. At the bridge of Kilmainham, where they were particularly troublesome, he contrived to dislodge them from the woods by his artillery, both himself and his men suffering from the rain which was pouring in torrents and which had swollen the streams. On the first of December he rode with Brereton to Waterford, reducing the castle of Kildare on their way.

The rebel chief, after burning Trim and Dunboyne, not far from the capital, proposed a truce till after twelfth night, in which the deputy studious of his ease gladly acquiesced. O'Moores, O'Conors, O'Briens and O'Neils committed occasional marauds to the great distress of the unarmed inhabitants, but the depth of winter was devoted to rest and preparation. Fitzgerald now tenth earl of Kildare strengthened his castles of Maynooth, Rathanagan, Portlester, Lea, Carlow and Castle Dermot. Ossory took Athy and incited Clanrickard to keep O'Kelly engaged, whilst he sowed such strife in Munster between McCarthies and Geraldines that they destroyed each other.

The war, if not sanguinary or marked by any engagements of consequence, fell without mercy on the helpless and unarmed. In February the garrisons destroyed thirty or forty of the neighboring villages. A few weeks later the deputy invested Maynooth, chief abode of the Kildares, the richest under the crown in its plenishing, and supposed impregnable, but Skeffington by well planted batteries silenced the guns on its donjon battlements, and affecting a breach in its lower walls the besiegers worked their way into the court-yard, slaying sixty of the experienced gunners to whom its defence had been committed. Of the prisoners, one was hung, perhaps Wafer, who killed the archbishop, or Paris, charged with betraying the fortress; twenty-five were beheaded, and two spared who sung well in the choir. As the unfortunate proprietor was hastening to its relief with seven thousand men collected in Connaught, the gloomy tidings of its surrender created profound discouragement. Many abandoned his banners, and after an unsuccessful skirmish he withdrew with sixteen personal attendants into Clare. He still indulged the hope of succor and of being able in the course of the season with ten thousand men promised him by the emperor, and more from Scotland, to take the field. With what force he could collect he hovered about the pale, but having no guns and but ten muskets the castles proved a formidable impediment. By stratagem he enticed their garrisons to sally forth, now by herds of cattle temptingly displayed before the walls of Rathanagan, now by rumors circulated that he was near by with a small force. Ossory not idle meanwhile took all his strong holds but Crom and Adare and gained over O'Moore.

The hold which the house of Kildare still retained upon the hearts of the people gathered other armies. In consternation at the approach of O'Brien, O'Kelly and O'Conor Faly to the pale, Allen master of the rolls, and Aylmer chief baron, were despatched to England for assistance. On the twenty-eighth of July, 1535, a year from the slaughter of the archbishop, Leonard Gray, sixth son of Dorset, arrived as marshal of Ireland. He found his work already accomplished. Rebellion, if not yet suppressed, had nearly died out by exhaustion, the torch more cruel than the sword having left little to destroy. Three-fourths of Kildare, six of its eight baronies, and Meath lay depopulated and waste.

The septs accustomed to select their leaders from middle life, after a while lost confidence in a youth who, however brave and intelligent, had little experience in war, and gained no battles. Ossory also their kinsman, knew well how to sap their allegiance and detach them from a cause which they knew to be hopeless. All the Ulster chiefs except Con and Manus, O'Moores, O'Carrols and McMorroghs, even O'Byrnes and O'Tooles in turn deserted, and when about the end of August, O'Conor was forced to submit, Kildare called a parley and yielded himself up to Grey upon assurance under the most solemn sacraments that his life should be spared. Carried to London by the marshal, he was imprisoned in the tower. The king was embarrassed for a time by the pledge given at his surrender, as is frankly acknowledged in the royal correspondence. But the machinations of his enemies, and the implacable resentment of the six kinsmen of the murdered archbishop, whose intrigues had materially contributed to the ruin of his father, finally overcame all scruples, and lord Thomas after sixteen months confinement left his cell for the scaffold.

During the absence of the marshal on this errand, Ossory and his son, by order of the king, proceeded into Munster to settle the disputed succession to the earldom of Desmond. Thomas the twelfth earl, 1454–1534, had recently deceased. His widow Catherine Fitzgerald of Drominagh was that "old countess" said to have survived her husband seventy years and then to have had her life shortened by an accident at the age of seven-score. The son of his first wife Celia MacCarthy, sister of Cormac Oge ninth lord of Muskerry, died in 1520, leaving a son, James Fitzmaurice, who educated at the

35

English court and a page to the king, had recently returned
and married Mary daughter of Cormac. That powerful chieftain
supported him in his rightful pretensions to the succession, which
was disputed by his great uncle John, upon the pretence of some
informality in the marriage of his father Maurice with the daughter
of the white knight. Sir John, who for a time wielded the power
of the house, played fast and loose with the government, but was
generally by them considered unreliable. He certainly took part
with the league, who ostensibly engaged in measures in the interest
of Gerald, were maintaining a correspondence with France and the emperor, as also with James the Fifth of Scotland, two thousand of whose
subjects had settled in Antrim. The Butlers took Dungarvan, occupied Youghal, and after parley with Cormac received hospitable entertainment from the authorities of Cork. While in that city James of
Desmond was presented to them by his father-in-law, and submitted
his claims to their adjudication.

Thither also came the lord Barry to complain of another son-in-law
of Cormac, MacCarthy Reagh of Carberry, and grandson of the eighth
Kildare, for depriving him of his possessions. But that chieftain, another Cormac, in a spirit unlike that of his kinsman and more characteristic of his lineage, English as well as Irish, declined any interference in his quarrels. He declared he would "hold by the
sword what his sword had won." At Limerick, whither the army
proceeded by Mallow and Kilmallock, came Sir John Desmond in
the same haughty temper, declining any controversy with "the boy,"
but finally consented to meet Cormac Oge before the council at
Youghal. Grey, upon his return in October, was ordered to arrest
the five uncles of Kildare, three of whom had taken but little part
in the rebellion, and long before its close had given in their submission. It is said they were inveigled by the marshal into his power
and seized at a banquet to which they had been invited. Of this
want of good faith there is no satisfactory proof, but on the contrary

evidence to render it highly improbable. The earl, who had been dependent upon his companions in the tower for garments to cover his nakedness, was executed with his uncles at Tyburn, the third of February, 1537.

Grey had been likewise ordered to seize upon his nephew Gerald. By his second wife Elizabeth, sister of the marshal, the ninth Kildare left two sons Gerald and Edward, and three daughters, one of whom the fair Geraldine was the admiration of the unfortunate Surrey, and commemorated by him in his well known sonnet. Gerald, but ten years old, when, by his brother's execution, he became next in succession to the earldom, remained for a year in the care of his sister Mary, wife of O'Conor of Offaly. He was subsequently for a time in Carberry with his aunt Eleanor, widow of McCarthy Reagh, or with her daughter the wife of Dermod O'Sullivan Beare at Dunboy. In these wild regions, and Dermod with impunity had just punished capitally the officers of an English cruiser, who molested a Spanish fisherman off his coast, the boy could not be reached by his uncle, however much disposed. The importance attached to his safety by the chiefs from the eagerness of the king to obtain possession of his person, made him of consequence, and to his subsequent adventures we shall have occasion to allude.

When Skeffington died on the last day of the year 1535, lord Leonard Grey was chosen deputy by the council, and confirmed by the king. Whilst at court he had been created for his services in suppressing the rebellion viscount Graney, James Butler, the life of whose father was drawing to a close, receiving like rank as viscount Thurles. The new deputy, if stern and imperious, possessed abilities of a high order, and sagacious in statesmanship, both his civil and military experience fitted him for his official duties. There was much in the condition of affairs to try his temper, and at the same time to bring out the resources of his character. The little court at Dublin seethed with corruption. Officials of low aims and sordid objects

steeped in intrigue, sought their own aggrandizement, striving to supplant their rivals by subserviency to power, and by crushing down
without hesitation whatever blocked their path that was weak.

The home government if directed by abler counsels was equally
unscrupulous, and beyond the reach of public opinion or compunction of conscience yielded itself without reserve to the
domineering temper of the king. If during the earlier period of his
reign only two instances had occurred of the death penalty for political offences, he was entering upon a period when neither learning nor
sanctity, youth nor sex were to be spared. Fisher and More, his
queens, their relatives and paramours, his aged kinswoman Margaret
of Salisbury, fell victims in turn to his sanguinary disposition. The
Geraldines immured in the tower were preparing for the block. It is
to be hoped that no guilty sense of having betrayed them to their fate
troubled Grey when four years later he tasted the bitterness of death.
When we study the course of events during his administration and
realize how entirely his natural wish to further the interests of his
sister's child coincided with his prevailing policy, it seems difficult to
doubt that the restoration of Gerald to the lands, rank and power of
his ancestors, as a political necessity indispensable to the preservation
of the island to the realm, was what he sought to bring about, and
only abandoned or deferred when he found that Con O'Neil was plotting independence and to become himself sole monarch of the land.

If any such considerations in reality affected his course, placing in jeopardy if betrayed, office and life and the end at which he
aimed, the deputy deserves admiration for his prudence and persist-
ency, for the masterly tact with which he pursued his object yet
avoided its perils. It was disloyal to administer the government in
opposition to the known wishes of the king who had entrusted it to his
keeping, and to use power delegated for another purpose to further
family interests was not to be palliated. But believing that under
existing circumstances English rule would be strengthened by re-

establishing the ascendancy of the Leinster Geraldines, and that the preservation of the island to the crown concerned not only Henry and his ministers, but the nation at large to whom he was also responsible, he hardly deserved the headman's axe for a policy which redounded to their advantage. No selfish or personal motives sullied his career; and with an empty treasury and inadequate forces, by his sagacity to conciliate the animosities of the contending septs, and pave the way for their consolidation under English rule, at least entitled him to gratitude from his own countrymen. He had able men to contend with and many discouragements, but he proved equal to his task.

His first parliament convened in April, 1536, manifested unwonted loyalty, passing the act of supremacy, confirming the divorce of Catharine of Aragon, and before it was over, the deposition of Ann Boleyn her successor. O'Neils and O'Conors were never at rest, but military movements were delayed for want of funds to pay the soldiers who were mutinous or discontented. Still the deputy in June proceeded to Dundalk and exacted professions and pledges of loyalty from Tyrone, and the month after joined the Butlers at Kilkenny where James Fitz John of Desmond, whose father had just died, promised to meet them. He failed to appear, but there gathered a goodly company, O'Moore, Gilpatrick, McMorrogh, O'Byrne and O'Carrol, with some of the English lords from Munster, those of Leinster remaining at home from fear of incurring the resentment of the Geraldines, in the event of their regaining power. Not meeting Desmond at Cashel or Limerick, the deputy afterwards took the castle of Carrigogunnel and gave it to Donogh O'Brien, son-in-law of Ossory, from whose men it was soon retaken. In August, led by Donogh by secret paths, they attacked the bridge ten miles up the Shannon and which was defended at either end by a strong castle of hewn marble some distance from the shore, with walls twelve feet thick. The connecting arches had been broken down, but the spaces were filled with fagots, over which the troops marched to the assault. The garrison escaped into Clare and the bridge was demolished.

Returning to Limerick they again took the castle of Carrigogunnel, putting the garrison with few exceptions to the sword, but the army still continuing mutinous further operations were given up. The deputy prorogued the parliament, which had followed his march and held its sessions at Cashel and Limerick, to January. Their bill of attainder against the Geraldines was held valid notwithstanding the death just before of Richmond the lord lieutenant, and upon complaint that absentees left their estates in incompetent keeping, titles held by Norfolk, Berkely, Shrewsbury, the heirs of Ormond, abbots of Furness, St. Austin at Bristol, priors of Christ Church, Canterbury, Llanthony and Cartinel, of the abbots of Kenlesham, Oseney, Bath and St. Thomas of Dacres, were vested in the crown. Notwithstanding their own experiences on the march of the danger to the country and themselves from the discontented spirit of the unpaid soldiers, they could not be persuaded to grant subsidies of the twentieth of temporal and ecclesiastical revenues or to resume the customs granted away by the crown.

Although O'Tooles, O'Byrnes and Cavanaghs had been long peaceably disposed, in 1537 the council decided to expel them from their possessions between Waterford and the capital. Before attempting to carry out this project, Grey marched into Offaly, through the countries of Mulmoy, Melaghlins and Macgeoghans, taking the castle of Bracknel and extending to the garrison the " pardon of Maynooth," or indiscriminate slaughter. He also destroyed Dengen. Cahir was made chief in place of Brian who withdrew into Ely. In July with the men of Leix and Ossory the deputy reduced O'Carrol and O'Meagher to terms, Brian suing for peace which was promised if approved by the king who was secretly advised not to grant it. Brian soon recovered the chieftainship, and when in November the deputy again marched to Bracknel and followed him into Regan he kept the English at bay. The campaign ended without other result than the capture of Killeigh and Castle Geashil from which was carried off as spoils a pair of organs and glass enough to glaze the college and castle of Maynooth. In February the O'Conors, now reconciled, made their peace with the deputy upon favorable terms.

Commissioners sent over to inquire into the condition of affairs, held a conference at Clonmel with James Fitz John of Desmond, who promised future obedience to the king as also to help secure his kinsman Gerald. He gave his son as hostage, but at the same moment secretly corresponded with the confederate chiefs. In April, 1538, Grey invaded MacMahon, and after hastening to Drogheda then menaced by Con O'Neil who retreated, marched into Cavan and received professions of amity from its chieftain. The young Gerald was at the time at Kilbrittan with his aunt Eleanor. To strengthen his position she now consented to marry Manus chief of Tyrconnel, who had recently lost his first wife, sister of Con O'Neil, her cousin. They were escorted by her son MacCarthy Reagh, and by O'Brien and Clanrickard to his abode, and the league formed to re-establish Gerald in his estates, or to worry the English till this was accomplished, soon embraced nearly all Ireland except the Butlers. The deputy naturally favored what would promote the interests of his nephew, and now that events were ripening for some demonstration in his behalf, the course he pursued was calculated to awaken doubts as to his loyalty.

The chiefs whom he upheld stood staunch for Gerald; their competitors, when any there were, the Butlers befriended; and resentment found frequent vent in representations home to his disadvantage. In June he was entertained at the abbey of Monasteroris by Brian O'Conor and wrested from the rival candidate in Ely Birr and Modren. In that part of Ormond ruled by O'Kennedy, came to him John of Desmond and the two Burkes, and at Limerick both clergy and laity took the oath of supremacy. Castle Clare and Bally Connel surrendered. A quarrel between Conor O'Brien chief of Thomond who died the next year and his brother Morrogh first earl of

Thomond, was peaceably adjusted; but another fraught with fatal consequences, in relation to some hostages of Mulryan, with Desmond, led to the latter drawing up his men to attack the deputy, when Sir Thomas Butler interposed and persuaded him to leave the camp. Ulick Burke entertained Grey at Galway; O'Conor Roe visited him in Hy-Many. Passing through the territory of O'Madden across the Shannon by the Mac Coghlans and Mageoghans he proceeded to Maynooth, which he reached on the twenty-fifth of July, 1538.

Henry realizing the importance of a good understanding between the deputy and the Butlers at a time when the Irish, all of one mind, were becoming dangerous, ordered them to lay aside their enmities. This was more than even the king could enforce. Piers Roe who the year before had resumed his earlier title of Ormond, and James his eldest son lord Thurles, were more ready than Grey to make advances though they insisted upon guarantees of safety in attending court. When the council remonstrated with the deputy for not receiving these advances with courtesy, he charged Ormond and Thurles with giving help to the enemy. This led to reflections by them upon his official conduct, and their several recriminations reduced to writing and sent home created impressions to his prejudice. Rumors that he was to be superseded inclined him to conciliation, and his troops and the Butlers united in humiliating the Cavanaghs. The council in October in communicating this event to the king represented the island as more tranquil and obedient than for a century. But it proved a false appearance. All the septs were leagued together at the time, ostensibly to restore Gerald, but with many ulterior objects, and among them with the boldest national independence.

Hopes were entertained of the restoration of the ancient monarchy, and that O'Neil, Gerald's cousin, would ascend the throne of his ancestors and be proclaimed at Tara. This combination was formidable, and if held together might well have led to independence;

and now that the Kildare Geraldines were powerless, Barrys and Fitz-gibbons at war, English rule was in peril. Ormond and the lords of the pale alone stood by Grey, who himself was doubted, for one object of the league was the restoration of his nephew.

Whatever his own inclination to further the interests of his sister or her son, there is no evidence or probability that the deputy by overt act or guilty intent swerved from fidelity to duty. In the confidence of all parties sufficiently to comprehend their designs, it was far from his wish that the hold on the island should grow weak. At the same time in his friendly relations with the chiefs and sense of what justice demanded, he discountenanced all schemes for taking advantage of their peaceable behavior. To extend the pale in Leinster by expulsion of such as were no longer strong enough for resistance was as impolitic as wicked, arousing the more formidable and less immediately menaced to combine against like encroachment later. They were wise enough to perceive that the first opportunity would be improved for their subjection, and the league formed for the restoration of Gerald constituted their best safeguard against molestation.

What was discussed in the council or embodied in state documents could not be kept secret, and projects not only for extirpating the septs of Leinster, but for occupying in force all the towns and strongholds over the land, were freely broached. The English reënforced were to war upon the septs till their subjugation was complete, and their subsistence consisting of corn and cattle destroyed, they should cease to exist. Such atrocious counsels from distinguished officials taint the reports of the period, and if not approved or transpiring, gave color enough to the courses actually adopted, to create jealousy, encourage combination and justify the prudence of timely resistance. Estimating aright the strength of the people united for security against farther aggression, the consummate tact of the deputy knew when and how to render abortive projects that tended toward separation.

36

His policy if resolute was nevertheless generally conciliatory. Obedient to his instructions he moved his force from one part of the island to another, but not so much to employ it as to inspire respect for authority. Indeed this was one motive for the military expeditions of the period, which often ended without bloodshed or even maraud. Certainly in two instances recorded, large forces on either side were drawn up in array, and treaties such as that of Sil Murray between Burkes and O'Donnel prevented an engagement. The recent league produced a sense of common interests, which appeased the old hereditary feuds, even inspired the hope that the septs might again consolidate into one nationality. Grey from his relation to the young Kildare shared in the general good fellowship, a popularity to cost him his life, for Ormond Allen and Brabazon hated him, and already were contriving his recall.

Winter closed upon an unwonted spectacle; hardly a ripple disturbed the profound repose. The septs were at peace with one another, and Henry assured by his council that no previous king was more loved and respected or better obeyed. Yet there were circumstances of a suspicious character ominous of the coming storm. At the south, James Fitzjohn, still angry with the deputy about the hostages, in possession of the Desmond dominions, and of the estates of Kildare in Munster which had been forfeited to the crown, stood fast by the league, and ingratiating himself with his neighbors of either race, was more powerful than any earl of his house within mortal remembrance. An English palace was a poor school for an Irish earl, and the pretensions of the court page, though the rightful heir, were little regarded now that Cormac Oge, his father-in-law, no longer lived to support them.

It seemed an inconsistency for all Ireland to combine to restore Gerald to the earldom of Kildare, and to manifest such indifference to the stronger claim of James Fitz-Maurice to that of Desmond. But as the favorite of the king and sure to carry out his policy, his restoration would have been an embarrassment. Gerald, by his personal graces and amiable character, justified the affection inspired both by his misfortunes and by the injustice that deprived him of his inheritance. Chiefs of Ulster and Connaught thronged the halls of Tyrconnel, over which Eleanor presided. Bards sang the praises of her nephew at the banquet. The chiefs in council concerted measures for the coming campaign. Selection of some one leader and general plan of operations were stumbling-blocks with so many opinions and rivalries; but a rising as early as September, when reinforcements from the isles and main land of Scotland were expected, seems to have been determined upon. Desmond and O'Brien were to engage the Butlers; the O'Byrnes and O'Tooles the forces of the pale, while the main force invaded Meath. The chief leaders at the north were Con and Manus, and it was their jealousy which seems to have defeated the enterprise. Whatever had been decided was revealed in June to the deputy by intercepted messengers.

In April, O'Neil and O'Donnel had promised the deputy to meet him on the plains of Carric-Bradagh and bring Gerald with them. They probably never intended to keep their appointment, and in his vexation Grey laid waste Tyrone. Con lay beyond reach of his resentment behind the Broadwater, where sixty years later Hugh, his successor in the earldom, for a winter held at bay the forces that conquered at Kinsale. Soon after, on the twenty-first of August, the eighth Ormond died, and his son James was assailed by Desmond and O'Brien. This formed part of the plan arranged by the confederate leaders, which was somewhat disconcerted by the Scots not appearing as agreed. The chiefs of Tyrone and Tyrconnel had already assembled their clans; they spoiled Meath, and obtaining rich booty from Ardee and Navan, drew up their troops at Tara in grand array. But returning elate they were attacked unprepared at Belahoe by the deputy, four hundred of their men being slain. Macginnis taken prisoner was subsequently put to death. It is evi-

dent that these hostilities were premature. Cowley wrote Cromwell "that Clanaboy, O'Rourke, MacCoghlan, Kane, Maguire,
Neil Conelagh, MacDermot with Scots from the isles and main,
and many more were to have joined Con and Manus, but the deputy by discomfiting the northern chiefs had prevented their junction."

Still in doubt as to what impended, Grey in October gathered his
forces at Trim, and bringing O'Reilly to terms, entered Lecale, over-
ran the domains of the Savage, taking eight castles, among them the
strong fortress of Dundrum.   He is said in this expedition to have
burnt the cathedral of Down and demolished the monuments of St.
Patrick, Bridget and Columbeille, but he stood fast by the faith of his
fathers, and heard several masses the same day before the statue of the
Blessed Virgin at Trim, which was soon after destroyed by order of
Browne, who succeeded Allen as archbishop of Dublin.   He hastened
early in November to join the new Ormond, now assailed in greater
force by Desmond and O'Brien, and determining "to pluck from the
latter all his forces and wings east and south of the Shannon,"
they took Roscrea from the O'Meaghers ; Modren from the O'Carrol who killed Ferganim.   Mac-i-brien-ara, Mulryan of Owney,
O'Dwyer of Kilnamanna promised allegiance and to pay tribute.

At Thurles, Gerald MacShane and the white knight joined them,
and at Youghal, whither they proceeded by Cashel, Clonmel and
Dungarvan, the three sons of Gerald of Desmond.   At Imokilly
they delivered to James Fitz-Maurice who had come over from
England, all the castles from Cork to Waterford appertaining to
Desmond, and at Kinsale, Kerrikurriky.   McCarthy Reagh and
Muskerry promised to keep the peace.   Whilst in the O'Callaghan
country on his way to Limerick, waiting to cross the Avonmore now
known as the Blackwater, then swollen by recent rains, James Fitzjohn with a large following on the other side, gave the deputy to understand that O'Brien and himself and the other chiefs were opposed to
Ormond.   Grey " sore moved by these words " and having but eight

hundred men, went back to Cork and thence to the pale. Con
O'Neil now declared his design to be inaugurated at Tara. He
promised to meet Grey at Dundalk, on the twenty-second of January, 1540. But his forces invaded Felim Roe of the Fews who was
friendly to the English, whereupon the deputy took and burnt
his castle of Dungannon. This pretension of Con to the crown
aroused the jealousies of Manus who had long entertained like
aspirations. It was fatal to the cause of Gerald, who embarking in
March as a wild Irish boy in a saffron shirt sailed for St. Malo.
Finding his way into Italy it was his good fortune to receive there
an excellent education, a fitting preparation for his prosperous
career later, when in the two following reigns he regained land and
earldom. His aunt suspecting her husband had designed to betray
Gerald to the English government, deserted him, and as she lived
long after his next wife Margaret MacDonnel died in 1544, they may
have been legally separated.

The Irish parliament long proved obstinate in refusing the ecclesiastical twentieth, and it was only in 1537 after the proctors from
the bishops had been expelled, that it passed that bill as also another
for dissolution of the monasteries. Disputes arose as to the appointments to vacant sees, but the reformers were not strong enough to
enforce the new laws. The deputy staunch for the old religion
stood in the way of reform, and requesting his recall that he might
inform the king of the state of affairs and marry a wife, he was
ordered home. Allen, Brabazon and Ormond were summoned over
at the same time to represent the opposite side. They proved too
powerful for him. He was thrown into the tower, and upon ninety
charges, with little exception frivolous, such as aiding his nephew to
escape, the favor shown by him to certain chieftains, traversing
Thomond with slender escort, he was condemned to death and
executed on Tower Hill in June, 1541.

In 1539 ended the life and reign of Conor O'Brien king of Thomond, son by Joan, daughter of the eighth lord Kerry of Turlogh Don, who died in 1528. By his first wife Anastacia Burke, Conor had Donogh second earl of Thomond, by his second Alice daughter of Maurice Baccagh, tenth earl of Desmond, Sir Donal, tanist after the death of his uncle Morogh the first earl. Conor took part with Silken Thomas and sheltered Gerald from the attempts of the deputy to obtain possession of his person, and later refused to surrender to the king the plate of the proscribed family which had been entrusted to his keeping. Before his death, however, he made peace for a year; his sub-chiefs, Kennedy of Ormond, Carrol of Ely, Meagher of Ikerrin, MacMahon of Corcavaskin, Conor of Corcumroe, Loghlin of Burren, Grady of Kineldonal, O'Brien of Arra, Mulryan of Owney, Dwyer of Kilnemanna, MacBrian of Oonagh, also giving in their submission. Conor was the last king of Thomond. His brother Morrogh who succeeded him surrendering the territory to Henry, and receiving it back as first earl, with remainder to Donogh, son of Conor.*

An incident mentioned by the Four Masters at this period forms an interesting episode amidst the marauds and sanguinary conflicts they relate. Not without precedent for we have already had occasion to advert to similar gatherings in Hy-Many and Offaly. From Bryan elder brother of Nial of the nine hostages of the fourth century, through many kings of Connaught, descended Mulroona, chieftain of Moylurg in Roscommon about the time of the battle of Clontarf. From him derived the Clanroona embracing the MacDonoghs of Tirerill and from which branched the MacDermots Roe, their progenitor Dermot being brother to Conor prince of Moylurg in 1300. One of the principal abodes of the elder line first erected a century earlier stood upon an island in Lough Kee, which was covered throughout its extent, except a large central court they enclosed,

---

* The ancestral line from Turlogh back was Tagd, Torlogh, Brien, Mahon, Murtogh, Turlogh, Tagd, Conor, Donogh, Donel More, Torlogh, Dermod, Torlogh, Tagd, Brian Born, whose wives in the reverse order were taken from the houses of Molloy, MacCarthy, MacMorrogh, O'Kennedy, Macnamara, O'Moore and Burke.

with buildings well adapted to repel attack. This sheet of water in the barony of Boyle, one of the many laying on either side of the Shannon, a river which through seventy tributaries great and small drains a valley of two hundred and thirty-four miles in length, is nearly circular and more than three miles in extent. Spreading out from the easterly base of the Curlew mountains, which of gentle acclivity are now cultivated nearly to their summits, it is studded with twenty islands, several of them occupied by remains of abbies and churches, castle and fortalice. As not infrequent in Ireland, the lake served as a social centre for the tribe, and seat of government for the chief, and when the convent bell mingled its echoes with the harp and song, and its shores and islands resounded with the mingled murmur of a numerous population, it must have been a pleasant place for dwelling. Its ancient structures, now in picturesque decay and mantled with ivy, harmoniously combine with many abodes of modern elegance which lay about the lake, Rockingham castle, the residence of Lord Lorton, being especially conspicuous, to lend variety to a scene of great natural beauty.

Here through many centuries ruled and dwelt the Macdermot chieftains, substantially independent. From the frequently repeated incursions of the Kinel Konel into Moylurg, especially after the O'Conors lost supremacy in Connaught, it is evident that though the princes of Tyrconnel claimed sovereignty over them, they never acknowledged fealty nor paid tribute, unless under coercion by force they could not resist. Their peculiar official relation earlier to the O'Conor, putting on his shoe at his coronation at Cairnfraich, was less a token of personal subjection than of mutual obligation. They took an active part in the wars with their neighbors, and were more exposed from their advanced position in the path of war.

This long line of chieftains, often mentioned by the annalists with distinguished respect for their prowess, culture and munificence, were represented in 1540 by Rory, who with his spouse, daughter of his neighbor Burke of Clanrickard, gave that year a general invitation of hospitality to the scholars of Ireland, and to all who sought gifts, to share in the festivities of the Rock, as this castle on the lake was called.   Here flocked in large numbers whatever was eminent in erudition or ability, and who many of them were is plain from the names embalmed in their native annals as then renowned.   They were generously entertained by their honored hosts, who allowed none to go unsatisfied away.   Offshoots from the parent stem of the Macdermots have since done honor to the name, and one who bore it by marriage, not by birth, watched tenderly over the happiness of the blind minstrel O'Carolan, 1670—1738, and it was at her home at Alderford that he died.   His funeral obsequies were largely attended, taking place in the abbey church of Kilronan, near by.   In our own day the race exhibits its pristine vigor and culture by freshly gathered laurels in law and literature.

XXX.

REIGN OF HENRY VIII.—1509-1547.—(Continued).

The direct and most immediate influence at work to separate England from the catholic church is generally admitted to have been the settled purpose of the king to repudiate Catherine and marry Ann. Ten years before this second marriage which took place privately in 1532, his latin treatise against Luther obtained for him from Leo the tenth the title of defender of the faith.   However conversant with scholastic divinity, his religious opinions, which never varied much from Roman standards, hardly reached his character or conscience, and little of the saint entered into his life or nature.   His love of sway and domineering temper brooked no control, and what claimed his veneration, provoked his hostility.   The manners of his youth were gracious, his presence pleasing, and his constitutional vigor and

open-handed profusion attached to him his people. Their affectionate loyalty yielded slowly to his later developed traits of cruelty and
self-indulgence, and they took ready part on his side in a controversy
which seemed to involve his conjugal happiness.

His unfortunate marriage justly claimed commiseration; but such
trials befall all conditions. The sanctity of the tie for better or
worse is the corner stone of our social structure as of civilization
itself and he was bound to submit. It is creditable to the firmness
and consistency of Clement, if prompted by such considerations, he
withstood the urgent appeal of Henry, but his obduracy is generally
attributed to unwillingness to displease Charles the Fifth, nephew of
the queen. He temporized by authorizing cardinals Wolsey and
Campeggio to inquire into the facts. But Wolsey with aspirations
for the papal throne and disposed to conciliate the emperor, thwarted
his master, who, when the court closed and the case was recalled
to Rome, more resolved than ever to effect his purpose, replaced him
by Cromwell and threw off allegiance to the sovereign pontiff.

But other and higher motives contributed to the renunciation of papal authority and to the independence of the English church. For at
least two centuries Englishmen had been found disposed to think
for themselves. Now that the sacred scriptures, no longer a sealed
book to the laity, through the recent invention of printing were extensively read, differences of interpretation and inference took fast
hold of inquisitive minds. Freedom of thought revolted against
dictation in matters of faith, and growing enlightenment recognized
no such sanctity in the life or conversation of the hierarchs of the
sixteenth century as constituted them infallible guides in christendom.
If English ecclesiastics had been more generally like Fisher and
Cromer the king would not have ventured to disturb them. Neither
Wolsey nor Browne were favorable samples of christian character.
The cloister still served as an asylum for the feeble and unfortunate,
travellers within their gates received hospitable welcome, but neither

37

regular nor secular inspired respect by their piety or asceticism. Tenacious and grasping they did not realize how far they had survived their usefulness, and unable or unwilling to accommodate themselves to the spirit of the age, the march of human progress which they vainly sought to stay, marched over them. They disappeared as they are now disappearing in other lands, to be perhaps revived in later days under happier auspices in closer accordance with the needs of a purified faith.

Still neither ecclesiastical corruption nor religious speculation, so much as the claim of the church to control in affairs temporal as well as spiritual, hastened separation. Dogmas widened the breach, imputed abuses greatly exaggerated quickened disaffection, but it was papal interference in politics, attempted subordination of state to church that brought about the reformation. In the acrimony engendered what characterized the ancient faith shared in the growing prejudice, and much was sacrificed to its iconoclastic temper protestants regret. Rites and observances, sacred by immemorial custom and endeared by habit, were discarded, to which among many there is a disposition to return. The beliefs common to christendom are vastly more important than their specific differences. However earnest not to lose sight of its essential truths in outward form, their recognition seeks expression in accordance with our complex nature. What serves to keep them paramount or aids devotion commends itself to whoever estimates aright our dependence or the mysteries involved in revelation.

Providence if inscrutable follows rational paths. Emancipation of the Germanic races from their old leading strings, when able to read and think for themselves, was one step in human progress, not to be ascribed to any earthly potentate. The six articles enjoining transubstantiation, sanctioning communion in one kind, celibacy of the clergy, monastic vows, private masses and auricular confession were passed in 1539 at the instance of Henry. The pil-

grimage of grace which desolated the kingdom and other persecutions
instituted by Cromwell were rather to maintain his supremacy than
punish heresy. When after Jane Seymour died in childbed of Edward in 1537, and Cromwell had fallen from grace by inducing the
king in 1540 to marry Ann of Cleves, soon after divorced for
Catharine Howard a catholic beheaded two years later, protestants
were proscribed. What actuated him was a headstrong will impatient of restraint. Instances in his house of papal resentment counselled him to keep beyond its reach. The closing of the court of the
cardinals in 1531 virtually ended England's connection with the Roman church, except for the few years of the reign of his daughter
Mary, and was followed by decrees for his excommunication.

Not easily intimidated, Henry was ever jealous of plots against his
throne. Whilst the church retained its possessions, reaction might set
in and his life be endangered. Two centuries before the vast estates
of the Templars, upon charge of similar abuses to what were now
imputed to the ecclesiastical bodies, had been confiscated. His wars
and pageants, the expenses attending his divorce, the avidity of his
ministers had drained his treasury. The eighteen hundred thousand
pounds Empson and Dudley had accumulated for his father having
been squandered, the church property offered to the king, when in
doubt how to replenish his coffers for the indulgence of his extravagant habits and appetites, temptations not easily withstood.
By advice of Cromwell nearly four hundred religious houses in
England were suppressed in a single year, Henry to disarm opposition founding colleges and sharing the spoil with his nobles.

The Four Masters in presenting the view taken of the early periods
of the reformation by the Irish themselves under date of 1537, say
that "a heresy and new error springing up in England through pride,
vain glory, avarice and lust, and through many strange sciences,
the men of England went into opposition to the pope and to Rome.
They at the same time adopted various opinions and among them

the old law of Moses, in imitation of the Jewish people; and they
styled the king the chief head of the church of God in his own
kingdom.   New laws and statutes were enacted by the king and
parliament according to their own will.   They destroyed the orders,
to whom worldly possessions were allowed, namely the monks, can-
ons, nuns, brethren of the cross and the four poor orders, minors,
preachers, carmelites and augustinians; and the lordships and livings of those were taken up for the king.   They broke down the
monasteries, and sold their roofs and bells, so that from Arran of
the saints to the Iccian sea there was not one monastery that was
not broken and shattered, with the exception of a few in Ireland, of
which the English took no notice or heed.   They afterwards burned
the images, shrines and relics of the saints of Ireland and England;
they likewise burnt the celebrated image of the blessed virgin at
Trim, which used to heal the blind, the deaf and the crippled and
persons affected with all kinds of diseases; and also the staff of
Jesus which was in Dublin, performing miracles from the time of
St. Patrick down to that time, and had been in the hands of Christ
whilst he was among men.   They also appointed archbishops and
sub-bishops for themselves, and though great was the persecution of
the Roman emperors against the church, scarcely had there ever
come so great a persecution from Rome as this; so that it is impossible to narrate, or tell its descriptions, unless it should be narrated
by one who saw it."

Many monasteries were beyond reach and escaped molestation till
within a recent period; a few remain on their ancient foundations.
The number suppressed under Henry has not been ascertained.
Grey who had set at liberty prisoners arrested by Brown for infring-
ing the ordinances, wrote Cromwell in May, 1539, requesting that
six houses should be exempted from the general suppression—St.
Mary's Abbey and Christ Church, Dublin, Grace-Dieu in Fingall,
Connell Abbey in Kildare, Kells and Jerpoint, Kilkenny, "for in

these houses commonly and such like in default of common inns which are not in this land, the deputy council and Irishmen coming to the deputy have been lodged at the cost of said houses ;" "young men and childer both gentlemen childer and others, both of mankind and woman kind, were brought up in virtue, learning and the English tongue, the ladies all in the nunneries of Grace-Dieu, the young men in other houses. St. Mary's Abbey was the hotel of all people of quality coming from England, and Christ Church was at once the parliament house, the council house and the common resort in their time for definitions of all matters by the judges." "The abbot of St. Mary's pled we verily be but stewards and purveyors to other mens uses for the kings honor, keeping hospitality and many poor men soldiers and orphans."

The abbeys of Beetive, St. Peter's at Trim, Dousk, Duleek, Holmpatrick, Dunbrody, Tintern, Ballybogan, Hogges, and Fernes were immediately confiscated, and many besides, at later periods. Thomas Court fell to Brabazon, ancestor of the earls of Meath, Grace-Dieu to Barnewall of Trimlestown, the O'Briens received Ellenesrane and others in Clare, Gilpatrick baron of Upper Ossory, Aghevo and Hagmacarte. The royal supremacy over the church had been recognized in the session of 1536, papal authority declared at an end, and penalties attached to disregard of these decrees. Priests who refused to surrender church property were slain at the altar. These sequestrations and arbitrary proceedings took time, and attracted less attention then, than after their consequences were felt and they were better understood.

Upon the departure of Grey Sir William Brereton was selected for the administration. Mac Morrough, O'Toole and O'Connor harried the settlements. Active correspondence went on as before, between the Ulster chiefs and Spain and Scotland. Upon rumor that all the septs were to muster for a general council or hosting at Foure in West Meath, bishops, peers and judges, all conditions of

men in the pale, to the number of ten thousand, collected, but finding there no trace of any such gathering they amused themselves for
twenty days as long as their provisions lasted, with destroying corn,
castles and dwellings in Offaly. Such marauds soon left little for
destruction. Both Con and Manus had grown weary of this perpetual strife and devastation when no longer bolstered up by the hope
of consolidating the strength of the septs for independence. They
wrote the king expressing their willingness to become good subjects;
but requesting various grants and favors in return. Con's letter was
in Latin under his seal and accompanied by gifts.

In August, 1540, arrived Sir Anthony St. Leger, one of the ablest
statesmen ever entrusted with the government, which remained for
the most part for the next twenty years in his charge. His arrival
produced early fruits. MacMorrough, after Idrone in Carlow his
only remaining possession had been ten days wasted by Ormond,
gave up that title as chief, and promised for himself and his successors to be known thereafter only by the name of Kavanagh.

Leix and Offaly were overrun. Accompanied by Ormond, the
deputy then proceeded to the south. At Cahir, the castle of Sir
Thomas Butler, his friend, James Fitz John, now through the murder or manslaughter by his brother Maurice A'Totan at Leacain in
Kerry of the court page thirteenth Desmond, the rightful earl,
accepted terms of amity, renouncing his hereditary privilege granted
to the seventh earl of not attending parliament or entering any walled
town except at his own pleasure. He entertained St. Leger and Ormond at his castle of Kilmattock, where no English governor had
been for a century, and in parting expressed his disposition to visit
the king at London, which in 1542 he accomplished. At Limerick
Morrogh king of Thomond by tanistry remained three days in conference with the deputy, from whom his request to rebuild the bridge
over the Shannon and regain his dominions east and south of the
river met with little encouragement.

His wings were indeed clipped. Donogh, son-in-law of Ormond and eldest son of the late king Conor, still continued devoted to the powers of the pale. His maternal uncle Ulick Na Cean, chief of Clanrickard, was of like mind; and his territory interposed between Thomond and Tyrconnel prevented Morrogh and Manus combining if disposed. Ulick is represented by the deputy to the king as "a goodly man, desirous of coming to civil order, and sooner to be brought to conformity by small gifts and honest persuasion, than by taking anything away from him or by rigor," praise not in character with his name "of the heads," given him from the piles heaped up of what he had chopped from his enemies. Before the summer was over, O'Byrnes requested that Wicklow should be made shire ground. Their neighbor Turlogh O'Toole, who when the pale was menaced from Ulster volunteered to defend it, declaring when their assailants were beaten off he should resume hostilities, grew less lofty when harried by the deputy and Ormond, and made peace. He requested leave to visit the king and twenty pounds were advanced him for his charges. Upon his return he was slain by his kinsman another Turlogh, who did not lose favor for the deed with the government. How it chanced that the deputy with inadequate means in a few weeks effected so much can only be accounted for by his coming at an opportune moment.

There were many abuses for him to reform. Cowley, who had been sent over not long before to investigate what became of the king's Irish revenues, reported that no books or accounts were kept of them. They were disbursed by Brabazon and Agard as they saw fit, or left in charge of officials who embezzled directly or indirectly the larger part. Much went to support garrisons too weak and widely dispersed for efficient service, who lived in riot and pillaged loyal subjects. The commander of castle Jordan was away taking his pastime when O'Conor took possession of it without resistance. The recommendation of Cowley that commissioners, neither needy nor

greedy, should examine into these irregularities and confidence be
placed in men of character and property of the pale, who should
be trusted and employed, rather than officials sent over without
sympathy for the people or interest in their prosperity, had its
weight.   One of the Plunkets was created baron of Dunsany, another of Louth ; Edmund Butler, of Dunboyne near Dublin ;
William Bermingham of Carbry ; John Rawson viscount of Clontarf,
and Thomas Eustace of Baltinglass.   From their power and dignity
as hereditary law-givers their influence was extended, and of like
views and associated in public duty, they were too independent to
be reached by the baser sort who sought office for pelf.   They had of
course objects of their own to answer, to keep their estates and lessen
public charges.   But these objects were best promoted by honest
administration, by good understanding among themselves, and encouraging in the septs friendly dispositions toward the government.

Indeed, not only several of the chiefs of Ulster and Connaught,
but O'Briens, McCarthys, McMoroughs, O'Dempseys, Mulroys,
M'Laghlins, M'Geoghans, even the O'Connors, O'Moores and
O'Tooles professed their willingness to accept the actual condition of
affairs and give in their allegiance to Henry as king, a title conferred
upon him in 1541 by the Irish parliament.   At this session attended
not only Barry and Roche, Kerry and Athenry, but Cavanaghs,
O'Moores, O'Reillys and Clanrickard.   Ormond translated the
speeches of the chancellor and speaker to the many of English race
as well as Irish who understood no English.

The differences which had long embittered the relations of Desmond and Ormond were now adjusted by cross-marriages between
their children, the latter relinquishing all claim to the earldom of
the former which he had previously urged in right of his wife, only
child of the eleventh earl.   Roche and Fitzgibbon, whose domains
touched and who were constantly at feud, were captured and imprisoned in the castle, and occupying the same bed became good friends.

O'Neil and O'Donnel first held back, but before another year was over Con accepted the title of earl of Tyrone, and his son of Lord Dungannon. On the first Sunday in July, 1543, also at Greenwich, with religious rites and splendid ceremonial, followed by a banquet, Morough O'Brien was created earl of Thomond for life with the barony of Inchiquin intail; Donogh the son of Conor his elder brother, baron of Ibreckan intail, with the reversion of the earldom; Ulick de Burgh, Donogh's maternal uncle, earl of Clanrickard and baron of Dunkellin.

The new lords surrendered all claim to their old titles and sovereignty as chiefs, as also to their lands, which they took back under English tenure. There were of course many disappointments. O'Donnel wished to be made earl of Sligo or Tyrconnel, McNamara of Clancuilen. The latter with O'Grady and O'Shaughnessy, as also two of the Maginneses, received the honor of knighthood. Gilpatrick was created lord of Upper Ossory; O'Reilly, viscount Cavan. O'Conor of Offaly promised baronial rank appears not to have obtained it. The king ordered them supplied with robes and money and residences at Dublin. They all were sadly in need of decent attire. Some even of the great English proprietors wore saffron shirts and shaggy kernogues, and O'Rourke begged for common clothing.

Cut off by the disturbed condition of the times from sources of supply, and expending whatever means they possessed in coats of mail and implements of war, the deputy describes chiefs and lords of either race as poorly clad for occasions of peace. O'Donnel was an exception. His active hostings replenished his coffers, and constant intercourse with other lands his garments. His dress consisted of a coat of crimson velvet with twenty or thirty pairs of golden aiglets, and over that a great double cloak of crimson satin, bordered with black velvet; and in his bonnet a feather set full with aiglets of gold. To him as to the rest were presented parliamentary robes. The modest apparel of the chieftains and their scanty wardrobes as ob-

38

served by St. Leger and reported home were accidental. Taste for brilliant colors and various material led in Ireland as in other countries at the period to extravagance, which during this reign was sought to be restrained by statute.

The conciliatory policy of the king, if kindly intended and with no ulterior design, struck a fatal blow at Irish independence. It sowed seeds of discord, spread plentifully the spores of distrust and disaffection. Preference to O'Brien and O'Neil created jealousies amongst disappointed expectants of similar honors, who after waiting in vain for fulfilment of their hopes settled down into more hostile dispositions than before. The land was in a ferment. For the chief to accept an earldom was surrendering the right of the sept to self-government, virtual abandonment of all its usages and traditions. In some instances it was regarded as abdication of the chieftainship which was filled by new selection. But whilst refusing to recognize the power of the chief to surrender land or jurisdiction, the dangerous consequences of even pretension to exercise it were obvious enough for alarm.

If these titular distinctions had been more generally bestowed opposition might have gradually disarmed. The superior dignity and influence of English earls and barons had worked prejudicially to the septs, and this and disputed successions under brehon law were an admitted evil. If the two countries were to be consolidated into one realm, and distinctions of race to be effaced, to admit both on equal terms to rank and privilege, as to right before the law, was an important step. Judiciously planned, and carried out with due regard to vested interests, the change would have worked its way to general acceptance. It was a favorable moment for such an innovation. On the brehon code had been engrafted many feudal ideas borrowed from the long established institutions around them. The social and political systems of both races in their pyramidal structure were sufficiently alike for this distribution of rank and legislative function not to be embarrassing. No prejudice existed to be shocked, no rankle would have been left, for each sept would have participated in the honors bestowed upon its chief. Neither peerage nor parliament would have been swamped by numbers, since the roll if extended under Cromwell had been greatly reduced by recent attainders.

The case here, when our American colonies severed their destinies from the mother land, was different. Though of the same race, faith and political institutions, in the general equality of condition that prevailed hereditary rank would have been out of place. Republican sentiment had already reached a development that revolted against domination by a privileged class, especially from over the sea ; and though the struggle for independence originated in an impatience of arbitrary power, that the objectionable measures proceeded from a government so constituted, widened the breach. That it produced such sentiment needs little proof. Washington ranked high as an officer, he had saved the army of Braddock from destruction, but as a provincial was refused a commission in the regular service. Such unjust discrimination festering in the minds of influential leaders rendered impossible common nationality for people of the same kindred where geographically remote, and it must work less kindly where of different race in close proximity and intermixed.

Surrender of the territory to the crown and regrant upon English tenure, if of any validity, involved consequences if not of deeper, of more immediate import than simple recognition of sovereignty. That the sept ignored in Thomond by electing after the death of Donogh, the second earl, in 1558, Sir Donald his brother as tanist. It was not attempted, probably not contemplated to disturb vested rights. But if carried out to its legitimate consequences, all such rights were at the pleasure of the lord paramount and no one would be safe. The consent of the sept had not been obtained or requested, and the whole transaction revolutionary and simple usurpation threatened to deprive them against their will of their inheritance. The regrant back being to the chief and his lineal heirs, if they failed, the territory vested absolutely in the crown.   For kinsmen within the degrees there was claim for the succession or to be elected tanists.   Farther down in the scale there were a great variety of vested rights to be swept away.   Even fuidhirs and bondsmen of the lower sort and all the expectant heirs entitled by gavelkind to a share of estates held by their parents or kinsfolk, could not tell where this modification of their ancient tenures might stop.

If both essentially differing from the allodial and absolute ownership known to our law, both Irish and feudal tenures had their general resemblances in the complicated duties and reciprocal obligations of lord and vassal, chief and sept.   In other respects they were greatly dissimilar.   What they actually were under the brehon law is still somewhat a matter of conjecture and dispute.   The Senchas Mor, Book of Aichill, Conus Beesna and other tracts recently translated, of great antiquity, long continued in authority as guides for the brehons, upon whom devolved the charge of regulating conveyances and contracts, reducing them to shape, recording and giving them force.   With the breaking up of the monarchy and legislative institutions consequent on the invasion, power vested more in the chief, and changes in custom and law assumed form and sanction from adjudications by brehons or stipulations entered into by concession or compulsion according to chance and circumstance.   Occasion no doubt was improved, when the ollavs and brehons assembled, to revise them, and as these functionaries were hereditary and belonged to a few families, such frequent consultation would naturally tend to prevent innovation and ensure uniformity.

What relation the chief held by law either to land or sept is not susceptible of precise definition, as it underwent many changes and varied in different tribes.   That the territory belonged to the clan, a term conventionally employed to embrace all the inhabitants, or

to the sept, consisting of the descendants from its ancient chiefs
in certain restricted degrees, rather than to the chieftain himself, is
a formula generally admitted. He had property of his own by
inheritance, castles and domains which appertained to his office,
power to dispose of estates vacated by death or forfeited for rebellion, of the common lands for the general benefit. Redistribution
upon decease of a clansman, or at stated intervals as not unknown in
our New England settlements for meadow lands held in common, had
led to inconvenience and been abandoned. But apportionments and
grants in severalty were regulated by law and not at the mere pleasure of the chieftain. Clansmen were not his tenants but the tribe's.
What they paid him to defray the charges of administration or expenses incident to his position was rather tax than rent, and for the
most part applied for the general benefit, not for his family needs or
private indulgence.

His time and thoughts were devoted to the public. Constantly
employed in official duties as ruler or judge, commander in war
and in peace, surrounded by the dignitaries of his court; his
gates ever open in hospitality to his humblest clansmen, few purely
selfish considerations could have entered his mind. His course
open to public scrutiny, depending on popularity for retaining his
hold on the loyalty of the clan, he was constrained to be just and
generous, and magnanimity was hardly an effort or a virtue. His
power if not absolute was not often disputed, it was necessarily
exercised with caution, and he rarely presumed to infringe upon
the rights of his subordinates as defined by law or regulated by
custom. Instances occur where lands taken from one were transferred to another, younger sons provided for by grants of territory
under obligation of fealty. His cosherings might sometimes prove
oppressive; his coyne and livery, risings out or compulsion to
military service, bonaght or claim to quarters for his soldiers.
These were incidents of vassalage, often pressing heavily on farm

or village.   But nowhere would a chieftain have ventured upon the
theory that the territory of the sept was his individual estate to use
as he pleased.   His subordinate flaths and bothachs, his ceille
bond or free, held their lands by grant or prescription by right as
sacred and secure as he his castle or demesne.

Why Tyrconnel failed to share in this distribution of honors is not
easily explained, for he was willing to acknowledge the royal supremacy.   Henry possibly may have denied to others conjugal liberties
he indulged himself.   Eleanor had been replaced by Margaret
Macdonnel daughter of Angus, and the king had cause to be jealous
of the growing power of the Scots in Ulster.   In 1542, the year his
rival Con exchanged his chieftainry for the earldom of Tyrone,
Manus made peace with the deputy, who received him with great distinction and respect, and they together passed through Tyrone to
break down the castle of Enniskillen, when Manus, with his sons
Calvagh and Hugh, went into Connaught to collect his tribute.
With O'Rourke and O'Kane he crossed the Bann, killed or houghed
vast herds of cattle, driving as many off, the despoiled MacQuillins buying their peace with horses, armor and many other things
beautiful and precious.   He gave Tura and Lurg to his son-in-law
Maguire, receiving in return the rising out of Fermanagh.

But his power had its limits and he probably felt that to deprive his
tributaries of the selection of their chief by giving up his position as
O'Donnel, and accepting instead an earldom, would have put his rule
in jeopardy.   His brothers were numerous and powerful.   Hugh,
learned in many sciences, distinguished "for his munificence and
prowess in the field and gap of danger and expected from his steadi-
ness of character to obtain the chieftainship," had died in 1538.   Two
other brothers Donogh and John of Lurg, discontented resorted to
arms, when John being captured was hung, Donogh and Egneghan
kept in fetters.   The year after, at the great council at Dublin the
chief was persuaded to set them at liberty, and he made friends with

his brother Con, who dwelt at the English court and was about to return, with whom his relations had been unfriendly.

Manus had also to experience filial ingratitude. He had entrusted his strong castle of Lifford to the O'Gallaghers, who in 1543 disloyally held it for his second son Hugh. Incensed at this treachery and unable to reduce the castle without ordnance, he wreaked his resentment by devastations and taking many prisoners, exacting pledges from O'Doherty who had violated his jurisdiction by killing his kinsman Cahir. Calvagh eldest son of Manus applying to the deputy for guns and gunners to reduce the castle, they were furnished and the hostages of Hugh were made over to their allies. Soon after one of the gunners being slain, perhaps contrary to such rules of war as were then recognized, one of these hostages Cahir was put to death, when, to save the life of the other Turlogh son of Felim Finn, Lifford was surrendered. Whether growing out of these animosities or from some other ground of resentment, in 1546 another brother of the chief, Donnell, was slain by O'Gallagher and his wife Honora at Ballyshannon" to the great grief of the land, for of all the descendants of Conel son of Nial, there was not one of his years from whom more was expected by the multitude."

That same year Brian O'Conor, brother-in-law of the Kildares Thomas and Gerald, who had been the happiness and prosperity of that half the island where he ruled, was driven out of Offaly into Connaught. Twice did the deputy harry his country, and after inviting the chiefs of Offaly to come in, which they did, he treacherously plundered them of thousands of cows. O'Conor and O'Moore were proclaimed traitors and their territories transferred to the king. What became of Brian will be related in the next chapter.

The Clan Colman his neighbors were likewise sore distressed. War and devastation prevailed throughout their land, cold and famine, weeping and wringing of hands throughout their habitations. Kedagh had been inaugurated in opposition to Rury who plundered

Delvin, whereupon O'Maddens and MacCoghlans pursued and slew thirteen of his kinsmen. The contest if brief while it lasted wrought innumerable evils, and ended in the death of Rury killed by Dalton in the interest of Kedagh.

Whilst the land was generally quiet, war between the O'Kanes and MacQuillins, dwelling on either side of the Bann in Ulster, disturbed its repose. The latter with their allies from Scotland were defeated in 1543 and driven into the river, but regaining courage, and helped by Brabazon governor in the absence of St. Leger, stormed Limavady the castle of the enemy. O'Donnel interposed, and taking Loughlan a fortress of great strength commanding the fisheries, gave it to O'Kane. Occasional feuds occurred among the O'Rourkes, MacSweenys and O'Boyles, rival aspirants for their respective chieftainships embruing their hands in fraternal blood. Con and Manus found frequent cause for dispute, but they both consented in 1543 to relinquish sovereignty over the border septs outside of their respective countries.

When the next year Ulick Burke the new earl of Clanrickard, "the most valiant of the English in Connaught," died, succession to his honors and domains was contested between Richard his son by Grace O'Carrol, and another by Maria Lynch named John, who claimed that Grace had not been legally separated from the Melaghlin her former husband. Ormond was sent with other commissioners to settle the question of legitimacy and decided in favor of the elder son, who being under age for rule, Ulick son of Richard Oge was made captain of the county. Irritated at Ormond for this decision, the sons of Richard defeated him at Athenry, Archdeacon or MacOda anglicised Cody and forty more being slain.

Later in the year the king engaged in war with France applied to the Irish council for three thousand kerns; but was forced to content himself with one third that number. Ormond provided two hundred, Desmond six score, Tyrone ninety, O'Briens, Carroll, Moore, Magnire, Rourke, Mulmoy, Melaghlin, none. Reilly supplied eighty-nine, Conor thirty-eight, Cahir Cavanagh only twenty-one, and the deficiency was made up by lords of the pale. No galloglasses, mailed warriors armed with battle axes, were sent; but the kernes who were, the deputy represented to the king to be excellent gunners. Their daring and efficiency in the field extorted admiration from their foes, who inquired if they were devils or men. After many feats of valor at the siege of Boulogne, a Frenchman of great strength and stature challenging any of the opposite side to single combat, one of the kerns Nichol Welch swam over, cut off his head and returned with it in his teeth.

In earlier times when safety depended upon mutual support and due subordination, chiefs of inferior power were content to admit their obligations of fealty and pay tribute when it could not be avoided. Under changed conditions such relations grew irksome, and now that they could be cast off with impunity, appeal to English tribunals resulted in decrees absolving from future dependence. Maguire, Magennis, Tyrconnel were set free from any such relation to Tyrone, Manns being still however held to pay sixty cows each year to Con, for Inishowen. Two of the Cavanaghs, Charles MacArt and Gerald Mac Cahir, contending for supremacy preferred resort to the old arbitrament of arms. After there had fallen in the fight a hundred warriors on either side, the former prevailed, retaining his ascendancy till under Mary he was created baron of Balian.

Brian Gilpatrick, unable to repress the turbulent spirit of his son a distinguished captain, sent him to Dublin with a statement of his crimes, where he was put to death at the request of his father. The O'Driscols on the south shore of the island were less inclined to amity or acknowledgment of English rule. The waters near by their abode at Baltimore afforded them sources of revenue, and they asserted their maritime rights with vigor. A Waterford ship laden with wines from Portugal, driven by stress of weather into their

39

haven, for some cause not stated was seized. The merchants of Waterford sent two ships and a galley with four hundred men to make reprisals, who plundered their country and razed to the ground their principal fortress.

The MacCarthies and their kindred chieftains were not inclined to conciliate royal favor or share in the honors bestowed. Eleanor after her ill omened marriage with Manus of Tyrconnel had returned to her home at Kilbrittain. Her four sons, Cormac-na-haoine, Florence, Donogh, and Owen, each in turn ruled over Carbery. They had intermarried with the daughters of Cormac Oge of Muskerry, MacCarthy Mor, Maurice Fitzgerald, brother of the earl of Desmond, and Dermod O'Callaghan. Her daughters, Catharine wife of the ruling chief of Blarney, Julia of the prince of Beare, Eleanor of Connor O'Meagher of Ikerrin, extended her influence, which in the next generation, then or afterwards, gained additional strength from alliances with O'Driscols, O'Donovans, O'Donoghues, Powers, Barrys and Fitzgibbons. These all powerful families in Munster shared in her resentment against the king for the execution of her brothers and her nephew. Expectations were indulged that Gerald with fifteen thousand men would soon effect a landing on the coast. But he was engaged in Malta or fighting the Moors, and not appearing there or in Ulster, where it was also supposed he might come, their zeal gradually abated. Eleanor herself became discouraged, and too sensible to persist against hope to the prejudice of her children made overtures for reconciliation. Her letter to the king in 1545, proffering allegiance, and requesting pardon, received a favorable response. How much longer she survived does not appear, but as her marriage with Donal Reagh must have taken place near the beginning of the century she was no longer young.

In the November following her submission, an expedition against Dunbarton under Ormond and Lennox left Dublin, but met with a storm, and when they gained the Scotch coast the adherents pro-

mised were not there. When Iver Mac Donald lord of the isles
joined them with his fleet, such formidable preparations had already
been made to oppose them that they returned to Carrickfergus, and
from thence fought their way by land through hostile septs to Dundalk.

Great expectations having been entertained of success, this inglo-
rious termination of a costly enterprise afforded the enemies of
Ormond in the council an opportunity they were not disposed to forego.
Allen lord chancellor an intriguer stirred up strife between the earl
and the deputy. "English power was then greater in Ireland than
ever before. Leath Mogha was in bondage." Precious metals from
America had not yet reached Europe in sufficient quantities to meet the
growing need, and copper coin was compelled to be taken as silver.
Pieces bearing the national emblem of the harp were broken up. The
people were generally impoverished and excitable. The council proposed a tax, which was supported by Allen and the deputy and
opposed by Ormond. Angry contention led to complaint home, and
the three were summoned to court. After a hearing before the
council, Allen, who had declared that only one of them should return to Ireland, was condemned for equivocation and on other charges
and imprisoned in the Fleet.

Ormond and St. Leger were reconciled, but the former at a splendid banquet at Ely House in Holborn with thirty-five of his followers partook of meats that were poisoned, which proved fatal to
half their number, and among them to the earl. He was greatly lamented by his countrymen and would seem to have merited their
affection, though his readiness, in 1534, with his father to throw
off allegiance to the church, lessened their regard. In 1543 he had
been directed to visit Tipperary, Waterford, Cork, Kerry, Ormond
and Desmond, imprisoning whom he saw fit, and his exercise of this
authority provoked complaint, but he was generally not only prudent
and politic, but generous and of a nature highly honorable and loyal.

His mother "great countess of Ormond," sister of Eleanor and of

Alice wife of Tyrone, daughters of the eighth Kildare, after fifty-five years of married life was dead. As maternal traits often descend, the following tribute by Stanihurst to this remarkable woman may prove of interest. "Her husband," the seventh earl Pierce Roe, "was himself a plain and simple gentleman, saving in feats of arms; and yet, nevertheless, he bare out the honor and charge of his government very worthily through the wisdom of his countess; a lady of such port that all the estates of the realm crouched under her; so politic that nothing was thought substantially debated without her advice; she was manlike and tall of stature; very liberal and bountiful; a secure friend, a bitter enemy; hardly disliking, where she fancied, not easily fancying where she disliked." Her six daughters, by marriage with persons of rank and power increased the influence of the Ormonds, and the poisoned earl's wife Joan, the only child of the eleventh Desmond, added Clonmel and other important possessions to his extensive domains. Joan married after his death, Sir Francis Bryan and Gerald sixteenth earl of Desmond, the last of whom she left a widower in 1562. From her seven sons by James who was the ninth Ormond descended a numerous posterity.

Cromwell as domineering as Oliver,* his nephew thrice removed, made many enemies. It was a sad blunder for him to have selected for political objects so unhandsome a wife for the king as Ann of Cleves. Arrested at the council table by Norfolk, in July, 1540, ten years after the death of Wolsey, he had expiated both this blunder and numberless cruelties and crimes in the pretended cause of religion on the scaffold. Catherine Howard two years later followed him to the block, and the sixth royal venture in matrimony, Catherine Parr, widow of Lord Latimer, before another twelvemonth occupied her place. She paid dearly for her elevation in what she had to endure from the irascible temper of her husband, but luckily survived him. Norfolk and Surrey his son retained their influence till

---

* Richard Williams son of his sister assumed her maiden name, and was great-grandfather of both Oliver Cromwell, and of John Hampden.

near the close of the reign. Norfolk labored assiduously to reform
the old religion without destroying it, but the council of Trent in
1540 and establishment of the inquisition in Flanders barred the door
against England's return within its fold. He in turn lost favor, and
with his son was cast into the tower. The fiat for his execution, actually issued, was stayed by the royal demise, but he did not recover
his liberty till Mary was queen.

Majesty swoln with indulgence and racked with pain its penalty,
savage and furious, an object of resentment at the many hearths
he had left desolate, of dread to all within compass of his ire,
never, as Raleigh says of him, having spared woman in his passion,
or man in his wrath, brutal and wretched and universally abhorred,
the sorry spectacle offered a gloomy contrast to the brilliant
promise that greeted him as he mounted the throne thirty-eight years
before. Denny had courage to tell him his death was nigh; Cranmer arrived but in season to obtain some slight recognition as he
passed, and England was relieved from her burden.

The people of the sister island had little more cause to mourn the
loss of a monarch under whose arbitrary rule they had so long been
groaning, and which but for dissensions amongst themselves they
might have shaken off. They possessed religious institutions
well suited to their needs to which they were attached. Not
one in twelve, even in England, were then protestants. Across
the channel his supremacy as head of the church had been recognized,
but few had changed their faith. The suppression of the conventual
establishments, if welcome to chiefs sharing in their confiscated
property, proved an unmitigated calamity to the people. The substitution menaced of English prayers for Latin, to which use had associated a meaning, would virtually operate to exclude them from participation in religious worship, and if addicted to war they were still
devout. They would be deprived of a principal enjoyment, since
church festivals formed an important part of their life.

In the earlier part of his reign, new foundations, or pious gifts to those already established proved the religious sentiment in full glow. At its close, monks and nuns with saddened hearts were driven from the cloister into a world strange and unnatural. Their ancient abodes fell into dilapidation or were changed into fortresses. Finglas, chief justice in 1534, in his breviate recommended that Tyntern, Dowske, Baltinglas and Graney be given with baronies to young men to guard the marches, as also the castles of old Ross in Bantry "a living for a lord," Leaghlin, Carlow, Fernes, Keating, Powerscourt, Wicklow and Arklow; and that the territory east of the line from Dublin to Waterford be taken from the Cavanaghs, Byrnes and Tooles who had not more than four hundred horsemen among them. There were then in Ireland five hundred castles outside the towns, a large share held by Englishmen, whose armor and weapons were superior to their enemies, and Finglas suggests that the army be made still more efficient. Hostings should be divided into wards, front, rear and middle, and led by captains chosen annually by their soldiers, who should be enjoined not to stray from their banners of which the number was too large, and who should practise with bow and arrow on holidays.

The customs and excise or livery he says required reform. The latter should be collected by the royal harbinger, and his bills have as a distinctive mark a horsehead. Hides ought not to be exported except in exchange for cargoes of wheat, salt, iron or wines, nor wheat when more than a shilling a peck, nor hawk nor horse. Bread, ale and whiskey might be sold to the Irish, the latter perhaps to make them easier to conquer. The adulterated coin should be called in and replaced with what was equal to five pence a groat. The scarcity of money is shown by ale selling two pence a gallon, which was also the price for a full meal for a soldier. He recommends merchants' wives not to frequent ale houses, but weave and spin wool and linen at home. He says the Irish respected their laws made on the hillside, but the English forgot and violated theirs after eight days. To another work of the period representing grievances of the people from the forced visits of their landlords, allusion has already been made.＊ There were other troubles. Tempests of extraordinary violence in 1515 prostrated walls at Clonmacnois, other monasteries and churches, and many buildings of lesser worth. Dearth of provisions, sixpence of the old money in Connaught, in white money in Meath, buying only one small cake of bread, also created distress.

The prevalence of letters at this period among the people and their habits of study, are curiously illustrated by Campion, who writes a few years later that "Irish scholars spoke Latin like a vulgar language, learned in their common schools of physic and law, whereat they began as children and held on sixteen or twenty years, coming by rote the aphorisms of Hypocrates, the civil institutes of Justinian and a few other parings of these two faculties. Chairs did not abound where devastations were so perpetual, and ten students in a chamber prostrate on couches of straw, their books to their noses, chanted their lessons by piece meal, being the most part lusty fellows of twenty-five years and upwards."

Familiar names of poets, brehons, ollavs and other learned men who receive brief notice as they pass serve also to show that very far from lapsing into barbarism the country found time in the intervals of war to cultivate the arts of peace. The year after the accession of Henry are mentioned Farrel O'Fealan, distinguished professor of poetry, and Owen Higgin its chief preceptor throughout the island. In that which followed, Duigenan, "affluent and learned in history, and MacBrady, twenty years bishop of the Brefineys, the only dignitary both races obeyed, a paragon of wisdom and piety, enlightening laity and clergy by his instruction and preaching, a faithful shepherd ordaining priests and consecrating churches and bountiful to poor and mighty:" O'Clery, O'Daly of Corcumroe and Hosey, poets who kept houses of hospitality. In 1519 died Martin Mulconry, ollav of Sil

＊ See p. 123, *ante*.

Murray, selected by the Geraldines and other English as their legal adviser who obtained all the jewels and wealth that he asked for; O'Curran the confidential friend of O'Rourke. In the next ten years are noted Cassidy ollav in physic to Maguire and O'Breslen his ollav in judicature; O'Corcoran learned in canon law, Con and Gilla O'Clery, adepts in history, poetry and literature, of great consideration, wealth and power; MacEgan head of Leath Mogha in fenachas and poetry.

Another decade embalms the memory of MacWard, a learned poet, surpassing all others in humanity and charitable deeds; MacKeogh intended ollav of Leinster, skilled in various arts, killed accidentally by the O'Tooles his uncles; another O'Higgin, chief preceptor of poetry in Scotland as well as in his own country; in the last under Henry, MacWard ollav to O'Donnel in poetry and superintendent of schools, not excelled in poetry or other arts; Mac Namee rich and affluent, proficient in poetry and literature, "cursed by O'Rourke for striking the great cross;" Mulconry "by whom many books had been transcribed, poems and lays composed, of great wealth and influence, who had kept many schools, several in his own house, superintending and teaching;" Morrissey, another master of schools and general lecturer, and Donnel son of Mac Gonigle, great official in Donegal; O'Colby also a preceptor taken prisoner by the English, who would have been put to death for attachment to his own countrymen, had he not after confinement for eighteen weeks effected his escape.

Some few ladies mentioned when they died by the annalists, afford some notion of what in those days constituted the standard of feminine excellence. Graine, mother of Maguire, was noted for her bounty and generous hospitality; Mary O'Malley, wife of Mac Sweeny Fanad, best wife for a constable or soldier; Gormley, daughter of Hugh Roe O'Donnell, and wife of Hugh O'Neil, who bestowed many gifts on the orders and churches, literary men and others, which was to be expected, as she had a mother worthy of her; Evelyn, daughter of the knight of Glynn, wife of O'Conor Kerry; Catharine, daughter of Con O'Neil, whose husbands were O'Reilly and O'Rourke; Finola, daughter of Conor O'Brien, wife of Hugh Roe O'Donnel, "who had regarded body and soul, and gained more renown than any of her cotemporaries, having spent her life and wealth in acts of charity:" Rose O'Boyle, charitable and hospitable; Julia O'Fallon, "a beautiful woman," wife of Carberry; Mary MacSweeny, daughter of O'Boyle, killed by being thrown from her horse at her castle gate; Judith, daughter of Con Mor O'Neil, at the age of forty-two in 1535, wife of Manus O'Donnel, pious and devout; and in 1544, Margaret, daughter of Angus Mac Donnel of the isles, his third wife; Celia his daughter, wife of O'Boyle, and Mary Magauran, wife of MacClancy.

These names have been preserved. Many more over the land of either sex of equal claim to be remembered for culture, refinement and estimable trait might be collected to remove impressions studiously conveyed by English writers. What race, if uneducated, impoverished and trampled upon, but becomes wild and savage? Greeks and Romans became degenerate. If battles and hostings averaged three a year, more than one hundred independent sovereignties had their quarrels as larger states. Chance medleys, where injustice provoked resentment, explain in part "the one hundred and sixty-eight murders in a generation." Wherever men went armed as in Scotland, and in England down to the last century, wearing swords as part of their apparel, deaths by violence from temper or depravity of nature occurred in like proportion.

If not well lodged, Tyrconnel's abode, O'Connor's at Dengen, McCarthys' were noble piles, and the poorer clansmens as good as they could get and keep. A great nation across the channel prevented effective resistance to systematic plans of conquest, which stretched through the centuries, improving opportunity for force, or as bishop Rokeby wrote in 1520, for politic practices more efficacious, enfeebling

40

the septs "by getting away their captains and putting division between
them." Anglo nobles racked their tenants, farmers, masons and carpenters, exacting coyne and livery, foy and pay, codies and coshies,
bonaghts, myrtieght and kintroisk of beeves, blackmen and black
money, mustrons and carriages, for private purposes, bread and butter
for their dogs when they hunted, sheep and cows, when sons went to
England, daughter married or neighbor came to visit. They regra-
ted and forestalled, impeded navigation by weirs, took fee or fine for
fishing, tapped casks as they crossed the ferry; held no courts, and
mulcted whoever sought justice anywhere else. Tormented both by
feudal and brehon impositions, the lands of English yeomen were at
last left waste, and becoming themselves armed retainers they were
little better than bandits of Italy or Greece.

Convents in England were much demoralized, but no such charge
was pretended against the Irish. Under Henry, six had been founded,
five of them Franciscans, one by O'Rourke, another by O'Neil and
two by MacDonnel. Of the suppressed, three hundred of the rule
of St. Benedict or St. Augustine afforded shelter for the peaceable
or infirm, male and female; nearly two hundred of the mendicant
order, Franciscan and Carmelite, supplied preachers for the poor and
sorrowing, with whom they prayed. Seventy-two long escaped
notice. None of them were rich. Their movables realized less than
three thousand pounds instead of one hundred thousand as expected.
Stipends of less than thirteen hundred were allowed the dispossessed, of
which five hundred went to the grand prior of Jerusalem. At that
time the whole revenue of Ireland fell short of eight thousand
pounds, three-quarters of which came from crown lands. The official salaries of the pale, twenty miles square, exceeded the compensation to the orders expelled. Irish convents and English on the
island, though alike in faith and rule, had never been friendly disposed towards each other, and excluded from fellowship those of
opposite race.

No distinction was now made. All were driven forth. The mendicant orders, pious and devout, still continued their vocation. They were welcome in every cot. Gaelic was the one tongue and that they understood as well as Latin. Machiavelli wrote, the nearer to church the less christianity; there was misery enough to need divine assistance, and it could be implored with as much fervor on the hill top as kneeling at the altar. The decree of 1539 despoiled alike not only English and Irish, but those who administered to the necessities of others as well as those who subsisted on alms themselves. There was some resistance. The monks of Monaghan, Cornelius bishop of Down, a Geraldine celebrated for his pulpit eloquence, father Robert of Atheree, the prior of Limerick, were slaughtered refusing to surrender their temporalities, but for the most part resistance was seen to be useless and the superiors released to the crown as they were bid.

XXXI.

REIGN OF EDWARD VI.—1547-1553.

Henry VIII. closed his feverish life and reign January 28, 1547, two years more than a century before his gr. gr. nephew, the unfortunate Charles, expiated his arbitrary rule on the scaffold. This husband of six wives, two of whom he beheaded, left three children, Edward, Mary and Elizabeth, who each in turn succeeded and died childless. During their reigns, what remained of Irish independence virtually ended. The reformation confiscated the property set apart for religious uses, banished, tortured and hung the priests. Substitution of English titles for ancient chieftainries, surrender of land and rule and grants back on English tenure cut off collateral heirs, fomented jealousies and endless war. Capable but unscrupulous governors, St. Leger, Bellingham, Sussex, Sydney, FitzWilliams,

Grey, Perrot, Russell, Borough, Essex, Mountjoy, held successive sway as lords lieutenant, deputies or justices.   Perrot, Felton, Malby, Drury, Norris, Bingham, Clifford, Carew, were presidents of Munster, or Connaught. Bellingham, Norris, Bagnal, Essex commanded the forces, and other personages more or less famous, Morrison, Raleigh, Harvey, Norris, Randolph, and Zouch, took part in military movements. It was a stirring and interesting period. Poor Ireland was in its last throes, and it is sad to see how often she might have escaped her fate had her children been as united as they were courageous·

Edward ascended the throne at the age of nine, in gentleness and amiability a marked contrast to his father. As his reign ended in his sixteenth year, when he died of consumption, in July, 1553, he exerted little influence over events. The sixteen councillors appointed by the late king's will to administer affairs during his minority consisted of Cranmer, Southampton, St. John, Russell, Hertford, Lisle, Tonstall, Browne, Paget, Forth, Montague, Bromley, Denny, Herbert and the two Wottons, and they selected Hertford, created duke of Somerset as the president of the council, and soon after constituted him protector of the realm and guardian of his nephew. His arbitrary proceedings, unscrupulous appropriation of lands and material taken from sacred edifices he destroyed to build Somerset House, the persecution of his accomplished brother Thomas of Sudely whose death warrant he signed with his own hand, lost him favor with king and people, and Northumberland and his other enemies, depriving him a second time of power he had abused, brought him to the scaffold. Ireland was little affected by these contentions in the English council. St. Leger was continued as deputy for the first year of the reign, making way for Sir Edward Bellingham in May, 1548.

Allen, again returned, in order to supplant or displace St. Leger, alleged that under his rule the pale had been neither extended nor strengthened nor the royal writ caused to be respected beyond its limits; that the chiefs under professions of obedience had but grown more formidable. Leinster was not reformed. Ulster chiefs allowed to carry on hostilities unmolested were gradually reducing to their obedience the smaller septs in their neighborhood. Compacts were not enforced,—no roads constructed as stipulated,—their old laws and customs were retained. To which the deputy in his defence responded that the horsemen of the Cavanaghs and O'Connors were reduced to a fourth of what they were before he came, and that all the country of the O'Moores could not muster as many as rode in daily attendance on their late chief; that the O'Tooles were utterly broken, and where, when he took charge of the government, no man could travel from Cashel to Limerick without a pass, or payment of a crown for every pack, now nothing was paid, and sheriffs duly chosen executed process. An O'Toole was sheriff of Dublin, the O'Byrnes had one of their own. That it had been proposed to dispossess these septs, and likewise the Cavanaghs, but it was considered more prudent to conciliate them than raise a general ferment by their expulsion. Allen further insisted the Irish were faithless to their promises, to which St. Leger replied that the Englishmen did not keep theirs.

When the deputy resumed his office, two nephews of the late earl of Kildare harried the pale burning Rathanagan, but with fourteen other leaders they were captured and executed. Kellys and Maddens were at feud, O'Connors and O'Moores. Richard and Thomas Fitzeustace with their father viscount Baltinglas, staunch catholics, incensed at interference with their religious rights, took up arms but soon yielded to the superior force arrayed against them by the deputy. Edward Bellingham sent over with a thousand men as marshal, twice invaded Offaly and Leix, drove the inhabitants into Connaught, declaring their territory forfeited, and had the credit of being the first since Henry III. to extend the pale. These two countries were near the capital and often harried without provocation. Their soil fertile and well tilled, when their crops were destroyed and their habitations, which elicited admiration from their invaders, were burnt, retaliation naturally followed. Their neighbors of the pale who coveted their possessions easily contrived to put them in the wrong. The marshal was rewarded by knighthood, and soon after by the intrigues of the council against St. Leger, whose integrity of character and moderation thwarted their projects, appointed deputy.

Gilpatrick O'Moore and Brian O'Conor, after holding out for a twelvemonth surrendered to Sir Francis Bryan. Their surrender was on their own terms, but "it proved a poor protection." Carried to London by St. Leger they were thrown into prison. When released they were allowed annuities of one hundred pounds each, but not permitted to return home. Their confiscated dominions were parcelled out by the crown among Bryan and his kinsmen, who erecting castles at Dengen and Campo, leased the lands as of their own inheritance, driving out the inhabitants. O'Moore died before his annuity could avail him. O'Conor survived to return under Mary, from whom the intercession of his daughter Margaret and influence of her Geraldine kinsfolk obtained his release.

This confiscation without precedent in later years, for Morogh and Donogh in accepting English titles had relinquished their claim to Thomond east and south of the Shannon, inaugurated anew the policy of conquest. The right of the septs to their territories, which for the first century after the invasion had been disregarded, had since with rare exception been respected, not from any scruple but because they were too powerful to disturb. Propositions had occasionally been entertained for their extermination, but not attempted to be carried out. They had at last been persuaded to recognize the supremacy of the English monarch, and this confiscation was its first fruits. They perhaps awoke slowly to the full extent of what it portended, but their confidence in the honest intentions of English rule sustained a rude shock. It suggested to those who reflected what was to follow and justified animosities, which have ever since embittered the relations of the two races and frustrated the well meaning but inadequate measures to consolidate them into one nationality.

The deputy was prudent and active. He tore from his fireside at Kilmallock the fourteenth Desmond who would not come when summoned, and carried him to Dublin. The earl was compelled to conform his manners, apparel and behavior to his estate and degree, and down to his death in 1558 giving no further trouble, daily prayed for the good Bellingham. Notwithstanding the vigor of his administration, perhaps from not being sufficiently subservient to the schemes of the council, he made enemies and was recalled. Sir Francis Bryan, who had extensive grants in Leix and Offaly, and whose wife, widow of the ninth Ormond was daughter of the eleventh Desmond, and subsequently wife of the fifteenth, was appointed in his stead. Upon his death in 1549 at Clonmel, Brabazon succeeded, receiving the submission of O'Carrol and adjusting disputes between the earls of Desmond and Thomond about their boundary.

In the following September St. Leger came back as lord lieutenant, and to him MacCarthy made professions of amity, and Charles MacArt Cavanagh who had been proclaimed a traitor submitted, the four earls of Desmond, Tyrone, Thomond and Clanrickard, Richard, brother of the ninth Ormond, now lord Mountgarret, and lord Dunboyne, being present. Cavanagh had better have fought on, since he was stripped of most of his territory. St. Leger, accused of lukewarmness in the cause of the reformation, was replaced in May, 1551, by Sir James Crofts, who for the next two years retained the office of deputy, making way towards the close of the reign of Edward for Sir Thomas Cusack, successor of John Allen as chancellor, and Gerald Aylmer as lords justices.

O'Melaghlin, in 1548, invited Edmund Fay with an English force into Delvin. Fay sent back to Dublin one of the sept, who had accompanied him, as a hostage. Kincora and Gallen were cap-

tured, and the chief found he had brought a rod into his country to
his own hurt, for Fay banished him and his people out of Delvin,
as also Cormac MacCoghlan from his portion of the territory.
Cormac in May returned in force, with the Hy-Many, slaying among
others O'Shiel hereditary physician of the MacCoghlan, but that
chief then in alliance with Fay defeated them on the Blackwater and
there fell sons of O'Kelly, O'Fallon and MacNaghtan. Some were
drowned, the survivors beheaded, and their heads were carried to
Bailie Mac Adam, Fay's castle in Ely O'Carroll, and elevated on poles
as trophies. Fay besieged Feadan castle, and after eight days Cormac
surrendered it giving hostages and entering into gossipred with his
enemies. But soon after Cormac declining a proposal to join
Fay in a maraud against O'Carroll, war was renewed, and O'Carrol
whose kinsman Calvagh had been seized at Dublin and MacCoghlan
drove Fay out of Delvin, taking his castles of Kincora and Kilcom-
mon. He hastened for aid to the deputy, who entered Delvin and
encamped at Stonestown, but returned on the morrow with little
booty. The Irish destroyed Banagher, Moystown and Cloghan castles
of Ely and Delvin, that they might not fall into possession of the
English, who were defeated by O'Carrol losing sixty of their force.
That chief burnt Nenagh and Magh Corrain, drove the Saxons out
of the monastery of Abington in Limerick, and finally ordered them
all out of his borders except a few warders, who held the round tower
of Nenagh. Cahir Roe O'Conor captured by Burke was put to
death.

Calvagh O'Donnel inherited with the vigor and great abilities of
his race their imperious temper; and some cause of discontent with
his father Manus led in 1548 to hostilities between them. He was
defeated by Manus at Ballisofey, near the river Finn in Donegal, his
ally O'Kane being killed. That same year Shane O'Neil invaded
Clanaboy, and Brian son of Nial Oge son of Nial son of Con son
of Hugh Boy, a successful and warlike man, bountiful and hospita-

ble, the star of his tribe fell in its defence. O'Melaghlin had his house burned over his head by rival chieftains of his family, incensed at his friendly relations with the English.

Of Shane who was to take so conspicuous a place in the history of Ulster we obtained a glimpse in 1531, when the castle of his foster father O'Donnelly* was demolished by his cousin Neil Connelagh, and with horses and other spoils he himself carried off into captivity. What life he led as a youth does not appear, but it was probably in consequence of his unruly behavior that Ferdoragh was put in the patent of the earldom in his place. For so proud a spirit it must have been a sore trial to have been set aside in favor of one who had no claim whatsoever to his ancestral inheritance.

Con Baccagh, first earl of Tyrone, was now growing old, for in 1498 he had reached sufficient maturity to avenge his father's death. He was son of Con by the sister of the eighth Kildare, whose daughter Alice he had married. By her he had three sons: Shane, whom Froude, with strange inaccuracy, calls illegitimate; Phelim and Turlough, and a daughter Mary, wife of Sorley Roy, father of the first earl of Antrim. The son of Alison, wife of O'Kelly a blacksmith at Dundalk, Matthew or Ferdoragh, whom he supposed his own, from paternal partiality, he had had included in the patent as baron Dungannon. Con, when displeased with English rule, had pronounced a curse on any of his posterity who should conform to English manners or associate with the Saxon race. When disposed to correct his mistake in the preference of Ferdoragh, the deputy, it is intimated at the instigation of the latter, who took advantage of the unguarded words and courses of his father to denounce him, contrived in 1551 to

---

* Gilla O'Donnelly, chief of Feara Droma, slain at Down in battle with Sir John De Courcey in 1180, was twenty-second from Nial of the nine hostages, monarch of Ireland 406. In the sixteenth century, their chief having possessions near Dungannon commanded a following of at least two hundred men. When Shane O'Neil was killed at the banquet by MacDonnell in his tent, his foster brother Dudley O'Donnelly was there with him, defended him, and shared his fate. Members of the family in later years have gained high social position, and O'Donovan in the Four Masters says of them that they were remarkable for their manly form and symmetry of person, and that even the peasants who bore the name exhibit frequently a stature and an expression of countenance which indicate high descent.

41

gain possession of Con and his countess and to imprison them in Dublin. Shane, indignant at this treatment of his father, assisted by his brother-in-law McDonnel, commenced hostilities against Ferdoragh and Crofts, who that year had replaced St. Leger, wasting Tyrone and Dungannon over an area of sixty miles by forty.

Crofts signalized his first autumn by a hosting into Ulster, despatching a force to Rathlin which was cut off, Bagnal the only survivor of the combat being exchanged for Sorly Boy Macdonnel,* son-in-law of Tyrone. Reinforced, a second attempt resulted in the loss of two hundred men, and a third the next year in no better success. Hugh of Clanaboy defeated his vanguard at Belfast, Savage of Ards being slain. The army of Ferdoragh, hastening to join him, attacked by Shane at night in his camp were cut to pieces. In the autumn Crofts once more invaded Ulster. The chiefs not perhaps prepared to offer him effectual resistance, withdrew into their fastnesses, and all he accomplished was the destruction of a few corn-fields, amply requited by devastation of English settlements by O'Reilly.

English tenures had weakened Irish resistance more than English swords. Brothers and kinsmen were set at strife, old feuds rekindled from their smouldering ashes, and many of the Leinster septs if not engaged in internecine warfare, were in arms against each other, or their common foe. Taking advantage of some contention between Melaghlins and MacCoghlans, the English seized upon Delvin. O'Carrolls whose chief was imprisoned at Dublin were restless. He promised to be quiet and was released; but incensed at fresh injustice, allied himself with Kellys, some of the Melaghlins, Mac Coghlans and O'Connors, and Morrogh, chief of the Kavanaghs. War raged from Dublin to the Shannon. Athlone garrisoned by the English protected their movements, and the clans were finally wearied out. O'Carroll made peace for them at Limerick, being himself created baron of Ely. Instead of making common cause other

---

* Born 1505, died 1586, father of Randal first earl of Antrim.

septs were torn by internal dissensions for the chieftainship. Among
them O'Ferralls, McSweenys, O'Rourkes, O'Reillys, O'Sullivans
Beare and O'Briens were occasionally at feud.

Fire arms were gradually beginning to supersede the older weapons
of warfare, but prudence in using so explosive a material as gunpowder was not immediately learned. An instance is recorded by the
Four Masters of an accidental explosion of a keg of powder at Dunboy, which proved fatal to the chieftain himself. Dermod the thirty-
fourth from Oliol and eleventh lord of Bear and Bantry son of Donnal son Donnal, son of Dermod Balbh, each of whom in turn ruled
over the country, is described as a kind and friendly man but fierce and
dangerous to his enemies. He married a daughter of Eleanor,
and gave asylum to her nephew Gerald. Auliffe the tanist succeeded, but soon after being killed, made way for Donal, son of Dermod,
and father by Sarah, daughter of Sir Donald O'Brien of that Donal
O'Sullivan Beare, who took a leading part in the Catholic war.

Under Morogh Thomond was at peace which was greatly disturbed
when he died. Valiant in attack and formidable on the defensive,
wealthy and influential, in some respects resembling in character his
great progenitor Brian Boru, his wisdom and moderation curbed the
restiveness of his people with whom he was deservedly popular.
For a few years whilst his brother Conor still lived, the government
of the sept devolved upon him, and closely allied with Manus of
Tyrconnel and Con of Tyrone, he took the lead in arranging for the
proposed meeting at Fore in Meath in 1540, which the activity of
Brabazon the deputy caused to be abandoned. When the conviction
was reluctantly forced upon him, that national independence was no
longer to be hoped for, he submitted to what he could not avert.
He requested that he might have confirmed to him whatever had
formed part of Thomond with rule over the same, not seeking to have
this vested in his own descendants, but certainly assenting to, if not
furthering its transfer as prescribed by ancient custom after his own

life to the heir of his elder brother.   Such suppressed abbies as had
been promised, he begged might be duly conveyed to him and an abode
assigned him in the capital; and furthermore that the English law
should supersede the brehon within his borders, and "Irishmen educated at Oxford or Cambridge, not infected with the poison of the
bishop of Rome, be sent to preach the gospel."   How far this petition was his own composition is open to doubt, for he understood no
English.   It was for the most part granted, and with the earldom
the king bestowed upon him the plate of Kildare, which had been entrusted to his brother Conor by "Silken Thomas."   For the nine years
he held the earldom he proved himself a loyal subject, his people if
dissatisfied with the new settlement being forced to acquiesce in it by
the vigor of his character.

Donogh his nephew and successor had lost favor with the Dalgais,
when to use his own expression, "he married the daughter of
Ormond,* and forsook father, uncle, friend and country to do
the king service."   This disaffection gained fresh strength when upon
his succession he took out a new patent to himself and his heirs of
Thomond and the earldom, including what belonging to earl Morogh
by its limitation for life had vested in the crown.   His mother was
Anabella Burke, daughter of Clanrickard.   His brother Sir Donald,
child of a second marriage of his father with Ellice daughter of Maurice Baccagh, tenth earl of Desmond, was son-in-law of Morogh.
Donogh had assigned Ibrickan to his brother Donald, but taken it away,
and though ordered by Crofts to give him equivalents had neglected
to do so.   In the angry contention which ensued Mahon lost his life,
and also the new earl, assailed in Lent 1552 in his castle of Clonroad by his brothers.   The town was burnt but the castle held out.
Some authorities state that the earl was killed in the assault, others
that he died a natural death the Saturday following.   His son Conor,
who succeeded him as third earl, and the sons of Morogh were no bet-

---

* The ninth earl.

ter liked than himself. Dermod second baron of Inchiquin, survived his father but a year, and his son Morogh being too young to rule, Sir Donald known as Donald Mor was inaugurated chief of the Dalgais as if no surrender had been made. His troubled career to be noticed under the two next reigns ended in 1579, the year before that of his nephew Conor the third earl.*

Gerald son of the last earl of Kildare, upon his escape from Donegal with his faithful followers, Walsh and Leverous, had taken refuge in France. When Chateaubrian informed Francis I. of his arrival the king sent for him to Paris and placed him with his son. England remonstrating, he was sent to the imperial court at Brussels and thence to his kinsman, cardinal Pole at Rome, and later pursued his studies at Verona and Mantua. It was rumored in 1544 that he was in Brittany prepared to take part in an invasion of Munster by a French army. Reaching his eighteenth year the cardinal gave him his choice of study or travel, and preferring the latter, he visited Naples, and with some knights of the order of St. John to which order had belonged two of his uncles, went to Malta, serving with credit against the Turks and Moors in Barbary. Entering the service of Cosmo de Medici at Florence as master of horse he remained there three years, making the acquaintance of his Italian kinsfolk, kept up afterwards by correspondence and presents. Hunting with one of the Farnese near Rome he fell into a pit. His horse killed by the fall, he remained in this predicament three hours, when his Irish greyhound leading his companions to the place, he was rescued.

* The male line of Donogh O'Brien became extinct on the death of Henry the eighth earl in 1741. Dissuaded by the king from leaving his estates to his next male heir, the sixth viscount Clare, who commanded soon after in 1745 the Irish brigade at Fontenoy, he entailed them, already under Cromwell shorn of their grand proportions, on Morogh son of the ninth baron and fourth earl of Inchiquin, who died in the lifetime of his father without issue, with remainder over to Percy Wyndham, son of Catharine Seymour, his wife's sister and daughter of the sixth duke of Somerset by Elizabeth Percy. Young Wyndham was created earl of Thomond, and upon his death unmarried in 1774, they passed to his nephew, third earl of Egremont, and from him to his nephew, the fourth and last; upon whose decease in 1845 they went to his cousin George Wyndham lord Leconfield. The ninth baron and fifth earl of Inchiquin was created marquess of Thomond in 1800, and on the death of the third marquess in 1855, the other honors became extinct, but the barony of Inchiquin under the original limitation of 1542 devolved on Sir Lucius brother of the well known Smith O'Brien, tenth generation from Moroghs younger son Donogh of Lemenagh, three centuries having passed since the death of Morogh. The original territories of the race had nearly all long before passed away not only from the name but from the blood of the O'Briens.

After the death of Henry he ventured to London in the suite of
an ambassador, and at a masque at the palace met Mabel Browne,
step-daughter of his sister the fair Geraldine. He married her, and
Sir Anthony her brother being a favorite at court, through his influence Gerald was restored in 1552 to the estates of his father in
Ireland. Leverous and Walsh who had accompanied him into Italy
were rewarded for their devotion. Queen Mary appointed the former,
whose sermons had delighted Crofts, bishop of Kildare, the latter
bishop of Meath, but they were deprived upon the accession of Elizabeth. Cardinal Pole who had generously befriended him in his exile
died in 1558 archbishop of Canterbury. Gerald in 1554 was restored
by Queen Mary as eleventh earl of Kildare. After her death he conformed to the new religion. He was reputed the best horseman of his
day and possessed of many other gentlemanly accomplishments. He
was courteous and brave, honorable though covetous. For thirty years
that he held the earldom the part which he took in affairs was prominent and creditable alike to his good sense and rectitude of purpose.

So long as hope could be indulged that Edward would outgrow
the native delicacy of his constitution and reach to manhood, his
union with his cousin Mary queen of Scots, five years younger than
himself, offered too many advantages not to be agitated. The consolidation of the two nations under one rule would conduce to their
mutual security, prosperity and power. But differences of faith were
insuperable obstacles and the Scotch regency objected to the match.
The handsome queen educated in France wedded in 1558 Francis
II., who died in less than two years afterwards. Disappointment at
the rejection of the proposal to marry her to Edward led to animosities
ending in war with Scotland, in which some of the O'Conors with a
brigade of kernes from Leinster were employed.

France taking part with Scotland improved the known disaffection
of the catholic chieftains. Henry II. despatched Forquevaux who had
won laurels in war, with Monthue his prothonatary, to Ulster by the

way of Scotland to negotiate. From Dunbarton where they met
Paris and Fitzgerald with one of the O'Moores on a similar errand
to the O'Byrnes and O'Carrols of Leinster, they proceeded to Lough
Foyle, which they reached according to Mageoghan in February
1553, but three years earlier according to Wright. At Culmor fort,
a large square stone tower in charge of the son of O'Dogherty a dependent of O'Donnel, Waucop the blind bishop of Armagh visited
them, and at Donegal, Tyrone and Tyrconnel "for themselves and
their brother chieftains promised to place their lives, fortunes and
possessions under protection of France, so that whoever was king of
France should be king of Ireland." Peace between the belligerents
rendered the compact of no avail, and moreover betrayed it to the
English government.

Confiscation of religious houses went on. Catholics intimidated
under Henry by the pilgrimage of grace and other measures as stern,
not to sacrifice or endanger their property, conformed. Small stipends saved the dispersed orders from actual destitution, but thousands of the aged and infirm had depended on conventual alms.
Poor laws of savage ferocity, punished poverty as a crime. Within
the fold men were not of one mind. Ingenuity exhausted all possible
shades of dogma, and the spirit of controversy created discord, which
knowing no moderation grew bitter and vindictive. The protector inclined to Zwingle, apostles of other opinions fond of display, contention and power swarmed from the continent stirring up strife. Under
Edward there was little actual persecution in either land unto death.
Cranmer of Lutheran tendencies instigated the burning for heresy of
Joan Bocher a crazy fanatic, a moral mistake expiated by his own
similar fate under Mary.

When his prayer book, much of it translated from the missal, was
forced upon Ireland and read in the cathedrals at Dublin, masses were
being chanted at the altars in the chapels. Its adoption was not
unopposed. Dowdal, who in 1543 at the suggestion of St. Leger,

had succeeded Cromer in Armagh, at a conference in the hall of St. Mary's abbey proposed with a view to harmony by Crofts the deputy, urged the impropriety of forcing upon an unwilling people prayers, which even the English race could not understand. The new liturgy was introduced on Easter Sunday, 1551, at Christ Church, and the six articles of Henry being repealed, the forty-two articles now reduced to thirty-nine were constituted the rule of faith. Penalties for non-compliance were not at first pressed with rigor, the court contenting itself with divesting Armagh of the primacy of all Ireland in favor of Dublin.

Brown the new primate was not of very exemplary character. Bale of Ossory, testy and crapulous, pronounced him "slack in things pertaining to God's glory, an epicurious archbishop, brockish swine and dissembling proselite." Browne accused Staples of Meath, who had defended the new liturgy at the conference, of "preaching so that the three mouthed Cerberus of hell could not have uttered it more viperously." Titular bishops, nominated at Rome, contested the several sees with those appointed by the crown. The blind jesuit Waucop claimed Armagh from which Dowdal although catholic had felt forced to flee. The garrison of Athlone despoiled Clonmacnois and other shrines of bell, book and candle, carrying off relic, plate and painted glass. Suppressed abbies bestowed from favor or from motives of policy were passing into hands of laymen, but persecution in Ireland under Edward did not slay priests at the altar or hang friars for intimidation, as chanced when his father was king.

John Bale, whose literary accomplishments had placed him in charge of the education of Edward, had cause to rue his elevation from a country living at Bishopstoke in Hampshire to the vacant see of Ossory. Reaching Dublin early in 1553, he refused to be consecrated by the catholic rite as proposed by Brown and Lockwood, the dean of St. Patrick, that he might be more acceptable to his diocese, and stayed the office until bread replaced the wafer on the table.

Twelve discourses at St. Canace incensed his clergy, and after Easter
he withdrew to Holmes Court his episcopal residence, a few miles out of
Kilkenny.   On the twenty-fifth of July, popular rejoicings announced
the death of Edward on the sixth, and Jane Grey was proclaimed in
that city as at Dublin.   Bale in his "vocation," an interesting account of his experiences, says the chiefs proposed to drive out the
English and proclaim a king of their own, but were better content when
some weeks later they learned that Mary was enthroned.   Catholic
services went on in the cathedral whilst he occupied the pulpit, but he
caused "the comedy of John the baptist" and "tragedy of Gods promises," miracle plays and compositions of his own, to be performed.
The resentment of clergy and laity, including the lords Mountgarret and Upper Ossory, menaced his safety ; and after five of his
servants had been killed and his horses driven off, the mayor and
four hundred men volunteering as his escort, he took shelter in Kilkenny for a few days, and then proceeded to Leighlin castle and
from thence to Dublin.   Captured by a Flemish ship when he left the
country for Scotland, he repaired when released to Geneva, and there
remained so long as Mary was queen.

In May, 1553, chancellor Cusack in a report home on the state of
the country says that Desmond, Roche, Barry, Fitzmaurice and
many more, in commission as justices of the peace, held sessions and
decided causes.   MacCarthy Mor, brother-in-law of Desmond and
"the most powerful Irishman in Ireland" in 1556,* to be created earl
of Clancarre, conformed to order.   Garrisons at Leighlin, Fernes
and Enniscorthy held under due restraint the Kavanaghs of Leinster ;
O'Byrnes with eighty horse and as many foot obeyed the deputy.
Thomond was at peace as were MacWilliams, Mac-I-brien-ara, and
Mulryans of Limerick or Tipperary, Kennedys, O'Briens of Coonagh,
O'Dwyres and Carrols.   The chancellor states that he had brought
to terms Richard the young earl, and Ulick the captain of Clanrick-

* Extinct Peerages, other authorities say 1566.

42

ard, which wasted by their contentions was again under tillage, and
cattle and plough might be left safe in the field. O'Kelly paid cess
for a hundred galloglasses, fourpence a day for each. Between Athlone and Offaly, O'Byrnes, MacCoghlans, Fox, Molloys and
Mageoghans made restitution of three hundred pounds for preys
taken of their neighbors; O'Reilly with his seven sons commanding
four hundred horse, two hundred galloglasses and a thousand kerne,
four hundred. Tyrone, sixty miles by twenty-four, three years before well inhabited, lay desolate from the rivalries of Shane and Ferdoragh. A garrison at Armagh, where stood "the best church in
Ireland," prevented marauds, and earl Con and his countess being
prisoners in Dublin, Ferdoragh curbed the restiveness of Tir-Owen.

In the opinion of Cusack the honors bestowed and late visits
to court of the chieftains had worked well, and if Leix and Offaly were
divided into counties and granted in fee farm, the rest of the island
reduced to shire ground, lands held of the crown, presidents appointed
in Connaught, Munster and Ulster, preachers sent over to inculcate
obedience to God and the king, affairs would stand better still.
Preaching there was none, without which the ignorant could have no
knowledge, but Irishmen had never been so weak or English subjects
so strong. His suggestions were put to the test. They effected their
object so far as concerned the English interest. The rightful owners
of the soil were crushed beneath its iron heel and driven out to perish,
and another historical crime of Christendom was perpetrated.

This is a sad accusation but not to be denied or extenuated. Might
does not make right. O'Conors and Moores had manifested a disposition to be peaceable subjects if left unmolested. Their territory
they had held for a thousand years. Their own annals and English
authorities afford abundant proof that they cultivated the arts of
peace and civilization. Their chiefs were allied with Graces and
Geraldines. Meath paid O'Conors five hundred pounds for protection from more distant septs, Kildare twenty. When their

annual payment stipulated by government was withheld. Delvin the
deputy became their prisoner. In 1537, not disposed to yield to a
demand made upon them for eight hundred cows, their principal castle
of Dengen was demolished. Grey repenting of "their cruel and
extreme handling" in a personal interview engaged that their rights
should be respected. Their possessions had been included in the
forfeitures of Kildare without pretension to justice : grants were made
of them in 1540; they resented it, capturing and destroying
castle Jordan in reprisal for Dengen. Barringtons, Houndens and
other adventurers were put in possession of Leix and Offaly by
Bellingham and his army of forty-five hundred men, and forts were
commenced for their security. Driven to desperation, resistance was
reasonable enough, but to little purpose.

The chiefs surrendered on their own terms, but these were disregarded and no mercy was shown. Their expulsion, an error
alike in morals and politics, engendered antagonisms, and arrested
the progress, already considerable, of fusion between the races, which
working down from castle to cot, would in time have rendered the
people, forced by geographical conditions into one nationality, homogeneous. If not all of the same religious opinions no rancor for
wrong would have kept them asunder, or prevented their gradually
drawing closer to common standards of faith and practice.

Whether it was that the church had proved domineering or exercised too faithful a sway over men's consciences, neither its spoliation
nor the act of supremacy had much affected the growing disposition
towards consolidation. The country would have been in excellent
condition to maintain her independence if united, but that was no
longer to be hoped. If consolidation signified protection from earls
and petty satraps, whose delight seemed in havoc and destruction
without other idea of government than to use it to their own advantage, the chiefs showed their wisdom in giving in allegiance to the
crown. But it was still an inexcusable blunder, after experience of

such perfidy and outrage, to repose confidence where it had been ever disappointed. Up to this time the country had been overrun, but neither subjected nor conquered. If now her clans could have treated in arms as often in their power, and secured terms of union, guaranteeing rights and liberties, their moral position would have been stronger in the subsequent conjunctures. Deceived by their own honesty of purpose and professions made to them, they took for granted that in becoming British subjects they would enjoy equal rights. Too late, when helplessly enthralled, they found themselves mocked. England not only withheld these rights, but exercised over them the power of a conqueror, not as regulated by public opinion and the law of nations, but a tyranny grinding and merciless and wholly unparalleled.

From what actually took place must be inferred a compact. If the people through their chieftains by general acquiescence consented to consolidation, it was conditioned on the extension to them of all privileges vouchsafed by the crown to their fellow subjects. Among them were the undisturbed enjoyment of vested right to land and property, of their peculiar local customs and institutions, representation in making laws and levying taxes, fair distribution of official preferment, and all such immunities and safeguards by charter or statute as formed integral part of the national constitution. Liberty of conscience in faith and worship, according to preference or conviction, was of course qualified by the prevailing insanities of the age, but the reformation was too recent for the bigoted intolerance and sanguinary persecutions of its later stages to be anticipated. How far these obligations on the part of England were sacredly regarded, or Ireland absolved by their violation from her allegiance, depends upon subsequent events, and for any just or reasonable conclusion as to present claims of reparation, or to what has been right or wrong in the past, they must be subjected to careful scrutiny.

If wanton destruction of life and property, eviction of whole

clans from their inheritance, were simply retaliation for outrages
warranting reprisal against nation or sept, if transfer of the soil from
one race to the other proceeded from superior wisdom and industry
in one, vice and improvidence in the other, however much to be de-
plored, the result accorded with natural laws and was not to be
controlled. But if brought about by arbitrary acts and systematic
plunder of the least powerful, it was an infringement of the terms
on which the compact was made. No lapse of time can remove the
reproach or limit the claim to redress, so long as the consequences
are still felt. That both government and influential classes of
English subjects, by such laws and spoliation, by superior military
force, did defraud and deprive the Irish of their birthright is generally
admitted, and indeed is too plainly written over all the pages of their
history to be questioned by impartiality or candor.

XXXII.

REIGN OF MARY.—1553-1558.

Nearest to the throne of England stood four daughters of the
house of Tudor. Mary and Elizabeth excluded by act of parliament, Mary of Scots objectionable on other grounds, the dying
monarch, in the interest of the reformation, named by will to the
succession, Jane Grey, grand niece of his father, under the persuasion of Northumberland, whose son Guilford Dudley she had
married. She was proclaimed; and the duke gathered a force of
ten thousand men to support her pretensions, which were received
with little fervor or favor. Convinced of his mistake he strove to
retrieve it by joining at Cambridge in the acclaim for Mary. This
proved of little avail. Before another month was over, he was beheaded on Tower Hill, the estimable victim of his ambition lady
Jane, her husband and others sharing his fate. Hastening to the

tower soon after her accession, the queen set at liberty the aged
Norfolk, Somerset, Courtney and Gardiner, the former of whom had
been incarcerated since her father's death, which alone had saved him
from the block.

Cranmer, deposed from the see of Canterbury, which he had held
for twenty years, was reserved for a more cruel death. His eminent
abilities were clouded by traits of character, by practices and policy,
not to be commended; and his life became him less than its close.
He first attracted Henry's notice by advocating the divorce, and helped
to relieve him of Ann Boleyn when she ceased to please. His religious
views were modified by expediency, and he possessed little natural
aptitude for the role of martyr which he was forced to assume.
In 1539, he urged the passage of the bloody act of the six articles,
and subsequently prosecuted those who obeyed it. In the late
reign though of avowed Lutheran tendencies, they became Zwin-
glian whilst Somerset was in the ascendant; and the thirty-nine
articles drawn up under his direction, curiously exemplified his controlling principle of being all things to all men, in reconciling the
various points of controversial belief. That he should have participated in the religious spoils accorded with the spirit of the times.
In his recantation with the hope of saving his life, he evinced less
firmness than Sir Thomas More or lady Jane Grey, but when the
fagots were ablaze about him at Cambridge in 1556, he made a
noble end.

Goodacre of Armagh was dead, Bale says poisoned by the priests.
Dowdal resumed his archepiscopate, restoring the catholic faith at
his synod in Drogheda. Brown of Dublin, Lancaster of Kildare,
Travers of Leighlin, Staples of Meath were deposed; Bale of Ossory
and Casey of Limerick had fled, and their places were respectively
filled by Curwin, Leverous, O'Fihely, Walsh, Thonery and Lacy,
whilst Rowland Bacon or Fitzgerald continued archbishop of Cashel.
The queen was disposed to be tolerant. She soon renounced all

pretension to religious supremacy. The English parliament, first insisting that church confiscations granted to laymen should not be
disturbed, repealed the laws against papal jurisdiction. Ireland
with slight exception catholic welcomed the restoration of the ancient
rule and rite. There was no occasion for persecution, as the people
were all of one mind; and the priests simply resumed their functions.

Grants made by Brown to his children were later avoided, but no
effort was made to divest others of church property. Although catholic rites were again established and the pope to be supreme in matters
ecclesiastical, he was given to understand* that he was not to interfere with the church spoliations, that title to land was grounded only
upon the laws and customs of the realm and could only be impleaded
in the queen's courts; and that all persons having the site of the
late monasteries or other religious places should keep and enjoy the
same according to the interest or estate they held by existing laws.
Bulls and decrees would be received, if not containing matter contrary or prejudicial to the authority, dignity or preëminence royal
and imperial of the realm. The queen appointed the bishops and
distributed with lavish hand church sequestrations when no disposition of them had already been made. Grants passed from the crown
of tithes to Sir John Travers, at Leix to Matthew King, of Fucul-
len to Brian O'Toole, of the farm of Swords to Brewerton, of St.
Catherines and Mothill in Waterford to Patrick Sherlock; of St.
Johns near Kells, St. Mary's near Drogheda, rectories of Rathayne,
Rathryan and Athsie and parsonage of Sidon; and later in the
reign of the monasteries of St. Mary in Urso, Athassel and Gran-
ard, Abbeys of Jerpont, Callan, and Tulliophilen, houses of
Augustines and Carmelites and hospital of St. Lawrence at Drogheda. The restoration of the priory of St. John of Jerusalem at
Kilmainham, of which Owen Massingberd was appointed prior at
the instance of Pole, may be ascribed to the frequent residence there

* By the act 3 and 4 Philip and Mary, chapter 8.

of the deputies, for whom it afforded from its military and ecclesiastical character combined a safe and convenient abode.

Beyond legislative permission to grant land for twenty years in mortmain, little provision was made for restoration of parochial churches or construction of new, for the support of the secular clergy or religious instruction of the people. Yet whilst Latimer and Ridley "were lighting such a candle in England as they trusted in God's grace would never be put out," and were soon followed to the stake by Cranmer and throngs of other martyrs to the new learning, persecution for heresy found few advocates in the pale, where protestant opinions predominated.

Toleration ruled, and it is even said that thirty thousand English protestants sought refuge in the island from persecution and privately worshipped undisturbed. Harvey, Ellis, Edmunds, Haugh and other respectable families from Cheshire with Jones their pastor, settled in Dublin. Towards the close of the reign, Cole, dean of St. Paul's, sent over to institute prosecutions for heresy, exhibited his commission at Chester on his way, to his hostess. To save her friends she substituted for it, whilst he was sleeping, a pack of cards, which, after explaining to the Irish council with much solemnity the object of his mission, to his confusion and their amusement he drew out from his packet and displayed in its stead.

Charles the fifth, tormented by gout and tired of power and grandeur, not pleased that protestants should have recognized rights within his imperial borders, was about to withdraw from the throne to the cloister. Ambition for his children still retained a hold, and Mary had been but six months queen when Egmond and Montmorency appeared at the English court to solicit her hand for his eldest son, Philip, then at the age of twenty-seven, she being ten years older. In July, 1554, they were married. Charles, two years afterwards, bestowed upon Philip the throne of Spain, living on as much longer himself, when fatigue at rehearsing his own obsequies accelerated his dissolution. Soon after the marriage cardinal Pole, esteemed for his many virtues, arrived as legate from Julius the Third, and more vigorous measures were adopted for the restoration of catholicism. Ambassadors proceeded to Rome, and after some hesitation as to their reception, since Mary had without papal permission assumed the title of queen of Ireland. Paul then pontiff, to assert his prerogative, in 1555, issued his bull constituting the island a kingdom.

St. Leger, for the sixth and last time deputy, received in November 1553 the sword of state from Cusack and Aylmer, who had shown their zeal by suppressing in Louth a rising of the O'Neils and defeating in Offaly Donogh son of Brian O'Conor. From his long experience in Irish administration and friendly relations with the chiefs, his appointment encouraged hopes of a policy moderate, efficient and conciliatory. The queen was disposed to reduce her force in the island to five hundred men. Such was the state of affairs that this could be but partially accomplished, six hundred foot and four hundred horse being retained.

O'Melaghlin, from some displeasure not explained, had slain at Ballina his tanist Nial "warlike and experienced, the best of his tribe," when returning home from court at Mullingar. Nugent, baron Delvin, with English troops from Athlone expelled the chief, taking possession of Clonlonan his principal castle. The baron then wasted Dealna, and soon after joined Gerald of Kildare in a raid into Ulster to help Shane his kinsman against Felim Roe son of Hugh. Kildare exacted from the MacCoghlans an eric of three hundred and forty cows for his foster brother Robert Nugent, who had been killed by Art, son of Cormac, the death of which Cormac heir to Dealna is recorded the same year. Charles Kavanagh, whose wife Alice was sister of Gerald, sharing with him the royal favor became baron Balyan, but died in 1554.

Gerald, restored by Mary to the remainder of his paternal inheritance and to the earldom of Kildare, had returned with his brother Edward

43

to Ireland, and with him came Thomas Duv, tenth earl of Ormond, who but fourteen years of age when his father was poisoned in 1546, was still quite young. They had taken an active part in the elevation of Mary to the throne, and in the suppression of the rising of Wyat. With them also came Brian son of Fitzpatrick, lord of Upper Ossory, the accomplished friend of the late king. Ormond, upon his return was employed against the chief of Thomond, Kildare against O'Neil of Clanaboy, Con being engaged in war with that branch of his name, Donald O'Brien with the Burkes of Clanrickard. Tyrone was defeated, losing three hundred men. Sir Donald, when chosen to the chieftainry upon the death of his brother Donogh, after driving the earl of Clanrickard from the castle of Benmore, had made his hosting into Ely, taking hostages from O'Carrol. He then proceeded into Leinster and held a conference with the English at Campa in Leix, parting friends.

In a war of the MacCoghlans with O'Molloy a peasant slew three warders of Clonony, seizing that castle, and in another with the Clancolman the castle of Rachra was demolished. This same year sanguinary conflicts at Kinsellagh in Donegal took place between the clan Sweeny of the Tuathas and another sept of the name. Sir Donald O'Brien besieged the earl Conor in his castle of Doon in Bunratty in Clare, but was driven off by Ormond. The next week he invaded Clanrickard, the disaffected kinsmen of that earl attending him into Galway and receiving from him fosterage and wages. Two years afterwards he marched to meet the deputy in Hy Regan, again making peace for all the Dalgais.

Hugh O'Madden, chief of Sil Anmachadha or Longford, was succeeded by John slain by Breasil, when two chiefs divided the sept. Brian O'Connor, who, after his release from durance in London, had been detained in Dublin as too dangerous to be at large, in 1555 regained his freedom, to fall in an attempt to recover the rule of his sept from his son Donogh.

Calvagh O'Donnel, again at feud with his father, in 1555 repaired to Scotland for aid, and returning with a force under Archibald Campbell, and with the gonna cam or "crooked gun," battered down the castles of Eanach and Inishowen. At Rosreagh he took Manus prisoner and kept him captive while he lived. Two years later Shane O'Neil with Hugh O'Donnel son of Manus, marched a large army into Tirconnell. "Their spacious and hero thronged camp" was first pitched at Carricleith between the rivers Finn and Mourne. They passed their time pleasantly in buying and selling mead, wine and rich clothing. When Shane received information that the Kinel Connel had betaken themselves with their horses and herds to the fastnesses of the country, he declared he would pursue them into Leinster or Munster till they submitted to his authority, and there should be but one king in Ulster for the future. Calvagh consulting his father, a cripple from age and infirmity, and then residing at the castle of Lifford, as to what course to pursue, Manus advised him not to attack Shane in the open field, but strive to take him unawares in his camp.

The Kinel Owen marched on with all expedition across the Finn to Balleaghan, where they constructed their booths and tents. Calvagh, near by, with his son Con and a small force of MacSweenys and Maguires on the hill of Binnion, despatched two trusty men to reconnoitre. Gaining the hostile encampment and not being recognized, as the army was numerous and variously composed, they went from one camp fire to another till they reached Shane's tent. A huge torch thicker than a man's body was flaming near the fire, and sixty grim galloglasses armed with sharp battle axes, and as many stern looking Scots with broad and massive swords were on guard. When the time came for the troops to take their repast and food was distributed, the spies held out their helmets with the rest for their share of meal and butter, and then took their departure unobserved for their own camp.

Calvagh, after hearing their report, immediately ordered his men to arms, and his son Con giving him his own horse, they made a fierce onslaught upon their enemies. "Both sides proceeded to kill, hack and mangle one another with their polished sharp axes and well tempered, keen edged, hero befitting swords, so that many warriors were wounded and disabled." When Shane heard the noise of the heavy troops and clamor of the bands, he passed through the western end of his tent unobserved. The night was rainy, heavy showers followed by silent dripping, and rivers and streams were flooded. His army after desperate resistance were defeated with great havoc. Shane with two of Hugh O'Donnel's men and Felim O'Gallagher swam the Deal, Finn and Derg, and borrowing a horse of Mongan erenagh of church in Omagh he at last reached Clogha in Tyrone. The Kinel Connel passed the night feasting and carousing, quaffing the wines of their defeated foes. Con had for his share of the spoil eighty horses, besides Shane's own steed called Mac-an-iolair, son of the eagle. Arms and coats of mail and costly apparel were found in the camp in great abundance, and scarcely so much booty had been obtained when Hugh Oge, in 1522, vanquished O'Neil at Knocavoe.

His forces utterly routed Shane lost popularity with his sept whilst Ferdoragh gained. Jealous of his rival, in 1558, Shane it is said being himself actually present, three of his foster brothers, the Donnellys, raised hue and cry near by the castle where Dungannon was passing the night, who sallying forth at the clamor was slain. The earl of Tyrone, not displeased at the event, for he had been imprisoned at Dublin in 1553 at the instance of Ferdoragh, restored Shane to favor, put him in positions of trust, and when he died the year after the death of Mary, Shane found little difficulty in obtaining from the Kinel Owen the chieftainry.

St. Leger was too independent to please either the magnates of the pale or the ghostly advisers of the queen for any length of time. If paying some outward observance to the ruling faith, he was well

known as indifferent if not a scoffer, and verses of his composition
irreverent of the eucharist had transpired. For this and other causes
he had been again, and for the last time, summoned home. Thomas
Ratcliffe, viscount Fitzwalter, at the age of thirty, "brave and constant," and "who hated the gypsey Leicester," appointed lord lieutenant, received in the spring of 1556 the insignia of office from his
predecessor. With him came his brother-in-law, also Dudley's, Sir
Henry Sydney, who for the next twenty years took a leading part
in Irish administration. Desmond held the post of treasurer for life,
and Sydney was appointed treasurer for the war. They brought
over twenty-five thousand pounds for use in military movements.
No time was lost. The Kinsellgh raided the pale. Seven score of
their troopers, driven into Powerscourt, surrendered to Stanley and
were half of them hung.

Parliament in June, 1556, convened at Dublin for the first time
since 1542. Chancellor Cusack read to the assembly on their knees,
a bull from Pole the legate extending full absolution for the past,
confirming disposition of benefices, marriages, dispensations and
land grants during the schism, and enjoining the restoration of
glebes and repeal of all laws against papal supremacy. This was
followed by a Te Deum in the cathedral and other thanksgiving for
reunion with Rome. Acts passed declaring the queen born in lawful wedlock, punishing treason and heresy, repealing all acts against
the holy see since 1529, reëstablishing the papal authority, discharg-
ing the payment of first fruits to the crown, restoring the rectories
and other church property, reserving only lands granted to the laity.
A subsidy of thirteen and four-pence for every ploughland was
granted to drive out the Scots. It was constituted high treason to
invite them into Ireland, and felony to intermarry with them without
license from the deputy. Leix with Upper Ossory, a portion of Offaly
west of the Barrow, Portnahinch belonging to O'Dunn, Tinnahinch
to O'Dempsey, was made Queen's County, with Maryborough for

its shiretown ; Offaly, east and west, belonged to Kildare; but Ely and Delvin and other portions of the O'Connor territory, Geashill, Warrenstown and Coolistown, with upper and lower Phillipstown, or Dengen for its shire town, into Kings. Power was given the deputy to make grants with such reservation of rent as he judged expedient. A commission was authorized to view other waste parts of the island, to reduce them into counties and hundreds. Poynings law as then amended, so that after parliament met new measures approved by the crown could be introduced, remained unchanged down to the union in 1800.

The October before William Fitzwilliam, John Allen and Valentine Browne had been sent over as commissioners of crown lands, and grants were soon made of the new counties. Donogh O'Conor now chief of Offaly and Connal O'Moore, indignant at the confiscation of their domains and dominions, flew to arms. Arrested they were released upon the interposition of Kildare and Ormond, but soon after again captured O'Moore with MacMorrogh his ally and several O'Connors were executed at Leighlin. MacCoghlan in Kings and O'Maddens from Connaught took Fadden; but driven out, and posted at Meelick, the deputy, with cannon boated down the Shannon from Athlone, forced them to give hostages and garrisoned the place. He then attacked the O'Conors and O'Moores, O'Carrols and Mulloys and in the forests of Fircal in Kings and vanquished them, O'Carrol owing his escape to the speed of his horse.

Scots from the Hebrides attacked Clanaboy, killing Hugh O'Neil its lord, whereupon the English, to weaken the sept, divided the country between two chiefs, Phelim Duv and Baccagh. Fitzwalter soon after his arrival vanquished the Scots at Carickfergus, the young Ormond and Stanley, lord marshal, gaining distinction in the fight. After visiting Munster and receiving submission from MacCarthy and other chieftains, and in September making peace with Shane O'Neil, and the O'Conors at Dengen, he devastated in October the country about Dundalk, Newry and Armagh. Called to England in 1557 he first took hostages from O'Carrol, O'Molloy, Mageoghan, Dunn, MacCoghlan and the two O'Maddens of Silanchie.

During his absence Sydney with Curwin the archbishop assumed charge of affairs. As soon as the mass which prepared them for their duty was over, Sydney marched again into Fircal against Arthur O'Molloy, and giving him neither rest nor peace drove him into exile, setting up his brother Theobald in his place. Again war raged from the Shannon to Dublin and Cork. O'Carrol took Leap, but soon again sought safety in flight.

In April, 1558, O'Reilly, Hugh son of Maelmora and Margaret daughter of Hugh Duv O'Donnel, lord of East Brefny or Cavan, visited the deputy at Kilmainham and entered into an agreement not to harbor O'Moore or O'Connor, but to keep the peace. It was farther stipulated that English money should be received within his possessions at its due value. In 1567 Hugh entered into another agreement of similar import. His death and that of his wife Isabella Barnwall are mentioned as taking place in 1583, when Cavan was divided among four descendants of his father Maelmora. His son John was knighted, but the statement of Moore, that he himself was created in 1560 baron of Cavan and earl of Brenny as promised by Henry VIII., would appear to be an error. Edmund was chosen chieftain in 1598 after the death of John. Shane O'Neil also that year went to Kilmainham for a friendly conference. Donogh O'Conor submitted at Dengen, but he soon after was again driven into hostilities, and in 1558 his death at the hands of O'Dempsy " left the Hy-Faly feeble, the Barrow and all Leinster in grief."

Returning with reinforcements in April, 1558, Fitzwalter, now earl of Sussex by the death of his father, marched to the relief of Conor earl of Thomond, then at war with his uncle Donald, taking Clonroad, Bunratty and Clare from the latter, whom he banished, and established the earl in his place, "greatly to the consternation of Banba,* and grief of the descendants of Con, of Cathoir, of Ith and Ir, of Heremon and Heber."

Proceeding to Limerick, he stood sponsor to James Sussex, infant son of Desmond by Honora daughter of MacCarthy Mor. To the child he presented a chain of gold, and to Dermod, lord of Muskerry, gilded spurs with the honor of knighthood. Desmond not long surviving this festal occasion was much lamented, for whilst he lived need had been none to watch cattle or close door from Dunquin by the western sea to where Suir, Nore and Barrow mingled their waters. It was not he but his brother Maurice that killed the court page, to whose taking off he owed his elevation. Known in his earlier years by the English as the traitor earl, he had been since generally peaceable and kept to the last the treasurership of the island. He had repudiated his first wife Joan Roche, on the score of consanguinity, bestowing on Thomas Ruagh his son by her, Killnataloon and Castlemore, whilst his second son Gerald by Mora O'Carrol succeeded as fifteenth earl to forfeit twenty-five years later life and land.

In September the lord lieutenant left Dublin by sea for the north, encountering a severe gale on the coast. He drove off the Scots from Rachlin and then laid waste Cantyre and Arran, the Scotch territories of the MacDonnels, and on his way back harried their settlements in Ulster. Two of their captains Donald Campbell and Dowell MacAllen had been in the service of Calvagh of Tirconnell, and for fame and booty had invaded Connaught. Marching through Carbury, Tireril, Gailenga and Tirawley, Mac William oughter of Mayo joined them. When Richard second earl of Clanrickard heard of their approach he gathered an army, clad for the most part in mail and supplied with ordnance, and drove them into the Moy. Both Donal and Dowell fell in the battle, " which was a loss as their ransom would have been great." The power of the Scots in the land was greatly reduced by this disaster to their arms.

* An ancient name of Ireland.

Reference has already been made to two defeats sustained by William O'Carroll from the English at Kincorea. Teigue his elder brother, created in 1551 baron of Ely, had lost his life in contention with his cousin Calvagh son of Donogh for the chieftainship, and William had avenged his death. Their mother, daughter of the ninth Kildare, was sister of the existing earl. William had recovered the family castle of Leap, and rule over Ely, but was not permitted in peace to possess them, and at Kincorea in 1558 barely effected his escape. "Many youths and warriors were there slain, and among them Morogh MacSweeny of Banagh, constable of the Dalgais, an office different members of that warlike race held under various chieftains, not only in Ulster but in other portions of the island. The next year making a captain's expedition against Mac-I-brian-ara*, O'Carrol devastated his country from Ballina to Arderony, slaying his brother Morogh. The chief of Ara retaliated, but all his fighting men were cut off including Heremon MacSweeney his constable, and he himself taken prisoner was held to ransom. William† later making his peace with the English, was knighted and acknowledged captain of his country by Sydney in 1561, but that position was his for a quarter of a century, and transmitted by him to his natural son Calvagh.

Whatever sanguine expectations chief or sept had early indulged that a queen of their own faith would respect their rights and promote their welfare, were speedily and rudely dispelled. Mary, engrossed in affairs at home, by foreign war or diplomacy, could hardly be held responsible for Irish administration. Her only idea was to increase her revenues, expel the Scots and plague the rebels. The government had little changed in its objects or policy, and the Irish were more harshly and unjustly treated than ever. Even

---

* Turlogh, son of Murtogh son of Donnel, son of Turlogh, son of Murrogh na raithnigne.

† Vide page 242. His grandson Roger was deprived by Cromwell, but his son Charles received from James II. sixty thousand acres in Maryland; his grandson Charles of Carrolton 1737–1832 was the signer of the declaration of American independence, and grandfather of Lady Wellesley and dutchess of Leeds—his brother John first catholic bishop of Baltimore; and a scion of this ancient stock is the present governor of Maryland.

44

Sussex in bad company fell into evil courses. In October, 1557, on a visit to Louth and the Plunkets he sent out troops from Dundalk to gather a prey from Shane O'Neil. He encamped in the cathedral of Armagh, which with three other churches as well as the town itself were plundered and burnt. The burning was probably accidental and the loot went to his men. But when after fruitless search for an enemy they had gathered in the flocks and herds and were on their way home, he divided the spoil with the rest.

The wretched queen, gloomy in temperament and with more fear than faith in her religion, afflicted by a complication of disorders, heart broken at the desertion of her husband, mourning over the loss of Calais, the gates of France, as a personal bereavement, and visited probably by some compunction for the victims of an intolerance, which had defeated its object, lingered along to her forty second year. Death, on the seventeenth of November, 1558, came to her relief. Her cousin and father-in-law, the great emperor, Charles the fifth, had preceded her to the tomb but a few weeks; Pole died the following day. The earthly career of Stephen Gardiner, bishop of Winchester, who had also guided her policy and directed her conscience the first two years of her reign, closed in November, 1555, just one month after Latimer and Ridley perished at the stake. Narrow-minded and bigoted, "bloody Mary" obeyed her own sense of right in her cruelties, nor are these to be ascribed so much to Pole, whose character was mild and amiable, as to her husband, Philip of Spain. To that husband, called by protestants " the demon of the south," notwithstanding his unfeigned indifference, she clung with all a woman's fondness. She wasted the national treasure in his wars, pledging to please him her own credit and that of England for two hundred thousand marks. At his dictation the axe and stake desolated the homes of her people, to whom the catholic faith as represented by him became abhorrent.

The cardinal exerted what influence he might to stay her sanguinary proceedings. But accused by the pope of screening schismatics he was forced to be prudent, which his family experiences also counselled. His brother Henry in 1539, on suspicion of furthering his own preferment to the throne, his excellent mother Margaret of Salisbury in 1541 at the age of seventy for no other fault than that of being the last Plantagenet, her brother Edward in 1499 for no better reason, had all been beheaded on Tower Hill; whilst his grandfather George of Clarence in 1477 had been drowned by his brother Edward IV. in the butt of malmsey. His own death was timely. Had he survived and remained in England, popular clamor would have demanded his death as amends for that of his predecessor Cranmer; had he escaped, Rome would have afforded him no safe asylum.

XXXIII.

REIGN OF ELIZABETH.—1558–1602.

Contention for the crown and natural desire to keep it had proved as fatal to the royal families of England, as for Irish chieftainships to the roydamnas. Elizabeth, when in her twenty-fifth year she crossed the threshold of her long and brilliant reign, stood in the world peculiarly alone. She had few intimates, fewer kinsfolk. She was almost the solitary survivor of Tudor and Plantagenet. Henry Carey and his sister, lady Knollys, were her first cousins, the Howards more remote; whilst Mary of Scots, who alone disputed her right, as a catholic and dauphiness of France, though her nearest paternal relative, was more of kin than kind. Adversity and the exigencies of her position had made her wary, and her duplicity, the most conspicuous trait of her character, grew out of the instinct of self preservation. Her brother-in-law, Philip of Spain, long indulged the fond expectation of winning her consent to become his wife. But though not discouraging his suit, and turning it to account in conciliating the favor of her catholic subjects, three-fourths even in England of them all, and in seeking to persuade the Pope to recognize the validity of her mother's marriage and her own legitimacy, she finally gave De Feria his minister to understand that such an alliance would not be best either for herself or for England. Yet when Philip, after the treaty of Cambray had secured to her the prospective restoration of Calais and relieved her of solicitude as to war with France, married Elizabeth daughter of Henry II., she expressed surprise that he should not have waited a few months longer. Her court was eager for her marriage; and Ferdinand of Austria, Arundel, Pickering and Arran, next in succession after Mary to the Scottish throne, were in turn suggested for her hand. But an interview with the latter ended without the result anticipated, and what heart she had to bestow had been given at fifteen to Thomas Seymour, or later to Robert Dudley, with whom she had been intimate when they were together prisoners in the tower. Dudley's wife Amy Robsart, dying of cancer at Cumnor, was hurried out of life, as an impediment to their union, but the queen though still infatuated with her handsome lover was too sensible to entrust herself to his keeping.

Her earlier life of seclusion or confinement had not been idle. Her active mind found solace in literary pursuits, and her natural abilities had been developed and strengthened by familiarity with various languages, living or classical, by acquisitions in many branches of learning. Her training had not tended to render her conscientious or devout. She was a free thinker in religion, ridiculing the importance attached to dogma and rite, yet conforming to what opinion about her demanded as expedient or of good reputation. Vain, vacillating, mendacious, her wonderful tact, rather the inspiration of genius than the result of any process of reasoning, carried her through entanglements, which often foiled her wisest counsellors.

If those she selected afford the test, her sagacity can hardly be too highly commended. Sir William Cecil, afterwards lord Burleigh,*

* 1570.

her most trusted adviser as she ascended the throne, for forty years retained an influence over her mind rarely disturbed, and though governed implicitly by the advice of no one, unless where coinciding with her own convictions, to his wisdom and consummate statesmanship must in large measure be ascribed the glory attending her reign. It was his policy to attain his objects by yielding to obstacles where not easily surmounted, and his peculiar traits and habits of thought in their long and intimate intercourse, had their effect in shaping her own. His brother-in-law, Sir Nicholas Bacon, as chancellor shared with him in her confidence, and Walsingham, though crafty and even less scrupulous, was perhaps for that better fitted for her schemes. They were all protestant, even bigoted protestants, but not to the degree of punishing religious contumacy with death.

For a time the cabinet of England, employed in foreign politics, paid little heed to Ireland. As soon as pacific relations with France and Spain, whose mutual jealousies fretted by diplomacy constituted her safety, permitted the attempt, parliament, reduced to sixty-three lay peers, only one half of whom and rarely more than ten prelates were often in attendance, and the commons representing the nation, neither in numbers, influence or faith, repudiated catholicism. In Scotland the reformation was gaining ground, when the death of Francis II., in December 1560, six months after his accession, brought home the widowed queen. Affectionate loyalty deepened by her misfortunes changed into detestation, when six years later, her third husband, Bothwell, murdered her second, Darnley, and what little reverence remained for her faith became chilled. Rome parted reluctantly with her subject nations. Ireland continued true and had besides other grounds of disaffection. It was through her that England was most vulnerable, and though her consolidation in faith, laws, letters and loyalty involved many embarrassments, this was the task the queen and her ministers were set upon accomplishing.

When Elizabeth succeeded in 1558 all Ireland was Catholic. Leix

and Offaly had been added to the pale. The rest was occupied by
the septs, or by English earls who held but limited allegiance. Con-
or of Thomond was loyal, and all the McCarthies. Had toleration
and respect for right evinced at this period the most distant idea of
religious obligation, or what christian faith and precept demanded,
Ireland might have been spared her misery, England her shame.
But Sussex on his return under orders of the queen called a packed
parliament, which disingenuously meeting on St. Bridget's day, when
the catholic lords greatly in the ascendancy were not notified, and
did not suspect the design, reëstablished Protestantism, imposing
heavy penalties for disobedience on a whole people of the opposite
faith.

Con Baccagh, earl of Tyrone, after a life of more than four score
years, spent without blemish or reproach, died as Elizabeth came to the
throne. For nearly forty years he had ruled over Tyr Owen with
good sense and judgment; and if often in arms, hostilities were less
of his seeking than forced upon him by his neighbors. He is represented as illiterate from having affixed his seal, and not his signature
to an address; but there is evidence enough of the aspersion being
groundless. In 1551 he procured, and entrusted to Dowdal, archbishop
of Armagh, the life of John de Courcy, to translate, and with an
English mother and wife, daughters of earls, it seems fair to suppose
that he was not only a good penman but familiar with English, Latin
and Gaelic, then the language of his sept. After the death of Alice
Fitzgerald, he married Mary MacDonnell, daughter of Alexander
of Lecale. Her two brothers sent by him to collect rent of the
MacArtans were slain by Brereton, engendering animosities still
rank a dozen years after. Mary was detained a prisoner in Scotland,
not long before the death of her husband. Dungannon for centuries
the home of his forefathers had been abandoned to Ferdoragh, the
castles of Dundrum, Fedan and Benburb, seven miles north of Armagh, taking its place.

No time was lost, and Shane received the suffrages of the sept as lord of Tyr Owen as his father passed. What opportunities were either allowed or improved by him for education, can only be conjectured from his correspondence and course. Both indicated culture highly respectable for the period. Represented as an untutored savage by prejudiced historians, whilst three fourths English in race, his barbarisms if running in the blood must have been derived from the Geraldines, not from Irish progenitors, from either Con, from Henry or Owen, all refined in character and noble in nature. It was the policy of England to crush him as dangerous, and what could not be easily effected by honest warfare, dagger or poison, was attempted by calumny and misrepresentation. Gerald of Kildare, his cousin, was his steadfast friend. Sydney and Sussex evidently respected him, and his intimacy after his visit to the queen, with the principal leaders of her court, has left its mark in letters that speak well for his talents, scholarship and character. He was sufficiently astute to baffle the queen and her cabinet in negotiation, and the points he raised were not easily answered.

Sussex came and went. He did not like Ireland, but his importunities to be recalled had little effect. Sydney held sway, when in the February after the accession of Elizabeth he proceeded to Dundalk, forty miles from the capital, near the gates of Ulster, to fortify the pale and confer with Shane. His own invitation declined, Shane proposed instead that he should visit him at Fedan six miles out of the town and stand godfather for his child, as Sussex had the year before for Desmond's, and be his gossip. It was the eldest son Henry by Mary O'Donnel. The lord justice was hospitably and sumptuously entertained. After the ceremony he expressed regret that Shane was not more peaceably inclined. O'Neil urged as his ground of dissatisfaction, the disposition to recognize Brian son of Ferdoragh as chief of Tyrone. Ferdoragh was at least illegitimate, and as he thought, spurious, in all probability being the son of Kelly the blacksmith of Dundalk. That his father's surrender of what did not belong to him but to the sept was void under Irish law, and that English law had never been extended to Tyrone ; that he was himself the lawful heir and chosen by the sept, and among its other members would fall the succession in the event of his removal. These suggestions had weight : they were later submitted to English lawyers, who in vain sought to resist their force, but set up as rendering valid the grant to Con and Ferdoragh, the concession to Con Mor of English rights, at his own solicitation.

The queen recognizing either the strength of his position or the reasonableness of his demands, acquiesced, and for a year Shane afforded no cause for discontent. Early in 1561 some of his men pursuing Felim Roe O'Neil, who after depredations had taken refuge in the pale, burnt three villages belonging to lord Slane. Sussex was not friendly, and correspondence ensued more frank than courteous. Upon his representations home, he was ordered to proceed into Ulster and substitute Brian in Shane's place. Whilst the queen was thus directing Sussex to invade Tyrone, secretly practising upon the earl of Argyle, James MacDonnel and his brother Sorley Boy to render aid, and sending robes and coronets to create Calvagh earl of Tyrconnel, and O'Reilly lord of Cavan and earl of Brenny, in order to enlist them in the cause, she was urging Shane to pay her a friendly visit at court that his complaints might be considered. The wife of Calvagh, Julia Maclean, widow of the third earl of Argyle, arrived in Donegal at the same time with two thousand men to further her designs. This double dealing could not escape the vigilance of Shane, and to be beforehand with his enemies gathering for his overthrow, he marched speedily into Tyrconnel in May, capturing Calvagh and his wife at the monastery of Killodonnel on Lough Foyle. Sussex forthwith collected an army and proceeded to Armagh, which he garrisoned and strongly fortified, and when it was menaced by Shane, marched back to its defence.

Shane whilst constructing new castles, one on Lake Neagh, strongly fortified, which he called Foonegal or "Hate of Englishmen," wrote an earnest and manly letter to the lord lieutenant not to wage an expensive and useless war against him, and declaring that he could not ask for peace or truce until all troops were withdrawn from his country. Towards the close of July an engagement took place resulting in a triumph for him. Sussex, who was not present but attending the sick bed of Ormond, wrote that "never before durst Scotch or Irishman look an Englishman in the face in a plain three miles from any wood, but with half their number Shane had charged the whole army, and the fame of the English so hardly gotten had vanished.' Utterly demoralized Sussex withdrew all his forces but the garrison at Armagh. Such a decided victory over an invading army more numerous than his own was an occurrence too rare not to create a sense of elation and power, and Calvagh his prisoner, Tyrconnel subjugated, Shane assumed command of the north from Drogheda to the Erne, and might well regard himself as having reached the acme of his ambition, and all but in name king of Ulster, as had been his progenitors.

The Irish earls, Ormond, Thomond, Desmond and Clanrickard, hastened to camp. Sussex corrupted Shane's seneschal and Neil Gray his messenger to assassinate him, which he mentions the 24th of August, as if nothing remarkable to the queen, who so far from expressing disapproval or indignation at the proposition regretted its miscarriage, and the next year the council recommended that the attempt should be repeated. This vile plot to make way by assassination with an enemy not to be conquered in the field, seems not to have been immediately divulged to its intended victim, and it is quite possible that seneschal and messenger while not unwilling to learn what might be designed by the viceroy, and yet aware of the danger to themselves of betraying his confidence, kept their own counsel till the danger was past, without swerving from fidelity to

45

their chief. This was not a solitary instance of like perfidy in Irish
administration. A few years later occurred another of the kind, in
which the crime was consummated, and many more varying in character, and oftener on a grander scale, equally flagitious, are found in
its annals.

Embittered against O'Neil, possibly from not having been able to
effect his purpose, and averse to any temporizing policy, believing,
as he wrote Cecil, " that if Shane were overthrown all could be settled, but that if any settlement were made with him all that was
settled would be overthrown," the lord lieutenant prepared for a general hosting. Unwilling that the chief should regain favor with the
queen, his despatches were kept back, and he effectually intrigued
to stir up strife between him and his subordinates. After waiting
awhile for money and men, for his troops were discontented from
three years arrear of pay, he marched north early in September,
sweeping Glenconkine in Tyrone of four thousand kine and numerous horses, without meeting opposition, though Shane the next
month retaliated by raiding the pale and burning four villages. Kildare sent over to negotiate and invite Shane to court at last reached
the camp, and on parley prevailed upon him to come to terms. On
the nineteenth of October, the council consenting that Armagh should
be evacuated when he went, and money advanced to pay his way,
the chief agreed to go over to London as requested, Gerald becoming surety for his safe return.

Suitable garments for court demanded time for preparation. The
money promised, three thousand pounds, came slow. Calvagh and
his wife were his prisoners at Benborb. Some years before Shane had
been an unsuccessful suitor to a sister of Argyle, whether the sister-
in-law Calvagh had recently married is not stated. Shane had then
soothed his disappointment by espousing Mary daughter of Calvagh,
by whom he had two sons Henry and Art. One principal vexation of
his life had been the preference of Ferdoragh to himself in the patent

of the earldom to his father, and now as reward for coöperation in his attempted overthrow, his father-in-law and feudatory O'Reily were to be made earls, and an interloper perhaps forced upon his own rightful inheritance. The attempt to assassinate him still farther fretted his temper, though he speaks of it in his letters with indifference. This may have been feigned. It did not prevent his repairing to court where Ormond twenty years before had been poisoned.

Daily harassed by the queen's waywardness, if cruel to Calvagh, allowance must be made. We are told by the annalists that Mary his wife " died of horror, loathing, grief and deep anguish, in consequence of the severity of the imprisonment inflicted on her father by Shane in her presence." She could not have survived long to suffer, for by the ninth of August, Shane had been long enough a widower to propose to Sussex, as one mode of preserving a good understanding between them, to take his sister Frances to wife. Mary may have been feeble in health, and distress at angry words or cruel treatment of her parent may have hastened her death, but the " Four Masters " compiled in Donegal are less reliable when commenting on what concerns their own princes and may not have been exact as to dates.

Though at last ready to take his departure, and meeting as agreed, Ormond and Kildare at Carrickabradog the English garrison still remained at Armagh. His cousin Gerald, whose professions of friendship he had no reason to distrust, urged him to waive for a while his claim to its being withdrawn, giving him assurance that it should not during his absence harm either his people or chiefs. When actually in English power he was subjected to the indignity of handcuffs on his wrists, probably a precaution against his changing his mind. Crossing over in December he was received by Cecil and other members of the council and the ceremonial arranged for his reception by the queen.

On the sixth day of January, 1562, attended by a band of galloglasses, armed with axes, bareheaded, their long curling hair about their shoulders, in saffron shirts with long sleeves, short coats, and hairy mantles or wolf skins on their backs, and led by his constable MacSweeny, "O'Neil the great, cousin to St. Patrick, friend to the queen of England, enemy to all the world besides," proceeded from his lodgings through the streets of London to the royal presence, and there after customary homage before the court and foreign ambassadors stated the injuries which had goaded him to hostilities. The queen received him with becoming courtesy, but deferred her answer till the baron of Dungannon should arrive. When the delay alarmed him and he proposed to go home relying on his protection, he was given to understand that that document had been carefully worded and mentioned no time for his return. He was equal to the occasion, and his letters to the queen and her ministers, his intimacy with the Spanish ambassador and a boldness that defied so gross an injustice and departure from propriety, had their effect. And when news came in April, that Brian the baron of Dungannon, depredating upon his territory, had fallen in battle with Turlogh who ruled over Tyrone in his absence, the queen concluding that nothing was to be gained by his longer detention, since Turlogh next in succession would be quite as hostile, he was permitted to go. Yet before his departure, on the twenty-sixth of May, he was forced to sign agreements extorted by duress, but which left him substantially supreme in authority over Tyrone.

He had improved his opportunity not only to make many friendships, maintained long afterwards by correspondence and gifts of horse, falcon and hound, but to learn with Robert Dudley and other gallants of the court to hunt, ride and dress after English modes. His two thousand pounds promised but not all paid, melted rapidly away in such companionship, and three hundred more were advanced to defray his charges. A widower, his ambition was an English wife of the queen's selection, but Frances Ratcliffe, sister of Sussex, afterwards lady Mildmay, remained his choice. He had had little time

amidst the busy scenes and incidents of war, the death of Mary
O'Donnel, and preparation for his visit to London, to pay court to
his earlier admiration, countess of Argyle and wife of Calvagh, of
whom he had been the unsuccessful suitor, and his unfortunate intimacy with her was doubtless of subsequent date.

When he returned he was more often in her company, and when
no English wife offered, and rumors reached him from the pale that
Frances Ratcliffe had been sent over to Dublin, to entrap him into
her brother's power, who wrote him that if they liked each other on
farther acquaintance he should not oppose their marriage, constant
intercourse between him and the countess may have led to liking not
easily withstood. Calvagh is described as of noble presence, sagacious and brave, stern to foe, but kind to friend, so estimable that
no good act of his created surprise, but either then or on previous
occasions growing out of the intimacy of family relations it is said
the countess had formed an attachment for Shane, whose prepossessing qualities and more active spirit gave him an advantage over her
staider husband. She was highly accomplished, spoke Latin, French
and Italian with fluency, and under conditions where there was little
female society, if they erred, though we would not extenuate their
error, some allowance must be made. He was steadfast to her and
she was with him at his death, and their son Hugh Gar-valoch grew
up to be executed in early manhood by Hugh, then earl of Tyrone,
brother of Bryan, slain at Carlingford.

The suggestion of a recent writer that Victoria would have given
her daughter with more readiness to the king of Dahomey, than Sussex
his sister to the Irish chieftain, is a gratuitous insult to the memory
of Shane. In blood even by English standards, in social position,
as an independent prince, as general and statesman, Sussex had no
advantage over him, and certainly not in character. Ferdoragh had
perished in a legitimate stratagem of war, Bryan in combat of his
own seeking; Shane had never attempted to remove his enemies by

dagger or by draught. His illicit love, the one stain upon his name, was of later date, and paralleled in those days in the instance of nearly every king in christendom. To the countess of Argyle he remained for a long time constant, and through her conciliated the support of her countrymen. If less temperate than became the ruler of men, carousing after days spent in the open air, in campaigning or sylvan pursuits, was the vice of that period, and not unknown even centuries later at the tables of the great.

Hugh O'Donnel, brother of Calvagh, joined Shane immediately after his return from London, and in July they invaded Fermanagh of which Shane claimed the sovereignty, as recognized in the treaty with the queen. Maguire appealed to Sussex and went himself to the pale to implore assistance, but upon his return in November they again raided his territory, "leaving neither house nor corn unwasted, church nor sentory unrobbed." He had stored his valuables in his islands, which boats were being provided to spoil. He wrote in English, praying Sussex to reply in that language and not in Latin, as that could be read. He closes by saying that Shane once possessed of Fermanagh could not be driven out and all Ulster would be at his disposal. Shane was also by his subordinate septs worrying Dundalk. Sussex and Kildare wrote him a joint letter, urging a conference at that place, but he refused, claiming their covenants made with him had been broken, and he should persevere till he had recovered sovereignty over all Ulster, the birthright of the O'Neils. The Catholic powers, with whom Shane was in correspondence, were plotting against the queen, there was danger of war with France, rumors were rife of a general rising, and he felt his strength.

The ancient Manus O'Donnel held for thirty years the chieftainship of the north-west corner of the island. When his death is noticed by the Four Masters under date of 1563, he is described as "lord of Tyrconnel, Inishowen, Kinnel-Moen, Fermanagh and lower Connaught; as a man who never suffered the chiefs in his neighborhood to encroach upon his superabundant possessions, fierce, obdurate, wrathful and combative toward his enemies and opponents, until he had made them obedient to his jurisdiction; as mild, friendly, benign, amicable, bountiful and hospitable toward the learned, the destitute, poets, ollavs and the church; as learned, skilled in many arts, gifted with a profound intellect and knowledge of every science." This was written in Donegal, but he seems to have been an estimable character, though grown testy and disqualified by age and infirmity for ruling over his turbulent subjects. When deposed by the clan, he had been succeeded by Calvagh, duly chosen in his place. This was not without opposition, and Calvagh, to reduce the refractory to obedience, had brought over a force from Scotland.

The new year found Sussex busily employed in practising upon Turlogh O'Neil, O'Reilly, and Con O'Donnel to desert Shane, against whom in April, proclamation was made; and the month after the army proceeded from Armagh, through bogs and forests, to Clogher, taking a distant view of the Troughs. Eight thousand kine had been driven to places of security, but a thousand remained to be gleaned. Neither kine nor kern sufficed for their contemplated objects, and resorting again to negotiation, at the end of July, Ormond and Kildare obtained a personal interview with the chieftain, who in September explained to the queen why the articles signed by him in London could not be carried out. He complained of various wrongs and depredations committed upon his territory, that his letters and presents to Dudley had not been forwarded by Sussex, and that treacherous attempts had been made upon his life. He renewed his suit for Frances Ratcliffe, his constancy to whom would seem to indicate attachment. Whilst these negotiations were pending, John Smyth, a creature of the lord lieutenant, often in his company, sent Shane a present of poisoned wine, which very nearly effected its purpose. The queen on the fifteenth of October expressed her indignation at the detestable attempt, but her correspondence with

Sussex in August, urging "his bearing some burden rather than force her to pardon Shane without submission" and similar phrases, suggest the impression that the attempt may have proceeded from a wish to please her.

Sussex did not favor the negotiation, but Kildare and Cusack the chancellor persuading Shane to moderate his pretensions, after long correspondence and discussion, the new articles of pacification, revoking all others before, were signed by the chief at his castle of Benborb on the eighteenth of November. He was to retain the title of O'Neil and all that it implied, with supreme rule over Tyrone and all subordinate chieftains, who had ever acknowledged allegiance to his predecessors, till parliament should determine upon his claim to the earldom. The garrison of Armagh was to be withdrawn at All Saints, and disputes were to be adjusted by arbiters, two chosen by the chief and two by the deputy. Calvagh was to be released, and Loftus, archbishop of Armagh, allowed to have and keep possession of his church and lands. This treaty, if an acknowledgment of English rule, was still a triumph for Shane. It conceded nearly all he demanded as his right, and if kept inviolate by the government it would perhaps have been equally respected by him.

Calvagh, after nearly three years captivity was set free upon payment of a large ransom by the Kinel Connell. In the autumn, the deputy with a numerous army escorted him through Tyrone to Lough Foyle, and entering Tyrconnel reinstated him in his lands and castles. Proceeding thence across the Erne into Carbury to take possession of Sligo, Calvagh caused his standard to be displayed from its battlements, and upon the lord justice inquiring whose standard it was, Calvagh replied it was his own, and that the town had belonged to his ancestors from a remote period, whereupon the keys were delivered to him.

In 1564 Calvagh and O'Boyle repaired to Dublin and were received with great honor. Upon their return, O'Donnel went into Fermanagh.

O'Boyle had not been long at home, when in May Con, son of Calvagh, requested him to go to Donegal, then possessed by Hugh, son of Hugh Oge, who upon their coming consented that Con should enter his castle, but not O'Boyle. Two other O'Donnels, sons of Hugh Boy, had agreed to betray the castle to Con, and with him proceeded to demolish the town in which Hugh then was, when suddenly Shane and Hugh, brother of Calvagh, called to the rescue with numerous forces, broke in upon them in the darkness of the night and routed them, taking Con prisoner. His father greatly distressed at the loss of his son sought to obtain his release. Shane insisted upon the surrender of his castle of Lifford, and it was yielded as ransom for Con.

Pride his besetting sin, Shane grew more bold and exacting with each fresh success, and vexed at the dilatory proceedings of parliament as regarded the earldom, expressed his displeasure. His demands received no response unless in the form of menace. This provoked his resentment. His troops invading Tyrconnel carried off ten thousand head of cattle, whilst he attempted to surprise Armagh, Loftus the archbishop having offended him by misrepresentation. In answer to the lord lieutenant who represented Ulster as verging on some great explosion, the queen wrote, that "his suspicions of Shane should give him no uneasiness, that he should tell his troops to take courage, and that his rebellion may turn to their advantage, as there will be lands to bestow on those that need them." Cusack again contrived to bring Shane to reason. He had disaffected his kinsman Turlogh, next to himself in power in Tyrone, and who had taken advantage of his absence at court to gain popularity and seek the chieftainship, but his hold upon the sept was not easily weakened, and the government, though not conceding what he asked, showed no disposition to drive him to extremities. Sussex himself as he was leaving Ireland wrote him in terms of courtesy and kindness; and both queen and chief seemed inclined to carry out in good faith the articles of Cusack of 1563.

46

Had he exhibited like sagacity and forbearance in his conduct to his neighbors as to the statesmen of the court, his reign might have been greatly prolonged and prospered. But such was not his temper. Not far from Sligo ruled O'Rourkes, from one of whose early kings killed in 1172, had been carried off Devorguil mother of Eva. Its chief Owen with Margaret his wife, daughter of Conor-na-srona, king of Thomond, founded in 1508, Carrigpatrick, for Franciscans, in which order twenty years after he died. His son Brian Ballagh, whose principal fame was as patron of poets, and of their works he possessed the best collection of his day, in 1540 constructed the castle of Leitrim and subdued Moylurg. After thirty-four years rarely disturbed by war or intestine dissension, his son Hugh Gallda succeeded, and then in 1564 another son Brian. O'Neil, in furtherance of his ambitious projects, set up Hugh Boy, whom two years later the Kinel Connel slew in battle or by means less lawful, and reinstated Bryan, nephew of Calvagh and who resenting the interference with his rights proved a dangerous foe. Sydney said of Bryan, he was the proudest man with whom he had to deal as deputy. His noble deportment and manly beauty charmed the queen, but did not prevent her putting him to death in 1591, when entrapped in Scotland, for extending shelter to Spaniards shipwrecked in the Armada. At this particular epoch when by his pride, exactions and exorbitant pretensions Shane was losing popularity with the other chiefs about his borders, he had better have left Bryan alone.

But he was never at rest. When Macdonnels and other clans from Scotland, extending their possessions in Antrim, rejected his claims to supremacy, and his overtures to alliance, he decided to bring them to terms. His treaty in London with the queen had stipulated that what he conquered from them should be annexed to his dominions. In August from the castle of Corcra in Tyrone, he communicated his designs to the deputy and council, who expressed their approval. A few weeks later he constructed a castle in Colerane on the east side of the Bann, taking possession of a monastery across the river. It sustained an attack lasting for twenty-four hours, in which Sorley Boy was wounded. Occasional raids sweeping over their settlements with fire and sword, gave the Scots further intimation of what was impending, and which they did not disregard. Three hundred young men selected from the best families of the clan, carefully trained in martial and athletic exercises, constituting the Luchtach or body guard of MacDonnel and commanded usually by his heir or tanist, were sent over to Lecale. After solemn celebration of Easter at Fedan, in April Shane marched by Dromore, and cutting a pass through the forest twelve miles long, for ten men abreast, to near Edenduffcarrick, the forces of Clanaboy and his best troops there came to join him. Repairing an old fortress at that place he continued his march, defeating Sorley Boy who disputed a pass, and burnt James Mac Donnel's castle at Red Bay.

That chief had been making preparation, and when the beacon fire on Torr Hill gave the signal, he crossed the channel, reaching Cushindun bay as the melting mists ushered in the May day morning of 1565. His burning castle and Sorley Boy in full retreat towards him were not encouraging, and expecting their other brother Alexander Oge with reënforcements from the isles, they withdrew with precipitation to Ballycastle and encamped at the foot of Glentow giving its name to the fight which ensued, the river Tow being Anglicised Taisi. Alexander that evening left Scotland with nine hundred men to arrive the day after the battle, only again to hurry home.

Shane who had himself passed the night at Bailecashlein or New Castle, Sorley Boy's town, at five in the morning of the second, marshalled his array, and exhorting his troops to be of good courage, and true to their prince, made his onset, giving the MacDonnels a complete overthrow, slaying seven hundred, and capturing James desperately wounded, Sorley Boy, the young MacLeod their brother-in-law, and nineteen other chiefs. James offered Shane all his lands and chattels in Scotland and Ireland for his ransom, but O'Neil answered that as he was acting for the queen it was for her to determine; and when Mary of Scots, the earl of Argyle and the island lords earnestly besought him to release the two brothers, he made the same reply.

Without delay he reduced Dunsverick and besieged Dunluce, belonging to Sorley. The latter held out three days, but the garrison, informed that their chief was to have neither meat nor drink till the place capitulated, surrendered. Having thus killed or banished the Scots, he returned to Glenulla in Clanaboy, whence he sent James to his castle of Corcra to die of his wounds in a dungeon. James is described as " a paragon of hospitality and prowess, wise, bountiful and munificent, without peer in the Clandonnel, who would have paid his weight in gold for his ransom." Shane is said to have given him honorable interment in Armagh. The night of the battle of Glentow he wrote the lord justice Arnold and the council an account in Latin of his victory, and a month later his secretary Fleming wrote Cusack further details of the campaign. The acknowledgments of the council were presented to Shane for his success. It was hailed in England as a victory also for the queen, who still with the usual crookedness that marked her policy took him to task.

Alarmed at the growing strength of O'Neil and fretted that he refused to surrender his prisoners, the queen sent over Sydney as deputy who wrote to request an interview at Dundalk. In his reply the chief, who by the articles of 1563 was absolved from any obligation to wait upon the viceroy, declined, stating as reasons why his people would not suffer him to come : that his father refusing to deliver up Turlogh who had spoiled Tyrone, and visiting Dundalk, the deputy threatened to cut off his head, and after good service against the Scots entertaining the deputy at Armagh, he was carried off to Dublin, the repast untasted : that he had himself by agreement with St. Leger rendered aid for which he was to have three thousand pounds : this Sussex refused to pay : that he had agreed to go into England, if the garrison was removed from Armagh, which it was not, and he was taken there as a prisoner handlocked.   He had been unlawfully detained and constrained to give nineteen of his best pledges before he was released, and upon his return his life had been attempted by dagger and poison, and though he was assured of the friendship of the deputy his people were timid.

In March Sydney wrote Leicester that Shane was the only strong and rich man in Ireland, that he had sent Stukeley and Dowdal to bring about an interview with him to no purpose.   He received them kindly : but when the wine was in him he spoke his mind freely, "that he cared not to be made an earl unless he might be better and higher than an earl, for that he was in blood and power better than the best of them, unless it were his cousin Kildare who was of his house. They had made a wise man of MacCarthy Mor, but he kept as good a man as he.   The queen was his sovereign, but he never made peace with her but at her seeking.   When he came to Sussex he offered him the courtesy of a handlock.   The queen said it was true he had a safe conduct to come and go, but it did not say when he might go, and he was kept till he had agreed to things against his honor and profit that he would never perform.   That made him make war and he should do it again.   He could bring to the field one thousand horse and four thousand foot, and march to the walls of Dublin and back unfought.   His ancestors were kings of Ulster, and that Ulster was his and should be ; that O'Donnell should never come into his country, nor Bagnall into Newry, nor Kildare into Dundrum or Lecale.   They were now his.   With his sword he had won them and with his sword he would keep them."

It would not be just to infer from the allusion to the habits of the chieftain that he was intemperate beyond what was the custom of the times.   His repasts, as his progenitors' and those of all other ruling princes of the island as of other lands at that period, were taken at the head of his long and hospitable board, where his kins-folk and chiefs, his hostages and retainers bore him company, and where they all shared in the festal entertainment of harpist or trou-badour, whose hereditary function it was to render agreeable the hours passed in the banquet hall. It is impossible that one as am-bitious as Shane O'Neil, and of his strength of character, and dependent upon the esteem of his clansmen for retaining his position, if occasionally warmed as in the above instance by the wine which he shared with his guests, ever degenerated into a sot. When op-probriously charged by Stanihurst with excess in wine of which his cellars at Dundrum held two hundred tuns, this and his cooling off its effects in an earth bath are generally considered inventions.

Campion, who wrote in 1570, tells us "that Shane ordered the north so properly that if any subject could prove loss of money or goods within his precinct he would force the robber to restitution, or at his own cost redeem the harm to the loser's content. Sitting at meat, before he put one morsel into his own mouth he used to slice a portion and send it to some beggar at his gate, saying it was fit to serve Christ first." A work by Matthew O'Connor says of him: " that by the natural vigor of his mind he raised armies, erected forts, besieged fortified towns, defeated regular troops led on by ex-perienced generals, and made a resolute stand against the first nation of the world in riches, in arts and in arms. He was often victorious and never vanquished." His letters, many of which remain, to Eng-lish nobles whose acquaintance he had made on his visit to the queen, exhibit much culture and appreciation of what was of good report and meritorious in English institutions. His many defects of character and errors in conduct were exaggerated by English writers. It should be borne in mind that his ulterior motive throughout appears to have been the independence of Ulster, possibly of Ireland, and that his eagerness to reduce to his sway the neighboring septs was mainly to further this end.

In 1566 he had gained possession of all Ulster, Maguire and Calvagh O'Donnell taking refuge in Dublin. He invaded Connaught, wasting and destroying, received tribute or hostages from its principal chiefs as recognition of his sovereignty, devastating Clanrickard and carrying four thousand cattle back to Tyrone. He put away the wife of Calvagh and sought to marry the widow of James Macdonnel. Incensed at the duplicity of the queen who sent him the ratification of the Cusack articles whilst plotting his overthrow, he fortified Lifford in the north and Dundrum in Lecale threatening Dundalk. He wrote in April to Charles the IX. and Lorraine proffering allegiance if five thousand men were sent to his aid. In an engagement with Caffar brother of Calvagh he slew him and one hundred and forty of his men, and treating with Hugh O'Donnel, then with him, for several castles in Tyrconnel, he obtained possession of them. In July he entered the pale with fire and sword and on the twenty-ninth besieged Dundalk, but was repulsed by Fitzwilliam. He broke down the cathedral at Armagh, occupied Fermanagh. He wrote Desmond that he had burnt Meath, and then or never was the time to strike. Alexander Oge with twelve hundred men from Cantyre sided with the queen and wrote from the Glynns that he was ready to enter Tyrone.

Col. Randolph an able officer with a thousand men held Derry, and though the army of Tyr Owen quadrupled his force in numbers, they were powerless against its walls. In a sally towards Knocfergus in November Randolph, well supplied with artillery, in which arm O'Neil was deficient, gave Shane a check, but fell himself in the combat near Derry, which place, in April demolished by an accidental explosion of its magazines, was abandoned, and its garrison in their march to the pale much harassed. Shane, after defeating the English at the battle of the Sagums, killing four hundred, again invaded Tyrconnel, Connaught, Fermanagh and the lands of Bagenal in Newry and Brefney. Sydney, deputy since the recall of

Arnold in 1565, marched against him, but discouraged by the seven thousand men, fifteen hundred of them Scots, whom Shane had under his command, or as also said his supplies exhausted, withdrew ; but early in the spring before he could well be expected, passed round Tyrone into Connaught, establishing Hugh in Tyrconnel, restoring Brefney to Brian O'Rourke, in place of the chief friendly to O'Neil, and Fermanagh, its chief dying on the way, to his kinsman equally loyal to the English. Cavan was raided, and Benborb burnt.

Calvagh, son of Manus,* in the beginning of the winter, on the twenty-sixth of October, shortly after his return from England had fallen dead from his saddle in the midst of his cavalry, "without the slightest starting, stumbling, shying or prancing of his horse." Not his son Con, but his brother Hugh was chosen chief. This event not known in Dublin for some weeks changed greatly the posture of affairs. It added little to the strength of O'Neil who still persevered in his hostile operations. His renewed appeals to the cardinals produced no effect ; his present of the costly suit, given by Henry VIII. to his father Con when created earl, to the religious and puritan Argyle, did not help his cause ; and the desertion of the timid and time serving, even among his most trusted followers, Hugh O'Neil Mor of the Fews, Maguire, McGrath and McArdle, president of his council, foreboded his approaching downfall. Had Hugh O'Donnel stood fast to their earlier friendship, they could have together set at naught any army Elizabeth had to oppose to them, but with their conflicting claims to rule no sooner did Hugh become chief of Tyrconnel than forgetful of all obligations to Shane he made his inaugural hosting into his territory. Con, son of Calvagh, who had been described in his youth by Sussex as " wise, valiant and civil, the likeliest plant that ever sprang in Ulster whereon to graft a good subject," and whose character is rated high by the annalists under 1583 when he died, was set at liberty and put by Shane in possession

---

* Son of Hugh Duv, son of Hugh Roe, son of Nial Garv, son of Turlogh.

of Ballyshannon and Balleek, and this still further widened the breach.

Before the winter was over, Hugh made a second expedition into Tyrone, wasting and destroying, driving off cattle and ravaging Strabane. Shane gathered his clans to retaliate. Hugh, early in May, near the fords of the Swilly in Kilmacrenan with a small army, seasonably reënforced from the neighborhood, observing the Kinel Owen in hosts and squadrons crossing the ford, the tide out, sent his son Hugh with horse to engage their van, while he posted his infantry in a secure position where they could not be surrounded. Many fell in the cavalry encounter, and among them Magroarty who had charge of the sacred Cathach of Columkille. The troop withdrew discomfited, but MacSweenys, Tuath, Fanad and Banagh came to their relief. O'Donnel addressed them complaining of the wrongs they had sustained from the Kinel Owen, and dwelling especially on the loss of his fortress of Lifford given in ransom for Con.

Shane was promising himself submission or an easy victory, when the Kinel Connel came up. His men seized their arms and moved rapidly and in order to the combat. "Fierce and desperate were the grim and terrible looks that each cast at the other from their starlike eyes. They raised the battle cry aloud and their united shouting when rushing together was sufficient to strike with dismay and turn to flight the feeble and unwarlike. They continued to strike, mangle and cut down one another for a long time, so that many men were laid low, heroes wounded, youths slain, and robust warriors mangled in slaughter." At last the Kinel Owen defeated abandoned the field, and the tide having risen over the beach, crossed in the advance and by which lay their retreat, they plunged into the swollen sea. Countless numbers were drowned or slain by their pursuers, many of the Clan Donnell, O'Coinnes and O'Hagans, and Dudley O'Donnelly, Shane's faithful foster brother was killed. The loss of life is variously estimated from thirteen hundred to three thousand.

47

Thus were avenged the wrongs of Calvagh and Mary O'Donnel. The chief, broken hearted, escaped up the Swilly under guidance of ⋅the O'Gallaghers, possibly hostile to Hugh, and travelled on by retired and solitary ways, regaining his own domains to find Sydney approaching against him in force.   Bewildered and losing his wonted prudence, he sent messengers to Scotland to invite Alexander, brother of James mortally wounded at Glentow, to his assistance.   Come he did without delay to Cushindun, and there pitched his camp.   Taking Sorley boy, no longer prisoner, Shane repaired thither, and was received with apparent kindness.   But at the banquet, Aspuck son of Agnes, sister of the Mac Donnels and whose father had also fallen at Glentow, for the express purpose, it is presumed, of provoking a quarrel, entered into an angry altercation with the secretary of Shane, asking him if he had said that his aunt the lady Cantyre would consent to marry him who had killed her husband.   The secretary responded that Shane was fit match for Mary Stuart herself.   On this Shane interposing, Aspuch withdrew, and stirring up his men who may possibly have been prepared for the conjuncture, and only waiting for the preconcerted signal, they rushed into the tent, and though his few followers and one of the O'Donnellys fought bravely to defend him, Shane was quickly despatched.   Wrapped in a kerns shirt, he was interred near by in a ruinous church.

Sydney, as also Piers governor of Carrickfergus who rivalled majesty itself in taste and talent for indirection and who received ample equivalents for the head of Shane sent to decorate the battlements of Dublin castle, claimed what credit there was for his betrayal and death.   His active nature that knew no weariness, great practical sagacity, insatiable ambition and indomitable pride, with the vicissitudes of fortune, extreme and varied, that attended his career, invest Shane with peculiar interest.   Had he been less selfish and by justice and forbearance towards his brother princes won their regard, had his aim been his country's independence from a foreign yoke, or even the

preservation of its ancient faith, his fame would have stood out in
bold relief as a national hero. Or could he have escaped the too
easy fascinations of Calvagh's wife, or when free made her his own,
there would have been less to censure. But instead of reparation,
when in his power, he provoked the resentment of her kindred by
overtures for the hand of her step-daughter, widow of that James
Macdonnel who fell on the field of his triumph to miserably perish
in his dungeon at Corcra. The Nemesis that haunted his paths sped
swiftly to his undoing, and his strongly marked character and tragic
end afford rich material for dramatic treatment.

His sons by Mary O'Donnel, Henry and Art, were children,
and Turlogh Lineach, great-grandson of Con Mor, invested at
Tullaghoge, succeeded with the acquiescence of the English government to the chieftainship. Objection was made to his claim of
sovereignty over the border princes outside of Tyrone*; and this pretention he renounced; he likewise stipulated to leave Hugh, son of
Ferdoragh baron of Dungannon in quiet possession of his private estates. The lull in the affairs of Ulster that ensued, Sorley before the
new year returned in force from the isles to disturb, and Turlogh incensed that Hugh should be supported by the English as chief of
Tyrone, threw off his allegiance, proclaiming himself hereditary prince
of Ulster, and entered into alliance with Sorley, whose army in Antrim,
now augmented to four thousand men, set at defiance all opposition.

Turlogh, though no longer young, sought in marriage not
unsuccessfully the widow of James MacDonnel. Their nuptials
did not take place before the summer of 1569, when at Raghlin off
the northeastern coast of Ulster, not far from the Giants' Causeway,
the festal occasion was attended by a large concourse. To
strengthen still further this powerful combination, Ineen Duff,
daughter of this lady of Cantyre and Tyrone, became the wife of
Hugh, chief of Tyrconnel. Though Turlogh made his usual abode

* McMahons, Magennis, Maguire, O'Hanlon, and Hugh McNeil Mor of the Fews.

later at Strabane, his hereditary castles of Toome and Castleroe lay further north, as also Dunnalong, his principal residence on Lough Foyle, which stood six miles above Derry, and about that distance from Lifford the favorite abode of O'Donnel.

Sydney without defeating O'Neil had contrived to weaken his power by management and disaffecting his neighbors, and certainly proved a most efficient ruler. He was very popular among his own nationality in Ireland, and by the strict military discipline he maintained, administration of the finances and politic courses, paved the way for subjugation. His strong sense, energy of character, cheerful and kindly disposition, thorough knowledge of the queen and equanimity under her chidings to which he had always a ready but respectful response, fixed him firmly in her favor; and the friendship of Cecil, whose daughter was for a while the destined wife of his son Philip, stood him in stead whenever his brothers-in-law Sussex or Leicester took offence or grew jealous. His denunciation of the "cowardly policy" of breeding dissension between septs and chiefs to weaken their power, exemplifies the honesty of purpose which generally constituted his sterling trait. When exposure in the field had undermined his constitution, and with the death of Shane his main object was accomplished, he requested the grant of Athlone and the abbey lands of Connaught for his guerdon, and repaired by permission to court to further his quest by his presence. He went over in October, 1567, Weston the chancellor and Fitzwilliam, vice treasurer and also his brother-in-law, administering affairs for the twelve months that he was absent.

The result of his deliberations with the queen and Cecil upon Irish affairs appears in the correspondence with the lords justices, and assumed more definite shape in his instructions for his future government when he went back. Substitution of English law for brehon, establishment of the reformed religion, a general system of grammar schools as recommended six years before by James Crofts, appropriation of sept lands and their distribution amongst English settlers and soldiers, presidencies in Munster and Connaught formed part of their proposed policy. Legislation was needed and no time lost in carrying out these measures by the requisite enactments.

Sydney's parliament, convened January, 1569, was a sham. The Irish were not represented, nor do we find mention made of it in their annals. Where there was any show of election, government by intrigue and corruption secured the return of its creatures. Mayors returned themselves; nominees of no character, education or estate, sate for places they had never seen. Stanihurst presided, and Hooker, who continued Hollinshed and had represented Exeter in the English commons, having come over with Carew was member for Athenry. From his account the parliament was neither legally called nor decently conducted. It was simply a bear garden, noisy and disorderly. He framed rules for its proceedings, and after opposition of no avail against the majority, Shane O'Neil was attainted, the queen claiming an older title to Ireland than Heremon or Heber's. Half Ulster, Tyrone, Clannaboy and the Fews, Coleraine of the Kanes, Routa of the McQuillans, Glins of the McDonnels, Iveach of the Maguinnis, Orior of the Hanlons, Farney, Uriel, Lochta and Dartry of the four branches of the McMahons, Turrough of the McKennys, Clanbressail of the McCanns were declared forfeited. Portions were subsequently restored, but the whole proceeding was a mockery on legislation. Captainries were abolished unless granted by patent, imposts laid upon wines, free schools established, the deputy empowered to fill vacancies in the church in Connaught and Munster; fosterage with Irish, and keeping idle retainers were prohibited.

The Ulster triumvirate of Sorley, Turlogh and Hugh might well view with composure this ostentation of power. Hardly a rood of the land thus confiscated passed from its lawful owners. All attempts to colonize ended in disaster, and only in the next reign were attended

with other result.   The act attainting Shane set forth what he had
done or left undone, much that was untrue ; but except in retaliatory
raids on the pale or Dundalk, and burning the Armagh cathedral
when Loftus traduced him, there had been no violation on his part of
the articles unless in self-defence.   What appears to have been
uppermost in the minds of its framers as unpardonable were the
three occasions, on which deputy and council for several days together
assembled in solemn conclave to receive Shane summoned to their
presence, when by the articles he was under no obligation whatever
to obey their bidding and staid away.   He had conquered the Scots
as the queen requested.   The moment after he became crippled
by his defeat in Tyrconnel, Sydney in force crossed his border
and English emissaries compassed his death.   It was now proposed to
appropriate Ulster as already Leix and Offaly.

But if baffled in reaping the fruits of her rapacity, the queen was
greatly relieved that this vexatious war was at an end.   Her first sixteen years of Irish administration cost half a million of pounds
sterling, three-fourths out of the English treasury.   More than a
fourth had been wasted in violating her treaty with Shane in fruitless
hostings and official embezzlements, and thirty-five hundred men had
perished by battle or disease, without laurel or loot, unless it were
cattle found unguarded on the hill-side and driven within the pale.

Parliament had confiscated Ulster.   Taking possession was another matter.   To Sir Thomas Smith had been granted Ards in
Down, and his son to civilize the natives led there a colony, but
O'Neil of Clannaboy slew him, leaving him little time to carry out
his benevolent purposes.   Essex with the queen had planned to
send out two thousand settlers, and the earl raising ten thousand pounds
on his English estates, proceeded to possess himself of Glyns, Routa
and Clannaboy, partly occupied by the Scots.   With a brave following of lords and knights, full purse and numerous and well
appointed force, Essex started on his ill-starred quest.   To better

learn his purpose or perhaps not suspecting his design, Brian, lord of Clanaboy, received him kindly, but soon no longer in doubt, prepared for resistance by gathering his clans and calling in his allies. From Con O'Donnel son of Calvagh who came to greet him, Essex wrested Lifford, his principal castle, taking him prisoner without the slightest pretext or provocation.

Courtiers soon wearied of the hardships of campaigning and went home. For the next two years war waged with alternate fortune, now Mcdonnels and O'Neils for many hours together subjecting Essex to repulse and mortification, then driven themselves across the Ban with considerable slaughter. The earl had begun hostilities, whilst guest of Bryan, by seizing his flocks and herds. These disappeared from his bawns in the darkness of the night. When later superiority of weapons turned the scale, his troops scoured Clanaboy destroying its harvests, wasting in a single day six thousand pounds in value of its grain. The country till then abounding in every growth was changed to a desolate wilderness. The earl proposed that the chief should become his farmer. Grim humor mingled in the offer, and also in Bryan's reply, that man and beast swept off, it would not pay for cultivation. Every proposition of the chief to compromise, was met by treachery, and whilst receiving the hospitalities of Brian who represented the eldest branch of the Hy Nials, Essex seized him, his wife and brother, and they were hung and quartered at Dublin. Sorley Boy he enticed into submission, and at the same time sent Norris to Raghlin with six hundred men and guns.

There Sorley Boy six years before had built from the woods of Antrim pleasant halls for Turlogh's wedding, and there had gathered Ulster and Cantyre in high festival, for an occasion auspicious of future safety. The castle, though strong and garrisoned with two hundred men, yielded to artillery, and the constable stipulating for his own safety, his wife's and child's, made it is alleged no terms for his men. They were massacred by the English soldiers, and three hundred other inhabitants of the island, old and young, found in caves and coverts, shared their fate. Perhaps Essex if present might have spared even the garrison, but his willingness to appropriate the property of others, his bad faith to Bryan and Sorley inspire a doubt, and he mentions with like complacency the wholesale slaughter of Raghlin and that of the two hundred shot down unarmed when he sent Bryan and his wife to death in Dublin. His settlement did not prosper. He hastened home to solicit aid from the queen. She refused it, though she appointed him lord marshal. He came back again in a few months to be poisoned soon after his return in September, at Dublin, it is surmised by Leicester who repudiated his own wife, daughter of Howard, earl of Effingham, to marry his widow. Smith wasted some thought and money on Ards, but to little use, for King James taking it away from his heirs gave it to one of his Scotch favorites. Some remains of that of Essex in Cavan are still held by his descendants of another name.

XXXIV.

REIGN OF ELIZABETH.—1558-1602.—(Continued.)

Thus far to avoid confusion Ulster has been dealt with apart. But all over the island the times were stirring and strong passions working themselves out in events of historical importance. Within the pale, as the field offered richer harvests, intrigue grew rank, and corruption became so open and intolerable as to call down printed denunciations from students at colleges and inns of court, and from anonymous sources, sometimes supposed to be Parker master of the rolls, sometimes Kildare, but probably Bermingham.

Gerald, received upon his return in 1554 with enthusiastic demonstrations of attachment by the people generally, retained hold of the devoted loyalty of his Irish kinsfolk as well as of the many powerful friends and adherents of the Leinster Geraldines. Whether he cherished or not any such aspirations himself, they regarded him as destined at no distant day to occupy the position of his father, grandsire and more remote progenitors, as viceroy. He had smoothed the way for his preferment by acknowledging the royal supremacy in matters ecclesiastical as well as temporal, and by embracing outwardly if not from conviction the new rites and tenets. His affection for his cousin Shane, for O'Connors and O'Carrols and all indeed allied to him by ties of consanguinity, was rarely disguised, and warmed into renewed vigor the long cherished partiality of the septs for his house. This often found imprudent expression, greatly distorted and exaggerated when it reached the queen. He found little difficulty, however, when in her presence in removing her distrust, the good offices of his sister, the fair Geraldine, now wife of Lincoln, lord high admiral, and her especial favorite, being a help. His success in bringing Shane to terms and to court, his services against O'Reilly, O'Coghlans, O'Moores and O'Conors, confirmed her confidence in his loyalty. He had however many enemies. Influential counsellors had lost their anticipated share of the spoils by his restoration to his paternal inheritance, and John Allen, formerly chancellor, now one of the commissioners of crown lands, near akin to the archbishop who perished in the rebellion of his brother lord Thomas, harbored towards him a spirit of revenge, watching its opportunity with unrelenting rancor.

Fitzwilliam loved him not, and in 1560 accused him of ambitious schemes, rudely demanding his follower Daly whom Kildare gave up. When at war with the O'Reillys, some of the Geraldines robbing the marshal, Stanley, of "a keg of drink," a battle ensued, threatening serious consequences, when the earl interposed to separate the combatants. In 1565, Oliver Sutton, a gentleman of the pale, and one of his neighbors in Kildare, wrote Cecil twenty pages, complaining of his taking coyne and livery against the law, keeping three hundred Irish to attend his horses, and forty messengers to go

48

his errands, and raising supplies for five hundred guests who came to visit him at the Christmas and Easter festivals; and that when captain of Annaly, an office which Sydney had taken away from him, he quartered the eight hundred men who rode in his company on English colonists. Little heed was paid to these charges; but when that year the earl arrested Tyrrel for slaying Gerald Nugent, uncle of Delvin, the lord justice advised Leicester that the queen should give him the garter. In reply she commended his good dispositions and advised that he should dislodge Shane from Lecale, but was as cheery of her honors as of her gifts. He accompanied Sydney from Drogheda in the march to Clogher, burning twenty-four miles about that city; and there seems little doubt that he continued loyal, and prudent enough to avoid suspicion.

When Shane ceased to trouble, the queen restored to him whatever belonging to his father remained in the crown, and parliament reversed his attainder. To make him president of Ulster was even under consideration. In the early summer of 1572, he persuaded Rory O'Moore to submission, Byrnes and Cavanaghs, and in 1573 with Essex held parley with Desmond and his brother at Waterford. The next year John Allen and Keating, two of whose kinsmen his people had waylaid and slain by his orders but under instructions from Fitzwilliam then deputy, accused him of complicity with rebel chiefs, but carried over by Fitton, at the examination before the privy council the evidence produced betrayed its inspiration. After nine months incarceration his wife Mabel joined him. He was released in 1576, and two years after, when his eldest son Gerald had married the daughter of Sir Francis Knollys, own cousin of the queen, permitted to go home.

For a while his enemies, disheartened, left him in peace. Baltinglas in 1579 sought to engage him in the catholic cause, and, though refusing, he did not escape suspicion. To a general muster of the troops of the pale gathered at Tara, not long before, he rode in his company; and on his way back with Loftus was thought to have screened Baltinglas from notice under circumstances somewhat suspicious. Certain secret interviews with him later appeared equivocal, and when requested to arrest him he excused himself on the ground that he was his near kinsman, and such a step would weaken his influence in Leinster. When the catholic rising took place a few weeks afterwards, with his son-in-law Delvin also compromised, he was again sent prisoner to the tower, recovering his liberty not long before his death in 1585. His large possessions and extensive influence constituted him a power in Leinster, and though somewhat in anticipation of the course of events, this sketch will serve to explain the part he took in its affairs.

Elizabeth, like most well disposed rulers when first clothed with power, appreciated her obligations and opportunities. Under healthy influence in Cecil's, and prompted by her own sense of duty, she strove hard to amend whatever was amiss in Irish administration or working prejudice to the general welfare. It was no easy task. Selfish officials, more concerned for their own emoluments than for the public, thwarted plans she was forced to abandon or defer. In others she persevered. The currency consisting of " harps " or other coins, debased one fourth below English standards, she called in by proclamation, and though merchants bought them up, sixty thousand pounds weight, three ounces fine, issued from the tower mint in London, and found their way into circulation. Whether working the mines of Wexford, parcelling out Leix and Offaly, regulating trade by imposts or defending her cess, she looked sharp to her regal rights, and her own gains by the proceeding were estimated at two thousand pounds. Twenty years afterwards she adulterated the smaller coins, and just before her death the larger. As she was at that time feeble in mind and body, perhaps she herself had less to do with it than Robert Cecil, whom experience in this particular had made wiser than his father. In 1602 royal proclamation was made that the good coin had been sent out of Ireland in such quantities to purchase arms and munitions of war for the rebels that little was left, and that return to coin of inferior alloy had become a necessity.

Whilst replacing where she could catholic bishops by protestant, it was not till pope Pius V. in 1569, issued his decree excommunicating and deposing the queen, and absolving her subjects from allegiance, that their liberty to worship as they pleased was seriously infringed. So long as her encouragement of Alencon, heir presumptive to the French throne, as her suitor, kept at bay the Spaniards, it was her policy to be tolerant. When his death placed Henry of Navarre, a protestant, one step nearer to the throne, and the massacre of St. Bartholomew brought into more intimate alliance Philip and the Guises, then in the ascendant, she lent strength to William of Orange to readjust the balance for her own security. Realizing that Ireland was the portion of her dominions most open to attack, from its religious beliefs, she redoubled her efforts to change them. Her English subjects in the island stood in her way. Of the twenty-eight Irish peers,* consisting of seven earls, four viscounts, and seventeen barons, nearly all English in race, Ormond Kildare and Fitzpatrick had conformed or were lukewarm, the rest for the most part continued catholic. Penal laws but proved of little avail. Priests and jesuits driven into exile, and fines imposed upon the laity for not attending church, converted indifference into zeal.

But confiscation of church property, dispersion of the monastic orders left little revenue for maintenance of churches or priest. The former had fallen into decay, and if regular or secular performed

---

* Students of history are frequently at a loss for the family names of persons designated by titles of rank or office. The upper house of the Irish parliament besides a score of bishops, consisted at this time of the Fitzgeralds, earls of Kildare and Desmond; Butlers Ormond, Montgarret, Dunboyne and Cahir; McCarthy, Clancarre; O'Brien, Thomond; Burke, Clanrickard; Barry, Buttevant; Roche, Fermoy; Bermingham, Carbury and Athenry; De Courcy, Kinsale; Fitzeustace, Baltinglas; Preston, Gormanstown; Nugent, Delvin; Fleming, Slane; St. Lawrence, Howth; Plunkets, Killeen, Louth and Dunsany; Barnewal, Trimlestown; Fitzmaurice, Kerry; Power, Curraghmore; Fitzpatrick, Upper Ossory; and O'Neil, Dungannon.

his functions, it was without observation or by stealth. Active manhood enjoyed its freedom from irksome restraints, and immoralities and disregard of religious obligation prevailed. No state authorities entitled to respect, and such was the natural consequence of destroying existing religious institutions, when the whole people were opposed to what were to be substituted in their stead. Eloquent preachers, and among them John Knox, sent over to convert in a strange language produced no effect. Not sixty out of two millions of whom the Irish consisted, according to Mageoghan, embraced the new doctrine. That request should be made to allow the clergy to officiate in latin, as that alone could be understood, shows how generally the old rites must have rendered it familiar.

The queen, obstinately set upon her object rather from policy than conscience, insisted that all her subjects should be catholic. Fines were imposed upon whoever refused to attend the protestant service, the roll was called in the churches of the cities and towns under English control, persistent contumacy constituted treason, forfeited substance and life, but men's minds were not to be convinced upon compulsion. Masses were attended, priests harbored and a feeling of bitterness engendered at this absurd spirit of dictation, rendering of no effect either persuasion or force. It was no excuse that catholic prelates and potentates had set the example. A christianity professing nearer approach to its precepts should have been more enlightened. Worldly considerations attached exclusively to neither race nor faith. Still grace quickens under persecution. Walsh dispossessed administered the sacraments, kept alive what remained in the island of catholicism as a church. Hundreds of priests and all but four bishops sufficiently conformed to retain their preferments. When Gregory in 1576 absolved Ireland also from allegiance, Loftus urged sterner measures and heavier penalties. A star chamber in Dublin with secret sessions, instruments of torture and no law, imposed summary punishment on political or religious offenders, and public attention, on the stretch for what it portended, fretted and fevered.

Correspondence preserved from this period proves that with its religious turmoil christianity had little to do. Saints and martyrs, lay or cleric, were out of place in that cold pitiless selfishness, which shaping opinion and governing men's lives, usurped its name. Scramble for church dignities or confiscations, or for other valuable possessions, vesting in the crown and yielded up to favor or importunity with wasteful prodigality, demoralized, as the chance rotations of that later wheel of fortune now proscribed by enlightened nations. All alike, from deputy and primate down through all grades of civil and ecclesiastical administration, were beggars, and public policy had often to withhold its hand, lest in gratifying one, hosts of disappointed supplicants should become disaffected. For the church this was a poor school for the growth of christian grace. Self-denial, self-surrender, consecration of life to duty and the welfare of others, a contrite spirit accepting providence however disagreeable without repining, not for heaven or from fear of losing it, but to answer the divine will and purpose, such may well have been more generally the religion of persecuted priests, beset with peril, guiding passing souls from pain and poverty to joy and rest, than of prelates of the new church lapped in luxury and ease, caring little for their flocks unless to shear them.

In the many parishes they controlled, if the sacred edifice had sufficiently escaped dilapidation, the new service in an unknown tongue suggested no single familiar association. Where from habit parishioners resorted with beads and rosaries to their accustomed devotions within its walls, chilled by the change they found there they went saddened away. In Meath out of two hundred and twenty-four parishes, the glebes of nearly half were alienated or leased to farmers. Curates appointed by non-resident incumbents read the service, but only eighteen understood English. The rest were for the most part Irish priests, who may have openly conformed to perform in secret their ministrations. But in many places, English clerics, where they could without apprehension, occupied the pulpits and preached or prayed to empty walls. Their wives, if their stipends allowed, flaunted their rich attire in towns and villages to the astonishment and scandal of devout catholics, to whom a married clergyman was an abomination.

In remoter sees, catholic bishops were undisturbed. Thomas O'Herlihy of Ross, M'Congal of Kilfenora, Hart of Achonry retained their posts, the latter rounding his century in 1603. Curwen, chancellor and primate, old and infirm, in 1567 surrendered Dublin to Loftus, who was translated from Armagh, and accepted instead the bishoprick of Oxford. Lealy superseded Bodkin in Tuam. Magrath who had submitted to the pressure of the time, occupied Cashel, whilst his competitor Dermod O'Herlihy appointed by the pope, Gregory XIII., arrested at the earl of Ormonds, after torture of peculiar aggravation, was hung in Dublin in early morning to avoid disturbance. Kildare's influence could not save from deprivation the companions of his exile; Brady taking the place of Walsh in Meath, and Leverous giving way to Craik, who as dean of St. Patrick's put up the first clock in the capital. He soon wearied of his post as the people of his preaching, and having from want of judgment parted with lands and manors belonging to his see for tithes of little value, was cast into the Marshalsea or debtors' prison for not paying his first fruits to the crown. Foley renounced the pope but without advantage, Cavanagh taking his place in Loughlin. Thonery successor of Bale in Ossory made way in 1566 for Gaffney; Skiddy held Cork and Cloyne for nine years, and a brother of O'Neil kept M'Caughwell out of Down. Maurice son of the chief of Ara retained Kylalloe. Lismore had a Catholic bishop to 1585, Clogher, Raphoe and Derry later.

Of the prevailing disorders ecclesiastical revenues partook. The archiepiscopal see of Dublin, in olden times the richest see under the crown, yielded but four hundred pounds. The greater part of the protestant bishops regarded the diocesan property as their own; and by long leases and heavy fines impoverished their successors. Allen of Fernes and Lynch of Elphin by ruinous alienations supplied their immediate needs, and others from improvidence exchanged what had been spared in the general confiscation of church property for inadequate considerations. The new faith was on its trial. It is not surprising that it attracted no converts. Ware and Spenser and the most prejudiced protestant authorities admit that greedy hierarchs and a clergy neither devout nor instructed dishonored their profession. To remedy the latter evil, Loftus proposed in 1563 St. Patrick's in the capital should be appropriated for a university, greatly to the disgust of Curwen the existing incumbent of the see, but his views underwent modification when he himself succeeded.

Among the magnates of the pale detraction was rife and venomous. Of one mind in appropriating what belonged to the septs, they were in perpetual contention amongst themselves as to the spoils. Bermingham censured Sussex for his extravagance, promising to save thirty thousand pounds in the annual expenses if allowed. Sussex and Sydney indulged in mutual recriminations. Arnold and Fitzwilliam judged and were judged. Sir Thomas Cusack happily escaped calumny, and by his wisdom and moderation, and especially as a peacemaker secured the esteem he deserved. He pacified O'Neil, reconciled Ormond and Desmond, interposed between Chevers and Carew, and though occasionally himself a petitioner for royal grants his memory stands out in bold relief amidst the frets and avidities of a corrupt age. Thomas Elyot, master gunner for thirty years, in charge of the artillery which battered down feudal strongholds and established English ascendancy, likewise stood high in the general estimation, and Draycot master of the rolls deserves mention for arranging and preserving the records in the castle.

Leinster was only comparatively quiet. The dispossessed chieftains from their mountain retreats watched for opportunity to wreak their resentment on the usurpers of their ancestral abodes, hovering about their settlements and inflicting what injury they could. For eighteen years Rory O'Moore, allowed even by his foes many estimable qualities, kept his clan organized in out of the way places, the dread and scourge of the colonists, losing no occasion of molesting them and baffling every attempt at pursuit. O'Connors and O'Carrols continued their marauds, O'Byrnes and O'Tooles, and Sir Edmund Butler, representative of Ormond then absent in England, and the Graces warred with Oliver Fitzgerald. Another grievance complicated the turmoil: Sir Peter Carew set up a stale claim to half Cork, to Idrone in Carlow belonging to the Cavanaghs, and also to Macleitham in Meath held by Chevers.

Born of an influential family in Devon, Carew after adventures in many lands returned to study up this traditional pretension to Irish estates; and gaining favor with the queen persuaded her and Cecil to allow its adjudication not in the courts of law but by the Irish council. His ancestor sixteen generations before married a daughter of Bigod, earl of Norfolk, who had inherited Carlow through an heiress of Eva, but the grandson of Bigod surrendered his lands to the crown for an annuity of one thousand pounds. Moreover any title derived from this source had been long forfeited under the act against absentees. In the next generation, William Carew is stated to have married Elizabeth daughter of Robert Fitzstephen, grantee with Cogan of Cork; but Robert left no lawful issue as proved in 1333, when the same claim on a grant made nearly two centuries before, of the larger portion of which there had not been even constructive possession, was advanced and disallowed.

Two generations later in the pedigree comes William, added by Hooker from ancient documents, upon which it is intimated little dependence can be placed. The grandson of this William is said to have

49

married the daughter and heiress of Digon, baron of Idrone, which their son John who died in 1324 did not long retain. Recovered by the Cavanaghs its rightful owners it had been for two hundred and fifty years in their undisputed possession, when this claim was advanced and strange to say allowed by the council. Chevers not being able to show any fee in himself in six sevenths of the land in dispute which he held in Meath, was glad by a small payment to compromise and confess judgment, receiving back the whole, which confirmed his title. As will be seen later the claim of Carew to half Cork, was to as little purpose, his death at Ross by disease in 1575 and that of his cousin of the same name, four years later in battle, putting an end to this proceeding. Sir George, afterwards president of Munster and earl of Totness, brother of the second Sir Peter, and natural guardian of his niece, who grew up to marry two husbands, Wilford and Apsley, had the good sense in her behalf not to pursue it.

The early death of the original claimant one year before that of Essex, and his cousin's, to whom he left his estates, so soon afterwards, suggests the fatality attending the De Burghs and Mortimers, and so many other landloupers of earlier days in the island. Many died natural deaths, none of course preternatural as intimated by chroniclers. But it was a wicked age. When the queen could connive at the assassination of Shane, deputy and earl take off the Keatings, Smith the apothecary of Dublin, who received for his mysterious reward a day's pay of the governor and army, may have been put occasionally to such uses as drugging Ormond's cup or platter at Ely House, or that choice wine which sent by one of his name, colonist of Ards, to O'Neil, all but succeeded in relieving administration of an embarrassment.

When the council decided that Idrone belonged to the claimant, the Cavanaghs naturally rose to defend this remnant of their once extensive possessions. Too near Dublin for effectual resistance, Carew stationed at Leighlin dispossessed them with relentless cruelty,

slaughtering hundreds unarmed, besides women and children.
Possibly as some security against similar pretensions, Mac I'Brian
Ara, Ferral and forty subordinate chiefs in Annaly, some of the
Cavanaghs, Gilpatricks, McFallons, Mageoghans, McShanes and
many other chieftains surrendered their estates to the crown, taking
back regrants on English tenure. In 1562 Annaly, the home of
the Ferrals, had been created the county of Longford, and not long
after Monoghan of the Ulster Mac Mahons, was made shire ground.
Philipstown and Maryboro', already two years before licensed as
market towns, were erected into boroughs in 1569. Parliament had
appointed commissioners to parcel out the new counties into baronies,
to be planted each by nine score planters. O'Mores were to have
Leix beyond the bog, each chief to be answerable for his sept, and
hold of the fort. Freeholders were to cause their children to learn
and speak English, keep open the fords, destroy the strongholds and
cut the passes. They were not to marry or foster with any but of
English blood without license from the deputy, and in every town
were to build a church within three years. This was easier to order
than carry out, and little progress was made.

In 1575, drought and intense heat brought with them the plague,
which raged virulently in Dublin, Naas, Ardee, Mullingar and
Athboy. Before the year had ended, Sydney returned for the last
time to find the country one scene of warfare and intestine commotion. He reconciled the Kinel Connel and Kinel Owen, and the
annalists say compelled Essex to go home. Con O'Donnel escaped
with Con O'Neil from the castle. The next year Mary Nugent jealous of her husband, Hugh O'Reilly, burnt the monastery of Cavan
and the town from the castle of Tullymongan to the river. O'Rourke
was busy in raiding Annaly. O'Carrol surrendered his estates,
taking them back on English tenure, and the chief of Offaly by
persuasion of the deputy accepted the actual situation of affairs, and
though stripped of the larger and more valuable portion of his dominions pledged himself to peace.

Rory O'More, recently yielding to the urgency of Kildare, had also agreed to be quiet. His grandfather Connal in 1557 had been hung at Leighlin. The territory of his ancestors had been parcelled out amongst strangers. He had himself been hunted down by the English as a wild beast of the forest. Yet wearied of incessant warfare he longed for rest. The constant encroachments and interference of Francis Cosbie seneschal of Leix, an official grasping and of harsh and unpleasant disposition, fretted his temper and provoked hostilities, till every colonist, whose home was not a castle and protected by artillery, was forced to abandon his newly acquired possessions, and seek shelter in the pale or the larger towns of Leix. In an engagement which took place between Rory and the English, Rory captured Alexander, son of Cosbie, and Harrington one of the council, and held them for ransom.

It chanced that the huntsman of Rory, subjected by his chief to punishment for some misdemeanor, went over to the enemy and persuaded Harpol, seneschal of Carlow, to attempt their rescue. Harpol with two hundred men under guidance of the huntsman, one stormy night, surrounded Rory's abode, which protected by a rampart with two entrances, lay in the densest part of the wood. There Rory was sleeping, his wife, cousin of Ormond, and an old man being with him, and near by him his prisoners bound. When the net was spread and the avenues guarded, guns were fired, which rousing the chieftain from his slumbers, he seized his arms and taking for granted that it was a plot of his prisoners, he slashed at them with his sword, wounding Harrington severely in the arm. Cutting his way through the foe he escaped unharmed into the forest. The soldiers killed his wife and the old man, and relieved Cosby and Harrington of their bonds. Rory naturally stirred to revenge by the fiendish murder of his wife, devastated Carlow, and bursting at night upon Naas, sat on a stone in the market place whilst his men gave the town to the flames. Not long after, Fitzpatrick baron of Ossory went with five hundred English and Irish in pursuit of Rory, who, while reconnoitring and watching their movements, taken at disadvantage was slain. His sept enraged at the loss of their beloved chieftain thereupon rushed upon the army of Ossory, and, though inferior in numbers, routed them with great slaughter, their leader effecting his escape by the speed of his horse.

The death of Rory afforded some equivalent for their discomfiture, whilst his sept and subordinate chieftains realizing how much they were weakened, now that he was no longer their leader, considered the conjuncture propitious for favorable terms and entered into negotiations for peace. Their overtures accepted without hesitation, and never dreaming of treachery, the chieftains of the seven septs of Leix, O'Mores, Kellys, Lalors, Devoys, Macaboys, Dorans and Dowlings with some hundred of their principal followers repaired, on the public faith and under protection of the government, to the rath of Mullamast, five miles from Athee in Kildare, for a conference; and there surrounded by a large force of infantry and cavalry were slaughtered in cold blood. Harry Lalor, as he was entering the rath, having the wit to discover what was intending, shunned the snare by timely flight and warned others on their way.

Responsibility for this massacre of unarmed men invited to a friendly conference, rests primarily and in all probability exclusively upon Cosbie and Harpol, Piggots, Bowens, Hovendons, and others, catholics as well as protestants, of whom there were then not many in Ireland. It may have been in retaliation for inroads upon their grants from the crown of land wrested from the septs. It is alleged that it was with the knowledge and assent of Sydney, and if so casts a cloud on a character generally estimable. If true it must have been one of his last acts before leaving Ireland forever, and he might well bemoan his twenty years service, which had made him twenty thousand pounds poorer, left him five thousand in debt, and loaded his memory with reproach. Although a supplicant for royal favors it is to his credit he did not enrich his family with Irish lands, and that Sir Philip, his son, had no part or work in Irish conquests.

That no mention is made of it in cotemporary public records has suggested doubt if this fiendish massacre ever took place.   In 1577 a plan for extirpating the rebels was entertained, as Sydney states in his letter to the council, in which the cost of the war against the O'Mores and O'Conors is estimated at two hundred thousand pounds.   In the same communication he mentions the rescue by Harpol of Cosbie on the eleventh of October 1577, and in the July following in another the death of Rory the thirtieth of June.   The massacre is here described as related by the Four Masters, compiled in 1636 at Donegal, and by Philip O'Sullivan in his history published in 1621.   Dermod, son of Dermod, prince of Beare and Bantry, and father of Philip with whom the author was residing in Spain when writing his work, died at the age of one hundred years after a busy life in military service about the time of its publication.   He must have known the truth of what actually occurred, and it is unhappily too abundantly corroborated by tradition and other sources for reasonable doubt.   If no distinct trace is found in state papers of the event, they were in the keeping of English officials, who may not have cared to preserve what reflected upon the honor of their own countrymen, and if known might justify or provoke retaliation.

Evidence fortunately exists to exonerate Sydney from complicity. A memorial[*] of Thomas Lee, referring to this affair at Mullamast, says, " They have drawn unto them by protection three or four hundred of the country people, under color to your majesty's service, and brought them to a place of meeting where your garrison soldiers were appointed to be, who have there most dishonorably put them all to the sword, and this hath been by the consent and practice of the lord deputy for the time being.   If this be a good course to draw these savage people to the state, to do your majesty service, and not

* In the Desiderata Curiosa, vol. ii. page 91, and dated 1596.

rather to enforce them to stand upon their guard. I humbly leave to your majesty." Lee, connected by marriage with Eustace, lord of Baltinglas, took part in his rebellion, but was reformed and sent into Flanders. His position was favorable for accurate information as to events. His expression of "deputy for the time being" evidently points at Drury, who succeeded Sydney the first day of September, 1578, two months after the death of Rory, and whose administration of a twelvemonth closing with his death made way for Sir William Pelham's, who surrendered the government to lord Grey in August, 1580.

At this period began to be agitated a grievance sensibly felt by the lords of the pale, which reminds us here of one of our own, which led to our national existence. Impositions levied from necessity, at first with some degree of moderation and submitted to without a murmur, had grown into exactions, oppressive and arbitrary, no longer to be patiently borne. A cess for support of the vice-regal household and the army, more intolerable even than coyne and livery, rested heavily upon proprietors within reach of government process, who finding no other redress, sought relief from the throne. In 1576, Baltinglas, Howth, Delvin, Sarsfield, Nenagh, Trimlestown, Talbot and Killeen petitioned the deputy and council to abandon or modify this system of purveyance, subjecting them to an annual damage of about seven thousand pounds, one third of which enured to the benefit of the court. For beeves worth twenty shillings not one half was allowed, for sheep a single shilling, when their value was half a crown, and no more for calves that sold in the market for five times as much. No satisfactory answer vouchsafed to their remonstrance, they despatched Netterville, Sherlock and Burnell, all able lawyers, to the queen who listened at first graciously to their complaint, expressing her fear that she had committed her flocks not to shepherds but to wolves, but privately instructed by Sydney, at the same time with her usual inconsistency, threw the envoys into prison for their audacity in questioning her prerogative. She also ordered the arrest of the petitioners who had sent them. Sydney proposed to commute the cess for four marks for each town-land, but that was declined as too much like a rent charge. After several hearings on the subject and consultation with Kildare, then again in favor, and due humiliation, they were set free, and composition made for seven years purveyance.

Had the queen been more loyal to her pledges, held out no encouragement to be disappointed, she would have better attained her ends. To Mulmora O'Reilly and the chiefs of Tyrone and Tyrconnel earldoms were promised. The patents passed the seal, robes were sent to the chiefs, and some of the three thousand royal garments, sometimes only the front of one of them, to their wives, to keep them in a state of expectation, whilst on one frivolous pretext or another the honor was deferred. To remove one obstacle in the way of Turlogh's preferment, it was proposed that the young baron of Dungannon, who had repudiated the daughter of Brian Mac Phelim O'Neil to take Judith O'Donnel, sister of Hugh, should marry his daughter. This plan now encouraged and then "impedited" stirred up strife as intended, and furnished a pretext for delay. Such courses did not increase the loyalty of the chiefs, who realizing that they were merely amused and trifled with, easily drifted into hostilities, when good faith would have secured their adherence at critical moments.

Bryan, son of that Cahir Mac Art Cavanagh who was created baron of Balian, son-in-law of Eustace, lord Baltinglas, and nephew of Gerald, earl of Kildare, " a brave and acomplished nobleman," killing Robert Brown lord of Malranken for having insulted him, and being too formidable a neighbor to be left unmolested, Devereux and the principal inhabitants of Wexford assembled for the purpose of avenging the death of Brown, and curbing his power. An engagement ensued in which the Cavanaghs gained a decisive victory, Devereux and thirty of his officers and many soldiers falling in the fight. For ten years Bryan representing his ancient lineage, so long kings of Leinster, sustained his reputation as a distinguished warrior. His abode at Borris has passed since through eight generations of his descendants, of scarcely diminished lustre, to the present proprietor, in whose veins commingles the blood of Ormonds, Mac Carthies, through the branch of Muskerry, and Mac Morrogh.

XXXV.

REIGN OF ELIZABETH.—1558-1602.—(Continued.)

What relates to Munster, in the earlier years of Elizabeth, had few connecting links with affairs elsewhere in the land. Broken up into small but virtually independent sovreignties by mutual jealousy and from their political condition, intercourse discouraged by the dangers besetting its paths and mainly dependent, except in favored localities along shore, by the Shannon or about the lakes, upon minstrels, priests or merchants itinerant, hostings or raids, the south presented what in degree, greater or less, was observable of the whole island at that period, a curious epitome of those larger theatres, continents or embracing the earth, over which history has woven its web. They fought, intrigued and variously combined for mutual protection or to re-adjust the balance of power, with like restless activity as grander potentates. Pent up by their insular position, from their impassioned and fervid temper they formed a seething cauldron, which if occasionally cooled down by infusion of more phlegmatic elements from over the sea, soon resumed its more natural ebullition when pressure was removed.

Under Mary, they had enjoyed unwonted tranquillity. Distinction of race obliterated by consanguinity, common language, habits and interests, their religious rights respected, under hereditary rulers to whom they were attached, lightly taxed and exposed to no confis-

50

cations, the states of Munster had good reason for content. But they were now entering upon a period of strife and calamity, which before the century closed and Tudor dynasty ended subjected them to an unscrupulous despotism, wasting farm and city, whoever survived, if not absolutely bereft of their possessions, left in bondage to taskmasters, strange and pitiless. The anarchs of misrule, whose personal animosities unbarred the gates for all this misery, overwhelming one and his house with irremediable ruin, were the same Geraldines and Butlers, who commenced that subjugation four centuries before, which another century was destined to consummate.

James the fifteenth Desmond whose death in 1558 has been noted, setting aside Thomas Ruagh, his eldest son by Joanna Roche who stood towards him within prohibited degrees, left the earldom to Gerald his second son by Mora O'Carroll. The new earl took his oath of allegiance at the end of November to the dead Mary, tidings of whose demise nine days before had not yet reached him. Teigue O'Brien, son of the first earl of Thomond, when his brother-in-law, Sir Donald, chief of Dalgais had been driven out by the help of Ormond, had taken refuge in Desmond. His cousin Conor, the third earl, in 1559, laying siege to Inchiquin his family castle, where his brother Donogh then was, he persuaded Gerald to go to his relief. Conor withdrew to effect a junction with his friend and kinsman, earl of Clanrickard, and their forces had united at Ballyally, near Ennis, when Desmond came up. "The two camps were not far asunder that night." In the morning, the opposing armies skirmished and manœuvred for position, till they reached the ridges of Spancil Hill, four miles off. Here the combat was long and obstinate. The Dalgais, say the chroniclers, had been accustomed to drive the Geraldines, and ascribe the change of fortune that day to the presence of Teigue with its enemies. Gerald gained the summit of the hill for which they were contending, and routed his brother earls, who lost on that bloody field many chiefs of Sil Aedha, seven of the Mac

Sweenys, including both constables of Thomond and Clanrickard, and with them the flower of their force. Leaving Teigue and Donogh in possession of Inchiquin, Gerald returned home after victory in triumph.

Another Teigue O'Brien, son of Sir Donald, most distinguished of his age for agility, strength, martial feats and horsemanship, died that year in Fermanagh; and Eveleen, widow of the late earl of Desmond, already remarried to Conor, earl of Thomond, a "charitable, humane, friendly and pious countess," was laid not long after among her kindred, the MacCarthys, in the abbey of Mucruss. When Christmas came, the two Geralds, earls of Kildare and Desmond held their festivities at Limerick, the varied experiences of the former in his earlier days in Italy and intercourse with Geraldines of Florence, doubtless forming for them both an interesting subject of discourse.

Irish earldoms in the sixteenth century were no sinecures; and for men in the vigor of life, energetic and more fond of glory and power than studious of their ease, afforded opportunities which might have been better improved by the heads of the two branches of the Geraldines now together at Limerick, than they were. But with such pressure from without and discordant elements within, although able and well disposed, such laudable intentions had they entertained them would have proved of little avail. Desmond claimed supremacy throughout an extent of one hundred and forty miles over a medley of either race, who paid tribute when coerced, filled his marshal array if the object pleased them, but were too jealous of his authority to improve their condition at his dictation. They were content with their independence. Yet if these petty autocrasies, under his lead or that of an Irish chieftain, could have formed a federal system for common objects, government might have exercised its legitimate functions for liberty and not oppression, and proved a blessing, not a curse. With their inheritance of misrule, however well disposed or fitted under happier auspices to meet the responsibilities of such a leadership in Munster, the embarrassments that attended the career of Desmond, if not his traits of character, hopelessly discouraged any such aspirations for him.

One of the most turbulent of his subjects was his uncle Maurice Duff, who twenty years before slew the court page, and who had received as his portion of the family domains, Kerricurrihy west of the cove of Cork. In 1560 his sons, James Fitsmaurice who afterwards occupied a conspicuous position in the history of Munster, and Thomas, invaded their neighbors, the Mac Carthys Reagh of Carbery, then ruled by Finnin, whose brother Donogh, father of Florence and their own brother-in-law, collecting a fine body of galloglasses under Turlogh Mac Sweeny of the Tuath branch of the name, pursued them to the Bandon, and at Inishowen defeated and slew two or three hundred. Gerald took umbrage at this procedure, either from its compromising his peaceable relations with so great a power as Carbery, or else from not brooking this disrespect shown to his authority. The resentment it occasioned if genuine was not easily appeased; but correspondence home from Dublin represents it as feigned and for ulterior objects, one of them a wish not to be called away from his own dominions which demanded his care.

Naturally of an overbearing temper, and elated by his recent victory, he bore with little patience what he regarded as encroachments upon his rights. His neighbor Ormond, distantly related to the queen and a protestant, stood high in her favor and had received the appointment of lord treasurer, an office held for life by the late Desmond and to which his son was naturally disappointed in not succeeding; without much reason, as the father of Ormond had been the predecessor of his own. He had a grant of Oonagh for years of which Ormond was seeking the fee. There existed another and more serious source of contention between them. Joanna, only child of the eleventh Desmond and mother of Ormond, after the death of her second husband Sir Francis Bryan, was now Gerald's wife. By devise or family settlement, she had received upon the death of her father the baronies of Clonmel on the Suir, Kilfeacle and Killethan. What were the terms of the grant does not appear, but Ormond claimed them before the death of his mother in January, 1564, by some more ancient title, although through her he could have derived none whilst she lived. In 1560, their respective pretensions by mutual defiance were about to be committed to the arbitrament of arms on the great road from Cashel to Tipperary, their whole musters confronting, when reflecting on the consequences or Sussex interposing, they parted without coming to blows. A few months after, in August at Clonmel, Sir Thomas Cusack, Stanley the marshal and Parker master of the rolls decided in favor of Desmond.

Not content to accept their decision as any settlement of the controversy, Ormond waylaid with hostile purpose his adversary, as they were returning home from Tyrone: but desisted when Sussex forbad. He wrote the deputy in February that Desmond had burnt a town and much corn, fallen out with his neighbors, and that his people had robbed one of his own near Limerick of five hundred pounds. Soon after at Waterford, they promised Fitzwilliam, lord justice in the absence of Sussex, to go over to court, as requested, at Easter. Desmond was directed not to exert any authority over Barrys, Kinsale, Kerry, Decies, MacCarthies, Sullivans, Donoghues or Callaghans, but only over his own kindred. When the earls reached London, as O'Neil was taking his leave, Desmond, least in fault, was placed in custody of the treasurer, the queen assuring his wife she meant him no harm and nothing but kindness. Yet at the same time reversing the award of the commissioners, she vested the disputed baronies in Ormond, insisting that they should be friends before suffered to depart. Desmond requested in September passports for himself and his thirty-seven attendants, but though Ormond was allowed to go home in January, he was detained a year longer. Joanna besought the queen for his release, stating that in their quar-

rel she had been strictly impartial between her husband and son.
The queen remained inflexible, though releasing him from confinement, inviting him to court, lending him money when four pounds
was all he had left.   It was not till his health had become seriously
impaired, Cusack had entreated, and Cecil and Sydney extorted a
promise that bonaghts, risings out, brehon law, rhymers, bards and
dice players should be suppressed, subsidies regularly levied, crown
rights to wardships and marriages enforced, and fourpence " cowe "
agreed to be paid, that requesting artillery to reduce the chiefs to
civility and leave to arrest offenders, he was permitted in December,
1653, to repair to his dying wife, who survived but a few weeks after
his reaching Clonmel.

Various points in the controversy still left undetermined, Cusack
that summer reaffirmed, certainly in part, the judgment of the commissioners, for Desmond later complained, and that after the death of
Joanna, that Ormond had collected rents in one of the baronies in
dispute.   The prisage of wines in Kinsale and Youghal was adjudi-
cated also to him, though given ten years afterwards to Ormond by
the queen.   Whilst these questions were pending, a messenger from
France was arrested and upon him found a free pass for hounds and
hawks sent from Desmond and O'Neil to the king, and though in
time of profound peace, it gave color to surmises, which lost nothing
in circulation.   Desmond was ordered to lend no aid to Sir Donald
O'Brien against Thomond.   Before the year closed Ormond wrote
Cecil, that he had prohibited coyne and livery in his palatinate, but
encroachments by Desmond compelled him to resume them.

Not long after his return home, Desmond's uncle, Maurice Duv,
although over eighty, made an incursion in which he lost his
life, into Muskerry.   Dermod chieftain of that country, also
son-in-law of Maurice as was Donogh of Carbery, overtook and routed him, and whilst pursuing his men left the old man, whom he had
captured, in charge of four of his own followers.   Maurice a trouble-

some captive was slain by them, " though the profit of sparing him would have been better than the victory gained by his death." As the thirteenth earl of Desmond his cousin whom he slew, had taken his bride from Blarney, this termination of his earthly career savors of retribution. Dermod being especially loyal and the friend of the deputy, this invasion of his territory by the near relatives of Gerald might have created fresh complications for him, had not Maurice been too headstrong and lawless for any one to be held accountable for his proceedings.

In February, 1565, the feud assumed more serious proportions. Desmond claiming sovereign rights over Decies, Sir Maurice Fitzgerald of Dromanagh, its lord, sent for Ormond to protect his cattle from cess: who surprising Desmond with an inferior force at Affane in Wexford attacked him. Pride forbade retreat. The unequal combat ended in disaster, and when Gerald borne wounded from the field on a litter by his foes was asked in derision " where was now the great earl of Desmond," he made his often quoted response, " where he ought to be, on the necks of the Butlers." Ormond accused him of treason, the deputy of harboring Cormac of Offaly a declared rebel, Thomond and Clanrickard with wasting their lands, and in April he was carried over by Liverpool to London, while Elizabeth heaped upon her favorite Ormond whom she styled her black husband, honor and possessions, abbey lands of Holy Cross and Athassel, releasing him from large arrearages to the crown.

Desmond had for companion across, his brother-in-law Donald Mac Carthy Mor, 1518–1596, upon whom the queen now proposed to confer the titles of earl of Clancarre and baron of Valentia. Chief of his name, from Pallis, on the river Lawne near Killarney, his rule extended over a wide range of country, fertile and picturesque, and he claimed supremacy over the various branches of the Eoghanacht, sometimes conceded and as often denied. In June surrendering his domains and dominions, he received them back to hold from the crown, and requested to be appointed vice-admiral upon his own

shores, to have the patronage of all spiritual promotions within his
county of Clancarre, and to have the appointment of head sheriff of
his own realm and an abode within the pale.   Prince and earl of
Desmond thus proceeding together under such different auspices to
the English court, offers one of the strange vicissitudes of Irish
history ; the chieftain, lineal representative of the ancient kings of
Munster, to receive such honor as the queen had long promised to
bestow,—Gerald, of the powerful earls who had usurped and abused
its sovereignty, with gloomy presentiments of what awaited him.
Near kinsmen and closely connected,—for besides many ties of similar sort in that and former generations, Donald's wife, Honora, was
sister of the earl, whose father's had been Donald's sister,—they
were alike staunch catholics, and since 1490, when the tenth Desmond slew in battle the then chieftain of Clancarthy, friendly relations
between their two houses had been rarely disturbed.   No immediate
or important conflicting interest now existed to divide them, and probably neither divined the motive which governed the queen in seeking
to weaken Geraldine power and influence in Munster, by raising up
a formidable competitor for its supremacy.

In the same ship, intended for similar honors, went Owen
O'Sullivan, chief of Beare and Bantry, an area stated to measure
forty-two miles by twenty-four, which he also surrendered, receiving it back with the honor of knighthood.   His elder brother
Donel, son of Dermod whose death in 1549 at Dunboy has been
mentioned, had been slain in 1563 in some contention or contest by
one of his race "lord of the Reeks."*   Donel, "worthy son of

---

* After the invasion, in the thirteenth century, the O'Sullivans, defeated near Cork in an
ambuscade in which fell eight of the ten sons of their chief, withdrew from Clonmel and
Knocgraffon their former possessions to Bantry and Dunkerron.   Their chieftain, Donald
More, gave when he died one third of his territory to his grandson, " child of his affections
and of his goods," whose descendants, lords of the Reeks, lofty mountains in Kerry, assumed the surname of Macgillicuddy, thus anglicised from Gil Mochuda or followers of
that good bishop of Lismore of the seventh century, adopted for the patron saint of the
sept.   They shared in the misfortunes of their country.   Their chief, who in the days of
Cromwell preferred to burn his castle rather than surrender it, or perhaps his son, commanded the Irish regiments sent into Germany by William III.   They still retain considerable portions of what Donald Mor gave his grandson more than six centuries ago, which
Richard the late chief held forty years, and upon his death in 1866, which descended to
another Richard his son.

a renowned father," left children, but too young to rule, and Sir Owen as tanist had succeeded. Owen displayed less consideration for the eldest representative of his house than Morrogh of Thomond, ancestor of the younger Donnel, taking back the estates entailed upon his own sons, the eldest of whom in later years married Joan daughter of Desmond. During his life, which ended in 1593, he remained through all the disturbances loyal to the crown.*

Off Galway bay, the isles of Arran from time immemorial had been inhabited by a branch of the O'Briens, freebooters of the sea, who infested the neighboring shores exacting tribute or striking by their daring exploits consternation in places more remote. In 1560 Mahon, their chief, with marauding intent visited Desmond, but the hospitable welcome he received changed his purpose and some of the inhabitants accompanied him back when he went as his guests. Upon his return voyage, his vessel driven at night by a furious tempest past Dun Angus, his abode, to the Moycullen coast, struck on a rock and foundering, all of the company, more than one hundred, perished, except himself and three more. Tuathal O'Malley, whose kinswoman Grace, then wife of O'Flaherty we shall have occasion again to mention, "the best pilot of a fleet of long ships of his day," went down with the rest.

Ever since St. Brendan a thousand years before made his famous seven years voyage to the land opposite conjectured to be America, and penetrated its interior, till water flowed west, fondness for maratime adventure found opportunity, not only all round the island, but on distant shores. Mention is frequently made by the annalists of bold navigators, who issuing out from the deep bays of the western

---

* His son Dermod married Desmond's daughter. Many other of his children by Elena Barry daughter of lord Buttevant influentially connected retained their possessions till most of them were taken away under Cromwell or William of Orange. His daughter married Nicholas Brown cousin of Lord Bacon; his descendants the earls of Kenmare, have been since large proprietors in Kerry. Near by their hereditary abode on the Lake of Killarney dwell the Herberts, whose ancestor derived large possessions, by similar devise to that of the last earl of Thomond in 1741 to the Wyndhams, from his kinsman, Charles McCarthy Mor, representative of Clancarre, being the g. g. g. grandson of his daughter Ellen, and who died in 1770.

coast, like vi-kings for conquest, or buccaneers for spoil, often on quests of more legitimate commerce, wandered over the seas. At this particular epoch Spaniards from their harvest fields of gold finding convenient refuge from tempest or hostile cruisers in its havens, carried on a lucrative trade in which the mariners of septs on the ocean participated in their own vessels. Elizabeth regarded this traffic with jealous eye, not pleased that catholic powers should gain any such hold over her Irish subjects, and eager besides to divert a portion of the profits into her treasury, by monopolising this commerce for English bottoms. Her orders proved of little avail, for in that wild country there were no revenue officers or coast guard to enforce them, and the four pounds on each tun of wine she requested when at last granted by parliament could not be collected.

Conor, earl of Thomond, speedily recovered from his defeat at Spancill Hill in 1559 and the campaign after in West Connaught, chased the O'Flahertys into the Joyce country. Their chief, Morrogh of the battle axes, withdrew beyond his reach, and for many years after, from amidst the twelve peaks of Bennabulla, lofty and inaccessible, made what war opportunity offered against O'Briens and all who supported English rule till Desmond's death in 1583 led to his submission. Teigue O'Brien, son of Morrogh, whilst at Limerick a few weeks afterwards was arrested and sent to Dublin at the instance of the earl, but effected his escape to wreak his resentment. The earl in 1562 invaded O'Connor Kerry and the knight of Glynn on the other side of the Shannon. Soon after his uncle Sir Donald, returned home from Ulster with his brother Teigue,* who with Donogh, son of Morrogh, his brother-in-law, pounced upon Conor at Ballymacregan, in the barony of Inchiquin, taking much spoil. They were opposed at first with success, and retreated to Scamhall, but there they rallied defeating the earl. The campaign of 1563 at first resulted in Conor's favor, and Ballyally, where dwelt the sons of

---

* Founder of the O'Briens of Ballycorick.

Morrogh, and Ballycar had been demolished, when Sir Donald and his brother invaded Clancuilen, near Rosrae the favorite abode of the earl, and after their maraud made good their escape across the Fergus with their prey.

Soon reinforced by the Clansheehy and Clansweeny from Desmond, who left behind them when they went fewer cattle than they consumed or drove away, they reduced the earl to extremities, who was glad to compromise " for peace that winter," and as amends for depriving his uncle Donald of the chieftainship five years before, by bestowing on him Corcomroe, its rents, customary services and church livings. Thereafter Donald, too prudent to hazard his possessions by revolt, continued at peace, an energetic and sagacious ruler, sometimes punishing with severity such as deserved it. When one branch of the Dalgais slew their kinsman Mahon, he pursued and captured them and taking them in fetters to Ross near the places of their atrocity, "that their anguish might be the more," according to the annalists, hung some and burnt the rest.

Towards the close of 1565, the queen ordered that all claims of Desmond and Ormond should be submitted to chancery, and upon issue joined, to commissioners: disputed lands to be left pending the controversy in charge of indifferent persons. She wrote Sydney that they were reconciled and about to go home, but that Desmond must be detained at Dublin till his dues were paid. Cecil impressed upon the deputy in May that he must be favorable to Ormond, or the queen would not suffer the suit to proceed. When Warham St. Leger, president of Munster, met Desmond at Loch Girr and imparted to him what the queen intended, he expressed his indignation and wrote Sydney that he had received great wrong, that he desired the benefit of the law and royal orders, and should distrain for his rents if withheld. St. Leger in consideration of his resolution and power advised ending the controversy, but Elizabeth recalling the president as too partial to him, urged in reply that

Ormond and his friends should be encouraged to resist him and that the rebels he harbored should be apprehended. In August she wrote from Kenilworth that he should not have a renewal of his lease of Oonagh, but that it should be given to Ormond.

The royal temper thus perverted, ten thousand pounds lost to him by her injustice, and O'Neil soliciting his aid, disaffection would have had its excuse. But he did not yield to his resentment. He invaded the territory of his brother-in-law, the sixteenth lord of Kerry,* but soon after joined the general hosting with him, St. Leger, the white knight, Dunboyne and Corraghmore against the O'Reillys. Whilst on this service the Butlers brothers of Ormond and the sons of Dunboyne, depredated his territory. Instead of punishing them, orders came over in March from the queen to commit the earl to Dublin castle, and place his brother Sir John in charge of Desmond. The ostensible ground for this procedure was the old charge, that he had harbored traitors, which had received some confirmation from Cahir O'Conor, one of the very chiefs of Offaly he had befriended but who was now making his peace.

Late in January, 1567, the deputy proceeding towards the south, found Leix peaceable and its tillage improving; the Butler domain in Kilkenny in excellent condition and increasing in wealth; that of the Fitzpatricks "in indifferent good order," Florence and Geoffry, younger sons of its lord, "evil doers," and engaged in depredations upon their neighbors; Ely well ruled by William O'Carrol, who wished to surrender and be made a baron; Ikerrin of the O'Meaghers wasted; Tipperary in frightful disorder from contentions between Ormond and Dunboyne, the latter of whom was also at strife with his brother. Sydney determined the dispute with Ormond in his favor, imprisoning the others with their wives who had stirred up the tur-

---

* Thomas son of the tenth lord of Leixnaw. Tidings of his unexpected succession to his brother and nephews had been brought to him in Italy in 1540 by his faithful nurse Joanna Harmon, when his kinsman Gerald after him in the line, not knowing he was alive, had claimed the inheritance. He married daughters of Desmond, McCarthy More, and Sir Donald O'Brien. His daughter Joan was first wife of Conor third earl of Thomond, and his eldest son, nephew of Clancarre, son-in-law of David Roche lord Fermoy.

moil, and quieted the land by his severities. The Butlers were law-less, and Desmond, little disposed to be aggrieved and not retaliate, had raided Killethan to collect his rents, as also Oliver Grace. The brothers of Ormond are described as "wanting both in justice and judgment and stoutness to execute," for when directed to bring in the O'Kennedys, chiefs of Upper Ormond, the region between the But-lers and the Shannon opposite Thomond, as likewise some of the Burkes, the deputy had to go himself in pursuit of them and bring them to submission.

Clonmel, Cashel and Fethard were greatly depopulated, the in-habitants not daring to issue from their gates. After reforming abuses, regulating their governments and dispensing stern justice to offenders. Sydney summoned chief and freeholder to meet him at Waterford. Warham St. Leger had maintained order there whilst he staid, but the country had been since worried by the Powers. Corraghmore enjoined to arrest the chief malefactors produced but two, who were hung, and the baron for his remissness sent to the castle. From Dungarvan passing on to Youghal the deputy found it in evil case. Desmond there pled his own cause, but one is in-clined to suspect from the terrorism of Tudor reigns that the judg-ment against him, not final or covering all the points, was a foregone conclusion, and not from any folly or fault of his own.

When this decree was rendered " he did not a little stir and fell into some disallowable heats and passions, but was taught to understand his duty to your majesty, obedience to your laws and reverence for such as sate by your authority." Sydney adds that from that time forward he showed himself wayward and unwilling to further the weal of the country or the service of the queen. He was retained under various pretences and placed under guard. Naturally incensed at this treatment, for Cusack the chancellor had twice decided in his favor, he strove to discourage the great lords of Cork from coming in to the deputy. Barry, Roche and Courcy, Clancarre and

O'Sullivans, Mac Carthies, Reagh and Muskerry, nevertheless appeared, complaining of his exactions, "with open mouths and held up hands, crying for justice, and that it might please the queen to cause her name to be known among them with reverence and her laws obeyed, offering to submit themselves, life, land and goods."

Not only were the towns decayed and dilapidated, but the whole country from Youghal to Limerick, pleasanter naturally than any Sydney had ever seen, was wasted and desolate, as if war had swept over it. Fire, sword, famine and incessant extortions, had left everywhere their mark; villages burnt, churches in ruins, castles and towns; bones and sculls, women and mothers quick with child ruthlessly murdered, and Desmond sitting at meat with the perpetrators of these atrocities. Marriage was little regarded, perjury, robbery and murder counted allowable, no consciousness of sin or of future life or grace to gain it if any there had been.

As they advanced further into Desmond, the earl chafed at his detention, threatening he would not put down his idle men or gallo-glasses, nor relinquish coyne and livery, but would keep five men for every one, and by midsummer have a thousand afoot. The deputy had ordered him to produce his base brother Thomas Ruagh and the white knight, and at Kilmallock one of his abodes, in presence of the chiefs of Cork and others who accompanied their march, reproached him with calling together his forces. This Desmond excused as the only mode of securing their presence. His countess, daughter of Dunboyne, an admirable woman and wife, recently a mother, he naturally wished to be near. Six hundred of his men laying west towards Limerick not South towards Youghall, where his wife then was, exciting suspicion, the deputy who had'with him but two hundred men-at-arms, charged him with treasonable designs, and threatened that if any outrage were offered on their way to Limerick he should die. Sydney says the earl fell on his knees and confessed his fault. This frequently mentioned of Irish chiefs looks much like a figure of speech. It seems difficult to understand that the proud earl had occasion or mood for any such humiliation, or Sydney the bad taste to require it.

Entrusting Cork, Kerry and Limerick to Sir John the earl's brother, the deputy dismissing the chiefs and lords who had attended his progress, reached Limerick in safety, escorted by three hundred men who came out to meet him. That city had been despoiled both by Desmond its neighbor on the south and from over the river by Thomond, whose lack of judgment and insufficiency to rule would have tempted the deputy to remove him could there have been found one loyal or reasonable enough to take his place. Galway guarded its gates day and night against the earl of Clanrickard, whose two sons by different mothers, both alive, contended for his succession and arrested were taken to Dublin. The earl, whom Sydney pronounces as wise to rule and obedient to law but under control of his wife, fretted by his unnatural progeny, worried by the Oughter branch of his name in Mayo and the O'Flaherties, "notwithstanding intentions of the best found himself often constrained to do the worst." Galway and Athenry with four only left of three hundred good householders suffered in consequence. His own baronies in the south of Connaught were well tilled and manured, and though Shane had not long before collected of him tribute by violence were prospering. Clancarre had no power or influence to govern, and Sydney is severe on all the four earls of Munster except Ormond, though entertaining more favorable impressions of the chiefs of Muskerry and Carbery. He recommended presidencies there and in Connaught, and resolved to send Cusack, whose experience, faithfulness and willingness he had cause to commend, to pacify their disputes, deprecating as already mentioned breeding of dissension as cowardly and bad policy, inasmuch as the population, not one fifth of what it should be, in their distress were never in more forwardness to reformation. Hugh O'Donnel and Donogh O'Conor Sligo at Galway renewed their

pledges of allegiance, and surrendered their lands, the latter proposing to visit the queen.   The deputy with his prisoners Desmond and
the sons of Clanrickard returned home through the country of the
O'Kelly and by Athlone, reaching Dublin on the sixteenth of April.
His second visit to the south ten years later had sadder stories to tell.

Sydney and St. Leger were alike reproved by Elizabeth for ex-
cusing Gerald.   She ordered that he should be indicted in Ireland
before being sent over, and should bring but six attendants in his
suite.   In August, Fitzwilliam with the master of the rolls and
justice Fitzsimmons passed nineteen days at Kilkenny the chief abode
of Ormond, hearing the causes between the two earls.   Sydney went
over to England in October, Weston now chancellor and Fitzwilliam taking his place as lord justices.   Desmond was detained in
the hope of securing the apprehension of his brother.   The efforts to
entrap him finally succeeded.   Sir John had been left by Sydney
in charge of the Desmond palatinate and had no reason to suspect any
designs upon his own liberty.   But upon his arrival in Dublin on
the twelfth of December, 1568, to take leave of his brother, he was
hurried on board the ship and they were carried over to London,
where for the next four years they remained prisoners.   Dunboyne,
father-in-law of Gerald, was to have accompanied him to England,
but had died in May in the castle at Dublin.

Commissioners appointed for Munster summoned its great chiefs
to the council, but they would not come unless the countess of Desmond came too.   She wrote from Kilmallock in January, 1568, "that
the country was in such disorder that few could trust, father, brother
or son.   Scarcely abiding two days in one place, she trudged about
day and night for safety, and the people were so worn out by cess she
could not collect their dues for her husband's necessities."   Lacy bishop
of Limerick brought her to Cork, and by her help James Fitzmaurice,
to whom the earl had confided the charge of Desmond, and Thomas
Ruagh again contending for the earldom, were apprehended, but

set free. Meanwhile the earl examined at court by Knollys, Mildmay and Gerrard, admitted he had taken Kilfeacle and collected rents in Killethan, but pled pardon for his other transgressions. He made his respectful submission, expressing his willingness that the queen should deprive him of portions of his land for the more quiet government of the rest, and gave recognizance in twenty thousand pounds. He was still, however, detained in the tower, suffering from cold in the same small comfortless apartment with his brother. His letters home, sometimes as many as nineteen in a day, were intercepted and perused by the ministers, Walsingham having a special fondness for that kind of reading. Money was supplied for his subsistence, but in prison he remained until the countess came over in 1570, when they were placed in charge of Warham St. Leger, whose house at London or castle Leeds in Kent then became their abode.

James Fitzmaurice able and active invaded the territory of the lord of Kerry, and ordered to desist, repeated his maraud. The inhabitants took refuge at Lixnaw with their herds. Intense heat and drought rendered the river brackish, and man and beast suffered from thirst and want of food. Coming up with a much more numerous army than theirs, James posted O'Connor Kerry with the Clan Sheehy on the east of the town, marching round, himself, to gain position on the west. Edmund Mac Sweeny constable of Clanmaurice and John O'Mally, with fifty men on a visit, were there, and when the baron consulted them as to what should be done, replied, that "in their situation life was near unto death, that no mercy could be expected from the foe, and as he wished not to give hostages, he must trust to fortune and take for his portion of Ireland, the land under the feet of his enemies ; that he should first attack the Clan Sheehy*

---

* Two septs of this name existed in Kerry one of Iveragh descendants of Core: king of Munster, and Conary monarch of Ireland ; the other originally of Coreagniny beyond Tralee and later in one or more patches of territory farther east near the brehons, Egans and Clancy, from Eogan Mor. Like the Mac Sweenys they were professional soldiers, and constantly at this period engaged in fighting where any was going on.

which especially deserved their resentment." Following the advice
thus bravely tendered, the lord of Lixnaw marshalled his men and the
Clan Sweeny in the van marched steadily against his adversaries,
who welcomed his approach assured of victory.   Both sides fought
gallantly, " making trial of the temper of their sharp spears, strength
of their battle axes, keenness of their swords and hardness of their
helmets."

The struggle proved long and desperate, but the fine army of the
Geraldines was at length worsted.   Three hundred fell, and among
them O'Connor Kerry, "the mournful loss of the Clan Rory, the
burning brand of his tribe and race ; a youth upon whom devolved
the chieftainship in preference to his seniors ; a sustaining prop of
the learned, distressed and the professors of the arts ; a pillar of
support in war against his neighbors and foreigners."   Edmund Mac
Sheehy, chief constable of the Geraldines, affluent and as famous for
his hospitality as for his dexterity, also fell, and O'Callaghan, the
sons of O'Dwyer and of the white knight, and many more perished.
The defeated Geraldines speedily rallied from their discomfiture, and
in October captured the baron.

The next year brought fresh cause for agitation.   The decision in
favor of Carew enraged wherever it menaced, and Clancarre, Butlers and Fitzmaurice were quickly in arms.   Clancarre, though not
of much force of character, was wise enough to perceive that to
wrest away the territory of his race and trample out its faith was the
policy of the queen and her ministers.   By uniting all the catholic
elements of resistance, these designs might be frustrated.   Supported by O'Sullivan Mor and other chiefs of the Eoghanacht he renounced
his English title and resumed that of McCarthy Mor, at the same
time asserting his claim to be king of Munster as his ancestors had
been for many generations.   Desmond was a prisoner, and his power and possessions might pass to strangers, and unless the opportunity
offered were improved, no other equally propitious might recur.

With O'Donoghues, Keefes, Macawleys, the son of O'Sullivan
Mor and Edmund Mac Sweeney, he spoiled Fermoy and Muskerry;
Edward Butler, brother of Ormond, whose castle of Killogrenan
had been seized by Carew, Ely with eight hundred men. Thomas
Ruagh joined Fitzmaurice, and the country completely disorganized "no Geraldine was quiet or Butler content." Unable to
reduce Kilkenny where Carew commanded in force, they harried
above and below from Dublin to Waterford, and stripped, with the
inhumanity usual on both sides, the fair of Enniscorthy of its horses
and herds, gold, silver and foreign wares and of whatever else it had
that was precious.

At a conference of all the principal leaders of Munster except
Decies, Roche, and Barrymore, Maurice Reagh Fitzgibbon, titular
archbishop of Cashel and the bishop of Ross were sent into Spain
to request aid of Philip II., which was promised at Easter.* As
two hundred Spanish vessels every year came to fish off the shore,
rumors were rife that forty with guns had arrived. Citizens of Waterford opened their gates to relieve eleven hundred people in seeming
distress, who breaking in tore down their houses and committed great
havoc. Kerricurrihy given up in part to St. Leger was spoiled, the
abbey of Tracton beset by half as many reduced, and its warders slain,
Cork besieged by James with four thousand men. Pollard sent
with Peryam to keep order was crippled with the gout and could not
go, and though Desmond and Sir John begged Fitzmaurice and
Thomas Ruagh to be still, Sydney wrote in June that rebellion raged
all over the realm but within the pale.

By her prerogative the queen could do no wrong. Yet by setting
aside the judgment of the commissioners as to the baronies out of
partiality for Ormond, coercing her prisoner in the tower, to give

* McGrath was at that time archbishop of Cashel, but suspected of disaffection was translated to Down. Loftus wished to exchange Dublin for an English bishoprick. Bodkin of
Tuam was loyal. The catholic primate of Armagh a prisoner in London was accused by
the daughter of his jailer, but confronted with his accuser she retracted. Dixon of Cork
did penance in the cathedral of Dublin, and was deposed on a similar charge.

St. Leger Carrigolene in Kerricurrihy to alienate James Fitzmaurice, and helping Carew to Idrone and in his claim to half Cork,
Munster had been overwhelmed with calamity, and there was hardly a
faithful soul left within its borders who did not detest her. They
were obliged to be wary or the heads of her pledges in the tower,
the earl and his brother, would have dropped prematurely from their
shoulders.

With a quarrel so reasonable and disaffection wide spread, could
the chiefs have forgotten their quarrels, abstained from fresh provocation, been all of one mind, they could have discouraged Carew in
his Munster pretensions, enjoyed their religious liberties undisturbed.
But feuds and jealousies estranged many of their leaders. Fineen
of Carbery, "who had not placed his affections on this world or
knew how much he had laid up," had been succeeded in 1568 by his
brother Donogh, and neither that chief nor Dermod of Muskerry,
lately knighted by Sydney, loved their brother-in-law James Fitzmaurice. Sir Owen of Beare and Bantry opposed the movement,
as did his neighbor O'Driscol, lord of Baltimore, who had lately
surrendered. Fitzmaurice as a Geraldine and also from his overbearing temper, was not as popular then as later, and many whose
titles were menaced or whose attachment to the ancient church was
unabated, grew timid or lukewarm. Fermoy, the lord of Decies
and the Barrys were loyal to the queen, as also Thomas brother of
Gerald and John uncle to James Fitzmaurice. Thus dissensions,
ever Ireland's weakness, palsied all attempt at combination, and they
found themselves borne along to destruction by events beyond their
control.

Sydney joined by Ormond, sent over by the queen to detach his
three brothers from the league, marched with considerable force into
Munster. Ormond after accomplishing his object, his brothers Edmund, Edward and Pierce submitting without hesitation, probably
upon promise of pardon, though this was not at once granted, crossed

the Suir, and by Coshlea passed on to Loughlene. He demolished
a strong castle of O'Sullivan Mor on an eminence at the mouth of
the gap of Dunloh, doing much havoc. Opposition not strong
enough to contend melting away, and the chiefs generally professing
loyalty, the lord deputy placed a garrison under Humphrey Gilbert
at Kilmallock, and himself repaired to Athlone. After establishing
Fitton as president of Connaught including Clare, he thence proceeded
toward Ulster, as Turlough O'Neil about to join the movement at the
south was accidentally wounded as it was said by a jester at his table.
During the winter of 1570 James Fitzmaurice spoiled Kilmallock,
and the following year in February with Mac Sweenys and the Clan
Sheehy took and utterly destroyed the place, removing its treasures
which belonged to Desmond. They are represented to have been of
priceless worth, that being his favorite abode though Tralee was the
seat of his government.

Fitton proved a tyrant, and his arbitrary proceedings and overbearing insolence disaffected even the loyalty of Conor O'Brien who
captured his uncle Sir Donal on his way from Corcumroe to the
presidential court at Ennis. Ormond called in to appease the exasperated governor persuaded the earl to surrender as amends Clonroad,
Clare and Bunratty : but indignant at thus being dispossessed of his
castles and his power, Conor gathered his friends and adherents at
his remaining fortress of Moy in Ibrackan. They were not many to
come, for by accepting the earldom he had forfeited their support
and brought these misfortunes on himself and the Dalgais. Discouraged, and sensible he had nothing to expect from English
clemency, he escaped into France. Whilst at that court gaining the
friendship of Norreys, the English minister, and proving to him that
he had been greatly aggrieved by the president, through his good
offices his peace was made and he was allowed to return.

Richard earl of Clanrickard and Fitton at midsummer, 1570, laid
siege to Shrule, a castle on the borders of Galway and Mayo, with

an army composed of all the fighting men of Upper Connaught, of Macdonnels, Mac Sweeneys and Clan Dugald, and three hundred cavalry in mail. John Burke, chieftain of Mayo, gathered his clans to oppose them, and among them came from Benabulla Morrogh O'Flaherty of the battle axes and some Scots. Deciding to fight upon foot, they formed their array, agreeing not to depart therefrom or stop to succor whoever might fall. Fitton and the earl occupied defiles of great strength, their artillery and halberdiers with the clans posted in the line of advance, the cavalry held in reserve. Mac William marched on, and though taken in flank his army kept their ranks and routed and drove the enemy, though reinforced or replaced by fresh troops, two miles, and returned home in triumph. It was a mistake not to follow up their success, for the fugitives rallied on their reserves, regained the field, and that night occupying the camp also claimed the victory.

The representatives of the old kings of Connaught, shorn of their ancient splendor and by family feuds and division of territory reduced in power and consequence, still existed, though history had found little occasion to mention them for some generations. Fitton turned O'Connor Don out of Balintober his principal abode, and on the pretext that with O'Connor Roe and Mac Dermot he had committed hostilities against the O'Kellys, they were summoned to appear at the presidential court to be held in 1572 at Galway. Fitton wrote the council that by the coming Easter term the queen would be entitled to half Connaught.

This court the Dalgais and both Burkes attended. But Ulick and John, sons of Clanrickard, alarmed at what might be designed, went angry away. Thereupon the president carried their father prisoner to Dublin, and returning when they gathered in force, demolished a castle of O'Flaherty's. Burkes oughter and eighter, for once in amity destroyed castle and town from Burren to the Shannon, pillaging all friends of English rule. Passing into Westmeath they burnt Mullin-

gar and Athlone out from the bridge, seriously damaged Athenry and
raided West Connaught, all summer engaged in the like depredations.   James Fitzmaurice took part, seeking their help and the Scots
to reduce Castlemagne, which Perrot president of Munster after siege
the previous year ineffectually and for three months this, finally reduced not for want of defence but of food.

For twenty years presidential governments in the several provinces had been recommended as the sovereign remedy against Irish
independence.   The experiment was on trial also in Munster.   It had
been proposed for Ulster, but with few Englishmen to sustain it
recognized there as impracticable, and in Connaught simply served to
render English rule still more unpalatable.   Fitton in October, 1571,
prayed to be relieved of an office, "the duties of which were merely
to have to speak the queen's enemies fair, to give his friends leave to
bribe the rebels for their own safety, and to see the people spoiled
before his face."   The project in Munster had been thus far attended
with no better result.   Upon a plan well considered and adopted
ostensibly to check the outrageous oppressions there prevailing, Sir
Warham St. Leger had been appointed in February, 1566, president,
with a council to consist of the four earls, archbishop of Cashel,
Robert Cusack and Nicholas White, with Owen Moore as clerk of
the signet; the three last to give their continued attendance to its
administration.

The president was not to quit his province for more than four days,
to report monthly and with one of the council to hear all manner of
complaints, real, personal and mixed, civil and criminal, and any
castle kept with force against him to overthrow.   He was authorized
to punish for contempt, and all malefactors at his discretion if not
repugnant to law.   With the council he had power to examine by
torture and stay judgment, and was instructed to persuade all persons
to conform to the established religion, and cause parish churches to be
repaired.   They were to appoint attorneys and fix their fees, and if

needed authorized to apply fines to their own subsistence, to repair
castles or build gaols. It was enjoined upon them to secure rents
from crown lands especially from dissolved abbies to better the royal
revenues, and seven hundred pounds annually was allowed for the
presidential table. Warham St. Leger, first appointed president of
Munster, soon afterwards received his recall. Sir John Pollard not
able to serve was discharged in April, 1570. Peryam joined in the
commission proved of little account. The troubled state of the
province demanded no ordinary ruler, and few fit for the task cared
to accept an office of such responsibility, arduous service and inadequate recompense. Such the queen found in her illegitimate brother.

In February, 1571, Sir John Perrot natural son of Henry VIII.,
a man of great physical power and strength of purpose, was created
president of Munster, and set himself to work to hunt Fitzmaurice
out of his hole. It was not an easy task, for he was frequently cajoled
and discomfited, and his account of his adventures reads very much
like the dance Puck led the lovers in the play.

Reaching Waterford as James was burning Kilmallock, he was
detained at the capital for many weeks, but visited its ruins on the
first of May as he passed on to Limerick. James in his woody fastnesses of Aherlow at the northern base of the Galtee mountains,
held him at advantage, and though the president marched by night
and by day through bog and through thicket, sleeping on the cold
grass as a common soldier, and enjoying no rest from the constant
and rapid movements of his adversary, his quarry baffled pursuit by
intelligence received from his own camp. He at last settled down to
the siege of Castlemagne, a strong fortress of Desmond's near the
head of the bay of Dingle and the boundary of Clancarre; but
when the summer closed he went away without having made any
impression upon its walls.

In November he was badly defeated by Fitzmaurice, who perhaps
as a blind to his designs challenged him to combat, singly or with

fifty or half that number on a side. Perrot accepted the challenge and made due preparation, but at the same time wrote Ormond to despatch his brother Edward with all the force he could muster. It is not stated that for this Fitzmaurice failed to appear at the time and place appointed, which was Emly near Kilmallock, but if the case, it was reason enough. In June, 1572, the president again set to work to reduce Castlemagne, but though provided with artillery for a long time, without result. James in order to make a diversion and victual the place went into Connaught to the Burkes, taking part in their marands, in the hope of inducing them to aid in relieving the besieged fortress. For this Fitton kept them too busily employed. Still when their devastations were over and their troops disbanded in the autumn, some of their Scotch auxiliaries joined him and crossed with him the Shannon. Perrot with Clancarre, McDonogh, Muskerry and Carbery, Roche, Barry, Decies, Lixnaw, Poer, Sir Thomas of Desmond and Tibbot Butler attacked him at Killooge in Coonagh, killing a few of his men. Castlemagne was not relieved, and from want of provisions, after a siege of four months, forced to capitulate.

James, no longer able to keep the field, lurked with his scanty followers in the recesses of the forest, generally defeating all efforts of the English to learn his whereabouts, whilst he inflicted, as opportunity offered, what mischief he could upon them. "It is impossible," say the annalists, "to relate all that James encountered of perils and great dangers, from want of food and sleep." At the end of October the garrison of Kilmallock, which had been partially rebuilt, surprised his men at night in their cabins and tents, slaying thirty of them and carrying off horses and kine, weapons and apparel, but James not in force to contend made good his escape. Disheartened and prompted by the wish to expedite the return of Desmond, he concluded to seek peace, and two years from the burning of Kilmallock, on the twenty-first of February, 1573, the Seneschal of Imokilly

53

and Owen Burke appeared at the gates of Castletown Roche, where Perrot then was, to make terms.

Perrot proceeded forthwith to Kilmallock near by, and in its church spared from the conflagration, Fitzmaurice and his followers on their knees acknowledged their fault and made submission. The phrases read by him, for himself and them, dictated by the president, if not purely formal, were shaped to please the queen, whose Tudor love of domineering delighted in such humiliation. For a brief period strife ended. During its continuance, correspondence from France and Spain had come freighted with promises of aid to be disappointed, one of six thousand Spaniards. Had they come, so general was the disaffection and the English force so reduced by royal parsimony, Sydney wrote, the island would have been lost to the realm, like Calais. Sir John Fitzgerald now set free, resumed in May the command of Desmond, which he had quitted four years before, when inveigled to Dublin to take leave of his brother, he was carried off with him captive to London. Perrot, elated by his success in accomplishing his task, indulged in some arbitrary proceedings, among others, suggestive of the ancient adage, compelling all Munster men within his reach to trim their glibbes or long locks. He went home in the autumn to return later, and Sir William Drury after an interval of two years succeeded to the presidency of Munster.

The queen and her ministers had either become convinced of their injustice in detaining Desmond and his brother in captivity without sufficient cause, or else of its impolicy. They wisely concluded it easier and more economical to bring back Munster to order and tranquillity under their rule, than that of their more energetic kinsman. Their detention caused expense; reimbursement depended upon the earl's restoration to his estates, and in December they were sent over not to their own homes but to Dublin.

The promises the queen would have exacted from her prisoner indicate what she regarded as abuses to be reformed. He was to allow

no galloglasses bonaght, beg or bowe, permit neither coin and livery nor cuddy or kernety, nor use guns of greater calibre than that
prescribed. He was to hold no parliaments on hills, or dispense
brehon or cane law, levy black rents, cricks or other recompence for
murder or practice comerick ; but was to submit a book of his men,
and cause his people to know God and swear only by him. The
earl positively refused to relinquish his Irish customs or yield up the
liberties of his palatinate : but finally, in order to regain his freedom,
made many concessions. His brother, less firm or more politic, and
with little to surrender, accommodated himself to the situation and
without demur accepted the conditions.

John was released as above mentioned in May, 1573. Gerald was
detained some months longer at Dublin. Having occasion to believe
his life endangered, in November, when hunting and well mounted he
distanced his companions, and taking to his feet with some few of his
personal attendants, after three days reached the centre of his own
dominions.

Gerald again at home, indignant at the treatment to which he had
been subjected and absolved from his allegiance by the capricious
tyranny of the queen, yet aware of his inability to resist, should she
choose to crush, felt compelled to dissemble. Her garrisons held his
castles. His lieges withheld rent and tribute, rarely yielded but to
superior force. His territory lay waste from recent strife. To
supply his needs in captivity, he had borrowed money on mortgage of
Kerricurrihy from St. Leger, who selected his security probably to
create enmity between the earl and his kinsman. As reparation other
lands were substituted to hold till the debt was paid. His first object
to regain possession of his strongholds, Gerald drove out their warders,
and his people seized upon Castlemagne, which much to his displeasure had been victualled by Lixnaw and Clancarre. The territory
of the latter he claimed to be within the limits of his palatinate and he
had other cause of grievance against him.

Clancarre, not content to occupy any position subordinate to one so imperious as James Fitzmaurice, and considering himself entitled to supremacy in Munster, when he found the Eoghanacht would not support his pretentions or take part in the struggle to maintain their independence, saw the inutility of prolonging hostilities. He made peace, and in 1571, in the cathedral of Dublin, renewing his pledges of fealty had received his pardon. This defection and the example it set to his neighbors crippled Fitzmaurice, and materially contributed to his overthrow. It provoked the resentment of Gerald, who collected a force, defeated Clancarre for withstanding his pretension to sovereignty, Mac Fincen of Kerry, Maurice and Owen Mac Sweeny the bravest among his captains and many more being slain.

Disappointed of his reasonable expectation of strengthening his position south of the Shannon, Gerald entered into league with the O'Briens of Thomond and Clanrickard. A conference took place between them at Killaloe near Kincora, and it was rumored that they had despatched messengers to Turlogh O'Neil, O'Moores and O'Connors to gather in strength, and made earnest appeal to Spain and the Scots for assistance. Their efforts to conceal their proceedings led to suspicion, and their movements were watched and reported. Probably measures actually concerted were greatly exaggerated by designing men with an object, possibly from no dishonest motive, misrepresented. They seem hardly consistent with what is known either of Thomond or Clanrickard. But that the government was ready enough to believe them admits of no doubt. Whatever their truth, Desmond still kept up the show and tone of loyalty aggrieved, and in January, 1574, wrote the deputy from Dingle, that he would meet at Clonmel Edward Fitzgerald, sent to confer with him. Charges, seven in number, were preferred against him, to which he proudly responded, at the same time assuring Burleigh of his continued attachment to the queen. He urged redress and reparation for the wrongs he had sustained, and restoration of such of his castles as were still withheld.

For answer came peremptory orders to surrender all his castles to
Sir George Bourchier, sent to receive them, whom he took and
kept in durance till his kinsman Essex besought his release. The
queen instructed the deputy to temporize with Turlogh O'Neil till
Desmond and Clanrickard were disposed of. In April news of
Spanish preparation encouraging hostilities, Gerald gathered at Cahir
three out of twenty thousand he had promised, thence to march to
Tara. Proclamation issued against him which neither Gormanstown
nor Delvin would sign. The government intimidated resorted to
corruption, and to detach Sir John from Gerald, promised him a part
of his brother's lands. Ormond and Fitzwilliam the deputy took
Derrilair. Their show of power disheartened his adherents and allies,
and Gerald weakened by their desertion, was disposed to make terms.
In July, Essex and Kildare at an interview with him and his countess
at Waterford, persuaded him to keep the peace, give up his castles
to which he finally consented, and accompany them under their safeguard to Dublin, from whence he prudently soon after took his
departure. His countess wrote the queen in September that her
husband had become reconciled. The Spaniards had not come as
promised, and hostilities without them of no advantage, his only alternative was to submit.

Conor restored to grace, and the president removed to become
treasurer at war, feuds broke out among the Dalcasians for causes
not explained. Torlogh, brother of the earl, with Mac Sweenys,
Butlers and Geraldines marched from the Fergus by Inchiquin and
Corcomroe, maranding as they went, and plundering the church at
Kilnaboy which proved of ill omen to them. Their slumbers at night
were disturbed by the lamentations of those they despoiled. Donald
collected the clans Sheehy and Sweeny and what forces he could,
Ulick Burke and the son of earl Morogh among the rest, and to
quicken their courage exhorted them to remember what old men and
historians had taught, "that not by multitudes was victory won or

the issue of war to be foreseen. The invaders consisted of a medley of men with no object but booty, and to whom maintaining their ground or flying to save their lives was the same." On the morrow the two armies early astir marched on parallel lines to Knocachif, where the earl's army drew up in a strong position on the hill, but upon Donald's approach took to flight, the cavalry westward by the sea, the infantry southeast. "Many were slain, beasts and birds of prey feasting on their carcasses." Upper Thomond long reaped the benefit of this harvest of death, armor and ordnance, horses and herds and prisoners in great number falling as spoil to the victors. Strife led to strife, and in 1575 Conor and his brother raided Moyburk and Clonderalaw, burning houses, cattle and corn. Sydney interposed, and after hearing both sides, appointed Sir Donald governor of Clare with full powers, which he exercised with rigor, "hanging rebels and plunderers, so that cattle needed no watch, no door to be closed."

The next year passed without event in Munster. In the spring Fitzmaurice and Edward Fitzgibbon went over with their families to the continent and were kindly received, Henry III. of France writing the queen to deal graciously with the former. From his abode at St. Malo he watched events at home and abroad, turning to account whatever promised for his country restoration of its ancient faith, or escape from the injustice of English rule.

In September, 1575, Sydney for the third time lord deputy, and for the seventh head of Irish administration, receiving the sword at Drogheda, proceeded to adjust the disputes of Ulster. He then visited in turn the several provinces, reporting to the queen their condition. Newry held by Sir Nicholas Bagnall the Marshal, he commended for the beauty of its buildings and its excellent tillage, lord and tenant being prosperous and hospitable. The Fews of Phelim O'Neil and Oriel given by the queen to Chatterton were wasted by efforts to reduce them to possession. Maguire was dutiful. Beyond, land given to Malbie he reported devastated and almost depopulated, none but outlaws of either race daring to dwell there, Clanaboy uninhabited from the efforts of Essex to civilize it, Carrickfergus uninterruptedly for centuries in English possession a wreck. With Sorleboy lord of the Glynnes and Route he made a treaty of amity, and at Armagh entertained the wife of Turlogh, whom he describes as "very well spoken, of great modesty, good nurture, parentage and disposition, eager to have her husband ennobled and a good subject." Turlogh joined them requesting rule over his urraghs and passed two days in his company.

Louth he found impoverished and scourged by the plague, Meath by Molloys and Conors: east Breffney, the best ruled country in Ireland under its ancient chief, O'Reilly, "the justest of Irishmen;" Kildare, Carlow and Wexford overrun with outlaws; Moores and Cavanaghs carrying their spoils into Kilkenny, receptacle of innumerable cattle and stolen goods, but undone by its own idlemen. Rory O'Moore under safeguard of Ormond came in, promising "to live in better sort and worse he could not." The deputy thence proceeded to the south, reaching Waterford about the middle of December, "where he was received with all shows and tokens of gladness and pomp, as well upon the water as the land, and presented with the best commodities they had."

Entertained by Power at Corraghmore with great splendor he passed through Decies, badly governed, to Dungarvan where though much decayed he lay three nights, and passing by Youghal, too much damaged in the late strife to receive him, reached Cork two days before Christmas. Here for six weeks his court was attended by the earls of Desmond, Thomond and Clancarre, accompanied by fourteen lords of countries, archbishop of Cashel, bishops of Cork and Ross, viscounts Barry and Roche, barons of Courcy, Lixnaw, Dunboyne, Barry Oge, and Louth who of slender means by his culture and refinement of manner and life set a good example to other Irish chieftains. Thither came Donogh lord of Carbery and Cormac of Muskerry, neither of them but in respect of territory able to be viscounts, and he wished them to be made barons, for both were good subjects and the latter for obedience to law and disposition "the rarest man that was ever born in Irishry." The O'Sullivans Mor and Beare, Carrolls, Donoghues of Loughlene and Glenflesk, Callaghan, Mahonys and Driscols, McTyrnans and Mac Finnins, Macauleys, representatives of the five powerful MacSweenys, were there, besides the brothers of the earl of Desmond, Thomas, John and James, and the ruined relics of ancient English inhabitants, Arundels, Rochfords, Barrets, Flemmings, Lombards and Tyrnys and many more of English name. "And the better to furnish the beauty and filling of the city, all these principal lords had with them their wives during all the Christmas festivities, who truly kept very honorable, at least very plentiful houses, and widows of earls," among them doubtless the ancient countess of Desmond who dwelt at Inchiquin near by, "and others of good note and account."

His court was held with much magnificence and fitting ceremonial, to which many of the guests were unaccustomed, and led to the adoption of many improvements in elegance and refinement. The mornings after twelfth night were spent in judging and condemning dozens of malefactors, members of many of the most influential families in Munster. When the month was over, sleeping two nights at Castletown Roche and passing by Kilmallock, now restored in part to its former condition, he entered Limerick accompanied by Desmond, Louth and the bishops, "received with greater pomp than he had ever before had or saw yielded to any other in the land." Irish chiefs repaired thither requesting the benefit of English laws, in which the deputy, ever set on the main chance, saw promise of greater rents for her majesty than ever before. Ormond and Upper Ossory, Thomond, Sir Donald and other O'Briens, "near kinsmen" but "extreme enemies," and the two MacNamaras and the likewise sons of Clanrickard attended his court. As February ended, with the latter in his train, he passed through Thomond.

Sligo appeared prosperous, abounding in strangers who drove a traffic more profitable to themselves than to the queen's customs. Athenry presented a woful spectacle, college, church and all else of value burnt by the graceless sons of Clanrickard. Sydney partook of the hospitality of O'Kelly for a night, and having held his court for nine days at Athlone, where a Burke of distinction was condemned and executed, went on to Annaly. The old chief Hugh O'Reilly of Breffny was ill, and his approaching end threatened to breed dissension among his seven sons and their descendants, whose scramble for the throne resulted later in a division of the land, to the destruction of its independence and its final transfer to strangers. Holding sessions as he passed, by law common or martial, or flat fighting, Sydney claimed credit for hordes of men " taking food without the good will of the giver, some of the best, the rest trembling, who fight for their dinner and many lose their heads before they are served with their supper. Down they go in every corner, and down they shall go, God willing." He concludes this is not " a dainty dish to set before the queen " though a Tudor, or to stuff his letters withal.

At Galway he took into consideration all griefs and losses, complaints of murder, burning, sacrilege and spoils infinite and immeasurable that were brought before him. Much of the mischief attributable to the contention of Teigue, son of Morrogh, first sheriff of Thomond, and the earl, he exiled them both, and putting a brother of Conor in irons, appointed Sir Donal to rule over Thomond, now created the county of Clare. Connaught he divided into four counties, Sligo, Mayo, Galway and Roscommon. MacMahons, Macnamaras resorted to his court. Richard Mac William oughter of Mayo called the Iron, speaking Latin but no English, a lover of quiet and civility, desired to hold his lands of the queen, suppress extortion and keep out the Scots. He is described as ever clad in mail. His wife Grace O'Mally of Carrygahooly, famous by sea and land for her exploits, afterwards on a visit to the queen, declined to be made a countess, though her son

54

became viscount of Mayo.*   Both attended; and Flahertys, Kellys,
Maddens and Naghtans came in, professing for the time being their
attachment to Elizabeth and her representative.   The archbishop of
Tuam, bishops of Clonfert and Kilmacduagh and the baron of Athenry, a poor lord but honest and sensible, made also their obeisance.

Besides beheading a vast number of insurgents and bad subjects,
Sydney "abolished the custom of keeping poets and literary men,
public festivals, kernes, bonaghts or retained soldiers and their leaders."
From the peaceable disposition manifested during his progress, he
came to the conclusion that seven hundred foot and three hundred
horse would keep the country quiet unless in case of invasion.   A
church more disordered and overthrown by the ruin of temples, dis-
sipation and embezzlement of its patrimony, want of ministers,
nowhere existing where Christ was professed, he recommended that
the queen's farmers should repair its edifices, clergymen properly
qualified for its services, versed in English and Irish, be sent over
from England and Scotland, and commissioners of good learning
and religion inquire into its condition and provide for its reformation.
A chief justice and attorney general, acquainted with English law,
were needed; no lawyer in the island possessing sufficient skill to
fill these offices.

Pressure of affairs detained the ever active deputy for a few weeks

* The posterity of Fitz Adelmn, g. g. grandson of Harlowen de Burg and Arlotta mother
of William the Conqueror, progenitor of Burkes, Bourkes, de Burgs in Ireland, able, prolific and prosperous, rival the stars in multitude.   The eldest line, from which proceeded the
lords of Castleconnell and Brittas, ended with the third earl of Ulster in 1332, when two
brothers, grandsons of William Athenkip, brother according to Lodge of the first earl, changing their name and adopting Irish laws, habits and language, divided the family territory in
Connaught between them.   William the eldest, as Mac William Eighter, took in Galway,
of which his line, earls and marquises of Clanrickard, still hold portions; Edmund Albanach
the younger, Mac William Oughter in Mayo, dying an aged man in 1375.   Edmund left by
Sabina O'Malley, a son Thomas d. in 1402, from whose eldest son Walter d. 1449, derive
the present earls of Mayo, so created in 1785; his second son, Edmund the bearded,
pronounced by the annalists "the only Englishman in Ireland worthy to be chosen chief
for his resolution, proportions of person, generosity, hospitality, constancy, truth, gentility
of blood, martial feats and qualities by which a man might merit praise," was father by
Honora ot Clanrickard of Ulick.   Ulick and Sabe O'Kelly were parents of Edmond, whose
son David by Finola O'Flaherty was the father of this Richard an Iran mentioned in the
text as husband of Grace O'Mally.   He died in 1583, described by the annalists as "a plundering, warlike, unquiet and rebellious man, who had often forced the gap of danger, and
upon whom it was frequently forced."   His son Theobald created viscount of Mayo in
1627, still a child, his distant kinsman, Richard, son of Oliver, son of John, was installed
in his place.

in the capital. The expected arrival of the new chancellor Gerrard ; dealings with O'Rourke " the proudest man in Ireland " ; a new earldom of Clan O'Neil for Turlogh and barony of Iveragh for Maginnis ; the grants of Malbie and Chatterton to be revoked ; disputes of Ormond with O'Carrol about the dower claim of lady Giles to Dorow, occupied his time and correspondence, when his attention was claimed by fresh outbreaks in Connaught. When at Galway the sons of Clanrickard had demurely volunteered their submission, and promised to be quiet. The deputy nevertheless by a stretch of authority carried them off prisoners to Dublin. Having no just cause to detain them, he set them free, extorting a promise that they would not go home without his permission. Out of his clutches, regarding an agreement under duress as of slight obligation, and summoned by their father, they crossed the Shannon, and the elements of discord, there abounding, speedily betrayed them into overt acts. They set the new gates of Athenry in ablaze, and drove away the masons from their work. Sydney gathering his forces started at once for the west, reaching Athlone by the tenth of July. Pouncing upon the earl, he placed garrisons in his castles and sent him to Dublin, where, in close confinement, without a soul to speak to, he had long to remain. On his way back Sydney established Sir William Drury in the presidency of Munster, to which Clare was now added. Fitton was removed from Athlone, and his administration having created abhorrence, Sir Nicholas Malbie appointed colonel of Connaught took command of that province.

Ulick and John, sons of Clanrickard, enraged at the harsh treatment of a father to whom, if not always respectful or obedient, they were attached, had recourse to arms to expel the intruders, who masters of the fortresses in pleasant places and with superior weapons, retained their hold, and drove them back to the wild recesses of the forests and " rough topped mountains," the country ravaged by either party and countless herds destroyed.

Drury, cruel and unsparing, occupied himself with hanging gentle and simple, boasting when he left of the many hundreds of which this disposition was made. The deputy had advised the queen to deprive both Ormond and Desmond of their palatine rights, and Drury, instructed to carry out this policy as regarded the latter, proceeded to usurp the long vested rights of his progenitors, and to hold courts, civil and criminal, even at Tralee. As he approached the place with three score men as his guard, in the dense forest that then stretched down from the top of Brandon to its gates, his little party were surrounded by several hundred of the Geraldine forces, who swarmed around them, brandishing their arms and shouting their battle cry. The president with serried ranks, pressed directly on his course without other show of opposition, and reaching the gates, sounded his signal for admission.

At the opening portal appeared the countess, the admirable Elinor Butler. She endeavored to appease the wrath of the angry president by representing it merely as a rude welcome, and accounting for the presence of so great a multitude by an intended chase for deer. He with scant courtesy accepted the explanation and entered the castle. Down to the present century still stood, in all of its feudal grandeur, this ancient stronghold of the Geraldines, which for sixteen earls served as the seat of their judicial administration, though the pleasanter abodes of Askeaton and Kilmallock, Imokilly and Stracally, were their preferred residence. After indulging in his taste for the halter by suspending four score men by the neck, the president proceeded by Limerick to Cork, where he apprehended John of Desmond, for being on good terms with the Burkes whose sister he had recently agreed to espouse, and sent him a prisoner to Dublin.

The court at Ennis held for eight days by Drury in June, 1577, largely attended by both races, ended in disappointment. His efforts to persuade the Dalgais of their own free will to acknowledge the queen by feudal relations and payment of rent, came to naught, and he went back to Limerick leaving a force to reduce them to obedience. The earl went over to London to ward off the impending blow, but before his return arbitrary measures overcame their resistance, and a cess of ten pounds for each barony was acceded to by his subordinate chiefs.

The queen was gracious to him and disposed to favor his wishes, but not to give up the rents except of his own domains. She consented at his request to confirm the earldom in tail on his lineal heirs, but when he claimed the right, immemorial in the princes of Thomond, to make surnames, and after the decease of every chief, to nominate his successor, and also wardships and reliefs incident to feudal tenure, she demurred, leaving it to Sydney to grant him reliefs from the meaner freeholders, but wished the more powerful to hold directly from herself. The customs of Clare and Clanroad he might have, and " exemption from bonaght on his own lands as it had been abolished." She also gave him the moiety of the abbey of Clare, still vested in the crown, he already having the other, and what belonged to the abbeys of Ennis and Quin, but not the island of Scattery which might be wanted by the city of Limerick. His son Donogh had been brought up at court, and his daughter Margaret was about to marry James Butler second lord of Dunboyne, and her partiality for her distant kinsmen may account for her readiness to comply with his desires.

Donogh Reagh lord of Cabery, brother-in-law of James Fitzmaurice, ended his days in January, 1576, leaving a son Florence then fifteen years of age, whose career was destined to prove peculiarly eventful. His brother Owen,* under the brehon law, succeeded to the chieftainship. He left another son Dermod Moyle, who took also a conspicuous part in the subsequent turmoil, and a daughter Julia who became the wife of Sir Owen O'Sullivan Mor, prince of Dun-

* Owen by Helena O'Callaghan had a son Florence in 1599, from whom descended a branch of the name established at Rochelle in France, one of whom, Seigneur de la Martiere, was by Louis XVI. created vicomte McCarthy in 1786.

kerron. The decease of Donogh received due commemoration from
the annalists as "cause of lamentation to the chiefs, of sadness to the
husbandmen and farmers of his territory; he is said to have out-
shone his seniors and not to have been excelled by his juniors." His
remains were laid with those of his father Donal and his grandfather
Fineen in the monastery of Timoleague, which also served as the
burial place of the Mahonys amongst the most powerful of his
subordinate chieftains. The demise of another chieftain in Carbery, a
year later, led to a domestic tragedy.

Near the southern coast of Ireland, west of Kinsale, and along the
banks of the Bandon, which winds its way through the fertile lands
and picturesque scenery of Carbery, stood many of the twenty-six castles of the southern branch of the Mac Carthy chieftains. In the
fourteenth century, Cormac Don, son of Donald the handsome first
prince of Carbery by the daughter of the marquis of Carew, received from his father Glen-a-Chroim, consisting of fifty-seven
ploughlands, forming a considerable portion of east Carbery. Acknowledging no fealty to the McCarthy Reagh or bound to attend
his rising out, this sept growing more vigorous from not being often
molested, still formed part of his array. Their strong castles of
Dunmanway and Togher were famed for hospitality, and they ranked
high for power and influence. Whilst Drury was president of Munster, Florence, sixth in descent from the first lord, ended his days,
and though leaving sons his brother Cormac as tanist succeeded according to law, receiving the white wand as badge of his office.

From their seven score castles in Cork and Kerry, two thirds of all
that then stood, the Milesian chiefs thronged to his inauguration,
celebrated with the traditional festivities of the house. Neither
prince of Carbery nor lord of Glen-a-Chroim had ever surrendered,
but this abandonment of ancient tenure extensively prevailed around
among their neighbors, and rendered it less easy for the family of the
deceased to yield up their abodes with composure, and subside into

a position subordinate to that of their chief, who would ever regard them with distrust. When the guests had taken their departure, whether from simple ambition to rule, discontent at the provision made for their future, or under other extenuating circumstances, Cormac Don, eldest son of the dead Florence, killed his uncle the new chief in the halls of Dunmanway, and sent for by Drury to Cork was there tried and executed. His brother Tagh-an-Forsa claimed the succession, and to strengthen his hold proposed through Raleigh to surrender and take back the territory to hold under English law.

Fynin, son of the murdered chief, went also over to court, and in a petition drawn up by Florence Mor, then a prisoner in the tower, set forth his pretensions. It was decided that the title forfeited by the murder had vested in the crown, and the queen bestowed Glen-a-chroim on Tagh who was succeeded by his son Tagh-an-Duna. In 1652, when both father and son had passed to their account, their domains were thought too precious to be left to Irish ownership, and upon an alleged crime perpetrated ten years before, not by either of them but by their retainers, whereby two English merchants named Ford had been slain, the property was wrested away. Though partially restored to their heir in 1685, it was again confiscated in 1696 and the larger part of it vested in Sir Richard Cox the historian. The family afterwards continued impoverished for several generations, its lineal representative, another Dermod-an-Duna dying, in the last century, in the castle of Donovan, kindly cared for by its proprietors his distant kinsmen. They have regained prosperity and lustre in later years, one of the present generation having been governor of Ceylon, another author of the life of Florence Mor, who befriended Felim without effect against Tagh-an-Forsa the successful claimant under Elizabeth.

Chancellor Gerrard allowed no opportunity to escape, in discharge of his official functions of letting the full weight of his authority be felt, whether in procuring evidence against Sir John of Desmond and

Clanrickard, or establishing circuits to administer injustice. His active spirit found less dignified but more useful employment in weighing beef, and making bread, that the one might be heavy and the other light. O'Rourke, having a mint of his own or suffering coiners in his realm, Sydney insisted upon the royal monopoly of making light money, and Malbie, aided by some of his turbulent subjects, seized castles and towns, which were speedily recovered or restored. Either from climate or bad habit, grown infectious, human life was held of little worth. Drury, like Sydney and Cosbie, revelled in its destruction, boasting of the hecatombs hurried by axe, halter or like method to account, among them Morrogh son of the first earl of Thomond.* The Irish, quick, passionate and contentious, took pleasure in combat, and welcomed death in what they regarded as the field of glory, but their task-masters restrained by no sense of responsibility for their deeds inflicted it without compunction, as they had the mind. Cotemporary historians and correspondence preserved express no horror at what in our day would be considered barbarities, and which estop the dominant race from reproaching that forced to succumb for occasionally following their example.

Sydney in September, 1578, after reconciling Drury with Desmond whose professions of loyalty were not dissembled, gladly went out to use his own phrase like the house of Jacob from among a strange people. "With painful labor, by day and night, in foul and fair weather, in storm and tempest, in scarcity and penury, in danger of the enemies and peril of his life, continually studying, devising, travelling, toiling and laboring to do them good, so long as they felt the ease and comfort, they were contented and grateful." But for much else that was less to their taste, as the obsequious Hooker adds, "they would have torn out not one eye as the Lacedemonians did from Lycurgus for like efforts to civilize them, but both. Still few

* Ancestor of the lord Inchiquin, present representative of Brian Boru, unless the Mahons have the elder claim.

characters connected with Irish administration, for honesty of purpose, good temper, wisdom to plan or ability to execute, deserve more respectful and affectionate remembrance than his. At a period when all around him were mercenary and grasping, covetous of what belonged to other men or to the state, he was almost the solitary exception of disinterestedness and singularly free from selfish motive or personal consideration. His nearly twenty years of arduous service, not all continuous, left him twenty thousand pounds poorer, and five thousand in debt. It was to his credit that he did not enrich his family with Irish lands, and that his sons had no part or work in Irish conquests. He survived his return to Penshurst till October, 1586, dying immediately after his eldest son the gallant Philip fell mortally wounded at Zutphen, and nearly a century before his great grandson, the equally celebrated Algernon, lost his head at Tower Hill for alleged connection with the Rye House plot.

Clanrickard, accompanying him to London as a prisoner, in March vindicated his character and conduct from any taint of disloyalty, by an enumeration of his services to the queen and her predecessors. "Coming into Ireland under Edward VI. he recovered his territories at his own charges. Through his power and influence Kellys and Conors held back from the chiefs of Leix and Offaly, in consequence forced to submit; and he captured Cahir O'Conor who was executed. Under Anthony St. Leger, he crippled Donald O'Brien chief of Thomond, and with eight hundred men aided Sussex in 1558 to banish him and substitute the earl in his stead. When Cusack waged war with Offaly, he overthrew Mac Willam and the Scots at Cosliebh, and soon after took Meelick. Whilst Sussex raided Cantire in 1558, he defeated at the Moy twelve hundred Scots under Richard-an-Irain, slaying Donnel and Dowell, cousins of Argyle, few escaping his four days pursuit.

"He at a later period greatly strengthened Sussex, against Shane O'Neil, whom marauding in Sligo he drove off, and induced Hugh

55

O'Donnel to desert.   With Sydney he reduced Roscommon and recovered Birmingham's castle ; sided with Fitton in his quarrel with
Thomond and at Shrule, extricating him from the meshes of O'Flaherty ; and after killing, in 1561, two hundred Scots, took part with
him the following November in the subjugation of Connaught, winning castles, burning and spoiling, and exacting pledges.   Because
his sons and Fitton disagreed, he was imprisoned eighteen months at
Dublin.   When released he had hung his own son, his nephew, second cousin, one of his captains and fifty of his followers that bore
armor for their rebellious behavior."

In an admirably expressed letter to the queen he denied ever
countenancing his sons in any treasonable practices, prayed that if
any one accused him he might be permitted to prove his innocence,
and promised to be ever loyal.   His appeal proved unavailing.   His
enemies were many and powerful.   He was detained till June, 1582,
when he was released to die the month following, after an imprisonment of five years, for no ostensible or conceivable cause than that
he could not govern his wives and sons, or that some one coveted his
possessions.   Designated Sassanagh or Englishman by the Irish, his
fate curiously illustrates the arbitrary rule of Elizabeth.

XXXVI.

REIGN OF ELIZABETH.—1558-1602.—(Continued.)

These arbitrary measures : transfer from the Irish of Leix, Offaly,
Oriel, Idrone and the Fews ; grants to Essex and Smith ; the
Carew claim in Munster, if suspended awaiting only more favorable
conditions to push ; introduction of English law and courts, under
which they had no rights to be respected, whilst they were subjected
to every injustice, in place of the brehon, to which they were accustomed ; substitution of feudal tenure vesting the territory in earls

and barons for their old chieftainries, which left large liberties and
defined rights to every clansman : the fixed purpose of a protestant
queen and her ministers to impose upon a people, all catholic, forms
of faith and worship, which, from the corruption, hypocrisy and un-
christian practices that attended them, outraged whatever religious
sentiment they possessed, were generating one universal spirit of
abhorrence to English rule, warily watching its chance.

At catholic courts and especially at Rome, able representatives
were pleading their cause. Fitzmaurice traversed the continent with
various experiences, seconded by MacCreagh, O'Herlihy and other
prelates, who were long deluded by promises of aid, which dangers
nearer home prevented catholic monarchs from extending. Disappointment hardly chilled their ardor, and they persevered against
every discouragement. Success came, but proved so inconsiderable and inadequate, that it served only to precipitate the calamities
it was designed to avert. Men act from mingled motives. Even
in Fitzmaurice, if analyzed might be detected elements of worldly
aspiration, not all compact of religious zeal or generous patriotism.
In his principal coadjutor, when his whole career passes in review,
hardly one refreshing trait can be found but personal courage. He
was vain, self-seeking and unscrupulous, wholly occupied with
schemes for his personal aggrandizement, unwise as dishonest, and
yet from manner and address, talent for intrigue, and tact in management of men, far more influential than the staider and nobler
Fitzmaurice.

Thomas Stukely, from similarity of form and feature as well as
other resemblances, deepened the impression sustained by tradition,
that like Perrot he owed his being to Henry VIII. His reputed
parentage at Ilfracombe in Devon, if not attended with affluence, afforded him high social position for advancement which he knew how to
improve. His first employment in the household of a bishop did
little to elevate his character, and marrying a fortune that he

squandered of a lady he deserted, he sought to better his condition
by planting a colony in Florida, of which he was to be the governor.
When taking his departure he told the queen he preferred rather to be
sovereign of a molehill than the highest subject of the greatest king in
christendom, adding that he was assured of being a prince before he
died.   Elizabeth banteringly answered, I shall hear from you when
instated in your principalities.   To which he responded he would
write, and when asked by her in what language, rejoined, in the style
of princes—to our dearest sister.

Want of means blocked his American project, but he brought
into an Irish port some captured French merchantmen.   Little distinction was then made between piracy and buccaneering, and less
legitimate cruising yielded him yet better harvest.   In hostilities
ashore, his military talents and gallant bearing attracted the notice
of Sydney, who turned to account his diplomatic shrewdness in negotiations with O'Neil.   The queen distrusted him, and refusing him
the stewardship of Wexford, he cultivated the leading catholics, and
with credentials from them in 1570 went into Spain.   Philip at first
favored him, promising aid to the cause he represented, but soon
grew weary of his importunities and self-sufficiency, and Stukely
disappointed repaired to Rome.   Here again he made friends.   The
pope taking him at his own estimate and eager to retain what hold
he had upon Ireland, listened patiently to his representations; but
on longer acquaintance, recognizing his vanity and the emptiness of
his pretensions, amused himself by heaping upon him a multitude of
titles, creating him baron of Ross and Idrone, viscount Murrogh
and Kinsellagh, earl of Wexford and Carlow, marquis of Leinster
and general of the army of the holy pontiff.

It chanced then as often later that the states of the church were
infested with bandits and other malefactors, whom the pope gladly
pardoned on condition that they would go with Stukely, who selecting a thousand or more from their number, to be paid by the Spanish

king, set sail with them for Ireland in the spring of 1578. Putting into Lisbon to repair his vessels, he found the unfortunate Sebastian with two Moorish kings starting to dethrone the emperor of Morocco. Promised aid after their return for his own expedition, he consented to accompany them in their ill-starred enterprise. At the battle of Alcazar, stationed near the royal standard he endeavored to dissuade Sebastian from a charge at disadvantage, but without avail. They rushed to the encounter, which proved fatal to the three kings as also to himself, and ended in utter rout.

James Fitzmaurice, meanwhile zealously employed in Spain in procuring additional forces, when he heard of the disaster, hastened to collect the survivors, about eighty in all, and with a few Cantabrians, Dr. Saunders, Allen, and Ryan bishop of Killaloe, embarked in three small vessels, reaching Smerwick beyond Tralee in Kerry in July, 1579. Upon a rocky promontory connected with the main by a ledge, stood a small work which he strengthened, but had hardly disembarked his men and material, when a vessel of war under Courtney, coming round from Kinsale, entered the harbor and captured his ships.

John of Desmond and others came to welcome him, and the party soon distributed engaged in preparation against the enemy, whose coming they had reason to expect. As Desmond held aloof, John was doubted, but when urged to commit himself by some act of hostility, he assaulted at night Tralee where Arthur Carter the English marshal had taken refuge, and with him Henry Davels, sent to keep Desmond to his allegiance. Both were slaughtered, Davels, according to the evidence of a small boy, who slept in his chamber, by Sir John.

James started soon after for the abbey of Holy Cross to perform a vow or collect his promised adherents. With a small force commanded by Thaddeus McCarthy, crossing a river a few miles southeast of Limerick, he encountered his cousin Theobald of

Castleconnal, who with his brothers Richard and Ulick and a force superior to his own entered the water on the other side to dispute his passage. In the combat that ensued, James was struck by a ball, whereupon putting spurs to his steed he rushed upon the enemy, drove them from the ford, and overtaking Theobald clove his head with his sword, his two brothers being also slain. James, mortally wounded, sought shelter in the forest, and begging his companions when he was dead to cut off his head, that his remains might not be recognized or subjected to indignities, breathed his last, six hours after the engagement. His death was too great a relief to the English for his body to remain undisturbed, and exhumed it was after the fashion of the time quartered and exposed to gaze at Kilmallock. William the aged father of the Burkes was forthwith created lord of Castleconnel. At his investiture in May he swooned and soon died; whether from joy at his new rank, or grief for his sons, is differently represented by the historians.

The loss of James was a serious blow to the catholic cause. Desmond, either from unwillingness to hazard his possessions, or else from his growing infirmities, being unable to mount his horse without assistance, though appointed chief of the holy league by the pope, chose to preserve his neutrality, and the command devolved upon his brother, Sir John. The queen, alarmed at the tidings from Ireland, offered her favorite Ormond, then at court, the territory of Desmond if he would hasten to suppress the rising. Drury marched south with six hundred men under Bagnal, Malby, Wingfield, Waterhouse, Fitton and Masterson, joined by Kildare, Montgarret, Dunboyne and Upper Ossory with some hundreds more as he went. At Kilmallock he sent for the earl of Desmond, who with some hesitation obeyed his summons. He was soon set free, but his lands were given up to pillage, and his brothers soon flew to arms to stay or to resent it.

Sir John posted his men, who had rallied in goodly numbers to his standard, in an advantageous position, a portion in ambuscade, when a strong detachment of the English, under Eustace, Herbert and Price came up. Attacked in flank by the party hid in the wood, the captains with three hundred of their men were slain, and their army put to flight.

Reënforced by six hundred veterans recently arrived at Waterford, under Bourchier, Carew and Dowdal, and Perrot arriving at Cork with six vessels to protect the coast from Spanish armaments constantly expected, Drury marched into Connello. Destroying what he could and ill from excessive fatigue, he transferred the command to Malbie, and, carried in a carriage to Waterford, there died. We find it related that bishop O'Healy and his companion O'Rourke, who coming into the country, not long before Fitzmaurice, had been captured, were brought from their fetid dungeon before him at Limerick, and not able to persuade them to adopt the new faith, after cruel torture, he condemned them to death. As they left the apartment, Healy summoned his judge to meet them in two weeks, before a higher than earthly tribunal, and within that period they had all entered their appearance in that dread court from which nothing could be concealed. If they thus met, the martyred bishop probably grieved over his profanity, as Drury over his long and bloody record.

Malbie in command, leaving three hundred and fifty of his men in garrison at Kilmallock, marched to Limerick for reinforcements. They poured in. Ulick Burke, recently from his imprisoned father in London, and whose youthful daughter Honora* was then or about to be Malbie's wife, joined him with his brother John and the Lacies. As October opened, they proceeded in search of the Geraldines, and nine miles to the southwest, encamped near the abbey of Monasternena, still magnificent in its ruins, but standing in its pristine completeness till before his departure Malbie gave it to the flames.

* Ulick married Margaret Fitz Alan, daughter of the earl of Arundel, 1764. Malbie died 1584. His daughter Ursula became the wife of Sir Anthony Brabazon, 1581. After his connection with the Burkes he exerted his influence in various ways for the release of the earl.

Sir John of Desmond, that his troops might more effectively cope with their better disciplined adversaries, had availed himself of the officers from abroad to train them for the new methods of warfare. Their proficiency in the battle that ensued excited surprise, and Stanley the marshal wrote Walsingham that they came into the field as resolute to fight as the best soldiers of Europe, and later that the English had no advantage over them but discipline. Fitzmaurice had brought them arms. They had had little time to perfect themselves in the new drill and tactics; not all had become wonted to their new weapons; the foreign officers placed over them often needed an interpreter, and the system may have proved rather an embarrassment than a help.

Desmond would have gladly deferred the combat until better prepared. He had been reinforced that morning by six hundred men under his brother, James Sussex, and overruled by the persuasion of Allen he marched to meet the enemy. Whilst still at some distance himself, his van encountering their advance guard attacked them, and drove them to their camp. The fugitives discovering how scanty their numbers, sallied forth in great strength, and had already gained an advantage, when Sir John coming up his troops resumed their ranks, and the battle became general. Historians disagree both as to the incidents of the fight and its result. O'Haverty says, the Geraldines twice broke the ranks of the royalists, and compelled them to retreat in order to reform; Mageoghan, that both sides fought with equal bravery till the right wing of the English beginning to give way, and one of their principal officers killed, they were entirely routed, after an engagement of an hour and a half. O'Daly claimed the victory for his own countrymen, and that large guns, standards and other spoils fell into their hands. O'Sullivan, whose father Dermod was a principal leader in the war and near him when he wrote, counts it among the victories of the Geraldines. The Four Masters compiled when not safe to lisp a syllable against En-

glish rule or English history, follow Camden, " who wrote of events
he had not seen, according to the prejudices of his countrymen."

Malbie, on the tenth, wrote Walsingham that all the Geraldine captains were slain, except John and James, who marched off with the
papal standard in post haste through the woods. This would seem
an embellishment. The standard would have been a grand prize as
well as the brothers, if Malbie had dared to overtake them. The
loss was heavy on both sides, two hundred and sixty slain of the
Geraldines, and no less of the English. The two armies no doubt
were alike exhausted and demoralized, and neither of them inclined to
renew the combat when interrupted by some chance of the day. Malbie, rallying his troops in his camp on the ground, claimed the glory
of the victory, but continued to anticipate fresh attack from the
foe, who still hovered around his entrenchments. These variances
show how little dependence is to be placed on historical statements,
where national vanity or interest sway.

Papers on the person of Allen, killed in the fight, were said to
have compromised Desmond. With anxious interest as to the event,
with lord Kerry he had watched the battle from a neighboring height.
His brothers and kinsfolk were among the combatants ; his territory
had been lately devastated ; he had suffered other grievous wrong
from the queen, and his sympathies were naturally all with his own
people. But his only son was hostage for his peaceable behavior ;
he could not justly be held responsible for brothers beyond his control ; he had cautiously avoided himself every act of retaliation, or
word of resentment at which umbrage could be taken ; when
rudely summoned by the president to come to him, former acts of
treachery, when he had complied with like orders, warranted his
staying away. He was eager to obtain intelligence about the battle
and also as to what had betided his friends, and he wrote the next
morning to Malbie, inquiring if he had been really victorious.

The question may have been difficult to answer, and nettled the

56

English commander. That same day he despatched a force to Rath-
more, a castle of Desmond's not far from the battle-field, which with
the town was sacked and valuable documents carried away. On
the sixth, he spoiled Rathkeale, burning houses and corn, and the
day after encamped within the abbey of Askeaton. He defaced the
monuments of the earl's ancestors, desecrating the sepulchre of his
first countess Joanna, fired the abbey, town and corn round-abouts,
and shot at the warders within the castle walls. On the tenth Gerald
wrote Ormond that Malbie had broken and burnt his mother's tomb,
prayed that his own good services, enumerating them, might be cer-
tified to the queen and the council, and these unauthorized outrages
be punished. Rumors soon spread that he had joined the rebels, and in
a letter from Sir Owen O'Sullivan to Leicester, on the twenty-fifth,
complaining of Humphrey Gilbert, whom he had kindly received,
but who had requited his hospitality with injury, allusion is made to
them. Owen was himself obnoxious to suspicion, for his brother
Dermod was with the Geraldines.

Ormond had been instructed to seek an interview with Desmond,
and it took place on the thirtieth. In the existing relations between
them the pride of Gerald was not likely to bend. When demanded,
as condition of immunity for past transgressions, restoration of his
ancient privileges and other honorable terms, that he should seize and
surrender to the queen, as her subject, Dr. Saunders, his friend and
ghostly adviser, his reply, like one of Ormond's later, was doubtless
anticipated. He refused to betray a pious clergyman who had been
driven by his own people to seek refuge with the pope, and been attracted into Ireland by its sanctity and devotion to the faith.

Three days after this conference, Pelham, the new lord justice,
marching an army into his palatinate issued a proclamation, which
Gormanstown and Delvin refused to sign, declaring Gerald a traitor,
and appointed Ormond, his hereditary foe, governor of Munster.
No alternative remained for Gerald but recourse to arms. He was

buoyed up by expectation of Spanish aid, and that the catholic league
so termed in England as in France would unite in a general rising.
Possibly, as had chanced before in the annals of his race, he hoped
to procure better terms by prolonging the contest.

He knew well that his enemies were bent upon his destruction, and
as records reveal, that officials of the pale were ravening for his spoils.
Twelve months before, when the lords of Munster pledged themselves
to defend him against the injustice of Drury and all who coveted his
inheritance, he had conveyed his territory to trustees for his heirs to
prevent its forfeiture. Preferring the uncertainties of the future and
fortunes of war, to the humiliations proposed or dangers that menaced, without farther vacillation, he assumed command of the
Geraldines, harried Barry and Roche, on his way to regain possession
of his castles. After three days siege, at Christmas, aided from
within, he stormed Youghal, Dermod O'Sullivan, with six hundred
men from Beare, scaling its walls and overcoming its defenders.
The place was vigorously disputed and the besiegers lost one hundred
and eighty men. Gold and silver and much else had been removed.
What belonged to the earl was carried to Stracally and Lefinonen
the castle of Sir John; rich prey fell to the victors, and the town
was burnt. Ormond invaded Connello, then marched to Cork,
sweeping sad havoc, as he went with torch, sword and halter,
slaughtering old and young, sparing no Irish or catholic, burning
every house and stack of corn, till the land was bare as a floor. Returning south he sacked and burnt Lefinonen and wasted Coshbride
and all Imokilly, slaying the brother of its seneschal. In Cork he
took pledges from Clancarre, Barry Roche, Courey, chiefs of Muskerry and Carbery, O'Sullivan Beare, McDonoghue and Keefe, and
garrisoned Kinsale. His soldiers were worn with travel, sickly,
without money, food, or garments. He contrived to seize the mayor
of Youghal, who had helped Desmond to that place, hanging him at
his own door. The only living person he found within its walls

was a poor friar, who had brought the body of Davels a hundred miles from Tralee to give it christian burial at Waterford.

Early in the spring, Ormond and the deputy marched through Desmond's territory, leaving a desert where they passed. They met near Tralee and laid siege to Carrigafoyle, garrisoned by nineteen Spaniards and fifty Irishmen. It was battered down by five thirty-six pounders, landed from Winter's fleet, and its defenders hung or put to the sword. Alarmed by this new artillery against which stone walls were no protection, the neighboring castles of Desmond were abandoned, Ballyloughan being first destroyed, but the attempt to blow up Askeaton happily failed. Pelham, after forty days at Limerick, went back to Askeaton, occupied with putting to death sick and idiotic, women and children, Wall blind from his birth, and Supple a hundred years old. Well might he write the queen that all Limerick and Kerry were in rebellion. Clancarre, McCarthy Reagh, Fitzmaurice, even Muskerry at these horrors became disgusted and disaffected. Barry entertained John and James Fitzgerald. O'Neils and O'Donnels gathered their strength and Scots poured into Ulster.

Ormond left Cashel early in June, and proceeding through Kerry, losing many horses and men on his march, at Castlemagne met Pelham, who crossing the mountains, startled Desmond, his wife and Dr. Saunders in their covert. They barely effected their escape, leaving behind them cups and bells, crosses and vestments, with their repast untasted. Desmond, shattered in constitution and worn out by his wanderings, would have gladly sought reconciliation. The countess made an earnest appeal to the privy council, but Ormond protested against any mercy being shown. With Pelham he visited Dingle and Smerwick, where, the previous year, Fitzmaurice had landed, soon to be the scene of memorable carnage. They hastened home on tidings of impending danger. Baltinglas and the catholics of the pale were in arms. Ormond returned to Cork, prevailing on the Munster lords to join him, and applied for pardon for them all but Desmond. James Sussex, in August, marauding in Muskerry, was waylaid and captured by Cormac its chief, and surrendered to Raleigh at Cork, after imprisonment for a month, was hung and quartered at the gates of that city.

In August, 1580, lord Grey de Wilton, later one of the commissioners that condemned Mary queen of Scots, at Fotheringay, and who justified her execution, landed as lord deputy, and proceeded at once into Wicklow to attack the O'Byrnes, who with Cavanaghs, O'Tooles, one of the Fitzgeralds of Kildare and Eustace, lord of Baltinglas, were in arms. The van of his army fell into ambuscade in the pass of Glenmalure. This pass between high hills covered with heavy growth and thicket, in the county of Wicklow and about twenty-five miles from the capital, was boggy and full of slippery stones. Grey and Kildare, Wingfield and his nephew George Carew, a kinsman of the claimant of Idrone, remained on a woody eminence at the mouth of the glen, with a portion of the army, whilst the rest entered its gates. Their progress was slow, for the way was difficult, and when they had penetrated half a mile, volleys all around from an unseen foe against whom they could make no resistance, thinned their ranks. Thrown into confusion the Irish poured down upon them in overwhelming numbers, despatching them with spear and skein. Wingfield realizing the danger had endeavored to keep back Peter Carew, heir of his cousin, from entering the defile, but without success, and now in heavy armor, which embarrassed his flight, he fell exhausted and was speedily slain. More, Audley and Cosby the tyrant of Leix, shared the same fate. Few escaped, and the deputy, crest fallen and dismayed, retreated in all haste to Dublin. This black day for the defeated was a bright one for the conquerors, and the Irish catholics were greatly encouraged. Among those saved from the catastrophe was George Carew, brother to Peter, afterwards president of Munster, who was held back from entering the pass by his uncle. By his vigorous administration and collection of documents relating to it, preserved at Lambeth, his name is conspicuously associated with Irish history. Grey had little time allowed him to lament his disaster. Alarming tidings from the west called him in that direction.

Winter leaving the coast to refit, Sebastian San Josefo landed in August, at Smerwick, with seven hundred Spaniards, sending back his vessels for more. He brought money and arms for five thousand men, inspiring the Geraldines with sanguine expectations, which derived additional encouragement from Glenmalure. Ormond led his troops to attack Fort del Oro, as the Smerwick rock was now called, which had been greatly strengthened by Spanish engineers. A sally drove him off, and he marched back to Rathkeale, where Grey joined him with eight hundred men. After they started for Coreaguiney, Raleigh lingered behind, not in vain, to catch any rebels that according to wont might be attracted to the abandoned camp by curiosity, or for spoil. A kern with withes in his hand, being asked to what use they were to be put, replied to hang Englishmen, whereupon, Raleigh hung him.

Sebastian, summoned to surrender, replied disdainfully that Ireland had been granted to his king by the pope, and he should hold what he had and get more if he could. Guns from the fleets of Bingham and Winter, now back, battered for three days at the walls, when the place being small and without water, on the ninth of November, a white flag was displayed for parley. The interpreter is said to have deceived the Spaniards, who understood that their lives were to be spared. This the victors deny, and say that from the first, the besieged were refused any protection from the usages of war or law of nations, that they had no commission to show when demanded, and as allies of rebels they were not lawful enemies, or entitled to any terms better than unconditional surrender.

In the morning, troops under Raleigh and Macworth took posses-

sion. Either by them or by sailors, who entered independently from
the water, the garrison, from five to seven hundred in number, were
slaughtered.   Grey, whose reputation among the catholics for good
faith suffered from his alleged perfidy on this occasion, admits to the
queen the massacre was by his orders.   In her reply she regrets that
their lives had not been left to her justice or mercy.   An army of
four thousand men under Desmond to relieve the place had been
hourly expected. Grey was smarting under his recent defeat at
Glenmalure.   His temper sour and puritanical, tinctured by no
elements of amiability, he took to himself no reproach for what he
conceived as timely severity.   Raleigh, Macworth and the subordinates, who took part, should be judged by the inhumanities of the
times, the ways of warfare prevailing, which were cruel and merciless.   Edmund Spenser, there as secretary to Grey, defended his
course. Besides the poet and Raleigh, there was present a son of
Sir John Cheeke, famous as professor of Greek, another scholar of
repute at the time, though of less celebrity later, who was slain in
the attack.

The whole country, except Ulster, which enjoyed a brief respite of
repose, was up in arms.   The sons of Clanrickard, one year before,
fraternally disposed, fighting together at Monasternena against the
Geraldines, were again at strife between themselves.   They both
hated the intruders on their paternal inheritance, more than each
other as competitors for its succession.   John proffered implicit
obedience to his elder brother Ulick, and surrender of Leitrim,
Baltinlough and all claim to Loughrea, the principal residence of the
earls, in acknowledgment of seniority, if he would render his assistance in expelling them from the family dominions.   Ulick readily
consented, and they demolished the white castles of Clanrickard, not
sparing Loughrea or scarcely another from Clonfert to Kiltartan,
from Leitrim to Oban.   O'Briens, all but the young earl Donogh,
who that year succeeded his father, now after twenty-two years of

troubled rule, finishing his course at the early age of forty-five, and Turlogh, who had shortly before succeeded Sir Donald as lord of Ennistimmond and sheriff of Clare, marshalled their men. In 1581 the Burkes agreed to peace, on condition that there should be no tax, fine or other servitude imposed upon their country or their allies, they paying certain specified rents twice a year to the crown.

O'Rourke the proud, set at defiance Malbie, destroyed his castle of Leitrim,* that it might not harbor the foe, and when Malbie had done him the good service, not intended, of rebuilding it, compelled him to remove his warders. Calling to his aid his neighbors, the O'Connors of Connaught, they raided O'Naghtan near Athlone, and in December devastated Hy-Many, slaying the garrison of Lisdalon, where Hugh last chieftain of the O'Kellys, whose rule and life ended five years afterwards, made his abode.

In Leinster the catholics, greatly encouraged by their recent victory, swept havoc where they could, and Dunlaing† last inaugurated chief but one of the O'Byrnes plundered the pale up to the gates of the capital. Grey, surrounded by disaffection, knew not in whom to place trust. The catholic leaders of English race were sent to the tower. Nugent and forty-four more were executed; Kildare and Delvin put under arrest, and as already related sent to London. Wheat was twenty-five shillings the quarter, the war had already made havoc of the army, and though the queen counselled the deputy to be tolerant in matters of religion, his temper not conciliatory, fretted by his embarrassments, rendered his task difficult.

John of Desmond, deprived of the command when his brother, the

---

* There were two Leitrims, one a barony of Clanrickard in Galway, from which John Burke took his title of baron. The country of the O'Rourkes farther north lay east of the Shannon and constitutes the present county of the name.

† Descended from Cahir More of the second century. Five of the line were kings of Leinster before the English invasion. Their dominion as that of the O'Tooles at the time embraced large portions of Kildare, but they subsequently dwelt in the mountains of Wicklow, or by the sea. Dunlaing, twenty-seventh from Cahir More, had two sons whose descendants shared alternately in the chieftainry, Dunlaing in the text of the elder line being in the thirteenth generation from his namesake; Fiagh his successor in the fifteenth of the younger line. Fiagh was son of Hugh of Glenmalure, who invited treacherously to a conference in 1579, by the seneschal of Wexford, had been there put to death with a hundred of his youth and kinsfolk.

earl, throwing off his allegiance assumed it, had not been idle. Whilst
Gerald, in July, 1580, was hiding in the mountains, out of health and
despondent, he entered the woods of Aherlow, four miles south of
Tipperary, with less than one hundred shields and but thirteen horsemen. The Fogartys opposed him, but eighteen chiefs of that name
paid with their lives for their temerity. Gilpatricks, O'Conors of
Offaly, Moores and Carrols, his kinsmen, gathered to his call, and he
had soon an organized army. Sleeping on the cold ground, with a
stone for his pillow, roasting his meat on twigs by his bivouac fire,
and drinking from the palms of his hands water from the mountain
streams, he proceeded to wreak his resentment on the Butlers.
Abbey Leix, Maryborough, seven castles in a day, were given to the
flames, and horses, arms and armor procured for his followers.
Joining at Glenmalure the conquerors of the deputy, they spoiled
Leinster and Meath, and defeating the garrison of Kilmallock, which
came out to intercept their progress on their way to meet Eustace,
marched west too late for the relief of Smerwick. With his brother,
Eustace and Grace, Sir John attempted, at Bongonder, to waylay
Ormond on his march from Cork, who hurrying to reinforce the deputy avoided an engagement.

In May, he crossed the Suir, destroying Ardmayle and the monastery of Athassel, and at Lismore defeated a regiment of redcoats
from Berwick, that color having already been adopted for English
soldiers. Whilst collecting the spoils he was overtaken by a numerous force, three hundred of whom fell in the combat. A few weeks
later he marched into Kerry to take vengeance on the MacCarthies,
spoiling from Muskerry to Iveragh and driving his prey into Magun-
nihy. Not all the Eoghanacht sided with Clancarre. The chief of
Duhallow, Owen son of Donogh, died prisoner of the queen, as also
James Barry More* closely allied to them. Owen O'Sullivan Beare

* James d. 1581, was grandson of John, s. of William k. by his brother David, archdeacon of Cork and Cloyne in 1499, s. of Thomas who paid homage to Edgecombe, 1488, s. of
John d. 1485, s. of William, s. of James, s. of John d. 1402, s. of David, s. of David d.

was kept under guard of Fitton at Dunboy. The sept under his brother and nephew took an active part with the Geraldines. Zouche, left by Grey in charge of Kerry, on his way to Cork sent a force from Carbery under Turlogh Mac Sweeny and Dermot O'Donovan to plunder Donal, nephew of Owen and next in succession to the chieftainship. Donal overtook them with their spoil near the monastery of Bantry, and though inferior in numbers, in a warmly contested engagement defeated them, slaying several hundred, and among them Dermod son of Donal lord of castle Donovan.

It was a partisan warfare, and the incidents often bear close resemblance to what Froissart relates of the free lances of France two centuries before. A considerable force of English soldiers from Adare sallied forth for fight or booty, and caring little whom they despoiled, David Oge Purcel, who had done good service for the queen throughout the war, suffered from their depredations. David and his people fell upon the plunderers and left them "a heap of bloody carcasses." Akin, their captain, learning what had bechanced, proceeded forthwith in force to Ballycallane, a castle once of the O'Cathlains, then Purcells, and not finding David at home, killed all who were there, within or without, and with them one hundred and fifty women and children. David, not long after, with sixteen men crossed the Shannon from Kenry to Scattery. Turlogh Mac Mahon, from east Corkavaskin on the north shore of the river, entertaining some grudge against him, sailed over to the island, and set fire to the house in which he and his followers were sleeping. They rushed out unarmed, and speedily overpowered he hung them all but David, who, sent to Limerick, was put to death. Similar incidents about

1317, s. of David, s. of John, s. of Lawrence, first lord of Ibawne and Barry Roe (now or late in the family), s. of William and Joan, d. of second Kerry, s. of David Oge, son of David first viscount Buttevant, d. 1278, s. of David k. 1262, s. of Robert, son of Philip, brother of Robert k. at Lismore 1185, and of Geraldus Cambrensis the author, who were sons of William and Angaret, daughter of Nesta and sister of Robert Fitzstephen and Maurice Fitzgerald ancestor of the Geraldines. David s. of James and Ellen d. of Cormac McCarthy Reagh, paid a fine of five hundred pounds, and becoming loyal to the crown d. in 1617, and his grandson and successor David, 1605-1642, first earl Barrymore, m Alice Boyle, d. first earl of Cork. Upon the death of the eighth earl in 1824 the title became extinct.

the country suggest to an official writing home, resemblances this desultory warfare bore to the national sport of fox-hunting. It may have been animating, but it was attended with atrocities unparalleled.

Desmond, now lurking in glen and forest, now at the head of considerable armaments, wasting and destroying, ranging through Kerry and Limerick, one day at Cork and then knocking at the gates of the capital, baffled pursuit. In May, 1581, with Barry, Imokilly and Condon he invaded Decies, one of his southern tributary provinces, burnt thirty-six towns and carried off seven thousand kine. A few weeks later whilst encamped at Glen Aghadoe near Killarney, with two thousand men, he allowed himself to be surprised by Zouche with a smaller force. His army had been weakened by detachments sent to scour the neighborhood, that Clancarre feeling his strength might yield to its pressure and join the strife. All were sleeping, when one Sunday morning, before day break, Zouche stealthily approached. Sentinels off their guard were dispatched by concerted arrangement at their posts, and much mischief done before the camp startled from its slumbers. Desmond made what disposition the confusion allowed, but the captain not waiting for an engagement slipped away in the darkness, dragging off women and children. Pursuit rescued the captives, but the troopers, too well mounted to be overtaken, reached Castlemaine.

In September the earl marched down to the plains of Cashel, pillaging that city and its neighborhood, obtaining what his army much needed, horses, cattle, clothing, iron and copper. Troops from the neighboring garrisons of Cahir and Moyalif, hastily assembled, were dispatched to oppose him. They avoided an ambuscade he had prepared to entrap them, but attacked in the open field were badly cut up and four hundred of them slain. Sir John at Christmas removed from the castle of Kilfeacle near Tipperary whatever it contained of value, and demolished it.

Desmond looked for aid from abroad, and also from O'Neil. Unhappily for his cause, complications at home between the great chiefs of Ulster, notwithstanding their various ties of blood and affinity very like his own and Ormonds, deprived him at this critical moment of succor from that quarter. Con and John Oge, sons of Shane O'Neil by Julia countess of Argyle, had plundered east Brenny. Philip O'Reilly, son of its aged chief, recovered the prey, capturing Con and killing his brother. Turlogh in revenge compelled Con's liberation without ransom, and erick for John. Soon after, with Con O'Donnel at feud with his uncle Hugh, chief of Tyrconnel, Turlogh encamped at Raphoe with a numerous army. Hugh from friendly relations with the English government had lost popularity with his people, but mustered what force he could to drive out the invaders.

As Hugh, on the fourth of July, 1581, drew near, O'Neil inquired of Con and Turlogh Mac Sweeny, what they thought would be the result of the combat? Turlogh answered that if the Kinel Konnel drew breath or drank water, or in other words took time to advance leisurely and in order, they would gain the day. But that they did not. Confident of victory they rushed on tumultuously. The battle was desperately contested, as when kinsmen are opposed, and after heavy loss they were badly defeated. Mac Sweenys fell on either side, O'Gallaghers and O'Boyles on Hugh's. The abbot of Kilmacrenan attributed the issue to his imprecation on the O'Donnels, who had despoiled his abbey on their way to the battle field. The deputy hastened to the relief of Hugh, ordering Malbie up from Connaught to meet him. Early in August he made peace with Turlogh at the Blackwater, and returned vexed with Dungannon for not delivering up to him William Nugent. Not long after Turlogh with twenty-five hundred men went into Sligo threatening Malbie.

Taking advantage of this confusion the sons of lord Kerry effected their escape from Limerick castle. Their father, iritated at the devastation of his territory, entered into their plans, destroying Lixnaw, Listowel and other fortresses. William O'Carrol, released from the tower upon pledge of allegiance, fell victim to the hatred of his clan towards the rulers of the pale and all who favored them.

Envy, jealousy, personal animosities, and more than all else, greed for land and gain, color the official correspondence of the period, crippled the government, helped the catholics. Malbie, Wallop, Waterhouse, St. Leger, maligned not only each other, Desmond and Kildare, but Ormond came in for a large share of their tergiversation. Raleigh wrote Walsingham, that Ormond had been two years lord general of Munster, and there were a thousand more traitors than at his coming. His brother Gilbert had ended a rebellion not much inferior in two months, and he recommended him for the place. St. Leger represented that Ormond lost twenty Englishmen for one rebel slain. In a letter to the deputy the queen says that Ormond had promised with three hundred men to put down Desmond, and with fifteen hundred nothing had been done. Ormond replied that he had warded the castles of Barry Roe, but that David Barry complained that Raleigh and St. Leger, then in command at Cork, had procured warrant to kill him and garrison Barry Court, Castle Lyons and the other strongholds of his father, and driven him into rebellion. He further stated that five hundred and ninety-eight prominent personages and four thousand of the common sort had perished through his means. It was not enough. He was thought too lenient and recalled, and going over to court regained the royal favor, which rarely withstood his personal influence.

Cruelty did not propitiate the Irish. David Barry burnt his father's castles, lest Raleigh should possess them. His three brothers-in-law, Roche, Fynnen and Donnel McCarthy and Philip O'Sullivan with a force of six hundred men joined him, "becoming Robin Hoods." Archbishop Magrath of Cashel in March reported that Clancarre, all the O'Sullivans and McCarthy Reagh were disaffected. Walsh urged that the cause was not religion, but cess. Both were operating, but in different degrees in different minds. In the death of the estimable prelate, Dr. Saunders, the papal nuncio, the former lost strength. Devout and indefatigable, disease contracted from exposure and privations in his wanderings, as the spring opened, brought what must have been a welcome release, and four leading catholic warriors performed his funeral obsequies at dead of night in the forest, away from observation. Sensitiveness at indignities to the dead tended to provoke them, and secret burials of the eminent constituted a frequent experience of those troubled times.

War, pestilence and famine stalked about the land, claiming innumerable victims, thirty thousand perishing from disease alone. It was hardly necessary, as Wallop wished, that the survivors "should cut each other's throats, that better might be planted in their stead." Impoverishment reigned in castle as in cot or covert. Andrew Trollope relates " that Clancarre and Kerry came to Dublin in September, who for all their bravery, wore but russet mantles, leathern jerkins and brogues, not worth a noble. At night all ages and both sexes slept in one small apartment, and in the morning shook their heads and went their ways without prayer or toilet. They had not always meat, and lived on the three leaved shamrock, and would have starved but for food sent out from England. He considers the Irish, judging from his own standards of course, and blind to the faults common to all, and of which his own race had a few, as not christians, but savages, as lately at Dublin they had planned to cut the throats of all Englishmen. The church bells rang, but their was no service. Loftus, the archbishop of Dublin, had many daughters to marry, and sharing the profits of the faculty commission, was thought to have had too easy a conscience, and even good bishop Brady the report charges with some foibles not in character with his cloth."

Zouche, now governor of Munster, with Raleigh and Dowdal wintered at Cork marauding as opportunity offered. Raleigh with ninety men made a perilous expedition to Castletown and brought back with him lord Roche and his wife, who professing allegiance

were soon allowed to go home. Provoked, possibly at this unexpected defection, Barry and the seneschal of Imokilly raided Fermoy,
when some dispute led to estrangement, and their respective forces
separating confronted each other near the Blackwater in angry
menace. The earl and his brother lay north of the river in the
country of their faithful ally, Patrick Condon, and alarmed at their
quarrel, John went at once to make peace. Dowdal informed by a
spy of his intention, started with Zouche early in the morning, on
the fifth of January, 1582, as if for Limerick, and at Castle Lyons
learned that lord Barry had just before departed for the conference.
Disappointed in not meeting John on the usual route to the place
appointed, they laid in wait in the woods, through which they hoped
he might pass.

John with eight followers had crossed the mountains of Drumfinen,
and the evening air refreshing after his noontide ride, dismounted as
did his companions, who, thinking the English far off, moved unsus-
pectingly along, leading their horses. Suddenly their attention was
attracted by the appearance of Zouche and Dowdal whom they perceived rapidly approaching towards them with sixty troopers. All
immediately mounted, except John, who usually the most skilful
of them all, of great courage and strength, and peculiarly cool upon
sudden emergencies, to whom, to leap to the back of his horse ordi-
narily would have been an easy affair, was at the moment too much
overpowered by fatigue ; and when his steed, generally docile and
well trained, became restive, plunged and reared, lashing with his
feet, he found it impossible to mount. Ordering his men to leave
him he bade them farewell, saying his fated day had come. They
started for the covert, but his kinsman, James Fitzgerald of Sron-
cally, turned back refusing to desert " the bravest of men, under
whose lead they had so often conquered their unbelieving foe, and
by whose hand so many had fallen ; he should not die alone ; they
had often followed him through the ranks of the enemy, and he at

least would be his companion in death." Thus speaking or thinking, he dismounted, and on foot, near John, who was mortally wounded at the first onset by their assailants, they both fell, preferring to die rather than surrender. James recovered of his wounds to perish on the scaffold.

What was expected to result from killing John, may be measured by the general exultation at his death; the five hundred pounds set upon his head. Before the month ended, Grey begged for his estate. Propositions for reducing the army to three thousand men, one third of its number six months before, Wallop opposed, as likely to lead to a general massacre, not twenty Irishmen being friendly. Barry with Mac Sweeny, gained a victory in Carbery and another over Fitton constable of Bearhaven, whose army enticed from the abbey of Bantry was annihilated, and himself, after three days hiding among the mountains, barely escaping to Dunboy with his life.

In April the three sons of lord Kerry entered Ardfert and slew the commander of the place, and whilst besieging the garrison, their father, who had seen much military service on the continent in his early life, joined them. Zouche approaching in force, they withdrew into the woods. Desmond came to their aid, and returning they defeated the English. The few survivors found their way back to Cork, and for the rest of the year throughout the western territory of the Geraldines not a soldier remained. The warders were removed from Limerick, and Owen O'Sullivan set free at Dunboy.

Desmond, " stronger than ever before," occupied Aherlow and the region from Kilmallock to Castle Lyons, raiding the Butlers as occasion presented. The country uncultivated lay waste, " not the lowing of cow or voice of ploughman heard in all Munster from Dunquin to Cashel." In April, Condon and Imokilly slew four sons of lord Roche and their men, till only fourteen were left able to bear arms in Fermoy, which was nearly depopulated. In June, the sons and brothers of Ormond gathered what force they could, horse and

foot. at Fethard, and marched to Knocgraffon in pursuit of the earl,
who turned upon and defeated them with great slaughter, Colla
Mac Sweeny. chief constable of the Butlers, falling with the rest.

But the allies of the Geraldines were wearying of this continual
strife. David Barry, since the death of his father viscount Buttevant,
purchased peace by payment of five hundred pounds; Kerry came
in with his sons, and Donogh son of Mac-I-Brian-ara. Desmond
who had had the war forced upon him and been always disposed to
reasonable terms of reconciliation, thinking the moment propitious,
sent his wife to Dublin to propose a settlement. Her humble supplications to be permitted to go over to the queen were however
rejected, the terms he demanded considered inadmissible, and unconditional surrender insisted upon. Praying that her son Gerald, then at
Dublin, might be sent across to London to be educated, she returned
disappointed to her husband. He was forced to fight on. In the
autumn while in Kerry, his men foraging in Pobble-O-Keefe were
pursued by its chieftain Art with his clan. Gerald fell upon them as
they approached his camp and defeated them, taking Art and his son
captive.

Grey bettered his instructions. His faith of that sterner sort,
not unlike the great protector's, drew its inspiration rather from the
contention and carnage of holy writ, than from its gentler precepts.
O'Molloy, lord of Fircall, and chief justice Nugent fell victims to his
suspicious temper. Owing to his cruelties the queen grew impatient
lest nothing should be left in Munster for her to rule over but ashes
and carcasses. He did not relish his task, and longed to be recalled.
Both races felt equal relief with himself, when early in September,
1582, he surrendered the sword to archbishop Loftus and Wallop,
as lords justices, and disappeared.

Elena, still at Dublin when that month came to a close, besought
to be allowed to remain a few days longer, in the hope that the
queen might relent. She implored that her three daughters, Mar-

58

garet, Joanna and Catharine, with her son Gerald, might be taken
under protection and educated, but Elizabeth, ruled by Ormond,
proved inexorable.   Desmond with a considerable force of cavalry and
two thousand men, represented by Fenton as "stronger than ever,"
employed his October in gathering the harvests.   He threatened to
overrun Carbery, portions of which had already been granted to
St. Leger, whilst Imokilly sacked Ormond's castle of Carrig, and
laid waste Waterford.   Thomas Norris who had succeeded Zouche
in the nominal rule of Munster, was powerless to resist with his remnant of an army.   Loftus exhorted Burleigh to comfort a people
perishing with famine, by withdrawing the soldiers and pardoning
Desmond, who had intimated to St. Leger his peaceable disposition.
The earl was worth conciliating.   His men largely reinforced by the
Ryans and O'Briens, by "sharing the inn of the wolf, its bed and covering," from constant exposure to cold and wet, had become dangerously fierce and vigorous.   The elements were not propitious.   Much
tempestuous weather prevailed as we are told by the annalists.   Wind,
constant rains and thunder storms, interfered with the campaign for
both armies.   The bishop of Killaloe sent to Spain reported en-
encouragingly of foreign aid, whilst the vast amounts of money expended to little purpose fretted the frugal queen, who in December,
while appointing Ormond governor of Munster, authorized St.
Leger to treat.

The earl, after securing his winter supplies had gone into Kerry
to persuade Clancarthy, O'Sullivan and Fitzmaurice to a general
rising.   At Christmas he besieged Dingle.   A few days later Imokilly and Condon entered Youghal and nearly surprised Cork.   Ormond reached Waterford on the twenty-first of January, 1583, his
first demand for the custody of Desmond's territories indicating him
little disposed to further his restoration to grace.   He brought over
large forces which he judiciously distributed.   Sir George Thornton
had nearly succeeded, early in the month, in capturing Desmond not

far from Kilmallock and Kilqueene, when the roads were almost
impassable from mire and the streams swollen. The earl leaving
his bed, plunged into the river, and for hours remained concealed
under its bank, up to his chin in water, his wife bearing him company.
Fenton in March wrote Walsingham that he had urged the lord
general to have Desmond assassinated. The queen's injunctions to
Ormond had been to procure a conference with Gerald, but Lacy, sent
to sound him, reported that he still insisted upon life, land and liberty.
The countess came in under protection, saying that Gerald would
not yield himself to a Butler, his ancient enemy, but was willing to
go over to the queen. Expecting aid from abroad, he was not disposed to abate his pretentions.

Ormond, not very gentle, hung up the mother of Imokilly, but
with due respect to legal formalities. Walsingham advised him to
subdue or reclaim Desmond speedily, or the queen would adopt
another policy to lessen her charges. Gerald knew Ormond too well to
expect mercy, had he been willing to accept it at his hands. Still he
realized his inability to prolong the struggle, and entertained thoughts
of abandoning Ireland and taking refuge on the continent. At the
instigation of Elena he wrote Ormond in June to appoint some time
and place for an interview, making many protestations of loyalty.
Had Butler been sincerely inclined to carry out his instructions, he
could have easily persuaded Desmond, in his then state of despon-
dency, to accept terms, but the humiliation he proposed proved too
bitter a draught for the pride of the Geraldine, who is described, a
few weeks afterwards, by Ormond, as wandering unhappily from
place to place, forsaken by all men. Twenty-one hundred principal
noblemen and gentlemen of Munster had come in at Castlemagne,
among them Clancarre and the two O'Sullivans. In September
Ormond professed himself weary of so much bloodshed and denied
any wish to crowd Desmond, but actions spoke plainer than words,
and a thousand pounds offered for his head, no pains were spared
to capture him.

Good tidings that the pope was urging Philip to send ten thousand men, recently employed in reducing the Azores, to his assistance, may have colored his expectations; but he offered, in October, to yield if life and liberty were granted to himself, and after his death his son permitted to inherit.   The chiefs of Duhallo and Clanawley still befriended him, and his cousin Maurice, son of John had sixty swords in Aberlow.   But when it was bruited about that lord Roche had nearly captured him, with his priest and two kernes as his only companions, any disposition to jeopardize life and estate for a cause so utterly hopeless died out.

His kinsmen nearly all dead, abandoned at his own request by wife and children, this unhappy lord of a vast palatinate roamed stealthily through the wild scenes of his happier boyhood, not knowing where to lay his head.   All that remained of his once numerous following had shrunk to some few personal attendants, who watched tenderly over his security and provided such food and shelter as circumstances allowed.   Constantly on the alert they watched on the hill tops to apprise him of approaching danger, and keeping ever on the move, baffled his pursuers.   Food cooked in one place was eaten in another.   Caverns or the starry heavens canopied their rest, when no ruined cabin could be found.   The large price set upon his head was no temptation to them.   Among the most devoted proved Godfrey Mac Sweeny, offshoot of that remarkable stock in Donegal, who from their valor and military talent, furnished constables to nearly every sept and army of either race throughout the land, O'Neil and O'Donnel, Butler and Geraldine.   Godfrey had been constable of Desmond, and though all semblance of organized force had melted away, still continued steadfast to his chief throughout his adversities.

Whilst off on some quest for Gerald, he fell into the hands of Ormond.   Claiming protection as a reconciled rebel, evidence that he had been recently seen with the proclaimed earl, imperilled his life, which the lord general promised him, together with rich rewards, if

he would betray his master. Godfrey, practising on the simplicity
of Ormond, and meeting fraud with fraud, perhaps in this case to be
palliated, seemingly consented; but declared that to succeed in the
attempt to capture him, he must go alone. Rejoining the earl in his
lurking place he supplied his necessities by hunting or maraud, till
on some expedition of the latter sort, he was slain as the winter
was closing in. Cut off from all hope of flight or pardon, his
health broken and not sure of his daily food except from Him who
feeds the ravens that call upon him, the earl doubtless, at times, lamented that his father on slight pretext had ever disinherited, for his
benefit, his elder brother Thomas Ruagh, who during all this tumult
was dwelling in quiet at Castlemore or Kilnataloon.

On Saturday, the ninth of November, the earl left the woods near
Castle island, sending two of his horsemen and eighteen kernes to
bring in a prey. They carried off forty cows and nine horses from
the widow of one of the Moriartys, whom they stripped of all she
possessed. Her brother Owen and Maurice, whose deposition as to
what occurred, taken at the time, is still extant, were ordered by
Stanley to use the ward of Castlemagne and go in pursuit. Five of
that garrison joining them on their way, the party, then consisting of
thirty men familiar with the country, reached Tralee Sunday afternoon. Making no stop, they followed the trail so long as daylight
lasted, and then, the moon serving, entered Glenaginty on Slieve
Luachra. Climbing to the mountain top to discover, if they could,
any fire in the valley, they saw one beneath them not far off. Maurice
went to reconnoitre, but reported that there were no cattle there,
though a cabin and some people. As the day dawned, on Monday
morning, they cautiously approached the house, and as they entered
several persons were seen to escape through the rear door into the
woods.

On the floor before the fire lay a venerable personage, who,
being struck in the arm with a sword by Daniel O'Kelly, one of

the soldiers, all of whom had now gathered in the hut, exclaimed
"I am the earl of Desmond, spare my life." Maurice replied he
had already thrown that away, and should now be Ormond's
prisoner and the queen's. They proposed to take him down the
glen in turn, upon their backs, Donnel first, but soon the rest refusing lest a rescue should be made, Maurice ordered O'Kelly to cut
off his head which was done. It was carried to Castlemagne, but
an easterly storm prevailing, some weeks elapsed before it reached
London with the intelligence of his death. His body after two
months hiding was interred by his attached adherents and kinsfolk,
in a churchyard of the Geraldines, near the church of Kilmury.
The stone coffin in which it was laid, exhumed by a neighbor in the
present century, was found empty and broken up for the lime kiln.
The head of Gerald in an iron cage adorned till it mouldered London
Bridge.

Not long after the final catastrophe, appeared on the southern coast
of the island a Spanish corvet with money and munitions of war and
tidings that troops were on their way. A friar on board inquired
for Desmond or some one who represented him to receive what they
brought, but after being informed as to the posture of affairs they
sailed away. For a while Ulster expected these promised troops in
her ports, but Philip showed no disposition to venture without more
adequate promise of success.

With Gerald ended the rule of the Geraldines in Munster. The
growth of four centuries of wrong and robbery as many years had
sufficed to overthrow. From Youghal to Dingle extended the vast
possessions of his house, and a large part of Munster when its power
was in the ascendant yielded to its exactions. Too proud to be
pliant and conform as Butlers and O'Briens to royal caprice and the
course of events, he stood fast by the faith of his fathers, and his long
imprisonment and the partiality shown Ormond in their quarrels
rankled in his breast. It was not however before his dominions had

been devastated contrary to agreement that he committed himself to
hostilities, but when once compromised he persevered with vigor,
and without further vacillation. At various times at the instance
of his amiable and devoted wife, he thought of submission, but remembering how short a shrift Tudors gave their victims, and that
he had nothing to hope from queen or Ormond, he accepted his fate.
He may not have been very politic, but his character, composed of
many elements of strength both of temper and principle, is interesting as an historical study.

Human nature is infinitely various. Character dependent for its
form and pressure upon inheritance, imitation or circumstance,
neither in the master pieces of genius, nor distorted creations of fiction, can be studied to such good purpose as from actual life, in
historical personages like Shane O'Niel or Gerald. "That philosophy
which teaches by example" affords insight into the motives that
prompt and principles that govern, and it is not the great and good,
the faultless or utterly depraved, who yield its most profitable lessons. Where the elements of good and evil are more equally
commingled, and approach nearer to ordinary standards, where practical common sense and honesty of purpose are subjected to the fiery
ordeal of peculiar trial and temptation, much more is to be learned
for individual improvement.

In an age of unparalleled barbarities when rack, boot and thumb-
screw aggravated the pains of death on scaffold or at the stake for
woman or for martyr, the few acts of cruelty charged to Gerald are
disproved, or found to be grossly exaggerated by the prevailing spirit
of detraction. His numberless adherents testified their attachment
by devoted sacrifice. Not one could be tempted to betray him. Injustice without scruple provoked his resentment, but prudence
controlled his temper. When longer forbearance became pusilla-
nimity, he defended what he conceived his right with courage.
Armies of veterans ably led melted away before his judicious com-

binations, and for two years he inflicted heavier blows than he received. He realized the hardship of being exposed to the caprices of a woman, whose character he contemned, yet whose power to harm he could not control. But he met the courses of providence without repining, as his appointed cross. Always disposed for peace upon terms that were reasonable, he refused to submit to oppression. After his resources were exhausted and resistance ceased to be possible, he accepted his fate with composure rather then yield to humiliation.

His unwillingness to tamper with his religious convictions, refusal to betray Saunders for his own security, should protect his memory from the reproaches of cotemporary writers interested in his confiscations, from their being perpetuated, without motive, and against evidence, by modern prejudice. The vastness of his domains resulted from a vicious policy concentrating wealth and power in the few as an effective bulwark against popular commotion. Arbitrary rule, its natural outgrowth, he found rooted in the system which he was called to administer, and responsibility for its abuses rested not upon him. It could not be disturbed without ruin to the structure it supported. Not what was just or would conduce to the general welfare constituted its governing principle; but the gravitation, to which society owed its stability, consisted mainly of selfish interests and brute force. Their contagious influence corrupted the higher motives and nobler aims of the wiser and more beneficent rule it superseded, and little was left anywhere of what alone justifies authority, the maintenance of right and order, disinterested consideration for the public good. But for the Geraldines, English power would never have gained a permanent foothold in the island. Now that they had served their purpose and thwarted protestant views, their overthrow became a settled design. Not Desmond's defects of character but his nobler traits gave it effect, and led to the ruin of his house.

What became of the family of this " ingens rebellibus exemplar " the reader may be interested to learn. By Elena, daughter of Edmund first lord Dunboyne* and Julia daughter of Cormac Oge of Muskerry, he had two sons and five daughters. Thomas died young; Gerald became the sixteenth earl, and ended his days in the tower of London, in 1601, unmarried. Margaret became the wife of Dermod O'Conor of Connaught; 2, Joan, of Dermod O'Sullivan Beare and died 1619; 3, Catherine, successively of Maurice Roche lord Fermoy, and of Sir Donal O'Brien brother of fourth earl of Thomond and ancestor of the viscounts Clare, the fifth of whom commanded the Irish brigade at Fontenoy and gained that memorable victory; 4, Ellen, of Sir Donogh O'Conor Sligo, of Robert Cressy, and of her kinsman Edmund third lord Dunboyne; and 5, Ellis, of Valentine Browne of Ross. The widow of Gerald married for her second husband Sir Donogh O'Conor Sligo, and died according to one account in 1656, to others, which seem more consistent with probability, twenty years earlier. The last descendant of the male line of Thomas of Drogheda, eighth earl, died in 1787. Maurice, son of John Oge, son of John, son of the eighth earl, was one of the three surviving heirs to the earldom in 1601, the Sugan earl and his brother being the other two. After the death of Gerald he went into Spain.

Resistance had died out, septs at the south and centre subsided into discouragement. In diminished numbers they ranged the woods and mountains, fierce and famishing, or hovered about the settlements wresting from their neighbors what they conceived their own, and needed to save their families from perishing. Clansmen

* The several branches of the Butlers in Ireland are difficult to follow. That of Dunboyne descended from Thomas, brother of Edmond created first earl of Carrick in 1308, who married Sinolda le Petit heiress of Dunboyne in Meath. His grandson William son of Peter died in 1415; and his, Edmund son of James and Morna O'Brien, by Catherine Butler, left James who married Elenor McCarthy Reagh and died in 1508. Their son James who died 1533, by his wife Joan daughter of Pierce, earl of Ormond, was father of the Edmund created 1541 baron of Dunboyne mentioned in the text. James, the brother of Elena, deceased in 1601, left by Margaret Fitzpatrick of Upper Ossory five sons and three daughters and a widow another Margaret daughter of Connor third earl of Thomond. He was succeeded by Edward his grandson 1595-1640, who married his cousin Ellen, daughter of Elena, who died 1660. Theobald present and thirteenth baron was born in 1806. The Cahir branch, earls of Glengall, descended from third earl, were created barons in 1543, Theobald who married Mary daughter of the chancellor Sir Thomas Cusack being the first of the second creation. At the death of Richard second earl of Glengall and eleventh lord Cahir, b. 1794 d. 1858, these honors came to an end unless some heir existed to the elder title.

59

of high degree kept less aloof from the intruders, professing friend-
liness they had very little occasion to feel. Strong castles went
up in Offaly and Leix, the ancient inhabitants crushed out between
these tightening folds of "advancing civilization." Misery does not
tend to make men peaceable, and a dispute in September between
two O'Conors took a course unusual. They brought it for adjust-
ment before the lords justices, who to more effectually dispose of the
case and of the parties, proposed wager of battle, a process if then
known to the law practically obsolete. Seven days were assigned
for preparation, passed by one of them in pious offices, by the other
in training for the fight. At the time appointed, in the court of the
castle, the archbishop presiding and all the high officials, priests and
laymen, civil and military in attendance, the chiefs in their shirts,
with sword and target entered the lists, and the pleadings read and
oaths administered, at sound of trumpet, engaged in deadly combat.
Tagd the appellant, after valiant fighting by both of them, disarmed
Con his antagonist, and cutting off his head presented it to the
pleased archbishop.

Hooker, who describes the scene of which he was a witness,
observes that many present would have preferred that the whole sept
had taken part instead of only these two gentlemen. The affair
savored of the joust, but for its lack of steeds, and bare shirt offered
but sorry substitute for coat of mail. It bore resemblance to contests
in the arena which delighted the heathen, to bear bait or bull fight,
pleasant to christendom. It was well adapted to suit the fancy of
archbishop Loftus who tortured Hurley, and was rather worse than
the killing of Allen, all three of them venerable prelates. It was in
bad taste in this more than else, that the aggrieved race should have
thus afforded gratification to their enemies by quarrels among themselves, and constitutes a curious exemplification of the contentious
spirit which has ever been the perdition and bane of Ireland.

But if indecorous for the primate to preside over this sanguinary conflict, there were extenuating circumstances. Twelve months before the massacre of St. Bartholomew had tainted the air of France with the blood of thirty thousand Huguenots. Such horrors grown infectious whetted the appetite for more. Neither Catherine de Medici nor the archbishop were model christians or disposed to shrink from human shambles, where they conceived public policy concerned. Persecution of schismatics or non-conformists was not to save souls, but to uphold papal power or shake it off. Atrocities of deepest dye perpetrated alike by protestant and catholic must be attributed to a morbid spirit of dictation, or to carry out some cherished design. That design was often, sad to say, the gratification of malignant temper, personal resentment, or selfish greed. Blood was poured out like water, the most savage cruelties inflicted in the name of Christianity, when the actuating motive was to crush an enemy, or improve one's estate. During the Desmond war policy counselled toleration. Now that persecution could no longer strengthen opposition and would help along confiscation, the blood hounds were let loose.

Religious differences were adjusted by martial law or processes equally summary. Hurley papal archbishop of Cashel, learned and estimable, some few weeks before the death of Desmond, whilst employed in secretly administering the holy sacraments, had found himself at castle Slane at supper with another guest, judge Dillon. Conversation flowed on, when discussion arose as to controverted points of theology. The prelate held his peace not to betray himself. But when something advanced peculiarly offensive touched him to the quick, he expressed his views with an ability leading the judge to suspect him no ordinary personage. Ascertaining who he in reality was, Dillon denounced him to the lords justices, who caused his arrest under the roof of Ormond. After long imprisonment in a dank and murky dungeon, Loftus offered him his see, if he would renounce the pope and hold it of the queen. Declining, he was put to torture.

As there was no rack at the castle, his feet were placed in boots constructed for the purpose. Oil, wax and pitch, salt and butter were poured in with boiling water and fire applied. With untroubled mien the martyr sustained his excruciating torments. Remanded to his cell, Mac Morris his fellow prisoner, a jesuit physician skilled in medicaments, effected his partial cure, but the lords justices, with the sanction of the queen and fearing Ormond's interference, if delayed, ordered his execution without the walls, and at dawn, lest tumult should arise. Abbot Cullinan and another priest were also hung, and many more underwent a like fate.

The Burkes after their submission at the close of the campaign of 1581, had kept quiet for them. They awaited some act of grace from the queen to shield them from her wrath for their previous course. The loss of seven hundred of their followers, in the contest, two hundred of them their kinsmen, had diminished their strength, and humbled their pride. Their father, dying of consumption, longed for his native air, and exciting the commiseration of the queen and her council was released, and went home in the summer of 1582. He received, after his long absence, an enthusiastic welcome at Galway from neighbor and kinsfolk, and having reconciled his sons with each other and the queen, died and was buried at Loughrea. Ulick and John, born to him by different mothers, entered into similar contention for the earldom as their father and uncle, thirty years before. They left it in the first instance to Malbie to determine, who decided in favor of Ulick his father-in-law. John appealing to the council who affirmed the judgment of the governor, he was appeased by being created baron of Leitrim.

The death of John by violence the year after his father's, cast suspicion on Malbie, reproach on Ulick. Receiving the hospitalities of a kinsman, the castle keys were treacherously or surreptitiously abstracted from the keeping of the seneschal, to whose charge they were entrusted at night, and the warders drugged or inebriated at a feast provided for the purpose, the gates were thrown open and an armed band of Ulick's admitted. Two knights of distinction were killed in their beds. John, who slept in the adjoining chamber, awoke at the stir and hastily slipped on his breast-plate over his night dress, seizing what weapons were at hand. The door was closed against the intruders, but upon parley it was agreed that he should join his brother, then without the castle expecting him, assurance being given for his safety. He had hardly laid down his sword and doffed his armor before the assailants rushed through the opening door, and he fell pierced by many wounds.

Dissension arose still farther west, for Ballinahinch. Teigue son of the battle-axes held it ; but the descendants of Owen, another O'Flaherty, claimed. Pursued by their kinsmen to Arran, many were slain besides one of the Clan Maurice of Kerry their ally. They finally recovered the lands in controversy. As 1584 ended, Brian O'Rourke grandson of his chief, helped himself to the herds of Dartry. Their rightful owner, Mac Clancy, rushed to recover them, and at Benbo a mountain famous for its promise of gold, never realized, fought the despoiler who came as haughtily to the encounter as the proud O'Rourke himself. That chieftain, disapproving of the marauding propensities of his descendant and namesake, sent the men of Bremny to stay his proceedings. In Brian's pay were MacShechys late gal-loglasses of Desmond, whose iron morions and coats pierced with nails did not save them that day from slaughter. Brian carried off by his fellow clansmen paid the penalty for appropriating what belonged to his neighbor contrary to tribe usage, and incurring still further the displeasure of his chief was put to death.

Ulster aswarm with warriors preferring fight to feast, continued volcanic. Kilcote in 1581, as related, went against O'Donnel. Another year found his army and Turlogh's in large numbers confronting on Lough Foyle, whilst the chieftains held an amicable conference. This ended not without bloodshed, Scotch highlanders under O'Neil having an affray with the equally tempersome Mac Sweenys. The humiliation of having received the last blow rankled in the heart of Tyrconnel and he burned Strabane, the residence of Turlogh and near his own. Turlogh gathered his clan and some English to resent this indignity, and in June the rival chieftain concentrated his forces at Drumlean. Skirmishes ensued and reconnoissances in force. Turlogh's choicest cavalry crossed the Finn, and passing Lifford, Hugh despatched a large mounted force to drive them back. The obstinate and merciless encounter lasted long, but the invaders environed by superior numbers and badly cut up gave way, and unable in their haste and confusion to discover the ford rushed into the angry flood. Many were drowned, among them O'Gormly and O'Clery half brother of Turlogh and keeper of his treasures.

Desmond's career commencing with the reign of Elizabeth forms an epoch in Irish history which closes with his death. Allusion to that of some few of his cotemporaries mentioned by the annalists will suggest what then constituted claims to notice. O'Hara distinguished for horsemanship and hearty hospitality; O'Byrne versed in Latin and Irish civil and common law; O'Madden of similar culture, valorous in war and compassionate to the needy; Pierce Butler who obtained no property of the church; Gilla O'Shaugnessy esteemed for his many excellent traits by both races, and his mother Margaret O'Brien famed for her beauty; another of the latter name, wife of Clanrickard, respected throughout the land for her kindness to friend and kinsfolk; and yet another, daughter of the third earl, equally renowned for her integrity, purity and piety; Catherine Maguire wife of O'Boyle and the best any chieftain had in Ulster, ended their days.

During the next decade are noted John MacNamara lord of Clancuillen in Thomond, noble and magestic, favorite of dame and damsel for mirth and pleasantry; Sir Thomas Cusack thrice viceroy, and the excellent chancellor " not to be forgotten, as peacemaker, in Munster for a century;" Magrath ollav of Dalgais in poetry but also an

oracle in science and husbandry; Hugh Mac Clancy professor of
the fenachas and poetry, whose bins of choice wine added to his celebrity; and another of the same intellectual race, ollav of judicature;
Mac Ward ollav to O'Donnel in poetry, and president of his schools;
Johanna O'Boyle learning to swim in the river; Donal Mac
Gorman servant of trust; Meva daughter of Hugh Roe O'Donnel
wife first to Maclean and then to O'Kane, at the age of eighty-
seven, who had spent this long life, happily and in affluence, and
gained renown for her generous hospitality and graces of demeanor;
Abbot O'Dwyer from his virtue and culture, greatly lamented;
Teigue O'Brien son of the first earl, champion in battle, ursine in
vigor and fierceness; O'Duigenan of Kilronan, ollav of Tirerill, a
learned historian, who kept a thronged house, cheerful, affable and
endowed with the gift of eloquence.

Henry O'Neil son of Turlogh not long after the appearance in the
southeast in January of the wonderful comet with curved tail resembling bright lightning, the brilliancy of which illuminated the earth
around, and firmament above; Donnell O'Sullivan Mor; James lord
of Decies; Calvagh only son of Donnel of Sligo; John O'Doherty
lord of Inishowen, for whose ransom many horses and lands would
have been given; Con son of Calvagh O'Donnel accomplished,
sedate and hospitable, supporting pillar of gentle and simple, purchaser
of books, so illustrious among the descendents of Nial of the nine
hostages that after his death Kinnel Konnel might have been likened
to a harp without a string, ship without pilot, field without shade.
Murrogh O'Sheehy who died of grief at the death of Desmond; lord
Roche and his wife in the same month; Sir Cormac Mac Teigue* lord

* Seventh in descent from Dermod (113) b. 1310–1367, second son of Cormac Mor (112),
and first lord of Muskerry; sixth from Cormac (114) b. 1346 k. 1374; fifth from Tagd (115)
b. 1380 d. 1448; fourth from Cormac Laidir (116) b. 1411, k. 1495, who built Blarney; third
from Cormac Oge (117) b. 1447, d. 1536 and Catherine Parry; second from Tagd (118) b.
1472, and Catherine d of Donal Reagh by d. of eighth Kildare; son of Dermod (119) b. 1501,
d. 1570, and Helena daughter of Maurice Fitzgerald. Authorities disagree as to the successor of Cormac Mac Teigue the chief mentioned in the text. Four Masters say Cormac
son of Tagd son of Dermot succeeded, Cormac son of Dermot son of Tagd contending.
The latter b. 1552 d. 1616 eventually lord of Muskerry by Mary Butler d. lord Cahir

of Muskerry, high sheriff of Cork, rarest man among the Irishy, comely shaped, bright countenanced, who possessed, besides Blarney, of the builder of which he was g. g. grandson, more whitewashed edifices, fine built castles and hereditary seats than any one of the Eoghanacht; Conor O'Kennedy of Ormond, ready, tranquil and domestic, without reproach from his birth; Eveleen Roche wife of Donogh fourth earl of Thomond; Hugh O'Reilly chief of Brenny; Margaret O'Donnel daughter of Hugh Duv and wife of Maelmora O'Reilly, than whom not another female descendant of Gaedhal Glas then living gave away more presents, are selected from amongst the rest as indicating of what consisted the prominent individuals in the country at this period.

XXXVII.

REIGN OF ELIZABETH.—1558-1602.—(Continued.)

Nearly twenty years of the last reign of the Tudors remain for compression within brief space. A general view of an historical epoch often conveys more distinct idea of its form and pressure than details more minute. Readers engrossed with one subject or eager for information upon many have rarely taste or leisure for investigation out of their accustomed beat, and to them even this imperfect sketch of a period fraught with momentous consequences, not confined to the actual generation but perennial even to our own, may be of use. The difficulty of sifting truth from error, where

left a younger son Daniel of Carrignavar whose descendant represents the male line of this branch, and his eldest son Cormac b. 1564, d. 1640 cr. 1628 viscount Muskerry, who by Margaret d. of fourth Thomond left Donogh 1594-1666, cr. 1658 earl of Clancarthy, who by Eleanor Butler sister first duke of Ormond had Cormac k. in battle at sea 1665, and Callaghan 1630-1676, third earl, who by Elizabeth d. sixteenth Kildare, had Donogh, b. 1665, d. 1734 fourth earl, who for James II. forfeited lands since worth £200,000 a year, as alleged because his troopers tossed in a blanket, for reasons good or bad, a butcher of Cork. He married 1684, Elizabeth Spenser, d. earl of Sunderland, and their son Robert 1686-1770 died at Boulogne leaving two sons, who died without issue. The title of Clancarthy is now held by the family of Le Poor Trench descendants of John Power and Helena sister of Donogh first earl of Clancarthy.

authority and evidence are so various, conflicting and often inaccessible, can hardly be exaggerated.

Early in 1584 Sir John Perrot, whose previous experiences in
Irish administration qualified him for the task, had been commissioned as deputy. He was empowered according to precedent to make
war and peace, punish and pardon, fine, confiscate, declare martial
law, with royal privity assemble parliament, appoint all officers except
the chancellor, three chief justices and master of the rolls, and confer
all spiritual promotions except to the sees: in fine, to do whatever
relating to government and justice the queen could do if present.
He was active and vigorous, generally popular with the septs, and
his departure in 1572 had been "lamented by the poor, the widows,
the feeble and unwarlike of the country." But if humane for an
English governor and of an integrity of character that inspired and
merited confidence, the annalists say his word was as good as his
bond, he was quick to perceive and improve conjunctures propitious
to the main object of English policy, the reduction of the septs to
obedience to the crown.

After a few weeks of consultation at Dublin with the council, consisting of the late lords justices, the bishops of Armagh, Meath and
Kilmora, Ormond, Nicholas Bagnall knight marshal, Robert Gardiner
chief justice, the two Dillons, White master of the rolls, Fenton
secretary of state, Cowley, Waterhouse, Lestrange, Brabazon, Warham St. Leger and Valentine Browne, he proceeded into Connaught,
taking with him Sir Richard Bingham governor of that province, and
Sir John Norris, of Munster. Malbie learned in many tongues,
brave in the field, and able in council, had lately died, not without having reaped his reward in a gift from the crown of the town of Roscommon, of Ballinasloe from the Burkes. During his absence for
a year, his son-in-law, Edward Brabazon, cruel and unsparing,
ruled in his stead, and his successor in sternness and cruelty out-
heroded the bloody Fitton. The lord deputy held his court at
60

Galway, generally attended by the neighboring chieftains, and installing Bingham over the province now to consist of Galway, Leitrim, Mayo, Roscommon, Sligo and Thomond then as now Clare, proceeded leisurely towards Limerick. He occupied three days in his progress, passing his first night at Kilmacduagh, and his second at Quinn. There he caused Donogh Beg O'Brien, cousin of the earl, to be pounded at the cart tail with an axe, and suspended, with his bones broken and half dead, to the steeple of its church.

At Limerick where he instated Norris, tidings came that fleets from the isles were bringing reinforcements to Sorley Boy, who learning that the deputy had been instructed to expel him from the Route, which he had possessed for thirty years, had determined upon resistance. Perrot, ordering all troops from Beare to Boyne to collect at Drogheda, flew to meet the danger. He wrote home to the queen that having but nine hundred men at his immediate disposal he had summoned Ormond to his assistance; and to the privy council that Turlogh with the Scots and Spaniards, expected at Sligo, and the disaffected in Munster and Connaught had combined for a general rising. Dungannon had of late been on friendly terms with the English, but had gone to join O'Neil, and his uncle the Maguire, chief of Fermanagh, had become estranged. On his way at Dublin he wrote Walsingham, to propose turning St. Patricks into a court house and endowing two colleges out of its revenues.

Sixteen hundred Scots had come over with the sons of James Mc-Donnel and twenty-four hundred since. Not anticipating such vigorous proceedings on the part of the deputy, or else receiving orders from home as no war existed between the two countries, many of them reëmbarked. The Kinel-Owen not satisfied with Turlogh for calling in Englishmen and allowing himself to be beaten by Hugh at Drumleen, proposed to substitute Shane's son in his place. With Dungannon he took refuge with Perrot who reduced Donfert and Dunluce in Antrim, "the strongest piece in the realm, situate upon a rock hanging over the sea, divided from the main land by a broad, deep, rocky ditch, natural and not artificial, with no way to it but a small neck of the same rock, which was also cut off very deep." The garrison having no guns suitable for defence surrendered. Sorley Boy late lord of fifty thousand cows, now of fifteen hundred, took to his woods. He soon after submitted and then repaired into Scotland, Donnel Gorme, son of Agnes, being set up in his stead. Perrot improved the opportunity offered by this apparent submission, to divide Ulster into seven counties: Antrim, Armagh, Cavan, Coleraine, Donegal, Fermanagh and Tyrone, and appointed sheriffs and other officials. But as the inhabitants were not prepared to receive them, or admit either English tribunals or English rule, it was simply a decree; and without other result than to enable certain greedy and unscrupulous individuals, where they could with impunity, to harass and despoil the helpless and unprotected.

The energetic deputy having gone through all the provinces of the realm within less than a quarter of a year, was back in Dublin by the middle of October. He requested reinforcements of five hundred men to make his standing force twenty-five hundred, and fifty thousand pounds a year for three years to build seven bridges, as many towns and castles.* This shocked the economy of his royal mistress, who was expecting an invasion from the Spaniards. Perrot sent over to England for education Gerald, now sixteenth earl of Desmond, with the sons of Clanrickard and O'Rourke, "pretty quick boys," and with them the holy cross of Columbkille, "a god of great veneration with Sorley Boy and all Ulster," as a gift to Walsingham.

The winter passed in preparation for the new parliament. White was hanging in Leinster forty-eight out of one hundred and eighty-one prisoners. At Ballynecor at the mouth of the Glynn, Feagh

* Towns: Athlone, Coleraine, Sligo, Mayo, Dingle and the Newry. Bridges: Coleraine, Lifford, Ballyshannon, Dundalk, Broadwater in Munster, river Virdo on the Slewe Lougher, Kilsan Caneboy. Castles: Blackwater to be better fortified, Ballyshannon, Moyrick to be erected, Broadwater in Munster, Castle Martin upon the Route; Galim in the Queen's County and Kilcobran in Feagh McHugh O'Byrnes. By these the whole realm would be environed and strengthened, and all great waters made passable.

Mac Hugh of the O'Byrnes professed good intentions, but could not offend his captain. Cavan was erected into a shire. Perrot had ordered that Sorley Boy and his son should be assassinated, but Dantry wrote he could not bring it about. Valentine Browne thirty-five years in service, sent to survey Munster, found it wasted by famine, justice and the sword, not one in thirty left of its inhabitants. He suffered all sorts of hardship and discomfort, but did his work.

In the midwinter, an unwonted season for hostilities, two thousand Scots came over under Angus McDonnel and Sorley Boy and attacked Stanley and Bagnall, but were beaten off, Stanley being thrice badly wounded. Sorley in February declaring his good intentions, offered to pay the same rent for the Route and third part of the Glynns as previously for the whole, his cousin Donnal Gorme having now possession of the other two thirds. For answer his territory was devastated, and Angus returning by order of the king to Scotland, Sorley soon followed.

At the end of April the parliament met and presented an unwonted aspect. Chiefs in native costume flocked to the capital. Some reluctantly adopted the parliamentary robes, O'Neil begging that his chaplain might wear petticoats and share the ridicule. Besides Turlogh, Hugh came as earl of Tyrone. Hugh Roe O'Donnel, Cuconnaught Maguire, John Oge O'Doherty, Turlogh O'Boyle, Owen O'Gallagher, Ross McMahon, Rory O'Kane, Con O'Neil of Clanaboy, Hugh Magennis, Brian O'Rourke, John Roe O'Reilly and his uncle Edmund, William O'Ferrall Bane and Fachtna O'Ferall Boy, Hugh O'Conor Don, Teigue Oge O'Conor Roe, Donnel O'Conor Sligo, Brian Mac Dermot of Moylurg, Carbry O'Bierne of Tir Briuin, Teigue O'Kelly, Donnel O'Madden, Morrogh O'Flaherty of the battle axes, John and Dermot sons of Gilladuv O'Shaughnessy, Sir Turlogh O'Brien son of Sir Donald, John Macnamara, Boethius Mac Clancy, Ross O'Loughlin of Burren, Murtogh Mac-I-brien-Ara, bishop of Killaloe, Calvagh O'Carroll,

John McCoghlan, Philip O'Dwyer of Tipperary, Murtogh MacBrien of Carrigogunnell and Conor O'Mulryan were there.

Of the Eoghanacht Donnal MacCarthy Mor, earl of Clancarre, Owen McCarthy Reagh of Carbery, Donnel son of Cormac Reagh and Florence son of Donogh, Dermot and Donogh competitors for Duhallow, Owen O'Sullivan Beare and Owen O'Sullivan Mor of Dunkerron came, and also Conor and Florence O'Driscoll, Florence Mac Gilpatrick, Conla Mageoghan of West Meath, and Feagh O'Byrne of Glanmalure. None of the O'Mores of Leix or O'Conors of Offaly, MacGormans or Kavanaghs, Tooles, Dunns or Dempsys attended.

Many of the chieftains, who improved the occasion to visit the capital for the laudable purpose of meeting their acquaintance and enlarging their experience of the world, were not members. Thirty six towns were represented. In the upper house sat the four arch-bishops, Dublin, Armagh, Tuam and Cashel :* twenty bishops, two of whom, Clogher and Raphoe, were professed catholics : six earls, Ormond, Kildare, Tyrone, Thomond, Clanrickard and Clancarre : four viscounts, Buttevant, Gormanstown, Fermoy and Montgarret : fourteen barons, Athenry, Kinsale, Slane, Delvin, Killeen, Howth, Trimlestown, Dunsany, Upper Ossory, Louth, Curraghmore, Inchi-quin, Castleconnel, and Cahir. The session ended on the twenty-ninth of May, parliament having attainted James Eustace, viscount Baltinglass, and restored Lawrence Delahide whose ancestor had been attainted under Henry VIII. The proposition to suspend the Poynings act was defeated by the Anglo Irish members, and sixteen bills sent over from England thrown out. They refused to pass the usual subsidy, to vest the queen with lands of attainted persons without inquisition or office found, or to declare those guilty of trea-son who should rebelliously detain any of her castles. The recalcitrant members were much the same who had hounded Kildare, Netterville

* Loftus, Long, Leahy and Magrath.

the friend of Leicester, Burnell, Sutton, Garland and Edward Nugent. They persuaded O'Ferral Ban, Tirrel, Philip and Edmund O'Reilly members for Cavan, Sir Hugh Magennis and John Cusack to aid. Government instituted proceedings against them, when Gormanstown and other peers apologized to the queen for their audacity. The parliament in no amiable humor was prorogued to the twenty-eighth of April, of the following year.

The session over, as the deputy was starting for the north, he commissioned Bingham, the earls of Thomond and Clanrickard, lord Athenry, the knights Torlogh O'Brien, Richard Burke na-Irain, Donald O'Conor of Sligo, Brian O'Rourke, Morrogh O'Flaherty of the battle axes, and others to call before them all lords spiritual and temporal, chiefs and captains and propose to substitute ten shillings for each quarter of one hundred and twenty acres, bearing horn or corn, in lieu of all cess or taxation except for risings out and fortifications for the general benefit. It was kindly received, and an indenture dated the seventeenth of August was executed by sixty-seven* of the Irish chieftains, and several of the large English proprietors. This was not a surrender, hardly a recognition of fealty, but a composition for the claim to cess or tax, and yielded under duress, not of much obligation in conscience or law. At a session of the court of the whole province in the monastery of Ennis, five shillings for each quarter in Thomond except from the liberties or church lands was allowed to the earl, who gave up Inchiquin to Morrogh son of Dermot, son of the first earl, Corcomroe to Torlogh, son of Sir Donald.

* Forty one Macs: Mac William Eighter and Roe, Mac Namara, Finn and Reagh, M'Gilly, M'Glinaghee, Everhin, Hubbert, Oughe, Cremon, Walter, Hugh, Edmond, Gyramgh, Reamon, Thomas, Vavy, Walter, Dermots, Roe and Gael, Padyn, Tybbot, Philipen; Connel, Gloughe, Tyrnan, Kelly, Gerald, Reaman, Kelarny, Evily, Costello, Jordan, Murray, Enery, Loughlin, Grannill, Donoghs, Many. Twenty-one Oes: O'Rourke, Conors Sligo, Don and Roe, Kelly, Flaherty, Molly Heyne, Madden, Dowde, Hart, Poy and Reagh, Naughtan, Loughlin, Goff, Neylan, Murry, Maning, Cowchanon, Byrne, Flynn, Hawley, Harty, Loream, Flanegan and Mulryan.

Among others who signed in Clare were the bishops and deans of Killaloe and Kiltinora, Edward, Waterhouse, the two Mac Mahons of the Corcavaskins and Mac Namara of Moitullen. O'Briens of Drumleen and Clonoon, O'Deas of Tullyodea, Mac Gilleroy of Cragbrian, Bradie, son of the bishop of Meath, Edward White of Crotelagh, George Cusack of Dromoylan, O'Grady of Inchicronan, McClanchy of the Ulion, O'Brians of Ballicourey, Ballicassy and Caherceorcran and George Fanning of Limerick.

Inquisitions at Cork professed to discover that several lordships belonging to the crown had been usurped by persons without title, among them Kinelmeaky. Conogher O'Mahony to whom it belonged had perished in the rebellion. His ancestors one hundred and twenty-six years before, driving out the interlopers upon the territories of his sept, had divided them with McCarthy Reagh for their better security. It was pretended that Barry Oge had previously to this recovery by the O'Mahony chieftains, paid rent into the exchequer, and that consequently it was the property of the crown. Callen was claimed as occupied without title by Richard Roach. Lambert, constable of Dublin castle who had been badly wounded in the war, setting up a grant from Edward III. laid claim to Cloghroe, which with Ballea, Courtbreac and Castlemore had been settled on Cormac Mac Tagh of Muskerry some fifty years before. The claim of Lambert was pronounced untenable ten years later, but though no inquest had been held by the chief justice as coroner, as required by law, for the forfeiture of estates, where the proprietor had been killed in rebellion, the crown title to Kinalmeaky was upheld by the English tribunals, in direct violation of rules they had themselves constantly enforced, against the O'Mahonys.

As regarded this territory, no surrender or broken allegiance could be pretended. Prescription or constructive possession by payment of rent into the treasury, whilst the actual occupants paid none whatsoever to any one but their own chieftain, had no ground to rest upon. Title thus gained by rule of law had been by the same rule lost by adverse possession for a century without any such payment. The crown had no paramount claim under which to confiscate. If it had ever overrun, it had never subdued or held under subjection, and what feeble hold it had clutched, had been shaken off. Its papal pretensions were equally fanciful. What Adrian gave, Pius had divested. The principle that local law governs land titles lent them no strength, since their authority was never sufficiently established, either in fact, or by superior power to bind by legislation. This they admitted by accepting the surrenders. If in the pale and palatinates where Englishmen held from the crown, violated allegiance worked forfeiture and justified confiscation, if this applied to lands surrendered and the surrenders availed against the septs, it did not apply to O'Mahony who had not surrendered or ever been subjected.

Hastings found England in a measure feudal; king over earl, earl over thane. Authority and estate by subinfeudation extended down guarded by Saxon liberty. William after Ely in 1071 having crushed opposition, confirmed rather than established feudal tenures, appropriating fiefs to his own followers. No such feudal usages or feudal law existed in Ireland a century later. Its own complicated but enlightened system of land tenures vested an allodial estate in the septs, chief and clansmen holding by defined rules. The chief had hardly a freehold. Specific portions of property, held for life and descending to heirs by custom, appertained to office and depended on election. No incident of feudality, wardship or marriage attached to the soil. The brehon law in force, the chief could not surrender what belonged to his sept, and confiscation could not reach them. One chief was put down and another set up, but the boundaries remained unchanged. Respect for neighbors' landmarks was of peculiar sanctity. The same septs held for centuries, losing cattle or paying tribute, but were never disturbed in possession by neighboring lord or clan, but only by the foreign element, the English invader. In Connaught the proposition by Perrot to substitute fixed sums for cess was stretched in numerous instances into surrender, to be followed up with a regrant by patent occasionally withheld. By English rule, patents were to be enrolled in order to be produced in evidence. This was purposely neglected. Three thousand pounds, later appropriated to make good the oversight of patentees or covin of officials who received the money but disobeyed the law, vanished, and evidence required not forthcoming, lands were lost. The chiefs in surrendering were in a measure prompted by the conviction that conformity to English law under existing conditions was wisest and best, both for their clans and for themselves. But not many years had elapsed before their lands on one pretext or another were wrested away from them, their families died out or disappeared, and their clans became hereditary bondsmen to the dominant race, who by chicanery had outwitted their confiding and less astute victims. Thus in the inception of title, disregard of rules parliament had established and of principles recognized by the courts, there were fatal defects in all these transfers, which nothing but the law of limitations has cured. It is to be hoped that the landed interest will bear this in mind in generous concession, and avoid such retributions as befel the chieftains.

Long, consecrated lord primate of Armagh in July, 1584, in the place of Jones, found "the churches fallen into dilapidation, that children and laymen held livings and benefices with cure, and that clergymen were tolerated to have three or four pastoral dignities, who themselves unlearned were not meet to instruct others." Parliament endeavored to reform the court of faculties established to regulate the clergy, to stay ecclesiastical corruption, but Long says to little purpose; both clergy and laity going in a wild gallop to the devil. Hart, bishop of Achonry who had attended the council of Trent, having renounced the pope and his see, he wrote that if they did not use this people more for gain than for conscience, the Lord's work would be mightily preferred. He complained that the justices of the peace and lords of the pale would not take the oath of supremacy. Walsingham replied that the course of the deputy as regarded the reformation would have better suited the times of Henry VIII. when princes persisted in honorable attempts, than their own which had other manners of proceeding, and Perrot must conform. The plan of the deputy for appropriating St. Patrick's for a university angered Loftus. His other measures of reform alarmed the officials.

Representations were made for his removal, even a letter forged from Turlogh O'Neil, but both Long and himself were too strong in their integrity to shake.

Burkes and Binghams were over much for Connaught. The death of Sir Richard-na-Irain* led to a disputed succession. The new governor at first affected moderation, but this was not his natural temper. At a court held in January 1586, seventy men and women were put to death, Donnel O'Brien, Brian O'Hara, and many besides. Thomas Roe, one of the principal Burkes rudely summoned to his presence, was slain when refusing to come, and two of his followers executed. The chiefs, too much incensed and disgusted at these outrages to attend his court, he resorted to violence to compel them. The castle of Clonoon he took and demolished, Owen O'Brien† its chief falling in its defence. He then besieged Hag's castle, on an island in Lough Mask in Mayo, reputed one of the strongest in the west, into which Richard, brother of the Burke above mentioned, had thrown himself with a slender following. The governor, his men killed and his boats shattered by shot from the castle and himself thrown into the water, was forced to swim ashore for safety. Not sufficiently strong or provided with artillery to contend with such force as the irate commander could bring to bear against him, the chief and his warders crossed to the main land, where overtaken they also were executed.

---

* Allusion has been made to his wife, the bold buccaneer, and her visit to court in 1576, at the invitation of the queen, who proposed to make her a countess, an honor she declined as they were both princesses, but prayed the queen bestow what honors she pleased on her infant son, born on the voyage across. On her return she landed at Howth for provisions, and the gates closed as the family were at dinner, admittance was refused. The child of the lord of the castle was playing by the sea shore, and him she took on board her ship and carried off to Connaught, and refused to restore him till promise was made that the castle gate should never be closed again at dinner time. From her galleys that lay off her castle of Carrigahooly extended a rope into the apartment where she slept to apprise her of any hostile approach or prey worthy of her notice.

† Son of Turlogh bishop of Killaloe, son of Mahon, son of Mahon, fifth son of Torlogh Bog, king of Thomond, who died in 1459, and Catherine Burke of Clanrickard. Chief of Sliocht Mahon of which the present baronets of Castlegar are supposed head, " he was champion of the pope and great practiser with foreign powers for the invasion of Ireland," as was also Donogh his son, now represented by the head of the Carbally or Ennis branch, the eminent barrister of London. Bingham gave his territory to George son of chancellor Cusack, killed in 1599 by Turlogh, Owen's eldest son, who three years later was slain by John Burke in Hy-Many. By their kinsmen the Clanrickards this branch again rose to position. The name of O'Brien, dropped as usual when losing their inheritance, all the Mahons of the west descend from Owen.

Perrot disapproving these tyrannical proceedings bade the governor desist. But the council headed by Loftus, whose natural dislike to the deputy, for thwarting his plans and seeking to reform abuses, was aggravated by the proposed appropriation of one of his cathedrals for a college, sided with the governor, refusing Perrot permission to go into Connaught to restore order. The governor thus encouraged to persevere in his savage course, what little affection for English rule existed turned into implacable resentment, and the chiefs gathered in strength for resistance. Joyces, Clandonell and Clangibbon came to aid. Several thousand Scots landing at Inishowen marched through Donegal and Fermanagh to Lough Erne to join them. Bingham put to death his hostages and gathering his garrisons and summoning Ulick with his men from Clanrickard, kept out of view, till he had organized his army. The hostile force finding the bridge at Collony strongly guarded, crossed the river by a ford and encamped at Ardnaree. Not expecting attack, strong detachments went out to maraud. Bingham after a night's march broke in upon their main force at noon the next day, when their camp was in confusion. The men sleeping off their fatigues were aroused by the cries of their sentinels who were being slaughtered.

The Scots fought their best, but did not recover the effect of the surprise, and routed were driven in to the Moy, two thousand being slain. This victory gained by Bingham on the twenty-second of September, 1586, was followed by a court held at Galway in December, when still more men and women were indiscriminately put to death. His captains raided the province, O'Toole chief of Omey, an island off Connamara, was slain, and Edmund Burke a withered old man of respectable position and character executed. The deputy when he heard of the landing of the Scots and what they were doing marched to reinforce the governor, but when he learned the result of the battle of Ardnaree he returned home.

When parliament again assembled to attaint Gerald, the deed of trust of 1576, already mentioned, was urged as sufficient to protect his estates from confiscation. Upon this, articles of association, dated two years before, on the eighteenth of July, 1574, between himself and twenty-two of his tributaries and allies, wherein they pledged life, land and goods to resist any attempt of deputy or council to deprive him wrongfully of his property, were produced as treasonable acts, invalidating the subsequent conveyance. This plainly against law and precedent, as any such infringement of his vested rights by violence without due legal process, as that menaced, would have justified resistance, was resisted. An ex post facto law, constituting such combinations treasonable and making void conveyances, made as his had been, did not remove the difficulty. But the government, in no humor to regard constitutional objections, pressed the attainder, which after much legislation and protracted debate, finally passed, declaring all his lands and those of one hundred and forty of his kinsmen and dependents forfeited to the crown. The area embraced in these confiscations covered five hundred and seventy-four thousand six hundred and twenty-eight acres, or about a thousand square miles; the annual revenue, probably payable for the most part in kind or in service, being estimated at four hundred thousand marks. The Desmonds claimed supremacy, and exacted tribute when they were in power, over areas as large again as what was thus confiscated.

Of this vast territory large portions were restored to Condons, Fitzgibbons and other Geraldines. Less than half, two hundred and forty-five thousand acres, were granted in thirty-two seignories, to undertakers in parcels generally of twelve thousand acres, each grant conditioned on the settlement of eighty-six families. It was anticipated that thus twenty thousand English would avail themselves of the very reasonable terms to come over. Many came, especially from the southern and western counties, from Somerset, Dorset and Devon, younger sons of respectable families, some of them taking under several landlords.

According to Morrison, 30,569 acres in Kerry and Desmond, with yearly rents of 524 l. 3 s., were passed by patent to Sir William Herbert, Carol Herbert, Sir Valentine Browne, besides an uncertain portion to George Stone and John Chapman. In Limerick 90,165 acres, with yearly rents of 363 l. 4 s. to Sir Henry Billinsly, William Carter, Edmund Mannering, William Trenchard, Sir George Thornton, Richard Fitton, Robert Annesley, Edward Berkeley, Sir Henry Uthered, Sir William Courtney and Robert Stroude. In Cork 88,337 acres, with annual rents of 512 l. 7 1-2 s. to Vane Beecher, Henry North, Arthur Rawlins, Arthur Hide, Hugh Cuffe, Sir Thomas Norris, Warham St. Leger, Sir Thomas Stoyes, Master Spenser, Thomas Fleetwood and Marmaduke Edmunds. In Waterford and Tipperary 22,910 acres, with rents of 303 l. 3 d. to Ormond, Sir Christopher Hatton, Sir Edward Fitton and Sir Walter Raleigh.* These undertakers did not people their seignories with well affected English as covenanted, but either sold them to English papists or disposed of them to their best profit. Neither did they build castles, and her majesty's bounty turned not to strengthen but rather to weaken the government in Munster.

Desmond's confiscations had little warrant from precedent. His ancestors wrested portions of their vast domains from the septs, more had vested in their line by purchase, inheritance or grant. If in their veins flowed as large a measure of Milesian blood as of Nesta or Plantagenet, if to preserve what fell to their lot they were often engaged in rebellion, it was owing to the ties that bound Geraldines and Burkes to the Irish chieftains, that England retained what hold she had of the island. Often before English lords had been subjected to fine and forfeiture or even decapitation, but their

---

* Mageoghan adds to the above names John Holly, Captain Jenkin Conway, and John Campion instead of Chapman; in Cork, Hugh Worth and Thomas Say; in Cork and Waterford, Richard Bacon. Ormond, claiming all Desmond as his inheritance, besides the estates in Tipperary received also a large portion of the peninsula of Corkaguiney, later surrendered in whole or in part to the knight of Kerry. The rent fixed per acre for the settlers was three pence in Limerick, Conello and Kerry, two pence in Cork or Waterford, about twenty-five hundred pounds, no large return for such an extent of territory.

estates if sequestered were restored to their lineal heirs and pardon
speedily followed submission.   Gerald had been patient under injury
and insult.   Cast into prison, duped and trifled with by the queen and
her representatives, it was in self-defence that he was provoked to
resistance, and then under circumstances more excusable than had
often justified concession and forgiveness not to one race alone but
to both.   If smarting under wrong he hearkened rather to resentment than to more prudent counsels, no Geraldine experience in the
past foreshadowed the approaching catastrophe in the irretrievable
downfall of his house.

It was a fearful wreck.   Desolation brooded over Munster.   From
Tralee to Youghal extended a howling wilderness.   Famine and
pestilence were at work and wolves fattening on human flesh.   War
had penetrated far beyond any previous limits.   Artillery employed a
century earlier, now greatly improved, had battered down wall and
battlement.   Castles in dilapidation, towns and villages in ashes,
not even the cabin spared, what remained of the wretched inhabitants hid in caverns or clefts of rock among the mountains, to perish
of hunger and cold.   Younger sons and other adventurers from over
the sea eagerly responded to the call of undertakers to colonize what
once was the garden of the land, but dismayed at the misery that
surrounded them and the angry menace of the despoiled, speedily
forsook these sorry substitutes for the comfortable homes they had
left.

More sanguine spirits favorably circumstanced to avail themselves of the opportunities presented, bought cheap claims thus
abandoned, and when the country nearly depopulated offered safer
abode, others equally enterprising flocked in.   Several of the grantees
sold out to speculators.   The powerful at court were permitted to
retain without complying with the conditions.   Contrary to the stipulated restrictions, leases were made to native tenants who preferred
to till for others their ancestral lands than starve.   The old race soon

repossessed themselves as tenants at low rents of much of the land, and very little was accomplished by all this expense of money and conscience for the purposes intended. Later wars divested both them and their taskmasters, but numerous families still hold under titles derived from these Desmond confiscations.

Raleigh for a brief period took up his abode at Youghal, of which place he served as mayor. His house at Myrtle Grove, where he dwelt, and where he planted the potato brought from America, remains much as when he left it. The widow of the twelfth Desmond, 1464–1604, already aged, resided on his grant in the castle of Inchiquin. His restless spirit led to expense, and his forty thousand acres were sold to Richard Boyle first earl of Cork, who coming into Ireland with less than thirty pounds, had a rental when he died of forty thousand. Askeaton and Lismore, homes of the Desmonds, were his, and passed with much else of his vast accumulations through Cliffords to the dukes of Devonshire.

Not the least distinguished among the undertakers was Edmund Spenser, who at the age of twenty-seven in 1580 as private secretary attended lord Grey at the Smerwick slaughter. Six years later lord of Kilcolman Castle, and three thousand acres on the Mulla near Fermoy in Cork, part of the spoils, he there composed portions of his Fairy Queen, and entertained Raleigh, whom he accompanied to London to publish it in 1591. There again afterwards, while clerk of the Munster council, he wrote his view of Ireland, an able work, and took to wife an Irish maiden, one of his children perishing in the conflagration of his castle in the Tyrone war of 1598, which year he died poor in London, as Ben Jonson writes Drummond of Hawthornden.

His famous poem derived incident and illustration from his experience and observation in a land where knights errant, forlorn damsels and perilous adventure abounded ; where spectres and seemingly supernatural occurrences haunted the popular imagination ; and characters of noblest heroism or basest brutality combined with desperate conflicts, cruel martyrdoms and shattered thrones, amidst natural scenery of great variety and beauty, afforded material to be wrought into imperishable verse by his poetic genius. To delineate human nature in its best development by contrast or example under the influences of chivalric institutions, then coming to an end, was what he aimed to accomplish, and for this he was favorably placed, and the times opportune.

The most remarkable personage of the period was Hugh O'Neil. Whether his father Ferdoragh was son of the first earl of Tyrone or of the blacksmith of Dundalk has never been determined. If the latter hypothesis be correct, he was an O'Kelly of Breggia and the other parent of Hugh was Joanna Maguire of Fermanagh. Born about the time his father was created baron of Dungannon, natural endowments of a high order, an amiable disposition with prepossessing manners and attractive person, rendered the youth a favorite alike with his clansmen and with the queen and her court. The best schools afforded him advantages which he carefully improved, and long residence near the queen and her ministers inspired him with confidence which was strength in his power to cope with them. Certainly in duplicity and dissimulation he was fully their match. He had married early in life an O'Toole whom he divorced; Judith O'Donnel daughter of Hugh brought him seven children; his third wife, the beautiful Mabel Bagnal, in 1591 eloped with him; and his last who survived him, daughter of Magennis, lord Iveagh, was his companion in exile at Rome, where he died aged and blind in 1616.

During his early manhood, subjected to jealous scrutiny, it was only in the army of the queen that he could acquire experience in arms. In 1580 he took part in the expedition against the Spaniards at Smerwick, serving with distinction, and four years later with Perrot and Ormond in that against the Scots of Ulster. Standing high in royal favor in 1587 he was created an earl and placed in possession of Tyrone. Permitted to maintain in his pay six companies, he changed his men till the great body of his clan had become efficient soldiers. The lead imported for his new castle of Dungannon, in quantities sufficient to sheet the mountains, was run into balls. He made friends of the MacDonnels, fostered his son with O'Cahan, and conciliating his vassal chiefs was elected and inaugurated the O'Neill at the rath of Tulloghoge. The tragedy of Fotheringay quickening catholic resentment, wrecks from the armada strewed his shores. The rescued Spaniards found cordial welcome beneath his roof. While cautious not to excite suspicion by careless word or imprudent act, subsequent events proved plainly the nature of their conferences and what were already his designs.

Four score years had hardly chilled the ardor of Sorley. The massacre of his children ten years before at Rathleen had wrung his heart, and his son Aleck perished in these wars under circumstances not chivalric. Challenging an English captain to personal combat, the invitation was accepted, but the captain substituted in his own armor an antagonist more powerful than himself, who was slain, and then continued the fight with the help of Hugh O'Donnel son of Calvagh. Mac Donnel, mortally wounded, had strength remaining to swim across the Lough, but pursued, his head was cut off and sent to the capital. This blow, however much it may have agonized Sorley, yet taught him to dissemble. In June, 1586, he made obeisance to the portrait of the queen, swearing allegiance and receiving rich robes of crimson velvet and gold which she had sent him, and also restitution of Dunluce and other portions of his domains. Whilst at Dublin, an official invited him to look at Aleck's head on a pike at the castle gate. He exclaimed, horror stricken and groaning, "my son hath many heads." The brave old chieftain survived till 1589, when he died at his castle of Donanynie. His remains were carried down the slope of the castle hill past the harbor where he had so often welcomed the Clandonnel to the shores of Antrim,

62

and by the ford to the abbey of Bunnamairge, the Irish caoine and
Scotch coronach mingling in one wild wail for the dead. His wife,
Mary O'Niel, sister of Shane, had died in 1582, and Donnel and
Aleck had preceded him to the tomb. James succeeded, surviving
till 1601, when according to tradition he was poisoned by an emissary
of Cecil. Randal the third son, in 1620, was created first earl of
Antrim.

Perrot himelf, actuated by honesty of purpose and with hearty
contempt for officials who thwarted his efforts for their own sordid
ends, wearied of his work. "Neglected in England and denied the
support necessary for his government, mortified in various instances
by his royal sister, traduced by the unceasing malice of his enemies,
and insulted by his inferiors at the council board," his request even
to be recalled was refused. In May, 1587, a personal altercation with
the marshal, Nicholas Bagnall, in presence of high functionaries of his
court, in the course of which the lie was freely interchanged, would
have come to an actual breach of the peace, had not White and Fenton interfered. One of the best friends of the Irish ever deputy,
Perrot loved fair play, and strove to protect them from official depredations. He wrote the queen he could better please them than
her English subjects. The marshal had already acquired extensive
possessions in Ulster, but coveted more, and bent on the destruction of
the O'Neils, the deputy stood in his path.

Mary queen of Scots, on the eighth of February, lost that beautiful head of hers, baleful and bewitching as Medusa's, and Spain
bristled with vast preparation, to culminate another year in the invincible armada. Irish chieftains alive to what impended, and restless
with expectation, became objects of vigilance, and the deputy where
he could, exacted hostages to hold them under restraint. O'Donnel
too remote for coercion found plentiful pretexts for refusing such
pledges, which his clans would have regarded as badges of servitude.
The royal sheriffs were not allowed to come within his borders.

Joan his daughter had married the earl of Tyrone. Turlogh, aged
and infirm, from subservience to the pale had lost favor with his
people, who transferred their affections if not their allegiance to the
earl. Schemes for keeping Ulster weak by dissension, stale and no
longer efficacious, its two principal powers, at amity, might become
dangerous in the coming strife, unless hostages could be procured.
Recourse to compulsion would have been impolitic and precipitated
a rising, and the royal army was too weak for any such measures.
In his zeal, the deputy resorted to stratagem, leaving a stain on a
character generally estimable. After consultation with his council
he sent John Birmingham, a merchant of Dublin, in a bark laden
with wine and with fifty soldiers on board, to Lough Swilly, where
they anchored near Rathmullan, a castle of Mac Sweeny Fanad,
hereditary constable of Tyrconnel. Portions of the cargo carried
ashore attracted a concourse to purchase, and the hospitable chief
entertained the young nobles drawn thither by the natural fondness
of idle men for carousals.

Hugh Roe, son of Hugh O'Donnel, chief of Tyrconnel, by Ineenduf
daughter of James Macdonnel, then though only fourteen already
famed for his wisdom, noble dispositions and deeds, chanced to be
on a visit of recreation or devotion with his ollavs to the neighborhood,
where he had been brought up in fosterage by Owen Mac Sweeney
of Tuath.* His companions easily persuaded him to repair to Rathmullan, where he received a cordial welcome, but came late, for the
flagons were empty. Cupbearers despatched for additional supplies
were told that the wine not needed for the ship was all sold, but a small

* The third Donegal branch of the MacSweenys, that of Banagh, were in troubles of
their own. Brian Oge, its chief two years before had been slain by his brother Nial, who
banishing Donogh another brother succeeded to the chieftainry. Donogh had betaken himself first to the English and then to the O'Neils, but returning he laid in wait for Nial on
the strand in Boylagh, opposite Aran. A battle ensued at Derryness, in which Nial with a
great number of his followers and of the Clan Sweeny of Munster were slain, and Donogh
ruled in his stead. Some doubt exists as to this race. Some derive them from the De Veres,
others from the vikings of the Baltic; but Four Masters, p. 1851, cite Irwin 1697 as authority for the statement that this warlike sept, though an off-shoot from the O'Nials, came
into Donegal from Scotland where M'Swane's castle in Knapdale in Argyleshire was their
chief's abode.

party were invited aboard. Fanad, Tuath and Sir Owen O'Gallagher with Hugh, rowed over in a small boat, were conducted to the cabin and partook freely of the generous beverage, till their arms stealthily removed and the hatch closed, they found themselves prisoners. Sails were set and anchor raised. The people suspecting treachery flocked to the shore. There was no help. No vessels were at hand for pursuit. Fanad sent for his son Daniel as hostage for himself, Tuath for his son in whose stead appeared another boy in his dress, O'Gallagher for his nephew Hugh. Large ransom was offered for the young O'Donnel, but the vessel carried him and his three companions to Dublin.

Brought before the deputy and council they engaged him in conversation that they might learn what he was likely to prove when older. They then ordered him to be placed in confinement in the Birmingham tower where the other government hostages were kept, and where their only occupation to beguile their weariness was to lament their suffering and troubles and the cruelties practised on Irish chiefs. This capture was said to have delayed the rising of Ulster for several years, since so long as the life of his son might be endangered by hostilities, O'Donnel took care not to provoke the government of the pale, though not refraining from warfare nearer home.

Possibly Turlogh may have been held responsible for this act of perfidy. O'Donnel and the earl his son-in-law, in April, 1588, crossed the Mourne and Derg to Carricklee in Strabane with an army. Mostin from Connaught, Macsweenys from Munster, O'Flaherty with O'Gallagher joined Turlogh and his son Art to oppose them. Gallagher not deeming honorable a nocturnal attack as urged, distinguished himself in a fiercely fought battle on the morrow, which was May day, in defeating the earl, who left behind him on the field many men and horses, and much spoil for the victors.

Incenduf, like her mother Agnes, wife of Turlogh, with many feminine graces, united an energy of character befitting the times

and circumstances of her position as helpmate of a chieftain.
Hugh, son of Calvagh, had sided with Turlogh against her husband
and his son-in-law the earl of Tyrone. He had taken part in killing
her cousin Alexander, son of Sorley Boy, he was an object of her
aversion for his pride and arrogance, and she had moreover other
causes of enmity against him. Her Scotch auxiliaries had promised
to wreak vengeance upon her enemies, and when Hugh came to
Mongalvin, where she chanced to be, with a proud and exultant spirit,
the angry chieftainess, in whose veins coursed the hot surges of
highland temper, reminded them of this pledge. They attacked him
and his company with darts and bullets, leaving him lifeless.

Whether the queen needed him to fight against the Spaniard, or
official jealousy had finally effected its end, Perrot, in July, 1588,
left Ireland. He took the precaution before transferring the government to Sir William Fitzwilliam to persuade the chiefs, whom he
thought vacillating in their allegiance, to volunteer their hostages
and give assurance of their loyalty. Accompanied a second time
by the regrets of all the well disposed of either race, and attended
to the shore by the aged Turlogh who wept to part with him, he
went home to take his place at the council board. But presuming
on his relation to his royal sister, he spoke slightingly of her and
of Hatton, her "dancing chancellor." The latter was no enemy to
provoke with impunity. Through his means, though he did not live
to see the end, for he died himself in 1591, broken hearted at royal
ingratitude, inquiry was instituted into the conduct of the late deputy
in his Irish administration. His secretary bore witness against him
that he had favored the catholic clergy, and incited O'Rourkes and
Burkes to revolt. The charges were not even plausible, but he
frankly acknowledged that in moments of irritation he had let fall
expressions disrespectful to the queen and her advisers. Condemned
to death, some poisonous potion or like trouble to Hatton's, two years
later, saved him from the execution of his sentence.

XXXVIII.

Sir William Fitzwilliam had been for more than thirty years connected with the government, five times as lord justice, when now he was placed for the third time at its head as lord deputy.   Descended from the main stem of his name flourishing for centuries at Sprotborough in Yorkshire, the family estates had recently passed by an heiress to the Copleys who still hold.   His grandfather, a sixth son of a former lord, made a fortune in trade in London, and proved a faithful friend of Wolsey even in disgrace.   The deputy, born in 1526, had married a sister of Sir Henry Sydney, an alliance which proved useful to him in his official course and explains its success.   Not satisfied with his appointments as deputy, he was given to understand that the place was a preferment not a service, and it is to be hoped that the tradition of the modes to which he had recourse to turn it to account, may have been exaggerated.   His example, contrasting to his disadvantage with that of his predecessor, set free his subordinates from any restraint upon their cupidity, and no opportunity was lost to fleece the queen's flocks where powerless to resist.

Whilst assuming charge of affairs in Dublin, the vaunted armada approached the coasts of England.   Its menace had led to fitting preparation.   If neither Medina Sidonia nor Effingham possessed much nautical experience, they had captains under them who had won laurels in long maritime adventure.   If inferior in force, the English vessels were the best handled.   Gales, fire ships, shoals, collisions, and partial engagements dispersed or destroyed the bulky but unmanageable galleasses, and the Spanish admiral, convinced of his inability to cope with his more agile foe, fled round Scotland, strewing the shores of Ireland from Lough Foyle to Castlehaven with the wreck of eighteen of his larger ships, and when he reached San

Andero thirty of his best had foundered or gone to wreck, and ten thousand of his men had perished. O'Donnel, timid for his son, arrested the fugitives in his havens, but a thousand found welcome and cordial hospitality from O'Rourke. Their commander De Leva, entreated to aid against the English, deferred action to a more convenient season, and setting sail was lost with his men within sight of the shore. Other officers visited Dungannon and were courteously received.

Rich spoils fell to the wreckers. Iron safes strongly banded, which held the treasure, are still preserved, one not long since at Dunluce. Deputy and governor marched in November into Bretney to collect the plunder, but it had disappeared, and when they had devastated the country about, and Mac Sweenys above, they were not better off. Balked of his prize, the deputy seized upon O'Gallagher and O'Dogherty and carried them to the castle of Dublin, the former to die of the rigors of his imprisonment, the latter to recover his liberty, two years later, by a bribe. Twice in successive years these marauds were repeated, and in 1590, betrayed by his own disaffected chiefs, the proud O'Rourke sought safety in flight. He passed into Scotland, where arrested he was delivered up to Elizabeth, imprisoned in the tower, and in time put to death.

Upon the death of Rossa McMahon, chief of Monaghan in 1589, without sons, his brother Hugh succeeded as his heir by English and brehon law. Brian of Dartry and Ever of Farney contested his right. Hugh appealed to the deputy, offering him six hundred cows to be instated in his chieftainry. The deputy assented and accompanied him home to settle him in Monaghan. He there arrested him for collecting a rent two years before in Farney, had him tried by a jury of soldiers and hung at his castle gate. The territory he divided among his followers; Sir Henry Bagnal, in whose favor his father soon after resigned the marshalship, having a principal share, and Henslowe the chief's castle, the deputy for decorum remaining

content with payment in money from the rest. In his letter to
Burleigh in March, 1589, however, he denied having benefited himself by the fall of Mac Mahon, and he may have been maligned.

Another chief, Maguire of Fermanagh, died the same year, "a
lord in his munificence towards churches, ollavs, soldiers and servants, and a learned and studious adept in latin and his own tongue."
Conor Roe his kinsman claimed the succession. Hugh son of the
deceased sent for aid, to his relative, Donnel, son of Tyrconnel, "a
mighty champion and general in battle." Assigning Skea castle on
Upper Lough Erne, nine miles south east of Enniskillen, for their
rendezvous, O'Donnel there joined him, and using the slipper Conor
had left as a token of his pretensions, it served for the installation of
Hugh in the chieftainship. Donnel though the elder son of Tyrconnel, somewhat similarly placed in relation to the chieftainship,
and vexed that his younger brother Hugh should be preferred to
himself as successor to the aged chief, strove to displace him, and
Boylagh, Bannagh and MacSweenys of Munster favored his cause.
Incenduf assembled the Kinel Konnell, O'Doherty, Mac Sweenys
of Tuath and Fanad, and at Derrylahan in Banagh on the fourteenth
of December an engagement took place in which fell Donnel, several
of the chiefs and two hundred of his men.

One of Tyrone's Spanish guests when in Scotland, on his way
home, gratefully acknowledged the hospitable entertainment he had
received at Dungannon, and the generosity of character of his host
before Hugh na Gavaloch or "of the fetters," son of Shane by the
countess of Argyle. Gavaloch craftily volunteered to carry letters
for him to the earl, as he was about to go over to Ireland, and the
offer accepted, hastened to deliver what were entrusted to his care,
and which were somewhat compromising to O'Neil, to the council.
The earl learning what had chanced repaired in May to London, and
though imprisoned for coming over without permission of the deputy,
pled his cause so effectively that all but Burley adjudged him guilt-

less. In their power, pledges were demanded of him to keep peace
with the other septs, continue loyal, renounce the title of O'Neil,
promise that Tyrone should be made shire ground, and neither to foster with his brother chieftains nor league with the Scotch. He was to
compound for cess and tax as had been done in Connaught, make no
exactions from his neighbors, or inroads upon their country, unless
within five days from any prey. He agreed to repress depredators
and deliver them up, and not hang any man without leave unless by
martial law. His troop of fifty men were to be kept ready for service, and he was to answer hostings promptly. Spiritual livings
were not to be meddled with, no monks or friars to be suffered within
his borders, he was not to correspond with foreign traitors, or levy
black mail, but do what he could to compel his people to wear English garments and shave off their glibbes. He further stipulated
to sell provisions to the fort at Blackwater at reasonable rates. As
customary under brehon law, he was to be answerable for his brother
Turlogh of the Fews, and Turlogh Luineach so long as he lived was
not to be disturbed in his supremacy over Maguire and O'Kane. His
sureties were not to be imprisoned in the castle, but to be committed
to the charge of merchants or gentlemen answerable for their safe
keeping, and they might be changed every three months.

In July, Gavaloch appeared before the council denouncing him for
plotting with Spain against the queen. Tyrone denied the charges,
attributing them on the part of his accuser, who had taken advantage
of his having lost favor with the people by his loyalty, to gain popularity, to aspirations for the chieftainship which the queen wished to
abolish. Hatton and Ormond became bound for his good behavior, and, again in Dublin, he confirmed the articles, but deferred
performance till his neighbors did the same, since if they continued
free they might invade his territories, whilst restrained himself by
these obligations from defending them. Gavaloch before the year
ended fell into the power of his chief whom he had thus sought to

63

supplant, and tried by martial law, was condemned. Not finding any subject of his own to carry out the sentence the earl procured an executioner from Meath. The queen expressed her displeasure at his audacity, but Tyrone claimed that he had reserved the prerogative of punishing with death under martial law, and that the culprit was a notorious traitor. The following summer he attacked and wounded Turlogh, whom he claimed had commenced hostilities.

Mabel Bagnal, her father the old marshal having died, was spending the summer of 1591 with her sister lady Barnwall, at the ancient manor house of Turvey, seven miles from the capital, when Tyrone now a widower, having recently lost Judith O'Donnel, met her, and enamored of her beauty, won her affections. Where mutual inclination yearns for opportunities, they come, and after brief courtship their troth was plighted, the earl in token of his love presenting her with a gold chain, and a time for their marriage being appointed. Twenty days later, on the third of August, he came to Turvey and engaging in conversation with his host and the company present, his friend Sir William Warren, whose abode of Drumcondra was in the immediate neighborhood of Dublin, rode home with Mabel behind him. The earl, with ten gentlemen of his kinsfolk and acquaintance, English and Irish, to witness the nuptials, followed. Probably from the consideration that she had been brought up a protestant, and exception might be taken if the rites were performed by a priest, Tyrone had sent a messenger into the city for Jones, bishop of Meath, to come to him speedily upon a matter of moment, without specifying its nature.

Upon the arrival of the bishop at Drumcondra, the motive for his summons was explained, and he interrogated the maiden apart, as to her inclinations and wishes. Discovering that she had come of her own free will, lest her delicacy might be compromised and her happiness disturbed, if impediments were thrown in the way of their union, he tied the knot. Her brother the new marshal fretted and fumed.

He wrote Burleigh he could not but curse himself and his fortune, that his blood, which in his father and himself had so often been spilled in repressing this rebellious race, should now be mingled with it in marriage. Jones coming in for a share of his resentment, an explanation to the queen exonerated him from reproach. The marshal sought consolation in withholding his sister's estate, and in the bitterness of his tongue charging the earl with having another wife living.* Tyrone entreated the queen to intercede and bring about a more friendly feeling, but Bagnal hated on till killed, in 1598, at his memorable defeat at Blackwater. His sister died two years before him, a convert to the faith of her husband, not he to hers, as had been hoped.

Meanwhile the son of O'Donnel was wasting his young life in durance at Dublin. His companions, scions of noble stock, hostages for parent or kinsman, came and went with tidings of what was taking place outside their bars, of fetters, cruel as their own, forging for their countrymen. As the ignorant are more easily subjugated, education was withheld, an ungenerous policy which did not further its purpose. Hearts cankering under injustice became but the more envenomed against English rule, the more dangerous without the restraints that liberal culture might have fostered. Three years and as many months wore away, when aid came from an unexpected quarter. If tradition may be credited, the deputy himself connived at his escape. Whether bribed, as generally accepted, by the aged chieftain, disconsolate at the prolonged captivity of his favorite son, or prompted by better motive, Fitzwilliam removed a guard whose suspicion had been aroused by circumstances denoting what was intended, and placed in his stead one more open to corruption.

A wooden bridge spanned the castle† ditch before the windows of

---

* But from the daughter of Sir Brian Mac Felim O'Neil, his first wife, he had been divorced previous to his marriage with Judith.

† The castle formed an oblong quadrangle encompassed by a deep moat enclosing many buildings. Bermingham tower, built about 1321, now the record office, then served as the prison house for hostages and prisoners of state. It connected with Cork tower by a high

the common room Art Kavanagh and Hugh Roe occupied by day. At nightfall, just before they were to be removed to their cells, they fastened a rope to the window, and friends below to help, slid down to the bridge beyond the castle gate, which they fastened behind them on the outside by a billet of wood. Before their flight was discovered and the door opened by the neighbors at the call of the warders from the wall, they had left the city. Crossing the red mountain they entered a forest. Kavanagh proceeding on, Hugh, weary and lame, sent for succor to Felim O'Toole, whom he had reason to suppose friendly, but whose kinsfolk would not suffer him to compromise himself by giving shelter to the fugitive. Troops arriving in pursuit, they gave him up to them. Fettered and carefully guarded he remained several months longer a prisoner, when at Christmas another attempt proved successful. With the sons of Shane, his cousins, descending by an open flue connected with the ditch, he made for Wicklow. The weather cold and snow falling, they wandered three days in Glenmalure, till overpowered by fatigue and exposure they laid down to perish. One of the O'Byrnes discovered them nearly lifeless, and sending word to his chief, Fiach, the victor of Glendalough, took Hugh home. Art O'Niel, refusing to eat the leaves of the trees, had died from want of nourishment, and Henry his brother already gone into Ulster.

Tyrone apprised of the condition of his brother-in-law, whose feet had been frozen but who was slowly recovering, despatched one of

curtain wall. The entrance into the castle by a drawbridge on the north side lay between two round towers. Eighty-one windows or spickes on the outside walls served for light or defence. Sydney, in 1565, first occupied it as a viceregal abode, Thomas Court, Kilmainham or the archbishop's palace, serving previously for the purpose. Parliament and the upper courts also sat there under Elizabeth and James. The original city wall as then existing from Dame Gate to Birmingham tower was little more than a mile, extending thence to Stanihurst's 195 feet. Pole Gate and Genevilles lay next. From St. Nicholas gate the wall ran 312 feet to Sarsfield, thence to Sedgrave's 340, thence by Fagans to the New Gate, thence to Fitzsymons 180, to Gormond's gate 840, to Harberd's castle 308, to Usher's house near the Liffey 140. From thence to Pricketts it continued 843 feet, to Fians 356, to another Fitzsimmons 188, to Issolds 172, to Buttevants 166, to Bises 188, and thence to Dame Gate 108. The walls varied in thickness from 4 to 7 feet, in height from 15 to 28, the towers rarely exceeding 49 or 50 in elevation. The population of Dublin, now a quarter of a million, was in the sixteenth century densely packed. It was greatly fluctuating, but not one sixth as many as now. In the seventeenth century the castle was renovated chiefly under Ormond.

his retainers, Turlogh O'Hagan, in whose intelligence and faithfulness he could trust, to bring him to Dungannon.   Felim O'Toole of
Powerscourt, who on his former escape had surrendered Hugh to the
troops, now made amends, and escorted him with a force of cavalry
so far as prudence permitted.   The passes of the Liffey were carefully
guarded, but by one of its fords near Dublin too dangerous to be
often used, they crossed that river, and in a boat, the Boyne, near
Drogheda, and resuming their horses which O'Hagan had led through
the town, after a night at Mellifont and another at Armagh reached
the castle of the earl.   There O'Donnel rested several days in concealment till sufficiently recruited to proceed.   Maguire received him
tenderly, and furnishing him with "a black polished boat" to row
down Lake Erne, he arrived at home at Ballyshannon many weeks
after his escape, receiving an enthusiastic welcome from the Kinel
Konnel.

He was greatly needed.   His father with body and mind enfeebled
had suffered a few hundred Englishmen from Connaught to take possession of the monastery of Donegal and of one of his castles, and to
waste and to spoil all the country around.   Hugh Roe drove them
out, but, his constitution shattered by the exposures of his escape, for
months he remained under medical treatment.   When his health was
reëstablished, he repaired with his father to Kilmacrenan, where the
chiefs of Kinel Konnel time out of mind had been inaugurated.
There on the third of May, 1592, his father resigning in his favor,
the assembled chieftains elected him to rule over them, and by the
simple but significant forms common to such occasions he was installed in an office which, unlike that of the deputy, was a service not
a preferment.   In obedience to ancestral precedent when the ceremonial was concluded he marched forth with his gathered array to lay
waste Strabane.   Troops were sent to the aid of Turlogh, when
he again attacked him and drove his army to the castle of O'Kane.
That chief claiming forbearance on the ground of fosterage, he re-

turned to besiege Strabane, and burned the place to its castle walls.
Tyrone interposed, and accompanying his brother-in-law to Dundalk,
the deputy recognized him as lord of Tyrconnel, and thereupon several of his chiefs, who had previously held aloof, gave in to him their
allegiance.

Bagnal not abating in his hate for Tyrone reported to the council
his slightest indiscretions.   The deputy also viewed him with distrust,
which, undeserved, created disaffection.   When Maguire incensed at
their arbitrary proceedings was about to put to the sword the sheriff
Willis, whom Hugh Roe had driven out of Donegal the year before,
and his English posse, the earl interposed his authority to save their
lives, on condition that they quitted Fermanagh.   Accused of being
as was natural more considerate of his vassal chief, than of English
interests, he sent an envoy to the queen to disarm her displeasure.
Sheriffs were equally rapacious and overbearing in Breffny, and
O'Rourke flew to arms.   Maguire and chiefs of Tyrone and Tyrconnel
lent him their aid, and he invaded Connaught destroying Ballymote and
other towns.   In an encounter with Bingham at Tulks, Macgauran
then lately returned from Rome as archbishop of Armagh, and the abbot Cathal Maguire while engaged in ministrations, bodily and spiritual, to the wounded, were killed, as also Sir William Clifford on the
other side.   Bingham drew off and Maguire went home with his prey.
The deputy upon the news of this outbreak marched a force of four
hundred men into Fermanagh and attacked the chief at Enniskillen,
a strong post between the lakes of Erne.   Tyrone joined the deputy
and was wounded in the battle, in which the English artillery gained
the advantage after a desperate and prolonged engagement.

Hugh Roe, at the time on his march to aid Maguire, sent word to
the earl that if he did not take part with them, he should regard him
as an enemy.   Tyrone begged him to refrain so long as he remained
with the English army, his brother Cormac and four hundred men
with his sanction or of their own motion joining the Kinel Konnel.

Their approach in superior force discouraged the deputy from farther proceeding, and setting up Conor Oge Maguire in opposition to the legitimate chief of Fermanagh, he withdrew.

Turlogh was still an embarrassment. Whilst he continued at the head of the Kinel Owen supported by the queen, the earl even after his election at Tullahoge was trammelled. Hugh Roe a constant menace at Lifford to Turlogh at Strabane gathered his clans in the summer of 1593 with intention sufficiently manifest, when his superannuated neighbor consented to surrender the chieftainship to the earl, and the two Hughs ruled over all Ulster unless it were Antrim.

In the spring of 1594 the deputy reduced Enniskillen, but Hugh Roe declaring war combined with Maguire to recover it. The garrison by August had exhausted their supplies, and George Bingham with an army from Connaught reinforced from Meath sought to relieve them. He had reached a ford four miles from the place, when Maguire came down upon him and after a sanguinary engagement put his army to rout. The supplies for the fortress came acceptably to the victors, and from the quantity captured the battle became known as the Ford of the biscuits. Enniskillen soon surrendered, and what were left of its warders were allowed to depart. The conquerors entered Connaught, reduced Balleek, slaughtering the garrison, and, it is said, spared no one who could not speak Irish from fifteen to sixty, in retaliation for the cruelties practised upon men, women and children massacred at Enniskillen. They established Theobald son of Walter Burke, who commanded at Shrule in 1570, as the Mac William.

The Desmond confiscations ripened the long cherished project of a protestant seminary in the capital. Archbishop Curwin when it was proposed to appropriate St. Patrick for the purpose objected, on the ground "that a university in the capital would prove unprofitable, for the Irish enemy under color of study might send their friends thither, who would learn the secrets of the court and advertise them thereof; so that the Irish rebels should by them know the secrets of the English pale." The reformation created a demand for learned protestant clergymen, and Loftus inclined to favor the plan when the property of All Hallows, which had been given by the crown to the corporation of Dublin, was substituted for the site instead of his cathedral. It was chartered in 1591. Fitzwilliam dedicated it the year after, and the queen in 1597 endowed it with lands of the value of four hundred pounds, which with later acquisitions now yield over thirty thousand. It was opened for students on the ninth of January, 1593, and, though sharing in the vicissitudes of troubled times, it has been highly prospered, now numbering nearly fifteen hundred students.

XXXIX.

REIGN OF ELIZABETH.—1558-1602.—(Continued.)

The recall of Fitzwilliam was no great cause of lamentation. His tablet when he died five years afterwards rehearsed his praise, but he was not a model governor any more than his descendant lord Byron, admirable as a poet, was exemplary as a man. In July, 1594, came over to take his place Sir William Russell, youngest son of the earl of Bedford, whose earlier career on the continent had redounded to his fame as a soldier and statesman, which his administration did not tarnish. First ascertaining from the various officials the actual state of the country, on the eleventh of August he assumed the sword. He marched at once into Fermanagh, and his coming not expected he surprised Enniskillen and took possession of the place without opposition.

Tyrone, without compromising his independence as an Irish chieftain, had studiously avoided giving occasion for censure, and still suffering from his wound in the service of the queen, presented himself at the court of the new deputy without misgiving. The marshal virulent as ever against him, called upon the council for his arrest on charges of high treason in entertaining the late archbishop Mac-gauran, corresponding with O'Donnel, disciplining his troops, and manufacturing bullets. The earl defied Bagnal to prove his assertions by ordeal of personal combat, himself without armor, but his challenge was declined. His many friends at the council board prevented his proposed arrest, but Ormond advised him to leave the capital lest his liberty should be restrained.

Whether justly entitled to it or not, Hugh has been esteemed the cleverest man that ever bore the name of O'Neil. Historians generally concur in the conclusion, that his father was no son of Con but of the blacksmith, and consequently an O'Kelly of Bregia.* His maternal ancestors, princes of Fermanagh, were noted for noble trait, and if acquired habits of rule become aptitudes transmitted, this heirloom was his. His natural endowments quickened into best development by education he was now in his prime, and naturally regarded as entitled to the lead. The death, in 1595, at Strabane of Turlogh, whose munificence had gained him popularity, vested in the earl undisputed sway over Tyrone.

That incensed at the arbitrary proceedings of the government and encroachment upon the religious rights of his countrymen, he would have gladly removed the yoke from their necks even by transfer of allegiance to Spain, hardly admits of a doubt. Neither he nor any Irishman could feel under moral or honorary obligation or other restraint than prudence, to refrain from that course which would best protect their property from pillage, their highest privilege of worshipping God as they pleased from interference. If under pressure of force, submission or pledge had been extorted, English law attached no validity to promises under duress. Besides where faith had

* If so, his paternal line descended from Hugh Slane, monarch from 599 to 605, nine of whose race were kings of the island, but the name in Ulster had long sunk into comparative obscurity.

64

been so often broken with them. punctilio would have been out of place. Officials and adventurers hungry for their spoils, self-preservation justified all measures to circumvent them.

He knew too well the power of England to hope single handed to regain Ireland for the Irish, and after the armada might well despair of effective foreign intervention. To render Ulster and Connaught strong enough to discourage aggression, seemed all that remained. Fairly treated, he would have avoided strife, which if not attended with success must have proved pregnant with disaster. But goaded by injustice and aggrieved by unmerited distrust, he drew the sword and threw away the sheath. He still entered into the league now forming of the northern powers with less openness than the rest, so guarding his assent to their proceedings that it should not be used as evidence against him, in the event of reverse.

In other days, wise rulers and able generals had maintained the unequal struggle, and now the character and ability of the Ulster chiefs preëminently fitted them for the crisis. Both possessed extraordinary powers of physical endurance, indefatigable industry, mental qualities suited to grand undertakings, military knowledge of the best and personal prowess. They were alike wise and prudent. Tyrconnel more remote had less to consider, Tyrone nearer the pale was forced to dissemble and wait. Tyrconnel descended maternally from Macdonnels and Campbells, not so much of an Irishman, had his own claims to favor. Of his twenty-five years, four of the most precious had been passed in a murky prison house, but he had already asserted his superiority, and displayed among strong men of ripe experience qualities that forced its recognition. Fortunately he was both too young and too generous to enter into rivalry with Tyrone, whose amiable disposition and nobleness of nature relieved subordination of whatever might have rendered it humiliating under one more imperious and dictatorial.

Besides the personal qualities of Tyrconnel to inspire respect and conciliate affection, an ancient prophecy of St. Columkill, that one of his stock should reign ten years, during which the nation would be set free from bondage, had not been forgotten. What he had already achieved since his own liberation warranted its application to him, and his activity never grew wearied. In March, 1595, he led his troops through Leitrim into Connaught. Bingham left Roscommon, assembling at Boyle his garrisons from Tulks, Loughkee, Ballymote and Sligo. Hugh after sweeping off the herds of O'Conor Roe and O'Hanly, approached the Shannon, and when the governor strove to stay his further progress he repulsed him and escaped with his prey.

A few weeks after, with Maguire he entered Annaly. The O'Ferrals displaced by adventurers whom it was their aim to drive out, they burned the castle of Longford, Christopher Brown its usurper with his wife escaping by a rope from the flames that consumed fifteen of his hostages, whom he abandoned to their fate. Farney in Cavan, the queen had given to Essex. Talbot its seneschal awoke half suffocated, fleeing with his family horror stricken into the forest by the lurid light of his burning abode. They laid waste the land, one cloud of smoke darkening the heavens as they proceeded from the conflagration of houses and towns in possession of the hated race. Whilst thus engaged, two of the Geraldines of Kildare were stirring up strife further south.

Peter Fitzgerald, a protestant official of Leinster, who spared in his cruelty neither age nor sex, thirsted for the blood of his kinsman, Walter Riagh, who pursued by him to his castle of Gloran, barely effected his escape. In retaliation, the abode of Peter was burnt. Not to be outdone when least expected, a multitudinous host environed Gloran, Gerald brother of its lord falling in its defence. Unprepared to stand a siege, Walter broke through the besieging lines. He hovered around, soldiers scattered in neighboring villages were slain, when one evening he himself fell wounded, his thigh broken by a ball. George Moore, one of his company, fighting as he went, conveyed him to a place of concealment. Left in charge of an English prisoner, or, for the accounts differ, of a physician of his sept, in whom he reposed implicit confidence, but by whom he was betrayed, he was put to death.

Fiagh O'Byrne, one of the heroes of Glendalough, and known as "the firebrand of the mountain," moved by indignation at the cruelties of Peter, had taken part with Walter his son-in-law, and before the latter was wounded, the deputy, on the sixteenth of January, had marched to Ballinacor, his abode in Glenmalure. The chieftain, put upon his guard by a drumbeat, perhaps for parley at his gate, escaped through a postern, or some secret passage, in which castles of that period abounded. The deputy withdrew disappointed, but before the month ended Walter had burnt Crumlin, two miles from the capital, carrying off the church roof for bullets. Russell marched back into Wicklow, hung two brothers of Walter, and in April as above related, Walter himself. Fiagh submitted and was pardoned in November, but his castle was occupied by an English garrison. He surprised and demolished it the following August, and after many brave exploits in encounters with his enemies, fell mortally wounded in one of them, in May, 1597.

After the armada, persecution filled the prisons with catholic priests, and the war with O'Rourke and Maguire grew out of their harboring the Spaniards. Many important engagements had taken place since, but what is known as the fifteen years catholic war, and so termed by its cotemporary historian, Philip O'Sullivan,* though lasting from 1588 to 1602, attained a general character, even at the north,

* Grandson of Dermod chief of Beare and Bantry killed in 1549, and son of Dermod, born about 1530, who with his brother-in-law, Owen, Edmund and Maurice Mac Sweeny, joined James Fitzmaurice when he landed in 1569, and who took part in all these wars down to their close in 1603. Dermod died at Corunna in Spain, at the advanced age of over one hundred years. By Joanna, daughter of Donald Mac Sweeny Tuath and Margaret of the house of Mac Carthy More, he had seventeen children, four only of whom survived to accompany him into Spain. Daniel was killed in battle with the Turks, Helena drowned on the way to join her husband in Ireland ; Leonora became a nun. From an elegiac poem of nearly two hundred lines, in latin, by the historian, these particulars are gleaned. Philip's history was first published in 1621, and he was living at Madrid in 1634. His work is generally esteemed as the best source of information in relation to this period on the Catholic side.

only at this period, when Tyrone engaged in it. Munster still remained quiet, Leinster was but little disturbed, and Meath occupied by English plantations and garrisons, its Irish inhabitants were bound hand and foot, but the storm was gathering.

How it chanced that all catholics did not embrace the catholic cause, that so many of rank and position fought against it, is accounted for by its historian as retribution visited on the land for its transgressions. Calamity that had overwhelmed participants in former risings dissuaded many, others reflected that the queen was old and mortal and her successor might be catholic. If not, by their fidelity to the crown they would have at least earned a claim to have their religious liberties respected. Anglo-Irish feared that if the chiefs prevailed they should be driven out. Their priests even encouraged them to side against their faith. It was not protestant arms or valor that conquered, but craft. In war, persecution was stayed; peace raised the scaffold, lighted the torch and reduced to impoverishment. In war if chiefs deserted the queen, they were welcomed back, their derelictions forgiven and favors bestowed. But if in peace they betrayed the slightest disaffection, if they winced under injury or insult, forms of faith were preserved, but new crimes were invented and on the most shallow pretexts they were put to death. Penalties equally severe were visited upon catholics who had continued loyal, and on Irish protestants. Conformity to the reformed religion in the latter when they could no longer be used against the catholics, was not regarded as genuine, but merely a cover from fear or prudential considerations. Spanish tyranny was held up as a warning against accepting her sway. But Ireland was soon to experience from English domination refinements of cruelty not dreamed of by Torquemado.

Another device of the government was to destroy village and farm, field, flock and herd of the catholics whom they could not subdue, not sparing their own adherents, lest means should be left them for continued resistance. Base money was substituted for silver and gold to the grievous wrong of merchants, and all entitled to rent or tribute, from the persuasion that wars would not cease while food or money to buy it remained in the land, and that the true policy was to feed their own armies from England, and starve the Irish. But still as ever before the most effective weapon for subjugation was to stir up strife and jealousies, create contention for the chieftainships, and lending seasonable help, when opportunity offered appropriate to themselves the spoils. Nial in Tyrconnel, sons of Shane in Tyrone, Owen in Beare, Theodore O'Rourke, the English Maguire, Florence, Dermot and Donal in Clancarre and "six hundred other examples," went to show that a kingdom divided against itself must fall. The motives which led to embracing one side or the other in the struggle were various and operated without regard to geographical position, nationality or faith. Not even character or personal predilections governed, but son divided against sire, brother against brother, according to circumstances peculiar to each case.*

That under such unfavorable conditions the catholic forces should have so long proved victorious, soldiers unarmed defeat veterans amply provided with the best weapons, means so scanty for nearly fifteen years cope with the power and resources of the whole realm, was indeed a marvel. If the Anglo Irish, catholic and protestant, had not well understood that upon success depended the preservation of

---

* For the queen. Ormond, Buttevant, Dunboyne, Upper Ossory, Castleconnel, Theobald Burke, Athenry, Kildares, Howth, Gormanstown, Delvin, Slane, Thomond, Inchiquin, Mac Carthy Reagh and Muskerry, O'Connor Don, Melaghlin and the three Plunkets. For the catholics, Tyrone, Mac Gennis, Mac Mahon, Maguire, O'Kane, O'Hanlon, Macdonnels, of the Glynns, O'Donnel, the three Mac Sweenys, O'Dogherty, O'Boyle, O'Sullivans Beare and Mor, O'Connor Kerry, Mac Carthies of Duhallo, O'Driscol, O'Mahon, O'Donovan, both O'Donohues, O'Rourke, Mac Dermot, O'Kelley, Kavanaghs, O'Conors Offaly, O'Moores, O'Byrnes, Mageoghan, Roche, Mountgarret, Lixnaw, Butler of Cahir; Condon, Purcel, knights of Kerry, Valley and Fitzgibbon, Florence and Donal McCarthy, O'Conor Sligo, James sugan earl of Desmond, Raymond Burke, lord Leitrim, all lords of territories. Besides these, Nial O'Donnel, Cornelius O'Driscol, Dermod O'Sullivan father of the historian, Fiagh O'Byrne, Cormac O'Niel, Cornelius O'Reilly, Dermot McCarthy Reagh, William Burke, Bernard O'Kelly, Richard Tirrell, Bernard O'Moore, Walter Geraldine, Dermot O'Conor, Peter Lessius, Edmund O'Moore, James Butler, Magnus Maurice and Daniel Magnus Mac Sweeney, Ulick Burke, Richard Mageoghan, Maurice O'Sullivan, Thaddeus O'Mahon. Not all at the same time; if they had, it would have been less easy to conquer them.

their estates, or it had not been so ordered above, the struggle could hardly have been so prolonged or assumed proportions as formidable. It would still have been more politic to have followed the counsel of Sir William Russell, and distributed the church spoliations vested in the crown, among the nobility of both persuasions, in Ireland as in England, and they would then have held their religion as their land in capite and stuck to the queen as the great support of both. Which predominated, land or religion, as governing considerations in this strife, can only be conjectured. In numerous instances, no doubt, the latter influenced the more elevated characters, to keep what they possessed of the former or obtain what they coveted prevailing with the less generous.

When Desmond became endangered his friends and neighbors entered into covenants to shield him from injustice. Twenty years later, the northern chiefs united for mutual protection against religious persecution, intrusion of sheriffs, and like aggressions. Tyrone, though cautious to avoid committal, favored the league, if he did not originate it. How far this combination was known to the government is a matter of conjecture, but that the north was disaffected, united and strong was sufficiently apparent. What force the deputy had at his disposal consisted largely of Irish catholics upon whom no dependence could be placed. Urging reinforcements, Sir John Norris with laurels fresh from France and the Low Countries, a grandson of that Henry who died rather than accuse Anna Boleyn, brought over two thousand veterans who had served under him in Brittany and also one thousand new levies. A chain of fortresses across the island from Dundalk to Ballyshannon were to be constructed or strengthened to overawe Ulster and serve for base of operations. The hosting of the pale added to the numerical if not actual force, which under the deputy and Norris, both able generals, now menaced the north.

Tyrone demanded explanations, but his letters to court and the deputy were intercepted or delayed by the marshal, and not to be taken unawares, he gathered his army and reduced Portmore, three miles from Armagh and seven from Dungannon, which though his principal abode, he gave to the flames.   His sons-in-law, Bryan Mac Mahon and Arthur Magennis, lord of Iveagh, whose territories lay most exposed to the enemy, with O'Kane, came to his aid with their clans, and sending for O'Donnel and Maguire who were awaiting his call, he flung his banner, the red right hand on its snowy folds, to the breeze, committed himself to the chances of war, and marched to lay siege to Monaghan.   O'Byrnes and Kavanaghs with the Fitz-geralds were not less troublesome from their recent reverses in Leinster, and thus indirectly lent help to the northern chieftains.

Norris appointed general of the army in Ulster with power to par-don, a clause "in the absence of the deputy," added out of considera-tion for Russell, created confusion, and the divided responsibility tend-ed to produce estrangement and defeat the objects of the campaign. Whilst the marshal marched to relieve Monaghan pressed by Tyrone, general and deputy with their whole available forces left the pale in June for Dundalk.   Proclaiming the Ulster chiefs traitors as they went, they proceeded on to Armagh fighting their way through the Mowry pass, where later the general constructed a fortress named from himself, Mountnorris.   Their progress beyond Armagh was arrested by the appearance of Tyrone, who followed them back to that place. For fifteen days the two armies confronted without coming to blows. The intercepted letters, already adverted to, now received, changed to a certain extent the complexion of affairs, and the deputy not having force to contend or food for such as he had, labored to bring about, what one side termed peace, the other submission.

The invitation of Wallop and Gardiner, commissioners to negotiate, to the chiefs to meet them at Dundalk not being accepted, the con-ference took place midway between the armies.   Tyrone insisted upon full amnesty, free exercise of religion, payment by the marshal of one thousand pounds for Mabel's portion, restoration of his troop in the queen's pay, restitution of preys taken, and that no garrison or sheriff should come within his borders. O'Donnel claimed that Sligo should be restored and complained of his imprisonment; Mac Phelim O'Neil, that Essex had despoiled him of a barony; Maguire, of the garrison and sheriff who had slain one of his kinsmen in Fermanagh: Mac Mahon, of the execution of Hu h Roe. The terms proposed by the chiefs referred to the queen, and those demanded of them by the commissioners not accepted, negotiations were broken off. His supplies exhausted, the deputy left garrisons at Armagh and Monaghan, surrendered at Dundalk command of the army to Norris, and by the eighteenth of July was again in Dublin.* Early in September the chiefs were judicially condemned in form for high treason, and with them Cormac brother of Tyrone, Con his base son, Henry Oge and Turlogh his brother, other O'Neils.

Norris, in August, marching to relieve Monaghan, at Clontibret five miles from that town, encountered Tyrone with eight thousand men posted to dispute his passage over a stream, flowing between hills through a valley open but wet. Cavalry skirmishes and volleys of musketry were followed up by charges by Norris in force, twice repulsed by the catholics, for though his squadrons were the better armed, theirs excelled in dexterity. The Irish were also the best marksmen, which proved however of no advantage to either side, since in the queen's army they outnumbered the English. Whilst Norris whose horse had been shot, vexed at his discomfiture, was recalling his broken forces, the last himself to leave the field, James Segrave from Meath, of strength and stature above ordinary standards, requested permission of the marshal to charge upon Tyrone, who stood at the edge of the

* Among the battles mentioned by O'Sullivan as taking place at this period is that at the church of Kiloter, two miles from Armagh, in which Tyrone defeated the royalists and chased them back to the gates of that city. From his account, it would seem to have occurred when Russell and Norris strove to penetrate into the country beyond Armagh, and the date given by the editors of the Catholic History (Ed. 1850) is June 29, 1595. Mitchell in his life of Tyrone assigns this battle to the ensuing year, just before Stafford surrendered Armagh.

ford watching the fight and giving his orders. Bagnal consented, but Tyrone's body guard shot down many of the approaching squadron as they crossed the stream.

Segrave singled out the chieftain, and their spears shivering at the shock on each other's corslets, seized him by the neck striving to draw him from his horse. Grasped in deadly embrace, they fell together to the ground, struggling for mastery. As he lay prostrate, O'Neil drew his poniard and pierced the groin of his adversary with fatal effect. The peril of their leaders had for a moment stayed the combat, but the troops of Tyrone, assured of his safety, with a wild shout swept down upon their foe. The struggle was desperate but brief. The ground heaped up with seven hundred fallen combatants, eighteen knights in glittering steel about the lifeless form of Segrave. The general and his brother wounded, their standards taken and their army utterly routed, fled from the field. The next day a body of their men overtaken, attempted some resistance, when O'Hanlon, standard bearer of the queen alternately with O'Molloy, was slain. Con, son of Tyrone, was sent to take possession of Monaghan, Hinch with three companies that composed its garrison being suffered to go away unharmed.

During the absence of O'Donnel, George Oge Bingham, kinsman of the governor, with Ulick Burke, sailed round from Sligo to Lough Swilley, and rifled the abbeys of Rathmullan and Tory island of their relics and plate. Hugh Roe at this intelligence hastened home, but recalled, took part in the movements related. Immediate danger at an end with the rout at Clontibret, and tidings brought him that in consequence of some wrong or indignity Bingham had been slain by Ulick, who desired to surrender to him the castle of Sligo, he took leave of the earl, and speeded to regain possession of what he so eagerly coveted. Ulick was as good as his word, and his kinsmen, the Clandonnel, Sil Conor, Clan Mulroony, or Macdonoghs and Macdermots, flocking to welcome one they were quite willing to ac-

cept as their lord paramount, were reinstated by him in their respective
territories, of which the governor had deprived them.

Hearing that McLeod of Ara had landed in Donegal with six
hundred men from the isles, Tyrconnel engaged them in his service,
and returning through Leyny and Costello, reduced Castlemore and
Turlogh Mochair in Dunmore, eight miles north of Tuam. Bingham with fifteen companies followed him back, but Hugh covering his
rear with his cavalry moved on with his spoils to Glendallan in Leitrim.
The governor laid siege to Sligo, sending his nephew Martin in
pursuit of O'Donnel, who hoping to capture him placed four
hundred of his men in ambush and directed Felim Mac Devit with a
squadron to advance and then retreat in order to draw him into the
trap. Martin swiftly mounted had nearly overtaken and was about
to kill Felim, who, his horse being lame rode in the rear, when the
pursued turning took deliberate and deadly aim at the arm pit of his
enemy, which was exposed as he lifted his weapon. O'Donnel was
vexed that his plan should miscarry, but there was no one to blame.

Bingham pushed the siege of Sligo. Tearing down the screen and
wood-work of the church, he constructed a testudo or pent-house on
wheels, covered with skins, and rolled it filled with men to undermine
the foundations of the castle. But the garrison dropped large stones
torn from an interior wall on the heads of the sappers below, a heavy
beam guided by a rope did much execution, and many were shot
from the loopholes. Despairing of success, the governor went home
to Roscommon, and O'Donnel demolished the castle lest it should be
used against him.

For young men accustomed to an active life of adventure and enjoyment in the open air, confinement within stone walls became irksome, and one August evening when their guards were off duty and the
people of the town generally engaged at their principal repast, the hostages at Galway attempted an escape. They made their way through
the streets, but found the bridge when they reached it already occupied,

their flight having been discovered. Some of them plunged into the river, several were shot or drowned, and the rest driven back. Bingham was not of a nature to mitigate the penalty, and ordered the survivors to be executed. Among them were sons of Richard-na-Irain, O'Flaherty of the battle axes, O'Conor Roe, and Mac David. It would be hard to parallel in the whole annals of Irish cruelties any atrocity more utterly indefensible than this.

Balleck in Mayo besieged by Theobald Burke, John Bingham, brother of the governor, with captains Foal, Mensi and Tuite, sent to relieve it came late, for the place had already surrendered and they were slain. Several of Theobald's kinsmen, older and of greater dignity than himself, disputing the chieftainship, O'Donnel confirmed it to him, who being in the bloom of youth seemed best able to endure the toils of war. In presence of the assembled hosts of Mayo, he was inaugurated as the Mac William Iochtar, his competitors giving hostages and pledges of obedience. The ceremony over and Christmas at hand, the new chieftain entertained Hugh Roe, whose supremacy nearly all Connaught except Clanrickard was now inclined to recognize.

Hugh reducing thirteen castles of unfriendly chiefs, appointed Ferdorcha O'Kelly, lord of Hy-Many; Maurice Macdonogh, lord of Tirrerill; Rory of Corran; Conor Macdermot of Moylurg; O'Dowde and O'Hara over their respective septs. Russell at this time in Galway summoned the castle of Cloghan, held by O'Maddens, who refused to deliver it up, saying that if his army consisted of lord deputies, they would defend it. It proved an idle boast, for the royal artillery soon compelled them to surrender, forty-six of their men being slain in the defence and the rest thrown headlong from the walls. The sept enraged, destroyed all their castles except Longford, the abode of Donnel their chief, captured Kenovan, bishop of Clonfert, raided Delvin and Fircal beyond the Shannon, and only after they had testified their resentment by more extensive devastations would they be still.

Philip of Spain, decrepid with age and indulgence, survived, for ten years, his famous fleet. His wrath, less easily repressed, found vent rather in menace than performance. What projects he seriously entertained were disconcerted by rumors industriously spread by English envoys abroad, that Ireland subdued had submitted. When undeceived, his promises of assistance and exhortations to persist fostered expectations to which the arrival of three small pinnaces laden with powder and bringing two hundred men, gave new life. Tyrone rejected the pardon sent him in April, 1596, by Edward Moore, and his emissaries to Munster and letters to O'Byrne instigated war or at least preparation. O'Byrne, as mentioned, recovered Ballinacor. O'Moores, O'Connors, O'Tooles and Cavanaghs gathered in force, as also the dispossessed Butlers. They demanded restoration of their confiscated estates, wasting and destroying, the terrified usurpers imploring protection. Russell had learned the way to Glenmalure: Ormond endeavored to suppress his revolted kinsfolk: St. Leger found employment in Leix and Ophaly.

Impatient at the waste of the war and its ill success, the queen inclined to concession, which course Norris approved but not the deputy. Pride blinding her to the condition of affairs, Tyrone in April, 1596, met her commissioners,* only to hear his terms offered at Armagh rejected, and others proposed altogether inadmissible. What Morrison relates of the advantage taken of his presence explains his unwillingness afterwards to treat. He was called upon to sign preliminaries to negotiation sufficiently compromising. Copus and other envoys had arrived with proffers from Spain, and it is alleged Tyrone communicated them to the deputy, a statement not very probable if anything remained to be learned. Pardon was promised upon render of pledges, and the chief withdrew to renew hostilities.

Tyrone had friends among the queen's warders. In her garrison

* Norris and Fenton.

spearheads mysteriously disappeared, powder and ball from her guns, and one of her captains, terror struck by apparitions, registered a vow never again to desecrate catholic shrines, and resigned his commission and pay lest he might be tempted to break it. Nine Irishmen, part of the garrison of Carlingford, concerted with Tyrone to seize that place, and it was arranged that he should come at dawn to take possession. A favorable moment prematurely offering, they rose upon their companions, who instead of being overpowered, fled or were driven from the castle. Having reason to expect their return with a force not to be resisted, the catholics left the place, but not meeting the earl in the darkness to apprise him of what had occurred, he stationed himself as proposed near the gates, in vain waiting for their signal. Meanwhile as apprehended, the warders expelled drew near with what troops they could collect, and themselves unperceived, discovered the earl in the gloaming. Conjecturing for what he was waiting, they contrived to reënter the deserted walls, and he had to take his departure disappointed.

Forts judiciously constructed, duly manned and provisioned, could not be reduced, burned, or without artillery to batter their walls, be taken by storm. Armagh had used up its stores, vermin infested the place, famine and pestilence made havoc of its warders. O'Neil captured at night among the mountains three battalions of foot, and a squadron of horse, bringing relief. Sending his son Con with one portion of his force to a monastery outside the walls to abide his orders, another assuming the garments and armor of his prisoners approached in array the gates with the supplies. When within view of the sentinels on the walls, attacked by the rest with all the circumstance of an actual fight, Stafford in command sent out half his garrison to extricate his supposed countrymen. Assailed to their surprise by both contending parties, Con sallied forth from the monastery and cut off their retreat. Not long after, Stafford, his magazines exhausted, surrendered the city, on terms which were respected, and O'Neil dismantled its fortifications.

The commissioners had been empowered to make more ample concessions, and Tyrone showed a disposition to hearken at least with courtesy to their overtures, too wary, however, to place himself again in their power. He rather evaded than refused their propositions. He had no faith in the sincerity of their professions, they none in his, and though different times were assigned for a conference he did not appear. When nothing was to be accomplished in the field, correspondence afforded him opportunity to express his sense of the perfidious policy pursued towards his countrymen, to gain time, obtain information and also provide for reverses.

Dundalk and Newry sixteen miles farther north, continued throughout the war the base of operations against Ulster, and in May Norris lay before the latter place in great force out of reach of Tyrone. He had resolved to rebuild Armagh and started for the purpose, when pounced upon a few miles out at the church of Killoony by the earl, accompanied by Maguire, O'Kane, sons of O'Hanlon and other chiefs. It was past noon when the battle began. When it ended the general and his army were in full retreat for Newry, their loss in the engagement and rout six hundred, Tyrone's one third that number.

Advantage was taken soon after of the absence of O'Neil, to reoccupy Armagh with forces from Dundalk, and Henry Davers left in command. Norris proceeded to Portmore. But his march beyond was blocked by the army of Tyrone. In order to keep open his communications with Newry, the general constructed Mount Norris, his work greatly impeded by the foe. Many encounters took place, in which the English sustained the most loss. When sufficiently advanced to be tenable the general entrusted the new fort at Portmore to Williams and withdrew. Tyrone cut off its supplies. Norris marched back to its relief, encountering O'Neil at Molachbreac, in Orior. Twice thrown into confusion the English renewed the fight, but MacGuire with his cavalry decided the contest by a brilliant charge, Norris fell wounded by a cannon ball; and Ulster again triumphed. This was the last encounter between Tyrone and Norris, who proceeded when sufficiently restored from his hurt into Connaught.

There at Athlone he gathered his strength, and with an army of ten thousand men occupied the bank of the Robe, on the opposite side of which river O'Donnel encamped. Parleys by day were followed by skirmishes at night, sallies and surprises, and many men fell. Thaddeus O'Rourke joined O'Donnel. Norris for want of food at last broke up his camp, and followed close and hard pressed by the foe contrived an ambuscade which was fortunately discovered in season. O'Donnel rode speedily to the head of his columns and ordered them back just in time to save them. Norris lost in Ireland his reputation as a successful general, but his military abilities are generally conceded as also many generous and noble traits of character. Want of supplies baffled his movements, and orders sent over from the queen and her ministers were often based upon entire ignorance of the situation. Moreover, Essex all powerful was not his friend, and Russell provoked that he should be preferred before himself, often stood in the way of his success.

Bingham going home without permission, early in 1597, was sent back with Sir Conyers Clifford, appointed in his place, whose amiable temper and generous policy at this particular crisis saved English rule from extinction in Connaught. The earls of Thomond and Clanrickard remained loyal to the queen, and O'Connor Sligo who had married the widow of Desmond, recently returned from court, influenced his feudatories, Macdonogh of Tirrerill and O'Hart, to declare in her favor. Hugh Conor Roe and Conor Macdermot with Theobald of the ships, son of Grace O'Mally, established by the English as the Mac William Iochtar, instead of the other Theobald, son of Walter, lent strength to this confederacy. O'Donnel saw the danger. Sweeping the country of every head of cattle he collected his forces in Leitrim and again raided Tirrerill, Corran and Hy-Many, reduced Athenry, burnt up to the gates of Galway. His prey despatched over the Erne, he proceeded to Sligo, and there in February routed its chieftain, whereupon Macdermot and other chiefs who were wavering, returned to their allegiance.

Not all. O'Conor Roe, Hugh son of Turlogh, excited much distrust, and yet as O'Rourke befriended him he hesitated to bring him to terms. Encamping at Glencar, he invited that chieftain to join him, but without waiting for his arrival he entered O'Conor's territory and carried off his herds. O'Rourke, provoked at what he conceived this breach of good faith, made his peace with the governor. Maguire with his nephew Cormac O'Neil raided Mullingar; Macdermots Glinsk the abode of Mac David, who defeated them on their way home. The Irish Mac William plundered O'Mallies, kinsfolk of the queen's. Burkes of Castleconnel laid claim to Porterush and attacked the reapers of Margaret Cusack widow of lord Inchiquin, to whom it belonged. A fierce battle resulted in the death of many men of note on either side, among them Hugh O'Hogan, excellent and rich. O'Conor Don, long prisoner of Tyrconnel, set at liberty promised obedience, giving for pledge the sons of O'Beirne, O'Flynn, OHanly and his own.

Much no doubt to the grief of the economical queen, there exploded in March, on Winetavern street, in Dublin, one hundred and forty-four barrels of gunpowder sent over for the benefit of her loving subjects, causing great havoc. The buildings all around were demolished. It gave work to the carpenters, organized into a guild in 1583, and who at this time were receiving their charter.

In May, the deputy, his last feat before his administration ended, subdued O'Byrne, who dying in battle left two sons, Felim and Raymond, to inherit his courage, his zeal for the catholic cause and his death to avenge. Felim repaired to Tyrone, who lent him three hundred and fifty men under Brian, tanist of Leix, and after seven

66

successful battles he recovered his dominions, a large English force being cut to pieces in Wexford.   Owen and Edmund O'Moore, sons of Rory killed in 1578, had been carefully nurtured by Fiagh and trained for military service.   The eldest was elected chieftain by his sept.   At the battle of Stradbally bridge he defeated and slew Alexander and Francis Cosby, son and grandson of the infamous Cosby of Mullamast, who had usurped his inheritance, and later overcame St. Leger, who left on the field five hundred of his men.

In 1596 died Donald, who had been for thirty years earl of Clancarre, and as Maccarthy Mor, lord paramount of fourteen countries for forty.   His only legitimate son, lord of Valentia, left as a hostage for his father in the castle of Dublin, made his escape in 1588 into France and there died.   Another son, but illegitimate, named Donal, claimed succession to the chieftainship.   Ellen, his only surviving child born in wedlock, and his heir at least by English law, had become in 1588 wife of Florence Maccarthy of Carbery son of Donogh, through the good offices of O'Sullivan Mor his brother-in-law who had gained the consent of her parents to the alliance. The queen, minded to espouse Ellen to some Englishman of her court, manifested her resentment against Florence by imprisoning him in the tower of London, which with other places of confinement for nearly half a century as already mentioned was to be his abode. Clancarre mortgaged portions of his territory to his new son-in-law for Ellen's dowry of six thousand pounds, and much given to hospitality and sumptuous entertainments to English functionaries, other portions to Sir Valentine Browne his neighbor, for five hundred.   This last encumbrance on Cosmaigne, Glanerought and Ballicarbery, Florence was allowed to redeem in 1630 on payment of the loan.   In 1595 in Dublin he had offered his services to Russell against O'Neil, but they were not accepted.

Florence claimed Clancarre for his wife by family settlement and also under the patent from the crown.   Strange to say, no nearer

kinsman of the earl advanced any pretension either to estate or chieftainry, than the chief of Duhallo, descended from Donal-na-
Curragh who died nearly four centuries before. By the death of his
uncle Owen, in 1593, Florence had become tanist of Carbery, next
in succession to Donal-na-pipi, son of his uncle Cormac, who had
entered into bonds, with ten thousand pounds penalty, not to defeat
his succession, and upon Donal's death, which actually occurred in
1614, Florence if surviving was to succeed. Clancarre and Carbery
united, their chief would become as powerful as Tyrone. This would
have conflicted with English policy, and serves to explain the injustice
practised towards Florence, who if he had his faults, none to justify
robbing him and his descendants of their birthright.

During the last ten years many other personages of note mentioned by the annalists finished their course : John Coghlan famous
for his many well appointed abodes ; Thomas sixteenth lord Kerry,
best purchaser of wines, horses and literary works of his day ; Donnel Mac Sweeny constable of Muskerry, praiseworthy in the eyes
of English and Irish ; Turlogh Roe O'Boyle, at Ballyweel in 1591,
most distinguished of his tribe, sustaining pillar of the learned and
destitute, exalter of sanctuaries, churches and science, the personifi-
cation like Guaire a thousand years before of generosity ; Brian
Mac Dermot lord of Moylurg in 1592 ; Donnel Mac Namara Reagh
of West Clancuillan, sumptuous, warlike, bountiful, humane ; Catherine daughter of Donnell Reagh and wife of Muskerry, sensible,
pious, charitable ; Dermot O'Dwyer of Kilnemanagh in Tipperary,
succeeding his father Phillip ; Teigue Mac Mahon lord of east Corcavaskin ; Sir Owen O'Sullivan, deprived the year before by the council of Beare and Dunboy in favor of his nephew Donnel chosen by
the sept for their chief; Macon O'Clery ollav to O'Donnel in history,
learned and ingenious, an orator fluent and eloquent ; Hugh Magennis, of renown ; Turlogh lord of West Corcavaskin ; Sir John
O'Gallagher, of great name ; John O'Reilly, accidentally shot by the

O'Neils who had made him chief of Breffny, succeeded in 1597 by his uncle Edmund; Theobald Butler lord of Cahir, who possessed the largest collection of poetical compositions of any of English race in Ireland; Nial Mageoghan; Owen Mac Sweeny Tuath, influential and generous, who had never incurred reproach from the time he assumed the chieftainship, sumptuous, warlike, humane and bountiful, powerful to sustain and brave to make attack, and of good sense and counsel in peace and war.

XL.

REIGN OF ELIZABETH.—1558-1602.—(Continued.)

When events disappointed expectation recourse was had to change of rulers. Russell had already expressed a wish to be recalled. Essex and Norris, rivals for glory or preferment in continental warfare, eager to succeed him, were alike disappointed. On the twenty-second of May, 1597, Thomas de Bourgh, sixth baron of the English branch of his name, and whose brother John had won celebrity in the naval service, qualified as deputy. Of elevated character, great liberality and familiar with the science of war, he gained popularity with lords and chieftains near the pale by his frank and courteous demeanor. He proposed, doubtless in good faith and with the hope of effecting a peace, truce for thirty days, but meanwhile made every preparation against the possibility of hostilities being renewed. He sent Norris whom Essex did not like back to his presidency in Munster, with orders not to leave it, and there two months later, that veteran officer died in the arms of his brother in consequence of festering wounds, or broken hearted at unmerited disgrace. The deputy sent word to Clifford in Connaught to occupy the attention of O'Donnel, and follow him into Tyrone, and proclaimed a general hosting at Drogheda or the twentieth of July to march into Ulster.

Four days later, Clifford assembled his troops at Boyle. Clanrickard, Thomond, chiefs of Mayo and Roscommon, a numerous and gallant array, they proceeded by Sligo to cross the Erne, but O'Donnel had posted detachments at its several fords. At the falls of Athenllaine they effected their passage, losing many men washed down the stream, and lord Inchiquin was shot while in its midst endeavoring to save them. The army passed Sunday, the first of August, at Assaroe, waiting for their artillery sent by sea from Galway, and which they planted the next day against Ballyshannon. After battering its walls for three days, a strong force well protected by their shields and defensive armor, with machines for undermining the foundation, approached the castle. Crawford with his garrison of eighty men destroyed their works as fast as they were constructed, dropping down upon them large stones, heavy beams and wooden blocks, till finding the attempt without result the assailants were called off. In a cavalry skirmish Donogh O'Connor Sligo was badly wounded.

O'Donnell by Monday had gathered his troops and with them O'Rourkes and Maguires, and surrounding the besiegers poured into them such a constant fire that by the fifteenth the governor in despair held a council of war with a view of raising the siege. But even this was attended with danger, for the fords were all guarded. Starting at daybreak and leaving their guns and storeships as spoils for the enemy, the governor recrossed the Erne by the falls of Assaroe, many perishing before he got over. When intelligence of his flight reached the sleeping camp of O'Donnel, the alarm was sounded, and his troops hastily attired, the chief started in pursuit. The English army with their twenty-two battalions well armed, were drawn up in a strong position by the sea shore. They were compelled to yield ground, and fighting as they went and favored by torrents of rain which spoiled the powder of their pursuers whilst their own was protected by garments worn over their armor, they reached Sligo. They

did not dare to stop there, and the coming morning pushing on to
Boyle withdrew to their several homes, Clifford going back in humiliation to Athlone.

Meanwhile the deputy with an army largely composed of veterans
who had gained experience under Russell and Norris and which had
been reinforced from England and the pale, proceeded into Ulster.
Guided by Turlogh son of Phelim O'Neil, he crossed the Blackwater
unopposed. As O'Donnel suffered Clifford to cross the Erne, it may
have been strategy on the part of Tyrone to allow the deputy to
penetrate into his territory where he would have him more at disadvantage. Armagh and Portmore had been dismantled, and the deputy
razing a fort used for observation constructed another of larger dimensions, and placed it in charge of Thomas Williams with three
hundred men. He was on his way back to Dublin when he learned
that Tyrone had attempted to take the work by storm.

Turning back he found the catholics in two camps, one under Mac
Mahon and the sons of Tyrone, on the road to Benburb, James Macdonnel son of Sorleboy in the other with Tyrone himself, who kept
up night and day a continual fire upon his troops. To protect them
and strengthen his position, he endeavored to restore the Norris fort
to a defensible condition, Tyrone endeavoring to embarrass his
work. O'Donnel set free from Clifford and arriving with his cavalry
defeated Terence Mac Henry, another O'Neil, who had taken part
with the English.

During these operations, the deputy with several of his principal
officers ascended an eminence near his camp to reconnoitre, when
the enemy on the alert improving the chance offered by his imprudence, rushed up the hill and many were slain. On this occasion
or in a nocturnal attack by the catholics on the royal camp, the
deputy himself was mortally wounded. Lest this should discourage
his army or elate the foe, it was not suffered if true to transpire,
and carried off on a litter as if only ill, towards Newry, he died on

the way, before the thirtieth of August, about six weeks from the time he left Drogheda.

The command devolved upon Henry twelfth earl of Kildare, who "full of lightness and temerity" and vainly confident of his ability to effect what the deputy could not, with his best troops proceeded through woods and by obscure paths and supposed he had surmounted all the difficulties in his way, when the catholics gathering around brought him to battle. Sixty of his choicest troopers fell, and with them, Turner the treasurer of the army, Francis Vaughan brother-in-law of the deputy, and Thomas Walwyn. Kildare twice forced from the saddle by opposing lances was reseated by two O'Conors of Offaly, sons of his nurse and his own kinsmen, and badly shaken fled to die a few weeks afterwards, either from his wounds or grief for the loss of his foster brothers, who whilst engaged in remounting him had been surrounded and slain. Many of the royalists were wounded, and all who had come out on the expedition were either killed or driven back.* The royal army after having been engaged for nearly four months in battles and skirmishes between Benburb and Portmore, garrisons being left under Williams at the latter place and at Armagh, withdrew into winter quarters, and all the septs and chiefs whom Bourg had conciliated returned to their earlier and more natural fealty to Tyrone.

In response to appeal for assistance Tyrone had detached fifteen hundred men into Leinster, four hundred of them placed under Tirrell of Fertulagh in West Meath. A larger army under Barnwall lord Trimlestown was nigh, on its way to join the deputy. Not deeming

---

* Cox and the Four Masters mention two expeditions in 1597, by the deputy to the Blackwater; Lombard who wrote in 1600 but one, and one battle, in which Kildare and Bourg were both mortally wounded; O'Sullivan mentions but one expedition; but with Mageoghan states that Kildare succeeded to the command after Bourg was wounded. Two letters dated the third of August from Dublin mention Kildare's death as occurring on the second of that month, and Collins and Lodge concur substantially with them, but dates are not always reliable. The history of the house of Kildare and its supplemental volume in the text state that he died on the thirtieth of September at Drogheda. His brother William succeeded to the earldom and to his special command as a cavalry officer, but there seems no ground for believing that he took command of the army on the Blackwater after Bourg gave it up. That the deputy should have marched his army to the capital and then returned seems less consistent with what is known than that he started and came back.

so small a force worthy of his own steel, Barnwall sent his son with a thousand men to engage Tirrell ; but that able officer with O'Connor to aid found it easy to outgeneral the inexperienced youth. At a pass near his own abode, and since known by his name, he waylaid the approaching force, and utterly annihilated them, the leader himself being spared and sent prisoner to Tyrone. The hand of O'Conor, the hero of the day, was so swollen at night by his work that a file was needed to disengage it from his hilt.

Thomas Norris, summoned from the presidency of Munster, in which he had succeeded John, was elected by the council, lord justice, but grieving for the loss of his brother after a month resigned. Loftus and Gardiner, in November, were put in his place, and Ormond appointed lord general of the army. Tyrone seeking to starve out the garrison left at Armagh, encamped a mile beyond that city on the road by which he thought relief would be sent. His son Con, angry with him for reasons not stated, a few days before had joined the English, with whom his nephew Terence then was, and they conducted the marshal with his supplies by secret paths to victual the place. Thirteen hundred infantry and three troops of cavalry engaged Cormac O'Neil, brother of Tyrone, in battle, whilst the convoy entered the gates and returned.

Terence and Con, easily angered, thirsted for the blood of the earl, and also hating O'Hanlon still more, led Bagnal to the catholic camp, and to the tent where they supposed the latter was sleeping, but it proved that of the earl, twenty-four of whose mounted body-guard were slain, and O'Neil and those that were with him forced to flee half awake and half clad. The royalists took the abandoned tents, killing the attendants who were left. O'Neil gathered his forces and the day after pursued his despoilers, doing them some hurt ; but Bagnal was greatly elated at having relieved Armagh and driven O'Neil from his camp besides for the few that were slain.

In November Sir John Chichester holding Carrickfergus sallied forth, with five hundred men, to attack James Mac Donnel who having placed in ambush a part of his Highlanders at a cave four miles off, approached the town with the hope not disappointed of tempting him out. A combat with fire arms resulted in the discomfiture of the English, when Sir John bringing up his horse restored the battle. Macdonnel with his own cavalry charged upon Chichester and was thrice struck by the lance of his antagonist, which did not penetrate his corslet. Yielding ground, and seeming to retreat, Macdonnel drew Sir John towards the cave, and as they reached the spot, the concealed Highlanders emerging from their covert fell upon their foe and chased them for three miles, killing or wounding so many that scarcely one got back to tell the tale. Sir John taken prisoner was beheaded on a stone at the entrance of the Glynn. A monument having been erected to his honor in the family burial place, the church of St. Nicholas at Carrickfergus, a year or two after Macdonnel visited the church. His attention directed to the statue of Sir John forming part of the monument, he exclaimed, " where did he get his head again, he was sure he cut it off."

Ormond favored accommodation ; war absorbing her revenue, the queen wished it at an end. At her instance he opened negotiations and at Christmas Tyrone and Tyrconnel met him and Thomond at Dundalk. The presence of Fenton likewise commissioner must have discouraged much confidential communication, as he reported to court whatever beehanced. For three days they discoursed the situation, Tyrone protesting " on the knees of his heart " that injustice alone had forced him into hostilities and that he was ready to make peace on reasonable terms. A truce for eight weeks was agreed upon ; he promised to recall his troops from Leinster, hold no correspondence with Spain, allow Portmore to be provisioned. Mutual trade between Ulster and the pale was to be permitted. Tyrone undertook to procure the release from O'Moore of James, brother of Ormond, and

67

furnish forty beeves to the beleaguered fortress. His wrongs and claims were to be transmitted in a book to the queen. Peace seemed assured. O'Rourke, provoked with O'Donnel for raiding O'Conor Roe, and other western chiefs submitted to Clifford.

When on the fifteenth of March the negotiators reassembled to learn the queen's mind, its perversity proved in the ascendant. The chiefs were imperiously ordered to disband their troops and send away their allies, and betray all intercourse with Spain; Tyrone to renounce the title of O'Neil, exercise no authority over his uriaghts, rebuild at his own expense the bridge and fort at Blackwater, pay a fine, admit a sheriff, deliver up traitors, surrender the sons of Shane, and give his own eldest son as hostage. Freedom of worship was not to be tolerated and priests and friars were to be banished. His answer was sufficiently courteous, but not to be mistaken. He could not desert his confederates till they had time to submit; he was willing to relinquish the title of O'Neil, but not his power as chieftain. Shane's sons were his prisoners, not the queen's. One of his own people might be appointed sheriff, but that better be deferred. He would surrender refugees for political offences but not for conscience sake, and refused to give his son as hostage. Clanrickard and Thomond persuaded the queen to abate some of her pretensions, and on the eleventh of April his pardon passed the seal, but this he scornfully rejected and sent aid to O'Byrne, encouraged Raymond Burke against his uncle Clanrickard and O'Rourke to break with Clifford.

Reinforcements sent from home, the new levies placed in garrison relieved for the field the more experienced veterans. The justices divided their forces, three thousand invading Leix under Ormond who sent against Brian O'Moore a third of his men under his nephew James, a catholic. James fell, and his army routed would have been destroyed by Brian had not Ormond come up. Brian dying four days after of wounds received in the conflict, Owen

took command of the O'Moores, and with Raymond Burke lord of
Leitrim, deprived of his inheritance by his uncle Clanrickard who had
slain his father, with Dermod O'Conor Don and Richard Tirrell,
drove Ormond out of Leix.

Portmore still held out against O'Neil, whose forty beeves, duly
delivered, ten of them rejected and replaced, had been soon used up.
O'Donnel advised an assault.   Ladders to hold five abreast had been
prepared, but the garrison aware of what was being designed deepened
the ditch, and they fell short.   One hundred and twenty of the besiegers fell in the attempt.   Without artillery no impression could be
made upon the citadel protected by earthworks, and in a position almost impregnable.   Famine however was doing its work upon its
gallant defenders, who devoured their horses and gleaned the weeds
from the ditch.   The queen chided her council and officials for not
affording relief, and sent reinforcements with stringent orders no
longer to delay.

The marshal led a large army from Dundalk and Newry to the aid
of the beleagured fortress, by Armagh which was reached the third
day.   Bagnal skilled in military science, possessed what is rare in a
commander, sagacity, great presence of mind and prudence in prosperous circumstances, not losing courage in adverse, and was far less
overbearing to the conquered than most of his countrymen who were
not then noted for kindness of deed or word to prostrate foe.   Few
officers in the service equalled, none surpassed him.   His hatred to
O'Neil, not on public considerations, for his religion or for his hostility
to the queen, but on private grounds, was intense.   His army consisted
of forty-five hundred infantry under forty banners, five hundred
horse under eight commanded by Montague.   In the whole number
there were more Irish than English, but all veterans, the latter survivors of those who had served in France under Norris, been summoned
from the garrisons in the Low Countries, or who had learned the
methods of Irish warfare from the beginning of hostilities ; the former

content to learn their profession in the pay of the queen and who had
given frequent proofs of their bravery.

With the royalists, of noble birth, were Maelmora O'Reilly,
son of the prince of Breffney, of rare elegance of form, and called
" the handsome," from the beauty of his countenance, and also Christopher St. Lawrence, son of lord Howth, descendant of that Amory
St. Lawrence whose gallant achievements won Ulster four centuries
before.   Among them all not one was a novice in war or untrained in
any branch of its service.   Infantry, cavalry in mail, musketmen
with weapons heavy or light, girded with sword and dagger, helmets
on their heads, formed a brilliant array which glowed with colored
plumes, silken baldries and other warlike splendors.   Guns of polished brass drawn on wheels, powder and ball and bullets abounded.
Horses and oxen bore masses of meat and bread, not for the army
alone but for the relief of Portmore, with the usual impediments of
drivers, caterers and followers of the camp.

O'Neil striving to reduce Portmore by famine, lay with his army
about three miles from Armagh, when he heard of the approach
of the enemy.   He moved his camp within two miles of that city,
leaving a small force to prevent the garrison from sallying forth in
his rear.   The catholics that day numbered about forty-five hundred
foot and six hundred horse ;[*] O'Donnel with two thousand men, one
half from Connaught under Mac William, the rest his own Kinel
Konnel ; O'Neil surrounded by his brothers and kinsmen and chiefs
bound to him by ancient obligations, nearly all the noble youth of

---

* Neil Bryan of Upper Clanaboy, 80 foot, 30 horse ; Shane Mac Bryan of Lower Clanaboy, 80 foot, 50 horse ; Mac Rory of Kilwarlin, 60 foot, 10 horse ; Shane Mac Bryan Carogh
from Bannside, 50 foot, 10 horse ; Art O'Neil, 330 foot, 60 horse ; Henry Oge O'Neil, 200
foot, 40 horse ; Turlogh Mac Henry of the Fews, 300 foot, 60 horse ; Cormac brother of
Tyrone, 300 foot, 60 horse ; Tyrone, 700 foot, 200 horse ; Duffern White's county, 200 foot ;
Mac Artan of Down, 100 foot, 20 horse ; Macginness of Iveagh, 200 foot, 40 horse ; Mac
Murtogh from mein water, 40 foot ; O'Hagan of Tullahoge, 100 foot, 30 horse ; James Mac
Donnell, Route and Glynns, 400 foot, 100 horse ; Maguire, 600 foot, 100 horse ; Mac Mahons,
500 foot, 160 horse ; O'Reilly, 800 foot. 100 horse ; O'Cahan Lough Foyle and Bann, 500
foot, 200 horse ; from Tyrconnel, Hugh Roe, 350 foot, 110 horse ; O'Doherty of Inishowen,
300 foot, 40 horse ; Mac Sweenys, 500 foot, 30 horse ; O'Boyle, 100 foot, 20 horse ; O'Gallagher of Ballyshannon, 200 foot, 40 horse.   Total, 6780 foot, 1510 horse ; Total, horse and
foot, 8290 ; sent into Leinster, 1500 ; balance 6790.   Deductions of one third for garrisons,
hospitals and furloughs would leave the number in the text.

Ulster and many from Connaught. They were far inferior in weapons, for both horse and foot were lightly armed. " Few of them were clad in armor like the English, but they had a sufficient quantity of spears and broad lances with strong handles of ash; of straight keen edged swords and thin polished battle axes. They had besides javelins, bows and arrows and guns with matchlocks." O'Neil knowing well the efficiency of the enemy, the deliberate courage of their leader and their superiority in arms and strength, hesitated as a cautious general might, and would have retreated had not O'Clery, an interpreter of the Irish prophecies, pointed out a prediction of Saint Bearchan in ancient verse, that on that spot the heretics would be conquered.

O'Neil encouraged, exhorted his soldiers to fight as christians and brave men. What they had long earnestly sought by prayer and supplication, had at last by divine grace been granted. They had always implored the father and the heavenly hosts, that they might fight the protestants on equal terms. This had been all that they asked. Now they were not only equal but superior in number, and if when few they had routed their enemy surely they would now when they were superior in strength. Victory came not from lifeless armor or empty sound of artillery, but from living fearless souls. They must remember how many greater generals, stronger armies they had conquered, how often Bagnal himself when they were less well armed and disciplined. Englishmen at no time were comparable in valor with their own countrymen, who fighting with the enemy against their faith would be conscience stricken, whilst that faith would nerve their own arms in defence of religion, country, wives and children. Bagnal their most bitter enemy who sought their possessions and thirsted for their blood, who had assailed his own honor, should receive the punishment he deserved. The insult at their tents, their comrades slain at Portmore, cried for vengeance. That stronghold which had so long resisted their efforts must be reduced.

With God and his saints to help them, the victory promised by his holy prophet was at hand.*

The address of Bagnal to his army, if also the invention of the historian, indicates the temper of the times.   Trusting in their fortitude, he had selected them as his comrades, leaving the ignorant, inexperienced dregs of the army whose inefficiency might have encumbered their movements in the garrisons under Ormond.   With them he promised himself a glorious victory.   His experience of their courage left no doubt of their triumph.   He could not but think that they who had escaped safe from so many perils would not only that day wreath their own life with glory, but revenge their comrades slain under Norris and De Burgh.   Could it be that their enemies without armor would dare encounter men strong and brave, clothed in steel, armed with the best of weapons.   It seemed folly to doubt but that the coming battle would bring all Ulster under the yoke, subject Ireland to the queen, win vast spoils for themselves.   They should remember their valor as they bore relief to Armagh, drove O'Neil from his tent.   Whoever at evening should bring him the head of that chief or O'Donnel's should have for guerdon a thousand pounds in gold, and the deserts of all however many should be fittingly acknowledged both by the queen and himself.   But they should hasten on to battle and not delay their victory.

His harangue over, Bagnal before sunrise of the fourteenth of August, the day Ormond was receiving his repulse in Leix from Brian O'Moore, left his camp at Armagh.   His spearmen were in three bodies, cavalry and gunners before and behind.   Perry led the

* The address in the text is translated from the Catholic History. O'Clery, in his life of O'Donnel, gives the following as the speech of Tyrone, taken from the Gaelic version. Brave people, be not dismayed at the English on account of their foreign appearance, of their array and the strangeness of their armor and arms, the sound of their trumpets and tabours and warlike instruments, or of their great numbers, for it is certain that they shall be defeated in the battle of this day. Of this we are indeed convinced, for you are on the side of truth, and they of what is false, fettering you in prisons and beheading you in order to rob you of your patrimonies. We have indeed high expectation that this very day will distinguish between truth, as Moran the son of Maen says; There has never been found a more veritable judge than the battle field. Moreover it is easier for you to defend your own patrimony after being expelled from your native country which has been in your possession for twenty centuries (from 3500 A.M.), than win a home from others.

van followed by Bagnal's own regiment, then Cosby's and Wingfield's, Quinn's and Billings' bringing up the rear. Brooks, Montague and Fleming commanded the cavalry. They left in Armagh their impediments and whatever could encumber their march. It was a bright mid-summer morning, and with banners flaunting, trumpets sounding, fife and drum, in all the pomp and pageantry of war, man and horse pushed on through fields exuberant in their vernal splendor, eager for the fray. The road soon grew narrow, set with a thin growth of low junipers. About the seventh hour from behind these trees and flitting among them five hundred skirmishers, beardless youth, posted there by O'Neil, poured into their ranks a hail of bullets as far as the wood extended, overthrowing horse and man, and with the more safety for themselves that the royal cavalry could not, for the trees, either help their own or hurt them. The ground served well for those that occupied it, but was out of reach of the advancing foe.

From this strait Bagnal with difficulty disengaged his men, not a little damaged by this sharp skirmishing, the more vexatious from the boyish character of their assailants. Out of the junipers, the plain spread away towards the catholics and the royal cavalry charged at full speed against their advanced guards. O'Neil had taken the precaution to excavate frequent pitfalls and ditches about this open ground and the road they would naturally take, concealed from sight by grass spread over thin wattles or osiers; and into these hollows plunged the heavy armed troopers to the danger of their horses and with broken limbs for the riders, the catholic skirmishers not allowing their comrades to extricate them. By this device, when the royalists reached less treacherous ground their courage was abated by the loss already sustained. The troops of O'Neil fresh and in full vigor relieved their jaded comrades, and Bagnal's skirmishers and his heavy armed infantry engaged in the fight. Spearsmen agile and dexterous, swooped about, again and again rushing into the melee, inflicting wounds, goring their foes and were off. Cuirassiers fought

with spears six cubits long resting against their thighs, light horse
with longer lances on their right shoulders, used less than the javelins, four cubits in length and with sharp iron points, which they
cast.   Bagnal, often brought to a stand by these troublesome assailants whom he occasionally drove off after four hours incessant fighting, drew near the catholic entrenchments.   Here the ground with
bogs on either side contracted.   Tyrone had constructed a breastwork
six furlongs in length and four feet in height with ditch deeper within,
less to protect his own army than embarrass the foe, between whom
and this rampart exuded from the marshes streams of turbid water,
from which the battle field took its name of the yellow ford.   For
two hours, in which ancient and modern warfare raged side by side,
was fought by men of intrepid bravery, of the best training under
consummate leaders, amid volleys of artillery, showers of musket
balls, charges of cavalry and hand to hand encounters with axe and
sword, this memorable combat.   It was here that the strife was most
desperate, and its issue determined.

At the hottest moment of the contest an English gunner, his
powder expended, was replenishing, when his burning fuse exploded
the cask and two more, blowing into the air all who stood near.
One of the guns battering the earth work burst, scattering havoc
around ; another fastened in the marsh baffled all efforts to disengage
it.   The fire from the rest galled the unprotected ranks of the catholics, whose gunners and cavalry were powerless against its ravages.
In time the breast-work crumbled down to the plain.   Its defenders
driven off, two royal regiments poured in, one turning against O'Neil,
the other against O'Donnel, who commanded the left wing, some
ranks crossing the lines, whilst the third pushed up to their support.
The royal cavalry and musketmen rushed upon horse and foot of the
catholics driven from their entrenchments, and now on equal ground
in close conflict the fight thickened, muzzle to muzzle, hand to hand,
either side striving to dismount and overthrow their opponents.   The

catholic spearsmen removed from the fire of the batteries, observing that the guns no longer of use had been abandoned, took possession of them and turned them against their enemies.

At this moment Bagnal, oppressed by cuirass and helm which were of steel, bullet proof and of great weight, believing the victory won and eager to breathe more freely, raised his beaver better to see the happy turn of the contest, and fell lifeless, struck in the brow by a ball. Dismay seized the third column which he led. The other two in front, not aware of what had chanced fought valiantly on, the catholics no less. O'Donnel with his musketmen, the Kinel Owen in the midst of the peril. The issue hung in the balance, when Tyrone near by with forty horsemen and as many gunners ordered the latter to pour in their shot. Thrown into confusion by this attack from an unexpected quarter, the chief with his cavalry charged into the midst of the royalists. His infantry, raising his battle cry, with overwhelming power followed the paths he opened, and the enemy struck with panic wavered and fled. It was then an hour past noon. The right wing opposed to O'Donnel witnessing the rout and likewise demoralized, turned and rushed from the field.

Montague and his troopers took to their spurs, the musketeers to their heels. O'Neil, O'Donnel and Maguire who commanded the catholic cavalry kept close to their backs. Ditch and rampart more in their way than when advancing, they fell one over the other, trampled upon by the foot, bruised by the hoofs of the horses. The third column, saddened at the loss of their leader and dismayed at the general rout, had no help to render. The splendid O'Reilly exhorted his men to be of good heart and fight on, it being more honorable to die in battle than be slain unavenged, and that they might possibly not only sustain the attack but repel it. Emboldened by his words his young kinsmen renewed the combat, their commander ever present with aid to the hard pushed or imperilled. Abandoned

68

by the royalists, hemmed in by the catholics, they all fell covered
with wounds, the fall of "Pulcher" himself ending the battle.

An utter rout, straggling over the plain, among the junipers, they
were slaughtered, even up to the gates of Armagh. Within the sacred walls of its fortified cathedral, a thousand foot soldiers and half as
many troopers at last found refuge. The royalists lost twenty-five
hundred men, their general, twenty-three of his subordinates, besides
standard bearers, aids and adjutants, and thirty-four military standards, drums, cannon, vast quantities of arms, twelve thousand pounds
in gold, and all their provision. The fight was not bloodless to the
victors, two hundred being killed, thrice as many wounded. Armagh
was besieged. Montague breaking out at night with his cavalry,
Terence O'Hanlon from the camp of Tyrone pursued him, capturing
his baggage train and two hundred of his horses, killing three of his
officers. Romley, another, smoking his pipe of tobacco next day in
a thicket not far from the road was caught and killed. Armagh and
Portmore after three days surrendered upon terms. The garrisons
were set free, but whether from the almost romantic generosity which
marked Tyrone in his dealings with the conquered, prudence in case
of reverse, or to conciliate the favor of the queen, will be differently
interpreted by different minds.

It was a glorious triumph for the cause of national independence.
The chain was broken, and every catholic, every Irishman who did
not wish to be subjugated, be deprived of his property or say his
prayers at other men's dictation, felt himself free. Tyrone, champion of the faith, saviour of his country, not Ulster alone, but the
nation throughout all its tribes hailed leader and king. Dismay
paralyzed the pale, Ormond shut himself up in Kilkenny, adventurers
and undertakers trembled for land and life. Could the northern
chiefs have improved their victory and marched upon the capital, foreign domination might have tottered to its fall. That they did not,
cannot well be attributed to want of wisdom or courage. The re-

sources of England were unexhausted as the next two years proved. Bagnal's field pieces, Armagh's guns would have been powerless against stone walls. Their fallen braves were not to be swept into cavities in the earth like the holocausts of despotism, but reverently laid in the tombs of their ancestors with dirge and rite. Many minds were to be consulted, preparations made. What had been gained was too precious to risk by precipitate measures, and such moments of exultation in their perennial resistance to superior numbers, wealth and armaments, too rarely vouchsafed not to be enjoyed.

Our historical sympathies lean naturally to the victors who were defending their hearths and altars, for in the cause of human rights and independence they are excusable even where against our own countrymen if forging fetters for the free. There could be no justification for the attempt to reduce Ulster to a conquered province. It had been tried and signally failed. It had cost vast expenditures of life and treasure, and now except the trembling garrisons in Dublin and Cork, Ireland was Irish. Leinster chiefs levied tribute under the walls of the capital, and when O'Moore marched into Desmond the southern septs with Geraldines, Roches and Butlers rose in arms and joined him to expel the intruders.

Much remained to be accomplished before their strength would be consolidated and in condition to cope with English power now lashed into rage and resentment by reverses deemed not only disastrous, but attended with disgrace. The two great leaders of the north were admirably suited to the conjuncture. Owen O'Moore, Maguire and O'Rourke, Donal Maccarthy, Dermod and Donal O'Sullivan, Desmond and his brother John, were able and earnest in the cause. Ulster, menaced from without but not much endangered, within was of one mind. Connaught less united, with Clifford esteemed and both earls loyal, might prove in the crisis portending an element of weakness. Its charge naturally fell to Tyrconnel, who to be nearer his work bought of the Macdonoghs for four hundred pounds and three hundred cows the castle of Ballimote, south of Sligo, Clifford the governor competing for its purchase.

Hardly established with his creaghts about him in his new abode he raided Theobald of the ships, and after Christmas Clanrickard, carrying home unopposed whatever of value he found. In February after rallying his hosts he left part to prey such septs as were hostile at the north, and moved silently and rapidly with the rest under O'Rourke, Maguire, MacSwenys, Fanad and Banagh, O'Dogherty and O'Boyle, to Kilcolgan in Galway, which he reached at daybreak. Having rested his troops during the day, that he might take the country by surprise, they entered Clare at midnight in detachments, Maguire wasting Inchiquin, O'Donel himself proceeding by Kilnaboy to Kilfenora, directing the several parties to join him on his homeward march with their prey.

Whilst halting, a bard of the Dalgais who had been plundered of his herds, his principal belongings, came for redress to his tent, addressing him as the chosen agent of saint Columbkille, to avenge the destruction five centuries before of Oileach, the home of his royal progenitors, by Murrogh grandson of Brian Boru. This pleased the chieftain who gave him his cattle back. Not much of Clare suffered except Inchiquin and Corcomroe, the latter belonging to Torlogh of Enystimmond, son of Sir Donald, still friendly to the queen, which many other O'Briens, provoked at English tenures that deprived them of their lands or cut off their reasonable expectations, were not. Donogh the earl had been in England since the Christmas conference at Dundalk a year before with Tyrone and Tyrconnel, and lately returned was with Ormond helping him in Munster. Besides his early education in England, his second wife, daughter of Gerald eleventh earl of Kildare and Mabel Brown, attached him to the queen. But he was not a mere courtier, his efficiency in the field earned him the title of the great earl. He had left Thomond in charge of his brothers Torlogh and Daniel, sixty years later created first viscount

Clare, but another brother Teague was then, though soon after to change, in league with O'Donnel. When the earl heard of the raid to which his dominions had been subjected, he hastened home. Irritated that Mac Mahon of West Corcavaskin his subordinate chief should have presumed to make war against his brothers whom he had left in his place, he planted ordnance against Carrigaholt, one of his castles, hanging its warders to the neighboring trees, and reduced Dunmore another stronghold a mile off. He drove out the garrisons from Derryowen, Cloone and Lessofin, restoring the latter to Macnamara, Cloone to O'Grady.

XLI.

REIGN OF ELIZABETH.—1558-1602.—(Continued.)

Its climate favorable to vegetation and soil responsive to labor, even Leix, recovered by its rightful proprietors, bloomed like a garden. The dozen summers since the Desmond wars wrought changes farther south equally marked. Colonists with capital constructed better abodes than had been destroyed, and the people generally resumed their avocations. Plenty reigned and food abundant supplied their own needs, whilst many from Connaught and some from Leinster their country wasted came there to be fed. Had Munster possessed leaders as experienced in war and with resources as great as the two northern chiefs, Ireland might have regained her independence. Donnal son of Clancarre, bold and able, had at command no revenues and his birth worked to his disadvantage. With Dermot of Duhallo his competitor he submitted to its chiefs his claims to the chieftainship of Clancarthy, and was inaugurated Maccarthy Mor. James, son of Thomas Ruagh recently deceased, recognized as earl of Desmond by Tyrone, shared with him the lead. Termed the sugan or straw earl by the enemy, this new Desmond in presence and bearing noble as in character and disposition, sensible and prudent yet brave and daring, might have proved, had opportunity allowed, the commander that the crisis demanded. Donnal, too, displayed in his relations with his subordinates as later at court in London the shrewd good sense that marked his military movements.

Fortunately no conflict of interest, no jealousy divided them, and their united forces persuaded or compelled such chiefs as were not irrevocably pledged to the queen to become their tributaries or enter their ranks. They were more successful with O'Driscols by sea than with Donal lord of Carberry and his subordinate lords by land. Ormond had followed O'Moore with three thousand men, joining the president at Kilmallock. They marched together into Duhallo, but proved no match for their opponents who drove them to Mallow. But when Owen returned to the north, the earl anxious for his possessions also hastened home, whilst the president no longer assured of his safety betook himself to Cork.

William Burke of Castle Connel with Thomas Fitzgerald reduced Molatif held by Sir Nicholas Brown, defeating a body of redcoats and capturing the hunting dogs of the president, who having collected twenty-five hundred men was marching to place his raw recruits in Kilmallock, and to take thence the veterans for service in the field. Returning, Desmond, Montgarret, Cahir, Purcell, Burke and Tyrrel, about equal in number, drove him back with great loss, eight miles to that place. When they disappeared from his front, he again strove to reach Cork, and occupied Rochefort, abandoned by lord Fermoy who shut himself up in castle Roche near by.

The catholics not far off hastened to help. For twelve days the two armies confronted in equal strength, skirmishing with varying success. When the president appeared rather disposed to retire than advance, the catholics moved their position to block his path. Resolving to break through, he assailed their camps before daybreak with cavalry and seven hundred matchlocks. The sleepers rudely dis-

turbed, fled, panic stricken, when Burke from another part of the
camp promptly brought aid, and the fugitives returning to their
ranks forced the assailants back to their lines. The next day, his
baggage sent before, the president proceeded towards Cork pursued
by the catholics, who slew two hundred of his men at the monastery
of Mona.

Thomas, another of the Burkes, not long after reducing the strongholds of Muskerry Kurk, the president who lay near with twelve
hundred horse and foot on his way to Thomastown, encountered him
at Kittilly. Burke not strong enough to seek a battle would have
retired, but Norris not content that he should escape charged their
rear ranks, who turned upon their assailants : and John Burke hit him
through his visor with a spear of which the point stuck in his head.
The wounded president was carried to the splendid abode he had
erected at Mallow, and there died on the twentieth of June, fifteen
days after the battle. Dermot O'Connor marauding the baron of
Castle Connel and hemmed in by three hundred of his dependents
and as many royalists from Limerick, rushed upon them and put them
to rout, slaying their leaders the baron and his brother.

English settlers, dismayed at this general disaffection and left
unprotected, abandoned their estates and took refuge in the walled
towns or fell victims to the resentment of the catholics who ransacked
or demolished their dwellings, burnt their crops and swept off such
quantities of horses and cattle, that a cow in calf sold for sixpence,
a brood mare for three. "In the course of seventeen days they left
not within the length and breadth of the country of the Geraldines,
from Dunqueen to the Suir, which the Saxons had well filled with
habitations and various wealth, a single son of a Saxon whom they
did not either kill or expel. Nor did they leave a single head residence, castle or one sod of Geraldine territory, which they did not
put in possession of the earl of Desmond, except Castlemagne. Askeaton and Mallow."

His genius did not save Edmund Spenser from grief. For ten years he had been quietly possessed of Kilcolman and his three thousand acres, near Mallow on the Mulla. His castle burnt and one of his children perishing in the flames, he escaped with the other and some few of his manuscripts, to die in London impoverished and broken-hearted on the sixteenth day of the new year at the early age of forty-five. His abode at the north side of a beautiful sheet of water abounding in fish and the resort of water fowl, was surrounded by mountains commanding a view of half the breadth of the island. Near by flowed the Mulla, bathing as it went the castle walls of Buttevant, Doneraile and Roche, falling into the Blackwater at Bridgetown. St. Legers, Norrises and Roches were thus his neighbors, and his position as clerk of Munster and of its council board, brought him into intimate and pleasant relations with all its officials. Whether his great poem, portions of which were published in 1591, was ever completed is unknown; but quite probably it was still engaging his attention. His view of Ireland had been recently written, and escaped destruction, possibly from its having been sent to court, as its recommendations shaped the policy immediately afterwards adopted. Sir James Ware, into whose possession it fell, published it in 1633.

In this work, which deserves the study of both races whenever similar questions are under discussion, he was cautious not to offend English prejudice or thwart English plans. Conclusions often at variance with good judgment, justice and humanity from such a source must create suspicion, and charity suggests that he means the opposite of what he says, and that a vein of sarcasm lurked beneath his exaggerations. He inveighs in no measured terms against all Irish institutions, tanistry, erics, the whole brehon law as an obstacle in the way of English supremacy, and especially against the doctrine, that no chief could bind his sept beyond his own lifetime. Juries composed of natives would not render verdicts in favor of the crown or its subjects. Yet if consisting exclusively of strangers there would

have been clamor against partiality and injustice. When evidence
in court was shown to be false the orders of their chiefs were urged
as sufficient justification. But such abuses were confined to neither
race. Tipperary under Ormond was privileged ground for depredators, a receptacle of stolen goods. Obsolete laws capriciously enforced
made saffron shirts, hair on the upper lip, gilt bridles, coin and livery
felony, and landlord or traveller accepting meat or horse bait liable
to prosecution upon complaint of any hostile informer.

Their property consisting of cattle, herdsmen pastured on the
mountains, and their booths or huts the refuge of malefactors, they
themselves became demoralized, setting authority at defiance. Their
mantles served as fitting home for an outlaw, meet bed for a rebel,
apt cloak for a thief, his pent house in rain, his tent against the wind,
his tabernacle when it was freezing. Never heavy or cumbersome,
it could be worn loose in summer or wrapt close in winter, his screen
from the gnats, buckler against sword or spear. It concealed his
weapons and his plunder as also himself from observation, which latter
purpose the glibbes also served. From strangers was acquired taste
for bright colors, and horsemen and galloglasses learned from them to
use saddles, coats of mail to the calf of the leg and heavy axes. Their
kernes, valiant and hardy, bore without murmur cold, labor, hunger
and every hardship. They were active and strong of hand, swift of
foot, vigilant and circumspect in enterprise, undaunted in danger,
scornful of death. When abroad and disciplined and put to musket
or pike, soldiers of no other nation surpassed them in efficiency.

Spenser shows little sympathy for his fellow craftsmen, the poets,
whose profession being to set forth praise or honor, none dared to
displease them since their verses and songs formed part of festal entertainments. Their teaching he says was not edifying. They glorified
deeds of daring and rebellion, whatever worked prejudice against
government or tended to throw off its thraldom, inciting the young
not to eat meat unless won by the sword, to prefer night to day, to

69

light their way by the flames of other men's houses, not to woo by
harp or lay but by violence, by the lamentation of the aggrieved, by
clash of steel, and when dying their natural death of the battle-field,
" not to be bewailed by many, but to make many wail that dearly
bought their death."

Chiefs maintained numerous idlemen, horse boys and armor bearers ;
even the foot soldiers had lads to carry their arms. No inns or
hostlers existing on the road, these lads grew up to knavery, and
when employed by Englishmen learned the use of fire arms. Car-
roghs roamed from house to house living by cards and dice, gesters
by their welcome news. Cess was the pest of husbandry. Soldiers
quartered on the villagers quarrelled with their food, exacting better
and consumed whatever they found, and the government tables and
garrisons exhausted everything within reach. Annual leases led to
rack rent to the disadvantage of both landlord and tenant and discouraging all improvements people dwelt in squalid destitution.
Catholic priests imitating protestants took tithe and offerings, but
neither preached nor administered sacraments. In the English fold
gross simony, greedy covetousness, sloth and disorderly life prevailed, and the example was contagious.

Officers and soldiers, even governors, were loath to end the war,
lest they should lose their pay. They would occasionally cut off the
head of an enemy to please some rival, and send it to the capital in
proof of their zeal. Governors would not suppress evil for fear of
reproach, or lest if creating disturbance their successors by suppressing it might gain praise to their prejudice. Envy and jealousy
were the bane of administration. No steady policy, each new deputy adopted the opposite of his predecessor. Abuses were smothered
up, no one caring what came afterwards. The remedy recommended
was the sword, a powerful army in strong garrisons, to nip in the bud
disaffection, paid and fed by government, operating in winter, destroying the resources of the people, exterminating all who did not

submit, and if they did, sending them away from their homes into the interior.

This policy of destruction and extermination had worked well in Munster, a beautiful country stored with goodly rivers full of fish, pleasant islands, lakes like inland seas, woods for building houses and ships; if some princes had them they would be lords of the world; ports and havens inviting traffic for their excellent commodities, the fertile soil being fit to yield all kinds of fruit committed thereunto and the climate moist, mild and temperate. The clans he would banish from their lands which he would have given to Englishmen, who might retain a convenient number of natives for their cultivation. Corporate towns should be multiplied as a check upon insurrection.

Once subdued, and ten thousand men distributed in garrisons over the land with magazines well filled, fifty thousand pounds should be levied in rent or tax for their support out of that number of ploughlands. The two races should be intermingled, the refractory transported into Ulster. The old Saxon tything-men revived should be responsible each for his hundred, who at stated times should report themselves. Younger sons now left to seek their fortunes must be kept in check and put to employments, the rich and powerful giving pledge and being sworn to obedience. He recommended a general inquest to ascertain land titles, the disloyal to be deprived. Old names, O's and Macs, should be abandoned, and others assumed from employments or personal peculiarities. Idlers were to be put to trades, manual, intellectual or mixed.

Capable protestant clergymen were needed to preach and teach, like the zealots from Rome and Spain. Churches should be rebuilt, schools instituted, bridges supersede fords; roads one hundred yards in width be cut through the forests and provided with inns. Market towns which furthered civility by more frequent intercourse ought to be established, and cattle marked to detect and discourage raids. Lord lieutenants with the council should have power unrestrained, and rather imitate the sternness of Grey with whom he had come into Ireland as secretary, and whom he defends from reproach, than Perrot who befriended chiefs and slighted his own countrymen. But the crying evil of administration was the universal bribery and corruption which should be reformed. From the numerous reports upon the country in public archives of similar import, this view of the poet may have well been prepared to enlighten the government at home, and some of its suggestions were speedily improved upon and carried out.

XLII.

REIGN OF ELIZABETH.—1558–1602.—(Continued.)

Her armies annihilated, her ablest commanders defeated and slain, England determined to crush the catholics with whatever power she possessed. Bingham restored to grace was despatched as marshal to Dublin, where he died in a month, and then Sir Samuel Bagnal with two thousand men intended for Lough Foyle, but who landing at Dungarvan, reached the pale reduced in numbers by skirmishes on the route. Elizabeth had selected for deputy Charles Blount, who like Raleigh had qualities to win her favor. But Robert Devreux earl of Essex, later brother-in-law of Blount and already uncle of his children, persuaded the queen that he had neither the means nor experience for the charge. This he secured for himself, to the satisfaction of his rivals who rejoiced at his removal from court. Sir Francis Bacon his friend wrote out considerations for his government, counselling toleration for a time not definite, English colonization, and measures to cut off hopes of foreign succor as well as for fomenting feuds in order to divide and conquer.

Essex, as viceroy, left London towards the end of March, 1599, with twenty thousand men, to which were added at his request, upon his departure, two regiments of veterans. Arriving at Dublin he seemed about to invade Ulster where O'Neil with Tyrconnel ready to aid stood prepared to receive him, but contrary to expectation, with seven thousand men and nine hundred horse started for Munster. Traversing Leix, Owen O'Moore with five hundred foot assailed his rear, killing many and taking much spoil in a defile, since, from the feathers which adorned the dismayed royalists, and which were scattered over the scene of their disaster, known as the Pass of Plumes. Essex laid siege to Cahir, Desmond, Leitrim and his brother William contriving to drive away Vinkle from the bridge leading to its gates and reinforce the garrison by fifty men. The walls at last shattered by artillery, notwithstanding the efforts of Desmond to embarrass the besiegers, James Butler who was in command sallied out with his troops and effected his escape. Essex went on to Limerick and thence to Askeaton to reinforce its ward.

On his march with this design, Desmond and Donal Maccarthy with five thousand men endeavored to block his progress. William Burke and Dermot O'Conor were posted on the plain, Walter Tyrrell and Thomas Plunket in the pass, through which his way laid. The plan to surround the royalists as directed by Lacy was disconcerted by Plunket disobeying orders, a charge he however denied. Essex led his army in four bodies under Thomond, Clanrickard and Mac Phieris, passing Burke and O'Conor unopposed by them as arranged, and then into the open plain by Tyrrell and Plunket, who also allowed him to pass unmolested. O'Connor astounded at what seemed treachery in Plunket attacked the enemy, but forced to yield ground joined Burke, and at Rosver in Adare for three hours they continued the combat, doing less damage to the foe now out of the pass where they might have been checked.

Essex effected his purpose in strengthening Askeaton, the catholics making a nocturnal attack upon his camp but without result. Monday on his march south they attacked him at Finita along his whole line, Henry brother of the late president being slain as also many more of the royalists, and some of the catholics. The battle lasted eight hours, till five in the afternoon, when Essex reached Croom. For six subsequent days all the way to Decies Desmond followed Essex constantly skirmishing and thinning his ranks. Reaching Dublin at the end of July, "his soldiers wearied, sickly and their numbers more than a man can believe diminished," the lord lieutenant was mortified to find that six hundred of his troops left to watch the O'Byrnes had during his absence been routed with terrible carnage. Fretting over these repeated disasters, aggravated by the recapture of Cahir, he court-martialled the officers, decimating the surviving soldiers of the detachment for not succeeding better then he had himself.

In explanation of his mischance he wrote the queen that the Irish troops were more powerful and better disciplined than her own, stronger in body and more perfect in the use of arms. He advised that the priests should be hunted down ; Bacon's policy of fomenting dissensions adopted ; coasts be guarded, garrisons planted and the country laid waste. An invasion of Leix and Offaly without success, though Morrison says he brake them with ease, still further diminished his numbers, and requesting reinforcements that he might proceed into Ulster another thousand were sent.

Preparing to march north, he had ordered Clifford to occupy and rebuild Sligo, to hold in check O'Donnel, whom Donogh O'Conor strove to persuade the chiefs of Connaught to desert. O'Donnel too much for him drove him with some loss into Colloony, where besieged he held out for forty days, but was about from famine to surrender, when the governor hastened his movements on Sligo to relieve him. He ordered Theobald Burke of the ships to carry by water from Galway, food, guns, lime and other material for the works, whilst he marched by land. O'Donnel apprised of his design left four hundred of his foot under Mac Sweeny Fanad and Mac William in charge of Sligo, O'Boyle with two hundred horse to prosecute the siege of Colloony, O'Doherty to occupy the Corlew mountain over which Clifford must come. In one of its passes narrow and obstructed, he posted three bands in ambuscade to check the foe in their advance, in another more open, O'Doherty and himself with two thousand foot that had never known defeat, spread their tents. Theobald of the ships with twenty vessels reached Sligo, but not daring to land awaited the arrival of Clifford, who with an equal force of chosen troops and three squadron of horse, with O'Conor Don, Mac Sweeny Tuath still irate with O'Donnel, and lord Dunkellin son of Clanrickard, with thirty-nine banners, three of them horse, marched from Athlone to Boyle.

O'Donnel at Ballyboy, who had amused himself while waiting his approach, in chasing the stag, ordered trees to be felled in the way as an obstacle for the foe and protection for himself, and selecting that for his battle field, encamped a mile beyond. The day before, the eve of the assumption, had been passed in confession, fasting and prayer, and in the morning which was cloudy and wet the sacrament was administered. Under the impression that the enemy would not advance in the rain, he kept quiet, whilst Mac Sweeny, concluding that he would not leave the shelter of his tents of skin in such weather, persuaded Clifford to push on. The governor had left his horse under Sir Griffin Markham at Boyle, as of no use on the mountains, and with his foot alone took possession of the unguarded pass. Scarcely had the sacred rite ended, when scouts came in to report to O'Donnel that the enemy had already passed the fallen trees. Ordering his army to take their food the better to fight, he reminded them that by the help of the mother of God they had ever conquered the heretic, how much more now since in her honor they had passed the previous day in fasting and that were celebrating her feast. In her honor they should fight with her enemies, and by her help again they would triumph.

With these words his soldiers kindling with renewed ardor for the coming conflict, he despatched Owen Mac Sweeny Tuath and the O'Gallaghers to check the advance of the royalists, till he should come up with the spearsmen. The enemy ascended the hill out of the pass on to even ground, when the rain ceasing the musketeers were hastened up by O'Donnel. There on equal footing in a hand to hand encounter, between combatants in the fire of youth, midst showers of balls, wounds were given and received. The musket-men of Tyrconnel were giving way, when their leaders reproached them for not doing their duty, or fighting as should the warriors of the virgin mother. Shame forced them back to the battle.

With incredible courage, with the utmost constancy and skill, the infantry fought on both sides with their firelocks. The royalists driven back on to the spearmen overwhelmed by a stream of bullets, wounded, surrounded in front and flank, thrice turned in a circle, at a loss which way they should go. O'Rourke to complete their confusion brought up nine score fresh men to the catholics, and as they came in sight the whole army of royalists turned and fled, strewing the field with their arms, the catholics in pursuit. O'Donnel hastening up with his spearsmen came late to the fight, and the devout historian, whose account we render from the latin, adds that had not Heaven helped, the royalists would not have been beaten.

Clifford beguiled by two Irish soldiers to whom he promised large reward for his safety, was pierced through the side with a lance, and Dunkellin barely escaped. The felled trees and obstructed pass, where they had left a portion of their arms and garments, embarrassed the fugitives. Half a mile from Boyle, Markham with his horse met the routed army, driving off their pursuers, who were chasing them in disorder, killing as they went. O'Rourke rallied the catholics, restored their array and becoming the assailant, Markham wounded in the hand and thigh ordered a retreat, the foe in hot chase hunting them to Boyle. There perished of the royalists, besides

Clifford and his kinsman Henry Radcliff, fourteen hundred of his men, nearly all English or of English race from Meath. The troops of Connaught familiar with the country effected their retreat. Arms were lost, and standards, drums, baggage and many garments. O'Neil on his way to help the Kinelconnel was two days' journey off. Theobald of the ships, learning the death of Clifford, sailed back to Galway. O'Connor submitted at discretion ; O'Donnel restored his principality of Sligo, loading him with gifts but binding him by oath never afterwards to aid the protestants.

When at last as August ended Essex approached O'Neil, that chief appeared in force and sent O'Hagan to propose a conference. Essex answered that he would meet him the next day in battle array, and after some slight skirmishes with horse and musketry, a parley took place. At Anagelart then Ballyclinch on the Lagan, O'Neil rode into the river, the viceroy remaining on the opposite bank. For an hour or more in conversation too confidential with an enemy, Essex betrayed his schemes and his pretensions. They parted to meet again on the eighth of September, each of them accompanied by six of his officers, when a truce was agreed upon till May unless terminated by either side upon fourteen days notice. Freedom of religion, from interference in other affairs, restitution of lands, officials natives, half the army Irishmen, the terms demanded as preliminaries to negotiation by Tyrone, the viceroy thought sufficiently reasonable, and promised to use his influence to obtain.

And what better could he do. But four thousand of all his grand army left, many of these deserted when ordered north. Ulster alone had six thousand shot and fifteen hundred horse ; Leinster and Meath, twenty-five hundred men ; Munster, fifty-three hundred ; Connaught, three thousand ; a force of nearly eighteen thousand warriors, to which the lords of the isles threatened to add two or three thousand more. English soldiers for the most part raw recruits, unwonted to cold and wet, poorly clad and ill fed, if better

70

armed were less expert in the use of their weapons. Some of the
bands were filled up with Irishmen, in others often a third. They
carried off the guns given them to kill their countrymen, more of
which they purchased from the faithless followers of the camp.
Essex had shown military genius at Cadiz. Realizing that numbers
without discipline did not make an army efficient, he yet felt obliged
to conceal his weakness. Clifford slain and his army annihilated,
had O'Neil gained another victory English rule would have been
at an end. That the chieftain also inclined to peace may be attributed
to the Kinelconnel being still engaged in Connaught, and a more
favorable conjuncture anticipated, which never came.

The queen nevertheless in her vexation with Essex, little disposed to
make allowances and provoked at his course, expressed her displeasure
in able but bitter phrase. Trusting to his hold upon her affections and
to her sign manual when appointed authorizing him to return to
her presence should he have cause, on the twenty-eighth of September, delegating his post to Loftus and Carew, he hastened to court,
and to the morning toilet of his ancient queen, who received him with
tenderness, but on second thought put him under arrest. After a hearing in June before eighteen commissioners, Bacon not proving a
judicious friend if an honest one, he was convicted of the charges, and
escaping to stir up a crazy rebellion, another tribunal showed him no
mercy, and on the twenty-fifth of February, 1601, he perished on
the scaffold.

XLIII.

REIGN OF ELIZABETH.—1558–1602.—(Continued.)

Prejudice is the besetting sin of historians. Persistent misrepresentation by modern writers of events at this period and of the motives which brought them about, can only be explained by the many important links that connect the present with the past. It cannot however be doubted that candor would prove the better policy to avert discontents at times seriously threatening public stability. No Englishman deserves the name who thinks less well of the northern chiefs for aiming at religious liberty or national independence. Their measures were prudent, their courage heroic, and if striving with inadequate means to compass laudable ends, imperial consolidation is not helped by futile efforts to tarnish their fame. So long as the truth is systematically kept out of view or intelligent minds disincline to understand and admit it, neither danger nor just ground for solicitude grows less.

The imprisonment of Essex was not encouraging for any peaceable solution of affairs, and Tyrone in November issued an able appeal to his countrymen to unite in defence of their faith. Philip III. now king of Spain sent assurances of aid. When the government of the pale alarmed at rumors afloat, demanded explanation of his preparations for war and other courses creating suspicion, Tyrone for answer gave notice that the truce was at an end. He informed Dermot O'Conor who visited him in December of his intention to repair to Holy Cross near Thurles in Tipperary, and leaving his country well guarded he started as the new year opened with three thousand men on this pilgrimage. He wasted as he went Delvin, the baron submitting, and also the possessions of Dillon, and passing by the gates of Athlone, encamped nine days at Fircall. After ravaging Ely to punish O'Carrol for slaying some Mac Mahons in his service, he visited the venerable abbey, still much of it remaining, and which for five centuries had been the repository of a fragment of the true cross sent by Paschal II. to its founder.

Recently Baranova had brought him from Spain substantial aid and friendly promises, perhaps the phœnix plume sent by Clement VIII. in recognition of his regal claims, to be followed up in April by a papal bull in confirmation, and the following year by pardons and indulgences and twenty-two thousand pieces of gold by Cerda to pay his soldiers. Had the country boldly proclaimed him king at Holycross, it might have slipped its yoke. But English catholics shrank from Irish rule, Irish chiefs from subordination to any one of their own number. They had some years before entered into a league of which Tyrone as acknowledged head corresponded with the disaffected. They had bound themselves never to make peace or war with the English unless all its members were included. No chief was to imperil the cause by standing out when the rest had submitted, or to expose himself to danger, by presuming out of any pride or presumption to spend himself in his own quarrel. These covenants had been acted upon with much consistency of purpose and consolidated resistance, but had failed to conquer an invincible repugnance to one man power. Tyrone, qualified for an authority needed as he knew by the country, bore patiently his disappointment.

Moving south leisurely, he spent part of February among the O'Dwyers and friendly Butlers, Ormond and Thomond threatening but keeping aloof. Here James, his earl of Desmond, joined him and they proceeded together by the cromlech of Oliol Olum, near Gilbally in Limerick, through Clangibbon and Fermoy, wasting Barry who in the correspondence that ensued reminded Tyrone of his English descent, and that his allegiance was due to the crown. Crossing the Lee they pitched their camp between that river and the Bandon, at Inniscartha, and there remained for twenty days. Thither came Donal Mac Carthy More and his competitor for land

and rule, and also many more of that name, but not Cormac lord of Muskerry. Donal had lost power, and Florence substituted by the sept through the influence of O'Sullivan Mor in his stead, was duly installed in his office and recognized by Tyrone. O'Donoghues and other chieftains of the south attended or sent gifts.

Maguire, while foraging towards Kinsale, accompanied by two of his attendants and his chaplain, met accidentally or was waylaid by Sir Warham St. Leger with sixty horse. Between them, besides public grounds of hostility, existed a rivalry, each being respectively regarded by his own people as their especial champion for valor and skill. The chief of Fermanagh did not consider it consistent with his dignity to fly or to surrender, and putting spurs to his steed rushed upon St. Leger who shot him with a pistol as he approached, and who was himself pierced through the casque by the spear of Maguire, which nearly severed his head. The chief, though his companions were also wounded, leaving his spear in the body of his antagonist, turned and cutting his way with his sword through the enemy, escaped to die as he reached the camp. Warham survived fifteen days. O'Neil grieving for the loss of his best and bravest officer, took pledges from the southern chiefs, promising soon to return, and authorizing Dermot O'Connor to levy two thousand men in his pay, proceeded homewards by a route west of Cashel. Ormond and Thomond, without disturbing his march, hovered near, but by the middle of April he was safe back in Tyrone.

It was time. Charles Blount, created when the war ended earl of Devonshire for his services, but then lord Mountjoy, more sensible than Essex, had been in February installed in his place. He verified Tyrone's scornful prediction that he would lose opportunities waiting for breakfast, and reached Mullingar too late to intercept his march, which by rapid strides the length of the island baffled deputy and Ormond and vexed the queen. Ormond and Thomond repaired to the vice-regal court, separately returning into

Munster. With the latter, Sir George Carew, appointed president of that province in the place of Norris, left the capital, Monday, seventh of April, 1600, attended for two miles on his way by all the grand functionaries, and proceeded with eight hundred men by Naas and Catherlough to Kilkenny. The day after their arrival, which was the tenth, Ormond invited his guests to accompany him after dinner to a conference appointed with Owen O'Moore the young chieftain of Leix, to take place at Corronneduff, upon the borders of Idough eight miles off.

Accordingly, when their noon-day repast was over, the party, miscellaneously composed of about forty persons, seventeen mounted troopers and a few lawyers and merchants armed with their swords and on hacknies, left the castle. An escort of two hundred foot, which must have retarded their movements unless sent in advance, were left to await their return two miles from the place of parley, a heath near a ravine, surrounded by scrubby trees and boggy grounds. Owen Mac Rory with his body-guard of pikemen promptly made his appearance, some five hundred of his clan well armed and appointed, with twenty horse, being in view beyond the ravine half a culverin shot distant. The conference had already lasted an hour without result, when Ormond urged by his companions to withdraw begged first to see Archer the jesuit to whom was chiefly ascribed the consolidation of catholic resistance to English rule.

Conversation warmed into discussion, and soon the earl losing his temper called the priest a traitor, reproving him for embroiling her majesty's subjects in rebellion under pretext of religion. The gestures of the disputants grew menacing, and when Archer raised his staff, the lookers on naturally interested drew nearer and crowded about the wranglers as if at a fair. Suspicious of unfair dealing, which they had reason in their recent history to fear, many of the O'Moores crossing the ravine likewise gathered round. Thomond begged

their chief to send them back, the president besought Ormond to
retire. As they turned to depart, the latter was drawn from his
horse and hurried off into the woods. Carew says the chief laid
hands upon himself, but their powerful chargers trampling down whoever came in their way, bore him and Thomond, wounded in the back
with a pike, out of the throng. The royalists, eager to secure the
priest as pledge for the safety of Ormond, rushed upon him but
were driven off by Cornelius O'Reilly. Skirmishing continued
till nightfall ended the combat, and the next day both parties had
disappeared.

That no treachery had been intended is abundantly manifest.
The men of Leix so largely outnumbered the royalists that they
could have easily cut them off. Two months the earl continued in
captivity pressed by the priest to return to the faith of his fathers,
and he either dissembled or else was half persuaded to do so. At the
request of Tyrone, he was liberated in June, giving the eldest sons
of twelve of his principal vassals as pledges for the payment of
three thousand pounds that he would not resent his capture. Owen
was slain, the pledges escaped, and no ransom was paid.

Meanwhile when the fugitives reached the castle, the countess and
her only child, a maiden of eighteen, were sore distressed. Ormond,*
though destined to survive fifteen years longer, dying quite blind in
1614, was already advanced in years and constantly exposed in the

* This tenth earl Thomas Duff, captured by O'Moore, is said to have been of great parts,
admirable judgment, vast experience and a prodigious memory, comely and graceful, and
from his dark complexion called by the queen her black husband. The flower of his
country, he kept the greatest house, used the greatest hospitality, and his valor, wisdom and
liberality made him known in many lands. He repaired Kilkenny and Carrick at great
expense, made a deer park at Earlsrags near the former place, where he founded a hospital, and also erected a castle near Holycross. Since 1546 he had held the earldom, and lived
beyond fourscore. As he lost his sight, according to Lodge, fifteen years before his death in
1614, this calamity must have overtaken him at this time when he was about seventy. His
son Thomas died without issue in 1605, and Elizabeth, the only survivor of the family, married Sir Robert Preston, created, 1614, earl of Desmond. Their only child, born 1615, married
her kinsman, grandson of Walter eleventh earl, James first duke of Ormond, 1607–1688.
The second duke their grandchild, 1651–1745, was attainted in 1715, but the earl of Arran
purchased his estates under an Act of Parliament, which are still held in part by the present
marquisses created in 1825. They derive from Richard of Kileash, brother of the first
duke, and their claim to the earldom was allowed on the ground that an English attainder
did not affect an Irish peerage.

field to danger, his death would involve a disputed succession. His next brother Edmund not restored in blood, his nephew, Walter of the rosaries, who eventually succeeded as eleventh earl, and lord Mountgarret had also their claims. Five hundred men left to protect the countess, the president reached Waterford on the sixteenth. Desmond at Youghall blocked his way to Cork with forces superior to his own, the whole army of Munster then consisting of but three thousand foot and two hundred horse. By recourse to one principal means of success, he contrived to induce Power and Fitzgerald, natural son of Decies, to desert the enemy and come in.

Whilst disposed to admit all that his biographer claims of ability for Florence MacCarthy, his natural desire to recover his wife's inheritance proved a fatal stumbling-block in the way of Irish consolidation. To become powerful and feared parallel instances pointed out as the path to success; and this was the loadstone that influenced the devious paths which proved as fatal to himself as to his country. His wife discouraged his vacillations and politic courses. She was personally attached to the queen and a favorite at court. He had been eleven years a prisoner, three in the Tower in a cell in which he could not stand upright. But neither his character nor his good sense were improved by adversity. It simply rendered him crafty and selfish. His principal armed resistance to the crown, he defended as warranted by unjust aggression against his own people. He had in some way obtained possession of the old Head of Kinsale, the inheritance of the DeCourcies. His own patrimony was not far removed, and this now suffered maraud, possibly on his part provoked, since as a new chief he may well have inclined to signalize his elevation by the customary hosting.

Just before the president reached Waterford, captains Flower and Bostock had been sent by the commissioners with twelve hundred foot and two hundred horse to burn and spoil in Carbery towards Rosse. They took thirty-seven men of note prisoners. Florence

with two thousand bonoghs under Dermot O'Conor, laid in wait
for them on their return, at Awnsby bridge mid-way between Cork
and Kinsale. They lay concealed in a glen on the north side of the
river, and on the south in a scrubby wood, when Bostock in advance
espied the gleam of their morions and turned back. Perceiving they
were discovered, they emerged from their covert and fell upon the
foragers, who fled to a ruined castle half a mile off. In the pursuit
Lane posted in ambush slew the brother of O'Conor as he passed.
The catholics reached Kinalmeaky that night and stayed two days
with their wounded. Both sides claimed the victory. The attention
of the enemy thus occupied, the president reached his capital, visiting
Barry as he went. Lacy for six hours fought with Slingby and four
hundred men freebooting towards Kilmallock, Redmond Burke and
six hundred men with one of the O'Dwyers, friendly to the queen.

With seven thousand able and well armed foes serving for bonaght
or as clansmen inside his province, and thrice that number without to
aid them, Carew resorted to craft. The white knight not long
before denounced by Fitzthomas, held to ransom by Burke, and preyed
upon by Ormond, was angry and sore, and yielded easily to his
blandishments; Condon and Barret to his menaces in order to escape depredation. Florence, notwithstanding his late battle at the
bridge, ventured under safe conduct to Shandon, and though objecting to giving his eldest son as pledge, lest by disaffecting his followers his wife's inheritance now nearly recovered should be lost, consented even to that if the queen would confirm his right to Clancarre,
bestow upon him the earldom or recognize him as chief, and allow
him three hundred men in her pay. Threatened with fire and sword
if he persisted in hostilities, time was proposed for consideration, he
promising meanwhile to remain neutral, furnish intelligence and perform underhand service.

Acknowledged Maccarthy Mor and chief of his name by Tyrone,
his defection neutralized fifteen hundred of his immediate followers, and

71

as many more dependents of its other branches.   It worked greater
prejudice to the catholics that he remained their ostensible friend.
Their leaders at a loss to account for his conduct, yet reposing faith
in his professions, remonstrated and demanded explanation, but were
not disposed to break with one who constituted an important element
of their strength.   Honesty would have proved his better policy, and
historians concur in the opinion that he merited his fate.   But his
duplicity, if not to be defended, grew out of his position, and was
of a character with that of the queen and her ministers.   It was not
without parallel in the case of Tyrone, who, as will be remembered,
in climbing the giddy heights of his ambition, played fast and loose.

Maccarthies no longer dangerous, Geraldines remained to be crushed.
Lands had been confiscated but not hearts, and their loyalty baulked
of its natural object in the protestant prisoner in the tower, cen-
tred on James Fitzthomas, rightful earl but for the irregular marriage
of his grandsire.*   Margaret, wife of O'Connor general of the bonoghs, yearned for the restoration of her captive brother to the earldom, and the president, an adept in intrigue, improved this feeling for
his own purposes.   Like the evil spirit in the garden, he tempted the
wife and she her husband, poor but for his pay, offering them a thousand pounds to kill the Sugan or betray him into his power.   About
the same time he bought one Nugent, also in the catholic service, to
kill John the Sugan's brother.

His march for Limerick, announced for the sixth of May, the
catholics collected in force to intercept, but their supplies exhausted
before he appeared, they dispersed.   Two weeks later, when the way
was clear, he left Cork for Mallow, and at Kilmallock the white knight,
who had requested time to recover his pledges, came in.   Possession
was taken as they went of Brough, abandoned by Lacy, of importance to keep open the road to Limerick, now for nearly two years

---

* The first wife of James, fourteenth earl, was granddaughter of his brother Maurice.
Such marriages, by dispensation, have been sanctioned by the catholic church.

impassable, and likewise to watch Lochguire, three miles off on an island not easily approached, where John Fitzthomas then lay. Carew reconnoitred the place as he passed, and at Limerick where he rested three days its warden, Owen Graem, from the north, left in charge by Tyrone, offered to betray it for sixty pounds. This sum paid to an emissary it is pleasant to think never reached the traitor.

Nugent was already at work. When the army had passed, John left the island for Aherlow, where his forces were encamped, with Nugent whom he trusted riding as his companion, but who dropping to the rear, when he supposed himself unobserved aimed a double loaded pistol at his back. Coppinger, also of the party, seasonably discovering what he was about, struck up the weapon, and at his cry of treason Nugent fled. His horse stumbling he was caught, and when hung the next day confessed his design had been to kill both brothers, alleging that others had been employed by Carew for a like purpose. James, when twelve months later a prisoner, declared that this unexpected treachery prevented his brother and himself from ever sleeping under the same roof, or appearing together at the head of their men, lest the destruction of both should prove disastrous to the cause.

His army refreshed, the president raided the Burkes, lords of Clanwilliam and half-brothers of Lacy, who unlike their haughty sires bowed in the dust before the satrap, to escape plunder by his locusts, a fate which overtook Owny. Visiting Thomond at Bunratty to concert future operations, an armed vessel came in with ordnance to reduce the castles on the river. O'Donnell down again in Connaught, eight hundred men were detailed to drive him out. The president placed the rest of his forces in garrison, a step which, with so little effected, occasioned surprise, but it was to afford O'Connor opportunity to seize the Sugan, not easy when their armies were massed and which separated for subsistence whenever their foes did the like. To further the plot, Carew had addressed James a letter acknowledging pretended communications from him and his brother, confirming his assurance of a liberal reward if they betrayed O'Connor as promised. Dermot contrived a conference on the eighteenth of June, with his colleague in command, when altercation purposely provoked between their officers as to the disposal of camp hides, James to appease the quarrel sent off his followers. Thus left powerless, Dermot denounced him as a traitor, producing the letter of Carew, alleged to have been intercepted, and sent him as prisoner of Tyrone to the castle of Ishin, removing thence his own wife and hostages to Ballyallinan, a castle of MacShyhy.

Dermot had overreached himself. False and base he distrusted his confederate and had insisted on pledges for his blood money, and was not willing to lose hold of his prisoner until it was paid. Two sons of the archbishop of Cashel and two Powers, foster-brothers of his wife, selected to avoid suspicion, had been placed in his keeping, and one of the latter he now sent to the president to meet her at Kilmallock to consummate their infamous bargain. Carew waited there a week, but meantime the Sugan had been rescued. His brother John, Lacy, Fitzmaurice and William Burke gathered their forces, from eighteen hundred to four thousand as differently stated, and forcing the warden to surrender Ishin, carried off James in triumph. They then besieged Dermot. The president marched to his relief, but when three miles off the castle capitulated, and strange to say, either deluded by the representation that the letter was without his connivance, or his command of the bonoghs made it prudent to dissemble, on his promises of fidelity Dermot was taken again into favor. The wits at court insisted that Carew had been duped. He went back discomfited to Limerick, and thence by Askeaton seventeen miles to reduce Glynn, harassed as he went by Desmond, who encamped within striking distance had Carew inclined. O'Flaherty and Macwilliam now proposed to be neutral for a price, and O'Connor Kerry and the knight of the valley tendered submission. It being intended, however, to occupy their castles of Glynn and Carrigophoyle which commanded the Shannon, their submission was declined.

On the fifth of July the army reached Glynn. This was a castle about one hundred feet square. Advantage was taken of a parley to land their guns and take a position of strength. Two days later the knight of the valley came in on safe conduct to the earl of Thomond, but standing upon conditions was commanded to depart. His son, six years old, Carew threatened to kill, and the child was actually placed upon the gabions as a mark from the castle wall, but removed before the battery opened its fire. It was probably designed as bravado or menace, but the president had a natural love for deeds of atrocity. The constable of the castle came also under safe conduct to persuade the besiegers to stay the attack as the catholic army was near, but without changing their purpose.

Incessant fire after two days effecting a breach into the cellar beneath the great hall, Flower, sergeant-major, with five companies rushed in, and from the turrets above commanded the donjon to which the garrison had withdrawn. A sally at night was attempted and two warders escaped, but the constable was slain. The assailants fired the tower door. It burnt for two hours, and as the smoke cleared away the defenders proffered terms, not accepted, of surrender. Power, Slingsby, Nevil, Harvey with hundreds of men filed up the winding staircase to the battlements, where after a desperate engagement thirty of the English were killed and wounded, eighty of the garrison being either thrown over into the water or slain, twenty-three of them followers of the lord of the castle.

The knight of the valley had not been in arms, but had tendered submission which had been rejected. If civil war existed it should not have involved non-combatants, and this wholesale massacre in repeated instances, of prisoners or men defending their homes, burnt or cut to pieces by order of the president, was outrage without palliation. The treachery of Dermot paralyzed catholic action. John O'Connor yielded Carrigophoyle four miles down the river, the strongest castle in Kerry, earl Donogh giving him another and thirteen ploughlands in

Thomond, where he remained passive till the Spaniards came. The bonoghs, eager for home, crossed the Shannon with Dermot O'Connor, the Burkes of Clanwilliam attacking them as they passed and slaying sixty of their number.

After reducing various smaller castles, the president, again in Limerick on the sixteenth of July, refreshed his forces for a week, when Florence, who had been in camp with Desmond, strove to persuade Talbot, lieutenant of Stack, to surrender to him Liscaghan. The president taking umbrage marched with a thousand men down the north shore of the Shannon, and at Carrigophoyle crossed the river, there six miles wide, to raid Clancarre. Both Desmond and Carew wrote the recreant Florence to take sides with them, but he chose to preserve his neutrality. Fitzmaurice, his chief castle of Lixnaw taken, died of vexation on the twelfth, and his son Thomas, eighteenth baron, succeeded. Tralee was seized and Rathown the episcopal abode. When the president was about to enter Kerry he remembered that four thousand men could be there arrayed against him. It also came to his knowledge that Florence was bringing about a matrimonial alliance between the Sugan and the sister of Cormac MacDermot, lord of Muskerry. Leaving the command to Sir Charles Wilmot, he started for Cork to circumvent them.

He learnt on his way that Florence had sent to Tyrone for the release of his brother-in-law Owen O'Sullivan Mor, who refusing to pay bonacht to Dermot O'Connor had been carried by him to the north. Florence had consented to his capture, though not openly for he owed to him wife and chieftainship. Owen was now needed to bring out the strength of Dunkerron. Lacy tendered submission, but Carew had lost faith in others, and it is difficult to believe Lacy could have been false to the catholics. The white knight, when Harvey burnt his town by mistake, and made war upon his son who protested, hurting sixty of his men, probably wished he had himself kept steadfast. Sir William Fitzgerald, knight of Kerry, refusing to entertain the Sugan at Dingle, and for this raided by his catholic neighbors, was received into favor. But when the new lord of Lixmaw through his brother-in-law, the earl of Thomond, proffered submission, the conditions demanded, he wrote, stood not with his conscience or honor.

His wife, Honora O'Brien, displayed at this time the fiery characteristics of her race, owing to her husband's integrity immunity from any misconstruction. Maurice Stack, of small statue but fierce and overbearing, had been dining with her and her brother Daniel, first viscount Clare, at her castle, when taking him aside for some object of importance after the repast was finished, some indignity, word or deed, provoked her resentment. Summoning her guard they stabbed him with their skeins, and the next day her husband hung the brother of Stack who was in his keeping. The nature of the provocation never transpired. The earl, who sided with the queen as she with the catholics, according to English writers, condemned the conduct of his sister, but if so it was probably either from prejudice or not to lose favor with the party whose cause he had espoused. She did not long survive for regret or repentance, if occasion there was for either, for this year going home into Thomond she died.

Carew meanwhile had given orders through Wilmot, that the garrisons should secure what they could of the harvest and destroy the rest, a course pursued at this time throughout Ireland, creating the famine which the next year effected its subjugation. The superiority of English arms being in artillery, for fear the guns left by Essex at Cahir which James Galdie, brother of its lord, occupied, should fall into the hands of the rebels, Carew sent the baron, with Comerford the justice, to gain possession, threatening to destroy the castle if his orders were disobeyed. Dermod Mac Owen, of Duhallo, of great wit and courage, was won over, and his chiefs Macawley and O'Keefe, and Ardart after nine days' defence reduced.

The president lived in perpetual dread of Florence, "a Saul taller than his fellows," vigorous, of great ability, and notwithstanding his vacillations influential at the English court and among his own people. His wife Ellen at times resented his hostility to the queen, and it is said even shut him or his warders out of castle Lough, her patrimonial abode on Killarney. Kerry, mountainous, rich in its forest wealth, and valleys thick with herds and grain, had hardly been reached by the war, and defended by thousands of a warlike race set English rule at defiance. The Sugan had agreed to relinquish to Florence all chief dues over Beare and Bantry, the famous beeves of Carbery extorted when Geraldines were strong, Killaha, Quirinie, Carrigowan and Balliny near Cork. Carew endeavored, by taking into favor Donal, Ellen's base brother, to disconcert their schemes.

Raleigh advised the queen to send over from his English prison, James Fitzgerald as earl, who arrived at Youghal on the eighteenth of October in charge of Price, but their reception at Cork was discouraging, for they could not obtain shelter or food. At Kilmallock, a vast concourse assembled to greet him upon his arrival on Saturday, showering upon him wheat and salt in token of welcome; but when the next morning he attended not chapel but church, he was discarded by all. His friend, Thomas Oge, warden of Castlemayne, yielded up that fortress at his request, which had hitherto been held for his rival, and through his means an alliance planned by his mother for his sister Joan* with O'Donnel, was averted. Another between himself and Lady Norris had been projected, but was prevented by the queen who chose to dispose of him as her ward.

Eager to see his brother-in-law, Dermot O'Connor requested safe conduct into Munster. When within twenty miles of Limerick he was set upon by Theobald of the ships, son of Grace O'Mally, who chased him into an old church, set it on fire, killing forty of his men

---

* Joan afterwards married Dermod O'Sullivan Beare.

driven out by the flames, and cutting off his head. Theobald to his
countrymen excused the act as fitting punishment for betraying the
Sugan to the English, and to the English as righteous retribution for
Dermot having killed his own kinsman Bourke near Limerick. It
cost him his men and his pay, but not many future preferments after
the reign of the queen was over.

Carew, restless when not destroying, improved also the law to
glut his craving. He started from Kilmallock in November to execute what he terms exemplary justice upon rebels decoyed into his
clutch. At Limerick and Cashel his gaol delivery was the scaffold,
as also at Clonmel, where he strove to persuade Ormond, summoned to confer with him, to permit him to sweep his palatinate
with fire and sword. The aged earl no longer rioting in bloodshed,
as once when Gerald was his foe, evaded this solicitation by undertaking himself the unwelcome task, from which he was set free by
the loss of his countess. The president, as a terror to harborers of
traitors, burnt house and harvest in Owney, killed all mankind
in Muskryquirk where some kind friend had succored Lacy, and
in Aherlow left neither man nor beast.

Capturing a lad who had been recently servant to the Sugan,
he induced him by threat or promise of reward to betray his
master, and guide Thornton, Thomond and Harvey to the place
where he lay in Drumfinnin. Sentinels on the watch seasonably
signalled their approach, and the hunted earl fled barefoot from his
ruined cabin, MacCarthy, papal bishop of Cork, his companion,
clad as a churl, passing by them unregarded. Carew boasted to
the council that not a castle in Munster, not five rebels of seven
thousand when he came, held out against the queen, a pious work
to use his own expression to be attributed to God. John Berkeley
helped on the good cause. He seized a thousand cows and two
hundred horses from Macawley for extending hospitality common in

72

the land to the heart broken fugitives, and slew many who had sought safety in the bogs.

The towns making merchandize of the war had thriven. They wisely selected lawyers for their magistrates for their better protection against arbitrary exactions. One of the garrison of Limerick stealing a hatchet and cast into prison, the president demanded his release. This Galway the mayor resisting as contrary to their chartered rights, he was arrested, carried off to a neighboring castle, fined four hundred pounds and the citizens compelled to choose another in his stead. The fine was expended in repairing the city walls, but this excessive punishment for a slight offence provoked ill will, and the more when their agent sent to the queen to remonstrate, returned in humiliation and without redress.

Of "fifteen* thousand swordsmen" the president found in Munster when he came, two thousand he had placed beneath the sod. The rest he had disarmed by promises or dissimulation, by his skill in stirring up strife or creating fear for life or land. Ten thousand lest they should be compromised by their foes, he says were knocking at the gate for pardons, of which four thousand were actually issued. Not an O'Connor the deputy boasted had been left in Offaly, not forty O'Moores in Leix, and the indomitable Tyrrell ranged a fugitive in Ulster. The mountain chiefs near the capital, and among them Daniel Spaniagh, the border septs towards the north, O'Hanlons, MacMahons and O'Reillys, Ferney and the Fewes were subjected, and a strong garrison in the Brenny ever ready like the spider to pounce upon its prey, enabled Maguire, fighting for the queen, to sweep high up towards Loughfoyle.

Meanwhile James Fitzthomas, once more powerful than any Geraldine among his predecessors in rule, still strong in the hearts of the adherents of his house, wandered as his uncle Gerald twenty years before, lurking in glen and mountain evading pursuit. His

---

* This is in the Falstaff vein, but green was not then the color of their coat.

courage buoyed up by Spanish promises of aid, with nothing to hope from president or queen. noble and trustful he accepted his lot, inspiring affection and never betrayed by any clansman in whom he placed faith. Diligent search, stimulated by the offer of four hundred pounds set upon his head, led to the capture of his garments, but his faithful harper and devoted priest baffled the efforts of his pursuers by their shrewd devices. The hiding places of his uncle about Tralee were too well known, and he ranged from one concealment to another among the hills near Aherlow and the borders of Ormond, very frequently seeking refuge in Clangibbon, the territory of Fitzgibbon the white knight.

That he had been seen thereabouts was reported to the president. By recourse to his wonted unscrupulous procedure Carew succeeded in effecting his capture through the white knight, who, though not friendly to the Sugan. would not willingly have betrayed him, if for no other reason than that it would have called down upon him the detestation of his neighbors. But the president, instigated by Barry who had some inveterate grudge against Fitzgibbon, held him responsible for producing the earl, and on the twenty-ninth of May, in a cavern many fathoms in depth in the mountains of Slewgort he was found. Conviction in Ireland of treason being indispensable to confiscation of lands there, this was not delayed, and other indictments were draughted to be sent over with him to the queen. As his brother John would have succeeded to his pretensions if he were executed, his life was spared, and for eight years he remained a captive in the tower.

His competitor for the earldom soon realized that as a protestant his chance of happiness was small even if restored. But this, if seriously intended, had not worked to expectation. All the while he remained in Munster, Richard Boyle, afterwards earl of Cork. then clerk of the council and already proprietor, by purchase from Raleigh, of forty thousand acres of the Desmond confiscations destined to enrich his numerous posterity, had been employed to keep the earl in constant view, report who had resort to him, indeed his every word and act. James by his long imprisonment in the tower was ill able to cope with one so astute. It certainly was not for Boyle's interests that the project of restoring the earldom with its ancient prerogatives should prosper, and it did not. And besides he was only one of a score, then even more powerful than himself, whose interests were identical. To remain longer in Ireland became so distasteful to James that he longed to be set free from annoyances to which he was daily subjected, preferring, as he wrote, obscurity with independence, to any such restraint. He urged the queen to allow him free range and suitable maintenance, or else an adequate support near herself, with a wife of her own selection.

When the estates of Fitzmaurice then in rebellion were offered him, he honorably declined them, and glad to escape, had gone back in April to await such provision as the queen would make for him in England. He did not long survive, dying in the tower, just as Kinsale fell a few months afterwards, it is said of poison. If the draught were mingled by undertakers who dreaded his restoration, not an uncommon experience in Geraldine history, and they thus lose their grants, deeds as atrocious for less motive in those days of darkness were not without example.

Florence still hung like a dark cloud over the head of the president. Spain, indignant at English interference with her provinces, humiliated by the defeat of the armada, menaced with preparation which, if exaggerated by rumor, caused reasonable alarm. If from a prevailing sense of the inutility of premature resistance Munster remained quiet, Carew knew it was from no attachment to English rule and that it only waited opportunity. Even at Blarney close by the gates of his capital there were indications of disaffection, and if Muskerry joined the Eoghenacht he might be shut up within its walls. Florence, acknowledged as chieftain, in the prime and vigor of life, of noble presence and vigorous mind, trained in the best schools of diplomacy and war, with all the qualities but disinterestedness to be the leader of men, needed but gold and guns to imperil the hold on Munster. If Spain had not been dilatory and had come a twelvemonth sooner, this hold might have been shaken off.

This wide-spread disaffection was sufficiently logical. The wrongs of Florence were not solitary instances. If the queen and her ministers had been more honest they would have confirmed to him his wife's inheritance, hers not only by Irish rules but by the law under which Elizabeth held her crown. The settlement made by her grandfather in due form, invalidating the surrender beyond the life of her father, vested in her in the extinction of all male heirs for several generations the family estates. If the rights of the other septs and chiefs to land and liberty of conscience had been respected, opposition to English rule would have died out and a vast loss of life and treasure, much shame and guilt been spared. But this was not the disposition of the times, and the unjustifiable policy of colonizing without regard to the birthright of the people, impoverishment which had led to frequent mortgages of estates to pay the cost of resistance, had raised up a crowd of anxious claimants powerful at court.

Too weak to resist or resent, the chief was compelled to dissemble in the trust that to him as to others better times might come. Desmond's reverses in Aherlow left no alternative but to temporize, and at the end of October, under protection, with forty mounted attendants he appeared at the gates of Mallow and received courteous welcome from the president. He promised his son as his pledge, but Carew having other hostages, he went as he came. It was charged against him later that whilst under the roof of the president he wrote the warden of Castlemagne not to surrender that stronghold; to Redmond Burke in Ely to hold out, for aid would soon reach him from Ulster. He was again at Mallow in January, promising to surrender his son and take out his pardon. But

Nicholas Brown and Pelham were claiming his estates under mortgage, and he was not till long after permitted to redeem them. It was rumored that two thousand of his followers were organized and armed in the west, and as he was leaving Cork for his own country he was arrested and thrown into prison, on the pretext that he had promised to take out his pardon, and that the period specified would be at an end in two weeks. In August with Desmond he was sent over to the queen to remain in captivity, much of it in close confinement, till his death.

XLIV.

REIGN OF ELIZABETH.—1558-1602.—(Continued.)

Whilst the president at the south, by fraud rather than by force, reduced Munster to seeming acquiescence in English rule, the deputy, aided by Dowera, Morrison and Chichester in Ulster, by Savage in the west, and Lambert in the centre of the kingdom, employed the same weapons for the like objects. As the operations of these two years, by the application of three-fourths of the whole revenue of the royal treasury, effectually undermined and overthrew what remained of Irish independence, they claim especial notice. If, instead of relying upon foreign assistance, Irishmen had trusted to their own hearts and hands, and united had placed the direction of affairs in O'Neil who merited their confidence, even if consolidation of the two nations had been inevitable, they might as the Scotch have dictated the terms. Although the course of events at either extremity of the island had a reciprocal effect in bringing them respectively about, and alike conduced to the final result of the struggle, they were sufficiently independent for separate treatment. We now return to Blount, whom we left soon after his installation as deputy in February, 1600, disappointed at not having intercepted Tyrone on his way home from Munster.

His instructions chiefly relating to details of administration, limited his forces to twelve thousand foot and twelve hundred horse. He was to provide hospitals for the sick, take care that the soldiers should not sell their arms or leave their colors, and plant garrisons in the rebel countries. He was empowered to protect or pardon such as submitted, even Tyrone himself if assured of his sincerity; one test of such sincerity, in all cases, to be having drawn blood one upon another. In dealing with the northern chiefs there should be no exaction of profit, but simply of military service; and there should be no interference with religion till they were more completely subjected. Cities and towns were to raise and maintain forces for their own protection. Surveys were to be made of their shipping against its being needed for public service, and knighthood was not to be conferred without the queen's sanction.

Morrison, loyal to his master, represents Blount as estimable not only in his private relations, but as an accomplished general and able statesman. Success is not invariably the safe criterion of desert, and the conquest consummated under his sway was as much due to his policy of corruption as to his military operations or extraordinary wisdom. Thrice during the summer he approached the borders of Tyrone: early in May, in the middle of July and of September. His object in May, to engage the attention of the chiefs whilst Sir Henry Dowera effected his landing at Loughfoyle, was crowned with success.

This long contemplated measure, bridling the north with a chain of forts, if not carried out to the extent originally designed, favored by circumstances, notwithstanding various discouragements, proved efficacious beyond expectation. Towards the end of April three thousand foot and two hundred horse, under Dowera, left Chesterton to meet at Knockfergus another thousand of veterans from the garrisons, one-fourth designed under Morgan for Ballyshannon. Their landing on Loughfoyle was effected on the sixteenth of May, without opposition, for the fighting men were in camp with Tyrone

engaged against the deputy. In six days Culmore, surrounded by
river and bog, open to the sea but not assailable by land, afforded
them shelter and security, marauds into Inishowen fuel and food.
Advanced posts were established, one at Aileach home of the ancient
kings, another at Derry soon to be famous, where an area of forty
acres occupied only by ruined abbey and church, castle and episcopal abode, strong by nature and now further strengthened by works
of earth and stone taken from its dilapidated buildings, became his
principal headquarters.

When known in Ulster what was intending, the chiefs gathered
their clans. They marched five thousand strong with all speed to
meet Blount, who, to divert their attention from this operation, had in
May advanced to Dundalk, and on Whit-Sunday by the Moyry pass
to Newry. Southampton, still in command of the cavalry, on his way
to join the deputy, five hundred men were despatched under Blayny for
his protection. Their united forces encountered at Four-mile-water,
a ford environed by dense forests in the midst of the pass, an
enemy, of whose numbers they could not judge, and who, when
Blount marched down from Newry to effect a junction with the
cavalry, changed their position and with little vigor charged the
rear of Southampton who gained some glory in beating them off.

Tyrone with no powder to spare, presuming Blount intended
to penetrate further into Ulster for coöperation with the northern army,
had burnt Armagh, dismantled Dungannon, and constructed lines three
miles in extent at Loughlurken, where he hoped to repeat his late
victory. But when news came from Chichester, at Carrickfergus,
that the invaders were already entrenched, the deputy moved his army
by the pass of Carlingford, that of Moyry being less safe, and dis-
tributing it among the garrisons went back to the capital. The
chiefs set free hastened north, but in vain sought to tempt Dowera
from his walls at Cullmore, who, his army already wasted one-fourth
in skirmish and by disease, had begged to be permitted to defer the

expedition to Ballyshannon. Upon representations home to this effect, the deputy being at the time too busily occupied elsewhere to spare him any troops for the purpose, his request was granted.

Not cess alone but many other oppressive exactions the pale had still to endure from the soldiers. Howth and Barnwal sent to complain, chided like their predecessors twenty years before for coming without consent of the deputy, obtained but little relief. But no sooner was the army in Ulster than the tribes around burst over it like a tempest sweeping it clean. Blount, his diversion effected for the northern expedition, hastened home. The harpies had flown, but, perhaps to retaliate, in July he went back to spoil the crops he had left growing. Chichester at Knockfergus, Morrison at Dundalk, Bagnal at Newry emulated his example, not sparing a blade of grass they could destroy. Two of the MacMahons proffered submission, granted to each on condition he brought the other's head. Maguire came in and O'Connor Roe.

Early in July, Lambert with fourteen hundred men had relieved Phillipstown and planted a garrison at Togher to keep open its communications, and on the twelfth of August the deputy, upon his return from his maraud towards the borders of Tyrone, proceeding west, joined him on the sixteenth, both fighting, burning and destroying as they marched to meet. The next day they reached a dangerous pass to the magazines of Leix, where the foe in ambush let the van pass by and attacked the deputy. One hundred marksmen, Morrison relates, had been instructed by Tyrrell to shoot the general, whose horse was killed under him. O'Moore fell, and with him for a long period of years the power of his country to resist the yoke.

Ripening harvests, ten thousand pounds worth in a day, ruthlessly ravaged, "fields fenced and excellently tilled, towns frequently inhabited, both highways and paths well beaten, because until now beyond reach of the war," Leix was utterly wasted and left a desolation. Lambert spoiled Daniel Spagniah of a thousand cows and half

73

as many horses. Savage, governor of Connaught, strove in vain to join the deputy, but Keating came in and Kellies and Lalors, who holding Ormond's pledges gave them up to avert like depredations.

Royal missives to redress the abuses in the pale awaited the deputy, whose reply to Cecil silenced reproach. He was ordered to offer two thousand pounds for Tyrone alive, half as much for his head. But one of his countrymen could be tempted, and that his kinsman Henry Oge, by offer of the earldom. When an Englishman employed by the deputy to assassinate him gained his presence, the chieftain was too carefully guarded by his devoted followers to be endangered.

With no guns to batter down stone walls, and anticipating a more favorable conjuncture when the enemy was further reduced and straitened, O'Donnel impatient at enforced inactivity went down into Connaught. Brian O'Rourke, Donogh O'Conor Sligo, Hugh O'Conor Roe, Conor Mac Dermot of Moylurg, Mac William, Theobald son of Walter, joined them at Ballimote with their forces. Their march through Roscommon, Kiltartan of the O'Shaugnessys, by the O'Gradys to the Fergus was unopposed. His detachments ravaged from Kirwan's Crag to Balligowan. "Many a feast fit for a goodly gentleman or for the lord of a territory, was enjoyed at night in Thomond, under shelter of a shrubbery or at the side of a bush." Mansions and habitations were given to the flames, the clouds of smoke and vapor that marked their progress obscuring their way, which extended to within four miles of the gates of Galway. At the hill of the White Horse, between that city and Kilcolgan, the prey was divided and after a grand banquet the chiefs separated. O'Donnel with four hundred men proceeded to Loughrea, the chief residence of the earls of Clanrickard, whose territory he wasted, and then returned by Corren to Ballimote, and in September, home.

Sir Arthur O'Neil, son of Turlogh Lenagh, also promised the earldom of Tyrone, joined Dowera in June. He advised a maraud upon O'Kane across the lough. It was carried out successfully by Chamberlain, slain as the month ended in another battle with O'Doherty who had attacked Aileach. Early in July eight hundred men landing at Dunalong fortified the place, skirmishing with Tyrone whose camp lay two miles off. Maelmora MacSweeney in some moment of discontent had deserted his sept and gone over to London, and sent out with the expedition had command of one hundred English soldiers. Returning to his natural allegiance, O'Donnell upon his information swept off two hundred horses from the neighborhood of the fort. Dowera started in pursuit, and charging the marauders fell struck by a staff from his saddle, stunned by the blow. When three weeks later he counted his men, not one in five was fit for service.

MacSweeny, sent to Dublin to be punished for his treachery, evaded his guard, gaining the deck through a hatch left open to set beer, and leaping into the sea swam ashore. In August Rory, brother of the O'Kane, bringing meat to Culmore, requested command of eight hundred men for some notable service. Sir Arthur O'Neil at first was disposed to trust him, but his faith soon shaken put the general on his guard. The day after, Rory appearing at the waterside opposite the fort, offered ransom for two of his followers left in pledge for his fidelity, threatening that no Englishman in his power should be spared if harm came to them. For answer a gibbet was ordered to be prepared and his hostages hung up before his eyes.

Winter set in early for men unprovided against its rigors. Worn out by continuous labor and with but six days' provision left, the chiefs offered them safe passage home, and when they declined assailed their works. It was without effect, and the day after arrived supplies, six hundred men with frames and materials for two houses of which they stood greatly in need. Early in October, Nial Garve next in influence with the Kinelconnel to the chief, at Dowera's solicitation, and under his instructions promised all Tyrconnel if he would abjure his allegiance, came in and delivered up Lifford placed in his charge. The castle, dismantled, was repaired and rendered tenable.

When O'Donnel, again employed in extending his authority in Connaught and battling with Clanrickard and Thomond, heard of this desertion he hurried back. Several encounters took place near the castle which was strongly garrisoned by a thousand English soldiers. In one of them, Manus, brother of O'Donnell, being about to slay Nial Garve, Owen O'Gallagher fended off the blow through hereditary loyalty to the family of his chieftain, a sentiment his kinsman Cornelius did not share, for he slew Manus and was hung for it by O'Donnell. Rory, brother of Manus, roydamma of Tyrconnel and afterwards its earl, rushed lance in rest upon Nial, the head of whose charger thrown up by the bridle received the fatal blow intended for its rider.

" Woe is me," saith the chronicler, " that these heroes of Kinelconnel had not been united, for whilst at peace among themselves they were not driven from their territories." The English, their commander Heath mortally wounded, withdrew to Lifford, sustaining considerable loss on the way. The chieftain greatly grieved, hastened to the side of his dying brother, who, borne on a litter to Donegal, lingered for a week. Repenting his pride and evil thoughts, he forgave the man who had inflicted the fatal wound, declaring that he himself gave the first blow. Before the year ended, his father Hugh, then very aged, who, after twenty-six years of rule, had abdicated in favor of his son, eight years before, was also interred in the ancestral burial-place at Donegal, where the previous June had been deposited the remains of Joan Maguire, mother of Tyrone. She is eulogized by the chroniclers as " the pillar of support and maintenance of the indigent and mighty, of poets and exiles, of widows and orphans, of the clergy and men of science, the head of counsel and advice to the gentlemen and chiefs of Ulster, demure, womanly, devout, charitable, meek, benignant, with pure piety, the love of God and her neighbors."

Frequent reinforcements from home made good the waste from battle and disease. Dowcra could now muster an effective force of three thousand men. The southern army was as strong, and nine thousand remained under the deputy for garrisons and field operations. With half he encamped, on the fifteenth of September, at Faughard, and there lay several weeks "drenched to the skin by continual rains, storms blowing down his tents." He knew well, as Morrison relates, to guard himself from the weather by many garments. He was also provident of his men, and his hospitals and magazines were under cover at Dundalk three miles off. Tyrone, in the Moyry pass, was less favorably placed. His clansmen were without shelter and often famishing. To that they were used; but with no heavy guns, and scant ammunition for their matchlocks, they repulsed with difficulty the assaults of an enemy who could choose his own time for attack. On the eighth of October they were sore pressed and driven out of their works. Weakened by the defection of Sir Arthur O'Neil and his brothers, many of his best soldiers about Loughfoyle protecting their own neighborhoods from raids, O'Donnell but recently hurried home from Connaught to obviate the consequences of Nial's treachery, Tyrone not having men to lose or powder to waste without result, abandoned the pass.

The deputy, kept apprised of his movements by scouts, spies and perhaps traitors in his camp, learning that the pass was left unguarded, the twenty-first took possession of it, and levelling the entrenchments and cutting down the trees on either side, passed through to Newry where he rested his troops. Again advancing, on the second of November, eight miles towards Armagh, he there erected or rebuilt a fort upon a promontory surrounded by bogs, woods and the river. The spot had been selected for the purpose by Norris, under whom Blount had served, and by whose name it was called. Tyrone obstructed the work as far as he was able by constant skirmishes with detachments collecting material, but it was completed in a week, and the sergeant-major Blayney left in charge with four hundred men. It had been intended to fortify Armagh, eight miles beyond, but its

distance from the base of supplies and numerous garrison required
to hold it, rendered it inexpedient.

Shortening days and tempests increasing in violence, discouraging
further operations in the field with so large a force to feed and keep
effective, the deputy proclaiming a reward of two thousand pounds
for Tyrone alive, half that amount for his head, left Newry for his
march to the pale. Instead of returning by the Moyry pass, through
which he would have had to fight his way, he chose for his route the
pass of Carlingford, at which place had been collected supplies of
which his army stood in need. This pass terminating at its southerly end some half a dozen miles from Dundalk, led along the coast
and part of the way consisted of a beach between the mountains and
the sea, merely wide enough in some places for seven men to walk
abreast when the tide was out, and which became wholly impassable
when it was up; at which time a road through the forest, narrow
and deep, served for ordinary travel. Midway of the pass the hills
receded from the shore leaving an open space, encircled on the west
by the forests which covered the sides of the mountain, and bounded
on the north by a stream which sought its outlet across the beach.
The natural features of the scenery bear striking resemblance to the
description given by Grote of the more famous pass where Leonidas
and his three hundred Spartans for a while stayed twenty centuries
before Xerxes and his hosts. That shore ended in marshes bordering
on the gulf, the Carlingford beaches opened directly on the sea.

The royalists reached, on the twelfth, a larger stream above called
the Narrow-water, swollen by autumn rains, which the infantry
immediately crossed, the cavalry and gunners being sent round by
the Faddome, a ford higher up. Two days the men had fasted, but
the next morning refreshed by provisions, chiefly consisting of bread
and butter sent by water from Carlingford, the army resumed its
way, starting early that the tide might not impede their progress.
They had observed on the previous day their enemies crossing the

hills, and expected that their march would be harassed if not blocked
by them where the ground served. Tyrone, surprised when he learnt
of the change of route, hastened by secret paths to gain the Carlingford Pace. Little time was left for constructing lines of defence, or
under circumstances wholly unexpected, to prepare for an engagement with an army vastly superior in numbers to his own, better
armed, in perfect array, and organized for the occasion. Entrenchments were thrown up in front of the wood, which, except along the
sea, circled the open space. The small stream which bounded it on
the north served for a moat, and a barricado hastily constructed
along its southerly limits and extending from the water some distance
into the wood, constituted a formidable barrier if bravely defended.

His army about equalled in numbers that of Thermopylæ, including the auxiliaries. Both were less than they should have been in
consequence of the defection of their respective countrymen. Many
of the Greeks were in attendance on their sacred games. These the
Irish once had at Tailtan or the Curragh, which English occupation
had brought to an end. But many of them were engaged elsewhere
in military service. Both battles were bravely contested; but English foes were of tougher material than Medes or Persians, and
the superiority of arms was reversed. Tyrone drew up his infantry
and cavalry on the open space awaiting the coming of the hostile
columns, which, that day, consisted of two bodies, van and rear, each
two thousand strong, under experienced commanders, Berry, St.
Lawrence, Morrison and Bagnal. They soon appeared and crossed
the stream, though not without opposition. But when they reached
the plain the catholic army had disappeared from sight, the horse
into the forests, the foot behind their entrenchments, whence they
poured volley after volley in rapid succession into the dense ranks of
their assailants.

Many fell, but the English had learned much since their defeat at
Glenmalure, in forcing their way through defiles or dealing with

ambuscades. Such a contingency had already been provided for, and three strong detachments selected from the rest, under Billings, Esmond and Constable, rushed without hesitation at the several defences at the points assigned to them. The catholics did their best with pike and sword when their powder was expended, or the close struggle prevented reloading, but overwhelmed by numbers finally gave way and abandoned even the barricade lest their retreat should be cut off. Their chief directed their movements from an eminence on the edge of the wood, beneath which the fight was most hotly and fiercely contested, and an officer on whose shoulder he leant fell mortally wounded by a ball, intended for himself, fired by Blount's own henchman at his command.

The cavalry, retiring through the woods, gained the rear of the enemy, composed of Irish auxiliaries mounted, where Bagnal the marshal commanded. Caulfield, Constable and young Blount, despatched to strengthen what is apt to offer a vulnerable point for attack, maintained for half an hour the combat with them with varied success, when the catholic army emerging from the woods into a plain, were set upon by Davers and broke. This ended the battle, the royalists hastening their steps towards Dundalk, the catholics back to the north. Different accounts transmitted of the loss sustained on either side, lead to the conclusion that it was about equal, two hundred each. The catholics, in the campaign, lost eight hundred that ill could be spared; the royalist writers estimate their own killed and wounded at six hundred, soon made good by the cure of the hurt, or fresh recruits. Among the prisoners, Cormac, nephew of Tyrone and his designated successor as chief, fell into the hands of the deputy, who refused three thousand pounds offered for his ransom. Sad to relate, many Irish catholics fought that day against their own side, and one of them Conor Roe Maguire, whose valiant predecessor not long before had fallen, as related, in combat mutually deadly with St. Leger. The deputy provided winter quar-

ters for his army, and on the seventeenth, repaired to the capital in
great glory and honor. The queen wrote in terms of peculiar en-
dearment that he must never doubt her affection, or heed what ill
nature might say to his prejudice. *

Whilst the army was absent at the north, the neighboring septs
kept the suburbs of Dublin alarmed by frequent raids. Tyrrell, with
forces from the north, devastated Kildare, Carlow and Tipperary,
taking castles, prisoners and spoil, creating great havoc. The deputy
after a few weeks of official duty, again took the field. Giving
out that Leix and Ophaly were his objective points, he speedily
crossed the snow covered mountains to the abode of Phelim, chief
of the O'Byrnes, who escaped into the woods but left his family and
Christmas repast to the deputy. Twenty days were spent in wasting Ranelagh and Cashry, herds, houses and corn. Planting garrisons at Wicklow and Tullogh, Blount visited Kildare, then deserted,
Maynooth, occupied by Mabel the ancient countess of Kildare, and
the castle of Trim which he chose for his own abode. The next
month he passed through Meath to Athlone, tarrying as the guest of
Trimlestown, Delvin and Dillon, pressing heavily on their hospitality
as his escort consisted of five hundred men. He wrote Carew urgently for a thousand more, which the president might well spare,
since he held as pledges for the peace of his province the child or
next of kin of nearly all its chieftains, and recognizances from the
less powerful. On the nineteenth of March he reached Denoar, the
castle of Mageoghan, and after driving Tyrrell out of his fastnesses
into the borders of Leix, where he in vain endeavored to capture
him, he wasted Ferney, and four weeks later was upon his return
from Drogheda to the capital. By his activity, and that in winter,
he had disproved Tyrone's prediction of his military inaptitude, and
deserved the high estimate formed of his generalship by English
writers.

* She addressed him as her " dear kitchen maid."

74

The border chiefs exposed to aggression from the pale, with the sanction of Tyrone, submitted to the deputy, who, upon his return to Dublin, entertained them at the feast of St. George. O'Hanlon, Turlogh of the Fews, Ever MacCooly chief of Ferney, Daniel Spaniagh of the Cavanaghs, Felim O'Byrne, to reciprocate his Christmas banquet, and other chiefs were his guests; his colonels and captains serving the meal or tending upon the table. Blount, as representative of royalty on this state occasion, perhaps hoped to conciliate respect for authority, by such an example of subservience to the crown. It probably had its effect in flattering the pride of chieftains welcomed as equals of sovereignity. Could they have read the correspondence of the period and known that this welcome was one to hospitable graves, that in the field their clansmen were exposed to especial danger to thin their numbers, and that their host advised the queen to send them into foreign service, inasmuch as they could not there become better soldiers, but would in all likelihood perish and never return to plague her, they would have taken less pleasure in these festive splendors.

The destruction of the crops was already working its purpose. Before the year was over, families were perishing from famine, dying with their mouths green from the nettles and weeds on which they endeavored to appease their hunger. In the hope of quickening the work the queen, with Cecil to advise, called in all the coin of the English or debased Irish standard, substituting two hundred thousand pounds of what was greatly inferior in value, and which from doubt of what it actually was worth soon ceased to be taken even at that. The army first suffered, then the tradesmen. Confidence at an end in money, interchange of commodities one for another grew sluggish, and trade lost its animation. It wrought even greater prejudice to its inventors than those against whom it was aimed, for Irish trade with foreign lands was less interrupted, and Spanish gold extensively circulated through the seaports. But that it con_ tributed with other diabolical measures of the crown to create the wide-spread distress which crippled resistance, seems generally admitted.

Arthur O'Neil derived no personal advantage from betraying his country for his own aggrandizement. Fever killed him in October, and Turlogh his son accepted by government as heir to his promised reward when the war ended was forgotten, and Hugh remained undisturbed. Nial obtained no better treatment, for set aside on the pretext that he had swerved from his obedience, Rory succeeding his brother red Hugh, after his death, became earl of Tyrconnel. Nial deserved well his designation of rough and often gave offence. O'Donnel aware of his unpopularity, and thinking his enemies all venal, for he had bought a deputy himself when regaining his liberty, sent Hugh and Phelim Macdavid to Culmore with wares to dispose of, instructed if opportunity offered to propose to Alford in command to give up the place with Nial in it, for a large pension from Spain, with money and a gold chain in hand. Dowera received the chain, but the chief discovered in season that the trap was set for himself.

John Doherty dying at Christmas, O'Donnel, according to laws of tanistry, recognized his brother Phelim as chief, neglecting his son Cahir to the great indignation of the Macdavids by whom he had been bred and fostered. Notwithstanding their abortive intrigue with Alford they agreed with Dowera that if Cahir were confirmed as chief and made independent of O'Donnel, they and all they could influence would do good service. The promise was made, the services rendered and faith broken. Absolving Inishowen from fealty to Tyrconnel still further exasperated the irascible Nial. That was also his rightful inheritance, and he claimed into Tyrone, Fermanagh and Connaught, and whatever appertained to his chieftainry.

MacSweeney Fanad, separated by an arm of the sea from O'Doherty, spoiled by the royalists of a thousand cows, professed allegiance to recover them. Dowera, helped by Nial, reduced as the spring opened,

castle Derg in Tyrone. O'Donnel, in May, with fifteen hundred men
hoping to take the enemy unprepared, invaded Inishowen where the
partisans of Cahir had in guard at Binnen, on a tongue of land jut-
ting out towards Scotland and protected by the old castle of Cargan,
three thousand head of cattle belonging principally to the forts.
Contingents from Connaught declining to take their appointed place
in the front of his battle array, the chief with his own men broke
into the defences of the enemy. They contrived to escape to where
their cattle and men were defended by heavy guns and strong walls.
His own force reduced by desertion of his followers and powerless
against them without artillery, O'Donnel disappeared.

Still, whilst Tyrconnel could at will raid the west for food, or
join the Spaniards now expected there or further south in force,
the urgency of some stronghold, such as Ballyshannon, to clip his
wings became more than ever apparent. The country around
swarmed with doughty warriors. O'Rourke with eight hundred,
Redmond Burke with six hundred, O'Malleys and O'Flahertys as
strong, awaited in arms the signal to combine their colors. It had
not been given, and they were far apart when Flower despatched
by the deputy at an opportune moment. gathered on his way the
hostings of Thomond and Clanrickard, and in an encounter at
Quin, Teigue O'Brien and the MacWilliam, son of the black abbot,
were slain. Carew with the rest of his army lined the stream to
Athlone, and when the fugitives short of food, fearing to be
hemmed in by a superior force, were fighting their way down to
the boats of O'Madden to cross, they found their path blocked, and
on the eighteenth of May in passing over the Suck two hundred
were drowned and much of their baggage and munition lost. Disheartened the clansmen dispersed to their homes; the stranger chiefs
with their array shrivelling up under disaster, sought safety with
friends or in concealment. The country clear, Boyle and Athlone
were strengthened to facilitate the main design as the prospect
improved.

In May, Newton four miles from Lifford, another month Ainough
castle of the O'Kanes, were occupied, both the year after recovered
by the catholics, and in July the deputy sent for Dowcra to hasten
to meet him at the Blackwater, who having no matches for his matchlocks could not go. Tyrconnel and his chiefs lying in wait for his
coming had left the abbey of Donegal, near the sea, unprotected.
Nial Garve with five hundred English soldiers and other troops was
sent to take it. The deputy retiring, O'Donnel laid siege to the abbey
which on the sixteenth of September took fire. The garrison removed
food and powder to a corner out of reach of the flames which raged
through the night, the fight unremitted, and when the moment
seemed ripe O'Donnel burst in. The defenders fought bravely;
nearly a thousand perished. The catholics delaying to take possession of the burning building, they escaped by a hidden way to a
smaller monastery near, which they defended. Clanrickard sought
to raise the siege by an inroad upon Elphin, but O'Donnel went
to meet him and the earl went home. The Ulster chiefs in May
had sent O'Rourk, Leitrim and Duhallo with more than a thousand
men to help Desmond. Duhallo was slain by a ball from the way-
side, and it being rumored that Desmond was captured they stopped.
Clanrickard attacked them and died within fifteen days, it is said, of
wounds received in the combat. His son Richard, the fourth earl,
succeeded,* and it was him that O'Donnel drove home.

Eager to be doing, perhaps to keep them effective, Blount with
three thousand men on the twenty-fifth of May had marched to Faughard and constructed a fort. Three weeks later he proceeded by the

---

* Ulick, third earl, besides his daughter Honora, who married Malby, had by his wife
Margaret Fitzallen, whom he married in 1564, five sons, who grew to manhood. Thomas,
the third, commanded fifteen hundred foot in the army of Elizabeth; William, the fourth,
whose wife was daughter of Sir James MacSorleboy MacDonnel, was father of Richard,
the sixth earl, who died 1666, and of William the seventh, in 1683; John, the fifth, viscount
Clanmorris, died 1635. Richard, the second son, who succeeded his father as fourth earl,
called of Kinsale, from his services at the siege, married Frances Walsingham, widow of
Philip Sydney, killed at Zutphen, and of Robert, earl of Essex, beheaded Feb. 1601. His
son, Ulick, 1604-1657, created marquis 1644, played an important part in the Cromwellian
wars. He left an only child, Margaret, wife of lord Muskerry, killed in the sea-fight of
1665, mother of Charles, second earl of Clancarthy, who died young in 1666.

Moyry pass to Newry; thence he marched east into the territory of
Evagh MacGuinness, planting a garrison under Morrison at Lecale.
Seven miles beyond, the fortress of Dundrum, considered impregnable,
was surrendered by Phelim O'Neil, and he passed on through the
country of MacCartan, by Downpatrick, six miles to Ardglas.
Here he relieved Jordan who, for three years, had been shut up in
the castle.   Passing through Russeltown he encamped at Blackstalf,
and thence on the nineteenth marched by Five-mile-church to Car-
rickbane, north of Newry.   Tyrone occasionally appeared in sight,
but not opposing, probably holding himself in reserve against the
Spaniards came.

The fourteenth of July, the deputy at the Blackwater wrote Dowera,
as mentioned above, to join him from Derry.   Dowera came down
within sixteen miles on the north of Dungannon.   Blount approached
it somewhat nearer from the south.   It was too well defended for
successful attack, and the catholic authorities say he sustained a
severe repulse when he attempted it.   For want of matches Dowera
could come no nearer.   Tyrone, avoiding a pitched battle, kept aloof.
Skirmishes occasionally occurred, and in one Peter Lacy was killed.
On the twenty-second of August, the deputy was still at Newry, and
a few days later at Millifont, on his way to meet the council at
Trim.   On the fifteenth of September at Kilkenny, in daily expectation of the arrival of the Spaniards, he organized his army, largely
reinforced from England, to oppose them.   Three thousand he had
left at the north, to watch and block the movements of Tyrone.

XLV.

REIGN OF ELIZABETH.—1558–1602.—(Continued.)

The end approached. Rumors of succor from Spain were rife in the seaports, and assuming definite form occupy considerable space in correspondence preserved. Tyrone and Tyrconnel had proceeded together at Christmas to the western shores, to receive and divide gold and munitions of war, promise of more to follow with an army to aid. But absolute monarchies, if sufficiently arbitrary, are not always very prompt or energetic. Philip was easily beaten by Cecil in the game of European diplomacy. False reports purposely set afloat and industriously circulated, took time for contradiction, and the king, however eager to resent or retaliate interference with his own provinces, on the part of the queen and the protestants, was engrossed either with the duties and pleasures of his court, or with the affairs of his extensive dominions.

His subordinates, with their own objects to be furthered by delay, procrastinated where they could, and preparations for the Irish expedition grew fitful and sluggish. Vessels were equipped, food and arms collected, ten thousand troops levied or organized; but these extensive armaments melted away, diverted to other purposes, the men perishing by disease or wearied of the service deserting. Their place was to be supplied, and new recruits to be drilled and disciplined. As the case with the armada, the fitting moment flitted by unimproved. When the fleet sailed the force it carried was grossly inadequate to the undertaking, and when, after being shattered by storms on the ocean, the remnant reached the Irish coast and landed less than three thousand men, with a few small guns, an expression of utter disappointment the chiefs, who had long been fed with sanguine expectations of achieving independence through Spanish help, could hardly restrain.

What followed is variously represented by the authorities on either side. We follow principally the catholic historian of the war, 1587–1602, whose work, though not translated from the Latin, rests upon relations made to him by the leaders who took part, especially by his own father, one of the most efficient of them all. It has been generally accepted as a faithful account of what actually occurred. Whatever else exists available, Carew, Morrison and the calendars, has been compared with his statements, and where proceeding from sources of information not within his reach, has been interwoven in the narrative.

Early summer had found the expedition in readiness to take its departure under protection of a fleet, when peremptory orders came to the admiral, Brochero, to proceed forthwith to Terceira with his men-of-war, and convoy home the American treasure ships. Upon his return fleet and army rendezvoused at Lisbon, the troops, thirty-five hundred in number, in transports under command of Juan de Aquila, who had made many blunders and whose military record was not brilliant. There were forty-five ships in all, and when in mid-ocean, overtaken by heavy storms, they were dispersed. Seven vessels under Zubiar driven back, took refuge in Corunna. The rest gathering to the flagship, reached Kinsale on the twenty-third of September. Its harbor at the mouth of the Blackwater opened to the south, guarded on the east by the castle of Rincorran, on the west by the Castle-ni-Park, both of them separated from the town by the river. Had these strongholds been properly armed and garrisoned, approach from the sea would have been more difficult.

The town had greatly suffered in the Desmond wars. It contained about two hundred houses, several castles and churches, and was environed by hills of no great elevation. Its shattered walls poorly reconstructed, could afford little resistance to heavy guns. An island in the harbor might have been fortified, but its communications with the main were liable to interruption by a hostile fleet, and fresh

water could only be procured in sufficient quantity by pinnaces sent
up into the country. North of the town rose an eminence called the
Spittal, available to those who occupied it for assailing or defending
the place, for which latter purpose the river also proved of service.
The English garrison, consisting of about fifty men under Saxey, were
withdrawn to Cork upon arrival of the Spaniards. Aquila disembarking, marched his men under forty captains into the place, at the gates
of which they were cordially welcomed by the inhabitants, staunch
catholics, who put them in full possession of its defences. The commander, led to expect large and immediate accessions from home and
the neighboring septs, and to take the field without delay, made little
effort to strengthen the works. Four small guns were landed, as
also their supplies in much haste from the fleet, when it sailed away
to avoid attack for which it was ill prepared. A battalion with one
of these guns occupied Rincorran, but there was a deficiency of ordnance which by some fatality had been laden upon the ships blown
home by the storm, and their heavy burden probably explains their
not proceeding with the rest.

Aquila, and Ovieto, archbishop of Dublin, who accompanied him,
were not always of one mind, and the former possibly was not the
least in fault. His temper, irascible and unreasonable, offended and
discouraged the few chiefs who responded with alacrity to his call.
Donal Coom O'Sullivan,* prince of Beare and Bantry, sent him word
that he was on his way with two thousand of his followers, one-half
of whom only were armed, and requesting weapons for the rest that
he might engage the attention of the deputy and delay the siege until
the northern chiefs arrived. This was not in the power of the com-

---

* Donal Coom, 1560-1680, son of Donal, prince of Beare (killed 1563), by Sarah O'Brien,
daughter of Sir Donald and Slany, daughter of the first earl of Thomond, was elected
prince of Beare in 1592. His grandfather, Dermot, who died 1549, at his castle of Dunboy,
married Julia, daughter of Donal Reagh of Carbery, by Elinor, daughter of the eighth
earl of Kildare. By Ellen, daughter of O'Sullivan Moore and the sister of Florence Mac-
Carthy, Donal Coom had two sons. Dermot, count of Bearehaven, represented Spain in
1612 at Kilkenny, and according to Smith's History of Cork, his descendants were hereditary governors of the Groyne a century later.

75

mander to grant, as the arms intended for the Irish were likewise in the missing ships.

Blount, in a personal interview, had concerted measures with Carew, and when intelligence reached him that the Spaniards had disembarked, he proceeded south from Kilkenny, giving orders to collect the army.   Attended by a few of his council he reached Cork on the twenty-eighth of September, and after reconnoitering the enemy, advanced to Awnsby bridge, midway between Cork and Kinsale, where Florence fought his battle.   Both generals appealed to the people by proclamation to invite coöperation.   The insincerity of the inducements held out by the deputy is curiously displayed in his letters home.   The late desolating warfare had left large numbers of the chiefs and their followers without subsistence.   He proposed to take them into the queen's pay and use them hard against the Spaniards, and throw them over when they had accomplished their work. Paid in debased coin, it would be more rapidly circulated to the weakening of the country, which would be furthered by forcing them to obtain their own supplies.   If they declined to serve, when the war ended they would be more completely in their power.   When at last in sufficient strength to commence the siege, he advanced within half a mile of the town.   Cormac MacDermot, the new lord of Muskerry, joined him, and his adhesion was ostentatiously paraded.   Other troops from England or the north flocked in, and entrenching on the Spittal, on the twenty-sixth of October, his batteries sent by sea were planted, and soon after the month ended Rincorran surrendered.

Meanwhile O'Donnel, leaving the siege of Donegal on the first of October, with his brothers Rory and Calvagh gathered his allies, O'Rourke, O'Doherty, O'Boyle, MacDonoghs, MacDermot, Mac-Sweeny Tuath, O'Kelly, two sons of O'Connor Roe, O'Flaherties, Redmond Burke and his brother William, Donal O'Conor Sligo, Dermot Moyl brother of Florence, and others, with three thousand troops, four hundred of them horse, and marched to aid Aquila.   He

crossed the Shannon at Arteroch into Fircal, and at Moydrum, in
Ikerrin, halted twenty days for Tyrone. He had reached Holycross,
when Carew, sent from the camp of the deputy on the seventh of
November, having under his command, when reinforced by Barry and
Bourke, thirty-five hundred foot and four hundred horse, hearing at
Cashel of his approach endeavored to waylay him, blocking the
roads and passes with a view of bringing him to battle. Tyrconnel had other objects, and kindling wide-spread camp fires
to convey a mistaken impression of his numbers and position,
marched safely by the president, and sudden frost stiffening the bogs,
on the twenty-third of November crossed the mountains, thirty-two
miles in the night, by Owny and Crom, to the gates of Limerick,
and thence south-westerly into Hy-connel-gaura. He took possession as he went of Ardfert, Ballykealy and Lixnaw, their lord visiting Clanmaurice, his dominion, and John O'Conor Kerry repossessing
himself of Carrygophoyle. Tyrconnel again halted at different stages
of his progress, to effect a junction with O'Neil. Carew, outgener-
alled, not wishing to be cut off from Kinsale, hastened back.

After the surrender of Rincorran, a battery placed near by commanded the Spanish lines on that side of Kinsale. Thomond landing
at Castlehaven with one thousand reinforcements from England,
reached the camp on the fifteenth; on which day admirals Levison
and Preston with the fleet, and two thousand more, entered the harbor. The former with his men, much disordered by their voyage,
were ordered to Cork, and soon after, with his cavalry, the earl
himself joined Carew, returning with him and Clanrickard on the
twenty-fifth to the camp. Castle-ni-Park, commanded by the fleet,
after a vigorous defence had been forced to yield on the twentieth, and
the approaches, notwithstanding the severe frost and constant volleys
from the besieged, were drawn nearer to the town. The heavier
artillery of the royalists played incessantly upon the walls and battlements till their pieces were crazed with the heat, and sorties and

skirmishes were constantly taking place with varied fortune, two hundred of the Spaniards being killed in one warmly contested.

After an ineffectual summons on the twenty-eighth, batteries were planted against the gate and wall west of it, when the night of the second of December, which was rainy and dark, the Spaniards came out in force, but after heavy loss were driven back. When intelligence of the arrival of the missing ships with troops, at Castlehaven, reached the camp, confirmed by a Scotch captain who treacherously brought eighty of them into Cork, the fire was slackened, the guns withdrawn to protect the lines, and two additional works thrown up to complete the investiture of the town.

Early in December, Zubiar with his seven vessels approached too close the rock bound coast, near Castlehaven, for safety. The five O'Driscol brothers, sons of the chief, extricated them from their danger, and delivered up their castles, Dermod, who spoke their language, explaining the state of affairs. Levison with his fleet despatched from Kinsale, well armed, ably commanded and in greatly superior numbers, attacked the cruisers under the marquis of Santa Cruce, as well as the transports not designed for battle and out of condition from their recent voyage, as also the town and the castle which had no artillery to defend them. The English were about to land, when the Spanish commander realizing his danger wrote urgently to the prince of Beare to come to his rescue.

That chief with his uncle Dermod, an able officer with much experience in warfare, marched with five hundred foot and some horse from Bantry, fifteen miles distant, the same day, arriving as the English were leaping from their boats to crush the handfull of Spaniards ashore. O'Driscol Mor with his son Cornelius, O'Donovan and some of the Maccarthy chiefs joined them. Zubiar disembarking five of his guns battered the English fleet for two days, raking their ships from bow to stern with a heavy fire, penetrating their hulls with three hundred shot, killing sixty men in the flagship of the admiral, five hundred and seventy-five in all, when the fleet discomfited warped out, and the wind favoring, sailed away. O'Sullivan delivered up to Saavedra, with food for two months, his principal castle of Dunboy. It was supplied with guns, balls, powder, lead and gunrope, sent by water from Castlehaven. Its harbor, safe and frequented from ancient times by ships from Spain, from which circumstances, tradition says, it had derived its name of Bearhaven, was easy of access for friends but difficult for enemies. O'Driscol also admitted Spanish garrisons into his castles. After the fleet returned to Kinsale, stormy weather for the fortnight ensuing impeded siege operations, when on the twenty-first the scouts reported the approach of the army of relief.

O'Neil had not been dilatory, but various embarrassments had delayed his movements. He marched, the eighth of November, into Meath, and though opposed raided the country, English and Anglo-Irish, and in a combat provoked by Darsy Platen killed him, and having collected much spoil carried it home. He could not leave his dominions unprotected, or without adequate supplies of food and ammunition for those he left to defend them, or who were to accompany his march, since Dowcra had an effective force in Derry, and towards the pale the garrisons were numerous and aggressive. The winter had already set in when he at last started to march two hundred miles to Kinsale. MacMahon, Maguire, brother of the chief killed at Cork by St. Leger, Randal MacDonnel prince of Glynn, Fitzmaurice baron of Lixnaw, Richard Tyrrell and others of his family accompanied him, their whole force numbering twenty-six hundred foot and four hundred horse. Following O'Donnel into Barryorrery they encamped together at Belgooly, in Kinalea, organizing their array. Thither came Donal Coom, prince of Beare, with his clansmen and three hundred Spaniards from Zubiar, under O'Campo. With Donal came likewise O'Conor Kerry, Daniel son of O'Sullivan Mor, Daniel MacSweeny and other knights.

Without longer delay the catholic army advanced towards Kinsale, pitching their camp, protected by entrenchments, one mile and a half from the town on the road from Cork, where was then a wood about half a mile from the enemy. Thus cooped up between the besieged and the catholics, who cut off their supplies of provisions and prevented their marauds, the English could only venture far enough to hastily retreat, casting away their burdens when their enemy came in view. They soon abandoned all marauds by day, and soon after even at night. What they had was speedily consumed. Want, famine and at length pestilence wasted their army, whilst the Irish camp abounded in food. The besieged for many weeks had been supplied with what they brought with them, or the town afforded, secure from assault by their own valor, or by the defences which they had constructed.

The chiefs of Munster, hitherto neutral, took heart and promised to be no longer wanting to their country or faith, but rally their forces as speedily as they might. Irish soldiers in the English ranks gave intimation to Tyrconnell, that before three days they would come over to him, and justified their sincerity by deserting in twos or threes together, often ten at a time. If their desertion to the side to which they naturally owed their allegiance had been awaited in patience it would have been all over with the English army, for of the fifteen thousand troops with which they had commenced the siege, half had already succumbed to the sword, hunger, cold or disease. A large part of them, recent recruits from England, were sluggish and unaccustomed to toil or danger. Of the residue scarcely two thousand were English or protestant, so numerous in the ranks were Irish or Anglo-Irish. The deputy appalled by the discouraging posture of affairs, resolved to send off his cavalry if not to raise the siege, and betaking himself to Cork to defend its walls. Thus without combat or loss the catholics by patience would have been left victorious. Their historian piously ascribes the very different course of events to the sins of his countrymen.

Aquila. by frequent missives, urged O'Donnel to effect a junction
with him.   O'Neil, O'Sullivan and others thought it wise not to
precipitate affairs, but await the coming in of the expected deserters
and the retreat of the enemy.   This more prudent policy Tyrconnel
and the majority of the leaders opposed.   A day was appointed
when O'Neil, just before dawn, should draw near to the royalist
entrenchments, and Aquila sally forth to join him.   Letters intercepted or some traitor suborned by the deputy, betrayed their design.

O'Neil advancing with his forces drawn up in three lines to the specified point, found it to his surprise already occupied by the English,
who with drums and trumpets and firing of guns, appeared to be
engaged in combat.   Scouts from the town discovering the trick reported it to Aquila, who relinquished his part of the project.   O'Donnel led astray by guides ignorant or treacherous, wandered off in the
dark, and no information could be had of where he was.   O'Neil
and O'Sullivan, receiving an erroneous impression from what they
heard that Aquila had reached the place assigned for their rendezvous, hurried rapidly forward to his support.   Finding the English
had returned to their entrenchments and the camp silent, they also
at last surmised the deceit.   After some little delay they went cautiously on, in the gray of the morning, towards the place stipulated ; the
army of O'Sullivan, in advance, halting near the lines of the English
camp, but screened from their view by a hill.

As it became day, O'Neil surprised that the Spanish commander
did not come forward or give signal for commencing the fight, with
O'Sullivan and O'Campo ascended the hill, scanning with scrutinizing
gaze the camp below.   There it lay close by, in all its strength of
rampart, ditch, batteries and towers, soldiers under arms and horses
caparisoned.   Even in numbers they exceeded their own forces if
united, many of whom, and especially those from the south, had the
day before gone out to forage.   O'Donnel with his army did not
appear.   O'Neil, after a consultation with his officers, concluding to

defer the attempt to another night, ordered a retreat. Before they had retired four hundred paces, they met O'Donnel, greatly offended at their retrograde movement, who at this moment had encountered the English cavalry at the ford he was crossing and driven them back. The enemy renewed their attempt to cross the stream. O'Donnel supposing they could be easily crushed between the ford and his own troops, if he gained more space for evolution, drew back, when part of his own cavalry, either from accident or treachery, rode into the ranks of the rest creating confusion. This disorder extended to the infantry, whose lines, broken by the charges of the cavalry, took to flight, after a resistance in which they lost many hundred lives.

The panic spread. Ulster and Munster men, worn out by their long watching, not sufficiently instructed to realize that safety in battle was to keep cool and not break their ranks, and when thrown into disorder to reform with promptitude, repel cavalry charges in flank or rear as in front, lost presence of mind when the royalists moved rapidly down upon them. In spite of the efforts and entreaties of their officers to rally round their standards, they retreated. The royalist cavalry fearing this a snare to entrap them pursued with little vigor. Many Irish leaders on the royalist side endeavored to persuade the fugitives to renew the combat, promising their aid. Neither their efforts nor those of Tyrone and Tyrconnel availed. O'Sullivan, Tyrrel and the Spaniards prolonged the combat until they were overpowered by numbers. English writers say twelve hundred of the catholics were left dead upon the field. The catholic historian says one sixth of that number perished in O'Neil's army, probably in the retreat. Thomond and Clanrickard did good service. The latter, who had killed, in the engagement or retreat, twenty Irishmen with his own hand, and whose battle-cry was to spare no rebel, received from the deputy the honor of knighthood for his prowess on the field, where thanksgiving was rendered up for this unexpected victory.

It is easy to reconcile discrepancies between this and other accounts of the battle. According to the most reliable, the deputy learning from MacMahon what was designed, strengthened his outposts and kept his army ready for action. Towards daybreak, whilst in consultation with the marshal and president, Graham, in charge that night of the videttes, reported to them that his scouts had discovered the enemy's approach, from their matches flashing through the darkness. Putting his men under arms and sending word to Thomond, Blount ordered batteries to command the ford which the catholics must pass. Delcampo, eager to join Aquila within the walls with his eight hundred Spaniards, obtained leave from Tyrone to push on, but finding the ford thus guarded drew back.

The president sent to prevent sorties from the town, Blount advanced to where Tyrone had taken position beyond another ford on strong ground, with a bog in flank, his men still in disorder from their retrograde movement. The marshal, with Power and Clanrickard, drove in their skirmish lines, but the gross or main bodies on either side engaging, the royalists were repeatedly driven back. Godolphin, Graham, Mynshal, Barkley, Davers, Taafe and Fleming coming up with large masses of foot and horse, their charges were at first repulsed, but persevering, the catholics gave way, and covered by their cavalry, through the great exertions of their commanders, retreated in good order. Tyrrel, Donal Coom and Delcampo with the Spaniards, stood firm upon a hill to the right; when assailed by Roe they retired to an eminence beyond. Their numbers melting away under the withering fire, Delcampo and forty of his men surrendered, all that were left in his ranks of the eight hundred, and this, it is said, ended the strife.

Had the catholic king, or his ministers, heeded what Tyrone urgently wrote, this misery would have been escaped. "If sent to Ulster, four or five thousand men would be required, but if to Munster, they should send more strongly, because neither he nor O'Donnel

76

could come to help them." The event justified his foresight. For
with their utmost exertions the northern chiefs could not muster, and
leave their own country sufficiently guarded, more than six thousand
for coöperation at the south, and these inferior in arms and especially
in artillery.   In the open field, in mid-winter, without town or castle
for support or shelter, events they could not control baffled their
prudence.   They could neither select their ground nor a favorable
season for battle, and they were prematurely and without preparation entangled at great disadvantage.

This disaster, fatal to national independence, has been attributed
to the disloyalty of MacMahon, whose eldest son had been page to
the president, and who betrayed what was designed.   Occurrences
during the night are difficult to explain upon any other hypothesis
than treason in the ranks.   Besides, strange lights flitting about on the
lances of the English troops disturbed wanderers in a region not familiar,
whilst thunder and lightning, unusual at that season of the year, for
it was the day before Christmas,* increased their perplexities.

But divided councils, the ancient rivalry for command between
Tyrone and Tyrconnel, revived at this inopportune moment, and
assuming form as they left their entrenchments, proved the obstacle
to success.   From what is known of the condition of the royalists,
had either of them been allowed to control operations, victory would
have stood within their grasp.   The three armies, though not far
apart, acted without concert, and were a mutual embarrassment.   The
chroniclers tell us that few comparatively were slain, but that the
glory of the island for valor, chivalry and noble traits, its prosperity
and independence were thrown away in this battle.   It is recorded
that a prophecy was read to Blount from an old manuscript, and

---

* Old style. These dates may confuse. In 1582, Gregory abolished the Julian calendar and adopted the Gregorian, dropping ten days after the fourth of October. Protestants
were slow to accept an improvement emanating from Rome, and the English not before 1751.
In their works the date of the battle is as given in the text, the twenty-fourth of December,
by Spanish and Irish catholics the third of January. December then the tenth month, the
new year dated from the twenty-fifth of March. Elizabeth died March 24, 1602, old style;
by the new, April 3, 1603.

repeated to him by Thomond, that the Gael, or foreigner, was to gain a great victory at that time and place.

Tyrone lost heavily, yet still formidable in numbers, strove ineffectually to persuade his brother chieftains to resume their former methods of warfare, and taking at once some position of strength, to wear out their foes by famine and fatigue. But the other armies, more exposed had sustained greater loss than his own, and could not be reorganized in presence of an enemy emboldened by success. They withdrew, and the royalists doubting their own good fortune, or possibly conjecturing that appearances were deceitful, that the real design was to draw them away from their camp and afford Aquila a chance to attack it at advantage, did not pursue.

That night the broken troops reached Innishannon, near Bandon, demoralized. Reproaches mingled with their disappointment. They could not sleep. They sought no refreshment. All realized the extent of their calamity. Consultation among their leaders as to what course should be pursued to guard against perils impending, led to little conclusion, and the measures adopted were precipitate and not harmonious. O'Neil, whose advice if adopted would have averted the catastrophe, retained his wonted calmness and courage, advocating a bold course. But opposition from O'Rourke, from personal considerations, which at critical conjunctures in Ireland, as elsewhere, have often defeated wiser counsels, prevailed. Learning that his brother, left in charge of Brefny, had improved his absence to supplant him, he was anxious to hurry home. Randal of the Glynns also objected to remaining, and their example spread. It was determined to end the campaign, and defend their own borders until fresh succors came.

Donal Coom, of Beare, was directed meanwhile to take command of the troops, about three thousand, left in Munster. Tyrconnel, who had been wounded, with Redmond Burke and Mostyn sailed for Spain, on the twenty-seventh, from Castlehaven.

They reached in eight days Corunna, near that tower of Breogan, from which the great-grandsons of its builder had started twenty centuries before to resent the slaughter of their uncle and his companions, whom the Tuatha de Danaans, then possessors of the island, had inhospitably slain.

In the midst of winter, shut off by sea from reinforcements and supplies, the prospect of the besieged was not encouraging, and before the week ended their commander proposed a conference to arrange preliminaries for surrender. His demands, considering the changed aspect of affairs, were somewhat audacious, including a safe return home for his army, with treasure, guns and whatever else they possessed. These conditions were extended to cover Dunboy, Donneshed and Donnelong belonging to Sir Finnen O'Driscol, at Baltimore, and the fortresses of Sir Donogh at Castlehaven, with their respective Spanish garrisons. They were conceded after negotiation. The besiegers found themselves in no state to insist upon more rigorous terms, the besieged upon any more liberal.

Some weeks were needed to collect transports. Civilities, customary upon such occasions, were interchanged between the general officers, and a friendly intimacy grew up between Aquila and the president. This led later to expression in tokens of wine and fruit, returned by the crafty president, in horses, not of wood, but Irish pacers, the messengers conveying them instructed to ascertain what was intended and discourage it by misrepresentation. Fresh succor for the catholic cause in Ireland, to the extent of fourteen thousand men, prompted by the earnest solicitations of Tyrconnel, was already in preparation, and the king displeased at the precipitation of Aquila in surrendering Kinsale, upon his arrival threw him into prison where he died before many months.

XLVI.

REIGN OF ELIZABETH.—1558-1602.—(Continued.)

Tyrone realizing his danger, remote from his own possessions, which were seriously compromised by his reverses and heavy losses of men and arms, hastened north, it is said, on a litter from wounds received in the fight. Rory, on his way, encountered in Meath train bands from the towns, hastily collected and easily routed; but ill for several months, the royalists beset Ballyshannon, from which O'Gallagher after bravely defending it escaped. O'Dwyer, too ill to remove, had killed an Englishman in honest warfare, and on this pretext with three hundred women and children, was slain. Rory recovered, routed Lambert in the Corlew mountains driving him into Boyle, and mounting his musqueteers in croup behind his troopers, overtaking killed not a few. Lambert again sought to cross the mountains, but the chief and O'Conor Sligo blocked his path. When Guest, coming by sea, occupied Ballyshannon, Rory ordered the corn cut about the place. The garrison interfering, he drove them off, their loss amounting to three hundred killed and wounded.

Measures first taken for repairing Castle-ni-Park and Halbolin for protection of Cork, the deputy sent his kinsman George Blount to Tyrone to proffer terms of amity and pardon if he would make submission, assist in quelling the rebellion, disclaim the title of O'Neil and all rule over the uriaghts, release the sons of Shane and his other prisoners, admit sheriffs, pay rents, duties and arrears, and within six months deliver twenty thousand cows and build two forts. As assurance for his sincerity, he was to place in the hands of the queen his eldest son and four principal gentlemen of his blood. Sir Charles Wilmot, early in February, with two thousand men went back to his command in Kerry. On his march, between Askeaton and Glynn, he surprised at night Hugh MacSweeny, in wait to stay his passage over the Cassan. He took Carrigophoyle and Lixnaw, and at Ballyho, ten miles from Castlemagne, still held by his warders, defeated Sir William Fitzgerald, knight of Kerry, who, with Donal Clancarre bringing five thousand cows of his own, and William Burke, as a peace offering, four thousand belonging to O'Sullivan Mor collected as he came, tendered their allegiance.

Donal Coom not acknowledging the right to embrace his castles in the capitulation, took possession of them, entering Dunboy at night whilst the warders were asleep. Justifying his course to the king, he sent his eldest boy as pledge for his fidelity, with Dermod O'Driscol to solicit aid, resolved to keep the field till it came. His own adherents and two thousand auxiliaries,* constituted a considerable force; the more formidable from the mountainous character of the country which he controlled. He reduced, after a vigorous defence, Carriganass, the only castle his cousin Owen, always loyal to the crown as his father had been before him, retained. O'Donovan, who had deserted the cause, he attempted to win back by raiding within his borders, and shut up within their walls the royalists, whose numbers, their loss at the siege and detachments gone north with the deputy in pursuit of Tyrone, had greatly reduced.

Carew busily employed in embarking the Spaniards, part of whom were sent home in March and part in May, mustered at Cork what forces he could. Having but five hundred English soldiers, he depended mainly upon the Munster chiefs to assist him, who, staunch catholics, had little affection for a government arbitrary and tyrannical, and eager to spoil. Whilst hope could be reasonably entertained of success, many had openly or covertly manifested their natural sympathies; but now that it was extinguished, they readily embraced the opportunity extended of amnesty and protection for their property

---

* Dermot O'Sullivan, uncle of Donal Coom, and father of the catholic historian, Daniel, son of O'Sullivan Mor, Donal, son of Clancarre, MacSweenys, MacCarthies and O'Driscols, O'Connor Kerry, Lixnaw, knights of Kerry and Glynn, John Fitzthomas, James Butler, brother of Cahir, William Burke and Richard Tyrrel were under his command.

from confiscation, of their families from the fangs of their merciless
foes.* From the havoc of war, subsistence had become an embarrassment, and they greedily snatched at pay or ration offered by
Carew. It would have proved in the end a wiser policy if the four
thousand who responded to the call of the president had joined the
catholics.

With a considerable portion of these levies, Thomond was despatched, in March, to the west. Donal guarded the goat's pass
into Beare, where Cromwell fifty years afterwards constructed his
bridge part of which remains, declining an interview which the earl
requested. Thomond leaving eight battalions on Whiddy Island,
in the bay of Bantry, in a position of strength with competent supplies of guns, munitions and food, returned to Cork. After much
skirmishing and some partial engagements, the troops left were forced,
in May, to evacuate the island, and making their way to Bantry
were about to be cut off, when the president, who had hastened upon
the intelligence with his whole army to their rescue, coming into
view, the catholics, not in force to contend, retired. Dermot Moyle
MacCarthy, brother of Florence in the tower, had been sent into
Carbery to forage, where encountering Donal na Pipi, its chief,
they came to parley and parted ostensibly friends. The cattle generally in Munster had been driven by order of the president towards
Limerick or beyond Youghal. But those in Carbery, Donal had
pastured about Kinsale. Dermod, on the thirteenth, was gathering
his own from the herds into his castle, when the churls near by collected and setting upon his party he fell in the skirmish. He was an
able officer and highly esteemed, a great loss to the catholics, who
buried him with due solemnity at Timoleague.

Wilmot had just before received orders from the president to

* Thomond with O'Brien of Limerick, Maccarthies Reagh and Muskerry, Denis and
Florence, Barrymore, the white knight, Owen Beare, Dermot, brother of O'Sullivan Mor,
with many chiefs of Ormond joined Carew. Some of them near Cork had no alternative
but submission.

join him at Carew, or Downmark castle, two miles from Bantry
abbey.   This stronghold belonged three centuries before to the
marquis of Carew, to whose extensive claims to half Cork, derived
from Fitzstephen, Carew professed to be heir.   But what title had ever
vested had long before reverted to its more legitimate owners.   His
eagerness to establish his claim by act of possession, led the
president to disregard the dissuasions of Thomond and others from
an enterprise attended with great hazard and cost.   Wilmot obeyed
the summons, and crossing Killarney by Mucruss abbey over Man-
gerton mountain, effected a junction on the eighth with the main army,
already at their rendezvous, a strong detachment being sent to meet
him at Ardtully, the home of the MacFinnens.

Carew reinforced to three thousand effective troops, had started on the
twenty-third of April, to reduce the castles of Beare.   He took Baltimore on his march and reached Carew castle in a week.   On the
fourth of May, appeared in his camp O'Daly, whose ancestor had
received from the marquis, during his brief possession in Munster,
the country, towards the south, of Muinterbarra, to be held by himself and his descendants as hereditary rhymers of the Carews.   The
bard had been sent by Donal Coom as emissary to his cousin Owen,
chief of Bantry, to persuade him to join the catholics.   Owen reported
him to the president, who to retaliate offered bribes to two Spanish
gunners and an Italian in the garrison, to spike the guns and spoil their
carriages.   He sought also to persuade Tyrrel to a conference, but
Archer and the rest prevented what they feared might prove a temptation not to be resisted, Tyrrel having of late manifested an inclination to make peace.

After several weeks delay at Bantry, Carew's supplies and
artillery at last arrived in twenty vessels from the seaports.
Donal Coom laid wait for him about Glengariff, presuming his route
would be through the mountains which lay west of the bay.   But
breaking camp on the first of June, and leaving his sick on Whiddy

island, the president marched down to Kilnemanoge in Muinterbarra and passed over his army in detachments, on successive days,
having only boats for half his number at a time, to the island of
Beare, about twenty miles south of Bantry.

This island, seven miles in length, at its southerly extremity approached the main shore so nearly that a chain when raised closed
the entrance to the harbor.   Here with Castletown, or Bearehaven,
around it, stood the ancient castle of Dunboy, planted close by the
water-side to protect the haven, which enjoyed considerable trade from
foreign lands.   Its excellent fishing grounds, the resort of many
catholic nations, yielded its chief an annual revenue of five hundred
pounds.   The peninsula of Beare extends ten miles further to the
southwest, where Dursey island forms its continuation to the sea.

The castle itself, constructed of square masses of heavy mason work,
contained on its second floor the spacious banqueting hall, an essential
feature of both domestic and military life at this period.   Its windows
commanded wide views over the adjacent waters, but were so constructed
as to be easily barricaded against missiles from without.   On the
southwest of the castle, rose a circular tower to a greater elevation
than the principal edifice, and on it was mounted an iron falcon.
The bawn which, for guarding cattle or other purposes, surrounded
this medieval fortalice, had been filled up in part with mounds of earth
behind the walls, so that only eight feet were left in some places
between them and the castle, but from the correspondence of Anias, it
would appear that several buildings stood on the southerly side within its
limits.   From its barbican, sprung turrets mounted with artillery.   Hides and earth were heaped before the openings, and powder
mixed with balls ingeniously arranged to destroy storming parties.

The garrison of one hundred and forty-four men was commanded
by Magheogan; Taylor, who had married a niece of Tyrrel, succeeding him when he was mortally wounded.   Collins served as
chaplain, and we gather from the admirable poem on the siege, by

77

Mr. Sullivan, which follows the historical authorities with great exactness, that O'Daly had returned from his mission to cheer and inspire the garrison with his minstrelsy. Two or three miles north of Dunboy, stood a smaller fortress called Dermod, near by which opened Sandy Bay, the most practicable landing place above the haven, and a little to the north of it a small creek entered in among the hills. Opposite this castle and the bay lay the island of Deenish, not three hundred yards distant from the shore.

Carew passed two or three days on Beare island in organizing his army. Owen O'Sullivan, with his brothers, reduced the castle of Dunmanus, on the most easterly side of the Bantry peninsula, and on the fifth took place, with the assent of Donal Coom and the president, an interview between Thomond and Mageoghan to discover if any accommodation were practicable. The earl, under his instructions, insisted upon unconditional surrender. This was declined respectfully but firmly; but when Thomond proceeded to insult the noble chieftain by proposals to him to betray his trust, they were received with the scorn and contempt they deserved. Another event at this time exemplified the misery war brings in its train.

MacMahon, last chief of West Corkavaskin,* which lies along the north shore of the Shannon at its mouth, and from which Thomond had driven him out three years before, had captured an English merchantman at sea, which was now needed to expedite the promised succor from Spain. The urgency of the occasion justifying such an arbi-

---

* Moyarta, or West Corkavaskin, granted at this time by the crown to Daniel, brother of Donogh fourth earl of Thomond, and forfeited in 1690 by his g. g. son, was then granted to the Burtons who still hold. Daniel's attachment to the daughter of Teigue Cace, displeased her father, and on one occasion, the preconcerted signal being neglected or unheeded, the lover, surprised on a visit to Carrigaholt, escaped by swimming his horse across the bay. As the earl, in 1599, after taking the castle, hung the warders on the trees, Teigue was naturally irate (see page 541). Daniel married Catherine, daughter of Gerald, earl of Desmond (killed 1583), and must have been nearly ninety when created first viscount Clare in 1662. His g. g. son, sixth viscount, commanded the Irish brigade at Fontenoy. The representative of the Clonderala, or East Corkavaskin, branch of the MacMahons, was Stanislaus, or Terence, who in 1724 married at Bunratty castle g. g. daughter of 19th Lixnaw; his daughter, the head of the Macnamaras, of Rossroe, lately represented by Gen. Bourchier of Elm Hill. From another branch in France (ascending John, count d'Equilly, Patrick, Mortogh, Maurice, Mortogh, Bernard, Terence and Donatus who died 1472), its present executive chief is said to have descended.

trary proceeding, Donal. taking the chief with him, went to the river
to seize the vessel. As they approached, MacMahon ordered his
son Turlogh, in command, not to deliver it. Turlogh, in obedience
to the parental order, fired upon the assailants, a chance shot from
his own gun killing his father. The chroniclers in noting the catastrophe, pass high encomium upon the skill and generosity of the
deceased, and upon his taste for wine, horses and books.

Carew discovered a spot favorably situated for his batteries on the
opposite shore, screened by hills, which he thought he could reach without observation, and Sunday, the sixth of June, was the time fixed
for the attempt. Donal and Tyrrel, on the alert and apprized of the
intended movement, marched down to Sandy Bay, where they had
reason to believe the English would cross, and made their dispositions
to dispute their landing. Early that morning, which was foul and
stormy, the president, with one solitary attendant, rode forth to the
place where the boats lay ready for the embarkation. To gain a
nearer view of the coast he passed in the pinnace Merlin to the island
of Deenish, where, without being perceived, he could see the catholics in force at the bay, strongly posted. He ordered Fleming, the
captain of the pinnace, to land from it two falconets on the north end
of the island. When Thomond's regiment and his own coming over
disembarked as ordered, he marched them to that part of its shore
nearest the bay, within full view and musket shot of the catholics, as if
intending from thence to take a new departure across the few hundred
feet of water that separated them. The boats returned for the other
two regiments of Wilmot and Percy, who, making a feint to land at
the same place as the others, moved on rapidly to a point out of view
of the bay, and sufficiently remote to occupy and hold unmolested
until the boats crossed over the two other regiments from Deenish to
join them.

The catholics, surprised and disappointed, hastened to the attack,
but in their eagerness reached the ground in some disorder.

Against such odds, strongly posted and defended by artillery, their courage proved unavailing, and after considerable loss they were obliged to withdraw. Their disappointment was alleviated by intelligence that the day before a vessel had arrived at Ardea from Spain, bringing Donal twelve thousand pieces of gold to defray the expenses of the war, which he had previously borne out of his own resources. The vessel carried back Cornelius O'Driscol, to urge immediate reinforcements.

The royalists rested their first night near castle Dermod, and the following day advanced to within a mile of Dunboy, a creek separating it from their camp. Two falcons were planted to protect the lines, and on the tenth they drew nearer, the ordnance being safely transported under the guns of the castle by water. On the eleventh, now securely entrenched, the first shot was fired. Approaches were regularly made, culverings and demi-culverings mounted, and two minions landed and placed northwest of the castle. The night after, the catholics again attacked the entrenchments, but were a second time repulsed; the opportunity being improved to throw into the castle various supplies brought by the late arrival at Ardea.

Spanish engineers had thrown up ramparts of earth eighteen feet in thickness within the barbican, planting the guns on the top and lowering the castle to the vault only a dozen feet above the rampart itself. This solid embankment, whilst it shielded the lower part of the wall from the fire of ships, proved an embarrassment to the defenders in their sorties, and covered the approach of the besiegers from the castle guns. Constructing mounds and platforms twelve feet higher than the rampart, Carew directed his fire against the upper part of the castle, the besieged defending themselves as best they could from window and battlement.

Way having been made into the market place and trenches opened, platforms were constructed, and the guns mounted within seven-score yards of the walls. Mageoghan sallied forth to impede these operations, but to little purpose. Early on the sixteenth, all being prepared, they battered the devoted fortress for four hours, when the tower, not constructed to withstand artillery, toppled over on to the vaulted roof of the main building, burying in its ruins the falcon which had done good service. A messenger sent to propose terms of surrender was hung up by the arrogant Carew, upon the plea that the castle had not discontinued its fire.

After this battering for several days, the stones forced out of place, the outer walls grew weak, and a portion yielding the rest gave way. Through the breach the royalists rushed in. Large stones were hurled down upon them as they effected their entrance within the enclosure. Many fell pierced by the spear or hacked to pieces by the sword. The besieged fought bravely on amidst terrible carnage of themselves and their assailants, whilst wall after wall crumbled beneath the balls from the heavy guns of the besiegers, or with crash after crash fell in vast masses, dragging with them soldiers crushed by the ruins.

Gaining the barbican, with their immense superiority of numbers the besiegers fought their way into possession of one of the turrets, whilst the catholics, with several small pieces, from another opposite did much execution. Driven from that position, the battle continued in the space between the barbican and castle wall. There the besieged had the advantage, till some of the assailants who had gained the roof found a passage opened by the battering, to windows overlooking this area, when forty of the besieged sallying forth were slain, or taking to the water were drowned or killed by Harvey stationed there with three boats to cut off fugitives. The concentrated fire soon demolished what remained of the outer wall, and the defenders rushed towards the great hall of the castle, one half of which was already occupied by three battalions of the enemy, outnumbering what survived of their own reduced numbers. There hand to hand the combat fiercely raged till the royalists were driven out, removing their wounded.

Their ranks restored to order and strengthened by fresh troops in larger numbers, the three battalions increased to seven, more than could be formed to advantage in the limited space, they burst again into the large apartment. The floor heaped with carcasses, strewed with weapons no hands to wield them, streaming with blood. Nearly all the garrison were wounded, and at last their noble leader dropped bleeding at every pore, and all but lifeless among his fallen comrades. The survivors quitting the hall betook themselves to the vaults beneath, where still fighting with courage unabated and with desperation, often an incitement to a glorious death, they drove the enemy out, and not only of the hall but of the castle. Night alone suspended the combat.

The following morning, the president sent his summons for surrender, to which the besieged consented if allowed to quit the place with their lives, on the fifteenth of September; probably by that time expecting relief. Whatever terms, if any, were agreed upon, the English troops entered the castle, when Magheogan, still alive, endeavored to explode the magazine, stocked with nine casks of powder, to blow up the castle and his enemies, but seized fast hold of by Percy was slain before he could accomplish his design. Not many were taken alive, sixty that were, according to the humanity of the period, being hung in the market place to avenge the six hundred royalists who had perished. Twelve, including Taylor and Collins, had been reprieved for a few days. Tyrrel offered heavy ransom for their lives. The terms proposed in return involved a sacrifice of honor, and he had to abandon them to their fate.

The siege lasted from the seventh to the eighteenth, and considering the disparity of numbers and the powerful artillery arrayed against it, the place must have been both strong and ably defended. The president wrote, that a more obstinate and resolved defence had not been seen within the kingdom. Against so large an army of the royalists Donal Coom, at Glengariff, was powerless, and any further attempt to raise the siege might have ended in destruction of the force upon which the main dependence was placed to cover the landing of the expected Spaniards.

On the twelfth, a detachment sent to Dursey Island, occupied by the O'Driscols, had destroyed abbey, church and a castle built by Dermot, father of the catholic historian of the war, slaughtering old and young, women and children, infants and mothers quick with child, or pitching them down the rocks into the sea. Dunboy demolished, the president carried Collins, a priest, who with Archer had incited the garrison to hold out to the last, to Cork, where, after ineffectual efforts to allure him to apostacy, tortured and drawn by horses, his earthly career, in October, came to an end, at Youghal, his native town.

XLVII.

REIGN OF ELIZABETH.—1558-1602.—(Continued.)

After the fall of his castle, Donal, no way dismayed, followed with two thousand men the royalists to Cork, stripping on his way Carrignachor and Dundeary of lead and guns, and gathering into his ranks their dependents, compelled O'Donoghue of the valley to surrender Macroom. Wilmot and Bagnal on their march to the north, with forces more numerous than his own, came within a league of his camp; but heavy storms swelling the streams kept them apart, and Donal leaving sufficient forces to hold Macroom as he supposed, swept through the country carrying back rich spoils into Beare. The royalists besieged the castle. But when Cormac, lord of Muskerry, arrested on suspicion of correspondence with Spain, and put in chains for refusing to surrender Blarney, by help of Owen MacSweeny and his clansmen, effected his escape, the president alarmed lest his numberless retainers would be too many for him, ordered the siege to be raised if the place should not yield within twenty-four hours. The besiegers early in October were on the eve of retiring, when the garrison, without water to scald the swine for their food, kindled faggots to singe off their hair. A building near by in the bawn caught fire and the flames extended to the castle, which was burnt. This being a favorite residence of the lords of Muskerry, much that was precious was destroyed. The garrison, left exposed to the guns of the besiegers, cut their way out. Some of them perished, but more escaped into the woods.

Muskerry joined Donal who reduced Carrignaphoca, the stronghold of the sons of Teigue who had betrayed him, recovering the Spanish money paid them when professing allegiance. Donal delivered this castle and two more into his custody as their lawful proprietor, and raiding to the gates of Cork carried back much spoil to Glengariff. Wilmot holding Dunkerron, near Kenmare, with a thousand men, Donal, son of O'Sullivan Mor, put to the sword three battalions marching from Askeaton to reinforce him.

Meanwhile preparations in Spain for another expedition dragged slowly along. Squadrons blockaded its ports, and neither munitions nor ships could be collected. Tyrconnel, upon his arrival, had been kindly received by the king, begging him to send relief, but not to allow any chief to be placed over him or his dominions to be lessened. This promised,he returned to Corunna to accelerate operations, but in August, vexed at the delay and on his way to court, died at Simancas, supposed to have been poisoned by James Blake, of Galway, whom in June, the president wrote the deputy, he had sent to put him to death. Tyrconnel at first suspicious Blake in time ingratiated himself into his confidence, and Carew, in October, wrote Blount in cypher he no doubt had poisoned him.* Carew takes pride in having written, in the

---

* This method of disposing of a dangerous enemy seems, in the present state of public opinion, difficult to credit. But the assassination of Donal Coom, at Madrid, in 1618, by Bath who had gained his confidence, as Blake that of Tyrconnel, cannot well be explained on any other hypothesis. The disappearance of Henry O'Neil, eldest son of Tyrone, about the same time, can only be attributed to the secret machinations of unscrupulous power.

name of one of his officers, to Aquila and De Soto, letters covertly designed to discourage further aid, enclosing a letter of Tyrconnel to O'Connor Kerry begging him not to let the Spaniards learn of their reverses. This other poisoned arrow reached its mark. The blockade of the coast, tidings from Dunboy and murder of the chief by the president, staid farther preparation. This disappointment extinguished all hope of relief and broke the hearts of the catholics.

Tyrconnel's death produced profound consternation. Not thirty years of age, his military capacity and chivalric courage, his elevated statesmanship, aims and aspirations, high sense of justice and honor, with a disposition peculiarly amiable and affectionate, endeared him to his country whilst he lived, and his memory since has been justly cherished as one of its most precious heirlooms. His character won respect even from his foes, and elicits from the chroniclers unqualified eulogium. His funeral obsequies from the royal palace of Valladolid, attended with all the pomp and circumstance for which Spain was famous upon melancholy occasions, testified how high a place he occupied in the esteem of its king. Tyrone remained, but both were needed, and the death of red Hugh O'Donnel was generally recognized, for the time being if not forever, as the deathblow of national independence.

He never married.[*] Carew, who had defeated the alliance of the sugan with the sister of Muskerry, had interfered with like success to prevent his marriage with Joanna, daughter of the beheaded earl of Desmond. He was betrothed, when he died, to Julia, second daughter of Muskerry, later wife of Buttevant and of Sir Dermod O'Shaughnessy. His engagement to Julia probably had its effect

---

[*] According to one account he married a daughter of Tyrone, but it is not substantiated. His mother, Ina Dur, daughter of that James M'Donnel of Islay, who died 1565 prisoner of Shane O'Neil, married Hugh, chief of Tyrconnel, when her mother married Turlogh O'Neil. Her noble and heroic traits of character were transmitted to her children. Her daughter, Nuala, also honored, abandoned Niall Garv when he proved false to her brother, and went later, with Rory ... It was Rory or ... ... and honored Niall when he conspired with Sir Cahir O'Doherty. Niall ... ... rejected the title of baron Lifford, and passed the last eighteen years of his life in the tower of London.

78

in detaching her father from his allegiance to the crown, to whom both king Philip and pope Clement wrote urgently, even during the siege of Kinsale, to join the catholics, a step which his wife and her brother, James Galdie Butler, openly in rebellion, likewise exerted their influence to bring about.

But Cormac, if zealous in the faith, was politic. His wife and daughters were in custody at Cork, his eldest son, already betrothed to the daughter of Thomond, a student at Oxford, his second, Daniel, later head of the branch of Carrignavar, in pledge. Macroom his best abode had been destroyed, with five thousand pounds in value of his crops. Blarney and Kilcrea were in possession of the president. His dominions, the most valuable in Munster, stretched close up to the walls of Cork, and were peculiarly open to attack. Though he had one thousand men actually in arms and could muster thrice that number to his banners, and if chosen Maccarthy Mor, as he hoped, as many more, however much he desired the catholic cause to triumph he was not inclined to become a martyr. When tidings came that O'Donnel was dead, and the lateness of the season precluded all hope of succor before another spring, he wavered. His surrender of the castles confided to his keeping by Donal Coom, reflects discredit on his sense of honor, but with large and vulnerable possessions which Carew would have gladly appropriated under his stale pretensions, his course had its embarrassments.

Soon after his overtures to submission, Bagnal with a large force, ascertaining from one of the sons of Teigue, that Tyrrel with about one thousand men lay near, in an exposed position, made a nocturnal onslaught on his camp. By accident or design, a quarter of a mile before they reached the lines, some recruit stumbling his gun went off, and Tyrrel with his wife escaped. Eighty men were slain, forty chargers, four hundred beasts of burden, good store of Spanish money, household stuff, bolts of Holland, a piece of velvet uncut, gold and silver lace, good English apparel of satin and velvet, Tyrrel's own portmanteau, were the spoils. Tyrrel attributing this mischance to Muskerry, burnt his towns and villages, killed and hung many of his people, women and children. This exasperated and still further alienated the chief, whose power to hurt or help was too considerable not to conciliate.

He soon after submitted, and was pardoned. Donal of Clancarre, the knight of Kerry and Donal O'Sullivan Mor giving up the cause as hopeless, made overtures to peace. Tyrrel, denied forgiveness, led his bonies into Connaught. Donal Coom, his army reduced by these defections, fought on for four days with Wilmot at Glengariff. On the last day of December, 1602, with his uncle Dermot O'Conor and William Burke, in all four hundred, their wives having sought refuge as best they could, after a combat at Akaras which cost their foes dear, he started for the Shannon. On their second night at Ballyvourney, six miles west of Macroom, they offered solemn supplications commending themselves to divine providence. The Mac-Carthies, faithless sons of Teigue, who betrayed their chief and kinsman, the next day for four hours worried their march, but fled when charged. In Duhallo, without food, O'Keefes and Macawleys, who should have befriended them, disturbed even their repose. Near Limerick, they repulsed Cuff and Barry, burying their dead and carrying their wounded twenty miles to bivouac in Aherlow. With no other refreshment than roots and water, they started at dawn, and their path beset for eight hours by the dependents of the white knight, they proceeded, in a blaze of musketry the sky darkened by the smoke, to Ardpatrick, and passing four miles west of Tipperary, reached Sulchoid, where Donal confided to a faithful adherent his second son, Dermot, sent two years later to him in Spain.

The fifth night at Kilnemanagh, they kindled fires as the cold was intense, and appeased their hungry appetites on dead leaves. The next day, however, at Donahil, they found food which they devoured as if famished, and bravely anticipating the attack of forces sent by

Ormond, more numerous than their own, routed them. Daniel O'Malley and Thomas Burke, with sixty hungry soldiers, off without orders foraging, were waylaid, the former with twenty others being slain. Donal rescued the latter who was captured, with the loss of his arms but saving his helmet. In a chapel, at Latteragh, they slept alternately, the attacks of the garrison of the castle warded off by those on guard. On the sixth, showers of balls, now their daily experience, saluted them from every covert, the more vexatious that their successive assailants were always fresh and they weary. When they halted their foes retired, renewing the attack when their march was resumed. The strife only ended at night as they reached Brosnach, near Portland, on the Shannon.

There in the woods, girded about by felled trees and entrenchments, Dermot, uncle of the chief, built a boat of saplings, covered with the skins of twelve horses which they killed and ate. Stiffened by cross boards, flat to escape the rocks and shoals, this boat, twenty-six feet long, six broad and five high, the prow more elevated to contend with the waves, was carried, when completed, at night to the shore. Thirty crossed at a time, the horses swimming behind held by their halters. A smaller boat, constructed by O'Malley, when half over swamped with him and ten more. At daybreak, MacEgan, from Redwood a castle near by, would have seized their baggage, killed the boys in charge and thrown the women into the river. He paid for this temerity with his life. Thomas Burke, with twenty kinsmen, slew him and fifteen of his followers, routing the rest for the most part, hurt. The firing attracting the neighbors and creating alarm, too many crowded on board and the vessel upset as it approached the west bank. No one perished; and bailed out it brought over the rear guard and all but a few, who frightened by the country folk when they grew menacing, had concealed themselves. Lest it should help the foe in pursuit the corragh was destroyed.

Food obtained in Galway, they took up the line of march, eighty

in the van, the trains in the centre, Donal Coom with two hundred
bringing up the rear. At Aughrim, a spot destined for a less fortunate engagement for Irish independence ninety years later, they
encountered Richard Burke, Thomas, brother of Clanrickard, and
Henry Malby with a large force. The van broke and fled. The
rest, after being exhorted by their leader, proceeded to occupy a
suitable position for defence not far off, and had hardly reached it, in
some disorder, when the enemy, who had sought to anticipate them,
came up to receive a deadly fire of musquetry which killed eleven of
them. In the engagement which ensued, Malby, Richard Burke and
one hundred of the royalists fell: the rest taking refuge in the castle.
The catholic train, left unguarded in the conflict, was plundered, but
the victors found some compensation in the spoils abandoned by the
vanquished.

Passing swiftly through Hymany, near Kelley castle, they sheltered themselves in the forests of Ballinlough, in Roscommon, but
still in peril left their couches of stone in the darkness, and that
night hurried through the deep snow to Drambrach, where they finished their interrupted slumbers. Here the neighbors, generously
disregarding the penalty attached to giving food to rebels, provided
them with whatever they needed, and a horse for O'Connor, whose
feet were blistered and frozen, but who bore his excruciating agony
with great fortitude. Without guides, ignorant of their way, if the
night clear the stars screened by the thick branches, their dangers
multiplied. In the midst of their perplexities a man in linen garments, barefooted, with a white cloak about his head and staff in his
hand, presented himself and offered to guide them to Leitrim, castle
of O'Rourke, some twelve miles distant. Hesitating at first lest he
might betray them, reassured they placed themselves under his guidance, and their chief paid him two hundred pieces of gold, which he
courteously accepted. Sleeping that night at Knocvicar, in the
Curlew mountains near Boyle, the next morning their guide, telling

them that all danger was past, pointed out to them in the distance
their destination and dissappeared. Before noon they reached the
castle, but thirty-five in number, all that remained of the four
hundred who had left Glengariff twenty days before, the rest having
deserted or been disabled or slain by the way. Of these only eighteen were armed men. One of the party was Joanna, mother of the
historian, who had accompanied this march in the dead of winter,
and lived on, notwithstanding its exposures, for thirty years after.*
They were warmly welcomed and hospitably entertained by O'Rourke,
with whom they found Maguire, chief of Fermanagh, and MacWilliam, chief of Mayo.

There for some days they rested; when eager to aid Tyrone, Maguire, Donal Coom and Tyrrel, with three hundred men, started to
join him in Glenconquin. Their route lay south of lough Erne,
which was guarded by hostile forts, and three rivers over its tributaries were to be passed, which they effected by aid of boats covertly
provided by their friends. They had already crossed that at Beltur-
bet, when the English, Maguire, McLaughlin and Esmond with five
hundred men, not knowing they were over, ensconced themselves in
ambush near the ford to waylay them. They bivouacked that night
four miles beyond, and discovering on the morrow the camp of their
assailants about that same distance farther on, amply supplied with
herds and much else they valued, took possession, having despatched
the guard of fifty left in charge. Maguire, with two hundred men,
sallied forth in search of adventure, hoping to damage the foe, whilst
Donal Coom, setting fire to the tents, removed with the spoil into the
wood. The enemy informed by a scout of what had chanced, and
hastening back, prepared for battle. Donal drew up his small force
so disposed, even the women disguised as soldiers, as to give an im-

---

* Dermot and Joanna died about 1634 at Corunna, at an advanced age; Dermot over one
hundred, as stated in an elegy, at that time composed in latin, on their death, by his son
Philip O'Sullivan Beare, prefixed to his History of the War, ed. 1850.

pression of more formidable numbers, and the royalists not knowing Maguire was absent, wasted the day in doubt what to do.

At dusk the foragers returned laden with spoil. The royalists mortified at having been duped, and their supplies of food and powder appropriated, withdrew to defend their strongholds on the islands in the lake, till better able to contend. The shore too far off to reach that night, they betook themselves to an old dilapidated rath, in which the O'Neil, from time immemorial, had inaugurated the lords of Fermanagh. But when, about four hours after sunrise, they had reached the water and were about to embark, Esmond already off, they found themselves surrounded by their vigilant foes. Those that were able pushed on board the boats, some of which swamped, others leapt in their armor into the water and were drowned. Many clung by ropes to the vessels only to present a mark for volleys of musquetry from the shore. One bark, larger than the rest, crowded with fugitives within and hemmed around with others struggling to get on board, could not be loosed before many were slain. Con Maguire and his two sons found safety in a small boat that seasonably put off into the lake. Melaghlin, with four hundred, perished. Seven strongholds on the island captured, their defenders expiating the cruelties of Kinsale and Dunboy, Esmond and Con routed, the legitimate chief of Fermanagh was restored to much of his own.*

Avoiding the English garrisons, after three days they reached Gleneonquin to learn that Tyrone had submitted. Maguire, embraced in the terms of his surrender, was reinstated; O'Conor Kerry repairing to Scotland, finding favor with king James, being also restored to his territory. Tyrrel and William Burke, who had, ever since Kinsale, made repeated overtures for pardon, were pensioned. Don-

* The line from Con, d. 1605, brother of Hugh, killed by St. Leger, is as follows: ii. Brian, restored to Tempo 2000 acres in extent. iii. Hugh, m. O'Reilly. iv. Con, m. Magennis, killed with his whole regiment at Aughrim, after annihilating the second English cavalry. v. Brian, m. Nugent. vi. Philip, m. Morris. vii. Hugh, m. MacNamara, able, noble and generous. viii. Brian, m. Baker.

al Coom returned to O'Rourke, against whom, in March, Lambert
led three thousand men, and for twelve days vainly endeavored to
cross the Shannon, but they were driven back by that redoubtable
chief. Bostock contrived to transport seven companies to a peninsula convenient for raiding Leitrim; but was killed, with many of his
men, in a maraud, and the rest discouraged would have recrossed the
river, but the brother of O'Rourke, whose defection in Brefny broke
up the army before Kinsale, rose up against his brother, who died in
a few months of fever. Philip had sent by Cerda thirty thousand
pieces of gold with supplies for Tyrone and Rory, which arriving
after the surrender, were sent back, MacWilliam going in the same
ship, to die soon after in exile. Two thousand sent by Cornelius
O'Driscol into Munster, for Donal, were also returned.

When the chief crossed the Shannon with the remnant of his people, strife virtually ended in Munster. Lixnaw was in covert, and
his brother-in-law, Donal of Dunloh, eldest son of O'Sullivan Mor,
kept together a small following, south of the lakes of Killarney.
Wilmot upon his return, perhaps from his Christmas festivities,
found the camp at Glengariff abandoned to the wounded and sick
left to his compassion. This he showed by putting them to death.
With a garrison of one thousand men he still held the lately reconstructed castle of Dunkerron, near the now beautiful town of Kenmare, and under instructions from the president wasted Beare, sparing
neither man nor beast. He destroyed houses, boats, the ship reserved
to take the survivors to Spain, and every human creature in his path,
reducing Ardea and Carriganass, the last shelter of the women who
fled to the woods, forcing Ellen, wife of Donal Coom, and daughter
of Dunkerron, to seek refuge with her brother in Iveragh.

The president despatched Taafe and the white knight with six
hundred horse and the foot of Fermoy, in pursuit of the sons of
Owen, next after Florence in the succession to rule in Carberry, who

with Dermod O'Driscol, Mahon and some of the MacSweenys* were
in their own country but in arms.　Many fell on either side in skirmish, on one occasion the royalists being badly beaten.　On the
fifth of January, some of the Maccarthies cut off from their main
body were routed, when the white knight pursuing lost two of his
fingers in personal combat with O'Crowley "the fierce."　Mac-
Eagan, papal bishop of Ross, was slain in the fight, and another
ecclesiastic, Dermot Maccarthy, who had signalized his faith by care
of the wounded and dying of both sides, was captured.　Carried to
Cork, he was drawn at the tail of a horse through the villages, quartered and disembowelled, and half dead executed on the scaffold,
with the barbarity that marked the period.　The chiefs submitted and
were taken under protection.

Carbery ravaged, no power anywhere existed to curb the merciless
despotism which rioted in rapine and death over the land, crushing
in deadly folds the marrow from its bones, whatever remained of its
spirit or vitality.　The destruction of the crops the previous summer
had been so complete, that pestilence, which follows famine, found little
to consume.　The same desolation that marked the close of the Desmond war, twenty years before, again brooded over Munster.

Then, disputes growing out of the ill-starred dowry of Ormond's
mother and Desmond's wife, drenched their palatinates in blood.
Peter Carew, later, to gain Idrone slaughtered the Kavanaghs.　The
president, either for his niece or for himself, coveted, as his papers
show, what Henry II. four centuries before gave to Fitzstephen,
half the kingdom of Maccarthy Mor, extending from Limerick to
Lismore, all Cork and Kerry.　It did not signify that in 1333, by
English forms, Fitzstephen had been pronounced illegitimate and had
never married, that the marquis of Carew, neither as nephew or by
marrying his daughter, ever became entitled to inherit what he never

* The line of Tuath :—i. Maelmora.　ii. Donogh.　iii. Morogh.　iv. Donogh.　v. Turlogh.
vi. Edmund (1835).

79

possessed, or that for three centuries the present proprietors had held. Nor did it prove an obstacle to the recovery of Idrone, that links in the pedigree rested on conjecture or violent assumption. The same claim had been, then and since, asserted to all Munster, and it was well understood that if circumstances favored, it would be pushed. It was much as if the chiefs and clans dispossessed by Cromwell or Orange, should in some future change of political power claim to be reinstated. The chiefs menaced, while sufficiently wary to avoid committing themselves, naturally looked to Spain for protection from these monstrous pretensions, and loved their own faith the more for what they saw of protestant profligacy in this unscrupulous greed for what belonged to them.

Carew left no descendants, and his honored name has been too variously distinguished to suffer from his claims or crimes. Highly educated, of refined habits and polished manners, able and brave but arrogant and unscrupulous, he was utterly without moral sense, of a cold heart and malignant temper. His correspondence, which he took pains to preserve, proves that he employed Anias to make away, by assassination, with Florence, O'Conor with the sugan, Nugent with Sir John Fitzgerald, Blake with Tyrconnel. He hung prisoners, massacred women and children, tortured priests. That he should have been a favorite with the cold and cruel Tudor, whose favor he courted by the most abject subserviency, is less strange, than that he stood well with Cecil and Blount. Their record in Irish administration is by no means fleckless, still they had the grace at times to disapprove of what he did or intended. If allowance is to be made for the spirit of the times, there are bad men in power at all epochs, and will never be less unless duly stigmatized. He went, in January, to Galway to confer with the deputy, and in March proceeded to the couch of the dying queen. James created him lord Carew, Charles I. earl of Totness, and he lived on, variously employed, till 1629.

XLVIII.

REIGN OF ELIZABETH.—1558-1602.—(Concluded.)

Tyrone improved the months that he was left unmolested, in re-organizing his shattered army. Too wise and too noble to repine at events beyond his control, if not providentially ordained, he accepted his lot and applied himself to such measures of preparation as his judgment dictated, to fend off the blow he well knew impended. With others, he shared in the faith that Spain would speedily retrieve the disaster at Kinsale, and not leave a people in jeopardy she had encouraged to fight the battles of the faith and her own. Frequent intimations came over the sea that such indeed were her intentions, and rumors that armadas, more considerable than they actually were, would be soon on the way. But besides the war in the low country, her peaceable relations with France had become seriously compromised by revelations attending the conspiracy of Byron against Henry of Navarre ; an English fleet blockaded her ports, and besides knowing the pecuniary straits of the English treasury, much might be gained by delay. Whilst there remained assurance of aid, no course remained for Tyrone but to wait patiently and avoid rather than seek occasions which might lessen his numbers or impair their efficiency.

Why the deputy failed forthwith to follow up his victory, has been sufficiently explained by his heavy losses of men and material in the siege, and the necessity of leaving in Munster so large a portion of his force to reduce Dunboy. But another reason for his inactivity was the state of his health, undermined by exposure in his winter campaigns. Active operations necessarily deferred, he resorted to his old methods of weakening the enemy by detaching from him the border chiefs, and destroying the growing crops. As the war had already cost over three millions of money, and four hundred thousand were expended this very year, the queen was impatient for peace and wrote in August that she would gladly pardon Tyrone if he would spare her dignity by submission. The deputy even advised Carew to accept the overtures of Tyrrel to accommodation if he seemed to be sincere.

Early in June the president reached Dundalk, and on the fourteenth Armagh, crossing the Blackwater five miles eastward of Portmore. He employed Moryson in building a bridge and a castle, which he called Charlemont from his own name, placing it in charge of Caulfield, whose descendant took later from it his title of earl, one honorable in Irish annals. From this point there led a plain and open entrance into the country, and as he approached Dungannon, Tyrone set on fire his chief residence, and carried his creaghts into the woods. The deputy approached the place with a small force to reconnoitre, and after completing the works at the river returned there with his whole army on the twenty-seventh. Here Dowcra, who had advanced from lough Foyle to Owmy with large detachments, joined him, and after taking an island where Con, son of Shane, had long been incarcerated, he divided between him and his brother, Henry, the waste lands between the Blackwater and Newry. Effecting a junction with Chichester from Carrickfergus, he constructed another fortress at lough Neagh, called Mountjoy from his title, and in it placed a thousand men. He planted another garrison at Augher, the castle of Cormac O'Neil.

Tyrone took refuge in Slievegallen, a wide tract of moor and mountain extending from lough Foyle to lough Neagh, portions of what now constitute the county of Tyrone and Londonderry, and embracing Arachty on the Bann. Completely hemmed in by his foes, he kept up a brave heart, at castle Roe, setting at defiance the royal army now concentrating for his destruction. With the desire of liberty in a conquered nation to work upon, he maintained his ascendency over his devoted clansmen, not one of whom could be

tempted by bribes to betray him. Before July ended, the deputy
marched to Monaghan and wasted Dartry, leaving strong garrisons
there and in Fermanagh, under Con Maguire, Esmond and St. Lawrence, whom we have seen ineffectively trying to take in their toils
Maguire and Donal Coom. The country still abounded in herds
and grain. Dowera, Chichester and Moryson busy with the sickle
and the torch, utterly destroyed whatever was good for food. Houses
and stacks in flames darkened the sky with smoke, cattle slaughtered,
whose carcases, left to decay, tainted the air with pestilence and
death.

Magherlowny, the principal abode of Tyrone when not at Dungannon, and his principal magazine of military stores, as also Inis-
loghlin, near lough Neagh, where the chiefs of Ulster had deposited
for safety and concealment their plate and valuables, were reduced.
The stone chair in which were inaugurated the chiefs, at Tullaghoge,
home of the O'Hagans, was broken into fragments. Tyrone, realizing castle Roe was no longer tenable, quitted it for Glenconquin,
through which the Moyala flows into lough Foyle, and thence went
south into the wild and inaccessible forests near lough Erne, a
fastness which a handful of men could defend against an army. His
numbers had dwindled to six hundred foot and sixty horse, but here
for three months longer he kept at bay the thousands of troops that
dared not venture within twelve miles of his covert. O'Rourke still
unsubdued, occupied Lambert on the Shannon; Nial Garve, his
brother-in-law Rory, capturing Ballyshannon and destroying Enniskillen. Bryan MacArt, in Clanaboy, and O'Cahan held out for a
time, but finding resistance fruitless submitted; and when the news
came of O'Donnel's death, in October, his brother Rory, invited to
come in and promised not only amnesty but confirmation of his
principality, yielded.

Tyrone had urged Rory, O'Conors Roe and Sligo and O'Rourke,
to meet him at lough Erne, to concert measures for prolonged resis-

tance, or combine on terms to be proposed for accommodation. All
but the latter chieftain had already entered under protection. The
deputy, after his autumn sport of falconry, proceeded to Athlone,
which he advised in future should be the capital, and there, on the
fourteenth of December, Rory and O'Conor Sligo met him, and
keeping christmas at Galway, and sending for Carew, he extended
the royal amnesty to O'Conor Roe, O'Flahertys and MacDermots.

Again at the capital, his attention, and that of the council, was
occupied with the forlorn condition of the currency. The measures adopted or suggested, betrayed an amazing stupidity. The point
of debasement reached was one-fourth sterling, but impressions prevailed that the queen's coin was all base metal. She had thus tam-
pered with it to support the war, calculating that out of three
hundred thousand pounds manufactured for Ireland, two-thirds would
be net profit for her. But by constant return to the offices of
exchange on both sides the channel, it imposed an actual loss on the
treasury, whilst importers made two hundred per cent. on a trade
speedily exhausted, as there was no money to buy. Counterfeits
abounded. Penalties attached to decrying the coin, or even refusal
to receive it. Distrust became universal. Trade stood still, and
the people, their crops destroyed and unable to obtain food from
abroad, starved.

The terrible suffering of his people from famine and pestilence,
three thousand dying of starvation within his own borders, a thousand lying unburied between Toome and Tullaghoge, young children
in one instance feeding upon the remains of their mothers; aged
crones in another killing and devouring a poor girl who came, at
Newry, to their fire to warm herself, and similar tales of misery that
failed not to reach him, wrung the heart of Tyrone. He did not
feel justified in prolonging such agony from any feeling of pride.
Hope was a long time extinguished, and having done his utmost
to save his country from calamities, which verified his foresight, now

that no further effort of his could avail, he made overtures of peace. He wrote the deputy on the twelfth of November, to intimate his willingness to become loyal, provided submission involved no terms of humiliation. These were at first coldly received, but transmitted to Greenwich, appeared there at an opportune moment for their acceptance.

The approaching death of the queen had its embarrassments. What political convulsions might follow the event could not be foreseen ; there were rivals for her sceptre, catholic as well as protestant, and so many of the old faith remained in both islands, that Spain might well consider the conjuncture propitious for another invasion. The ministers were only too glad to be relieved of further anxiety about Ireland.

The preliminaries to negotiation assented to, Moore and Godolphin, appointed commissioners to arrange the terms, proved little exacting. Among them were full pardon, restoration in blood and removal of the attainder, full and free exercise of religion, confirmation to himself and the other Ulster chiefs of their respective territories, excepting the Fewes, held by Turlogh O'Neil, and the county held by Henry Oge. Six hundred acres were reserved on the Blackwater to be divided between the forts of Mountjoy and Charlemont. Tyrone, retaining his earldom, agreed to relinquish the title of O'Neil, his jurisdiction as chieftain, admit sheriffs and other officials into his territories, and recalling his son Henry from Spain surrender him as pledge for his fidelity. Not permitted to know that the queen had already expired, lest it should change his purpose, he was taken to Drogheda, and at Mellifont, on the thirtieth of March, made submission before the deputy on his knees, a humiliation then imposed as fitting retribution for resisting authority whether just or unjust.

They went together to the capital, and there the earl repeated his protestations of future fidelity to the queen, and after the ceremony was completed first became apprized of the royal demise. He regretted his precipitation, for at first it encouraged hopes to be bitterly disappointed in the sequel. Tears which started at the tidings were ascribed to affection for Elizabeth, but another construction to his grief was that he had not held out longer and made better terms. It was too late. He acknowledged fealty to king James, and wrote the king of Spain to inform him of his course and to request that his son Henry might be sent home to Ulster.

Nial Garve had to content himself with the title of baron which he resented, and denouncing the bad faith of England before the council, not recognizing his own which, with Sir Arthur O'Neil's, had ruined his country. The times were not rife for wholesale spoliation, and satisfied with subjecting the island, that was reserved for the fulness of time. Donal Coom was exempted from pardon, and going into Spain received monthly three hundred pieces of gold, and was created count of Bearehaven, Beare vesting in his kinsman, son of Sir Owen. Waterford, Cork and Limerick attached to the catholic faith, declared against king James, and reopened their chapels for its rites, but were soon suppressed, and a new era of Irish history commenced.

XLIX.

CONCLUSION.

In faith, race and nationality, neutral and impartial, we have endeavored to present the leading incidents of that momentous struggle for tribal or national independence, which at the commencement of the seventeenth century terminated in complete subjugation of the island to the English crown. After two centuries more of oppression and convulsion, what little of autocracy survived, merged at the union in the omnipotence of the British parliament. When another closes, its sense of right, no doubt, will have removed all ground of grievance, discontent or disaffection. For this desired consummation, both law and public sentiment must coöperate. Equal privileges, religious, social and educational, opportunities and preferment professional and in the public service, above all still further reform in land tenures, if nothing else prohibition of that usurious exaction, double rents, should leave no invidious distinction to create jealousy or justify resentment.

Might does not make right. That the strong man keepeth the house till a stronger than he cometh, may be the usage of the world, but it is a doctrine dangerous to progressive civilization, subversive of justice and order. Vested interests, although originating in wrong and robbery, cannot safely be disturbed. When Ireland was subjugated at the beginning of the seventeenth century, one half its area had already been transferred to owners of English birth, ancestry or name, largely under parchment titles which were to gain validity and force as English rule acquired stability and spread. Besides Meath and the pale, nearly all Leinster, half of Munster, small portions of Connaught and the east of Ulster had been wrested from Milesian chiefs and septs, and the actual tillers of the soil, as the inhabitants generally of the older race, were liable to be ousted at the will

80

of alien landlords. Resistance continued feebly and without other
effect than to bring down on the doomed land measureless calamity.

What remained in Irish ownership yielded slowly and steadily
to superior numbers, arms, education and cupidity ; to private greed,
legal chicanery and arbitrary legislation, till before the century closed
this too had for the most part followed, and the recent census reveals
the strange result that an inconsiderable portion of the island is vested
in other names than those of a race which, indicated by their patronymics, forms but a small portion of the whole population.

No reliable information has been transmitted as to their whole number, or that of the respective races, from the twelfth to the seventeenth
century, but probably the inhabitants of Ireland were not one to
four of the population of the sister kingdom, embracing England and
Wales. That they should against such odds have so long baffled
every attempt to subjugate them, when this disparity in numbers was
by no means their greatest disadvantage, speaks favorably not only
for their courage, but for the sagacious counsels that directed it.
No one can study their history or the character of their institutions,
without bias, and not come to the conclusion that their great misfortune was to have been placed geographically within reach of neighbors so aggressive, overbearing and powerful as the English.

Left to themselves, the septs, if occasionally at variance, and
compelled for security to form alliances and keep in working order
their military organization, were virtually independent. They were
governed by their own laws, and by chiefs to whom they were
devotedly attached, and their habits of life, when outside pressure
was removed, had elements enough of variety to prevent stagnation.
If not systematically industrious as Saxon yeoman or peasant of
France, they supplied their wants by tillage, and their numerous
herds constituted their wealth. As their laws contain rules for the
government of artificers of different kinds, the useful arts were not
neglected. Surrounded by the sea, frequent intercourse with

France and Spain afforded them, in exchange for their wool, wine and clothes.

For religious and secular education, this home rule seemed equally propitious. Public documents that remain emanating from their chieftains, annals and other works from the many writers of Irish birth whose names and productions have come down to us, abundantly indicate that not only in natural endowment but in culture they were quite equal to the Anglo-Normans, and fully as competent to govern themselves. Conventual establishments, if not now as useful, served then as asylums for the infirm and unprotected, kept alive a spirit of devotion, educated the young and refined their habits. The number, several hundred in all, recorded in the Apostolic Chamber, founded and endowed before the reformation in Ireland, testify not to the superstition of the age, but to the sense entertained of their value. In one instance, such a foundation was an atonement for assassination, but they generally proceeded from an enlightened piety. The larger proportion were erected by the chiefs, all the provinces contributing; and if we may judge from the exquisite remains of Holycross or Mucross Abbey, Roserea and Quinn, there may have been more costly and imposing edifices in wealthier lands, but few whose architectural beauty and adaptation to their intended use surpassed these and many others which might be mentioned mouldering about the old island of the saints.

Private abodes corresponded in elegance and convenience with these religious structures. Blarney Castle, dating from the middle of the fifteenth century, is still a delight to every beholder, and had civil war spared more examples of the taste of that period, they would have helped to disprove much that sounds harsh in recent criticisms. When castles were demolished in war and rebuilt in haste for protection, little heed was paid to symmetry or embellishment. Many ruined edifices remain haggard and ungraceful, but they were as often the work of English as of Irish men. The vulgar plainness

of some old Irish cities, in marked contrast to those of the continent,
speaks in terms not to be mistaken of the puritan notions of
Cromwell and his ironsides.   Disingenuously native chieftains
would be held responsible for hills and moors denuded of their
natural garniture.   This was not their work, but adventurers wishing
to realize, before their grants were reclaimed, cut off the forests.
Much was wasted or went to operate unprofitable mines.   If left to
the beneficent design of Providence mould would have accumulated,
and mountain slopes, now unsightly ledges, have furnished the best
of pasturage.

As an indication of the rudeness of manners prevailing at that
time in the principal abodes of the island, the habit is instanced of
housing cattle under the same roof with the master.   This precaution against predatory neighbors or siege was not peculiar to Ireland,
but to all lands exposed to disturbance.   In large castles, either
around or within their walls, capacious enclosures were provided into
which flocks and herds were driven at night, or when there was
apprehension of maraud.   It was a custom not unknown a few generations ago in New England, for in a house of the Wentworths,
near Portsmouth, the cellars were arranged for cattle or for cavalry
mounts at least half a hundred when Indian depredation was
imminent.

If daughters of noble degree hovered in light attire around the
family hearth in princely dwellings, the elegances of modern life
were not then common, if we may credit authority, even in kings'
palaces.   What few comforts Irish castles had to offer were at
the disposal of whoever came with friendly purpose.   Hospitality,
next to courage, was the cardinal virtue.   Two thousand persons,
rich and poor, as we have seen, partook of the Christmas banquet
at one castle; as many olavs, poets, historians and other learned
persons for several days on other occasions.   Harp and minstrelsy
and intellectual entertainments of high order afforded recreation to

the concourse assembled. The chief's hall was ever open to his clansmen or to strangers, and no one sent unsatisfied away. Whoever has examined the laws of Ireland, or is familiar with what has been transmitted of its chieftains, must admit they could not have been cruel task-masters, or oppressors of their clansmen. The relation was precisely that best calculated to produce the wise, just, efficient ruler; with character to stand the test of constant scrutiny; habits, not only of command and self-control, but of generous and unceasing consideration for kindred, near or remote, who of their own accord entrusted themselves to his leadership.

Sophistry and perversion of fact are near akin. That the Norman chiefs were born rulers of men, and therefore entitled to govern Ireland, is quite untenable in the light either of historical evidence or of moral principle. Their valor, clothed in impenetrable steel, may be conceded, and they possessed advantages for education which in itself is power. But as to their giving security to life or property, and enabling those who cared to be industrious to reap the fruits of their labors without fear of outrage or plunder, the protection they afforded was that of wolves to lambs. Under color of royal grants, readily procured from their influence at court, they despoiled the defenceless without mercy or compunction. The pretension that they strove to govern the country not as a vassal province but as a free nation, to extend to her the forms of English liberty, trial by jury, local courts, and parliamentary representation is utterly fallacious. The results abundantly show that the earnest request of the chiefs for one law for both races was frustrated through their intervention.

The imputation that life was so little valued that those who took it were allowed to make reparation by cattle, was not strictly true, for in the "Four Masters," the life of a chief's son is demanded in one instance as the fitting amends. Erics for murder were not peculiar to Ireland, but common as well to German and Saxon. This

lenity is certainly in contrast with the stern severities of English
law, under which seventy thousand persons were hung under the
Tudors, and poisoners boiled. In the last century, an Englishman
could commit one hundred and sixty offences punishable with death,
and his wife be burnt as a witch. Some of the Brehon regulations
seem irrational in the light of modern civilization, but our modern
statute books will not probably better stand the test in ages to
come.

In their taste for detraction, the works referred to berate both races
alike. They gloat over what has been said to the disadvantage of
either. Their seeming candor might mislead, did not the drift of their
strictures and defence of the harshest measures of English policy
betray their inspiration. Their object, however disguised, is obviously
to decry the old chieftains and foster in Irish minds, as education
opens their eyes and gives importance to their opinion, respect for
their present masters. They make no discrimination between Irish
birth and race. Silken Thomas, son of Kildare, who with his five
uncles were hung at Tyburn in 1536, had hardly a drop of Milesian
blood in his veins. His family were educated in England, Angliores
Anglis. He was near by when Archbishop Allen was slain, and this
is cited as proof of Irish barbarism. The English later betrayed
Catholic bishops and priests to torture and death by the score, they
subjected old men and women to thumb screw and boot, to lash and
starvation without mercy, but these are considered no crime.

If Ireland possesses few national works of art, the wealth that
should foster the genius of her children is squandered by absentee
proprietors; but Reynolds and Shea were presidents of the Royal
Academy. The mother of Goldsmith, whose "Vicar of Wakefield"
next to the Bible is the book most read in the language, derived from
the Dalgais; Wellington was Irish born and had no doubt Milesian
blood in his veins; certainly in those of the hero of Magenta, the
present sagacious ruler of France, trickles that of all the best stock

in Ireland of either race. Innumerable generals and statesmen in
every part of the globe have given good proof of their political
sagacity, lent lustre to honored names, showing it was not necessary
for their countrymen to seek for rulers amongst a people by nature
too domineering to be trusted with any such responsibility. Whilst
Irishmen bear in mind the O'Neils, O'Briens, McCarthys of earlier
times, or in those more recent, Burke, Sheridan and Moore, Curran,
Grattan and O'Connel, transcendant in eloquence or letters, they will
not be troubled by sneer or misrepresentation. Whilst such dispar-
agement perpetuates animosity, there will be no love lost between the
sister islands, and from incompatibility of temper, the only alternative
will be separation, home rule and such federal relations as work well
in Canada or Australia.

In the old manuscript records deaths in battle or by violence are
frequently mentioned, but this does not prove bloodshed more common than in France or England at the time, any more than laws
against murder on their statute-book indicate peculiar proclivities in
a people to that crime. Such annals record what is extraordinary.
If in an armed occupation of the country, as in those of other
nations, their pages reek with slaughter, it is to be attributed to
the false position of the English, who in utter disregard of all laws,
human or divine, were seeking to subjugate Ireland because they
chanced to be strongest. China and Japan prudently closed their
gates against European intrusion. Austria has the same claims to
Italy, Russia to Turkey, Turkey to Greece. But all, unless uphold-
ers of arbitrary power, who believe half the world booted and spurred
to ride hard the other half bitted and bridled, rejoice when the rider
is thrown.

Irishmen are reproached for their restlessness under injury and
insult, and with curious inconsistency that, while in number but one-
sixth of the population of the realm, disarmed, strangers on their
native soil, till lately cheated out of their just participation in industrial

pursuits, and of all opportunity for education or advancement, they
have not succeeded better in driving out their oppressors. Of English
origin and affection, Americans wish well to their mother country, but
as human beings such taunts, if they do not awaken the wish, raise
reasonable apprehension that retribution may be only delayed, and
that should poor Erin again resort to violence to vindicate her rights,
the responsibility will rest upon the heads of her ungenerous
defamers.

It may be idle to mourn over events growing directly out of human
infirmities, and constantly paralleled in other lands and ages. But
a candid consideration of the past yields the most valuable lessons to
statesmen who control the destinies of nations. Had England been
governed by a wise and generous policy towards Ireland, and respected the rights and liberties, civil and religious, of its people, she
would have been spared a vast effusion of blood and waste of treasure, a heavy responsibility for infinite misery and wretchedness.
For all these centuries Ireland was an expense to her treasury. If
its inhabitants had been permitted equal privileges with her other
subjects, they would in process of time have become loyal, and advancing in prosperity and civilization contributed in a larger measure
to her strength. To heap upon a favored few immense wealth which
added little to their enjoyment, the masses were reduced to a condition
of predial servitude.

The process, if slow, was steadily onward. Proscribed for their
religious beliefs, shut out from the advantages of education, of varied
employment and other civilizing influences, dispirited and broken-
hearted, they that could sought refuge in other lands. For such as
remained, labor without capital and consequently without enterprise,
permitted no abiding interest in the land it tilled, and withheld from
industries it preferred to benefit English rivalry—what more deplorable
condition can be conceived for any people—impoverishment, aggravated by early and prolific marriages nature and religion prescribed,

ate like a canker. Despair, inadequate nourishment, enforced idleness, if not always repressing their inherent gaiety, found temporary relief or oblivion in demoralizing indulgences, then common to both races and all conditions, but which, where there offered fewer recreations to take their place, were less easily abandoned. Already with us such reproach is rapidly ceasing to attach to any people, and in this great reform of the age, Celts march shoulder to shoulder with the Saxon in the front.

Refinements in life, in food or garments, are the growth of peace and plenty, of culture and education, intercourse with lands more advanced in these civilized arts. They were hardly to be expected where war, pestilence and famine had for generations wrought desolation, for a people by intolerance debarred from religious instruction, loaded down by rapacity with tithe and tax, whom unequal distribution of property through laws or customs of primogeniture, discouragement of industry, inadequate compensation for labor had disheartened or incensed. The unpleasant modes and usages Morrison witnessed at the beginning of the seventeenth century, probably in instances exceptional and extreme, are sufficiently explained by the events we have related. Sad to say, they may still be observed in many countries, even in his own, under similar conditions proceeding from equally efficient causes. Comforts and elegances that attend wealth may raise the standards around of taste, neatness and order, spreading, even where resources are limited for their indulgence, from palace to hut. But people ground down by poverty, enraged by injustice and struggling hard for subsistence, have little inclination, or temper, to be always nice in their necessary nourishments, habits or ways. It may be their misfortune, but the reproach does not always rest upon them.

Sydney Smith, an honored type of the best English development, in expressing, half a century ago, his admiration for their wit and eloquence, courage, generosity, hospitality and open-heartedness,

81

alluded to their love of display, want of economy and perseverance, eagerness for results without the slow and patient virtues that control them.   But he is frank to admit that their lack of unity among themselves, irritability, violence and revenge, disregard of law and its tribunals, of neatness and comfort among their poorer classes, were attributable to want of education, or the oppression to which they had been subjected.   He pronounces "the conduct of his countrymen towards Ireland to have been a system of atrocious cruelty and contemptible meanness, and that with such a climate, such a soil and such a people, the inferiority in civilization was directly chargeable to the wickedness of the government."

This strong language, applicable also, in some recent instances, to our treatment of the Indians, is borne out by the array of penal enactments which he cites in its support.   These laws have been for the most part repealed, but the history of the past cannot be understood without taking them into account.   Defects of character which retarded improvement or blocked the path to individual progress and prosperity, often charged as idiosyncrasies of race, were the natural and logical growth of their political condition. Certainly here, where properly trained, they display equal industry, frugality, steadfastness of purpose, loyalty to law and obligation with any other nationality.   So long as English opinion exasperates by arrogance, contumely or indifference, refuses to heed what is advanced in good faith in their defence, the realm will lose by their disaffection an element of strength, important for its security and also for the preservation of those representative institutions which we too have inherited as our birthright, and believe to have greatly improved.

The immunity of both countries from foreign assailants, may at times be dependent upon their political consolidation, but persecution has only served to strengthen the attachment of catholics to their faith, and there can be no loyalty to a government felt only in oppression. More liberal measures have already been adopted. Tenures have been made more permanent for those that till the soil, education more universal, suffrage extended, funds consecrated to religious instruction no longer one sixth only appropriated to the benefit of three-fourths of the people, but more justly divided. Much remains to be effected with regard to trade, taxation and official patronage, but all interested in the welfare of Ireland, or indeed of the empire from which we so largely derive our existence in this country, justly claim an interest in what conduces alike to the glory and honor of rose, shamrock and thistle. Rancor for ancient wrongs throws obstacles in the way of reparation, renders more insupportable existing restraints. But religious toleration, equality before the law, blending of nationalities are indispensable to tranquillity, progress and strength.

It behooves us to study the history of Ireland with peculiar attention. Its lessons and warnings teem with significance. For grievances far less bitter and intolerable than hers under Tudor and Stuart monarchs, we declared and asserted our independence. When we grow cold and indifferent to our political blessings, prize less our free institutions than our ancestors who planted them, its pages will teach us the danger we escaped in casting off a foreign yoke, the deplorable consequences of forfeiting our birthright, of relapsing under arbitrary rule. That rule may return, not in the guise of royal prerogative or alien legislation. Human nature unrestrained by principle or law is ever selfish and domineering. Despotism is equally detestable whether imposed from abroad, by party power or individual ambition, by infuriated mobs or communes, an absolute monarch or class control. Our best safeguards, if we would avoid the misrule of Ireland, subjection to tyranny or caprice of the arrogant, are the preservation of our constitutional checks and balances, just and equal laws faithfully administered by virtue and intelligence, a spirit of compromise and conciliation, which, respecting right and susceptibility in all, will disarm antagonisms such as have tormented, torn and impoverished lands beyond the sea. We may then defer to a later day, and may it be far removed, the study of how the republic of Rome succumbed to the Cæsars.

English writers discuss what concerns other nations without reserve, and especially our own, whilst Americans, firm believers in equal rights before the law and to political privilege, have rarely been zealous in making proselytes. But when appeal was taken to public opinion here, where multitudes had come to escape from conditions at home no longer to be endured, in cities of which the inhabitants of Irish birth or parentage form one-third of the whole population, when obloquy was cast on their own character and that of their fathers, on their history and traditions by writers of ability disposed, if not prejudiced, rather to dazzle than instruct, it suggested inquiry and prompted investigation confined to neither race nor sect. Out of that desire for fair play grew this volume, deriving its material from both ancient sources and recent publications, and it is believed to embody information scholars of Irish history on this side the ocean, at least, may find of value for the period of which it treats. If presumption for an American to venture upon such a field, or to controvert conclusions of authors of better opportunities and more widely known, the motive must justify the temerity.

INDEX OF NAMES.

82

INDEX OF BATTLES AND SIEGES.

ERRATA.

Page 10, line 16, *omit* " Trench and."
" 22, " 22, *read* Henry the Second's, *instead of* " John's."
" 23, " 5, " was for nearly, *instead of* " has been for."
" 25, " 8, " for, *instead of* " at."
" 25, " 16, " them, *instead of* " these."
" 26, " 29, " 1177, *instead of* " 1129."
" 27, " 28, " 1318, " " " 1217."
" 36, " 27, *add* are.
" 43, " 16, " 109 A.D.
" 70, " 12. *read* Carrigaphoyle.
" 71, " 19, " kings of the.
" 73, " 19, " Bath, *instead of* " Welsh."
" 95, " 32, " R. I. A.
" 102, " 16, " Duigenan.
" 102, " 21, " which, *instead of* " what."
" 103, " 28, " American edition by Mahoney.
" 104, " 3, " 1634 *instead of* " 1604."
" 107, " 24, " many, *instead of* " twenty."
" 108, " 13, " Joyce's Irish Names, Flanagan's Lord Chancellors, 1870, and Hart's
                        Irish Pedigrees, 1876.
" 149, " 2, " 1375, *instead of* " 1775."
" 157, " 20, " Edmund, *instead of* " Edward."
" 159, " 31, " elegances, *instead of* " elements."
" 233, " 14, " scion, *instead of* " sire."
" 240, " 11, " O'Donnel, *instead of* " O'Donnor."
" 279, " 13, " third, *instead of* " first."
" 294, " 26, " Kilmallock.
" 304, " 26, " country, *instead of* " county."
" 339, " 5, " who was kept.
" 375, " 8, " raged, *instead of* " waged."
" 378, " 10, " chary, *instead of* " cheery."
" 379, " 32, " no wiser.
" 421, " 1, " Judith, *instead of* " Joan."
" 496, " 17, " MacSweeny Banagh.
" 571, " 31, " soon after, *instead of* " already."

Note.—Gerald of Desmond, killed 1583, is most usually termed sixteenth earl of his line;
his son Gerald, who died 1601, seventeenth. The affix to the name of Burkes of Clanrickard is " Oughter" the upper; of those of Mayo, " Eighter" the lower.